Lecture Notes in Computer Science 8358

For further volumes:
http://www.springer.com/series/7407

Martín Abadi · Alberto Lluch Lafuente (Eds.)

Trustworthy Global Computing

8th International Symposium, TGC 2013
Buenos Aires, Argentina, August 30–31, 2013
Revised Selected Papers

Springer

Editors
Martín Abadi
Microsoft Research
Mountain View, CA
USA

Alberto Lluch Lafuente
IMT Institute for Advanced Studies
Lucca
Italy

ISSN 0302-9743 ISSN 1611-3349 (electronic)
ISBN 978-3-319-05118-5 ISBN 978-3-319-05119-2 (eBook)
DOI 10.1007/978-3-319-05119-2
Springer Cham Heidelberg New York Dordrecht London

Library of Congress Control Number: 2014933391

LNCS Sublibrary: SL1 – Theoretical Computer Science and General Issues

Printed on acid-free paper

Springer is part of Springer Science+Business Media (www.springer.com)

Preface

This volume contains the proceedings of TGC 2013, the 8th International Symposium on Trustworthy Global Computing. The symposium was held in Buenos Aires, Argentina, during August 30–31, 2013. It was co-located with CONCUR, QEST, and FORMATS, as part of the Buenos Aires Concurrency and Dependability Week. Informal pre-proceedings were available in electronic form to the participants. The papers in this volume have been further improved by the authors, in response to helpful feedback received at the symposium.

The Symposium on Trustworthy Global Computing is an international annual venue dedicated to safe and reliable computation in the so-called global computers, i.e., those computational abstractions emerging in large-scale infrastructures such as service-oriented architectures, autonomic systems, and cloud computing systems. It focuses on frameworks, tools, algorithms, and protocols for open-ended, large-scale systems and applications, and on rigorous reasoning about their behavior and properties. The underlying models of computation incorporate code and data mobility over distributed networks that connect heterogeneous devices, often with dynamically changing topologies.

The first TGC event took place in Edinburgh in 2005, with the co-sponsorship of IFIP TC-2, as part of ETAPS 2005. TGC 2005 was the evolution of the previous Global Computing I workshops held in Rovereto in 2003 and 2004 (see LNCS vol. 2874) as well as of the workshops on Foundation of Global Computing held as satellite events of ICALP and CONCUR (see ENTCS vol. 85). Four editions of TGC were co-located with the reviews of the EU-funded projects AEOLUS, MOBIUS, and SENSORIA within the FP6 initiative. They were held in Lucca, Italy (TGC 2006, LNCS vol. 4661); in Sophia Antipolis, France (TGC 2007, LNCS vol. 4912); in Barcelona, Spain (TGC 2008, LNCS vol. 5474); and in Munich, Germany (TGC 2010, LNCS vol. 6084). Further editions of TGC were held in Aachen, Germany (TGC 2011, LNCS vol. 7173) and in Newcastle upon Tyne, UK (TGC 2012, LNCS vol. 8191).

TGC 2013 solicited contributions in all areas of global computing, including (but not limited to) theories, languages, models, and algorithms; language concepts and abstraction mechanisms; security, trust, privacy, and reliability; resource usage and information flow policies; software development and software principles; model checkers, theorem provers, and static analyzers.

TGC 2013 carried out a fruitful collaboration with CONCUR 2013. Concurrent submissions to CONCUR and TGC were allowed, with the reviewing schedule of TGC slightly delayed with respect of that of CONCUR. Reviews were shared between CONCUR and TGC. Submissions accepted by CONCUR were automatically withdrawn from TGC. In all, 18 papers were concurrently submitted to CONCUR and TGC, out of which four were accepted by CONCUR and 14 were subject to further evaluation by TGC. Several of the papers rejected by CONCUR were found suitable for TGC, in part because of differences in evaluation criteria, and in part because the timeline of TGC gave authors several additional months to produce final versions of their work.

In addition to those concurrent submissions, TGC 2013 received 15 TGC-only submissions. In order to guarantee the fairness and quality of the selection process, each submission received at least three reviews.

The Program Committee selected 15 papers to be included in this volume and be presented at the symposium. The program was structured in sessions named "Security," "Pi-calculus," "Information Flow," "Models," "Specifications, and Proofs," and "Quantitative Analysis," chaired by Ugo Montanari, Mohammad Reza Mousavi, Hernán Melgratti, and Joost-Pieter Katoen.

Additionally, the program included three invited lectures:

- Luca de Alfaro (UC Santa Cruz, USA)
- Nobuko Yoshida (Imperial College London, UK)
- Jane Hillston (University of Edinburgh, UK)

All the invited speakers were encouraged to contribute a paper related to their lectures for these proceedings.

We would like to thank the Steering Committee of TGC for inviting us to chair the conference; the Program Committee members and external referees, for their detailed reports and the stimulating discussions during the review phase; the authors of submitted papers, the invited speakers, the session chairs, and the attendees, for contributing to the success of the event. We are also grateful to the providers of the EasyChair system, which was used to manage the submissions; to Microsoft Research, for sponsoring the event; and to Hernán Melgratti, Pedro D'Argenio, and the rest of the organizers of the Buenos Aires Concurrency and Dependability Week.

December 2013

Martín Abadi
Alberto Lluch Lafuente

Organization

Steering Committee

Gilles Barthe	IMDEA Software, Madrid, Spain
Rocco De Nicola	IMT Institute for Advanced Studies Lucca, Italy
Christos Kaklamanis	University of Patras, Greece
Ugo Montanari	University of Pisa, Italy
Davide Sangiorgi	University of Bologna, Italy
Don Sannella	University of Edinburgh, UK
Vladimiro Sassone	University of Southampton, UK
Martin Wirsing	LMU University of Munich, Germany

Program Committee Chairs

Martín Abadi	Microsoft Research and UC Santa Cruz, USA
Alberto Lluch Lafuente	IMT Institute for Advanced Studies Lucca, Italy

Program Committee

Gul Agha	University of Illinois at Urbana-Champaign, USA
Myrto Arapinis	University of Birmingham, UK
Luís Caires Caires	Universidade Nova de Lisboa, Portugal
Rocco De Nicola	IMT Institute for Advanced Studies Lucca, Italy
José Luiz Fiadeiro	Royal Holloway, University of London, UK
Andy Gordon	Microsoft Research and University of Edinburgh, UK
Radha Jagadeesan	DePaul University, USA
Matteo Maffei	Saarland University, Germany
Sergio Maffeis	Imperial College London, UK
Catuscia Palamidessi	Inria and École Polytechnique, France
Frank Pfenning	Carnegie Mellon University, USA
Sriram Rajamani	Microsoft Research, India
Tamara Rezk	Inria, France
Alejandro Russo	Chalmers University of Technology, Sweden
Davide Sangiorgi	University of Bologna, Italy
Carolyn Talcott	SRI International, USA
Emilio Tuosto	University of Leicester, UK
Sebastian Uchitel	University of Buenos Aires and Imperial College London, Argentina/UK
Martin Wirsing	LMU University of Munich, Germany

Additional Reviewers

Castellani, Ilaria
Charalambides, Minas
Giachino, Elena
Hennessy, Matthew
Mohsen, Rabih
Vandin, Andrea
Viswanathan, Mahesh

Contents

Invited Papers

Content-Driven Reputation for Collaborative Systems

Luca de Alfaro[1] (✉) and Bo Adler[2]

[1] Department of Computer Science, University of California, Santa Cruz, USA
[2] Facebook Inc., Menlo Park, USA
luca@ucsc.edu

Abstract. We consider collaborative editing systems in which users contribute to a set of documents, so that each document evolves as a sequence of versions. We describe a general technique for endowing such collaborative systems with a notion of content-driven reputation, in which users gain or lose reputation according to the quality of their contributions, rather than according to explicit feedback they give on one another. We show that content-driven reputation systems can be obtained by embedding the document versions in a metric space with a pseudometric that is both effort preserving (simple changes lead to close versions) and outcome preserving (versions that users perceive as similar are close). The quality of each user contribution can be measured on the basis of the pseudometric distances between appropriately chosen versions. This leads to content-driven reputation systems where users who provide contributions of positive quality gain reputation, while those who provide contributions of negative quality lose reputation. In the presence of notification schemes that prevent the formation of "dark corners" where closed groups of users can collaborate without outside interference, these content-driven reputation systems can be made resistent to a wide range of attacks, including attacks based on fake identities or specially-crafted edit schemes.

1 Introduction

In many collaborative systems, users can edit or modify the documents in the system, giving rise to a sequence of evolving versions for each document. We call such systems *collaborative editing systems.* The most prominent example of collaborative editing systems is wikis, but other systems can be similarly described. For instance, in Google Maps users can edit business listings, giving rise to a series of versions for the listings' content. A non-textual example consists in the process of uploading and revising 3D models to the Trimble 3D Warehouse [3]. Open software repositories and collaboration on shared documents are other examples.

We describe a general technique for developing *content-driven* reputation systems for collaborative editing systems. The idea behind content-driven reputation is simple: judge users by their actions, rather than by the word of other users.

M. Abadi and A. Lluch Lafuente (Eds.): TGC 2013, LNCS 8358, pp. 3–13, 2014.
DOI: 10.1007/978-3-319-05119-2_1,

In a content-driven reputation system, users gain or lose reputation according to how their contributions fare: users who contribute content that is preserved, or built-upon, by later users gain reputation; users whose work is undone lose reputation. Thus, content-driven reputation systems do not require users to express judgements on one another.

Reputation systems for collaboration provide an incentive for users to contribute constructively to the system. The power of reputation in motivating users is evident in many sites, such as Stack Overflow [4]. Another use of reputation is to help predict the future behavior of users; the predictive power of reputation has been demonstrated in the Wikipedia in [7,11]. Indeed, each time we use reputation to grant privileges to users, such as the ability to perform specific system actions, we trust in part the predictive power of reputation: if we did not believe that users who contributed greatly in the past are likely to continue to provide useful contributions, there would be little reason to grant such users additional privileges. A third use of reputation is to estimate content quality and identify vandalism [6,8,9].

Content-driven reputation systems have several advantages over systems that rely primarily on user feedback [7]. User-generated rating information can be quite sparse, especially in young editing systems. Gathering the feedback and ratings requires the implementation of user interfaces that are secondary to the goal of collaboration, and can be distracting or ineffective. Content-driven reputation comes "for free": it can be computed from content evolution information that is always present, without need for additional feedback or rating mechanisms. In content-driven reputation systems every user is turned into an active evaluator of other users' work, by the simple act of contributing to the system. By deriving the reputation signals from content evolution, rather than separate ratings, content-driven reputation prevents schemes such as *badmouthing:* a user cannot keep a contribution, while giving poor feedback on its author. Indeed, content-driven reputation systems can be made resistant to broad categories of attacks [11].

To endow a collaborative editing system with a notion of content-driven reputation, it suffices to provide a *pseudometric* on the space of document versions. A pseudometric is a function that satisfies the same axioms as a distance (positivity, symmetry, triangular inequality), except that distinct elements of the metric space (distinct versions, in our case) can have distance 0. The pseudometric between versions should satisfy two natural requirements:

- *Outcome preserving.* If two versions look similar to users, the pseudometric should consider them close. In particular, the pseudometric should assign distance 0 to versions that look identical or that are functionally identical.
- *Effort preserving.* If a user can transform one version of a document into another via a simple transformation, the pseudometric should consider the two versions close.

These two requirements are stated in an approximate way, and meeting them perfectly in a concrete collaborative editing system may not be possible.

However, the closer we get to satisfying these requirements, the higher-quality and harder-to-game the resulting reputation system will be.

For wikis, the outcome-preserving requirement means that the version pseudometric should be insensitive to differences in markup language that do not alter the way a wiki page is rendered. The effort-preserving requirement means that text that is moved from one place to the other in a document should yield a smaller pseudometric distance than separate, unrelated deletions and insertions of text. Pseudometrics suited to wikis have been analyzed in depth in [5].

Devising a suitable pseudometric is not necessarily trivial. Once a suitable pseudometric is available, however, we can use it to measure the quality of edits, by measuring how much the edits are preserved in future versions of the documents. We attribute positive quality to edits that bring the document closer to how it will be in the future, and negative quality to edits that make the document more different from how it will be in the future (these edits are thus reverted). This yields the foundation of the content-driven reputation system: users whose edits have positive quality gain reputation, while users whose edits have negative quality lose reputation.

We present and justify in detail the connection between version pseudometric distance and edit quality, and we describe how the resulting reputation system can be made resistant to broad types of attacks. The results we present are a synthesis of results from [5,7,11]. In those papers, the results were presented in the special context of text documents such as wikis. Here, we put the results in a general context, removing side-issues and complications that are particular to wikis, and showing how content-driven reputation systems can be adapted to broad classes of collaborative editing systems.

2 Collaborative Editing Systems

A *collaborative editing system* (CES) consists of a set $\mathcal{D} = \{D_1, D_2, D_3, \ldots\}$ of documents, where each document $D_i \in \mathcal{D}$ is composed of a series $v_0^i, v_1^i, v_2^i, \ldots,$ $v_{N_i}^i$ of *versions*. The version v_0^i is a null version, indicating that the document has not been created yet. Each subsequent version v_k^i, for $0 < k \leq N_i$, is obtained from r_{k-1}^i via an *edit* $e_k^i : v_{k-1}^i \rightarrow v_k^i$. We denote by $a(v)$ the author of version v, and for brevity, we denote by $a_0^i, a_1^i, a_2^i, \ldots$ the authors $a(v_0^i), a(v_1^i), a(v_2^i), \ldots$. In the following, we will often omit the superscript i denoting the document when clear from the context, or when not relevant.

We assume that the versions of the documents of the CES belong to a metric space $\mathcal{M} = (V, d)$, where V is the set of all possible versions, and $d : V \times V \mapsto \mathbb{R}_{\geq 0}$ is a pseudometric that is symmetrical and satisfies the inequality properties: for all $u, v, w \in V$,

$$\begin{aligned} d(u,u) &= 0 \\ d(u,v) &= d(v,u) \\ d(u,v) + d(v,w) &\leq d(u,w). \end{aligned}$$

We ask that d be a pseudometric, rather than a distance, because we do not require that $d(u, v) > 0$ for all distinct $u, v \in V, u \neq v$. Indeed, we will see that one of the desirable properties of the pseudometric d is that it assigns distance 0 to versions that are indistinguishable to users of the system.

The model of collaborative editing systems was inspired by wikis [7], but it can be widely applied to collaborative systems. For instance, the editing of business listings on Google Maps [2] and the editing of SketchUp models in the Trimble 3D Warehouse [3] can also be modeled as collaborative editing systems.

Wiki pages and their versions directly correspond to the documents and versions in a CES. As a pseudometric, we can use one of several notions of edit distance that satisfy the triangular inequality; see [5,18] for an in-depth discussion.

In the case of Google Maps, a business listing is comprised of various fields (title, categories, location, phone, and url, among others). Users can create new listings, and they can edit the values of the fields. The set of documents consists in the set of all business listings, and the user edits give rise to the sequence of versions. As pseudometric between fields, we can use the sum of the pseudometrics distances of the individual fields, perhaps using scaling factors that weigh the relative importance of each field. The physical distance between places on the Earth surface can be used as metric for locations; suitable distances for phone numbers and URLs consists in defining $d(u, v) = 2^{-\alpha m}$, where $\alpha > 0$ and m is the length of the longest common prefix of u and v. Distances for sets of categories are not difficult to define. These distances for the individual fields can then be combined in an overall distance for entire listings.

In the case of the 3D Warehouse of SketchUp models, the documents correspond to the designs that have been contributed by users. Users can upload updated versions of the designs, giving rise to the sequence of versions for each design. We can measure the distance between models by considering the edit distance between text descriptions of the vertices, planes, surfaces, textures, etc, comprising the designs.

In the next section, we describe some requirements of the psedumetrics that lead to useful measures of edit quality.

3 Measuring the Quality of Contributions

As a first step towards a reputation system for contributors to collaborative editing systems, we consider the problem of measuring the quality of each individual edit. We follow the idea that the quality of an edit can be measured by how long the edit survives in the subsequent history of the document [7]. To make this precise, we measure the quality of an edit $e_j : v_{j-1} \rightarrow v_j$ with the help of two versions: the previous version v_{j-1}, and a *judge* version v_k, where $j < k$. We define the *quality* $q(v_j \mid v_{j-1}, v_k)$ *of* v_j*, with respect to judge* v_k *and reference* v_{j-1}, as follows:

$$q(v_j \mid v_{j-1}, v_k) = \frac{d(v_{j-1}, v_k) - d(v_j, v_k)}{d(v_{j-1}, v_j)}. \qquad (1)$$

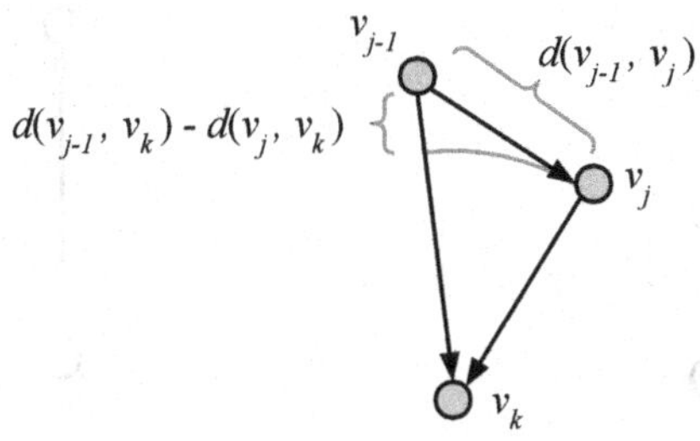

Fig. 1. The triangle of versions used to compute edit quality.

To understand this definition, it might help to refer to Fig. 1, and consider the situation from the point of view of the author a_k of v_k. Clearly, the author a_k prefers version v_k to any previous version of the document, since a_k contributed v_k. Thus, it is natural to assume that a_k will regard positively changes that bring the current version closer to v_k, and negatively changes that make the document more different from v_k. The quantity (1) captures this idea. The numerator $d(v_{j-1}, v_k) - d(v_j, v_k)$ measures how much closer the version has become to v_k due to edit e_j. The denominator $d(v_{j-1}, v_j)$ measures the total change caused by e_j. Their ratio $q(v_j \mid v_{j-1}, v_k)$ measures thus how much of the change introduced by e_j contributes to bringing the document closer to v_k.

From the triangular inequality, we have $q(v_j \mid v_{j-1}, v_k) \in [-1, 1]$ for all versions v_j, v_k.

- The maximum quality 1 is achieved when $d(v_{j-1}, v_k) = d(v_{j-1}, v_j) + d(v_j, v_k)$, which corresponds to Fig. 2(a). In this case, all the change done going from v_{j-1} to v_j is preserved in going to v_k.
- The minimum quality -1 is achieved when $d(v_j, v_k) = d(v_j, v_{j-1}) + d(v_{j-1}, v_k)$, which corresponds to Fig. 2(b). In this case, all the change from v_{j-1} to v_j is undone in the subsequent change from v_j to v_k: this corresponds to a reversion.

Choice of pseudometric. The definition of edit quality relies on a choice of pseudometric on the versions of the documents. To obtain a useful measure of edit quality, the pseudometric must be *effort-preserving* and *outcome-preserving*.

A pseudometric d is *effort preserving* if the distance between versions that can be easily obtained one from the other is small. An example of pseudometric that is not effort preserving is the text edit distance, measured according to the text diff tools commonly included in text revision systems, such as cvs or git [1]. The text differences computed by such tools do not model text transposition: when a block of text is moved, the resulting difference is large, even though the act of moving the text does not require much effort.

A pseudometric d is *outcome preserving* if versions that are similar to users are close in distance. In wikis, many changes to the whitespace (spaces, newlines, and so forth) do not result in visible changes of the corresponding document. If a user make changes to the whitespace of a document, these changes, having

(a) $q(v_j \mid v_{j-1}, v_k) = 1$ **(b)** $q(v_j \mid v_{j-1}, v_k) = -1$

Fig. 2. Edits having good and bad quality.

no effect, are unlikely to be reverted, even though they might not serve any purpose. If such whitespace changes resulted in non-negligible distance, they would provide users with an artificial opportunity for doing positive quality edits, while not contributing in any meaningful way to the wiki.

For wikis, the question of appropriate pseudometrics has been studied in depth in [5], where the quality of pseudometrics is measured according to the ability of the resulting reputation system to predict the quality of the future work of users. The pseudometrics that perform best are all insensitive to whitespace changes that do not affect the way in which the markup is rendered into HTML, in accordance with the outcome-presering requirement. Furthermore, unlike the Unix `diff` command, the pseudometrics that perform well track the movement of blocks of text across versions, and distinguish between text that is inserted and deleted, from text that is moved to another location in the document. This is in compliance with the effort preserving requirement: since block moves are easy to perform via cut-and-paste, they should give rise to small distances. Indeed, the best pseudometrics experimentally are those that explain the change from one version to the other via an edit list that contains a minimal amount of text insertion, deletion, and displacement: these functions measure thus the minimum amount of edit work required to go from one version to the other [5].

It is not difficult to devise appropriate pseudometrics for business listings, as previously mentioned. On the other hand, devising appropriate pseudometrics for complex domains, such as the 3D solids generated in SketchUp, is not an easy problem. The main difficulty lies in meeting the outcome preserving criterion, which requires the metric to consider close the designs that are visually similar.

4 Content-Driven Reputation

To construct our content-driven reputation system, we associate a reputation $r(a) \in \mathbb{R}_{\geq 0}$ with every author a. The initial value of user reputations corresponds

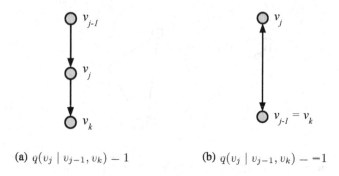

to the amount of reputation we can accord to users whom we have never seen in the system before, and it depends on how difficult it is to create new user accounts. In Wikipedia, where there are no restrictions to the creations of user accounts, WikiTrust gives new users reputation equal to 0: if we gave new users any larger amount $r > 0$, users whose reputation fell below r could simply open another account to get back to reputation r. In systems where users cannot easily create many accounts, we can afford giving new users some amount of reputation. This is akin to social interaction: when we deal with a perfect stranger hiding behind a nickname on the internet, we usually accord very little trust to the stranger, since obtaining such fake identities is essentially free. When we deal with a real person, whose name we know, we usually accord to that person some trust, since we know that the person cannot easily change identity if the person breaks our trust.

We update user reputation as follows. For each edit $e_j : v_{j-1} \to v_j$ done by a_j, we measure the quality of e_j with respect to set $F_j \subseteq \{v_{j+1}, \ldots, v_N\}$ of future versions; the precise rule for choosing F_j will be discussed later. For each version $v \in F_j$, we update the reputation of a_j via:

$$r(a_j) := r(a_j) + q(v_j \mid v_{j-1}, v)\, d(v_{j-1}, v_j)\, f(r(a(v))), \tag{2}$$

where $f : \mathbb{R}_{\geq 0} \mapsto \mathbb{R}_{\geq 0}$ is a monotonic function. Thus, the reputation of the author of e_j is incremented in proportion to the amount $d(v_{j-1}, v_j)$ of work done, multiplied by its quality $q(v_j \mid v_{j-1}, v)$, and multiplied by the reputation of the author of the reference revision v, rescaled according to a function $f(\cdot)$.

In (2), the version v has the role of "judge" in measuring the quality of the edit: the factor $f(r(a(v)))$ ensures that the higher the reputation of the author of v, the higher the weight we give to the quality judgement that uses v as reference. We rescale the reputation $r(a(v))$ using a monotonic function f to limit the influence of high-reputation users over the overall system. In most collaborative systems, including the Wikipedia, there is a group of long-term users who are responsible for a large fraction of the work; these users tend to accumulate large amounts of reputation. If in (2) we used $r(a(v))$ directly, this would give these top users an outsized influence over the reputation system. In the Wikipedia, we rescale reputations via $f(x) = \log(1 + \max\{0, \varepsilon + x\})$, where $\varepsilon \geq 0$ allows us to tune the amount of influence of new users on the system. Such a logarithmic rescaling function is a natural choice when the user contribution amounts and reputations follow a power-law distribution [10, 13, 15], and worked well in practice for Wikipedia editions in different languages [6, 7].

In order to choose the set F_j of reference versions, we first remove from $v_{j+1}, v_{j+2}, v_{j+2}, \ldots$ all the versions by the same author as v_j: we do not want a user to be a judge of his or her own work. Let $\sigma_j = v'_{j+1}, v'_{j+2}, v'_{j+3}, \ldots$ be the resulting sequence. One choice for F_j consists in taking the first K revisions of σ_j for some fixed $K > 0$; this is the choice followed in WikiTrust [7]. Another choice consists in taking F_j to be the whole σ_j, using geometrically-decaying weights for reference revisions farther in the future, to ensure that each edit causes a bounded change in the user's reputation. Under this choice, (2) becomes:

$$r(a_j) := r(a_j) + \sum_{k \geq j+1} (1-\alpha)\,\alpha^{j-k+1} q(v_j \mid v_{j-1}, v_k)\, d(v_{j-1}, v_j)\, f(r(a(v))) \quad (3)$$

for a geometric decay factor $0 < \alpha < 1$.

4.1 Truthfulness

A reputation system based on (2) or (3) is a *truthful* mechanism in the game-theoretic meaning of the term: if a user wants to modify a document, a dominating strategy (an optimal strategy for the user) consists in performing the modification as a single edit [11,17]. Users have no incentive to play complicated strategies in which the modification is broken up into a sequence of edits having the same cumulative effect. This property is fundamental in a reputation system. If users derived more reputation by breaking up edits into many small steps, or by performing every edit by first deleting the entire document, then replacing it with the new version, the evolution of the content in the collaborative system could be severely disrupted by users trying to maximize their reputation.

To prove the truthfulness of the reputation systems based on (2) or (3), we consider the case of an edit $e_j : v_{j-1} \to v_j$ being split into two edits having the same cumulative effect: $e'_j : v_{j-1} \to v'$ and $e''_j : v' \to v_j$; the general case is analogous. We analyze the case for (2); the same argument works also for (3). Consider a fixed version $v \in F_j$ used to judge e_j, and let $c = f(r(a(v)))$. For the edit e_j, the total amount of reputation gained by the author of e_j from judge v is:

$$\begin{aligned} c\,q(v_j \mid v_{j-1}, v)\, d(v_{j-1}, v_j) &= c \frac{d(v_{j-1}, v) - d(v_j, v)}{d(v_{j-1}, v_j)} d(v_{j-1}, v_j) \\ &= c\big[d(v_{j-1}, v) - d(v_j, v)\big]. \end{aligned} \quad (4)$$

When the edit e_j is split into e'_j, e''_j, the total amount of reputation gained due to judge v is:

$$\begin{aligned} & c\left[q(v' \mid v_{j-1}, v)\, d(v_{j-1}, v') + q(v_j \mid v', v)\, d(v', v_j)\right] \\ &= c\Big[\big[d(v_{j-1}, v) - d(v', v)\big] + \big[d(v', v) - d(v_j, v)\big]\Big] \\ &= c\big[d(v_{j-1}, v) - d(v_j, v)\big]. \end{aligned} \quad (5)$$

The result follows by comparing (4) and (5).

4.2 Resistance to Attacks and Dark Corners in Collaboration

The content-driven reputation defined by (2) or (3) is susceptible to attacks in which a user controls several user accounts, and coordinates the actions of these accounts in order to increase the reputation of a subset of these accounts; these attacks are broadly known as Sybil attacks or, less formally, sock-puppet attacks [11,12,14,16]. The accounts that are controlled by a user in order to enhance the reputation of the user's main account are known as *sock-puppet* accounts.

A detailed description of defense mechanisms that can be used in content-driven reputation systems against Sybil attacks appeared in [11]. We survey here the main idea, which consists in limiting the amount of reputation that can be gained from an interaction with other users, unless the contribution itself has stood the test of time.

The technique is applicable to the Wikipedia, and to other collaborative systems that, like the Wikipedia, have no "dark corners": all edits are viewed in timely fashion by honest users. More precisely, we say that a collaborative system has no dark corners within time constant T if there is a set U of *good users* such that, for every version v, v has been viewed by a user in U with probability at least $1 - e^{-t/T}$, where t is the time since the version was created. This set of good users must consists of users who are both well-intentioned, and willing to repair vandalism or damage to documents via edits. The Wikipedia, with its *recent-changes patrol* (or RC patrol), feeds of recent edits and page creations, and editors who subscribe to notifications to changes in pages, has no dark corners within a time constant of less than a day. When a collaborative system has no dark corners, a group of users cannot work at length in secrecy, hidden from view: every edit is eventually subjected to the judgement of users that do not belong to the select group.

In collaborative systems with no dark corners, the technique advocated in [11] calls for the author of a version v_j gaining reputation from a future reference version v, via (2), only in two cases:

- the reputation of the author of v is greater than the reputation of the author of v_j;
- the amount of time elapsed between v_j and v is longer than a pre-determined amount T, and for all versions v_i, v_k separated from v by less than time T, and with $i < j < k$, we have $q(v_j \mid v_i, v_k) > 0$.

These conditions ensure that a user can gain reputation only from users of higher reputation, or if no other users objected to the edits performed, for a pre-determined length of time T. Under these two conditions, [11] showed that if a user controls a set V of accounts, the user cannot raise the reputation of any account in U above the maximum $\max\{r(u) \mid u \in V\}$ already held, without performing work that is recognized as useful also by the broader community of users.

This result indicates how patrolling mechanisms such as notification feeds and the RC patrol contribute to the quality of a collaborative system, and how content-driven reputation can leverage such mechanisms and achieve resistance to Sybil attacks.

5 Conclusions

Content-driven notions of edit quality and reputation are well suited to a large class of collaborative editing systems, in which content evolves as a sequence of versions, each version produced by a user edit. These collaborative editing systems are common: examples include wikis, but also contributing to on-line shared documents, contributing to software repositories, collaboratively designing 3D objects, and editing business listings in Google Maps. Content-driven reputation systems provide a notion of user reputation that can be computed objectively, from the evolution of the content itself, without need for asking users for feedback on other user's work.

Two main requirements are needed for obtaining robust content-driven reputation systems. The first requirement is the ability to embed document versions in a metric space, so that the distance between versions is both *effort-preserving* (easy to do changes lead to close versions) and *outcome-preserving* (similar versions are close). Suitable metrics are available for text, and we believe can be developed in a great number of collaborative systems. The second requirement is the presence of patrolling mechanisms that ensure that the system does not have "dark corners" where users can work for a long time in secret, using various schemes to unduly raise their reputation. Under these two conditions, content-driven reputation systems can reward contributors whose work is preserved in the system, and are robust with respect to large categories of attacks, including Sybil attacks.

There is much research that needs to be done in furthering the use of content-driven reputation. One direction of work consists in identifying suitable notions of distance for more general collaborative editing domains. Another direction of work consists in studying the social consensus dynamics that the systems induce. For instance, the reputation-rescaling function f in (2) is used to prevent a class of users from deriving such high values of reputation, that their opinion trumps that of everyone else — creating a "reputation oligarchy". It would be of high interest to study under what conditions systems develop dominating sets of users, who cannot be replaced in spite of the constant influx of new users. A third direction of work consists in studying how to best integrate content-driven reputation with information derived from user-provided feedback and ratings.

References

1. http://git-scm.com
2. http://maps.google.com
3. http://sketchup.google.com/3dwarehouse/
4. http://stackoverflow.com
5. Adler, B.T.: WikiTrust: content-driven reputation for the Wikipedia. Ph.D. Thesis, University of California, Santa Cruz (2012)
6. Adler, B.T., Chatterjee, K., de Alfaro, L., Faella, M., Pye, I.: Assigning trust to Wikipedia content. In: WikiSym 08: Proceedings of the International Symposium on Wikis. ACM Press, New York (2008)

7. Adler, B.T., de Alfaro, L.: A content-driven reputation system for the Wikipedia. In: Proceedings of the 16th International World Wide Web Conference (WWW 2007). ACM Press, New York (2007)
8. Adler, B.T., de Alfaro, L., Mola-Velasco, S.M., Rosso, P., West, A.G.: Wikipedia vandalism detection: combining natural language, metadata, and reputation features. In: Gelbukh, A. (ed.) CICLing 2011, Part II. LNCS, vol. 6609, pp. 277–288. Springer, Heidelberg (2011)
9. Adler, B.T., de Alfaro, L., Pye, I.: Detecting Wikipedia vandalism using WikiTrust. In: PAN Lab Report, CLEF (Conference on Multilingual and Multimodal Information Access Evaluation) (2010)
10. Barabási, A.-L., Albert, R.: Emergence of scaling in random networks. Science **286**(5439), 509–512 (1999)
11. Chatterjee, K., de Alfaro, L., Pye, I.: Robust content-driven reputation. In: First ACM Workshop on AISec, ACM Press, New York (2008)
12. Cheng, A., Friedman, E.: Sybilproof reputation mechanisms. In: Proceedings of the ACM SIGCOMM Workshop on Economics of Peer-to-Peer Systems. ACM Press, New York (2005)
13. Clauset, A., Shalizi, C.R., Newman, M.E.J.: Power-law distributions in empirical data. SIAM Rev. **51**(4), 661–703 (2009)
14. Douceur, J.R.: The sybil attack. In: Druschel, P., Kaashoek, M.F., Rowstron, A. (eds.) IPTPS 2002. LNCS, vol. 2429, pp. 251–260. Springer, Heidelberg (2002)
15. Girvan, M., Newman, M.E.J.: Community structure in social and biological networks. Proc. Nat. Acad. Sci. **99**(12), 7821–7826 (2002)
16. Levine, B.N., Shields, C., Margolin, N.B.: A survey of solutions to the sybil attack. Technical Report 2006–052, University of Massachussets Amherst (2006)
17. Osborne, M.J., Rubinstein, A.: A Course in Game Theory. MIT Press, Cambridge (1994)
18. Sankoff, D., Kruskal, J.B. (eds.): Time Warps, String Edits, and Macromolecules: The Theory and Practice of Sequence Comparison. CSLI Publications, Stanford (1999)

Challenges for Quantitative Analysis of Collective Adaptive Systems

Jane Hillston(✉)

LFCS, School of Informatics, University of Edinburgh, Scotland, UK
jane.hillston@ed.ac.uk

1 Introduction

We are surrounded by both natural and engineered *collective systems*. Such systems include many entities, which interact locally and, without necessarily having any global knowledge, nevertheless work together to create a system with discernible characteristics at the global level; a phenomenon sometimes termed *emergence*. Examples include swarms of bees, flocks of birds, spread of disease through a population, traffic jams and robot swarms. Many of these systems are also *adaptive* in the sense that the constituent entities can respond to their perception of the current state of the system at large, changing their behaviour accordingly. Since the behaviour of the system is comprised of its constituent entities this brings about a change in the system, thus creating a feedback loop. For example, when a disease is spreading epidemically people adjust their behaviour to reduce contact with others; consequently the spread of the disease may diminish.

Increasingly IT systems are being build from large numbers of autonomous or semi-autonomous components which, together with a large population of users, makes a collective system. For example, in Edinburgh bus are equipped with GPS sensors, and bus stops have display boards, which inform users of the likely arrival time of the next bus on various routes. Bus users can choose which route to take for their journey based on the given information. As in this example, collective IT systems are often embedded in our environment and need to operate without centralised control or direction. Moreover when conditions within the system change it may not be feasible to have human intervention to adjust behaviour appropriately. For example, it would be desirable for a major traffic incident that re-routes some buses to be indicated on the information boards. For this to happen in general systems must be able to adapt autonomously.

What we are starting to witness is the establishment of what Robin Milner called the *informatics environment*, in which pervasive computing elements are embedded in the human environment, invisibly providing services and responding to requirements [20]. Such systems are now becoming the reality, and many form collective adaptive systems, in which large numbers of computing elements collaborate to meet the human need. The smart bus system described above is one example, and there are many others in the realm of "Smart Cities"

M. Abadi and A. Lluch Lafuente (Eds.): TGC 2013, LNCS 8358, pp. 14–21, 2014.
DOI: 10.1007/978-3-319-05119-2_2,

where information flows to and from users to enhance access and efficient use of resources.

Performance modelling aims to construct models of the dynamic behaviour of systems in order to support the fair and timely sharing of resources. Performance problems typically arise when there is contention for resources and this can impede the smooth running of a system and lead to user dissatisfaction. In the informatic environment, where the system itself is often almost invisible to the user, it is essential that the possible behaviour is thoroughly explored before systems are deployed. Performance analysis appears in many guises and may more generally be termed *quantitative analysis*, as it encompasses many quantified questions about the dynamic behaviour of systems. For example:

Capacity Planning: how many clients can the existing server support and still maintain reasonable response times? or how many buses do I need in order to maintain service at peak time in a smart urban transport system.

System Configuration: in a mobile phone network how many frequencies do I need in order to keep the blocking probability for new calls low? or what capacity do I need at the stations in a bike sharing scheme in order to minimise the extent to which bikes have to be relocated by truck to meet user demand?

System Tuning: in a flexible manufacturing system, what speed of conveyor belt will minimise robot idle time and maximum throughput whilst avoiding damaged goods? or what strategy can I use to maintain supply-demand balance within a smart electricity grid?

Markovian-based discrete event models have been applied to the performance prediction of computer systems since the mid-1960s and communication systems since the early 20th century. Originally queueing networks were primarily used to construct models, and sophisticated analysis techniques were developed. This approach is challenged by features of modern distributed systems, and there has been a shift towards the use of formal methods, in which formal language are enhanced with quantitative information such as durations and probabilities. Examples include Generalised Stochastic Petri Nets [1], and Stochastic Process Algebras such as EMPA [2], IMC [11] and PEPA [12]. From these high-level system descriptions the underlying mathematical model (Continuous Time Markov Chain (CTMC)) can be automatically generated via the formal semantics.

2 Progress in Recent Years

A key feature of collective systems is the existence of populations of entities who share certain characteristics. Attempts to model such systems without high-level modelling support are likely to be time-consuming and error-prone. In contrast, high-level modelling formalisms allow this repetition to be captured at the high-level rather than explicitly, and often support hierarchical and compositional development of models.

In particular process algebras are well-suited for constructing models of collective adaptive systems (CAS):

- These formal languages were originally developed to represent concurrent behaviour compositionally and CAS are highly concurrent systems.
- The compositional structure of the process algebra allows the interactions between individuals to be captured explicitly. In the context of CAS individuals of the same type may be regarded as a subpopulation with limited interaction between entities but all sharing the same pattern of interaction with other populations.
- Stochastic process algebras (SPAs) provide extensions of classical process algebras that allow the dynamics of system behaviour to be captured; moreover there are established mechanisms to automatically generate an underlying mathematical model from the process algebra description.
- In SPAs such as PEPA, state-dependent functional rates mean that the rate or probability with which an event occurs may depend on the current state of the system and this can allow adaptation to be captured [14].
- The languages are equipped with formal apparatus for reasoning about the behaviour of systems, including equivalence relations, formally defined abstraction mechanisms and mappings to model checkers such as PRISM [16].

As originally defined, an SPA model is equipped with a structured operational semantics which facilitates the automatic generation of a CTMC. In this case the global state of the system is the composition of the local states of all the participating components. When the size of the state space is not too large the CTMC is represented explicitly as an infinitesimal generator matrix, which is an $N \times N$ matrix, where N is the number of distinct states. Based on this matrix and linear algebra the CTMC can be subjected to a numerical solution which determines a steady state or transient probability distribution over all possible states. From this, performance indices such as throughput, utilisation and response time can be derived.

Alternatively the CTMC may be studied using stochastic simulation. This avoids the explicit construction of the entire state space, as states are generated on-the-fly as the simulation runs. Each run generates a single trajectory through the state space. Now, performance indices are derived from measurement of the behaviour of the simulation model and many runs are needed in order to obtain statistically meaningful estimates of performance measures.

Like all discrete state representations, performance modelling formalisms and CTMCs suffer from the problem of *state space explosion*: the mathematical structures required to analyse the system become so large that it is infeasible to carry out the analysis. As the size of the state space becomes large it becomes infeasible to carry out numerical solution of the CTMC and extremely time-consuming to conduct stochastic simulation. This poses a severe challenge for the analysis of collective systems, which by their nature typically contain very large numbers of entities.

The discrete state interpretation of SPA models is focussed on treating the instances of components as individuals. An alternative, more compact representation can be obtained if we move away from capturing each individual but instead work at the level of the subpopulations. This is clearly an abstraction,

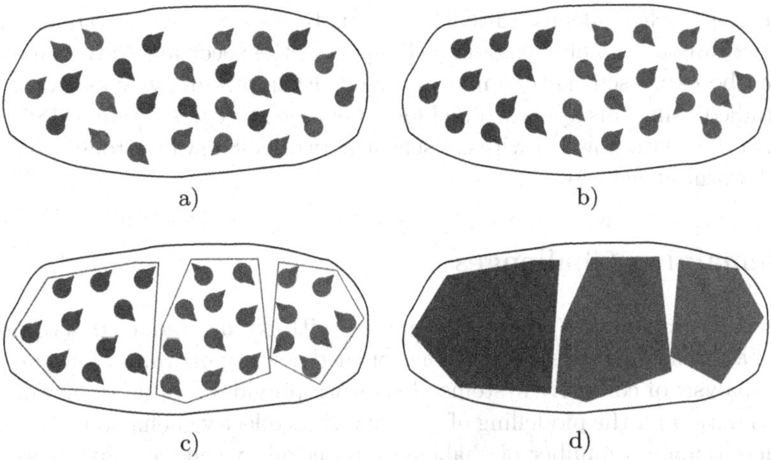

Fig. 1. Schematic representation showing the counting abstraction: a)–b)subpopulations are identified within the CAS; c)–d) rather than explicit counts, these are represented as proportions of the population as a whole.

and some information is lost, but it has the advantage that substantially larger systems can be considered.

The first step of our approach to analysing collective behaviour is to make a *counting abstraction* and view the system not in terms of the individual components but in terms of proportions within the subpopulations [15]. This is shown schematically in Fig. 1.

Initially this produces a *state aggregation*: a more compact discrete representation of the system. A further shift in perspective leads us to consider the evolution of the system as *continuous* rather than discrete. In this case the events in the system are aggregated, and captured by ordinary differential equations which represent the average behaviour of the system, in terms of the proportions of components which exhibit each possible local behaviour or state and how these proportions vary over time [13]. This is termed a *fluid* or *mean field approximation* [4].

Just as the discrete representation of the CTMC can be automatically generated from the structured operational semantics of PEPA models [12], the ODEs which give the fluid approximation of a PEPA model can similarly be derived from structured operational semantics [22]. Moreover the derived vector field $\mathcal{F}(x)$, gives an approximation of the expected count for each population over time and *fluid rewards*, from which performance indices can be derived, can be safely calculated from the fluid expectation trajectories [21]. Furthermore, vector fields have been defined to approximate higher moments [9], such as variance and skew, allowing more accurate estimates of the performance of a system to be derived and more sophisticated measures, such as passage times, can be approximated in an analogous way [10].

This approach is ideally suited to the analysis of collective systems, which would typically overwhelm existing techniques — the necessary state space could not even be expressed, never mind analysed. Examples of systems which have been studied using this approach include an emergency egress system [18], smart buildings [19], data flows in wireless sensor networks [8], swarm robots [17], and internet worm attacks [6].

3 Remaining Challenges

The fluid approximation approach coupled with formal model description in terms of a stochastic process algebra has opened new opportunities for quantified formal analysis of collective systems. This work provides a basic framework and firm foundation for the modelling of systems with collective behaviour. Nevertheless, there remain a number of challenges, especially when we consider systems which also consider adaptive behaviour. In particular, based on our experiences of modelling smart city applications within the QUANTICOL project[1] we would highlight:

- Spatial aspects;
- Richer forms of interaction and adaptation; and
- Extending model checking capabilities.

3.1 Modelling Space

Whilst fluid approximation of SPA models has been successfully used to model collective systems, it should be recognised that there is an implicit assumption within the approach that all components are co-located. This means that all components have the opportunity to interact if their specified behaviour allows it.

However, many collective systems, particularly in the context of smart cities, have behaviour which is partially governed by the spatial arrangement of the components. Interactions may only be allowed for entities which are within a certain physical distance of each other, or space may be segmented in such a way that even physically close entities are unable to communicate. Furthermore movement can be a crucial aspect of the behaviour of entities within the system. Capturing and analysing systems with characteristics like these require that space must be included explicitly within the modelling formalism, and the same component in different locations will be distinguished. This poses significant challenges both of model expression and model solution. There is a danger that as we distinguish subpopulations by their location, we no longer have a large enough population to justify the fluid approximation.

Initial work is exploring the use of time scale decompositions, partial differential equations and diffusion models but much more work is needed.

[1] www.quanticol.eu

3.2 Richer Forms of Interaction and Adaptation

The current work on collective system modelling with stochastic process algebras has made limited use of functional rates to capture adaptation. For example, in the modelling of emergency egress a functional rate is used to represent how occupants might alter their planned route out of the building when they encounter congestion in a stairwell. As this illustrates, a functional rate is able to model adaptation in the form of adjusting the rate or probability of certain events to reflect the current situation. However this is only a limited form of adaptation.

In general, real collective adaptive systems, especially those with emergent behaviour, embody rich forms of interaction, often based on asynchronous communication. An example of this is the pheromone trail left by a social insects such as an ant. In this case the message (pheromone) left by one ant will affect the behaviour of another ant in the same location at a later time. Moreover, the patterns of communication, who can communicate with whom, may change over time according to the state of the system. Languages like SCEL offer these richer communication patterns [7]. In SCEL components include a knowledge store which can be manipulated by the component itself and other components. Communication can then be attribute-based, meaning that a message is sent to all components that have a given value for an attribute.

Again this differentiation through attributes poses a risk to fluid approximation. Accuracy in the fluid approximation relies on having a large enough subpopulation with shared characteristics. Allowing components to have distinct attribute values creates distinguishing features amongst the members of the subpopulations. Within the QUANTICOL project we are exploring ways to overcome these problems.

3.3 Extending Model Checking Capabilities

Whilst many performance measures can be derived using the techniques of fluid rewards, more sophisticated interrogation of a model can be achieved through model checking. In stochastic model checking a suitably enhanced logic, CSL, specifies the query, and leads to a modification of the given CTMC. A naive approach based on fluid approximation would work directly with the vector field, but as this is deterministic this is amenable only to LTL model checking, and gives no indication of the inherent stochasticity in the system.

Recent work on *fluid model checking* develops an analogous approach for collective systems [3]. CSL properties related to a single component can be checked with respect to a population. In this approach the single component is left discrete and combined with a fluid approximation of the rest of the population, giving rise to a inhomogeneous time CTMC. This is then modified as in stochastic model checking, and solved numerically. Whilst effective, this approach can only be used to check the properties of one element of a population. In an alternative approach, based on a central limit approximation, the fraction of a population that satisfies a property expressed as a one-clock deterministic timed automaton can be checked [5]. Future work will seek to extend these to find scalable approaches to model checking global properties of collective systems.

4 Conclusions

Collective Adaptive Systems are an interesting and challenging class of systems to design and construct. Their role within infrastructure, such as within smart cities, make it essential that quantitive aspects of behaviour are taken into consideration, as well as functional correctness. Fluid approximation based analysis offers hope for scalable quantitative analysis techniques, but there remain many interesting and challenging problems to be solved.

Acknowledgement. This work is partially supported by the EU project QUANTICOL, 600708.

References

1. Ajmone Marsan, M., Conte, G., Balbo, G.: A class of generalized stochastic Petri nets for the performance evaluation of multiprocessor systems. ACM Trans. Comput. Syst. **2**(2), 93–122 (1984)
2. Bernardo, M., Gorrieri, R.: A tutorial on EMPA: a theory of concurrent processes with nondeterminism, priorities, probabilities and time. Theor. Comput. Sci. **202**(1–2), 1–54 (1998)
3. Bortolussi, L., Hillston, J.: Checking individual agent behaviours in Markov population models by fluid approximation. In: Bernardo, M., de Vink, E., Di Pierro, A., Wiklicky, H. (eds.) SFM 2013. LNCS, vol. 7938, pp. 113–149. Springer, Heidelberg (2013)
4. Bortolussi, L., Hillston, J., Latella, D., Massink, M.: Continuous approximation of collective system behaviour: A tutorial. Perform. Eval. **70**(5), 317–349 (2013)
5. Bortolussi, L., Lanciani, R.: Model checking Markov population models by central limit approximation. In: Joshi, K., Siegle, M., Stoelinga, M., D'Argenio, P.R. (eds.) QEST 2013. LNCS, vol. 8054, pp. 123–138. Springer, Heidelberg (2013)
6. Bradley, J.T., Gilmore, S.T., Hillston, J.: Analysing distributed Internet worm attacks using continuous state-space approximation of process algebra models. J. Comput. Syst. Sci. **74**(6), 1013–1032 (2008)
7. De Nicola, R., Ferrari, G., Loreti, M., Pugliese, R.: A language-based approach to autonomic computing. In: Beckert, B., Bonsangue, M.M. (eds.) FMCO 2011. LNCS, vol. 7542, pp. 25–48. Springer, Heidelberg (2012)
8. Guenther, M.C., Bradley, J.T.: Mean-field analysis of data flows in wireless sensor networks. In: ACM/SPEC International Conference on Performance, Engineering, ICPE'13, pp. 51–62 (2013)
9. Hayden, R.A., Bradley, J.T.: A fluid analysis framework for a Markovian process algebra. Theor. Comput. Sci. **411**(22–24), 2260–2297 (2010)
10. Hayden, R.A., Stefanek, A., Bradley, J.T.: Fluid computation of passage-time distributions in large Markov models. Theor. Comput. Sci. **413**(1), 106–141 (2012)
11. Hermanns, H. (ed.): Interactive Markov Chains: The Quest for Quantified Quality. LNCS, vol. 2428. Springer, Heidelberg (2002)
12. Hillston, J.: A Compositional Approach to Performance Modelling. Cambridge University Press, Cambridge (2005)
13. Hillston, J.: Fluid flow approximation of PEPA models. In: 2nd International Conference on the Quantitative Evaluaiton of Systems (QEST 2005), pp. 33–43 (2005)

14. Hillston, J., Kloul, L.: Formal techniques for performance analysis: blending SAN and PEPA. Formal Aspects Comput. **19**(1), 3–33 (2007)
15. Hillston, J., Tribastone, M., Gilmore, S.: Stochastic process algebras: from individuals to populations. Comput. J. **55**(7), 866–881 (2012)
16. Kwiatkowska, M.Z., Norman, G., Parker, D.: PRISM: probabilistic model checking for performance and reliability analysis. SIGMETRICS Perform. Eval. Rev. **36**(4), 40–45 (2009)
17. Massink, M., Brambilla, M., Latella, D., Dorigo, M., Birattari, M.: On the use of Bio-PEPA for modelling and analysing collective behaviours in swarm robotics. Swarm Intell. **7**(2–3), 20–228 (2013)
18. Massink, M., Latella, D., Bracciali, A., Harrison, M.D., Hillston, J.: Scalable context-dependent analysis of emergency egress models. Formal Aspects Comput. **24**(2), 267–302 (2012)
19. Massink, M., Harrison, M.D., Latella, D.: Scalable analysis of collective behaviour in smart service systems. In: Proceedings of the 2010 ACM Symposium on Applied Computing (SAC), pp. 1173–1180 (2010)
20. Milner, R.: The Space and Motion of Communicating Agents. Cambridge University Press, Cambridge (2009)
21. Tribastone, M., Ding, J., Gilmore, S., Hillston, J.: Fluid rewards for a stochastic process algebra. IEEE Trans. Softw. Eng. **38**(4), 861–874 (2012)
22. Tribastone, M., Hillston, J., Gilmore, S.: Scalable differential analysis of process algebra models. IEEE Trans. Softw. Eng. **38**(1), 205–219 (2012)

The Scribble Protocol Language

Nobuko Yoshida(✉), Raymond Hu, Rumyana Neykova, and Nicholas Ng

Imperial College London, London, UK
n.yoshida@imperial.ac.uk

Abstract. This paper describes a brief history of how Kohei Honda initiated the Scribble project, and summarises the current status of Scribble.

1 Introduction

Scribble is a language to describe application-level protocols amongm communicating systems. A protocol represents an agreement on how participating systems interact with each other [37,41]. Scribble was born in Paris in December 2006 Kohei Honda took his six month sabbatical. He started writing a seventy-page document of the first version of Scribble [17], based on his experiences as an invited expert for the W3 Web Services Choreography Description (WS-CDL) Working Group [8]. Since 2003, Kohei and the first author (Nobuko Yoshida) had been working for formalising WS-CDL in the π-calculus to guarantee deadlock-free communications by session types. Later, Marco Carbone joined the academic team of WS-CDL. Unexpectedly, it took more than five years for us to understand and formalise their core technologies due to complexity of the description: for example, to describe just a"hello world" protocol, WS-CDL requires the definition of Participant Types, Rolem Types, Relationship Types, Channel Types, Information Types, Tokens, Token Locators and finally Sequences with an Interaction and Exchange. During this work, Kohei proposed a much simpler, abstract version of choreography, which only focuses on signatures (or types) of CDLs. This is the origin of Scribble. He sent his first seventy-page draft to his close industry colleagues by e-mail together with his motivation:

> *Scribbling is necessary for architects, either physical or computing, since all great ideas of architectural construction come from that unconscious moment, when you do not realise what it is, when there is no concrete shape, only a whisper which is not a whisper, an image which is not an image, somehow it starts to urge you in your mind, in so small a voice but how persistent it is, at that point you start scribbling.*

This draft encouraged two of the members of WS-CDL WG, Gary Brown and Steve-Ross Talbot, to design and implement Scribble through Pi4 Technologies Foundations [35], collaborating with Kohei. The second version of Scribble document was written in collaboration with Brown in October 2007.

Interestingly, Scribble gave clues to solving the main theoretical open problem of the session type theory repeatedly posed by researchers and industry

M. Abadi and A. Lluch Lafuente (Eds.): TGC 2013, LNCS 8358, pp. 22–41, 2014.
DOI: 10.1007/978-3-319-05119-2_3,

partners at that time: that is whether original *binary* sessions [20,39] can be extended to *multiparty sessions*. This is a natural question since most business protocols and parallel computations in practice involve multiparty communications. Honda, Yoshida and Carbone formalised the essence of Scribble as the multiparty session type theory (MPST) in the π-calculus, and published in [22]. Since then Kohei has worked with several standardisation bodies [2,42] and open source communities [34,38]. Red Hat opened a new JBoss Project, Scribble [37]. More details about a history of his collaborations with the industry partners can be found in [19,21]. His last paper, which was mostly written by himself, is about Scribble [18].

The aims of this paper are to record his first draft [17] and to show the current status of Scribble project. Section 2 summarises the first version of Scribble draft; Sect. 3 outlines Scribble framework and its Python implementation; Sect. 4 discusses an extension of Scribble for subprotocols and interrupts; Sect. 5 shows another extension of Scribble for high-performance computations; Sect. 6 gives future works and Sect. 7 concludes.

2 Preamble of the First Scribble Document

This section presents extracts from the preamble of the first Scribble document as originally written in [17], and remarks how these initial ideas have been carried out.

2.1 Conversations and Protocols

This document presents concrete description examples of various interaction scenarios written in the first layer of Scribble (from [17, Sect. 1.1]). Scribble is a language for describing the structures and behaviours of communicating processes at a high level of abstraction, offering an intuitive and expressive syntax built on a rigorous mathematical basis. While the language can potentially be used for many purposes, our initial primary application area is description, validation and execution of the whole class of financial protocols and applications which use them.

Our central philosophy in designing Scribble, as a high-level language for describing communication-centred applications, is to enable description which is free from implementation details but which allows efficient and flexible implementation. The key idea to achieve these seemingly contradictory requirements is the use of the unit of abstraction called "conversation," known as *session* in the literature on theories of processes and programming languages.

A conversation in the present context means a series of interactions among two or more participants which follow a prescribed scenario of interactions. This scenario is the type (signature) of that conversation which we call *protocol*. A protocol is a minimal structure which guarantees type-safety of conversations, and has been known as *session. type* [7,14,20,25,43] in theories of processes which in turn is based on theories of types for programming languages [36]. At runtime, a conversation is established among its participants, and the participants get engaged in communications in its context following a stipulated protocol.

A single distributed application may be engaged in two or more conversations, even simultaneously. For example, during a commercial transaction, an application running for a merchant may be engaged in two conversations at the same time, one for a credit transfer and another for a debit transfer protocol. Another example is a travel agency who interacts with its customer electronically following a certain protocol and, to meet the demands of the customer, interacts with other service providers (for example airline companies), each following a distinct protocol. The agency's conversation with its customer and those with other services will interleave.

We specify a protocol using a type language of Scribble (just as types in ML are specified using a type language of ML). This type language constitutes the most abstract level of the description layers in Scribble. On its basis, the immediately upper layer of description defines what we call *conversation models* (which correspond to class models in UML). Conversation models serve many purposes including a foundation for a design-by-contract (DBC) framework, which starts from augmenting conversation models with assertions written in a logical language. Further we have languages for describing detailed behaviour, reaching executable descriptions, some of which may as well take the form of integration with existing programming languages. These languages as a whole contribute to flexible and comprehensive descriptions of the structure of message exchange (choreography) among communicating agents. Example descriptions in some of these languages will be treated in the sequels to the present note.

The language for protocols is the most abstract and terse: at the same time, it is also a rich description language for conversation scenarios, as well as offering a basis for the remaining layers. Protocols are also a basis of diverse forms of static and dynamic validation. Thus understanding this language is the key to understanding the present description framework as a whole.

2.2 Applications

The first and foremost objectives of Scribble is to allow scribbling of structures of interactions intuitively and unambiguously (from [17, Sect. 1.2]). Just like we are sure what is the intended behaviour of our programs and models for sequential computation, we want to be sure what our description for interactional applications means in a simple and intuitive syntax.

Scribble is based on theories of processes, in particular the π-calculus [27–29]. This is not a place to discuss the nature of this theoretical basis but it is worth noting that this theory enables us to mathematically identify what is the (interactional) "behaviour" embodied in a given description. Thus we can rigorously stipulate what each description means. While the meaning of sequential programs is relatively intuitive to capture, this may not be so for interactional software: thus this theory pins down the tenet of descriptions of interactional behaviour, bootstrapping all endeavours in the present enterprise.

Another theoretical underpinning of the design of Scribble is the study on session types [7,14,20,25,43] mentioned already, which present in-depth study of type languages for conversations and their use in static validation, abstraction concerns and runtime architecture.

Starting from clarity and precision in description, Scribble (together with its theoretical basis) is intended to be used for several purposes, some of which we summarise in the following.

- Describe protocols of conversations for applications clearly, intuitively and precisely; statically validate if the resulting descriptions are consistent; with unambiguous shared understanding on the meaning of resulting descriptions.
- Generate code prototypes and associated runtime parameters (e.g. an FSA (Finite State Machines) for monitoring) from stipulated protocols, with a formal guarantee that code/data exactly conform to the protocols.
- Describe conversation scenarios of a distributed application which use these protocols, as conversation models. Statically validate if the resulting models use protocols correctly, as well as other significant properties.
- Elaborate protocols and conversation models with assertions (logical formulae) to specify their properties, for enriched behavioural constraints/models.
- Develop (and debug) endpoint applications which realise given conversation models with incremental validation that the resulting programs conform to the stipulated protocols and conversation models.
- Statically validate if the applications have specific desirable properties (such as deadlock-freedom) leveraging high-level conversation structures.
- Dynamically validate (monitor) if runtime message exchanges of an application precisely follow the stipulated protocols/models: with a formal guarantee that all and only violations of the stipulated scenario are detected; automatically generate such a monitor from protocols/conversation models.
- Offer a tractable and unambiguous specification of software tools and infrastructure needed for achieving these goals.

We note that the central point of having a theoretical basis in Scribble is first of all to allow these ideas themselves (for example validation) to "make sense": we can share clearly what they mean and what they do not mean. And all of this should be built on the clarity of the behavioural description in the first place.

2.3 Remarks on the Preamble

The preamble ends with a "Caution" subsection. Kohei explicitly noted that "this compilation only lists *signatures* (or *types*) for conversations, *not* direct behavioural description. While it may look we are describing dynamic behaviour, what is indeed described is the static structure underlying dynamic behaviour, just as signature in class models extracts the static core of dynamic behaviour of objects." This became the basis for establishing a theory of multiparty session types [22]. In the rest of the document, the presentation is organised centring on concrete examples (use cases) described in Scribble. There are 29 divided into 11: the last section treats fairly complex examples from real world financial protocols. Many examples were obtained from his industry partners working in financial IT, which became valuable sources to not only implement Scribble but also extend the original theory [22]. For example, the work on exceptions [6], subsessions [10], dynamic multiroles [11] and asynchronous messaging optimisation [30] directly tackled the examples in [17]. Their results are reflected in the subsequent designs and updates of Scribble, as discussed in the next section. From the list of the applications in Sect. 2.2, we can observe that Kohei had a clear vision how Scribble should be used in future: in 2007, Kohei had even not known the Ocean Observatories Initiative [34] (cf. Sect. 3), but he had already an idea to apply Scribble for dynamic verification via generations of FSAs. About code generation, the Scribble team is currently working for generating type-safe, deadlock-free parallel algorithm implementations from Scribble (cf. Sect. 5). A conversation model mentioned in Sect. 2.1 is formalised as the DBC of MPSTs in [5] and its application to Scribble is on-going (cf. Logical Annotations in Sect. 6). The rest of the paper explains how the Scribble team has been working and developing Scribble, following his initial predictions.

3 Scribble

This section first describes the stages of the Scribble framework, explaining the design challenges of applying session types to practice and recent research threads motivated by this work. We then illustrate an example protocol specification in the Scribble language, and list a couple of extensions.

3.1 The Scribble Framework

The Scribble project [18,19,37,41] is a collaboration between session types researchers and architects and engineers from industry [26,38] towards the application of session types principles and techniques to current engineering practices. Building on the theory of multiparty session types [3,22] (MPST), this ongoing work tackles the challenges of adapting and implementing session types to meet real-world usage requirements. This section gives an overview of the current version of the Scribble framework for the MPST-based development of distributed software. In the context of Scribble, we use the terms *session* and *conversation* interchangeably.

The main elements of the Scribble framework, outlined in Fig. 1, are as follows.

The Scribble Language is a platform-independent description language for the *specification* of asynchronous, multiparty message passing protocols [18,19, 40]. Scribble may be used to specify protocols from both the global (neutral) perspective and the local perspective of a particular participant (abstracted as a role); at heart, the Scribble language is an engineering incarnation of the notation for global and local types in formal MPST systems and their correctness conditions.

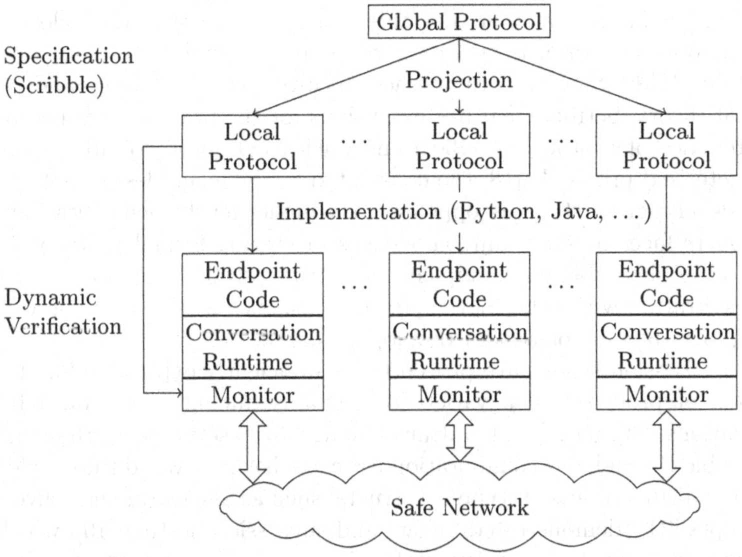

Fig. 1. The Scribble framework for distributed software development Scribble methodology from global specification to local runtime verification

The Scribble Conversation API provides the local communication operations for *implementing* the endpoint programs for each role natively in various mainstream languages. The current version of Scribble supports Java [37] and Python [26] Conversation APIs with both standard socket-like and event-driven interfaces for initiating and conducting conversations.

The Scribble Runtime is a local platform library for executing Scribble endpoint programs written using the Conversation API. The Runtime includes a conversation monitoring service for *dynamically verifying* [4,24,31] the interactions performed by the endpoint against the local protocol for its role in the conversation. In addition to internal monitors at the endpoints, Scribble also supports the deployment of external conversation monitors within the network [9].

3.2 Development Challenges of Scribble

The Scribble development workflow starts from the explicit specification of the required global protocols, similarly to the existing, informally applied approaches based on prose documentation, such as Internet protocol RFCs, and common graphical notations, such as UML and sequence diagrams. Designing an engineering language from the formal basis of MPST types faces the following challenges.

- To developers, Scribble is a new language to be learned and understood, particularly since most developers are not accustomed to formal protocol

specification in this manner. For this reason, we have worked closely with our collaborators towards making Scribble protocols easy to read, write and maintain. Aside from the core interaction constructs that are grounded in the original theory, Scribble features extensions for the practical engineering and maintenance of protocol specifications, such as subprotocol abstraction and parameterised protocols [18] (demonstrated in the examples below).
- As a development step (as opposed to a higher-level documentation step), developers face similar coding challenges in writing formal protocol descriptions as in the subsequent implementation steps. IDE support for Scribble and integration with other development tools, such as the Java-based tooling in [37], are thus important for developer uptake.
- Although session types have proven to be sufficiently expressive for the specification of protocols in a variety of domains, including standard Internet applications [23], parallel algorithms [33] and Web services [8], the evaluation of Scribble through our collaboration use cases has motivated the development of new multiparty session type constructs, such as asynchronous conversation interrupts [24] (demonstrated below) and subsession nesting [10], which were not supported by the pre-existing theory.

The Scribble framework combines the elements discussed before to promote the MPST-based methodology for distributed software development depicted in Fig. 1. Scribble resources are available from the project home pages [37, 41].

3.3 Online Travel Agency Example

To demonstrate Scribble as a multiparty session types language, Fig. 2 lists the Scribble specification of the global protocol for an Online Travel Agency example (a use case from [1]).

In this example, there are three interacting roles, named Customer, Agency and Service, that establish a session.

1. Customer is planning a trip through a Travel Agency. Each query from Customer includes the journey details, abstracted as a message of type *String*, to which the Agency answers with the price of the journey, abstracted as a message of type *Int*. This query is repeated until Customer decides either `ACCEPT` or `REJECT` the quote.
2. If Customer decides to `ACCEPT` a travel quote from Agency, Agency relays a confirmation to Service, which represents the transport service being brokered by Agency. Then Customer and Service exchanges the address details (a message of type *String*) and the ticket dispatch date (a message of type *Date*).
3. If Customer decides to `REJECT` a travel quote from Agency, Agency sends a termination signal to Service to end the interaction.

```
1 module TravelAgency;
2
3 type <py> "types.IntType" from "types.py" as Int;
4 type <py> "types.StringType" from "types.py" as String;
5 type <py> "travelagency.Date" from "Date.py" as Date;
6
7 global protocol BookJourney(role Customer as C,
8       role Agency as A, role Service as S) {
9   rec LOOP {
10    choice at C {
11      query(journey:String) from C to A;
12      price(Int) from A to C;
13      info(String) from A to S;
14      continue LOOP;
15    } or {
16      choice at C {
17        ACCEPT() from C to A;
18        ACCEPT() from A to S;
19        Address(String) from C to S;
20        (Date) from S to C;
21      } or {
22        REJECT() from C to A;
23        REJECT() from A to S;
24 } } } }
```

Fig. 2. A Scribble specification of a global protocol for the Online Travel Agency use case

The Scribble is read as follows:

- The first line declares the Scribble module name. Although this example is self-contained within a single module, Scribble code may be organised into a conventional hierarchy of packages and modules. Importing payload type and protocol declarations between modules is useful for factoring out libraries of common payload types and subprotocols.
- The design of the Scribble language focuses on the specification of protocol *structures*. With regards to the payload data that may be carried in the exchanged messages, Scribble is designed to work orthogonally with external message format specifications and data types from other languages. The `type` declaration on Line 3 a payload type using the Python data format, specifically the `IntType` definition from the file `types.py`, aliased as `Int` within this Scribble module. Data type formats from other languages, as well as XML or various IDL based message formats, may be used similarly. A single protocol definition may feature a mixture of message types defined by different formats.
- Lines 7–8 the signature of a global protocol called `BookJourney`. This protocol involves three roles, `Customer`, `Agency` and `Service`, aliased as `C`, `A` and `S`, respectively.

- Lines 9–24 the interaction structure of the protocol. Line 11 a basic message passing action. `query(journey:String)` is a message signature for a message with header (label) `journey`, carrying one payload element within the parentheses. A payload element is an (optional) annotation followed by a colon and the payload type, e.g. `journey` details are recorded in a `String`. This message is to be dispatched by `C` to be received by `A`.
- The outermost construct of the protocol body is the `rec` block with label `Loop`. Similarly to labelled blocks in e.g. Java, the occurrence of a `continue` for the same label within the block causes the flow of the protocol to return to the start of the block. The first `choice` within the `rec`, decided by `C`, is to obtain another quote (lines 11–14: send `A` the `query` details, receive a `price`, and `continue` back to the start), or to accept/reject a quote. The latter is given by the inner `choice`, with `C` sending `ACCEPT` to `A` in the first case and `REJECT` in the second. In the case of `ACCEPT` (lines 17–20), `A` forwards the confirmation to `S` before `C` and `S` exchange `Address` and `Date` messages; otherwise, `A` forwards the `REJECT` to `S` instead.

3.4 Scribble Projection and Verification

After the specification of the global protocols, the next step of the Scribble framework (Fig. 1) is the *projection* of local protocols from the global protocol for each role. In comparison to languages implemented from binary session types, such as Sing# [16] and SJ [23], this additional step is required to derive local specifications for the endpoint implementation of each role process from the central global protocol specification. Scribble projection follows the standard MPST algorithmic projections, with extensions for the additional features of Scribble, such as the subprotocols and conversation interrupts mentioned above [40].

Figure 3 lists the local protocol generated by the Scribble tools [41] as the projection of the `BookJourney` for the `Customer` role, as identified in the local protocol. signature. Projection preserves the dependencies of the global protocol, such as the payload types used, and the core interaction structures in which the target role is involved, e.g. the `rec` and `choice` blocks, as well as payload annotations and similar protocol details. The well-formedness conditions on global protocols allow the projection to safely discard all message actions not involving `C` (i.e. messages between `A` and `S`).

As for the binary session languages cited above, it is possible to statically type check role implementations written in endpoint languages with appropriate MPST programming primitives against the local protocols following the standard MPST theory: if the endpoint program for every role is correct, then the correctness of the whole multiparty system is guaranteed. The endpoint languages used in the Scribble industry projects, however, are mainstream engineering languages like Java and Python that lack the features, such as first-class communication channels with linear resource typing or object alias restriction, required to make static session typing feasible. In Scribble practice, the Conversation API (see Sect. 3.5) is used to perform the relevant conversation operations natively in these languages, making static MPST type checking intractable. In general,

```
module TravelAgency_BookJourney_Customer;

type <py> "types.IntType" from "types.py" as Int;
type <py> "types.StringType" from "types.py" as String;
type <py> "travelagency.Date" from "Date.py" as Date;

local protocol BookJourney_Customer at Customer
      (role Customer as C, role Agency as A,
       role Service as S) {
  rec LOOP {
    choice at C {
      query(journey:String) to A;
      price(Int) from A;
      continue LOOP;
    } or {
      choice at C {
        ACCEPT() to A;
        Address(String) to S;
        (Date) from S;
      } or {
        REJECT() to A;
} } } }
```

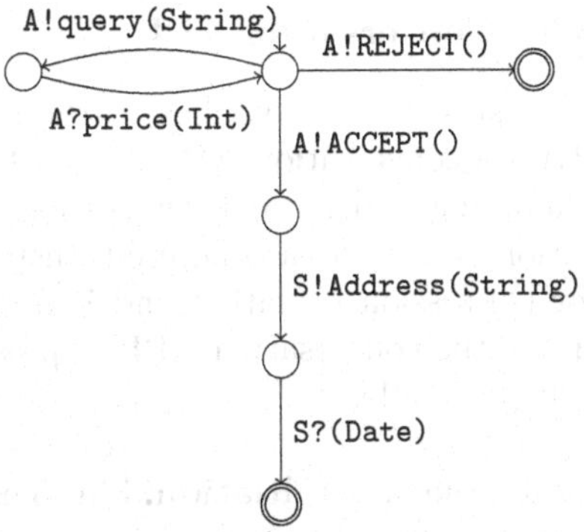

Fig. 3. (a) Scribble local protocol for `Customer` projected from the `BookJourney` global protocol, and (b) the FSA generated from the local protocol by the Scribble conversation monitor

distributed systems are often implemented in a mixture of languages, including dynamically typed languages (e.g. Python), and techniques such as event-driven programming, for which the static verification of strong safety properties is acknowledged to be difficult.

For these reasons, the Scribble framework, differently to the above session languages, is designed to focus on *dynamic verification* of endpoint behaviour [24]. Endpoint monitoring by the local Conversation Runtime is performed by converting local protocols to communicating finite state automata, for which the accepted languages correspond to the I/O action traces permitted by the protocol. The conversion from syntactic Scribble local protocols to FSA extends the algorithm in [12] to support subprotocols and interrupts, and to use nested FSM (Finite State Machine) for parallel conversation threads to avoid the potential state explosion from constructing their product. Figure 3 depicts the FSA generated by the monitor from the `Customer` local protocol. The FSA encodes the control flow of the protocol, with transitions corresponding to the valid I/O actions that `C` may perform at each state of the protocol.

Analogously to the static typing scenario, if every endpoint is monitored to be correct, the same communication-safety property is guaranteed [4]. In addition, since the monitor verifies both messages dispatched by the endpoint into the network and the messages inbound to the endpoint from the network, each conversation monitor is able to protect the local endpoint within an untrusted network and vice versa. The internal monitors embedded into each Conversation runtime function perform synchronous monitoring (the actions of the endpoint are verified synchronously as they are performed); Scribble supports mixed configurations between internal endpoint monitors and asynchronous, external monitors deployed within the network (as well as statically verified endpoints, where possible) [9].

3.5 Conversation API

This subsection describes Python endpoint implementation of Scribble. The Python conversation API offers a high level interface for safe conversation programming and maps basic session calculus primitives to lower-level communication actions on a concrete transport. In short, the API provides functionality for (1) session initiation and joining and (2) basic send/receive. Figure 4 illustrates the conversation API by presenting an implementation in Python of the Customer role.

Conversation Initiation. Line 5 initialises a new session, using the class named `Conversation`. When creating a session, we specify the protocol name `BookJourney` and a configuration file, holding the network addresses for all roles.

`Conversation.create` creates a fresh conversation id and sends an invitation message for each role specified in the protocol. The invitation mechanism is needed to map the role names to concrete addressable entities on the network and to propagate this mapping to all participants. In Line 6, after initialisation, the process joins (`joins`) the session as Customer role. By `conv.join`, it returns a

```
1  class Customer:
2    customer, A, S = ['customer', 'agency', 'service']
3
4    def book_journey(self):
5      conv = Conversation.create('BookJourney', 'config.yml')
6      with conv.join(customer, "\\address...") as c:
7        for place in self.destinations:
8          c.send(A, 'query', place)
9          msg = c.recv(A)
10
11         if msg.value<=self.budget()
12           c.send(A, 'ACCEPT')
13           c.send(A, 'Address', 'SE2 6UF')
14           date = c.recv(S)
15           self.save_the_day(date)
16           return
17
18       c.send(A, 'REJECT')
```

Fig. 4. Python implementation of Customer role

communication channel `c` to be used for the message exchange during the session. The explicit use of a conversation channel `c` in the program makes it possible to build the application logic with a clear understanding on the session control flow.

The next part of the code iterates over a list of travel destinations, following the interaction flow specified in the `BookJourney` protocol in Fig. 3. In each iteration Customer sends a message to `A` (line 8) and then it receives a reply (line 9) from `A` with the price for the booking. Then Customer can end the session in two ways: (1) tf the price for a `place` (`msg.value`) is acceptable (line 11), Customer completes the booking by sending an `ACCEPT` message (line 12) to `A`; (2) if none of the prices are good, Customer sends `REJECT` message (line 18) to `A` and the session ends.

Conversation Message Passing. The primitives for sending and receiving specify the name of the sender and receiver role respectively. All messages are sent or received as a tuple of an operation and a payload, accessible via the message attributes `op` and `value`. The API does not mandate how the operation field should be treated and allows the runtime freedom to interpret the operation name in various ways, e.g. as a plain message label, an RMI method name, etc.. A syntactic sugar such as an automatic dispatch on method calls based on the message operation is possible. The sending operation is asynchronous, meaning that a basic send does not block on the corresponding receive; however, the basic receive does block until the complete message has been received.

4 Extensions of Scribble: Subprotocols and Interrupts

The following gives two further examples to demonstrate additional features of Scribble motivated by application in practice.

The first example demonstrates the abstraction of protocol declarations as *subprotocols*, and the related feature of protocol declarations *parameterised* on payload types and message signatures. Figure 5 gives an alternative specification for the Travel Agency example that is decomposed into four smaller global protocols.

`ServiceCall` specifies a generic call-return pattern between a `Client` and a `Server`. The message signatures of the two communications are abstracted by the `Arg` and `Res` parameters, declared by the `sig` keyword inside the angle brackets of the protocol signature.

`Forward` specifies a generic forwarding pattern between three roles, from `X` to `Y` and then `Y` to `Z`. The intent is for `Y` to forward a copy of the same message, so the signatures of the two communications are abstracted by the same `M` parameter.

`CustomerOptions` is the main protocol in this version of the Travel Agency specification, with the same signature as `BookJourney` in Fig. 2. It starts with the `choice` of `C` to get another quote, to accept a quote or reject. The main interactions are now built by composing instances of the `Forward` and `ServiceCall`

```
1  global protocol CustomerOptions
2        (role Customer as C, role Agency as A, role Service as S) {
3    choice at C {
4      do GetQuote(C as Customer, A as Agency);
5    } or {
6      do Forward<ACCEPT()>(C as X, A as Y, S as Z);
7      do ServiceCall<Address(String), (Date)>(C as Client, S as Server);
8    } or {
9      do Forward<REJECT()>(C as X, A as Y, S as Z);
10 } }
11
12 global protocol GetQuote
13       (role Customer as C, role Agency as A, role Service as S) {
14   do ServiceCall<query(String), price(Int)>
15                      (C as Client, A as Server);
16   info(String) from A to S;
17   do CustomerOptions(C as Customer, A as Agency, S as Service);
18 }
19
20 global protocol ServiceCall<sig Arg, sig Res>
21       (role Client as C, role Server as S) {
22   Arg from C to S;
23   Res from S to C;
24 }
25
26 global protocol Forward<sig M>(role X, role Y, role Z) {
27   M from X to Y;
28   M from Y to Z;
29 }
```

Fig. 5. Decomposition of the BookJourney global protocol using subprotocols with message signature parameters

subprotocols. For example, do Forward<ACCEPT()>(C as X, A as Y, S as Z) on Line 6 states that the Forward protocol should be performed with the target roles X, Y and Z played by C, A and S, respectively, and ACCEPT() as the concrete message signature in place of the M parameter; C sends ACCEPT to A, who forwards it to S. After this, C and S engage in a ServiceCall subprotocol to exchange the Address and Date messages.

GetQuote performs the quote query case of the choice between C and A, and loops back to the overall start of the protocol. The quote exchange is specified by instantiating the ServiceCall with the appropriate role and message signature parameters. To return to the start of the protocol, we recursively do the main protocol CustomerOptions. The loop is thus specified by the mutual recursion between these two protocol declarations.

The final example demonstrates the Scribble feature for asynchronously interruptible conversations. Unlike the previous features, which involve the

```
global protocol InterruptServiceCall(role Client as C, role Server as S) {
  Arg from C to S;
  interruptible {
    Res from S to C;
  } with {
    cancel() by C;
} }
```

Fig. 6. Revision of the `ServiceCall` global protocol with a request cancel interrupt

integration of session types with useful, general programming language features (code abstraction and parameterisation), conversation interrupts require extensions to the core design of session types [24]. The motivation for interrupts comes from our collaboration use cases, featuring patterns such as asynchronously interruptible streams and interaction timeouts [26], which could not be directly expressed in the standard MPST formulations.

Figure 6 gives a very simple revision of the `ServiceCall` protocol that allows the `Client` to `cancel` the call by interrupting the `Server`'s reply. A key design point is that interruptible conversation segments do not incur any additional synchronisation over the explicit messaging actions (i.e. interrupts are themselves communicated as regular messages). Due to asynchrony between `C` and `S`, the interrupt can cause various communication race conditions to arise, e.g. `C` sending `cancel` before `S` processes the initial `Arg` or after `S` has already dispatched the `Res`. The Scribble Runtime is designed to handle these issues by tracking the progress of the local endpoint through the protocol (as part of the monitoring service). This allows the Runtime to resolve the communication races by discarding messages that are no longer relevant due to the local role raising an interrupt or receiving an interrupt message from another role.

5 Extensions of Scribble: Parameterised Scribble

This section presents Parameterised Scribble (*Pabble*) [32]. Pabble extends Scribble roles with indices, such that each role can represent multiple Scribble participants, and each of the participants can be addressed by its index. This extension is a result of applying Scribble to parallel programming, where programs are designed in a way that they can be scaled up to any number of participants, depending on parameters supplied at execution time. Figure 7 shows a simple Map-Reduce protocol in Pabble. This protocol distributes data from one participant (`Worker[0]`) to all other participants (`Workers`, which is a group role shorthand for `Worker[0..N]`), followed by a parallel reduction on the `Sum` operation. The results are sent to `Worker[0]`.

Parallel programming with Pabble starts by defining the global protocol. The global protocol is projected into endpoint protocols. However, in contrast to Scribble endpoint protocols, where a single global protocol will be projected to the same number of endpoint protocols as the number of participants, a Pabble

```
1 global protocol MapReduce(role Worker[0..N], group Workers={Worker[0..N]}){
2   rec MOREDATA {
3     Map(int) from Worker[0] to Workers;
4     Sum(int) from Workers to Worker[0];
5     continue MOREDATA;
6 } }
```

Fig. 7. MapReduce protocol in Pabble.

```
1  int main(int argc, char *argv[])
2  {
3    int rank, size;
4    MPI_Comm_rank(MPI_COMM_WORLD, &rank);
5    MPI_Comm_size(MPI_COMM_WORLD, &size); /* = N+1 */
6    // ... Setting up of data and custom communicators ...
7    MPI_Init(&argc, &argv);
8    while (/* moreData() */) {
9     MPI_Scatter(sndbuf0, sndcnt0, MPI_INT,
10                rcvbuf0, rcvcnt0, MPI_INT,
11                0/*Worker[0]*/, Workers_COMM);
12    MPI_Reduce(sndbuf1, rcvbuf1, count1,
13               MPI_INT, MPI_SUM, 0/*Worker[0]*/, Workers_COMM);
14   }
15   MPI_Finalize();
16   // ... Freeing memory and destroying custom communicators ...
17   return EXIT_SUCCESS;
18 }
```

Fig. 8. MapReduce protocol in MPI.

global protocol will convert to a single endpoint protocol. The endpoint protocol represents multiple endpoints grouped together. The details of the projection algorithm are explained in [32].

Then endpoint protocols are used to generate MPI (Message-Passing Interface) code, which makes up communication parts of the parallel application. An example MPI backbone code generated from the `MapReduce` protocol is given in Fig. 8. In Fig. 8, `Workers_COMM` is a custom MPI communicator, which groups together all processes from process id (called *rank*) `0` to `N`. This is declared in the Pabble protocol on Line 1, `group Workers = {Worker[0..N]}`. Line 9 of Fig. 8 corresponds to a map operation, which distributes data from the process with rank `0` (7 parameter of `MPI_Scatter`) to all other processes in `Workers_COMM`. Similarly, Line 12 of Fig. 8 is the reduction operation, collecting results of applying `MPI_SUM` to pairs of participants to the process with rank `0` (6th parameter of `MPI_Reduce`).

The significance of Pabble lies in the ability to represent scalable protocols, thus it is very useful in representing protocols used in high performance computing, involving hundreds of thousands process units (or participants) with relatively little effort. In Fig. 7, the protocol is designed such that `Worker` can be an arbitrary number of participants (`N`). In the generated implementation in Fig. 8, `size` on Line 5 represents the total number of processes, and this number is given at execution time by the MPI environment via a command line argument. The rest of the program body adapts based on `size` during the execution, for example, `MPI_Scatter` distributes data to all `N` processes, whatever the value of `N` is.

6 Future Work

The development of the Scribble framework and its application in real-world use cases is ongoing work. The two main use case projects mentioned above are:

Savara [38] is JBoss project developed by Red Hat and employed in a commercial setting by a Cognizant business unit [15]. Savara relies on Scribble as an intermediate language for representing protocols, to which high-level notations, such as BPMN2, are translated to perform endpoint projections and various refactoring tasks. Savara provides a suite of tools for testing of service specifications against the initial project requirements. The testing is based on simulations between the former, represented in Scribble, and the latter, expressed as sequence diagram traces.

The Ocean Observatories Initiative [34] is an NSF-funded project to develop the infrastructure for the remote, real-time acquisition and delivery of data from a large sensor network deployed in ocean environments to users at research institutions. The Scribble framework, including Conversation Runtime monitoring, has been integrated into the Python-based OOI platform. So far, the OOI cyberinfrastructure is mainly running on an RPC-based architecture. The current Scribble integration is accordingly primarily used for the specification of RPC service and application protocols, and the dynamic verification of the Python client/server endpoints.

Below, we summarise some of the active threads in regards to these projects.

Expressivity The Savara project is examining formal encodings between the specification languages commonly used in practice and Scribble (the current translation by Savara is not yet formalised), which is motivating further extensions to Scribble, such as dynamic introduction of roles during a conversation and fork-join conversation patterns. In general, adapting MPST and Scribble to graphical representations will increase the expressiveness of the protocol specification language. Using the native semantics of formal graphical formats for concurrency, such as communication automata [12,13] and Petri nets, to provide global execution models of conversations is an interesting direction for integrating Scribble protocol specifications with specifications of other system aspects, such as internal endpoint workflows.

Logical Annotations The current phase of the OOI project includes the development of a framework for actor-based interactions over the existing service infrastructure. To support the specification and verification of higher-level application properties above the core message passing protocol, Scribble is being extended with a framework for annotating protocols with assertions and policies in third-party languages. Annotations may be associated to individual messages, interaction steps, control flow structures, roles or protocols as a whole; examples range from basic constraints on specific message values and control flow (e.g. recursion bounds) to more complicated logics for security or contractual obligations of roles. The Scribble framework will accept plugins for parsing and projecting the annotation language, and evaluating the annotations at run-time. This allows the Scribble tools and monitors to be extended modularly with application- and domain-specific annotations, and the dynamic verification approach enables the enforcement of properties that would be difficult or impossible to verify statically without conservative restrictions.

Endpoint Implementations The Savara and OOI use cases implement the Scribble language, meaning the syntax, well-formedness (valid protocol) conditions and projections, as defined by the central language reference [41]. Both implementations also necessarily conform to baseline communication model of Scribble, namely asynchronous but reliable and role-to-role ordered messaging. The Scribble project is currently working on defining an accompanying Conversation Runtime specification. This will provide the reference for Scribble runtime libraries and platforms, including the specification of the key system protocols for conversation initiation, message formats (conversation and monitoring message meta data) and more advanced features such as conversation delegations [25]. This work is towards full interoperability of Scribble endpoints running on different platforms, such as the Java and Python platforms of the above use cases, supported by platform-independent monitoring. This interoperability will also extend to safely combining dynamically and statically verified endpoints within conversations.

7 Conclusion

While the Scribble project is actively proceeding with our collaborators, it is hardly believable that Kohei Honda cannot work anymore in this project. We conclude our paper with some words from Ocean Observatories Initiative Cyber Infrastructure Team (OOI-CI) [34] to Kohei:

A Rare Cluster of Qualities: *Kohei has lead us deep into the nature of communication and processing. His esthetics, precision and enthusiasm for our mutual pursuit of formal Session (Conversation) Types and specifically for our OOI collaboration to realize this vision in very concrete terms were, as penned by Henry James, lessons in seeing the nuances of both beauty and craft, through a rare cluster of qualities – curiosity, patience and perception; all at the perfect pitch of passion and expression.*

Acknowledgements. We thank Gary Brown for his comments. The work has been partially sponsored by the Ocean Observatories Initiative, VMware, EPSRC KTS under Cognizant, and EPSRC EP/K011715/1, EP/K034413/1 EP/G015635/1.

References

1. Web Services Choreography Description Language: Primer 1.0. http://www.w3.org/TR/ws-cdl-10-primer/
2. Advanced Message Queueing Protocols. www.amqp.org/confluence/display/AMQP/Advanced+Message+Queuing+Protocol
3. Bettini, L., Coppo, M., D'Antoni, L., De Luca, M., Dezani-Ciancaglini, M., Yoshida, N.: Global progress in dynamically interleaved multiparty sessions. In: van Breugel, F., Chechik, M. (eds.) CONCUR 2008. LNCS, vol. 5201, pp. 418–433. Springer, Heidelberg (2008)
4. Bocchi, L., Chen, T.-C., Demangeon, R., Honda, K., Yoshida, N.: Monitoring networks through multiparty session types. In: Beyer, D., Boreale, M. (eds.) FMOODS/FORTE 2013. LNCS, vol. 7892, pp. 50–65. Springer, Heidelberg (2013)
5. Bocchi, L., Honda, K., Tuosto, E., Yoshida, N.: A theory of design-by-contract for distributed multiparty interactions. In: Gastin, P., Laroussinie, F. (eds.) CONCUR 2010. LNCS, vol. 6269, pp. 162–176. Springer, Heidelberg (2010)
6. Capecchi, S., Giachino, E., Yoshida, N.: Global escape in multiparty sessions. In: FSTTCS 2010. LIPIcs, vol. 8, pp. 338–351. Schloss Dagstuhl (2010)
7. Carbone, M., Honda, K., Yoshida, N.: Structured communication-centred programming for web services. In: De Nicola, R. (ed.) ESOP 2007. LNCS, vol. 4421, pp. 2–17. Springer, Heidelberg (2007)
8. W3C Web Services Choreography Description Language. http://www.w3.org/2002/ws/chor/
9. Chen, T.-C., Bocchi, L., Deniélou, P.-M., Honda, K., Yoshida, N.: Asynchronous distributed monitoring for multiparty session enforcement. In: Bruni, R., Sassone, V. (eds.) TGC 2011. LNCS, vol. 7173, pp. 25–45. Springer, Heidelberg (2012)
10. Demangeon, R., Honda, K.: Nested protocols in session types. In: Koutny, M., Ulidowski, I. (eds.) CONCUR 2012. LNCS, vol. 7454, pp. 272–286. Springer, Heidelberg (2012)
11. Deniélou, P.-M., Yoshida, N.: Dynamic multirole session types. In: POPL, pp. 435–446. ACM (2011)
12. Deniélou, P.-M., Yoshida, N.: Multiparty session types meet communicating automata. In: Seidl, H. (ed.) ESOP 2012. LNCS, vol. 7211, pp. 194–213. Springer, Heidelberg (2012)
13. Deniélou, P.-M., Yoshida, N.: Multiparty compatibility in communicating automata: characterisation and synthesis of global session types. In: Fomin, F.V., Freivalds, R., Kwiatkowska, M., Peleg, D. (eds.) ICALP 2013, Part II. LNCS, vol. 7966, pp. 174–186. Springer, Heidelberg (2013)
14. Dezani-Ciancaglini, M., Mostrous, D., Yoshida, N., Drossopoulou, S.: Session types for object-oriented languages. In: Thomas, D. (ed.) ECOOP 2006. LNCS, vol. 4067, pp. 328–352. Springer, Heidelberg (2006)
15. Qualit e Cognizant business unit. Zero Deviation Life Cycle. http://0deviation.com/
16. Fähndrich, M., Aiken, M., Hawblitzel, C., Hodson, O., Hunt, G., Larus, J.R., Levi, S.: Language support for fast and reliable message-based communication in singularity OS. In : Proceedings of EuroSys'06, pp. 177–190. ACM (2006)

17. Honda, K.: Scribble Examples: (1) Protocols (2007)
18. Honda, K., Hu, R., Neykova, R., Chen, T.-C., Demangeon, R., Deniélou, P.-M., Yoshida, N.: Structuring communication with session types. In: COB'12. LNCS, Springer (to appear)
19. Honda, K., Mukhamedov, A., Brown, G., Chen, T.-C., Yoshida, N.: Scribbling interactions with a formal foundation. In: Natarajan, R., Ojo, A. (eds.) ICDCIT 2011. LNCS, vol. 6536, pp. 55–75. Springer, Heidelberg (2011)
20. Honda, K., Vasconcelos, V.T., Kubo, M.: Language primitives and type disciplines for structured communication-based programming. In: Hankin, C. (ed.) ESOP 1998. LNCS, vol. 1381, pp. 22–138. Springer, Heidelberg (1998)
21. Honda, Kohei, Yoshida, Nobuko, Carbone, Marco: Web services, mobile processes and types. EATCS Bull. **91**, 160–188 (2007)
22. Honda, K., Yoshida, N., Carbone, M.: Multiparty asynchronous session types. In: POPL '08, pp. 273–284. ACM (2008)
23. Hu, R., Kouzapas, D., Pernet, O., Yoshida, N., Honda, K.: Type-safe eventful sessions in Java. In: D'Hondt, T. (ed.) ECOOP 2010. LNCS, vol. 6183, pp. 329–353. Springer, Heidelberg (2010)
24. Hu, R., Neykova, R., Yoshida, N., Demangeon, R., Honda, K.: Practical interruptible conversations: distributed dynamic verification with session types and Python. In: Legay, A., Bensalem, S. (eds.) RV 2013. LNCS, vol. 8174, pp. 130–148. Springer, Heidelberg (2013)
25. Hu, R., Yoshida, N., Honda, K.: Session-based distributed programming in Java. In: Vitek, J. (ed.) ECOOP 2008. LNCS, vol. 5142, pp. 516–541. Springer, Heidelberg (2008)
26. Ocean Observatories Initiative. Scribble OOI derivalables. https://confluence.oceanobservatories.org/display/CIDev/Identify+required+Scribble+extensions+for+advanced+scenarios+of+R3+COI
27. Milner, R.: The polyadic π-calculus: a tutorial. In: Proceedings of the International Summer School on Logic Algebra of Specification, Marktoberdorf (1992)
28. Milner, R.: Communicating and Mobile Systems: The π-Calculus. Cambridge University Press, Cambridge (1999)
29. Milner, R., Parrow, J., Walker, D.: A calculus of mobile processes, Parts I and II. Inf. Comp. **100**(1), 1–40 (1992)
30. Mostrous, D., Yoshida, N., Honda, K.: Global principal typing in partially commutative asynchronous sessions. In: Castagna, G. (ed.) ESOP 2009. LNCS, vol. 5502, pp. 316–332. Springer, Heidelberg (2009)
31. Neykova, R., Yoshida, N., Hu, R.: SPY: local verification of global protocols. In: Legay, A., Bensalem, S. (eds.) RV 2013. LNCS, vol. 8174, pp. 358–363. Springer, Heidelberg (2013)
32. Ng, N., Yoshida, N.: Pabble: parameterised scribble for parallel programming. In: PDP, IEEE (2014, to appear)
33. Ng, N., Yoshida, N., Honda, K.: Multiparty session C: safe parallel programming with message optimisation. In: Furia, C.A., Nanz, S. (eds.) TOOLS 2012. LNCS, vol. 7304, pp. 202–218. Springer, Heidelberg (2012)
34. OOI. The Ocean Observatories Initiative. http://oceanobservatories.org/
35. Pi4tech home page. http://www.pi4tech.com
36. Pierce, B.C.: Types and Programming Languages. MIT Press, Cambridge (2002)
37. Red Hat JBoss. JBoss Community Scribble homepage. http://www.jboss.org/scribble
38. JBoss Savara. JBoss Savara Project homepage. http://www.jboss.org/savara

39. Takeuchi, K., Honda, K., Kubo, M.: An interaction-based language and its typing system. PARLE 1994. LNCS, vol. 817, pp. 398–413. Springer, Heidelberg (1994)
40. Scribble Team. Scribble Language Reference. https://github.com/scribble/scribble-spec
41. Scribble Team. Scribble Project github homepage. http://www.scribble.org
42. UNIFI. International Organization for Standardization 20022 UNIversal Financial Industry message scheme. http://www.iso20022.org (2002)
43. Yoshida, N., Vasconcelos, V.T.: Language primitives and type discipline for structured communication-based programming revisited: two systems for higher-order session communication. Electr. Notes Theor. Comput. Sci. **171**(4), 73–93 (2007)

Security

Dynamic Measurement and Protected Execution: Model and Analysis

Shiwei Xu[1], Ian Batten[2(✉)], and Mark Ryan[2]

[1] Wuhan Digital Engineering Institute, Wuhan, China
[2] School of Computer Science, University of Birmingham, West Midlands, UK
igb986@cs.bham.ac.uk

Abstract. Useful security properties arise from sealing data to specific units of code. Modern processors featuring Intel's TXT and AMD's SVM achieve this by a process of measured and protected execution. Only code which has the correct measurement can access the data, and this code runs in an environment protected from observation and interference. We present a modelling language with primitives for protected execution, along with its semantics. We characterise an attacker who has access to all the capabilities of the hardware. In order to achieve automatic analysis of systems using protected execution without attempting to search an infinite state space, we define transformations that reduce the number of times the attacker needs to use protected execution to a pre-determined bound. Given reasonable assumptions we prove the soundness of the transformation: no secrecy attacks are lost by applying it. We then describe using the StatVerif extensions to ProVerif to model the bounded invocations of protected execution. We show the analysis of realistic systems, for which we provide case studies.

1 Introduction

Modern hardware often includes security features that support the ability to *seal data to program code*. This allows a data owner to impose a policy (embodied as code) about how their data is to be processed: the hardware guarantees that the policy will be enforced. Sealing data to code is a very powerful mechanism that enables a wide variety of applications, in mobile computing and cloud computing alike. For example, mobiles can store cryptographic keys for exclusive use by certain applications, such as payment or banking applications. In the cloud, servers can guarantee to remote users that the data they uploaded is being processed only in accordance with their wishes.

This paper aims to analyse the specific mechanisms for sealing data to code provided on commodity processors from AMD and Intel. These processors already ship with off-the-shelf computers and are becoming ubiquitous. They allow code to be executed in a protected environment outside the influence of malware or untrusted software (including the operating system) that may be present on the host computer. Specifically, we analyse the architecture and mechanisms provided by Flicker [11]. The idea of Flicker is to define very small

M. Abadi and A. Lluch Lafuente (Eds.): TGC 2013, LNCS 8358, pp. 45–63, 2014.
DOI: 10.1007/978-3-319-05119-2_4,

programs that handle security-sensitive data, and are run in protected execution mode directly under the control of the hardware security features. The bulk of the software which is security-*in*sensitive runs on top of an operating system, as usual. For example [11], a *certificate authority* could be structured as a small secure base that handles the signing key, along with a bigger untrusted part that deals with I/O, the user interface, etc.

The hardware mechanisms which support this architecture are Intel's *trusted execution technology* (TXT), or the roughly-equivalent *secure virtual machine* (SVM) technology from AMD. Both of these technologies rely on the presence of a *trusted platform module* to store and use cryptographic keys. Our analysis therefore involves cryptographic protocols; and since the TPM uses persistent state registers called *platform configuration registers* (PCRs), it also involves statefulness.

For these reasons, we wish to use StatVerif [2] for our analysis; it is an extension of ProVerif which can deal with protocols that have persistent state. Unfortunately, StatVerif does not reliably terminate when the state space is infinite, such as in the case studies we are using in this paper. We therefore have to develop appropriate abstractions. There are two sources of infinite state in our application. The first one arises from an operation called PCR *extension*. We already found a suitable abstraction in earlier work [6], and we re-use it here. The second source of infinite state arises because an attacker can unboundedly often reset the hardware and invoke a new session that uses the hardware primitives. This paper is devoted to developing an abstraction to overcome this obstacle to the analysis; the details of our analysis are available as a technical report.

1.1 Contribution

A platform with a TPM and a processor that implements TXT or SVM supports *protected execution* and the ability to seal data to program code. We provide a formal model of this protected execution so that we can prove the security properties it offers. Specifically:

- We define TXML, a language with primitives for protected execution.
- We formalise a model for an adversary who is attacking protected execution.
- We state and prove a theorem that allows us to restrict attention to finite attacker strategies, paving the way to automated verification.
- We briefly describe the use of StatVerif [2] (which is an extension of ProVerif) to model some applications that use protected execution from the literature [11].
- We demonstrate that the applications indeed satisfy the security goals, in the context of our attacker model.

1.2 Attacker Model

Our attacker is a powerful attacker, inspired by the capabilities against a network protocol of a Dolev-Yao attacker. The attacker can:

- Perform arbitrary offline computation using their own resources in order to plan their strategy.
- Execute arbitrary code on the system they are attacking, including using supervisor, kernel or other privileged modes. This includes running either their own or the defender's code in a protected execution environment.
- Access the TPM as though they were the owner of the TPM, with full knowledge of the authorisation data.

The restrictions we impose exclude low-level hardware attacks on the platform, and assume that the hardware correctly implements the hardware design. We also assume that the cryptographic primitives are sound. Our attacker therefore cannot:

- Extract keys or other information from the TPM other than by using the published API. This excludes hardware attacks on the TPM, and assumes that the TPM correctly implements the API.
- Bypass the published protections of TXT/SVM by, for example, attacking the memory controller on the platform.
- Successfully guess cryptographic keys, perform offline decryption given only the cipher text, find collisions in hash functions.

1.3 Related Work

There have been previous formal analyses of TPM and dynamic measurement. Lin [10] uses the theorem prover Otter and the model finder Alloy to analyse the security of the TPM when presented with invalid sequences of API calls. Lin considered modelling PCR state, but was unable to do this with Otter. Gurgens *et al.* [9] describe an analysis of the TPM API using a finite state automata, but the model fragment given does not appear to consider PCR state and the analysis in the paper is predominantly informal. Coker *et al.* [3] focus on the analysis of TPM APIs for remote attestation, but their SAL model is not yet publicly available. Delaune *et al.* [5] analyse a fragment of the TPM, using the applied pi calculus as a modelling language and using the ProVerif tool to automate their verification, but they too do not consider PCR state.

Much of the previous formal work on dynamic measurement is abstract. Millen [12] uses LTL to model the roles and trust relationships in a dynamic measurement system; Datta [4] proposes a logic for reasoning about secure systems built on dynamic measurement; Fournet and Planul [7] reason in the cryptographic model about the security of sealed data. Our methods complement those of [4,7], because they are automatic and scalable. We demonstrate this with our case studies.

Arapinis *et al.* [2] extend the process language of ProVerif to allow the modelling of global state. Their work allows the description of the TPM and dynamic measurement in a process language with state, and the automatic generation of Horn clauses from this model. However, ProVerif will not terminate on these clauses. To assist termination, Delaune *et al.* [6] show a first-order model based on Horn clauses. This model focuses on PCR state and related API commands. They place an upper bound on the number of times a PCR needs to be extended between two resets. They show that if there is an attack using an unlimited number of extensions, then there is also an attack which requires a bounded number of PCR extensions. They also show that this upper bound is small enough to be tractable using ProVerif. Their model solves the non-termination problem caused by PCR extension; however, in some applications further termination problems are caused by multiple PCR resets as the result of multiple invocations of dynamic measurement. Bounding the number of PCR extensions does not solve the problem caused by multiple PCR resets, which we characterise and solve in this paper.

2 Background to Trusted Computing

Hardware Primitives. A TPM can provide evidence that a system is running in a particular configuration through the use of *platform configuration registers* (PCRs). The TPM only allows the PCRs to be reset to initial values by privileged instructions or at system reset. They can however be *extended* at any time. Extension involves hashing the current value of the PCR with another value; a PCR containing value p is extended with x by concatenating p with x, hashing the result and making this the new value of the PCR.

When a software module is loaded, its *measurement*, conventionally consisting of a secure hash of the code, can be extended into a PCR. A sequence of such extensions will result in a PCR value that is unique to the set of modules so measured, and the order in which they were measured, starting from an initial measure of trusted code loaded at boot-time.

Secret information can be *sealed* against a set of PCR values. The TPM encrypts the information using a key that the TPM controls, and the TPM will perform the matching decryption if and only if the PCRs are in the state against which the data has been sealed.

Only the loading of a unique sequence of modules will produce a particular PCR. Any change to any one of the modules will produce a different value. In practice, this limits the measurement of the whole configuration; the process of booting a general purpose operating system from initial power-on to user login has too many variable elements, and changes too frequently. Additionally, because code is measured at the point of loading, an attacker who can access memory (which is usually a reasonable assumption) can overwrite already-measured code without altering the PCR value.

To address these issues, version 1.2 of the TPM specification introduced the concept of a dynamic root of trust. Rather than tracing execution back to power-on, a privileged instruction can be used to reset PCRs in a new bank (17–22), which were initialised at power-on to all-ones (u_1), directly to all-zeroes (u_0). These *resetable* PCRs are then available to be extended with measurements from the reset onwards, rather than from power-on. This functionality is the basis for dynamic measurement technology, such as Intel's *Trusted Execution Technology* (TXT) [8] and AMD's *Secure Virtual Machine* (SVM) [1].

As the Intel and AMD technologies operate in a similar fashion, for simplicity we only consider the AMD SVM technology; the differences do not affect our argument in any material way. SVM provides a privileged command SKINIT, which creates a protected environment in which code can execute free from external influences. The unit of code to be executed with this protection is called a Secure Loader Block (SLB). When the SKINIT instruction is executed, interrupts and DMA are disabled to prevent access to the SLB and the resetable PCRs are reset. The SLB is sent to the TPM for measurement (using a hash function) and the result is extended into PCR17. The SLB is then executed.

Flicker Architecture. Flicker [11] provides a mechanism for executing pieces of code with specific guarantees of privacy and integrity by making use of dynamic measurement. It uses Intel TXT or AMD SVM technology to measure and protect an SLB, which consists of initialisation and clean-up (SLB Core) and application functionality (Pieces of Application Logic, PAL); the measurement allows the SLB to unseal private data, while the protection prevents interference or observation with manipulation of the private data. Appropriate kernel services are made available to enable execution.

Although their use is not mandatory, the standard SLB template provides some additional features. Firstly, it provides a standard mechanism for passing arguments in to the PAL and passing out results. Secondly, after execution of the PAL has completed, but before the SLB exits, the SLB measures the inputs and the outputs of the PAL and extends their value into PCR17, and then extends a fixed public constant into PCR17. One effect of this is to leave the PCRs in a state which is of no use to an attacker who is attempting to unseal confidential data; the extension with the fixed public constant leaves a value against which no data will have been sealed. It also provides a verifiable chain to prove the execution: PCR17 is left as the result of successively extending an initial u_0 with the measurements of the SLB, any inputs, any outputs and finally the fixed public constant. A later TPM_Quote operation on PCR17 provides an attestation as a verifiable link between the inputs, the outputs and the SLB for a verifier.

3 A Model of Protected Execution

In this section, we model the functionality of dynamic measurement and the TPM. We introduce a modelling language, TXML, along with its semantics. We describe a theorem that allows us to bound the length of traces such that models can be verified with available tools. To illustrate our model, we introduce a simple Flicker-based decryption oracle. We then formally define our model.

3.1 Simplifications and Abstractions

We simplify both Flicker and the TPM, but in ways which grant additional powers to the attacker. If the attacker cannot compromise our simplified system, he also cannot compromise the full system.

- We omit TPM authdata, normally required to authenticate access to the TPM. Permitting access to the TPM without authdata is equivalent to assuming that the attacker can obtain the authdata from the running machine; this is in keeping with our attacker model.
- We assume that all keys used in the model have been created and are permanently loaded in the TPM. This does not alter the power of the attacker but simplifies the model substantially.
- For simplicity, we consider a TPM with only PCR17, as it is sufficient to model the facilities we are using.
- Finally, as we are analysing the secrecy properties of the system rather than the correctness of attestations, we omit the SLB's extension of its input and output into PCR17. This allows the attacker to replay previous executions as though they were fresh.

3.2 An Introductory Example

Our introductory example is a decryption oracle implemented as an SLB. Any object supplied to the SLB is decrypted using symKey and returned to the user. The intent is that symKey is never revealed outside the oracle. In order to prevent the oracle being used to decrypt arbitrary ciphertexts, a check is made for the presence of a pre-arranged tag. Our concern is the privacy of the decryption key in the face of a powerful attacker, so the tag is made available to the attacker.

We represent the oracle SLB as slbD which receives as input the sealed symKey and an object which is to be treated as ciphertext. slbD attempts to unseal symKey. If that succeeds it uses symKey to decrypt the cipher-text. If that succeeds, and the tag is found in the plaintext, the plaintext is output. Finally, the public fixed constant fpc is extended into PCR17 to revoke access to the secrets.

Assuming the correctness of the TPM unsealing function, symKey can only be unsealed when PCR17 value is $\mathsf{h}(\mathsf{u}_0, \mathsf{slbD})$. Due to the operation of dynamic measurement, PCR17 can be set to $\mathsf{h}(\mathsf{u}_0, \mathsf{slbD})$ only by the execution of slbD with an SKINIT instruction. slbD itself uses, but does not output, symKey. Consequently, symKey is not exposed outside the decryption oracle.

3.3 Trusted Execution Modelling Language

We present a formal model of protected execution. This models a machine equipped with a simplified TPM which offers sealing, unsealing, resetting, reading and extension of the PCR. The machine also allows users to execute programs in the protected execution environment provided by dynamic measurement.

We introduce the syntax and semantics of a language, TXML[1]. This language describes actions that can be taken either by the attacker, as part of a strategy to attack the security properties of the defender's system, or by the defender, in order to implement protected execution. We model the decryption oracle example to show its use in describing a defender's SLB. We then define

[1] Trusted eXecution Modelling Language.

transformations from one strategy, which is used to model a list of commands in TXML, to another strategy. We show that the result of this transformation is both equivalent to the original and tractable for analysis.

TXML is not a complete language. It lacks any looping constructs, and has only rudimentary conditionals. The attacker would not design an attack strategy using TXML. However, any sequence of actions the attacker carries out can be retrospectively expressed in TXML. Any sequence of operations that involves loops or conditionals can be expressed, once the number of iterations in each loop and the outcome of each conditional has been determined, by a simpler sequence of operations that does not involve loops and conditionals, starting from the same initial state. The attacker is given the ability to perform arbitrary offline computation; this allows him to construct one or more sequences of TXML commands to perform their attack.

Syntax. Suppose sets N of names including 0, 1, $\mathsf{sk}_{\mathsf{srk}}$ (the storage root key of the TPM), tpmPf (the TPM Proof inserted into a seal so that the TPM can confirm that it was sealed on this TPM), ...; V of variables with typical elements x, y, z, ... The letters u, v, w, ... range over $\mathrm{V} \cup \mathrm{N}$. Typical constructor function symbols, including at least $\mathsf{h}/2$, $\mathsf{senc}/2$, $\mathsf{aenc}/3$, $\mathsf{pk}/1$ and $\mathsf{measure}/1$, are represented as f. These represent respectively the SHA1 hash function, symmetric and asymmetric encryption, the derivation of a public key from a private key, and the measurement with SHA1 of a fragment of program text. Typical destructor function symbols, including at least $\mathsf{sdec}/2$ and $\mathsf{adec}/2$, are represented as g. These represent respectively symmetric and asymmetric decryption. We define terms t_1,t_2,... over $\mathrm{V} \cup \mathrm{N}$ in the usual way. The rewrite rules $t_1 \rightarrow t_2$ where t_1,t_2 are over variables include at least $\mathsf{sdec}(x, \mathsf{senc}(x, y)) \rightarrow y$ and $\mathsf{adec}(x, \mathsf{aenc}(\mathrm{pk}(x), y, z)) \rightarrow z$, linking associated encryption and decryption operations.

The syntax of TXML is shown in Fig. 1 and described as follows:

- $x := \mathsf{f}(u_1, \ldots, u_n)$ and $x := \mathsf{g}(u_1, \ldots, u_n)$ are applications of constructors and destructors.
- $x := \mathsf{seal}(u, v)$, $x := \mathsf{unseal}(u)$, $\mathsf{extend}(u)$ and reset are the actions of sealing and unsealing data, extending a PCR and resetting the TPM.
- $\mathsf{check}\ u = v$ confirms the equality of two terms.
- skip is the null action.
- $x := \mathsf{SKINIT}\{\text{list(statement)}; \mathsf{rtn}\, u\}$ is a list of statements that are executed protected by SKINIT, which return u.
- $x := \mathsf{SUBR}\{\text{list(statement)}; \mathsf{rtn}\, u\}$ is analogous to $x := \mathsf{SKINIT}\{\ldots; \mathsf{rtn}\, u\}$. However, it does not modify the PCR value. SUBR is not available to the programmer or the attacker, and cannot appear in the definition of an SLB; it is present in TXML as a technical convenience that we use during transformation.

Semantics. We will be using TXML as the basis for our proof that we can bound the number of SKINITs used by the attacker. We therefore need to define its semantics. We consider configurations (K, p), where the attacker's knowledge

statement ::=
$x := \mathsf{f}(u_1, \ldots, u_n) \mid$
$x := \mathsf{g}(u_1, \ldots, u_n) \mid$
$x := \mathsf{seal}(u, v) \mid$
$x := \mathsf{unseal}(u) \mid$
$\mathsf{extend}(u) \mid \mathsf{reset} \mid$
$\mathsf{check}\ u = v \mid \mathsf{skip}$

command ::=
statement |
$x := \mathsf{SKINIT}\{\text{list(statement)}; \mathsf{rtn}\ u\} \mid$
$x := \mathsf{SUBR}\{\text{list(statement)}; \mathsf{rtn}\ u\}$
program ::=
list(command)

Fig. 1. Syntax of TXML

base $\mathsf{K} : \mathrm{V} \rightarrow$ ground terms is a partial function and p is a ground term. We assume K is extended to $\mathrm{V} \cup \mathrm{N}$, as the identity function on N. The initial configuration is $(\mathsf{K}_{init}, 1)$. Transitions between configurations are labelled by programs. We assume side conditions that $\mathsf{K}(x)$ is defined and r is non-deterministically chosen whenever we write $\mathsf{K}(x)$ and r. We also assume an injective function $\mathsf{measure} : \mathrm{TXML}^* \rightarrow N$ taking a sequence of TXML commands and returning a name.

$(\mathsf{K}, p) \xrightarrow{C} (\mathsf{K}', p')$ means that when the knowledge base is K and the PCR value is p, and the attacker performs command C, his new knowledge base will be K', and the new PCR value will be p'. The relations $\xrightarrow{C}$, which relates to individual commands, and $\xRightarrow{S}$, which relates to sequences of commands, are defined in Fig. 2. A PCR value of $\perp$ represents a PCR value against which no blob is sealed.

Figure 2 shows the semantics of each command in TXML. We clarify some of the more complex rules:

- A sealed blob consists of the encryption of (tpmPf, p, t), where tpmPf is a constant known only to the TPM, p is the PCR state which must be current for an unsealing operation to succeed, and t is the data which has been sealed. The encryption is done with a public key, whose private part is available only within the TPM. The rules for unseal add the secret t to the attacker's knowledge base if the required PCR value in the sealed blob matches the current PCR value.
- In the rule for $\mathsf{SKINIT}\{L; \mathsf{rtn}\, u\}$, we first compute the effect of L when run from knowledge base K and a PCR value reflecting the measurement of L.
- SUBR is similar to SKINIT, except that the final PCR value is p rather than p'. As mentioned, SUBR is not used in source TXML programs; we use it in our transformation.

Modelling the Introductory Example. Two objects are supplied to the decryption oracle: a sealed blob containing the symmetric key pre-sealed against PCR17 with the value of u_0 extended with the measurement of the decryption oracle's program, and some atomic message encrypted with the symmetric key.

$$(\mathsf{K}, p) \xrightarrow{\mathsf{skip}} (\mathsf{K}, p)$$
$$(\mathsf{K}, p) \xrightarrow{x:=\mathsf{f}(u_1,\ldots,u_n)} (\mathsf{K}[x \to \mathsf{f}(\mathsf{K}(u_1), \ldots, \mathsf{K}(u_n))], p)$$
$$(\mathsf{K}, p) \xrightarrow{x:=\mathsf{g}(u_1,\ldots,u_n)} (\mathsf{K}[x \to t], p) \text{ if } \mathsf{g}(t_1, \ldots, t_n) \to t_{n+1} \text{ is a reduc and } \mathsf{K}(u_i) = t_i\sigma \text{ and } t = t_{n+1}\sigma$$
$$(\mathsf{K}, p) \xrightarrow{x:=\mathsf{seal}(u,v)} (\mathsf{K}[x \to \mathsf{aenc}(\mathsf{pk}(\mathsf{sk}_{\mathsf{Srk}}), \mathsf{r}, (\mathsf{tpmPf}, \mathsf{K}(u), \mathsf{K}(v)))], p) \text{ if } \mathsf{K}(u) \neq \bot$$
$$(\mathsf{K}, p) \xrightarrow{x:=\mathsf{unseal}(u)} (\mathsf{K}[x \to t], p) \text{ if } p \neq \bot \text{ and } \mathsf{K}(u) = \mathsf{aenc}(\mathsf{pk}(\mathsf{sk}_{\mathsf{Srk}}), \mathsf{r}, (\mathsf{tpmPf}, p, t))$$
$$(\mathsf{K}, p) \xrightarrow{\mathsf{extend}(u)} (\mathsf{K}, \mathsf{h}(p, \mathsf{K}(u))) \text{ if } p \neq \bot$$
$$(\mathsf{K}, \bot) \xrightarrow{\mathsf{extend}(u)} (\mathsf{K}, \bot)$$
$$(\mathsf{K}, p) \xrightarrow{\mathsf{reset}} (\mathsf{K}, 1)$$
$$(\mathsf{K}, p) \xrightarrow{\mathsf{check}\ u=v} (\mathsf{K}, p) \text{ if } \mathsf{K}(u) = \mathsf{K}(v)$$
$$(\mathsf{K}, p) \xrightarrow{x:=\mathsf{SKINIT}\{\mathsf{L};\mathsf{rtn}\ u\}} (\mathsf{K}[x \to \mathsf{K}'(u)], p') \text{ if } (\mathsf{K}, \mathsf{h}(0, \mathsf{measure}(\mathsf{L}))) \overset{\mathsf{L}}{\Rrightarrow} (\mathsf{K}', p')$$
$$(\mathsf{K}, p) \xrightarrow{x:=\mathsf{SUBR}\{\mathsf{L};\mathsf{rtn}\ u\}} (\mathsf{K}[x \to \mathsf{K}'(u)], p) \text{ if } (\mathsf{K}, \mathsf{h}(0, \mathsf{measure}(\mathsf{L}))) \overset{\mathsf{L}}{\Rrightarrow} (\mathsf{K}', p')$$

Fig. 2. This defines the relation $\xrightarrow{C}$. Let S be a TXML program. The relation $\overset{S}{\Rrightarrow}$ is defined as $(\mathsf{K}, p) \overset{\emptyset}{\Rrightarrow} (\mathsf{K}, p)$ in the case that S is the null program. In other cases, $(\mathsf{K}, p) \overset{C;S}{\Longrightarrow} (\mathsf{K}', p')$ if $(\mathsf{K}, p) \xrightarrow{C} (\mathsf{K}'', p'')$ and $(\mathsf{K}'', p'') \overset{S}{\Rrightarrow} (\mathsf{K}', p')$.

Therefore, the initial knowledge base is:

$$\mathsf{K}_{init\_DO} = \{x_{sdata} = \mathsf{aenc}(\mathsf{pk}(\mathsf{sk}_{\mathsf{Srk}}), \mathsf{r}, (\mathsf{tpmPf}, \mathsf{h}(0, \mathsf{measure}(\mathsf{slbD})), \mathsf{symKey})),$$
$$x_{EncBlob} = \mathsf{senc}(\mathsf{symKey}, \mathsf{message})\}$$

where slbD is the program:

```
result := SKINIT {
  xSymKey := unseal(xSData);
  xMessage := sdec(xSymKey, xEncBlob);
  extend(fpc);
  rtn xMessage;
}.
```

The security property we are checking is the secrecy of the symmetric key symKey. To attempt to obtain the key, the attacker can adopt any strategy, as described in Sect. 1.2. The desired security property is therefore that there is no TXML program S, knowledge base K', PCR values p, p' and variable x such that $(K_{init\_DO}, p) \overset{S}{\Rrightarrow} (\mathsf{K}', p')$ and $\mathsf{K}'(x) = \mathsf{symKey}$.

Transformations of Strategies. The security property above requires reasoning over all possible TXML programs S. We show that it is sufficient to consider only programs involving a bounded number of SKINITs and resets. To achieve this, we transform any strategy S into a new strategy S' that is equivalent to S and has a number of SKINITs and resets which is bounded by a value derivable from the initial knowledge base. This allows us to use automatic tools to search for strategies that achieve a certain goal and model at most this number of SKINITs and resets; if none are found, we may conclude that there are no longer strategies that achieve the goal.

The transformation performs two changes. First, unseal operations that are not necessary are replaced by an equivalent assignment. An unseal operation is not necessary if there is another variable in the knowledge base that has the value of the unsealed item. Second, operations that reset the PCR, namely, reset and SKINIT, are removed if there is no necessary unseal operation between the current point and the next reset or SKINIT. This reflects the fact that PCR values are required to be correct only in order for unseals to work. The transformation uses configurations (K, p) as before, but with the extension that p may take the special value $\perp$ which signifies that any value will do; the PCR value is not needed. The transformation is such that $p = \perp$ if and only if there is no unseal between the current position in the program and the next reset or SKINIT.

The result of this transformation does not weaken the attacker. The attacker can perform computation with the defender SLB using any number of inputs. The attacker can run arbitrary code with the PCR in the state left by the execution of the defender SLB. The attacker can attempt to unseal data sealed by the defender. The attacker already knows the contents of sealed data sealed by the attacker. If the attacker wishes to obtain more results from the defender SLB, these are available to him from the transformed strategy.

The transformations we use are shown in Fig. 3. In the definition of $\xrightarrow[C]{C'}$, the truth or falsity of $p = \perp$ enforces a global constraint on the way the transformation works, and makes the transformation deterministic. The two rules for each of SKINIT and reset appear to be non-deterministic, but in fact only one of them may be chosen; which one is chosen depends on whether there is an unseal before the next SKINIT or reset, as expressed by the rule for unseal which requires $p \neq \perp$. The apparent free choice of whether $q = p$ or $q = \perp$ in the rule for unseal is similarly constrained by the remainder of the program S being transformed.

SUBR is introduced into S′ by the second rule for SKINIT, which is invoked if and only if there is no unseal between now and the next SKINIT or reset, as indicated by the $\perp$ value on the right hand side.

Bounding the Number of SKINITs and Resets. The ability to seal data against arbitrary PCR values is very flexible, and can lead to situations more complex than the simple sealing of one piece of data against one set of PCR values. A piece of data sealed against one set of PCR values can contain another piece of data sealed against another set of values. A piece of data may be sealed against an SLB which will only release the decrypted version once some other conditions are met. To reach a state where these conditions are true might include the decrementing of a counter, or transition through some state machine.

We define data as *boundedly sealed* if there is a finite bound to the number of SKINITs required to extract it.

The relation $(\mathsf{K},p) \xrightarrow[C']{C} (\mathsf{K}',p')$ indicates that when in configuration (K,p) the execution of command C yields the new configuration (K',p') and adds the command C' to the transformed strategy.

$$(\mathsf{K},p) \xrightarrow[\mathsf{skip}]{\mathsf{skip}} (\mathsf{K},p)$$

$$(\mathsf{K},p) \xrightarrow[x:=\mathsf{f}(u_1,\ldots,u_n)]{x:=\mathsf{f}(u_1,\ldots,u_n)} (\mathsf{K}[x \to \mathsf{f}(\mathsf{K}(u_1),\ldots,\mathsf{K}(u_n))],p)$$

$$(\mathsf{K},p) \xrightarrow[x:=\mathsf{g}(u_1,\ldots,u_n)]{x:=\mathsf{g}(u_1,\ldots,u_n)} (\mathsf{K}[x \to t],p) \text{ if } \mathsf{g}(t_1,\ldots,t_n) \to t_{n+1} \text{is a reduc and}$$
$$\mathsf{K}(u_i) = t_i\sigma \text{ and } t = t_{n+1}\sigma$$

$$(\mathsf{K},p) \xrightarrow[x:=\mathsf{seal}(u,v)]{x:=\mathsf{seal}(u,v)} (\mathsf{K}[x \to \mathsf{aenc}(\mathsf{pk}(\mathsf{sk}_{\mathsf{Srk}}),\mathsf{r},(\mathsf{tpmPf},\mathsf{K}(u),\mathsf{K}(v)))],p)$$

$$(\mathsf{K},p) \xrightarrow[x:=y]{x:=\mathsf{unseal}(u)} (\mathsf{K}[x \to \mathsf{K}(y)],p) \text{ if } \mathsf{K}(u) = \mathsf{aenc}(\mathsf{pk}(\mathsf{sk}_{\mathsf{Srk}}),\mathsf{r},(\mathsf{tpmPf},p',\mathsf{K}(y)))$$

$$(\mathsf{K},p) \xrightarrow[x:=\mathsf{unseal}(u)]{x:=\mathsf{unseal}(u)} (\mathsf{K}[x \to t],q) \text{ otherwise, if } \mathsf{K}(u) = \mathsf{aenc}(\mathsf{pk}(\mathsf{sk}_{\mathsf{Srk}}),\mathsf{r},(\mathsf{tpmPf},p,t))$$
$$\text{and } p \neq \bot \text{ and } (q = p \text{ or } q = \bot)$$

$$(\mathsf{K},p) \xrightarrow[\mathsf{extend}(u)]{\mathsf{extend}(u)} (K,\mathsf{h}(p,\mathsf{K}(u))) \text{ if } p \neq \bot$$

$$(\mathsf{K},\bot) \xrightarrow[\mathsf{extend}(u)]{\mathsf{extend}(u)} (K,\bot)$$

$$(\mathsf{K},\bot) \xrightarrow[\mathsf{reset}]{\mathsf{reset}} (\mathsf{K},1)$$

$$(\mathsf{K},\bot) \xrightarrow[\mathsf{skip}]{\mathsf{reset}} (\mathsf{K},\bot)$$

$$(\mathsf{K},p) \xrightarrow[\mathsf{check}\ u=v]{\mathsf{check}\ u=v} (\mathsf{K},p) \text{ if } \mathsf{K}(u) = \mathsf{K}(v)$$

Suppose $(\mathsf{K},\mathsf{h}(0,\mathsf{measure}(\mathrm{P}))) \xrightarrow[\mathrm{P}']{\mathrm{P}} (\mathsf{K}',p')$.

If P is a defender SLB:

$$(\mathsf{K},\bot) \xrightarrow[x:=\mathsf{SKINIT}\{\mathsf{P};\mathsf{rtn}\ u\}]{x:=\mathsf{SKINIT}\{\mathsf{P};\mathsf{rtn}\ u\}} (\mathsf{K}[x \to \mathsf{K}'(u)],p')$$

$$(\mathsf{K},\bot) \xrightarrow[x:=\mathsf{SUBR}\{\mathsf{P};\mathsf{rtn}\ u\}]{x:=\mathsf{SKINIT}\{\mathsf{P};\mathsf{rtn}\ u\}} (\mathsf{K}[x \to \mathsf{K}'(u)],\bot)$$

Suppose P is an attacker SLB:

$$(\mathsf{K},p) \xrightarrow[x:=\mathsf{SUBR}\{\mathsf{P}';\mathsf{rtn}\ u\}]{x:=\mathsf{SKINIT}\{\mathsf{P};\mathsf{rtn}\ u\}} (\mathsf{K}[x \to \mathsf{K}'(u)],\bot)$$

Fig. 3. Given a knowledge base $\mathsf{K}_{\mathsf{init}}$, a strategy S is transformed to S' if $(\mathsf{K}_{init},1) \overset{S}{\underset{S'}{\Rightarrow}} (\mathsf{K},\bot)$ for some K, where the relation $\overset{S}{\underset{S'}{\Rightarrow}}$ (S and S' are strategies) is defined from $\xrightarrow[C']{C}$ above as follows: $(\mathsf{K},p) \overset{\emptyset}{\underset{\emptyset}{\Rightarrow}} (\mathsf{K},p)$ where $\emptyset$ is the empty strategy; $(\mathsf{K},p) \overset{C;S}{\underset{C';S'}{\Longrightarrow}} (\mathsf{K}'',p'')$ if there exists (K',p') such that $(\mathsf{K},p) \xrightarrow[C']{C} (\mathsf{K}',p')$ and $(\mathsf{K}',p') \overset{S}{\underset{S'}{\Rightarrow}} (\mathsf{K}'',p'')$.

Definition 1. *1. A piece of sealed data B is* sealed against program *P if*

$$B = \mathit{aenc}(\mathsf{pk}(\mathsf{sk}_{\mathsf{Srk}}),r,(\mathsf{tpmPf},p,t))$$

and

$$p = \mathit{h}(\ldots \mathit{h}(\mathit{h}(0,\mathit{measure}(P)),t_2),\ldots t_n).$$

2. *A knowledge base* K produces K' *using* P *if*

$$\mathsf{K}' = \mathsf{K} \cup \{B \mid \textit{on inputs from } K\textit{, } P \textit{ can output } B\}$$

3. *We then define*

$$\overline{\mathsf{K}} = \bigcup_{K \textit{ produces* } K'} \mathsf{K}'.$$

where produces is the reflexive transitive closure of produces.* K *has only bounded seals if the number of sealed blobs in* $\overline{\mathsf{K}}$ *is finite.*

Theorem 1. Suppose knowledge base K has only bounded seals. Let m be the number of sealed blobs in $\overline{\mathsf{K}}$, as in the Definition 1. Let S be any strategy, and suppose that $(\mathsf{K}, \bot) \underset{S'}{\overset{S}{\Rightarrow}} (\mathsf{K}', \bot)$. We have the following properties:

1. $(\mathsf{K}, \bot) \overset{S}{\Rightarrow} (\mathsf{K}', p)$ implies $\exists S'.(\mathsf{K}, \bot) \underset{S'}{\overset{S}{\Rightarrow}} (\mathsf{K}', \bot)$.
2. S' simulates S; that is, $(\mathsf{K}, \bot) \underset{S'}{\overset{S}{\Rightarrow}} (\mathsf{K}', \bot)$ implies $\exists q.(\mathsf{K}, \bot) \overset{S'}{\Rightarrow} (\mathsf{K}', q)$.
3. S' uses only the data present in S that is, every name in S' is in S.
4. The number of SKINITs plus the number of resets in S' is at most m.

The proof of the theorem is given in Appendix A.

This theorem enables us to undertake practical verification of systems that use protected execution. Without the theorem, we would need to consider attacker strategies of unbounded length, or accept weak results based on a significantly weakened attacker who can only use strategies of a fixed length. Our theorem removes these restrictions.

The theorem allows us to bound the number of SKINIT operations that need to be considered to give the attacker access to the full range of PCR states. However, a typical SLB will perform some unsealing, and will leave the PCR in some new state, but it performs these operations in order to enable some calculation which returns a result. If we bound the attacker's ability to perform these calculations, then we substantially reduce their capability.

We therefore introduce the SUBR operation. Although it does not modify the PCR state (because we have shown that we can bound the number of such modifications we need to consider) it returns the same result as the corresponding SKINIT. So in the typical case where data is simply sealed so that we need only consider one SKINIT, the attacker can nonetheless make unlimited use of the SUBR to get results from the defender's SLB. Our theorem shows that it is sound to transform a strategy that uses an arbitrary number of SKINIT operations into a strategy which performs some bounded number of SKINIT operations, together with an arbitrary number of uses of the SUBR.

We are now in a position to verify the security properties of our decryption oracle. We have one piece of sealed data in our knowledge base, and by Definition 1 it is boundedly sealed: no sealed blobs are added to the knowledge base by the operation of the SLB. $\overline{\mathsf{K}_{init\_DO}}$ therefore contains only one seal, x_{sdata}. We apply Theorem 1 to K_{init_DO}, with $m = 1$.

A StatVerif model was constructed, which includes:

- A process modelling a TPM, complete with PCR state and seal, unseal, reset and extend operations;
- A process modelling the use of the SLB via SKINIT, which leave the PCR values in a deterministic state;
- A process modelling the use of the SLB via SUBR, which leave the PCR values in an indeterminate state.

This model is then bounded appropriately and run to test the secrecy property of the symmetric key. The property is confirmed.

4 Case Study: Password Authentication for SSH

Description. An additional authentication mechanism for OpenSSH is proposed by McCune *et al.* [11]. The goal is to prevent any malicious code on the server from learning the user's password, even if the server is compromised. The prevents an attacker from making use of the password to pose as the legitimate user.

A keypair is shared between the authentication SLB and the client. The private part of the keypair ($\mathsf{sk}_{\mathsf{slb}}$) is sealed against PCR17 with the value u_0 extended with the measurement slbA. The public part is conveyed to the user in a way which allows him to confirm the key generation was done correctly (see [11] Sect. 6.3.1 for details).

An authentication proceeds as follows. A nonce is generated by the server and sent to the client. The client encrypts this nonce and their password (pwd) using the public key that they hold and sends it to the server. The server sends the nonce and the cipher text to the SLB, together with the sealed key and the salt (salt) extracted from the password file.

The server invokes the SLB using SKINIT. The SLB unseals the private part of the keypair, and uses that to decrypt the message from the client. The nonce contained in that message is compared with the nonce supplied by the server to confirm freshness. The password extracted from the message is hashed together with the salt provided by the server to form a value that the server can compare with the copy of the hash from the password file. The plaintext of the password is not available outside the SLB; the hash is available more widely.

As with the decryption oracle, we can see that no sealed data is output. Although the output is not plaintext (it is the hash of a password together with some salt) it will does not contain the TPM proof and is not encrypted.

Modelling. We model the SSH password authentication application in TXML. As well as the salt and the public part of all keys, we assume that the attacker has the private part of $\mathsf{sk}_{\mathsf{slb}}$ sealed against u_0 extended with the measurement of slbA.

$$\begin{aligned}\mathsf{K}_{init\_SSH} = \{ & x_{salt} = \mathsf{salt}, \\ & x_{pksrk} = \mathsf{pk}(\mathsf{sk}_{\mathsf{Srk}}), \\ & x_{pkslb} = \mathsf{pk}(\mathsf{sk}_{\mathsf{Slb}}), \\ & x_{sdata} = \mathsf{aenc}(\mathsf{pk}(\mathsf{sk}_{\mathsf{Srk}}), \mathsf{r}, (\mathsf{tpmPf}, \mathsf{h}(0, \mathsf{measure}(\mathsf{slbA})), \mathsf{sk}_{\mathsf{Slb}})) \ \}\end{aligned}$$

where slbA is the program:

```
result := SKINIT {
  xsk_Slb := unseal(xSdata);
  xTemp := adec(xsk_Slb, xCipher);
  xPwd := fst2(xTemp);
  xNonce' := snd2(xTemp);
  check xNonce = xNonce';
  hash := md5(xSalt,xPwd);
  extend(fpc);
  rtn hash;
}.
```

Result of Our Analysis. Because slbA does not output any seals (it only outputs an MD5 hash), $\overline{\mathsf{K}_{init\_SSH}}$ contains only one seal (x_{sdata} from the initial knowledge). Therefore, we can apply Theorem 1 to K_{init_SSH} with $m = 1$.

We wrote a StatVerif model based on the above description. As previously stated, the SLB cannot output a sealed blob, as its only output is a hash of the password. We can bound the number bof extensions with the results in [6], and our theorem allows us to bound the number of resets and SKINITs. The complete StatVerif code for these examples, along with some supporting scripts to simplify the running of ProVerif and StatVerif, a description of the methodology used and some further background information, is available for download. The location is given in the bibliography.

5 Case Study: A Certification Authority

Description. This certification authority example is also taken from [11]. It consists of two SLBs, one to perform key generation, the other to perform key signing.

The key generation SLB constructs a keypair ($\mathsf{sk}_{\mathsf{SignKey}}$) suitable for use in signing other keys, and the private part of $\mathsf{sk}_{\mathsf{SignKey}}$ is sealed against u_0 extended with the measurement of the second SLB.

For the signing SLB (slbC), the client forms a certificate signing request (CSR) containing a public key along with details of the client's identity. The client submits this to the key signing SLB, which has access to the sealed form of its own private key. The SLB checks the signing policy, then unseals its private part of the keypair in order to sign the CSR. The result is returned to the client.

Modelling. We model the CA application in TXML, after making some abstractions. Firstly, we check that the signing SLB maintains the secrecy of any signing key with which it is used. This allows us to leave the key-generation SLB unmodelled and use a simple process that produces sealed keys instead. Secondly, as the required security property is the secrecy of the CA's signing key rather than the authenticity of the CSRs, the signing policy is not modelled.

We assume that the attacker has the public parts of the storage root key and the signing key $\mathsf{sk}_{\mathsf{SignKey}}$. We also assume that the attacker has the private part of $\mathsf{sk}_{\mathsf{SignKey}}$ sealed against u_0 extended with the measurement of slbC.

As in the previous example, we are able to determine that $m = 1$, as the application does not output any new sealed objects.

$$\begin{aligned}\mathsf{K}_{init\_CA} = \{&\\ &x_{pksrk} = \mathsf{pk}(\mathsf{sk}_{\mathsf{Srk}}),\\ &x_{pkSignKey} = \mathsf{pk}(\mathsf{sk}_{\mathsf{SignKey}}),\\ &x_{sdata} = \mathsf{aenc}(\mathsf{pk}(\mathsf{sk}_{\mathsf{Srk}}), \mathsf{r},\\ &\quad (\mathsf{tpmPf}, \mathsf{h}(0, \mathsf{measure}(\mathsf{slbC})), \mathsf{sk}_{\mathsf{SignKey}}))\\ \}&\end{aligned}$$

where slbC is the program:

```
result := SKINIT {
  xskSignKey := unseal(xSdata);
  xCert := sign(xskSignKey,xCSR);
  extend(fpc);
  rtn xCert;
}.
```

Result of Our Analysis. The security property we are checking is the secrecy of the CA signing key $\mathsf{sk}_{\mathsf{SignKey}}$. As a partial check that the model is correct we also check for the existence of certificates signed by $\mathsf{sk}_{\mathsf{SignKey}}$. The queries are written in the StatVerif calculus as follows:

$$\mathsf{query}\ \mathsf{att}(u, \mathsf{sk}_{\mathsf{SignKey}}) \qquad (F_5)$$
$$\mathsf{query}\ \mathsf{att}(u, \mathsf{sign}(\mathsf{sk}_{\mathsf{SignKey}}, x_{CSR})) \quad (F_6)$$

We bound the number of PCR extensions as in Sect. 4. ProVerif then terminates with F_6 reachable, which shows that the model does in fact produce signed certificates, and F_5 unreachable, which shows that there are no short attacks on the secrecy of the CA signing key $\mathsf{sk}_{\mathsf{SignKey}}$. Based on K_{init_CA} and slbC, the model conforms to the conditions of Theorem 1. Therefore there is no attack on the secrecy of $\mathsf{sk}_{\mathsf{SignKey}}$.

6 Conclusion

Protected execution on x86 platforms involves a stateful model with a state space that in unbounded in two ways. First, a PCR value may be extended with arbitrary data an arbitrary number of times. Second, the PCR value is reset each time a protected execution session is begun, and this too can happen an arbitrary number of times. We proved that it is nonetheless sound to consider only attacker strategies that are bounded in both these senses. This allows us to use StatVerif to analyse protected execution, which we have done for some examples.

Hardware-based security mechanisms, such as TPM, TXT, virtualisation and Hardware Security Modules are an important part of defending computing platforms. Formal analyses of their often complicated APIs are therefore timely. Developing abstractions of the kind described in this paper is a step in extending the ProVerif methodology to hardware-based security mechanisms. In future work, we intend to explore some more of these mechanisms.

The StatVerif files corresponding to our experiments are available for download at:

http://markryan.eu/research/projects/ProtectedExecution/

A Proof of Theorem 1

Suppose K contains B_1, B_2, ..., B_n. Let m be the number of sealed blobs in $\overline{\mathsf{K}}$, as in Definition 1. Let S be a strategy such that $(K, \bot) \overset{S}{\Rightarrow} (K', p)$. Then:

1 $\exists S'$ such that $(K, \bot) \underset{S'}{\overset{S}{\Rightarrow}} (K', \bot)$.

2 S' simulates S; that is $\exists q$ such that $(K, \bot) \overset{S'}{\Rightarrow} (K', q)$.

3 S' uses only data present in S, i.e. names$(S') \subseteq$ names(S).

4 The number of SKINITs plus the number of resets in S' is at most m.

We first prove a number of lemmas.

Lemma 1. $(K, \bot) \overset{S}{\Rightarrow} (K', p')$ *implies* $\forall p \exists p'' (K, p) \overset{S}{\Rightarrow} (K', p'')$.

Proof. We show this by induction on S.

Base case $S = \emptyset$. The proof is obvious, setting $p'' = p$.

Inductive case $S = C; S_1$. We have $(K, \bot) \overset{C}{\rightarrow} (K', p') \overset{S_1}{\Rightarrow} (K'', p''')$. Take any p.

Taking each case of C

$\mathsf{skip}, x := f(), x := g(), x := \mathsf{seal}(u, v), \mathsf{check}\ u = v$ We have $p' = \bot$, and $(K, p) \overset{C}{\rightarrow} (K', p)$. Apply IH with p to obtain p'', and we have $(K, p) \overset{C}{\rightarrow} (K', p) \overset{S_1}{\Rightarrow} (K'', p'')$, i.e. $(K, p) \overset{S}{\Rightarrow} (K'', p'')$.

$\mathsf{unseal}(v)$ This situation is impossible.

extend(v) We have $p' = \bot$ and $(K,p) \xrightarrow{C} (K', h(p,v))$. Apply IH with $h(p,v)$ to obtain p'', and we then have $(K,p) \xrightarrow{C} (K', h(p,v)) \stackrel{S_1}{\Rrightarrow} (K'', p'')$ i.e. $(K,p) \stackrel{S}{\Rrightarrow} (K', p'')$.

reset, *SKINIT*$\{P; rtn\, u\}$ We have $p' = 1$ and $(K,p) \xrightarrow{C} (K', 1)$, and $(K,p) \xrightarrow{C} (K', 1) \stackrel{S_1}{\Rrightarrow} (K'', p''')$, i.e. set $p'' = p'''$ and we have $(K,p) \stackrel{S}{\Rrightarrow} (K', p'')$.

Lemma 2. *$(K,p) \xrightarrow{C} (K',p')$ implies $\exists C'.(K,p) \xrightarrow[C']{C} (K',p')$.*

Proof. Consider each case of C in turn.

Lemma 3. *$(K,p) \xrightarrow{C} (K',p')$ implies $\exists C'.(K,p) \xrightarrow[C']{C} (K',\bot)$ or $(K,\bot) \xrightarrow[C']{C} (K',\bot)$.*

Proof. Consider each case of C in turn. For *unseal*, we prove the left disjunct. For all other cases, we prove the right disjunct.

Lemma 4. *If $p \neq \bot$ then $(K,p) \xrightarrow[C']{C} (K',p')$ implies $(K,p) \xrightarrow{C'} (K',p')$.*

Proof. Consider each case of C in turn.

Lemma 5. *$(K,p) \xrightarrow[C']{C} (K',\bot)$ implies $p \neq \bot, (K,p) \xrightarrow{C'} (K',p)$ or $\exists p'.(K,p) \xrightarrow{C'} (K',p')$.*

Proof. Consider each case of C in turn. For *unseal*, we prove the left disjunct. For all other cases, we prove the right disjunct.

Part 1 of Theorem 1

$(K,\bot) \stackrel{S}{\Rrightarrow} (K',p')$ implies $\exists S'.(K,\bot) \xRightarrow[S']{S} (K',\bot)$.

Proof. We prove something more general:

$(K,p) \stackrel{S}{\Rrightarrow} (K',p')$ implies $\exists S'.(K,p) \xRightarrow[S']{S} (K',\bot)$ or $(K,\bot) \xRightarrow[S']{S} (K',\bot)$.

Base case $S = \emptyset$ is obvious.

Inductive case $S = C; S_1$

Suppose $(K,p) \stackrel{S}{\Rrightarrow} (K',p'')$. RTP $\exists S'.(K,p) \xRightarrow[S']{S} (K',\bot)$ or $(K,\bot) \xRightarrow[S']{S} (K',\bot)$.

Expanding: $(K,p) \xrightarrow{C} (K',p') \stackrel{S_1}{\Rrightarrow} (K'',p'')$. By inductive hypothesis, $\exists S_1'$.

- either $(K,p') \xRightarrow[S_1']{S_1} (K',\bot)$. From $(K,p) \xrightarrow{C} (K',p')$, by Lemma 2, $\exists C'$. $(K,p) \xrightarrow[C']{C} (K',p')$. So set $S' = C'; S_1'$. Then $(K,p) \xrightarrow[S']{S} (K',\bot)$.
- or $(K,\bot) \xRightarrow[S_1']{S_1} (K',\bot)$. From $(K,p) \xrightarrow{C} (K',p')$, by Lemma 3, either $(K,p) \xrightarrow[C']{C} (K',\bot)$, so $(K,p) \xRightarrow[S']{S} (K',\bot)$, or $(K,\bot) \xrightarrow[C']{C} (K',\bot)$, so $(K,\bot) \xRightarrow[S']{S} (K',\bot)$ where again, $S' = C'; S_1'$.

Part 2 of Theorem 1

$(K, \bot) \underset{S'}{\overset{S}{\Longrightarrow}} (K', \bot)$ implies $\exists p'.(K, \bot) \overset{S'}{\Longrightarrow} (K, p')$.

Proof. We prove something stronger:

$(K, p) \underset{S'}{\overset{S}{\Longrightarrow}} (K', \bot)$ implies $\exists p'.(K, p) \overset{S'}{\Longrightarrow} (K', p')$.

We prove this using induction on S.

Base case $S = \emptyset$ is obvious.

Inductive case $S = C; S_1$. Inductive hypothesis: $(K, \bot) \underset{S_1'}{\overset{S_1}{\Longrightarrow}} (K', \bot)$ implies $\exists p'.(K, \bot) \overset{S_1'}{\Longrightarrow} (K', p')$.

We want to prove $(K, p) \underset{S'}{\overset{S}{\Longrightarrow}} (K', \bot)$ i.e. $(K, p) \underset{C'}{\overset{C}{\longrightarrow}} (K', p') \underset{S_1'}{\overset{S_1}{\Longrightarrow}} (K'', \bot)$.

- Either $p' = \bot$
  - either $p = \bot$: $(K, \bot) \underset{C'}{\overset{C}{\longrightarrow}} (K', \bot) \underset{S_1'}{\overset{S_1}{\Longrightarrow}} (K'', \bot)$, so by Lemma 4 and IH $\exists p''.(K, \bot) \overset{C'}{\longrightarrow} (K', \bot) \overset{S_1'}{\Longrightarrow} (K'', p'')$, i.e. $(K, \bot) \overset{S'}{\Longrightarrow} (K'', p'')$.
  - or $p \neq \bot$: $(K, p) \underset{C'}{\overset{C}{\longrightarrow}} (K', \bot) \underset{S_1'}{\overset{S_1}{\Longrightarrow}} (K'', \bot)$. by Lemma 5 and IH $\exists p''$.
    - * either $(K, p) \overset{C'}{\longrightarrow} (K', p), (K, \bot) \overset{S'}{\Longrightarrow} (K'', p'')$, Then by Lemma 1, $\exists p'''.(K, p) \underset{C'}{\overset{C'}{\longrightarrow}} (K', p) \overset{S_1'}{\Longrightarrow} (K''', p''')$, i.e. $(K, p) \overset{S'}{\Longrightarrow} (K''', p''')$.
    - * or $\exists p_1'.(K, p) \overset{C'}{\longrightarrow} (K', p_1'), (K', \bot) \overset{S_1'}{\Longrightarrow} (K'', p'')$. Then by Lemma 1, $\exists p'''.(K, p) \overset{C'}{\longrightarrow} (K', p) \overset{S_1'}{\Longrightarrow} (K'', p''')$, i.e. $(K, p) \overset{S'}{\Longrightarrow} (K'', p''')$.
- or $p' \neq \bot$ then $(K, p) \overset{C'}{\longrightarrow} (K', p')$ by Lemma 4, and so by IH $\exists p''.(K, p') \overset{S_1'}{\Longrightarrow} (K', p'')$, i.e. $(K, p) \overset{S'}{\Longrightarrow} (K'', p'')$.

Part 3 of Theorem 1

S' uses only the data present in S that is, every name in S' is in S.

Part 3 of the theorem is readily proved by inspection of the transformation.

Part 4 of Theorem 1

The number of SKINITs plus the number of resets in S' is at most m.

Part 4 follows from the facts that:

- at most m plaintext-distinct sealed blobs can be produced from the initial data;
- the transformed strategy S' runs at most one SKINIT for each blob sealed to a PCR value rooted in 0 (other invocations are run as SUBRs);
- the transformed strategy S' runs at most one reset for each sealed blob rooted in 1 (other resets are transformed into skips).

References

1. Advanced Micro Devices: Secure Virtual Machine Architecture Reference Manual. Advanced Micro Devices (2005)
2. Arapinis, M., Ritter, E., Ryan, M.D.: Statverif: verification of stateful processes. In: Proceedings of the 24th IEEE Computer Security Foundations Symposium, pp. 33–47. IEEE Computer Society Press (2011)
3. Coker, G., Guttman, J., Loscocco, P., Herzog, A., Millen, J., O'Hanlon, B., Ramsdell, J., Segall, A., Sheehy, J., Sniffen, B.: Principles of remote attestation. Int. J. Inf. Secur. **10**(2), 63–81 (2011)
4. Datta, A., Franklin, J., Garg, D., Kaynar, D.: A logic of secure systems and its application to trusted computing. In: Proceedings of the 30th IEEE Symposium on Security and Privacy, pp. 221–236. IEEE Computer Society Press (2009)
5. Delaune, S., Kremer, S., Ryan, M.D., Steel, G.: A formal analysis of authentication in the TPM. In: Degano, P., Etalle, S., Guttman, J. (eds.) FAST 2010. LNCS, vol. 6561, pp. 111–125. Springer, Heidelberg (2011)
6. Delaune, S., Kremer, S., Ryan, M., Steel, G.: Formal analysis of protocols based on TPM state registers. In: Proceedings of the 24th IEEE Computer Security Foundations Symposium. IEEE Computer Society Press (2011)
7. Fournet, C., Planul, J.: Compiling information-flow security to minimal trusted computing bases. In: Barthe, G. (ed.) ESOP 2011. LNCS, vol. 6602, pp. 216–235. Springer, Heidelberg (2011)
8. Grawrock, D.: Dynamics of a Trusted Platform: A Building Block Approach. Intel Press, Hillsboro (2009)
9. Gürgens, S., Rudolph, C., Scheuermann, D., Atts, M., Plaga, R.: Security evaluation of scenarios based on the TCG's TPM specification. In: Biskup, J., López, J. (eds.) ESORICS 2007. LNCS, vol. 4734, pp. 438–453. Springer, Heidelberg (2007)
10. Lin, A.: Automated analysis of security APIs. Ph.D. thesis, MIT (2005)
11. McCune, J., Parno, B., Perrig, A., Reiter, M., Isozaki, H.: Flicker: an execution infrastructure for TCB minimization. ACM SIGOPS Operating Syst. Rev. **42**(4), 315–328 (2008)
12. Millen, J., Guttman, J., Ramsdell, J., Sheehy, J., Sniffen, B.: Analysis of a measured launch. http://www.mitre.org/work/tech_papers/tech_papers_07/07_0843/07_0843.pdf (2007). Accessed 7 Dec 2011

Security Correctness for Secure Nested Transactions
Extended Abstract

Dominic Duggan[1(✉)] and Ye Wu[2,3]

[1] Department of Computer Science, Stevens Institute of Technology, Hoboken, NJ 07030, USA
ddugganⓐstevens.edu
[2] Tencent, Kejizhongyi Avenue, Hi-tech Park, Nanshan District, Shenzhen, China
wuye01@baidu.com
[3] Baidu Inc, 23F, MaoYe Time Square, Nanshan District, Shenzhen 518000, China

Abstract. Secure nested transactions have been introduced as a synthesis of two long-standing lines of research in computer security: security correctness for multilevel databases, and language-based security. The motivation is to consider information flow control for certain classes of concurrent applications. This article describes a noninterference result for secure nested transactions, based on observational equivalence. A semantics for secure nested transactions is provided based on an extension of the pi-calculus with nested transactions, the $\mathbf{Tau_{One}}$ calculus. A novelty of this semantics is a constrained labelled transition system, where local transition rules place logical constraints on the global state of the transactional context. This context is described by a notion of *logs*, an abstraction for factoring transactional state out of the usual description of concurrent processes. An advantage of this approach is that it allows the consideration of security properties such as noninterference independently of transactional properties such as serializability.

1 Introduction

The approach of secure nested transactions considers the synthesis of information flow control in databases and in programming languages [7]. In the realm of multilevel databases, correct information flow has been defined defined in terms of noninterference for transactional execution. Consider for example the following program, that contains a high transaction T_1 and a low transaction T_2:

$\mathtt{int}^{\mathsf{Low}}$ `X, Y, Z;`
T_1^{High}: `lock(X); while (1) ;`
T_2^{Low}: `(lock(X); Z=0;)` $\|$ `(lock(Y); Z=1)`

Preventing the writing of sensitive information to a "low" database variable is insufficient, since the use of locks to synchronize accesses to the database provides a covert channel. In this example, T_1 signals to T_2 by locking `X` but not `Y`. In multilevel databases, this leak is prevented by allowing the low transaction to

M. Abadi and A. Lluch Lafuente (Eds.): TGC 2013, LNCS 8358, pp. 64–79, 2014.
DOI: 10.1007/978-3-319-05119-2_5,

implicitly pre-empt the high transaction when the latter holds a resource that the former requires [2].

In the realm of programming languages, Volpano and Smith [24] noted that the certification of multilevel secrecy in programs [6] could be formulated as a type system, and this idea has been adopted by many researchers [21]. The key insight in this work is that noninterference can be related to the control flow in a program, so that indirect leaks through the control flow may be prevented via a type-based control flow analysis.

Ensuring noninterference in concurrent and distributed systems is still a challenge, as indicated by the example above. The approach of secure nested transactions [7] combines the language-based and database-based approaches to information flow control, using the framework of nested transactions [16]. The temporary shifting of security levels (the main concept in language-based information flow control for sequential languages) is modelled by nested of transactions, with potentially different levels. As with multilevel databases, synchronization leaks are prevented by allowing lower security level transactions to preempt higher security level transactions. The main point of interest is the use of *retroactive abort* to allow a high child transaction to be rolled back after it has committed, though before all of its ancestor transactions have committed.

This article considers a method for verifying noninterference for a system of secure nested transactions. Noninterference is defined in terms of observational equivalence, allowing it to be verified independently of transactional properties such as serializability. The main innovation is a constrained operational semantics where transitions in the semantics place logical constraints on the transactional state of the context.

Section 2 provides an informal introduction to $\mathbf{Tau_{One}}$, a formal language for describing the semantics of nested transactions with retroactive abort. Section 3 presents the semantics of $\mathbf{Tau_{One}}$. We verify noninterference for this nested transactional calculus in Sect. 4. We consider related work and conclusions in Sect. 5. Further details and proofs are provided in the full version of the paper [8].

2 Logs for Transactional State

In this section, we provide the syntax of our transactional language, and consider the most salient innovation in this language, the use of logs to record transaction state. We refer to the calculus of secure nested transactions presented here as $\mathbf{Tau_{One}}$.

We base our language on the asynchronous pi-calculus. This calculus must support communication paths from low to high processes, so the latter can receive data from the former. It might be assumed that with asynchronous message-passing, it is safe to allow low processes to "write up" by sending low security level messages to high processes. However as noted by Pottier [17], it is then possible for high processes to signal indirectly to low processes by consuming messages of low security level. There are alternatives to observational equivalence for process equality, that can allow messages to be transmitted asynchronously from low to high processes. For example the may-testing equivalence used by Hennessy and Riely [12] accomodates such communication. However may-testing equivalence is a weak notion of process equivalence that equates to trace equivalence, and does not consider the deadlock behavior of processes. We choose observational equivalence to avoid controversy.

Synchronization in message-passing calculi is usually implemented using message-passing. Because of the aforesaid issues with traffic analysis in message-passing, we add a special form of message, that we refer to as "locks[1]." Our notion of locks serves two purposes:

1. It represents the most familiar form of synchronization in distributed transactions to the lay reader, the one that is used in the description of nested transactions in every textbook on distributed systems.
2. As we have seen above, with a suitably refined notion of observational equivalence, we cannot allow "low" messages to be received by "high" processes, since this would allow leaks based on traffic analysis. "Locks" provide a safe form of communication, based on messages that the runtime ensures are handled linearly. This linearity in message-passing is also the key to ensuring noninterference for secure type systems

The extension of the pi-calculus with logs is intended to separate the mechanics of the language runtime from the conditions that are required for correct transactional execution. These conditions are defined as logical constraints entailed by log entries. This approach avoids defining a system that overspecifies the implementation of retroactive abort. Checking of conditions with respect to the logs in turn can be combined with two-phase commit, as is done in practice for distributed systems.

The syntax of the language is provided in Fig. 1. We assume the following spaces of variables and names:

$$\begin{aligned} a, b, c, \ldots, &\in \text{Channel name} \\ x, y, z, w &\in \text{Variable} \\ \overrightarrow{t} &\in \text{Transaction id} \\ k &\in \text{Event id} \end{aligned}$$

The only values in the language are channel names, represented by constants $a, b, c, \ldots$. As mentioned, some channels have special significance in their use as locks: they have the property that they are always released by a transaction, whether that transaction commits or aborts. Channels and locks have security levels, as explained in Sect. 4 when we introduce the type system. These security levels stratify channels into high and low channels, with high channels only usable by high processes and similarly for low channels and low processes. Locks are similarly stratified into high and low, but low locks may be acquired by high processes.

---

[1] Even if lock-based concurrency control is replaced by some other notion, such as optimistic concurrency control, we will still require messages from low to high processes to be handled in a special, *linear* fashion. Therefore we will still need a construct similar to these messages, whether we call them locks or something else.

$C \in$ Channel Type ::=	$(\vec{C})^{\ell}$	Message channel
|	$\mathsf{Lock}(\vec{C})^{\ell}$	Lock
|	Unit^{ℓ}	Unit
$\ell \in$ Security Level ::=	$\mathsf{High} \mid \mathsf{Low}$	
$T \in$ Type ::=	C	Channel type
|	$\mathsf{Trans}(\ell)$	Transaction type
|	$\mathsf{Event}(\vec{t}, \ell)$	Event type
$w \in$ Name ::=	$a \mid \vec{t} \mid k$	
$v \in$ Value ::=	$a \mid x \mid ()$	
$A \in$ Agent ::=	$\vec{t} P$	Agent process
|	$A_1 \mid A_2$	Composition of agents
|	$[\![\mathscr{L}]\!]$	Local log
|	$(\nu a{:}C)A$	Local name
$P \in$ Proc ::=	$\hat{v}\vec{v}$	Send message
|	$\check{a}\vec{x}P$	Receive message
|	$(v_1{=}v_2) \rightarrow P_1 [] P_2$	Internal choice
|	$P_1 + P_2$	External choice
|	$\vec{t}[P]$	Launch transaction
|	$P_1 \mid P_2$	Fork process
|	$(\nu a{:}C)P$	New channel
|	$\mathsf{repl}\ P$	Replicate
|	stop	Stopped
|	$\square$	Commit or abort
|	$\mathsf{await}\ t[\square]\ \mathsf{then}\ P$	Test status
$\square \in$ Status ::=	$\boxdot$	Commit
|	$\boxtimes$	Abort
$V \in$ Env ::=	ε	Empty env
|	$(a : C)$	Channel decl
|	$(t : \mathsf{Trans}(\ell))$	Transaction decl
|	$(k : \mathsf{Event}(\vec{t}, \ell))$	Event declaration
|	$V_1.V_2$	Append envs
$\mathscr{L} \in$ Log ::=	true	Empty log
|	$\mathscr{L}_1 \wedge \mathscr{L}_2$	Join logs
|	$k{::}\, \vec{t}\, \hat{a}\, \vec{c}$	Log send
|	$k{::}\, \vec{t}\, \check{a}\, \vec{c}$	Log receive
|	$k_1 \searrow k_2$	Mesg exchanged
|	$k\ \mathsf{undone}$	Undone receive
|	$k_1 \curvearrowright k_2$	Lock transferred
|	$\vec{t}\boxdot$	Trans commit
|	$\vec{t}\boxtimes$	Trans abort

Fig. 1. **Tau$_{\mathbf{One}}$** syntax

We assume the definition of metafunctions $bn(\_)$ and $fn(\_)$ for computing the set of bound and free names, respectively, in a syntactic term. We also assume the definition of the metafunction $fv(\_)$ for computing the set of free variables in a syntactic term.

Each transaction is identified by a sequence of transaction identifiers $\overrightarrow{t} = (t_1, \ldots, t_k)$ for some k. Here t_1 is intended to be the root transaction, and the complete path identifies a nested transaction and all of its ancestors. We denote the prefix relation between sequences by $\leq$, so we have:

$$\overrightarrow{t_1} \leq \overrightarrow{t_2} \text{ iff } \overrightarrow{t_2} = \overrightarrow{t_1}.\overrightarrow{t_1'}$$

where the period denotes sequence concatenation. Note that $\overrightarrow{t_1} \leq \overrightarrow{t_2}$ means that the former transaction is an ancestor of the latter. This is used extensively in what follows.

The syntax of types is provided in Fig. 1. We assume a security type system to prevent information flow leaks, by classifying data as High or Low. The details of this type system are provided in the full version of the paper [8]. These security levels ℓ decorate the types of message channels $(\overrightarrow{C})^\ell$ and locks $\mathsf{Lock}(\overrightarrow{C})^\ell$, and reflect restrictions on information that can be exchanged as a result of synchronization. Transactions are either "high" or "low," as reflected by their types, and can only have effects (sending and receiving of messages) based on their allowed security level. Whereas in sequential languages, a low thread can raise its security level to high in order to make high side effects, in our language a low transaction must spawn a high child transaction to have high effects. The most salient aspect of the type system is that we have the inclusion: $\mathsf{Lock}(\overrightarrow{C})^{\ell_1} \preceq \mathsf{Lock}(\overrightarrow{C})^{\ell_2}$ if $\ell_1 \preceq \ell_2$. Thus it is possible for both high and low transactions to compete for "low" locks, if we consider them as "low" messages whose security level can be elevated to "high." This is only safe because of the special handling of lock messages by the semantics. Ordinary message channels do not have this inclusion.

There are various forms of log rules added during evaluation:

1. A log entry of the form $k{::}\, \overrightarrow{t}\, \hat{a}\, \overrightarrow{c}$ requires the sending of a message or generation of a lock. If the former, the message is sent by a transaction operating within the transaction $\overrightarrow{t}$. If the latter, the type system requires that the lock be generated at top-level, outside the scope of any transaction ($|\overrightarrow{t}| = 0$).
2. A log entry of the form $k{::}\, \overrightarrow{t}\, \check{a}\, \overrightarrow{c}$ records the receipt of a message or acquisition of a lock by a process executing in the transaction $\overrightarrow{t}$.
3. A log entry of the form $k_1 \searrow k_2$ relates a receive event k_2 to the corresponding send event k_1. It has several purposes. One is to establish a failure dependency from the sending to the receiving transaction: If the former is aborted, the latter is required in turn to abort. Another purpose is to relate a receive event to the corresponding send event, so that if the latter is undone in the process of aborting a transaction, the corresponding message to be restored is identified.

4. A log entry of the form k undone denotes that the action logged with event identifier k in the logs has been undone. This corresponds to a message receive or lock acquisition event that has been undone because the corresponding transaction has aborted. This type of log entry is used to ensure that message receives are only undone once in the event that a transaction aborts.
5. A log entry of the form $k_2 \curvearrowright k_1$ denotes that the lock acquired in the event labelled with k_2 has been released (or "anti-inherited") from a transaction to one of its ancestor transactions, as a result of the former transaction having committed. The lock was then acquired by a descendant of that ancestor transaction, in a lock acquisition event labelled k_1. The actual anti-inheritance of locks up the transaction tree is implicit in the committal of ancestor transactions, and fresh log entries for a lock are only added when descendant of one of these ancestors (a "cousin" transaction) acquires the lock. A log entry reflecting the ownership of this lock by the cousin transaction is recorded in the logs with an event identifier k_1. It is the counterpart to the $k_2 \searrow k_1$, but where the lock has already been acquired in the transaction tree and now its ownership is being transferred within that tree.

Consider the following example (we insert semi-colons for readability):

$$A_0 = (\hat{a} \mid t_1(\check{a}; (\hat{a} \mid \boxdot)) \mid t_2(\check{a}; (\hat{a} \mid \boxdot)) \mid t_3(\check{a}; (\hat{a} \mid \boxdot)))$$

where t_1, t_2 and t_3 are top-level transactions. Assume that a is an ordinary communication channel. In this case, none of the transactions are nested.

This agent expression may evolve to the following:

$$A_1 = (t_2(\check{a}; (\hat{a} \mid \boxdot)) \mid t_3(\check{a}; (\hat{a} \mid \boxdot)) \mid [\![\mathscr{L}_1]\!])$$
$$\mathscr{L}_1 = k_0{::}\hat{a} \wedge k_1{::}t_1\check{a} \wedge k_0 \searrow k_1 \wedge t_1\boxdot$$

and then to:

$$A_2 = (t_3(\check{a}; (\hat{a} \mid \boxdot)) \mid [\![\mathscr{L}_2]\!])$$
$$\mathscr{L}_2 = \mathscr{L}_1 \wedge k_1'{::}\hat{a} \wedge k_2{::}t_2\check{a} \wedge k_1' \searrow k_2 \wedge t_2\boxdot$$

and finally to an empty agent expression $A_3 = [\![\mathscr{L}_3]\!]$, with

$$\mathscr{L}_3 = \mathscr{L}_2 \wedge k_2'{::}\hat{a} \wedge k_3{::}t_3\check{a} \wedge k_2' \searrow k_3 \wedge t_3\,\boxdot\,.$$

The logs record the receipt of a message by t_1, the receipt of an unrelated message by t_2, and the receipt of yet another unrelated message by t_3. Although these messages are unrelated, they establish failure dependencies between otherwise unrelated transactions. Since a transactions messages not visible until it commits, these failure dependencies are somewhat pointless at this point. A transaction can only establish a failure dependency on a transaction that has already committed.

Consider now the same example, but where a is a lock rather than a message channel. None of the transactions can "send" on the lock channel, since locks can only be sent at top-level, outside the scope of a transaction. Instead, by committing, they implicitly make the lock they have acquired available to other transactions, by anti-inheritance to their parent or to the top-level. So we rewrite the example as follows:

$$A_0 = (\hat{a} \mid t_1(\check{a};\boxdot) \mid t_2(\check{a};\boxdot) \mid t_3(\check{a};\boxdot))$$

This agent expression may evolve to the following:

$$A_1 = (t_2(\check{a};\boxdot) \mid t_3(\check{a};\boxdot) \mid [\![\mathscr{L}_1]\!])$$
$$\mathscr{L}_1 = k_0{::}\hat{a} \wedge k_1{::}t_1\check{a} \wedge k_0 \searrow k_1 \wedge t_1\boxdot$$

and then to:

$$A_2 = (t_3(\check{a};\boxdot) \mid [\![\mathscr{L}_2]\!])$$
$$\mathscr{L}_2 = \mathscr{L}_1 \wedge k_2{::}t_2\check{a} \wedge k_1 \curvearrowright k_2 \wedge t_2\boxdot$$

and finally to an empty agent expression A_3, with $A_3 = [\![\mathscr{L}_3]\!]$, with

$$\mathscr{L}_3 = \mathscr{L}_2 \wedge k_3{::}t_3\check{a} \wedge k_2 \curvearrowright k_3 \wedge t_3\boxdot\,.$$

The logs record the acquisition of the lock by t_1, transfer of the lock from t_1 to t_2, and then to t_3. This is tracing the history of the transfer of ownership of a single lock through the system.

A crucial point to note here is that acquisition of a lock by a transaction does *not* induce a failure dependency from transaction owning the lock to the transaction acquiring the lock. In the example in Fig. 2, if $\overrightarrow{t_1}$ acquires a lock from $\overrightarrow{t_0}$,then the abort of $\overrightarrow{t_0}$ does not induce the abort of $\overrightarrow{t_1}$. This is due to the restricted access to locks provided to transactions: a transaction cannot duplicate or destroy a lock. The type rules require that locks are generated at the top level, outside any transaction. Once acquired, a log entry records the holding of the lock by the transaction, until abort or commit of that transaction makes it available to other transactions. The release of the lock is guaranteed by the semantics of abort and commit of transactions. In effect we guarantee that locks are handled in a linear fashion: once acquired, a lock is always released.

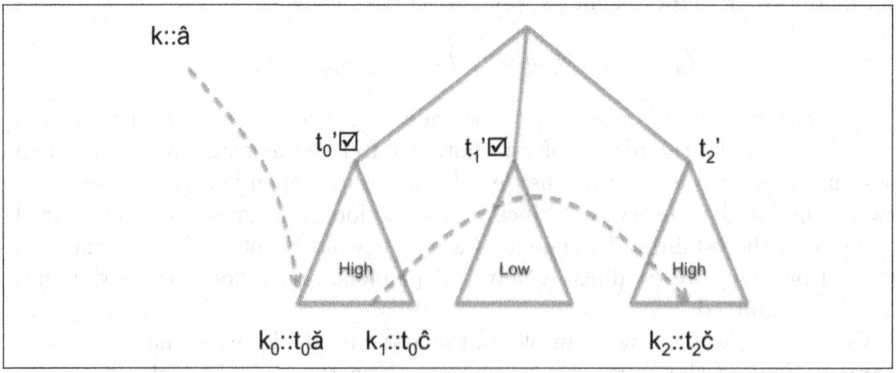

Fig. 2. Failure dependencies with retroactive abort

Table 1. Log judgements

$V, \mathscr{L} \vdash k{::}A$	Identifiable log entry
$V, \mathscr{L} \vdash A$	Anonymous log entry
$V, \mathscr{L} \vdash k_1 \searrow k_2$	Mesg or lock acquired
$V, \mathscr{L} \vdash k_1 \curvearrowright k_2$	Lock released
$V, \mathscr{L} \vdash k$ undone	Action undone
$V, \mathscr{L} \vdash \overrightarrow{t}$ $\mathsf{running}$	Transaction still running
$V, \mathscr{L} \vdash \overrightarrow{t}$ $\mathsf{aborted}$	Transaction aborted
$V, \mathscr{L} \vdash \overrightarrow{t}$ $\mathsf{committed}$ $\overrightarrow{t_0}$	Transaction committed
$V, \mathscr{L} \vdash k{::}A$ $\mathsf{terminal}$	Terminal lock ownership
$V, \mathscr{L} \vdash k{::}A$ $\mathsf{undoable}$	Undoable receive
$V, \mathscr{L} \vdash k{::}A$ $\mathsf{transferable}$ $\overrightarrow{t}$	Transferable lock
$V, \mathscr{L} \vdash k{::}A$ $\mathsf{preemptible}$ $\overrightarrow{t_2} \curvearrowright \overrightarrow{t_1}$	Preemptible trans
$V, \mathscr{L} \vdash k_1 \rightsquigarrow k_2$	Failure dependency
$V, \mathscr{L} \vdash k_1 \overset{*}{\curvearrowright} k_2$	Transfer of ownership

Rather than relying on linear types to statically enforce the linear handling of locks, we rely on the semantics of transactions to enforce this handling.

The operational semantics of $\mathbf{Tau_{One}}$ uses various judgements to check preconditions by reference to the log, as summarized in Table 1. The first five judgements correspond to simply looking up a log entry, while the remaining judgements are based on inferences drawn from the contents of the log. Further explanation for these judgements, including a inference system for infererences that can be drawn from logs, is provided in the full version of the article [8].

3 Constrained Operational Semantics

In this section, we consider the operational semantics of $\mathbf{Tau_{One}}$. An obvious and straightforward way to make use of logs is add preconditions to some of the operational semantics rules that check the logs for certain conditions. For example, a transaction should no longer be able to receive messages from other transactions if it has committed or aborted.

The complication is with our decision to use observational equivalence to reason about noninterference in the presence of concurrent processes with synchronization. We are forced to treat logs as local and distributed among the processes, rather than parameterizing the semantics by a single global log, because compositional reasoning about processes includes the ability to encapsulate local channel names within a process, preventing their "leakage" to outside processes unless they are explicitly communicated. *Scope extrusion* in the process equivalence rules is a fundamental aspect of the pi-calculus. Some log entries contain reference to channel names, so they cannot simply be globalized. Since transaction state, as represented by logs, is now local, compositional reasoning in turns requires some mechanism for constraining the possible contexts.

For example, if we allow a transaction to make progress because we assume it is still running, we must constrain the surrounding context to prevent any log entries that record it as committed or aborted, or record any causal dependencies on transactions that are committed or aborted.

The purpose of an LTS here is to give definitions of the reduction rules for the semantics that are purely local. The labels in the transition rules then specify logical conditions that must be satisfied by any context with which a process performing such an action is composed. For example, if a reduction rule requires as a precondition that a transaction is still running, then any context surrounding the application of that reduction rule must satisfy the conditions:

1. There are no log entries for abort of any transactions upon which that transaction is failure dependent.
2. No ancestor of that transaction can have committed.

We define a logic in which these conditions are specified, and statements in this logic are used as labels in the LTS to constrain contexts surrounding the application of the reduction rules of the semantics:

$$\begin{aligned}
\mathscr{F}^A &::= \overrightarrow{t_1} \rightsquigarrow \overrightarrow{t_2} \mid k_1 \overset{*}{\curvearrowright} k_2 \mid k{::}\,\overrightarrow{t}\,\hat{a}\,\overrightarrow{c} \mid k{::}\,\overrightarrow{t}\,\breve{a}\,\overrightarrow{c} \mid \\
&\quad\ \overrightarrow{t}\,[\Box] \mid k \ \mathsf{undone} \mid k_1 = k_2 \\
\mathscr{F} &::= \mathsf{true} \mid \mathscr{F}_1 \wedge \mathscr{F}_2 \mid \mathscr{F}_1 \vee \mathscr{F}_2 \mid \\
&\quad\ \forall X{:}T.\mathscr{F} \mid \exists X{:}T.\mathscr{F} \mid \mathscr{F}^A \mid \neg \mathscr{F}^A
\end{aligned}$$

We furthermore distinguish the positive and negative constraints:

$$\begin{aligned}
\mathscr{F}^+ &::= \mathsf{true} \mid \mathscr{F}_1^+ \wedge \mathscr{F}_2^+ \mid \exists X{:}T.\mathscr{F}^+ \mid \mathscr{F}^A \\
\mathscr{F}^- &::= \mathsf{true} \mid \mathscr{F}_1^- \wedge \mathscr{F}_2^- \mid \forall X{:}T.\mathscr{F} \mid \neg \mathscr{F}^A
\end{aligned}$$

Define:

$$\mathscr{F}_1^A \supset \mathscr{F}_2 \equiv \neg \mathscr{F}_1^A \vee \mathscr{F}_2$$

Positive constraints require the presence of particular log entries. Once satisfied, a positive constraint may be discharged. Negative constraints on the other hand prevent certain conditions from becoming true in the logs. They typically contain both universal quantifiers (quantifying over all log entries) and negative conditions (sometimes constraining the domain of a universal quantifier, and sometimes requiring that certain forms of log entries be absent). Since they are intended to constrain all expansions of the logs, it is not possible to discharge them. The key observation is that constraints concerning messages ($k{::}\,\overrightarrow{t}\,\hat{a}\,\overrightarrow{c}$ and $k{::}\,\overrightarrow{t}\,\breve{a}\,\overrightarrow{c}$) are always positive constraints, and thus can eventually be discharged. With transaction identifiers and event identifiers always globally defined, this allows local scoping of message channel and lock names. The latter in turn is important for reasoning about noninterference.

The use of negative conditions is restricted to checking the absence of log entries of particular forms (including failure and ownership dependency). This

$$
\begin{aligned}
\mathscr{F}(\overrightarrow{t}\ \mathsf{running}) &= (\forall \overrightarrow{t_0}.\overrightarrow{t_0} \leq \overrightarrow{t} \supset \neg \overrightarrow{t_0}\boxdot) \wedge (\forall \overrightarrow{t_0}.\overrightarrow{t_0} \rightsquigarrow \overrightarrow{t} \supset \neg \overrightarrow{t_0}\boxtimes) \\
\mathscr{F}(\overrightarrow{t}\ \mathsf{committed}\ \overrightarrow{t_0}) &= \exists t'.(\overrightarrow{t_0}.t' \leq \overrightarrow{t} \wedge \overrightarrow{t_0}.t'\boxdot) \wedge \forall \overrightarrow{t_1}.(\overrightarrow{t_1} \rightsquigarrow \overrightarrow{t} \supset \neg \overrightarrow{t_1}\boxtimes) \\
\mathscr{F}(\overrightarrow{t}\ \mathsf{aborted}) &= \exists \overrightarrow{t_0}.\overrightarrow{t_0}\boxtimes \wedge \overrightarrow{t_0} \rightsquigarrow \overrightarrow{t} \\
\mathscr{F}(k{::}\,\overrightarrow{t}\,\check{a}\,\overrightarrow{c}\ \mathsf{terminal}) &= k{::}\,\overrightarrow{t}\,\check{a}\,\overrightarrow{c} \wedge \forall k_0.(k = k_0 \vee \neg(k \overset{*}{\curvearrowright} k_0) \vee \exists \overrightarrow{t_0}.\overrightarrow{t_0}\boxtimes \wedge \overrightarrow{t_0} \rightsquigarrow k_0) \\
\mathscr{F}(k{::}\,\overrightarrow{t}\,\hat{a}\,\overrightarrow{c}\ \mathsf{undoable}) &= \mathscr{F}(k{::}\,\overrightarrow{t}\,\check{a}\,\overrightarrow{c}\ \mathsf{terminal}) \wedge \mathscr{F}(\overrightarrow{t}\ \mathsf{aborted}) \wedge \neg(k\ \mathsf{undone}) \\
\mathscr{F}(k{::}\,\overrightarrow{t}\,\check{a}\,\overrightarrow{c}\ \mathsf{transferable}\ \overrightarrow{t_0}) &= \mathscr{F}(k{::}\,\overrightarrow{t}\,\check{a}\,\overrightarrow{c}\ \mathsf{terminal}) \wedge \mathscr{F}(\overrightarrow{t}\ \mathsf{committed}\ \overrightarrow{t_0}) \\
\mathscr{F}(k_0{::}\,\overrightarrow{t_0}\,\check{a}\,\overrightarrow{c}\ \mathsf{preemptible}\ \overrightarrow{t_2} \curvearrowright \overrightarrow{t_1}) &= \\
&\quad \mathscr{F}(k_0{::}\,\overrightarrow{t_0}\,\check{a}\,\overrightarrow{c}\ \mathsf{terminal}) \wedge \\
&\quad \exists \overrightarrow{t_0'}.(\mathscr{F}(\overrightarrow{t_0}\ \mathsf{committed}\ \overrightarrow{t_0'}) \wedge \mathscr{F}(\overrightarrow{t_0'}\ \mathsf{running}))
\end{aligned}
$$

Fig. 3. Mapping log judgements to constraints

is sufficient for encoding the negative conditions that are required for some of the reduction rules in the semantics. We define the mapping from judgements of the log inference logic to logical preconditions in this constrained reduction semantics, in Fig. 3.

Given an agent expression A, then A^* denotes the logs underlying this agent expression, i.e., all log entries that are contained in log expressions in the agent expression.

The constrained semantics are specified using reduction rules of the form:

$$V \vdash A \overset{\mathscr{F}}{\Longrightarrow} A'$$

and using reaction rules of the form:

$$(V, A) \overset{\mathscr{F}}{\longrightarrow} (V', A')$$

The former rules denote "internal" reduction steps within a process expression, while the latter reaction rules denote computational steps that involve interactions with the surrounding context. In both forms of rules, the set V records type bindings of global channels, the agent expression A denotes the redex, and the agent expression A' denotes the reduct. The reaction rules include a constraint on the surrounding logs in the context, as already explained. We use $\left\{ \begin{array}{c} V \vdash A \Longrightarrow A' \\ (V,A) \longrightarrow (V',A') \end{array} \right\}$ as an abbreviation for $\left\{ \begin{array}{c} V \vdash A \overset{\mathsf{true}}{\Longrightarrow} A' \\ (V,A) \overset{\mathsf{true}}{\longrightarrow} (V,A') \end{array} \right\}$

The definition of a context $\mathscr{C}$ is given by:

$$\mathscr{C} ::= [\,] \mid (\mathscr{C} \mid A) \mid (\nu a{:}C)\mathscr{C}$$

An expression of the form $\mathscr{C}[A]$ denotes instantiating a context with an agent.

We also have a notion of *contextual constraint entailment*. We use the judgement form

$$V, \mathscr{L} \vdash \mathscr{C}[A] \rhd \mathscr{F}_1 \supset \mathscr{C}[\mathscr{F}_2].$$

The idea is that a computation step may have occurred with the agent A, in the context $\mathscr{C}$. The original set of constraints required to justify this computation step was $\mathscr{F}_2$. The constraint set $\mathscr{F}_1$ represents the result of simplifying these constraints under the context $\mathscr{C}$. For example, a positive constraint in $\mathscr{F}_2$ requiring the presence of a particular log entry may be discharged if that log entry is present in A. If the remaining constraints $\mathscr{F}_1$ are satisfied by the agent $\mathscr{C}[A]$, augmented by the log entries $\mathscr{L}$, then the original set of constraints $\mathscr{F}_2$ is satisfiable by the logs in A, the log entries added by the context $\mathscr{C}$, and the log entries $\mathscr{L}$.

Finally we have the following notion of repeated computation:

$$\begin{aligned}(V, A) \xRightarrow{*\mathscr{F}^-} (V', A') \text{iff}\, V = V_0, A = A_0, V' = V_n, A' = A_n,\\ (V_j, A_j) \xrightarrow{\mathscr{F}_j^-} (V_{j+1}, A_{j+1}) \text{ for } j = 0, \ldots, n-1\\ \text{and } \mathscr{F}^- \equiv \mathscr{F}_0^- \wedge \cdots \wedge \mathscr{F}_{n-1}^-,\end{aligned}$$

Once a reduction step has taken place, a negative condition may no longer be true in the resulting configuration. For example, once the receipt of a message by an aborted transaction has been undone, the absence of a log entry recording this undoing is no longer true. However the constraints on the reduction steps are intended to constrain the observer rather than the computation (once the positive constraints have been discharged). An allowable observer context is one in which all of the undischarged negative constraints are satisfied. Any changes to the logs that invalidates one of these constraints is internal to the process being observed.

4 Noninterference

In this section, we verify noninterference for the calculus of nested transactions, based on the security type system presented in the previous section. The verification is based on the observable behavior of processes. Because our calculus is asynchronous, we only consider observables arising from messages sent, since the receiving of messages cannot be observed directly.

Messages offered to the environment are defined in terms of barbs. Our definition of barbs differs from the normal case in certain important regards:

1. The definition of barbs is relativized to the transactional level at which an observation may be made. For example, a message cannot be observed at a certain level $\overrightarrow{t}$ until that message has become visible due to being committed by lower level transactions.
2. Barbs include a constraint on the context for the output to be offered. For example, a process may only offer a message to the context if any tranaction of which it is a part is still running.

3. Barbs may be offered not just by outputting messages, but also by relinquishing locks. Such locks are not manipulated explicitly by the processes, but are recorded in the logs and manipulated implicitly by commit and abort operations, and lock acquisition by other processes.
4. Barbs may be implicitly available, if they correspond to locks that are held by high-level processes that may be preempeted by low-level processes.

Definition 1 (Strong Barbs). *Define that the agent A in the environment V offers the* strong barb $\overrightarrow{t}a$ *with constraint $\mathscr{F}$, written $(V, A) \downarrow^{\mathscr{F}}_{\overrightarrow{t}a}$, if $V \vdash A \xRightarrow{\mathscr{F}_1^-} A'$ for some A' and $\mathscr{F}_1^-$, and there is a context $\mathscr{C}$ such that one of the following cases holds:*

1. $A' = \mathscr{C}[\overrightarrow{t_0}\hat{a}\overrightarrow{c}]$ *and* $\mathscr{F}_2 = \mathscr{F}(\overrightarrow{t_0}\ \textsf{committed}\ \overrightarrow{t})$*; or for some* $\overrightarrow{t_0}, \overrightarrow{c}$*; or*
2. $A' = \mathscr{C}[\overrightarrow{t_0}[\![\mathscr{L}]\!]]$ *and* $\mathscr{L} \equiv \mathscr{L}' \wedge k{::}\overrightarrow{t_0}\check{a}\overrightarrow{c}$ *and* $\mathscr{F}_2 = \mathscr{F}(k{::}\overrightarrow{t_0}\check{a}\overrightarrow{c}\ \textsf{transferable}\ \overrightarrow{t})$ *for some* $\overrightarrow{t_0}, \overrightarrow{c}$*; or*
3. $A' = \mathscr{C}[\overrightarrow{t}(\check{a}\overrightarrow{x}P_1 + P_2)]$ *and* $\mathscr{F}_2 = \mathscr{F}(k_0{::}\overrightarrow{t_1}\check{a}\overrightarrow{c}\ \textsf{preemptible}\ \overrightarrow{t_2} \curvearrowright \overrightarrow{t}) \wedge \mathscr{F}(\overrightarrow{t}\ \textsf{running})$*, and* $lev(V, \overrightarrow{t}) = \textsf{Low}$ *and* $lev(V, \overrightarrow{t_2}) = \textsf{High}$*.*

Furthermore we must have

$$V, \textsf{true} \vdash A' \rhd \mathscr{F}_2^- \supset \mathscr{F}_2$$

for some $\mathscr{F}_2^-$ such that $\mathscr{F} \equiv \mathscr{F}_1^- \wedge \mathscr{F}_2^-$.

This last condition states the log constraint $\mathscr{F}_2$ must be derivable from the agent expression A' (which may include log entries) and the remaining constraints $\mathscr{F}_2^-$ that arise from internal processing before the barb is offered.

Lemma 1. *Suppose $V \vdash A_1 \xRightarrow{\mathscr{F}^-} A_2$. Then $(V, A_2) \downarrow^{\mathscr{F}_2^-}_{\overrightarrow{t}a}$ if and only if $(V, A_1) \downarrow^{\mathscr{F}_1^-}_{\overrightarrow{t}a}$, for some $\mathscr{F}_1^- \equiv \mathscr{F}^- \wedge \mathscr{F}_2^-$.*

Definition 2 (Barbs). *Define $(V, A) \Downarrow^{\mathscr{F}^-}_{\overrightarrow{t}a}$ if $(V, A) \xRightarrow{*\mathscr{F}_1^-} (V', A')$ and $(V', A') \downarrow^{\mathscr{F}_2^-}_{\overrightarrow{t}a}$, and $\mathscr{F}^- \equiv \mathscr{F}_1^- \wedge \mathscr{F}_2^-$.*

Definition 3 (Barbed Bisimulation). *Define that a relation R is a* barbed bisimulation *if R is symmetric and, whenever $(A_1, A_2) \in R$, we have:*

1. *If for some V and $\mathscr{F}_1^-$ we have $(V, A_1) \xrightarrow{\mathscr{F}_1^-} (V_1', A_1')$, then $(V, A_2) \xRightarrow{*\mathscr{F}_2^-} (V_2', A_2')$ for some $V_2', A_2', \mathscr{F}_2^-$ such that $\mathscr{F}_1^- \equiv \mathscr{F}_2^-$ and $(A_1', A_2') \in R$.*
2. *If for some V and $\mathscr{F}_1^-$ we have $(V, A_1) \downarrow^{\mathscr{F}_1^-}_{\overrightarrow{t}a}$, then $(V, A_2) \Downarrow^{\mathscr{F}_2^-}_{\overrightarrow{t}a}$, for some $\mathscr{F}_2^-$ such that $\mathscr{F}_1^- \equiv \mathscr{F}_2^-$.*

Define that A_1 and A_2 are bisimilar, written $A_1 \stackrel{\bullet}{\approx} A_2$, if $(A_1, A_2) \in R$ for some bisimulation R.

A context $\mathscr{C}$ is a (V_1, ℓ_1)-(V_2, ℓ_2)-*context* if $V_2 \vdash \mathscr{C}\ \mathsf{agent}^{\ell_2}$ is derivable from $V_1 \vdash [\,]\ \mathsf{agent}^{\ell_1}$. An environment V is *closed* if it only binds names, and event and transaction identifiers. In particular it does not bind program variables.

Definition 4 (Barbed Congruence). *Define the barbed congruence $\approx_{V,\ell}$ by: $A_1 \approx_{V,\ell} A_2$ if*

1. $V \vdash A_1\ \mathsf{agent}^{\ell}$,
2. $V \vdash A_2\ \mathsf{agent}^{\ell}$, *and*
3. *for any closed V' and secrecy level ℓ', for any (V,ℓ)-(V',ℓ')-context $\mathscr{C}$, we have $\mathscr{C}[A_1] \overset{\bullet}{\approx} \mathscr{C}[A_2]$.*

Our main tool for reasoning about noninterference is an erasure of processes of high security level. We then show that any barbed congruences among low processes are unaffected by the erasure of the high processes. The complication with this is that there may be interactions between high and low processes. For example, a low process may acquire a lock that was released by a high process after it committed. The key insight is that erasure must be defined in such a way that it modifies the logs to remove any references to logs of high processes.

Recall the following example:

$$A_0 = (\hat{a} \mid t_1(\check{a}; \boxdot) \mid t_2(\check{a}; \boxdot) \mid t_3(\check{a}; \boxdot))$$

where we assume now that t_1 and t_3 are low transactions, and t_2 is high. Assume that a is a low-level lock, of type $\mathsf{Lock}(\ )^{\mathsf{Low}}$. As we have seen, this agent expression may evolve to $A_3 = [\![\mathscr{L}_3]\!]$, with

$$\mathscr{L}_3 = \mathscr{L}_2 \wedge k_3{::}t_3\check{a} \wedge k_2 \curvearrowright k_3 \wedge t_3 \boxdot .$$

The logs record the acquisition of the lock by t_1, transfer of the lock from t_1 to t_2, and then to t_3. In the erasure of the logs, we remove the dependency of the low transaction t_3 on the high transaction t_1 by rewriting the log entries to a dependency on t_1 instead:

$$\mathscr{E}^{L}_{V,\mathscr{L}}(\mathscr{L}_3) = \mathscr{E}^{L}_{V,\mathscr{L}}(\mathscr{L}_1) \wedge k_3{::}t_3\check{a} \wedge k_1 \curvearrowright k_3 \wedge t_3 \boxdot .$$

In the erasure, the logs for any high transactions have been removed, and the logs of any low transactions have been modified where necessary to remove any dependencies on the erased high transactions.

Consider now the above example where it is the transaction t_1, that initially acquires the lock, that is high. Both t_2 and t_3 are low. In the final configuration, we have the logs:

$$\mathscr{E}^{L}_{V,\mathscr{L}}(\mathscr{L}_2) = k_0{::}\hat{a} \wedge k_2{::}t_2\check{a} \wedge k_0 \searrow k_2 \wedge t_2 \boxdot .$$
$$\mathscr{E}^{L}_{V,\mathscr{L}}(\mathscr{L}_3) = \mathscr{E}^{L}_{V,\mathscr{L}}(\mathscr{L}_2) \wedge k_3{::}t_3\check{a} \wedge k_2 \curvearrowright k_3 \wedge t_3 \boxdot .$$

In this case, the logs for t_1 have been erased. These logs contain entries $k_1{::}t_1\check{a}$ and $k_0 \searrow k_1$. In the erasure, the log entry $k_1 \curvearrowright k_2$ for t_2 is translated to $k_0 \searrow k_2$. The transfer of the a lock from t_1 to t_2 is translated in the log entries into the acquisition of the lock at top level by t_2.

Theorem 1 (Noninterference). *Suppose V is a low-level environment, and $\mathscr{C}_0$ is a (V_0, High)-(V, ℓ) environment. If $V_0 \vdash A_1$ $\mathsf{agent}^{\mathsf{High}}$ and $V_0 \vdash A_2$ $\mathsf{agent}^{\mathsf{High}}$, then $\mathscr{C}_0[A_1] \approx_{V,\ell} \mathscr{C}_0[A_2]$.*

5 Related Work and Conclusions

A great deal of work on information flow control has been done in the concurrency community. Hennessy and Riely [11,12] develop a security π-calculus for which they study noninterference properties with respect to *may* and *must* testing. Honda and Yoshida [14] design a sophisticated system with linear and affine types for π-calculus to investigate noninterference expressed in terms of bisimulation. Boudol and Castellani [4] present a simple imperative language extended with parallelism to explore noninterference in a probabilistic setting. Ryan and Schneider characterize the absence of information flow in *CSP* [18] based on the notion of process equivalence. Piazza et al. [1] generalize an unwinding framework for the definition of a security property that entails a noninterference principle described in a simple concurrent language. Similar approach related to this line of work can also be found in [5]. Most of these works are focused on strong noninterference properties usually characterized by a partial equivalence relation in a typed process language.

To avoid termination leaks in concurrency, Smith and Vopano [22] investigated noninterference in a constrained multi-threaded language that does not allow high guard in `while` loops. Later, Smith, and independently, Boudol and Castellani [4] relaxed this constraint by allowing such a statement if only followed by a high statement, if any. Sabefeld [19] simulates such while loops as an effect of synchronization, in addition to the restriction above. High to low process synchronization is impossible due to the confinement of semaphores. In all these multi-threaded languages, variant conservative security type systems are constructed to rule out potential termination leak by restricting programs to certain behaviors. To enhance expressiveness, Sabefeld and Mantel [20] introduce encryption and more communication primitives in their multi-threaded language. In security process calculi, Hennessy identifies a similar problem in designing multi-security levels in [11], where the strong noninterference property cannot be achieved, because contention on different security level channels reveals distinct timing behavior to observers. Focardi et al. [9,10] propose a *program transformation* approach to mask such activity by including execution possibilities. Another trend in permitting secure communication such as synchronization and deadlock-freedom is to relieve the restrictions, such as in [11,12,17], where linear type systems are designed to enforce security properties. The goal of secure nested transactions is to provide a relatively simple and familiar type system, with the dynamic semantics enforcing properties that would in the aforesaid approaches be enforced using type-checking [13–15,25]. The relationship between our work and these other works is demonstrated by for example the fact that our proof technique for noninterference follows the technique used by Kobayashi for a system with linear types [15], where the latter is in turn based on the approach of Pottier [17].

Bertino et al. [3] consider noninterference for nested transactions. They are principally concerned with the issue of starvation of high transactions in multilevel databases. That work does not consider "mixed" nested transactions, consisting of both high and low transactions combined in a nested transaction. This consideration is central to the current article, proposed as the natural generalization of security-typed sequential languages to the concurrent, transactional context.

Stefan et al. [23] propose an alternative, mitigation-based approach to hande termination channels such as those motivating this work. Their approach relies on moving the computation would potentially view the leaked information to a separate thread, and dynamically raising the security level of that thread if information would otherwise leak. Both approaches share a philosophy of supplementing static type-based analysis with dynamic mechanisms (transaction-based pre-emption, thread-based mitigation) to prevent termination leaks in concurrent systems.

In related work [7], we have developed a "global" version of this semantics, where all logs are used at "top-level." This semantics is greatly simplified by avoiding the need for logical constraints on reaction rules in the semantics. Instead the logs are tested directly for preconditions. This simplification is possible because in the global system we are not concerned about reasoning compositionally about observational equivalence for the purpose of verifying noninterference. Using this system, we are able to verify serializability result, and to relate that global system to the local system presented here.

References

1. Piazza, C., Bossi, A., Rossi, S.: Compositional information flow security for concurrent programs. J. Comput. Secur. **15**(3), 373–416 (2007)
2. Atluri, V., Jajodia, S., George, B.: Multilevel Secure Transaction Processing. Kluwer Academic, Boston (1999)
3. Bertino, E., Catania, B., Ferrari, E.: A nested transaction model for multilevel secure database management systems. ACM Trans. Inf. Syst. Secur. **4**, 321–370 (2001)
4. Boudol, G., Castellani, I.: Noninterference for concurrent programs and thread systems. Theor. Comput. Sci. **281**(1–2), 109–130 (2002)
5. Crafa, S., Rossi, S.: A theory of noninterference for the π-calculus. In: De Nicola, R., Sangiorgi, D. (eds.) TGC 2005. LNCS, vol. 3705, pp. 2–18. Springer, Heidelberg (2005)
6. Denning, D.E., Denning, P.J.: Certifications of programs for secure information flow. Commun. ACM **20**(7), 504–513 (1977)
7. Duggan, D., Wu, Y.: Transactional correctness for secure nested transactions. In: Bruni, R., Sassone, V. (eds.) TGC 2011. LNCS, vol. 7173, pp. 179–196. Springer, Heidelberg (2012)
8. Duggan, D., Wu, Y.: Security correctness for secure nested transactions. Technical Report 2013–4, Stevens Institute of Technology. http://www.jeddak.org/Results/Stevens-CS-TR-2013-4.pdf (2013)

9. Focardi, R., Gorrieri, R.: Classification of security properties (part i: information flow). In: Focardi, R., Gorrieri, R. (eds.) FOSAD 2000. LNCS, vol. 2171, pp. 331–396. Springer, Heidelberg (2001)
10. Focardi, R., Rossi, S.: Information flow security in dynamic contexts. In: Computer Security Foundations Workshop, pp. 307–319. IEEE Press (2002)
11. Hennessy, M.: The security picalculus and non-interference. J. Logic Algebraic Program. **63**, 3–34 (2004)
12. Hennessy, M., Riely, J.: Information flow vs resource access in the asynchronous pi-calculus. TOPLAS **24**(5), 566–591 (2002)
13. Honda, K., Vasconcelos, V.T., Yoshida, N.: Secure information flow as typed process behaviour. In: Smolka, G. (ed.) ESOP 2000. LNCS, vol. 1782, pp. 180–199. Springer, Heidelberg (2000)
14. Honda, K., Yoshida, N.: A uniform type structure for secure information flow. In: POPL, pp. 81–92. ACM (2002)
15. Kobayashi, N.: Type-based information flow analysis for the pi-calculus. Acta Inf. (2003)
16. Moss, E.B.: Nested transactions: an approach to reliable distributed computing. Ph.D. thesis, Massachusetts Institute of Technology, Cambridge, MA, USA (1981)
17. Pottier, F.: A simple view of type-secure information flow in the pi-calculus. In: Proceedings of the 15th IEEE Computer Security Foundations Workshop, pp. 320–330 (2002)
18. Ryan, P.Y.A., Schneider, S.A.: Process algebra and non-interference. In: CSFW '99: Proceedings of the 12th IEEE Workshop on Computer Security Foundations, p. 214. IEEE Computer Society, Washington, DC (1999)
19. Sabelfeld, A.: Semantic models for the security of sequential and concurrent programs. Ph.D. thesis, Chalmers University of Technology and Gothenburg University, Gothenburg, Sweden, May 2001
20. Sabelfeld, A., Mantel, H.: Static confidentiality enforcement for distributed programs. In: Hermenegildo, M., Puebla, G. (eds.) SAS 2002. LNCS, vol. 2477, pp. 376–394. Springer, Heidelberg (2002)
21. Sabelfeld, A., Myers, A.: Language-based information-flow security. IEEE J. Sel. Areas Commun. **21**(1), 5–19 (2003)
22. Smith, G., Volpano, D.: Secure information flow in a multi-threaded imperative language. In: Proceedings of ACM Symposium on Principles of Programming Languages, pp. 19–21 (1998)
23. Stefan, D., Russo, A., Buiras, P., Levy, A., Mitchell, J.C., Mazières, D.: Addressing covert termination and timing channels in concurrent information flow systems. In: Proceedings of ACM International Conference on Functional Programming. Association for Computing Machinery (2012)
24. Volpano, D., Smith, G., Irvine, C.: A sound type system for secure flow analysis. J. Comput. Secur. **4**(3), 167–187 (1996)
25. Zdancewic, S., Myers, A.C.: Observational determinism for concurrent program security. In: Proceedings of the 16th IEEE Computer Security Foundations Workshop, pp. 29–43 (2003)

π-Calculus

Types for Resources in ψ-calculi

Hans Hüttel(✉)

Department of Computer Science, Aalborg University, Aalborg, Denmark
hans@cs.aau.dk

Abstract. Several type systems have been proposed for characterizing resource usage in process calculi, starting with the work on linear and unbounded names in the π-calculus by Kobayashi, Pierce and Turner. In this paper we use the general framework of ψ-calculi proposed by Bengtson, Parrow et al. to provide a general theory of type systems of this kind. We present a general type system that allows for a subject reduction property generalizing that of Kobayashi et al. and show how existing, quite different type systems for resource control can be expressed within our general type system. These are the original type system for linear names in the π-calculus, the graph types for strong normalization in the π-calculus due to Honda, Yoshida and Berger, a type system for termination in a value-passing calculus due to Deng and Sangiorgi and a type system for allocation and deallocation of generated names due to de Vries, Francalanza and Hennessy.

1 Introduction

Notions of resource usage are important in the study of program behaviour, and one that has been of particular interest is that of *linearity*. A resource is linear in a program if it will be used exactly once during any execution of the program.

In the setting of process calculi, several type systems have been proposed for characterizing linear resource usage. For the π-calculus, a first important contribution is the work on linear and unbounded names due to Kobayashi, Pierce and Turner [14]. Later work by Giunti and Vasconcelos [9] makes an explicit separation between the two ends of a channel and uses a simple notion of session types to give an account of linearity. More recently, the type system of Honda and Demangeon [5] introduces a notion of subtyping to the setting of a resource-conscious type system.

There is also work on resource-conscious type systems for other process calculi that extend the π-calculus. In the work by Maffei et al. [2] the authors introduce a notion of linearity which extends existing type systems for refinement types. And in work by Francalanza et al. [4] the authors consider the problem of resource-aware name generation using a version of the π-calculus with notions of allocation and deallocation.

All of these type systems have a rule for parallel composition of the form

$$\frac{\Gamma_1 \vdash P_1 \quad \Gamma_2 \vdash P_2}{\Gamma \vdash P_1 \mid P_2} \quad \Gamma = \Gamma_1 + \Gamma_2 \tag{1}$$

M. Abadi and A. Lluch Lafuente (Eds.): TGC 2013, LNCS 8358, pp. 83–102, 2014.
DOI: 10.1007/978-3-319-05119-2_6,

where we assume that the type environment Γ is partitioned into subenvironments Γ_1 and Γ_2 for typing the parallel components P_1 and P_2, respectively. This rule corresponds to the introduction rule for multiplicative conjunction in linear logic [8].

Just as type systems abound, so do process calculi with notions of names. In their seminal work, Bengtson et al. introduced ψ-calculi as a general account of the many extensions of the π-calculus that have been proposed [1].

The goal of the present paper is to use this general account of nominal process calculi to provide a general theory of resource-conscious type systems such as those mentioned above,

In an earlier paper [13], we showed how to use a general type system for ψ-calculi to give a general account of some seemingly very diverse type systems for variants of the π-calculus. In this paper we take a similar approach by using a resource-aware type system for ψ-calculi to give a general account of resource-aware type systems for variants of the π-calculus. Among the rules of our system is a general variant of (1).

We show how our type system subsumes the type system of [14] but is also able to capture certain liveness properties, including that of termination in the strongly normalizing π-calculus of Honda, Yoshida and Berger. To achieve this, we use the notion of assertions in the ψ-calculus framework to represent the graph types introduced in this setting. We also consider the allocation π-calculus due to Hennessy and Francalanza [4] and a type system for termination in a value-passing calculus inspired by Deng and Sangiorgi [6]. Every instantiation of our type system will satisfy a subject reduction property which generalizes that of [14].

The remainder of our paper is structured as follows. In Sect. 2 we present the syntax and semantics of ψ-calculi. In Sect. 3 we describe the type system. Sect. 4 describes the soundness result that holds for the type system, and sect. 5 presents a collection of instances of the type system.

2 Ψ-calculi

We here present the syntax and semantics of a typed version of the ψ-calculi introduced in [1].

2.1 Nominal Datatypes

Names are central to ψ-calculi, and the account of name bindings makes use of *nominal sets*. Informally, a nominal set is a set whose members can be affected by names being bound or swapped. If x is an element of a nominal set and $a \in \mathcal{N}$, we write $a\#x$ to denote that a is fresh for x; the notion extends to sets of names in the expected way.

In particular, we consider *nominal data types*. A nominal data type is a nominal set with additional internal structure. If Σ is a signature, a nominal data type over Σ is a Σ-algebra, whose carrier set is a nominal set (for the precise definition, see [7]). For our nominal data types we use simultaneous term substitution $X[\boldsymbol{z} := \boldsymbol{Y}]$. This is to be read as the substitution in which the terms in $\boldsymbol{Y}$ replace the names in $\boldsymbol{z}$ in X.

2.2 Syntax

A ψ-calculus has a set of *processes*, ranged over by $P, Q, \ldots$. Processes contain occurrences of *terms* and both processes and terms can contain *names*. We assume a countably infinite set of names $\mathcal{N}$ ranged over by $a, b, \ldots x, y, \ldots, m, n, \ldots, u, v, \ldots$. The set of names that appear in patterns (defined below) is called the set of *variable names* $\mathcal{N}_V$ and is ranged over by $x, y \ldots$. The set of other names, $\mathcal{N} \setminus \mathcal{N}_V$ is ranged over by $a, b, \ldots, m, n \ldots$.

For any process P, we let $\mathrm{n}(P)$ denote the support of P, i.e. the names of P, and let $\mathrm{fn}(P)$ denote the set of free names in P. These notions are also defined for terms.

Terms $M, N \ldots$ are elements of a nominal data type $\mathbf{T}$, *assertions* Ψ come from a nominal data type $\mathbf{A}$ and *conditions* φ belong to the nominal data type $\mathbf{C}$. These data types have the following operations:

$\otimes : \mathbf{A} \times \mathbf{A} \rightarrow \mathbf{A}$	composition	$\dot{\leftrightarrow} : \mathbf{T} \times \mathbf{T} \rightarrow \mathbf{C}$	channel equivalence
$\mathbf{1} \in \mathbf{A}$	unit	$\models \subseteq \mathbf{A} \times \mathbf{C}$	entailment

Terms. We assume that terms are built according to the following formation rules:

$$M ::= b \mid f(M_1, \ldots, M_k)$$

In the above, b ranges over a set of *basic terms* that includes the set of names. A term $f(M_1, \ldots, M_k)$ is a *composite term* in which f is a term constructor of arity k.

Assertions. For assertions, composition is assumed to satisfy the following axioms and rules.

$$\Psi_1 \otimes \Psi_2 \simeq \Psi_2 \otimes \Psi_1 \qquad \Psi_1 \otimes (\Psi_2 \otimes \Psi_3) \simeq (\Psi_1 \otimes \Psi_2) \otimes \Psi_3$$
$$\Psi \otimes \mathbf{1} \simeq \Psi \qquad \Psi \simeq \Psi' \Rightarrow \Psi \otimes \Psi_1 \simeq \Psi' \otimes \Psi_1$$

We say that an assertion Ψ is *idempotent* if $\Psi \otimes \Psi \simeq \Psi$.

We can define a preorder on assertions.

Definition 1. *We write* $\Psi_1 \leq \Psi_2$ *if there exists a* Ψ *such that* $\Psi_1 \otimes \Psi \simeq \Psi_2$*. We write* $\Psi_1 < \Psi_2$ *if* $\Psi_1 \not\simeq \Psi_2$*.*

We require this ordering to be a partial ordering up to $\simeq$ for all instances of our type system.

Finally, for every assertion Ψ and name x we assume the existence of the largest subassertion $\Psi \setminus x$ not containing occurrences of x.

Conditions. The entailment relation $\models$ describes when conditions are true, given a set of assertions, and is needed to describe the behaviour of a conditional process.

Channel equivalence. Channel equivalence tells us which terms represent the same communication channel; $\dot{\leftrightarrow}$ therefore appears in the rule describing communication. Note that we may have $M \not\dot{\leftrightarrow} M$; $\dot{\leftrightarrow}$ is only assumed symmetric and transitive.

Processes. We here present a typed version of the formation rules for processes.

$$P ::= \underline{M}(\lambda \boldsymbol{x})x.P \mid \overline{M}N.P \mid P_1 \mid P_2 \mid (\nu n : T)P \mid ! P$$
$$\mid \textbf{case } \varphi_1 : P_1, \ldots, \varphi_k : P_k \mid (\!|\Psi|\!)$$

The formation rules are typed, as the restriction operator $(\nu n : T)P$ assumes that the local name n is given type T; types are defined in Sect. 3.1. Most of the process constructs are similar to those of the π-calculus; an important difference is that, in a prefix, the object M can be an arbitrary term. Another important difference is found in the input construct $\underline{M}(\lambda \boldsymbol{x})N.P$, where the subject $(\lambda \boldsymbol{x})N$ is a *pattern* whose variable names $\boldsymbol{x}$ can occur free in N and P. Any term received on channel M has to match this pattern; a term N_1 matches the pattern $(\lambda \boldsymbol{x})N$ if N_1 can be found by instantiating the variable names $\boldsymbol{x}$ in N with terms. Finally note that assertions (see below) can also be used as processes in their own right.

2.3 Operational Semantics

We here give a typed, annotated semantics with labels. Transitions are of the form

$$\Psi \rhd P \xrightarrow{\alpha} P'$$

As every input or output action will consume resources, this is also the case for a communication. We therefore annotate action with the terms involved. In this way we can determine the resource usage involved in internal communications. The label set is

$$\alpha_V ::= \overline{M}(\nu \boldsymbol{a} : \boldsymbol{T})N \mid \underline{M}N$$
$$\alpha ::= \alpha_V \mid \tau@(\nu \boldsymbol{b} : \boldsymbol{T})(\alpha_V^1, \alpha_V^2)$$

In the label $\overline{M}(\nu \boldsymbol{a} : \boldsymbol{T})N$ the names in $\boldsymbol{a}$ are extruded using N. A composite label $\tau@(\nu \boldsymbol{b} : \boldsymbol{T})(\alpha_V^1, \alpha_V^2)$ should be read as stating that there was an internal communication in which the names in $\boldsymbol{b}$ were used in the subject channel, contributing with the resources $\boldsymbol{T}$.

For labels we define $\text{bn}((\nu \boldsymbol{b} : \boldsymbol{T})\overline{M}N) = \boldsymbol{b}$, $\text{bn}(\tau@(\nu \boldsymbol{b} : \boldsymbol{T})(\alpha_V^1, \alpha_V^2)) = \boldsymbol{b} \cup \text{bn}(\alpha_V^1) \cup \text{bn}(\alpha_V^2)$ and $\text{bn}(\alpha) = \emptyset$ otherwise (Table 1).

Table 1. Annotated labelled transition rules

(COM)
$$\frac{\Psi_Q \otimes \Psi \rhd P \xrightarrow{\overline{M}(\nu \boldsymbol{a}:\boldsymbol{T})N} P' \qquad \Psi_P \otimes \Psi \rhd Q \xrightarrow{\underline{K}N} Q' \qquad \Psi \otimes \Psi_P \otimes \Psi_Q \models M \dot{\leftrightarrow} K}{\Psi \rhd P \mid Q \xrightarrow{\tau @ (\overline{M}(\nu \boldsymbol{a}:\boldsymbol{T})N, \underline{K}N)} (\nu \boldsymbol{a} : \boldsymbol{T})(P' \mid Q')} \qquad \boldsymbol{a} \# Q$$

(CASE)
$$\frac{\Psi \rhd P_i \xrightarrow{\alpha} P' \quad , \Psi \models \varphi_i}{\Psi \rhd \mathbf{case}\ \tilde{\varphi} : \tilde{P} \xrightarrow{\alpha} P'}$$

(PAR)
$$\frac{\Psi_Q \otimes \Psi \rhd P \xrightarrow{\alpha} P'}{\Psi \rhd P \mid Q \xrightarrow{\alpha} P' \mid Q} \qquad \mathrm{bn}(\alpha) \# Q$$

(REP)
$$\frac{\Psi \rhd P \mid !P \xrightarrow{\alpha} P'}{\Psi \rhd !P \xrightarrow{\alpha} P'}$$

(SCOPE-1)
$$\frac{\Psi \rhd P \xrightarrow{\alpha} P' \quad b \# \alpha, , \Psi}{\Psi \rhd (\nu b : T)P \xrightarrow{\alpha} (\nu b : T)P'} \qquad \alpha \neq \tau @ (\alpha_V^1, \alpha_V^2)$$

(SCOPE-2)
$$\frac{\Psi \rhd P \xrightarrow{\tau @ (\nu c : \boldsymbol{T})(\alpha_1, \alpha_2)} P'}{\Psi \rhd (\nu b : T)P \xrightarrow{\tau @ (\nu c : \boldsymbol{T}, b : T')(\alpha_V^1, \alpha_V^2)} (\nu b : T - T')P'} \qquad b \in \mathrm{fn}(\alpha_V^1) \cup \mathrm{fn}(\alpha_V^2), \quad T' \leq_{\min} T$$

(IN)
$$\frac{\Psi \models M \dot{\leftrightarrow} K}{\Psi \rhd \underline{M}(\lambda \boldsymbol{x})N.P \xrightarrow{\underline{K}N[\boldsymbol{x} := \boldsymbol{L}]} P[\boldsymbol{x} := \boldsymbol{L}]}$$

(OUT)
$$\frac{\Psi \models M \dot{\leftrightarrow} K}{\Psi \rhd \overline{M}N.P \xrightarrow{\overline{K}N} P}$$

(OPEN)
$$\frac{\Psi \rhd P \xrightarrow{\overline{M}(\nu \boldsymbol{a}:\boldsymbol{T})N} P'}{\Psi \rhd (\nu b : T_1)P \xrightarrow{\overline{M}(\nu \boldsymbol{a}:\boldsymbol{T}, b:T_1)N} P'} \qquad b \# \boldsymbol{a}, \Psi, b \in n(N) \cup n(\boldsymbol{T}) \cup n(T_1)$$

In some of the rules, we need to extract the assertion information of a process P in the form of its *qualified frame* $\mathcal{F}(P) = \langle E_P, \Psi_P \rangle$, where Ψ_P is the composition of assertions in P and E_P records the types of the names local to Ψ_P.

Because types may contain names and appear in restrictions, in (OPEN) we write $\nu \boldsymbol{a} : \boldsymbol{T}, b : T$ to denote the typed sequence $\nu a_1 : T_1, \ldots, \nu a_n : T_n$ (with $a_1, \ldots, a_n = \boldsymbol{a}$) extended with $b : T$ and we extend the side condition of [1] to cover the case where an extruded name appears in the type.

There are two rules for restriction. In (SCOPE-2) the silent action involves terms that contain the bound name b. We therefore subtract some resources T' from the type annotation T; this T' must be a minimal resource component from T. Subtraction of types is defined in Sect. 3.1.

3 A Type System

We now describe our type system.

3.1 Types and Type Environments

In what follows, our set of types $\mathcal{T}$ is assumed to be a nominal datatype, since this will allow names to appear in types.

In our type system, types describe resources; we assume that resources have an additive structure. More precisely, we assume that a summation operation on types is defined, such that the set of types forms a type structure in the sense of Honda [11]. In a type structure, types are identified up to Kleene equality; we write $T \doteq T'$ if either T_1 and T_2 are both undefined or $T_1 = T_2$.

Definition 2 (Type structure [11]**).** *A* type structure *is a set of types* $\mathbb{T}$ *together with a partial binary operation* $+$ *on* $\mathbb{T}$ *such that* $T_1 + T_2 \doteq T_2 + T_1$ *and* $(T_1 + T_2) + T_3 \doteq T_1 + (T_2 + T_3)$ *for all* $T_1, T_2, T_3 \in \mathbb{T}$.

We write $T_1 \leq T_2$ if either $T_1 = T_2$ or there exists a T such that $T_1 + T = T_2$. We write $T_1 \leq_{\min} T_2$ if T_1 is a least type T such that $T \leq T_2$. Finally, we write $T_1 - T_2$ for the type T_3 such that $T_3 + T_2 = T_1$.

A type T is *unlimited* if $T + T = T$, that is, if T is idempotent under addition. This notion originates in the similar notion used by Kobayashi et al. [14]. Here, the idea was that a type T is unlimited if it is non-linear in one of two ways: names of an ω-type T can be used arbitrarily often, while names of a nullary type cannot be used at all.

We allow types to contain type environments; for a type T we let Γ_T denote the type environment associated with T.

Definition 3 (Type environment). *A type environment* Γ *is a finite map from names to types.*

We only consider well-formed type environments, i.e. ones in which all names mentioned are assigned types exactly once.

Definition 4 (Well-formed environment). *A type environment* Γ *is well-formed if whenever* $\Gamma(x) = T$ *then* $\forall y \in \mathrm{dom}(\Gamma_T) \cap \mathrm{dom}(\Gamma). \Gamma_T(y) = \Gamma(y)$ *and* $\forall z \in \mathrm{n}(T) \setminus \mathrm{dom}(\Gamma_T). z \in \mathrm{dom}(\Gamma')$.

Addition of type environments is a partial operation defined in a pointwise fashion.

Definition 5 (Addition of type environments [11]**).** *Let* Γ_1 *and* Γ_2 *be well-formed type environments. The sum of* Γ_1 *and* Γ_2 *is defined as the type environment* $\Gamma_1 + \Gamma_2$ *that is given by*

$$(\Gamma_1 + \Gamma_2)(x) = \begin{cases} \Gamma_1(x) & x \in \mathrm{dom}(\Gamma_1) \setminus \mathrm{dom}(\Gamma_2) \\ \Gamma_2(x) & x \in \mathrm{dom}(\Gamma_2) \setminus \mathrm{dom}(\Gamma_1) \\ \Gamma_1(x) + \Gamma_2(x) & \textit{otherwise} \end{cases}$$

Addition is only defined if the resulting environment is well-formed.

Note that this notation makes it easy to express that type information can be extended. If $x \notin \mathrm{dom}(\Gamma)$, then Γ extended with the binding $x : T$, written $\Gamma, x : T$, is simply $\Gamma + x : T$. We write $\Gamma_1 - \Gamma_2$ for the type environment Γ which satisfies that $\Gamma_2 + \Gamma = \Gamma_1$.

A type environment Γ is *unlimited* if $\Gamma + \Gamma = \Gamma$.

As in the case of types, we can define an ordering on type environments. We require this ordering to be a partial order.

Definition 6 (Ordering of type environments). *$\Gamma_1 \leq \Gamma_2$ if there exists a Γ such that $\Gamma_1 + \Gamma = \Gamma_2$.*

A *minimal* type judgement is one that uses the least resources and assertions.

Definition 7 (Minimal type judgement). *Minimality of term and pattern judgements is defined by*

1. *$\Gamma, \Psi \vdash_{\min} M : T$ if $\Gamma, \Psi \vdash M : T$ and for every $\Gamma' \leq \Gamma$ and $\Psi' < \Psi$ we have $\Gamma', \Psi' \nvdash M : T$.*
2. *$\Gamma, \Psi \vdash_{\min} (\lambda \boldsymbol{x})N : \boldsymbol{T} \to U_o$ if $\Gamma, \Psi \vdash (\lambda \boldsymbol{x})N : \boldsymbol{T} \to U_o$ and for every $\Gamma' \leq \Gamma$ and $\Psi' < \Psi$ we have $\Gamma', \Psi' \nvdash (\lambda \boldsymbol{x})N : \boldsymbol{T} \to U_o$.*

3.2 Typing Assertions, Conditions and Terms

Our type judgments are all relative to a type environment Γ and a global assertion Ψ. Type judgments for assertions and conditions are of the form

$$\Gamma, \Psi_1 \vdash \Psi \quad \text{and} \quad \Gamma, \Psi_1 \vdash \varphi$$

Type judgments for terms are of the form

$$\Gamma, \Psi \vdash M : T$$

In the above, T denotes the type of M.

We always assume that the global assertion is *well-formed*, that is that $\mathrm{n}(\Psi) \subseteq \mathrm{dom}(\Psi)$.

Since arbitrary terms can be used as channels, we need to assume that some natural conditions hold for channel types.

For *channel equality*, we require that equivalent channels have the same type in environment Γ and wrt. assertion Ψ, if they are equivalent under Ψ:

$$\text{If } \Gamma, \Psi \vdash M : T \text{ and } \Psi \models M \dot{\leftrightarrow} N \text{ then } \Gamma, \Psi \vdash N : T \tag{2}$$

Finally, we introduce a notion of channel *compatibility*. This is a predicate that describes which types of values can be carried by channels of a given types. We distinguish between output compatibility $\leftrightarrow\!\!\!\!\!\!\!P^{+}$ and input compatibility $\leftrightarrow\!\!\!\!\!\!\!P^{-}$. If $T_1 \leftrightarrow\!\!\!\!\!\!\!P^{+} T_2$ and $T_1 \leftrightarrow\!\!\!\!\!\!\!P^{-} T_2$ we write $T_1 \leftrightarrow\!\!\!\!\!\!\!P\, T_2$.

Since terms received by an input are instantiations of patterns, we introduce the following type rule for message patterns:

$$\text{(PATTERN)}\ \frac{\Gamma, \boldsymbol{x} : \boldsymbol{T}, \Psi \vdash M : U}{\Gamma, \Psi \vdash (\lambda \boldsymbol{x})M : \boldsymbol{T} \to U}$$

When an input abstraction has type $\boldsymbol{T} \to U$, it can receive any term of type U if this term contains pattern variables of types corresponding to $\boldsymbol{T}$.

3.3 Criteria for Type Rules

We require the following conditions to hold for any instance of our type system. We let $\mathcal{J}$ range over all judgements in our type system.

Firstly, we require *assertion invariance* for typing. In other words, whenever we have a valid type judgement $\Gamma, \Psi \vdash \mathcal{J}$ and $\Psi \simeq \Psi'$, then the type judgement $\Gamma, \Psi' \vdash \mathcal{J}$ is also valid.

Secondly, we require *substitutivity.*

Property 1 *(Substitution property for judgements). Suppose $\Gamma + \boldsymbol{x} : \boldsymbol{T}, \Psi \vdash \mathcal{J}$ with $\boldsymbol{x} \cap \mathrm{dom}(\Gamma) = \emptyset$, $\mathrm{fn}(\mathcal{J}) \subseteq \boldsymbol{x}$, and $\Gamma_i, \Psi_i \vdash M_i : T_i$ for all $i \in [1, |\boldsymbol{x}|]$. Then $\Gamma_0, \Psi_0 \vdash \mathcal{J}[\boldsymbol{x} := \boldsymbol{M}]$ where $\Gamma_0 = \Gamma + \sum_{1 \leq i \leq |\boldsymbol{x}|} \Gamma_i$ and $\Psi_0 = \Psi \otimes \bigotimes_{1 \leq i \leq |\boldsymbol{x}|} \Psi_i$.*

And finally, in ψ-calculi, the empty assertion $\mathbf{1}$ serves as the empty process. We therefore require that $\Gamma \vdash \mathbf{1}$ if and only if Γ is unlimited. In other words, an empty process cannot consume resources.

3.4 Type Rules for Processes

Type judgments for processes are of the form

$$\Gamma, \Psi \vdash P$$

The type rules defining them are found in Table 2; we here explain the most important ones.

For a parallel composition, the rule (T-PAR) describes that resources (typed names and assertions) are distributed among the parallel components. This rule is essentially that of [14]; our side conditions $\Psi'_{P_1} \leq \Psi_{P_1}$ and $\Psi'_{P_2} \leq \Psi_{P_2}$ express that it is possible (but not required) to use the assertions found in other parallel components.

Likewise, the rules (T-IN) and (T-OUT) are resource-conscious (and are also inspired by [14]) in that resources are distributed between the prefix and the continuation.

For (T-RES) we require that the assertion of the conclusion must not contain free occurrences of x and that subassertions containing x are removed from Ψ, resulting in the new assertion $\Psi \setminus x$.

The rule (T-REP) states that for a replicated process, all resources must be unlimited for the process to be well-typed.

We also allow for non-structural rules for weakening assertions. This is captured by (T-WEAK), which is a schema for finitely many rules that allow us to add additional assertions whenever the assertion Ψ satisfies a criterion wrt. P that is specific to the concrete instantiation of the ψ-calculus.

Table 2. Type rules for processes

(T-IN) $$\frac{\Gamma_1 + \boldsymbol{x} : \boldsymbol{T}, \Psi_1 \vdash P \quad \Gamma_2, \Psi_2 \vdash_{\min} (\lambda \boldsymbol{x})N : \boldsymbol{T} \to U_o \quad \Gamma_3, \Psi_3 \vdash_{\min} M : U_s}{\Gamma, \Psi \vdash \underline{M}(\lambda \boldsymbol{x})N.P} \quad \begin{array}{l} U_s \leftrightarrow_{\rho^-} U_o \\ \Gamma = \Gamma_1 + \Gamma_2 + \Gamma_3 \\ \Psi = \Psi_1 \otimes \Psi_2 \otimes \Psi_3 \end{array}$$

(T-OUT) $$\frac{\Gamma_1, \Psi_1 \vdash_{\min} M : T_s \quad \Gamma_2, \Psi_2 \vdash_{\min} N : T_o \quad \Gamma_3, \Psi_3 \vdash P}{\Gamma, \Psi \vdash \overline{M}N.P} \quad \begin{array}{l} T_s \leftrightarrow_{\rho^+} T_o \\ \Gamma = \Gamma_1 + \Gamma_2 + \Gamma_3 \\ \Psi = \Psi_1 \otimes \Psi_2 \otimes \Psi_3 \end{array}$$

(T-PAR) $$\frac{\Gamma_1 + \Gamma_{P_2}, \Psi_1 \otimes \Psi'_{P_2} \vdash P_1 \quad \Gamma_2 + \Gamma_{P_1}, \Psi_2 \otimes \Psi'_{P_1} \vdash P_2}{\Gamma, \Psi \vdash P_1 \mid P_2} \quad \begin{array}{l} \Gamma = \Gamma_1 + \Gamma_2 \\ \mathcal{F}(P_1) = \langle \Gamma_{P_1}, \Psi_{P_1} \rangle \\ \mathcal{F}(P_2) = \langle \Gamma_{P_2}, \Psi_{P_2} \rangle \\ \Psi = \Psi_1 \otimes \Psi_2 \\ \Psi'_{P_1} \leq \Psi_{P_1} \\ \Psi'_{P_2} \leq \Psi_{P_2} \end{array}$$

(T-RES) $$\frac{\Gamma + x : T, \Psi \vdash P}{\Gamma, \Psi \setminus x \vdash (\nu x : T)P} \quad x \# \Gamma$$

(T-REP) $$\frac{\Gamma, \Psi \vdash P}{\Gamma, \Psi \vdash ! P} \quad \begin{array}{l} \Gamma \text{ unlimited} \\ \Psi \text{ idempotent} \end{array}$$

(T-ASS) $$\frac{\Gamma, \Psi_1 \vdash \Psi}{\Gamma, \Psi_1 \vdash (\!|\Psi|\!)}$$

(T-CASE) $$\frac{\Gamma, \Psi \vdash \varphi_i \quad \Gamma, \Psi \vdash P_i \quad 1 \leq i \leq k}{\Gamma, \Psi \vdash \textbf{case } \varphi_1 : P_1, \ldots, \varphi_k : P_k}$$

(T-WEAK) $$\frac{\Gamma, \Psi_1 \vdash P}{\Gamma, \Psi_1 \otimes \Psi_2 \vdash P} \quad \mathcal{C}(P, \Psi)$$

4 Safety Results for the Type System

The main result about our type system is that it provides a safe approximation of the use of resources: the result generalizes the subject reduction result of [14].

4.1 A Subject Reduction Result

The subject reduction theorem tells us that whenever a labelled transition emanating from a well-typed process has a well-typed label with minimal resource usage, then the remaining resources can be used to type the continuation process.

We therefore need to define what it means for a label to be well-typed.

Definition 8 (Well-typed label). *We say that $\Gamma, \Psi \vdash \alpha$ if*

- *Whenever $\alpha = (\nu \boldsymbol{a} : \boldsymbol{T})\overline{M}N$, then $\Gamma_1, \Psi_1 \vdash M : U_o$ and $\Gamma_2, \boldsymbol{a} : \boldsymbol{T}, \Psi_2 \vdash N : U_s$ and $U_o \leftrightarrow^{P+} U_s$ for some $\Gamma = \Gamma_1 + \Gamma_2$ and $\Psi = \Psi_1 \otimes \Psi_2$.*
- *Whenever $\alpha = \underline{K}N\{\boldsymbol{x} := \boldsymbol{M}\}$ then for some $\Gamma = \Gamma_1 + \Gamma_2 + \sum_{1 \leq i \leq |\boldsymbol{x}|} \Gamma_3^i$ and $\Psi = \Psi_1 \otimes \Psi_2 \otimes \bigotimes_{1 \leq i \leq |\boldsymbol{x}|} \Psi_3^i$ we have that $\Gamma_1, \Psi_1 \vdash K : U_o$ and $\Gamma_2, \Psi_2 \vdash N : \boldsymbol{T} \to U_s$ with $U_o \leftrightarrow^{P-} U_s$ and $\Gamma_3^i, \Psi_3^i \vdash M_i : T_i$ for all $1 \leq i \leq |\boldsymbol{x}|$.*
- *If $\alpha = \tau @ (\nu \boldsymbol{b} : \boldsymbol{U})((\nu \boldsymbol{a} : \boldsymbol{T})\overline{M}N_1, \underline{K}N_2)$ then there exist $\Gamma_1, \Gamma_2, \Gamma_3, \Gamma_4$ and $\Psi_1, \Psi_2, \Psi_3, \Psi_4$ such that*

$$\Gamma = \Gamma_1 + \Gamma_2 + \Gamma_3 + \Gamma 4 \qquad \Psi = \Psi_1 \otimes \Psi_2 \otimes \Psi_3 \otimes \Psi_4$$

and such that

$$\Gamma_1, \boldsymbol{b} : \boldsymbol{U}, \Psi_1 \vdash M : U_s \qquad \Gamma_2, \boldsymbol{a} : \boldsymbol{T}, \Psi_2 \vdash N_1 : U_o$$
$$\Gamma_3, \boldsymbol{b} : \boldsymbol{U}, \Psi_1 \vdash K : U_s \qquad \Gamma_4, \boldsymbol{a} : \boldsymbol{T}, \Psi_1 \vdash N_2 : U_o$$

with $U_s \leftrightarrow^{P} U_o$.

We write $\Gamma, \Psi \vdash_{\min} \alpha$ if the type judgments for the subject and object terms of α as given above are minimal in the sense of Definition 7.

Note that the clause for well-typed τ-labels states that the subject types agree. The name bindings $\boldsymbol{b} : \boldsymbol{U}$ describe types of the bound names that were needed for typing the subject channel, whereas the name bindings $\boldsymbol{a} : \boldsymbol{T}$ describe the types of the bound names that were extruded.

Theorem 1. *Subject reduction. Suppose that $\Psi_0 \rhd P \xrightarrow{\alpha} P'$ and that $\Gamma, \Psi \vdash P$ for some $\Psi \leq \Psi_0$ and that $\Gamma_1, \Psi_1 \vdash_{\min} \alpha$ for some $\Gamma_1 \leq \Gamma$ and $\Psi_1 \leq \Psi$. Then there exists a Ψ' such that $\Gamma', \Psi' \vdash P'$ where $\Gamma' = (\Gamma - \Gamma_1) + \Gamma_\alpha$.*

5 Instances of the Type System

In this section we describe some instances of our type system. These instances show how the type structure and the assertions can be used to control the use of resources. In all instances, the substitution property Property 1 is easily seen to hold.

5.1 Linear Channels

We first consider the type system by Kobayashi, Pierce and Turner [14] for linear channel usage in a polyadic π-calculus with replicated input. The formation rules for processes are

$$P ::= x(\boldsymbol{y}).P_1 \mid \overline{x}\langle \boldsymbol{y}\rangle.P_1 \mid ! \, x(\boldsymbol{y}).P_1 \mid P_1 \mid P_2$$
$$\mid (\nu x : T)P_1 \mid \mathbf{0} \mid \text{if } x = y \text{ then } P_1 \text{ else } P_2$$

The only form of replication is thus that of replicated input. In the type system every type is equipped with a capability p that tells us if names of this type can be used for input, output, both or neither and a multiplicity m that tells us if names of this type are linear (1) or unlimited (ω).

The formation rules for types are

$$T ::= p^m T$$
$$p ::= \emptyset \mid \{!\} \mid \{?\} \mid \{!, ?\}$$
$$m ::= 1 \mid \omega$$

As in [14], addition is defined by (where either $m = \omega$ or $p \cap q = \emptyset$ and $m = 1$):

$$p^m T + q^m T \stackrel{\text{def}}{=} p \cup q^m T$$

The unlimited types in this system are thus those with multiplicity ω or capability $\emptyset$.

The syntax of [14] is easily represented in our type system, and the same holds for the type rules. In particular, the type rule for replicated input

$$\frac{\Gamma, \boldsymbol{y} : \boldsymbol{T} \vdash P \quad \Gamma \text{ unlimited}}{\Gamma + x : ?^{\omega} T \vdash ! \, x(\boldsymbol{y}).P}$$

can be expressed as a derived rule in our type system using (T-REP) and (T-IN).

Let $\vdash'$ denote the typability relation of [14] and let $[\![P]\!]$ denote our representation of process P. The following representation result is immediate.

Theorem 2. *Suppose* $\text{dom}(\Gamma) = \text{fn}(P)$. *Then*

$$\Gamma' \vdash' P \iff \Gamma, \mathbf{0} \vdash [\![P]\!]$$

5.2 Control in the π-calculus

In a series of papers Berger, Honda and Yoshida use an asynchronous π-calculus to encode the simply typed λ-calculus [16,17]. The goal is to show strong normalization for this calculus by using a π-calculus type system that soundly characterizes of strong normalization together with a typed version of Milner's encoding of the λ-calculus.

We adopt their formulation from [16], in which type judgments are of the form $\Gamma \vdash P \triangleright A$, where A is a so-called *action type*. An action type should be thought of as a finite directed graph whose vertices are polarized names px and whose edges describe the causal input/output dependencies between names.

Polarities and Action Types The underlying idea of the type system is to ensure strong normalization by ensuring that action types do not have cyclic dependencies between inputs and outputs and that inputs and outputs alternate.

We have the polarities

$$p ::= \downarrow \mid \uparrow \mid ! \mid ?$$

Here $\downarrow$ denotes linear input, $\uparrow$ denotes linear output, ! denotes replicated input and ? denotes an output to a replicated input. We use $\bot$ to indicate that a linear channel is capable of both input and output. The polarities have duals, such that $\overline{\uparrow} = \downarrow$ and $\overline{!} = ?$.

Since inputs and outputs should alternate, types are given by the formation rules

$$\alpha ::= \langle T, \overline{T} \rangle \qquad T_I ::= (\boldsymbol{T_O})^{\downarrow} \mid (\boldsymbol{T_O})^{!}$$
$$T ::= T_I \mid T_O \qquad T_O ::= (\boldsymbol{T_I})^{\uparrow} \mid (\boldsymbol{T_I})^{?}$$

In the above, $\overline{T}$ is the dual type of T, found by dualizing all capabilities in T.

Action types are defined by the following formation rules.

$$A ::= !x \to ?y \mid \downarrow \to \uparrow y \mid px \mid A_1, A_2$$

We write $px \in A$ if A contains a vertex px. An action type A is well-formed if no name in it occurs twice. If px occurs in A we say that x is *active* in A if there is no y on which x depends, i.e. there is no edge $qy \to px$. We let $A \setminus \boldsymbol{x}$ denote the action type found by removing all nodes whose names are in $\boldsymbol{x}$. Also let $A \cup B$ denote the graph union of A and B.

Action types can be composed as follows. First, define composition of polarities by $\downarrow \odot \uparrow \stackrel{\text{def}}{=} \bot$ and $? \odot ? \stackrel{\text{def}}{=} ?$ and $! \odot ? \stackrel{\text{def}}{=} !$ and let us say that action types A and B are composable, written $A \asymp B$, if whenever $px \in A$ and $qx \in B$, then $p \odot q$ is defined, and there are no circular dependencies in the union of edges from A and B, i.e. if $p_1x_1 \to \overline{p_2}x_2 . p_2x_2 \to \overline{p_3}x_3, \ldots, p_nx_n \to \overline{p_{n+1}}x_{n+1} \in A \cup B$, then $x_1 \neq x_n$. Then whenever $A \asymp B$, the action type $A \odot B$ is defined as follows:

- The vertices are given by: $px \in A \odot B$ if either $px \in A$ and $x \notin \text{fn}(B)$ and vice versa, or $qx \in A$ and $rx \in B$ with $p = q \odot r$.
- The edges are given by: $px \to qy \in A \odot B$ if $px, qy \in A \odot B$ and $px = r_1z_1 \to \overline{r_2}z_2, r_2z_2 \to \overline{r_3}z_3, \ldots, \overline{r_n}z_{n+1} = qy$

In other words, the edges of the composed action type correspond to the paths that can be followed by causally dependent communications.

Table 3 shows the original type rules of [16]. In the rules $A \amalg B$ denotes the action type that corresponds to the disjoint union of the underlying graphs of A and B.

Representing the Type System. In the original type system, all linearity information is kept in assertions, so in our version the additive structure of types is trivial; we let $T + T = T$ for every type T.

Table 3. Type rules of the type system for strong normalization in [16]

(ZERO) $\Gamma \vdash \mathbf{0} \rhd \mathbf{0}$

(PAR) $$\frac{\Gamma \vdash P_1 \rhd A_1 \quad \Gamma \vdash P_2 \rhd A_2}{\Gamma \vdash P_1 \mid P_2 \rhd A_1 \odot A_2} \quad A_1 \asymp A_2$$

(RES) $$\frac{\Gamma, x : T \vdash P \rhd A}{\Gamma \vdash (\nu x : T)P \rhd A/x} \quad px \in |A|, p \in \{?, \bot\}$$

(IN-$\downarrow$) $$\frac{\Gamma \vdash x : (\boldsymbol{T})^{\downarrow} \quad \Gamma, \boldsymbol{y} : \boldsymbol{T} \vdash P \rhd C^{-x}}{\Gamma \vdash x(\boldsymbol{y} : \boldsymbol{T}).P \rhd (\downarrow x \rightarrow A) \amalg B} \quad C/\boldsymbol{y} =\uparrow A \amalg ?B$$

(IN-!) $$\frac{\Gamma \vdash x : (\boldsymbol{T})^{!} \quad \Gamma, \boldsymbol{y} : \boldsymbol{T} \vdash P \rhd C}{\Gamma \vdash x(\boldsymbol{y} : \boldsymbol{T}).P \rhd (!x \rightarrow A)} \quad C/\boldsymbol{y} = ?A$$

(OUT-$\uparrow$) $$\frac{\Gamma \vdash x : (\boldsymbol{T})^{\uparrow} \quad \Gamma, \boldsymbol{y} : \boldsymbol{T} \vdash P \rhd C}{\Gamma \vdash \overline{x}(\boldsymbol{y} : \boldsymbol{T})P \rhd A \odot \uparrow x} \quad C/\boldsymbol{y} = A \asymp\uparrow x$$

(OUT-?) $$\frac{\Gamma \vdash x : (\boldsymbol{T})^{?} \quad \Gamma, \boldsymbol{y} : \boldsymbol{T} \vdash P \rhd C}{\Gamma \vdash \overline{x}(\boldsymbol{y} : \boldsymbol{T})P \rhd A \odot ?x} \quad C/\boldsymbol{y} = A \asymp ?x$$

(WEAK-$\bot$) $$\frac{\Gamma \vdash x : \downarrow, \uparrow \quad \Gamma \vdash P \rhd A^{-x}}{\Gamma \vdash P \rhd A \amalg \bot x}$$

(WEAK-?) $$\frac{\Gamma \vdash x : ? \quad \Gamma \vdash P \rhd A^{-x}}{\Gamma \vdash P \rhd A \amalg ?x}$$

The first central insight is that we can represent type graphs as assertions and define the composition operator in the appropriate fashion. Thus, a type judgment $\Gamma \vdash P \rhd A$ is represented by the judgment $\Gamma, \Psi_A \vdash P$ where Ψ_A is the assertion corresponding to the type graph A.

The second central insight is that only action types of certain shapes appear in the type system.

The assertions are given by the formation rules

$$\Psi ::= \downarrow\rightarrow k \mid\uparrow x \mid !x \rightarrow k \mid ?x \mid px \rightarrow qy \mid \Psi_1, \Psi_2 \mid (k)\Psi_1$$

where $k \in \mathbb{N}$. The idea is that these numbers act as unique root connectors, such that e.g. $\downarrow\rightarrow k \otimes (k)\Psi_1$ denotes that $\downarrow\rightarrow$ can only be connected to the root of the graph represented by Ψ_1. We say that a number k is fresh for an assertion if it does not occur in it.

Composing assertions. We define assertion composition as the free algebraic structure closed under the composition axioms and use the assertions to encode action types as follows.

The following translation is defined relative to a type environment Γ. The final clause applies to the cases not cover by the first four.

$$\llbracket(\downarrow x \to A_1) \amalg A_2\rrbracket = \downarrow x \to k \otimes (k)\llbracket A_1\rrbracket$$
$$\text{where } \Gamma(x) = \boldsymbol{y}, k \text{ fresh}, A \setminus \boldsymbol{y} = \uparrow A_1 \amalg A_2$$
$$\llbracket A_2 \odot \uparrow x\rrbracket = \uparrow x \otimes \llbracket A_1\rrbracket$$
$$\text{where } \Gamma(x) = \boldsymbol{y}, A_1 \setminus \boldsymbol{y} = A_2, A_2 \asymp \uparrow x$$
$$\llbracket !x \to A_2\rrbracket = !x \to k \otimes (k)\llbracket A\rrbracket$$
$$\text{where } \Gamma(x) = \boldsymbol{y}, A \setminus \boldsymbol{y} = ?A_2, k \text{ fresh}$$
$$\llbracket A_2 \odot ?x\rrbracket = ?x \otimes \llbracket A_1\rrbracket$$
$$\text{where } \Gamma(x) = \boldsymbol{y}, A_1 \setminus \boldsymbol{y} = A_2, A_2 \asymp ?x$$
$$\llbracket A_1 \odot A_2\rrbracket = \bigotimes_{px,qy \in A_1 \odot A_2, px = r_1 z_1 \to \overline{r_2} z_2, r_2 z_2 \to \overline{r_3} z_3, \ldots, \overline{r_n} z_{n+1} = qy} px \to qy$$

Type rules for messages. The only message terms are names; there are four type rules for names seen i Table 4.

Table 4. Type rules for names

(LIN-OUT)	$\Gamma, \uparrow x \vdash x : T$ if $\Gamma(x) = (\boldsymbol{T})^{\uparrow}$
(LIN-IN)	$\Gamma, \downarrow x \to \bullet \vdash x : T$ if $\Gamma(x) = (\boldsymbol{T})^{\downarrow}$
(UNLIM-OUT)	$\Gamma, ?x \vdash x : T$ if $\Gamma(x) = (\boldsymbol{T})^{?}$
(UNLIM-IN)	$\Gamma, !x \to \bullet \vdash x : T$ if $\Gamma(x) = (\boldsymbol{T})^{!}$

Other rules. The assertion weakening rules are captured by the non-structural weakening rules that we allow.

For the structural rules, we must take into account the notion of asynchronous output. A derived type rule would be

$$\frac{\Gamma_1, \Psi_1 \vdash x : \mathbf{Ch}(\boldsymbol{T}) \quad \Gamma_2, \Psi_2 \vdash \boldsymbol{y} : \boldsymbol{T}}{\Gamma_1 + \Gamma_2, \Psi_1 \amalg \Psi_2 \vdash \overline{x}(\boldsymbol{y})}$$

Theorem 3. *Let $\vdash'$ denote the typability relation in [16]. Then*

$$\Gamma \vdash' P \rhd A \iff \Gamma, \llbracket A\rrbracket \vdash \llbracket P\rrbracket$$

5.3 A Type System for Value-Passing

We next describe a type system similar to those of Deng and Sangiorgi [6] which guarantees termination in a value-passing process calculus without name-passing.

In the ψ-calculus that we consider, terms have the syntax

$$M ::= x \mid f(\boldsymbol{M})$$

Again, we shall assume that the calculus uses replicated input only.

The underlying idea of the type system is that every composite term is typed by its constructor depth. The only possible source of non-termination is that of replicated input; termination is guaranteed by the requirement that underneath a replicated input, we only encounter outputs of terms that have strictly lower constructor depth.

A syntactic constraint that will be ensured by the type system is that all channels are names – that is, subjects of inputs and outputs are always names.

The types of names are given by the formation rules

$$T ::= \mathsf{Ch}^n \mid n \mid c$$

so terms either have channel type, carrying terms of type n, are terms of index $n \in \mathbb{N}$ or terms of constant type c, where $c \in \mathbb{N}$. The additive structure of types is again the trivial one: for every type we let $T + T = T$.

Assertions are closed intervals of natural numbers.

$$\Psi ::= [m, n] \quad \text{where } m, n \in \mathbb{N}$$

For terms we let judgments have the form

$$\Gamma, [l, r] \vdash M : T$$

Composition of assertions is defined as the least encompassing interval:

$$\begin{aligned} [0, r] \otimes [0, r] &= [0, r] \\ [l_1, r_1] \otimes [l_2, r_2] &= [l_3, r_3] \quad \text{otherwise} \\ &\quad \text{where } l_3 = \min(l_1, l_2), r_3 = \max(r_1 + 1, r_2 + 1) \end{aligned}$$

This operation is easily seen to be commutative and associative.

We then let channels be typed in one-point intervals only, as seen from rule (Chan). Other terms are typable in intervals of length 1.

We always type a process in the interval $[0, n]$ for some $n \in \mathbb{N}$. The compatibility relation tells us that $\mathsf{Ch}^n \leftrightarrow_P n$; that is, channels of type Ch^n can carry terms of index n.

The type rules for terms are given below; they introduce a notion of simple subtyping. The rules guarantee that $\Gamma, \Psi \vdash M : n$ if the depth of M is at most n.

$$\text{(NAME)} \quad \Gamma, [n-1, n] \vdash x : T if \Gamma(x) = T$$

$$\text{(CHAN)} \quad \Gamma, [n, n] \vdash x : \mathsf{Ch}^{n+1} \qquad \text{if } \Gamma(x) = \mathsf{Ch}^n$$

$$\text{(COMP-1)} \quad \frac{\Gamma, [n_i - 1, n_i] \vdash M_i : n_i \quad 1 \leq i \leq |\boldsymbol{M}|}{\Gamma, [n-1, n] \vdash f(\boldsymbol{M}) : n'}$$

$$where \quad n \geq n' \geq 1 + \max_{1 \leq i \leq |\boldsymbol{M}|} (n_i)$$

In type judgements for processes, $\Gamma, \Psi \vdash P$, we have that Ψ is a bound on the channel type depth.

A replicated input is now typed as follows (this is a derived rule):

$$\frac{\Gamma_1, [n_1, n_1] \vdash M : \mathsf{Ch}^{n_1} \quad \Gamma_2 + x : n_1, [0, n_1 - 1] \vdash P}{\Gamma, [0, n_1] \vdash !\, M(x).P}$$

Note that the definition of assertion composition ensures that all terms in the continuation must have types less than that of the subject M.

Theorem 4. *If $\Gamma, n \vdash P$ then every transition sequence of P terminates.*

The proof that the type system ensures termination uses the following proposition.

Lemma 1. *$\Gamma, n \vdash P$ and $\Psi \rhd P \xrightarrow{\alpha}$ then $\Gamma, n \vdash \mathsf{s}(\alpha) : n$, where $\mathsf{s}(\alpha)$ is the term communicated by α.*

In other words, every labelled transition will communicate a term of constructor depth at most n. Together with Theorem 1 this ensures termination.

5.4 A π-calculus for Allocation and Deallocation

In [4] de Vries, Hennessy and Francalanza consider the Resource π-Calculus, a process calculus with notions of allocation and deallocation.

The syntax of the Resource π-Calculus is given by the formation rules

$$P ::= u(\boldsymbol{x}).P \mid \overline{u}\langle \boldsymbol{v} \rangle.P \mid \mathbf{0} \mid !\, P \mid P_1 \mid P_2 \mid \mathsf{if}\ u = v\ \mathsf{then}\ P\ \mathsf{else}\ Q \mid (\nu c : s)P$$
$$\mid \mathsf{alloc}(x).P \mid \mathsf{free}\ u.P$$
$$s ::= \top \mid \bot$$

The syntax mentions names $(u, v \ldots)$ which can be channels $(c, d, \ldots)$ or variables $(x, y, \ldots)$. The state s describes if a channel is allocated $(\top)$ or deallocated $(\bot)$.

In the reduction semantics of the Resource π-Calculus configurations, a function $\sigma : \mathsf{Chans} \rightharpoonup \{\top, \bot\}$ describes the allocation state of free channels. The new reduction rules are

$$\text{(ALLOC)} \quad \sigma \rhd \mathsf{alloc}(x).P \to \sigma \rhd (\nu c : \top) P\{^c/_x\} \quad \text{where } c \notin \mathrm{dom}(\sigma)$$

$$\text{(FREE)} \quad \sigma, c \mapsto \top \rhd \mathsf{free}\ u.P \to \sigma, c \mapsto \bot \rhd P$$

The type system uses types whose formation rules are

$$T ::= [\boldsymbol{T}]^a$$

where $\boldsymbol{T}$ denotes the types of names carried on channels of this type and a denotes the multiplicity. A multiplicity can be 1 (which here means affine), $(\bullet, i)$ (meaning that a name of this type will be uniquely allocated after i steps) or ω (unbounded). A name of type $(\bullet, 0)$ is a name that is uniquely determined now.

A simply notion of subtyping is assumed, defined by

$$(\bullet, i) <: (\bullet, i+1) \qquad (\bullet, i) <: \omega$$

$$\omega <: 1 \qquad \frac{a_1 <: a_2}{[\boldsymbol{T}]^{a_1} <: [\boldsymbol{T}]^{a_2}}$$

Some of the central typing rules are

$$(\textsc{In}) \quad \frac{\Gamma, u : [\boldsymbol{T}]^{a-1}, \boldsymbol{x} : \boldsymbol{T}}{\Gamma, u : [\boldsymbol{T}]^a \vdash u(\boldsymbol{x}).P} \qquad (\textsc{Rev}) \quad \frac{\Gamma, u : [\boldsymbol{T_2}]^\bullet \vdash P}{\Gamma, u : [\boldsymbol{T_1}]^\bullet \vdash P}$$

$$(\textsc{Alloc}) \quad \frac{\Gamma, x : [\boldsymbol{T}]^\bullet \vdash P}{\Gamma \vdash \mathsf{alloc}(x).P} \qquad (\textsc{Free}) \quad \frac{\Gamma \vdash P}{\Gamma, u : [\boldsymbol{T}]^\bullet \vdash \mathsf{free}\ u.P}$$

The rule (Rev) states that any name whose name is fixed now can be assumed to have any other type as well.

We can represent all this in our ψ-calculus setting as follows.

The idea is that assertions are used to track the allocation state of channels. Our assertions are given by the formation rules

$$\Psi ::= c@x \mapsto \top \mid c \mapsto \bot \mid \mathbf{0} \mid c@\mathbf{1} \mid \Psi_1, \Psi_1$$

and composition is given by

$$c@x \mapsto \top \otimes c \mapsto \bot = c@\mathbf{1} \qquad \mathbf{0} \otimes \mathbf{0} = \mathbf{0}$$
$$\Psi_1 \otimes \Psi_2 = \Psi_1, \Psi_2 \text{ otherwise}$$

Our conditions are of the form $u = v$ and we define $\Psi \models u = u$ for all names u. Channel equivalence is defined by

$$\Psi \models c \dot{\leftrightarrow} c \quad \text{if } c@x \mapsto \top \leq \Psi, c \mapsto \bot \neq \Psi$$

The new constructions are represented by

$$[\![\mathsf{alloc}(x).P]\!] \stackrel{\text{def}}{=} (\nu c : T_x)(c@x \mapsto \top \mid [\![P]\!]\{^c/_x\})$$
$$[\![\mathsf{free}\ c.P]\!] \stackrel{\text{def}}{=} (c \mapsto \bot \mid [\![P]\!])$$

The types are given by the formation rules

$$T ::= \mathbf{Ch}^a(\boldsymbol{T}) \mid T_x$$

We define addition of multiplicities by

$$\omega + \omega = \omega \qquad\qquad (\bullet, i) = 1 + (\bullet, i + 1)$$

and addition of types is defined by $\mathbf{Ch}^a(\boldsymbol{T}) + \mathbf{Ch}^1(\boldsymbol{T}) = \mathbf{Ch}^{a+1}(\boldsymbol{T})$.

Subtyping is captured by defining a notion of subarities:

$$(\bullet, i) \leq (i, i+1) \qquad\qquad (\bullet, i+1) \leq \omega$$
$$\omega \leq 1$$

Below we present two of the rules for terms. The first, (PSI-REV), is our representation of the (REV) rule. The second, (PSI-SUB-1) is one of the rules that captures the subtype relation.

$$(\text{PSI-REV}) \; \frac{\Gamma, \Psi \vdash u : \mathbf{Ch}((\bullet, 0))\boldsymbol{T_2}}{\Gamma, \Psi \vdash u : \mathbf{Ch}((\bullet, 0))\boldsymbol{T_1}}$$

$$(\text{PSI-SUB-1}) \; \frac{\Gamma, \Psi \vdash u : \mathbf{Ch}(a_1)\boldsymbol{T_1}}{\Gamma, \Psi \vdash u : \mathbf{Ch}(a_1)\boldsymbol{T_2}} \quad a_1 <: a_2$$

For assertions, the interesting rule is that for the assertion $\mathbf{0}$.

$$(\text{NIL}) \quad \emptyset \vdash \mathbf{0}$$

The type rules for processes in our representation of the Resource π-calculus are instances of our general rules. The rule (IN) is represented directly using our rule (T-IN) because of the definition of addition of types. Also note that assertions play no part in any of the original rules and are therefore also of no importance in our representation.

Theorem 5. *Let Γ' be a type environment as in [4] and let Γ be given by $\Gamma(x) = [\![\Gamma'(x)]\!]$ for all $x \in \mathrm{dom}(\Gamma')$. Then $\Gamma' \vdash' P \iff \Gamma, \mathbf{0} \vdash [\![P]\!]$.*

6 Conclusions and Further Work

In this paper we have presented a resource-conscious type system for ψ-calculi. The type system satisfies a subject reduction property which describes how resources will be consumed by well-typed transitions.

The study of properties of bisimilarity is a next topic to consider. In their original work, Kobayashi et al. [14] described how to develop a theory of barbed congruence for their linear type system for the asynchronous π-calculus. It would be interesting to see to what extent the results of [1] carry over to our setting and if we can give a general account of the results on confluence and determinacy described in [14].

Another important topic to be studied is that of notions of behavioural types. This includes the notions of usages employed by Kobayashi in his work on type systems for deadlock freedom [15] and, notably, the work on dyadic session types [10,12]. In the setting of session types for ψ-calculi one would expect the calculus syntax to be enriched with the usual session primitives of session channel generation, selection and branching. More interestingly, the notion of duality of session types must be dealt with for channels that can be composite terms. Moreover, a theory of session types for ψ-calculi should offer a smooth generalization of the type system presented here.

The notion of *linearized types* is of special interest here; a linearized type T occurring in a reduction sequence has the property that at any given configuration of the sequence there is precisely one term occurrence that has type T. However, unlike the case for linear types, there may be several distinct terms of type T that appear during the computation. As was already pointed out in [14], this notion is a special case of that of session types. As Dardha et al. have shown [3], it is now possible to encode session types directly in a linear type system. We would therefore expect any reasonable representation of session types for ψ-calculi to satisfy a similar, more general property.

References

1. Bengtson, J., Johansson, M., Parrow, J., Victor, B.: Psi-calculi: a framework for mobile processes with nominal data and logic. Logical Meth. Comput. Sci. 7(1), 11 (2011)
2. Bugliesi, M., Calzavara, S., Eigner, F., Maffei, M.: Resource-aware authorization policies for statically typed cryptographic protocols. In: Proceedings of CSF 2011, pp. 83–98. IEEE Computer Society (2011)
3. Dardha, O., Giachino, E., Sangiorgi, D.: Session types revisited. In: Proceedings of PPDP, pp. 139–150. ACM, New York (2012)
4. de Vries, E., Francalanza, A., Hennessy, M.: Uniqueness typing for resource management in message-passing concurrency. In: LINEARITY. EPTCS, vol. 22, pp. 26–37 (2009)
5. Demangeon, R., Honda, K.: Full Abstraction in a Subtyped pi-calculus with Linear Types. In: Katoen, J.-P., König, B. (eds.) CONCUR 2011. LNCS, vol. 6901, pp. 280–296. Springer, Heidelberg (2011)
6. Deng, Y., Sangiorgi, D.: Ensuring termination by typability. Inf. Comput. **204**(7), 1045–1082 (2006)
7. Gabbay, M.J., Mathijssen, A.: Nominal (universal) algebra: equational logic with names and binding. J. Logic Comput. **19**(6), 1455–1508 (2009)
8. Girard, J.-Y.: Linear logic. Theoret. Comput. Sci. **50**, 1–102 (1987)
9. Giunti, M., Vasconcelos, V.T.: A linear account of session types in the Pi calculus. In: Gastin, P., Laroussinie, F. (eds.) CONCUR 2010. LNCS, vol. 6269, pp. 432–446. Springer, Heidelberg (2010)
10. Honda, K.: Types for dynamic interaction. In: Best, E. (ed.) CONCUR 1993. LNCS, vol. 715, pp. 509–523. Springer, Heidelberg (1993)

11. Honda, K.: Composing processes. In: Proceedings of POPL 1996, pp. 344–357 (1996)
12. Kähkönen, K., Kindermann, R., Heljanko, K., Niemelä, I.: Experimental comparison of concolic and random testing for Java card applets. In: Pol, J., Weber, M. (eds.) Model Checking Software. LNCS, vol. 6349, pp. 22–39. Springer, Heidelberg (2010)
13. Hüttel, H.: Typed ψ-calculi. In: Katoen, J.-P., König, B. (eds.) CONCUR 2011. LNCS, vol. 6901, pp. 265–279. Springer, Heidelberg (2011)
14. Kobayashi, N., Pierce, B.C., Turner, D.N.: Linearity and the pi-calculus. ACM Trans. Program. Lang. Syst. **21**(5), 914–947 (1999)
15. Kobayashi, N.: A new type system for deadlock-free processes. In: Baier, Ch., Hermanns, H. (eds.) CONCUR 2006. LNCS, vol. 4137, pp. 233–247. Springer, Heidelberg (2006)
16. Yoshida, N., Berger, M., Honda, K.: Strong normalisation in the π-calculus. In: Proceedings of LICS 2001, pp. 311–322. IEEE (2001)
17. Yoshida, N., Berger, M., Honda, K.: Genericity and the π-calculus. Acta Inf. **42**(2/3), 83–141 (2005)

A Sorted Semantic Framework for Applied Process Calculi (Extended Abstract)

Johannes Borgström(✉), Ramūnas Gutkovas, Joachim Parrow, Björn Victor, and Johannes Åman Pohjola

Department of Information Technology, Uppsala University, Uppsala, Sweden
johannes.borgstrom@it.uu.se

Abstract. Applied process calculi include advanced programming constructs such as type systems, communication with pattern matching, encryption primitives, concurrent constraints, nondeterminism, process creation, and dynamic connection topologies. Several such formalisms, e.g. the applied pi calculus, are extensions of the the pi-calculus; a growing number is geared towards particular applications or computational paradigms.

Our goal is a unified framework to represent different process calculi and notions of computation. To this end, we extend our previous work on psi-calculi with novel abstract patterns and pattern matching, and add sorts to the data term language, giving sufficient criteria for subject reduction to hold. Our framework can accommodate several existing process calculi; the resulting transition systems are isomorphic to the originals up to strong bisimulation. We also demonstrate different notions of computation on data terms, including cryptographic primitives and a lambda-calculus with erratic choice. Substantial parts of the meta-theory of sorted psi-calculi have been machine-checked using Nominal Isabelle.

1 Introduction

There is today a growing number of high-level constructs in the area of concurrency. Examples include type systems, communication with pattern matching, encryption primitives, concurrent constraints, nondeterminism, and dynamic connection topologies. Combinations of such constructs are included in a variety of application oriented process calculi. For each such calculus its internal consistency, in terms of congruence results and algebraic laws, must be established independently. Our aim is a framework where many such calculi fit and where such results are derived once and for all, eliminating the need for individual proofs about each calculus.

Our effort in this direction is the framework of psi-calculi [1], which provides machine-checked proofs that important meta-theoretical properties, such as compositionality of bisimulation, hold in all instances of the framework. In this paper we introduce a novel generalization of pattern matching, decoupled from the definition of substitution, and introduce sorts for data terms and names.

M. Abadi and A. Lluch Lafuente (Eds.): TGC 2013, LNCS 8358, pp. 103–118, 2014.
DOI: 10.1007/978-3-319-05119-2_7,

The generalized pattern matching is a new contribution that holds general interest; here it allows us to directly capture computation on data in advanced process calculi, without elaborate encodings. We evaluate our framework by providing instances that are isomorphic to standard calculi, and by representing several different notions of computation. This is an advance over our previous work, where we had to resort to nontrivial encodings with unclear formal correspondence to the standard calculi.

1.1 Background: Psi-calculi

A psi-calculus has a notion of data terms, ranged over by K, L, M, N, and we write $\overline{M}\ N \,.\, P$ to represent an agent sending the term N along the channel M (which is also a data term), continuing as the agent P. We write $\underline{K}(\lambda\widetilde{x})X \,.\, Q$ to represent an agent that can input along the channel K, receiving some object matching the pattern X, where $\widetilde{x}$ are the variables bound by the prefix. These two agents can interact under two conditions. First, the two channels must be *channel equivalent*, as defined by the channel equivalence predicate $M \leftrightarrow K$. Second, N must match the pattern X.

Formally, a *transition* is of kind $\Psi \rhd P \xrightarrow{\alpha} P'$, meaning that in an environment represented by the *assertion* Ψ the agent P can do an action α to become P'. An assertion embodies a collection of facts used to infer *conditions* such as the channel equivalence predicate $\leftrightarrow$. To continue the example, if $N = X[\widetilde{x} := \widetilde{L}]$ we will have $\Psi \rhd \overline{M}\ N \,.\, P \mid \underline{K}(\lambda\widetilde{x})X \,.\, Q \xrightarrow{\tau} P \mid Q[\widetilde{x} := \widetilde{L}]$ when additionally $\Psi \vdash M \leftrightarrow K$, i.e. when the assertion Ψ entails that M and K represent the same channel. In this way we may introduce a parametrised equational theory over a data structure for channels. Conditions, ranged over by φ, can be tested in the **if** construct: we have that $\Psi \rhd \textbf{if}\ \varphi\ \textbf{then}\ \mathrm{P} \xrightarrow{\alpha} P'$ when $\Psi \vdash \varphi$ and $\Psi \rhd P \xrightarrow{\alpha} P'$. In order to represent concurrent constraints and local knowledge, assertions can be used as agents: $(\!|\Psi|\!)$ stands for an agent that asserts Ψ to its environment. Assertions may contain names and these can be scoped; for example, in $P \mid (\nu a)((\!|\Psi|\!) \mid Q)$ the agent Q uses all entailments provided by Ψ, while P only uses those that do not contain the name a.

Assertions and conditions can, in general, form any logical theory. Also the data terms can be drawn from an arbitrary set. One of our major contributions has been to pinpoint the precise requirements on the data terms and logic for a calculus to be useful in the sense that the natural formulation of bisimulation satisfies the expected algebraic laws (see Sect. 2). It turns out that it is necessary to view the terms and logics as *nominal* [2]. This means that there is a distinguished set of names, and for each term a well defined notion of *support*, intuitively corresponding to the names occurring in the term.

1.2 Extension: Generalized Pattern Matching

In our original definition of psi-calculi [1] (called "the original psi-calculi" below), patterns are just terms and pattern matching is defined by substitution in the usual way: the output object N matches the pattern X with binders $\widetilde{x}$ iff $N = X[\widetilde{x} := \widetilde{L}]$. In order to increase the generality we now introduce a function MATCH which takes a term N, a sequence of names $\widetilde{x}$ and a pattern X, returning a set of sequences of terms; the intuition is that if $\widetilde{L}$ is in $\text{MATCH}(N, \widetilde{x}, X)$ then N matches the pattern X by instantiating $\widetilde{x}$ to $\widetilde{L}$. The receiving agent $\underline{K}(\lambda\widetilde{x})X\,.\,Q$ then continues as $Q[\widetilde{x} := \widetilde{L}]$.

As an example we consider a term algebra with two function symbols: enc of arity three and dec of arity two. Here $\texttt{enc}(N, n, k)$ means encrypting N with the key k and a random nonce n and and $\texttt{dec}(N, k)$ represents symmetric key decryption, discarding the nonce. Suppose an agent sends an encryption, as in $\overline{M}\ \texttt{enc}(N, n, k)\,.\,P$. If we allow all terms to act as patterns, a receiving agent can use $\texttt{enc}(x, y, z)$ as a pattern, as in $\underline{c}(\lambda x, y, z)\texttt{enc}(x, y, z)\,.\,Q$, and in this way decompose the encryption and extract the message and key. Using the encryption function as a destructor in this way is clearly not the intention of a cryptographic model. With the new general form of pattern matching, we can simply limit the patterns to not bind names in terms at key position. Together with the separation between patterns and terms, this allows to directly represent dialects of the spi-calculus as in Examples 4 and 5 in Sect. 3.

Moreover, the generalization makes it possible to safely use rewrite rules such as $\texttt{dec}(\texttt{enc}(M, N, K), K) \to M$. In the psi-calculi framework such evaluation is not a primitive concept, but it can be part of the substitution function, with the idea that with each substitution all data terms are normalized according to rewrite rules. Such evaluating substitutions are dangerous for two reasons. First, in the original psi-calculi they can introduce ill-formed input prefixes. The input prefix $\underline{M}(\lambda\widetilde{x})N$ is well-formed when $\widetilde{x} \subseteq \text{n}(N)$, i.e. the names $\widetilde{x}$ must all occur in N; a rewrite of the well-formed $\underline{M}(\lambda y)\texttt{dec}(\texttt{enc}(N, y, k), k)\,.\,P$ to $\underline{M}(\lambda y)N\,.\,P$ yields an ill-formed agent when y does not appear in N. Such ill-formed agents could also arise from input transitions in some original psi-calculi; with the current generalization preservation of well-formedness is guaranteed.

Second, in the original psi-calculi there is a requirement that a substitution of $\widetilde{L}$ for $\widetilde{x}$ in M must yield a term containing all names in $\widetilde{L}$ whenever $\widetilde{x} \subseteq \text{n}(M)$. The reason is explained at length in [1]; briefly put, without this requirement the scope extension law is unsound. If rewrites such as $\texttt{dec}(\texttt{enc}(M, N, K), K) \to M$ are performed by substitutions this requirement is not fulfilled, since a substitution may then erase the names in N and K. However, a closer examination reveals that this requirement is only necessary for some uses of substitution. In the transition

$$\underline{M}(\lambda\widetilde{x})N.P \xrightarrow{\underline{K}\ N[\widetilde{x}:=\widetilde{L}]} P[\widetilde{x} := \widetilde{L}]$$

the non-erasing criterion is important for the substitution above the arrow ($N[\widetilde{x} := \widetilde{L}]$) but unimportant for the substitution after the arrow ($P[\widetilde{x} := \widetilde{L}]$). In the present paper, we replace the former of these uses by the MATCH function, where a similar non-erasing criterion applies. All other substitutions may safely use arbitrary rewrites, even erasing ones.

1.3 Extension: Sorting

Applied process calculi often make use of a sort system. The applied pi-calculus [3] has a name sort and a data sort; terms of name sort must not appear as subterms of terms of data sort. It also makes a distinction between input-bound variables (which may be substituted) and restriction-bound names (which may not). The pattern-matching spi-calculus [4] uses a sort of patterns and a sort of implementable terms; every implementable term can also be used as a pattern.

To represent such calculi, we admit a user-defined sort system on names, terms and patterns. Substitutions are only well-defined if they conform to the sorting discipline. To specify which terms can be used as channels, and which values can be received on them, we use compatibility predicates on the sorts of the subject and the object in input and output prefixes. The conditions for preservation of sorting by transitions (subject reduction) are very weak, allowing for great flexibility when defining instances.

The restriction to well-sorted substitution also allows to avoid "junk": terms that exist solely to make substitutions total. A prime example is representing the polyadic pi-calculus as a psi-calculus. The terms that can be transmitted between agents are tuples of names. Since a tuple is a term it can be substituted for a name, even if that name is already part of a tuple. The result is that the terms must admit nested tuples of names, which do not occur in the original calculus.

1.4 Related Work

Pattern-matching is in common use in programming languages (e.g. Lisp, ML). LINDA [5] uses pattern-matching when receiving from a tuple space. The pattern-matching spi-calculus limits which variables may be binding in a pattern in order to match encrypted messages without binding unknown keys (cf. Example 5). In all these cases, the pattern matching is defined by substitution in the usual way. In more recent languages, such as Scala and F#, pattern matching may involve computation, similarly to this paper.

The Kell calculus [6] also uses pattern languages equipped with a match function. However, in the Kell calculus the channels are single names and appear as part of patterns, patterns may match multiple communications simultaneously (à la join calculus), and pattern variables only match names (not composite messages) making forwarding and partial decomposition impossible.

Sorts for the pi-calculus were first described by Milner [7]. Hüttel's typed psi-calculi [8] admit a family of dependent type systems, capable of capturing a wide range of earlier type systems for pi-like calculi formulated as instances of psi-calculi. However, the term language of typed psi-calculi is required to be a free term algebra (and without name binders); it uses only the standard notions of substitution and matching, and does not admit any computation on terms. The sophisticated type system of typed psi-calculi is intended for fine-grained control of the behaviour of processes, while we focus on an earlier step: the creation of a calculus that is as close to the modeller's intent as possible. Indeed, sorted psi-calculi gives a formal account of the separation between variables and names in typed psi-calculi, and Hüttel's claim that "the set of well-[sorted] terms is closed under well-[sorted] substitutions, which suffices". Furthermore, we prove meta-theoretical results including preservation of well-formedness under structural equivalence; no such results exist for typed psi-calculi.

In the applied pi-calculus [3] the data language is a term algebra modulo an equational logic, which is suitable for modelling deterministic computation only. ProVerif [9] is a specialised tool for security protocol verification in an extension of applied pi, including a pattern matching construct. Its implementation allows pattern matching of tagged tuples modulo a user-defined rewrite system; this is strictly less general than the psi-calculus pattern matching described in this paper (cf. Example 2).

Fournet et al. [10] add a general authentication logic to a process calculus with destructor matching; the authentication logic is only used to specify program correctness, and do not influence the operational semantics in any way. A comparison of expressiveness to calculi with communication primitives other than binary directed communication, such as the concurrent pattern calculus [11] and the join-calculus [12], would be interesting. We here inherit positive results from the pi calculus, such as the encoding of the join-calculus.

1.5 Results and Outline

In Sect. 2 we define psi-calculi with the above extensions and explain the necessary change to the semantics. A formal account of the whole operational semantics and bisimulations can be found in an appendix. Our results are the usual algebraic properties of bisimilarity, preservation of well-formedness, and subject reduction.

We demonstrate the expressiveness of our generalization in Sect. 3 by directly representing calculi with advanced data structures and computations on them, even nondeterministic reductions.

2 Definitions

Psi-calculi are based on nominal data types. A nominal data type is similar to a traditional data type, but can also contain binders and identify alpha-variants of terms. Formally, the only requirements are related to the treatment of the atomic symbols called names as explained below. In this paper, we consider sorted nominal datatypes, where names may have different sorts.

We assume a set of sorts $\mathcal{S}$. Given a countable set of sorts for names $\mathcal{S}_\mathcal{N} \subseteq \mathcal{S}$, we assume countably infinite pair-wise disjoint sets of atomic *names* $\mathcal{N}_s$, where $s \in \mathcal{S}_\mathcal{N}$. The set of all names, $\mathcal{N} = \cup_s \mathcal{N}_s$, is ranged over by $a, b, \ldots, x, y, z$. We write $\tilde{x}$ for a tuple of names $x_1, \ldots, x_n$ and similarly for other tuples, and $\tilde{x}$ stands for the set of names $\{x_1, \ldots, x_n\}$ if used where a set is expected.

A sorted *nominal set* [2,13] is a set equipped with *name swapping* functions written $(a\ b)$, for any sort s and names $a, b \in \mathcal{N}_s$, i.e. name swappings must respect sorting. An intuition is that for any member T it holds that $(a\ b) \cdot T$ is T with a replaced by b and b replaced by a. The support of a term, written $\mathrm{n}(T)$, is intuitively the set of names affected by name swappings on T. This definition of support coincides with the usual definition of free names for abstract syntax trees that may contain binders. We write $a \# T$ for $a \notin \mathrm{n}(T)$, and extend this to finite sets and tuples by conjunction. A function f is equivariant if $(a\ b)(f(T)) = f((a\ b)T)$ always. A *nominal data type* is a nominal set together with some functions on it, for instance a substitution function.

2.1 Original Psi-calculi Parameters

Sorted psi-calculi is an extension of the original psi-calculi framework [1].

Definition 1 (Original psi-calculus parameters). *The psi-calculus parameters from the original psi-calculus include three nominal data types: (data) terms* $M, N \in \mathbf{T}$, *conditions* $\varphi \in \mathbf{C}$, *and assertions* $\Psi \in \mathbf{A}$; *and four equivariant operators: channel equivalence* $\dot{\leftrightarrow} : \mathbf{T} \times \mathbf{T} \to \mathbf{C}$, *assertion composition* $\otimes : \mathbf{A} \times \mathbf{A} \to \mathbf{A}$, *the unit assertion* $\mathbf{1}$, *and the entailment relation* $\vdash \subseteq \mathbf{A} \times \mathbf{C}$.

The binary functions $\dot{\leftrightarrow}$, $\otimes$ and the relation $\vdash$ above will be used in infix form.

Two assertions are equivalent, written $\Psi \simeq \Psi'$, if they entail the same conditions, i.e. for all φ we have that $\Psi \vdash \varphi \Leftrightarrow \Psi' \vdash \varphi$. We impose certain requisites on the sets and operators. In brief, channel equivalence must be symmetric and transitive, the assertions with $(\otimes, \mathbf{1})$ must form an abelian monoid modulo $\simeq$, and $\otimes$ must be compositional w.r.t. $\simeq$ (i.e. $\Psi_1 \simeq \Psi_2 \implies \Psi \otimes \Psi_1 \simeq \Psi \otimes \Psi_2$). For details see [1].

2.2 New Parameters for Generalized Pattern-Matching

To the parameters of the original psi-calculi we add patterns X, Y, that are used in input prefixes, a function VARS which yields the possible combinations of binding names in the pattern, and a pattern-matching function MATCH, which is used when the input takes place. Intuitively, an input pattern $(\lambda \widetilde{x})X$ matches a message N if there are $\widetilde{L} \in \mathrm{MATCH}(N, \widetilde{x}, X)$; the receiving agent then continues after substituting $\widetilde{L}$ for $\widetilde{x}$. If $\mathrm{MATCH}(N, \widetilde{x}, X) = \emptyset$ then $(\lambda \widetilde{x})X$ does not match N; if $|\mathrm{MATCH}(N, \widetilde{x}, X)| > 1$ then one of the matches will be non-deterministically chosen. Below, we use "variable" for names that can be bound in a pattern.

Definition 2 (Psi-calculus parameters for pattern-matching). *The psi-calculus parameters for pattern-matching include the nominal data type* $\mathbf{X}$ *of (input) patterns, ranged over by* X, Y, *and the two equivariant operators*

$$\begin{array}{ll} \mathrm{MATCH} : \mathbf{T} \times \mathcal{N}^* \times \mathbf{X} \to \mathcal{P}_{\mathrm{fin}}(\mathbf{T}^*) & \textit{Pattern matching} \\ \mathrm{VARS} : \mathbf{X} \to \mathcal{P}_{\mathrm{fin}}(\mathcal{P}_{\mathrm{fin}}(\mathcal{N})) & \textit{Pattern variables} \end{array}$$

The VARS operator gives the possible (finite) sets of names in a pattern which are bound by an input prefix. For example, an input prefix with a pairing pattern $\langle x, y \rangle$ may bind both x and y, only one of them, or none, so $\mathrm{VARS}(\langle x, y \rangle) =$

$\{\{x, y\}, \{x\}, \{y\}, \{\}\}$. This way, we can let the input prefix $\underline{c}(\lambda x)\langle x, y\rangle$ only match pairs where the second argument is the name y. To model a calculus where input patterns cannot be selective in this way, we may instead define $\text{VARS}(\langle x, y\rangle) = \{\{x, y\}\}$. This ensures that input prefixes that use the pattern $\langle x, y\rangle$ must be of the form $\underline{M}(\lambda x, y)\langle x, y\rangle$, where both x and y are bound. Another use for VARS is to exclude the binding of terms in certain positions, such as the keys of cryptographic messages (cf. Example 5).

Requirements on VARS and MATCH are given below in Definition 5. Note that the four data types **T**, **C**, **A** and **X** are not required to be disjoint. In most of the examples in this paper, the patterns **X** is a subset of the terms **T**.

2.3 New Parameters for Sorting

To the parameters defined above we add a sorting function and four sort compatibility predicates.

Definition 3 (Psi-calculus parameters for sorting). *The psi-calculus parameters for sorting include the sorting function* $\text{SORT} : \mathcal{N} \uplus \mathbf{T} \uplus \mathbf{X} \to \mathcal{S}$, *and the four compatibility predicates*

$$
\begin{array}{ll}
\underline{\propto} \subseteq \mathcal{S} \times \mathcal{S} & \textit{Can be used to receive} \\
\overline{\propto} \subseteq \mathcal{S} \times \mathcal{S} & \textit{Can be used to send} \\
\prec \subseteq \mathcal{S} \times \mathcal{S} & \textit{Can be substituted by} \\
\mathcal{S}_\nu \subseteq \mathcal{S} & \textit{Can be bound by name restriction}
\end{array}
$$

The SORT operator gives the sort of a name, term or pattern; on names we require that $\text{SORT}(a) = s$ iff $a \in \mathcal{N}_s$. The sort compatibility predicates are used to restrict where terms and names of certain sorts may appear in processes. Terms of sort s can be used to send values of sort t if $s \mathrel{\overline{\propto}} t$. Dually, a term of sort s can be used to receive with a pattern of sort t if $s \mathrel{\underline{\propto}} t$. A name a can be used in a restriction (νa) if $\text{SORT}(a) \in \mathcal{S}_\nu$. If $\text{SORT}(a) \prec \text{SORT}(M)$ we can substitute the term M for the name a. In most of our examples, $\prec$ is a subset of the equality relation. These predicates can be chosen freely, although the set of well-formed substitutions depends on $\prec$, as detailed in Definition 4 below.

2.4 Substitution and Matching

We require that each datatype is equipped with an equivariant substitution function, which intuitively substitutes terms for names. The requisites on substitution differ from the original psi-calculi as indicated in the Introduction. Substitutions must preserve or refine sorts, and bound pattern variables must not be removed by substitutions.

We define a subsorting preorder $\leq$ on $\mathcal{S}$ as $s_1 \leq s_2$ if s_1 can be used as a channel or message whenever s_2 can be: formally $s_1 \leq s_2$ iff $\forall t \in \mathcal{S}.(s_2 \mathrel{\underline{\propto}} t \Rightarrow s_1 \mathrel{\underline{\propto}} t) \wedge (s_2 \mathrel{\overline{\propto}} t \Rightarrow s_1 \mathrel{\overline{\propto}} t) \wedge (t \mathrel{\underline{\propto}} s_2 \Rightarrow t \mathrel{\underline{\propto}} s_1) \wedge (t \mathrel{\overline{\propto}} s_2 \Rightarrow t \mathrel{\overline{\propto}} s_1)$. This relation compares sorts of terms, and so does not have any formal relationship to $\prec$ (which relates the sort of a name to the sort of a term).

Definition 4 (Substitution). *If $\widetilde{a}$ is a sequence of distinct names and $\widetilde{N}$ is an equally long sequence of terms such that* $\text{SORT}(a_i) \prec \text{SORT}(N_i)$ *for all i, we say that $[\widetilde{a} := \widetilde{N}]$ is a* substitution. *Substitutions are ranged over by σ.*

For each data type among $\mathbf{T}, \mathbf{A}, \mathbf{C}$ we define substitution on elements T of that data type as follows: we require that $T\sigma$ is an element of the same data type, and that if $(\widetilde{a}\ \widetilde{b})$ is a (bijective) name swapping such that $\widetilde{b}\#T, \widetilde{a}$ then $T[\widetilde{a} := \widetilde{N}] = ((\widetilde{a}\ \widetilde{b}).T)[\widetilde{b} := \widetilde{N}]$ (alpha-renaming of substituted variables). For terms we additionally require that $\text{SORT}(M\sigma) \leq \text{SORT}(M)$.

For substitution on patterns $X \in \mathbf{X}$, we require that if $\widetilde{x} \in \text{VARS}(X)$ and $\widetilde{x}\#\sigma$ then $X\sigma \in \mathbf{X}$ and $\text{SORT}(X\sigma) \leq \text{SORT}(X)$ and $\widetilde{x} \in \text{VARS}(X\sigma)$ and alpha-renaming of substituted variables (as above) holds.

Intuitively, the requirements on substitutions on patterns ensure that a substitution on a pattern with binders $((\lambda\widetilde{x})X)\sigma$ with $\widetilde{x} \in \text{VARS}(X)$ and $\widetilde{x}\#\sigma$ yields a pattern $(\lambda\widetilde{x})Y$ with $\widetilde{x} \in \text{VARS}(Y)$. As an example, consider the pair patterns discussed above with $\mathbf{X} = \{\langle x, y\rangle : x \neq y\}$ and $\text{VARS}(\langle x, y\rangle) = \{\{x, y\}\}$. We can let $\langle x, y\rangle\sigma = \langle x, y\rangle$ when $x, y\#\sigma$. Since $\text{VARS}(\langle x, y\rangle) = \{\{x, y\}\}$ the pattern $\langle x, y\rangle$ in a well-formed agent will always occur directly under the binder $(\lambda x, y)$, i.e. in $(\lambda x, y)\langle x, y\rangle$, and here a substitution for x or y will have no effect. It therefore does not matter what e.g. $\langle x, y\rangle[x := M]$ is, since it will never occur in derivations of transitions of well-formed agents. We could think of substitutions as partial functions which are undefined in such cases; formally, since substitutions are total, the result of this substitution can be assigned an arbitrary value.

Matching must be invariant under renaming of pattern variables, and the substitution resulting from a match must not contain any names that are not from the matched term or the pattern:

Definition 5 (Generalized pattern matching). *For the function* MATCH *we require that if $\widetilde{x} \in \text{VARS}(X)$ are distinct and $\widetilde{N} \in \text{MATCH}(M, \widetilde{x}, X)$ then it must hold that $[\widetilde{x} := \widetilde{N}]$ is a substitution, that* $\text{n}(\widetilde{N}) \subseteq \text{n}(M) \cup (\text{n}(X) \setminus \widetilde{x})$, *and that for all name swappings $(\widetilde{x}\ \widetilde{y})$ we have $\widetilde{N} \in \text{MATCH}(M, \widetilde{y}, (\widetilde{x}\ \widetilde{y})X)$ (alpha-renaming of matching).*

In the original psi-calculi equivariance of matching is imposed as a requirement on substitution on terms, but there is no requirement that substitutions preserve pattern variables. For this reason, the original psi semantics does not preserve the well-formedness of agents (an input prefix $\underline{M}(\lambda\widetilde{x})N\,.\,P$ is well-formed when $\widetilde{x} \subseteq \text{n}(N)$), although this is assumed by the operational semantics [1]. In contrast, the semantics of pattern-matching psi-calculi does preserve well-formedness, as shown below in Theorem 1.

In many process calculi, and also in the symbolic semantics of psi [14], the input construct binds a single variable. This is a trivial instance of pattern matching where the pattern is a single bound variable, matching any term.

Example 1 Given values for the other requisites, we can take $\mathbf{X} = \mathcal{N}$ with $\text{VARS}(a) = \{a\}$, meaning that the pattern variable must always occur bound, and $\text{MATCH}(M, a, a) = \{M\}$ if $\text{SORT}(a) \prec \text{SORT}(M)$. On patterns we define substitution as $a\sigma = a$ when $a\#\sigma$.

2.5 Agents

Definition 6 (Agents). *The* agents, *ranged over by* $P, Q, \ldots$, *are of the following forms.*

$\overline{M}\,N.P$	Output
$\underline{M}(\lambda\widetilde{x})X.P$	Input
$\mathbf{case}\ \varphi_1 : P_1 \,[\!]\, \cdots \,[\!]\, \varphi_n : P_n$	Case
$(\nu a)P$	Restriction
$P \mid Q$	Parallel
$!P$	Replication
$(\!\vert\Psi\vert\!)$	Assertion

In the Input any name in $\widetilde{x}$ *binds its occurrences in both* X *and* P, *and in the Restriction* a *binds in* P. *An assertion is* guarded *if it is a subterm of an Input or Output. An agent is* well-formed *if, for all its subterms, in a replication* $!P$ *there are no unguarded assertions in* P, *and in* $\mathbf{case}\ \varphi_1 : P_1 \,[\!]\, \cdots \,[\!]\, \varphi_n : P_n$ *there are no unguarded assertion in any* P_i. *Substitution on agents is defined inductively on their structure, using the substitution function of each datatype based on syntactic position, avoiding name capture.*

In comparison to [1] we restrict the syntax of well-formed agents by imposing requirements on sorts: the subjects and objects of prefixes must have compatible sorts, and restrictions may only bind names of a sort in $\mathcal{S}_\nu$.

Definition 7. *In sorted psi-calculi, an agent is* well-formed *if additionally the following holds for all its subterms. In an Output* $\overline{M}\,N.P$ *we require that* $\textsc{sort}(M)\ \overline{\propto}\ \textsc{sort}(N)$. *In an Input* $\underline{M}(\lambda\widetilde{x})X.P$ *we require that* $\widetilde{x} \in \textsc{vars}(X)$ *is a tuple of distinct names and* $\textsc{sort}(M)\ \underline{\propto}\ \textsc{sort}(X)$. *In a Restriction* $(\nu a)P$ *we require that* $\textsc{sort}(a) \in \mathcal{S}_\nu$.

The output prefix $\overline{M}\,N.P$ sends N on a channel that is equivalent to M. Dually, $\underline{M}(\lambda\widetilde{x})X.P$ receives a message matching the pattern X from a channel equivalent to M. A non-deterministic case statement $\mathbf{case}\ \varphi_1 : P_1 \,[\!]\, \cdots \,[\!]\, \varphi_n : P_n$ executes one of the branches P_i where the corresponding condition φ_i holds, discarding the other branches. Restriction $(\nu a)P$ scopes the name a in P; the scope of a may be extruded if P communicates a data term containing a. A parallel composition $P \mid Q$ denotes P and Q running in parallel; they may proceed independently or communicate. A replication $!P$ models an unbounded number of copies of the process P. The assertion $(\!\vert\Psi\vert\!)$ contributes Ψ to its environment. We often write **if** φ **then** P for **case** $\varphi : P$, and nothing or $\mathbf{0}$ for the empty case statement **case**.

2.6 Semantics and Bisimulation

The semantics of a psi-calculus is defined inductively as a structural operation semantics yielding a labelled transition relation. The full definition can be found in our earlier work [1]. We here only comment on the one change necessary to accommodate the generalized pattern matching. The original input rule reads

$$\frac{\Psi \vdash M \leftrightarrow K}{\Psi \rhd \underline{M}(\lambda\widetilde{y})X.P \xrightarrow{\underline{K}\, X[\widetilde{y}:=\widetilde{L}]} P[\widetilde{y} := \widetilde{L}]}$$

and means that the instantiating substitution $[\widetilde{y} := \widetilde{L}]$ is applied both in the transition label and in the agent after the transition. Our new input rule is

$$\frac{\Psi \vdash M \leftrightarrow K \quad \widetilde{L} \in \text{MATCH}(N, \widetilde{y}, X)}{\Psi \rhd \underline{M}(\lambda\widetilde{y})X.P \xrightarrow{\underline{K}\, N} P[\widetilde{y} := \widetilde{L}]}$$

Here the matching with the transition label and the substitution applied to the following agent may be different. The MATCH predicate determines both the former (by designating the term N) and the latter (by designating the substitution), but there is no requirement on how they relate. As explained in Sect. 1.2 this means we can introduce evaluation of terms in the substitution or in the matching.

Theorem 1 (Preservation of well-formedness). *If P is well-formed, then $P\sigma$ is well-formed, and if $\Psi \rhd P \xrightarrow{\alpha} P'$ then P' is well-formed.*

Proof The first part is by induction on P. The interesting case is input $\underline{M}(\lambda\widetilde{x})X.Q$: assume that Q is well-formed, that $\widetilde{x} \in \text{VARS}(X)$, that $\text{SORT}(M) \underline{\propto} \text{SORT}(X)$ and that $\widetilde{x} \# \sigma$. By induction $Q\sigma$ is well-formed. By sort preservation we get $\text{SORT}(M\sigma) \leq \text{SORT}(M)$, so $\text{SORT}(M\sigma) \underline{\propto} \text{SORT}(X)$. By preservation of patterns by non-capturing substitutions we have that $\widetilde{x} \in \text{VARS}(X\sigma)$ and $\text{SORT}(X\sigma) \leq \text{SORT}(X)$, so $\text{SORT}(M\sigma) \underline{\propto} \text{SORT}(X\sigma)$. The second part is by induction on the transition rules, using part 1 in the IN rule.

Note that well-formedness implies conformance to the sorting discipline; therefore this theorem shows a kind of subject reduction property.

The definition of strong and weak bisimulation and their algebraic properties are unchanged from our previous work [1]. The results can be summarized as follows:

Theorem 2 (Properties of bisimulation). *All results on bisimulation established in [1] and [15] still hold in sorted psi-calculi with generalized matching.*

Theorem 2 has been formally verified in Isabelle/Nominal by adapting our existing proof scripts. The main difference is in the input cases of inductive proofs. This represents no more than two days of work, with the bulk of the effort going towards proving a crucial technical lemma stating that transitions do not invent new names with the new pattern matching. We have also machine-checked the proof of Theorem 1. Unfortunately, in Isabelle/Nominal there are currently no facilities to reason parametrically over the set of name sorts. Therefore the mechanically checked proofs only apply to psi-calculi with a trivial sorting (a single sort that is admitted everywhere); we complement them with manual proofs to extend these to arbitrary sortings.

3 Examples

Several well-known process algebras can be directly represented as a sorted psi-calculus by instantiating the parameters in the right way. With this we mean that the syntax is isomorphic and that the operational semantics is exactly preserved in a strong operational correspondence modulo strong bisimulation. There is no need for elaborate coding schemes and the correspondence proofs are straightforward.

Theorem 3 (Process algebra representations). *CCS with value passing [16], the unsorted and the sorted polyadic pi-calculus [7, 17], and the polyadic synchronization pi-calculus [18] can all be directly represented as sorted psi-calculi.*

The list can certainly be made longer, though each process algebra currently has a separate definition and therefore requires a separate formal proof. For example, a version of LINDA [5] can easily be obtained as a variant of the polyadic pi-calculus. To illustrate the technique, the only difference between polyadic pi-calculus and polyadic synchronization pi-calculus is about admitting tuples of names in prefix subjects.

More interestingly we demonstrate that we can accommodate a variety of structures for communication channels; in general these can be any kind of data, and substitution can include any kind of computation on these structures. This indicates that the word "substitution" may be a misnomer — a better word may be "effect" — though we keep it to conform with our earlier work. The examples below use default values for the parameters where $\mathbf{A} = \{\mathbf{1}\}$, $\mathbf{C} = \{\top, \bot\}$ and $M \leftrightarrow N = \top$ iff $M = N$, otherwise $\bot$. We let $\mathbf{1} \vdash \top$ and $\mathbf{1} \nvdash \bot$. We also let $\underline{\propto} = \overline{\propto} = \mathcal{S} \times \mathcal{S}$, $\mathcal{S}_\nu = \mathcal{S}_\mathcal{N}$, and let $\prec$ be the identity on $\mathcal{S}$, unless otherwise defined. Finally we let $\text{MATCH}(M, \tilde{x}, X) = \emptyset$ where not otherwise defined, we write $\preceq$ for the subterm (non-strict) partial order, and we use the standard notion of simultaneous substitution unless otherwise stated.

Example 2 (Convergent rewrite system on terms). We here consider deterministic computations specified using a rewrite system on terms containing names. This example highlights how a notion of substitution restricts the possible choices for $\text{VARS}(X)$; see Examples 3 and 4 for two concrete instances.

Let Σ be a sorted signature, and $\cdot \Downarrow$ be normalization with respect to a convergent rewrite system on the nominal term algebra over $\mathcal{N}$ generated by the signature Σ. We write ρ for sort-preserving capture-avoiding simultaneous substitutions $\{\widetilde{M}/\tilde{a}\}$ where every M_i is in normal form; here $n(\rho) = \mathrm{n}(\widetilde{M}, \tilde{a})$. A pattern (term) X is stable if for all ρ, $X\rho\Downarrow = X\rho$. The patterns include the stable patterns Y and all instances X thereof (i.e., where $X = Y\rho$); such an X can bind any names occurring in Y but not in ρ.

REWRITE($\Downarrow$)
$\mathbf{T} = \mathbf{X} = \mathrm{range}(\Downarrow)$
$M[\tilde{y} := \widetilde{L}] = M\{\widetilde{L}/\tilde{y}\}\Downarrow$
$\text{VARS}(X) = \bigcup\{\mathcal{P}(\mathrm{n}(Y) \setminus \mathrm{n}(\rho)) : Y \text{ stable} \wedge X = Y\rho\}$
$\text{MATCH}(M, \tilde{x}, X) = \{\widetilde{L} : M = X\{\widetilde{L}/\tilde{x}\}\}$

As a simple instance of Example 2, we may consider Peano arithmetic.

Example 3 (Peano arithmetic). Let $\mathcal{S} = \mathcal{S}_{\mathcal{N}} = \{\mathtt{nat}, \mathtt{chan}\}$. We take the signature consisting of the function symbols $\mathtt{zero} : \mathtt{nat}$, $\mathtt{succ} : \mathtt{nat} \to \mathtt{nat}$ and $\mathtt{plus} : \mathtt{nat} \times \mathtt{nat} \to \mathtt{nat}$. The rewrite rules $\mathtt{plus}(K, \mathtt{succ}(M)) \to \mathtt{plus}(\mathtt{succ}(K), M)$ and $\mathtt{plus}(K, \mathtt{zero}) \to K$ induce a convergent rewrite system $\Downarrow^{\mathrm{Peano}}$.

The stable terms are those that do not contain any occurrence of $\mathtt{plus}$. The construction of Example 2 yields that $\widetilde{x} \in \textsc{vars}(X)$ if $\widetilde{x} = \varepsilon$ (which matches only the term X itself), or if $\widetilde{x} = a$ and $X = \mathtt{succ}^n(a)$.

Writing i for $\mathtt{succ}^i(\mathtt{zero})$, the agent $(\nu a)(\overline{a}\, 2 \mid \underline{a}(\lambda y)\mathtt{succ}(y) \,.\, \overline{c}\, \mathtt{plus}(3, y))$ of $\mathbf{REWRITE}(\Downarrow^{\mathrm{Peano}})$ has one visible transition, with the label $\overline{c}\, 4$. In particular, the object of the label is $\mathtt{plus}(3, y)[y := 1] = \mathtt{plus}(3, y)\{^1/_y\}\Downarrow^{\mathrm{Peano}} = 4$.

Example 4 (Symmetric encryption). We can also consider variants on the construction in Example 2, such as a simple Dolev-Yao style [19] cryptographic message algebra for symmetric cryptography, where we ensure that the encryption keys of received encryptions can not be bound in input patterns, in agreement with cryptographic intuition.

Let $\mathcal{S} = \mathcal{S}_{\mathcal{N}} = \{\mathtt{message}, \mathtt{key}\}$, and consider the term algebra over the signature with the two function symbols $\mathtt{enc}, \mathtt{dec}$ of sort $\mathtt{message} \times \mathtt{key} \to \mathtt{message}$. The rewrite rule $\mathtt{dec}(\mathtt{enc}(M, K), K) \to M$ induces a convergent rewrite system $\Downarrow^{\mathrm{enc}}$, where the terms not containing $\mathtt{dec}$ are stable.

The construction of Example 2 yields that $\widetilde{x} \in \textsc{vars}(X)$ if $\widetilde{x} \subseteq \mathrm{n}(X)$ are pair-wise different and no x_i occurs as a subterm of a $\mathtt{dec}$ in X. This construction would permit to bind the keys of an encrypted message upon reception, e.g. $\underline{a}(\lambda m, k)\mathtt{enc}(m, k) \,.\, P$ would be allowed although it does not make cryptographic sense. Therefore we further restrict $\textsc{vars}(X)$ to those sets not containing names that occur in key position in X, thus disallowing the binding of k above.

SYMSPI
As $\mathbf{REWRITE}(\Downarrow^{\mathrm{enc}})$, except $\textsc{vars}(X) = \mathcal{P}(n(X) \setminus \{a : a \preceq \mathtt{dec}(Y_1, Y_2) \preceq X \vee$ $(a \preceq Y_2 \wedge \mathtt{enc}(Y_1, Y_2) \preceq X)\})$

As an example, the agent $(\nu a, k)(\overline{a}\, \mathtt{enc}(\mathtt{enc}(M, l), k) \mid \underline{a}(\lambda y)\mathtt{enc}(y, k) \,.\, \overline{c}\, \mathtt{dec}(y, l))$ has a visible transition with label $\overline{c}\, M$.

Example 5 (Pattern-matching spi-calculus). A more advanced version of Example 4 is the treatment of data in the pattern-matching spi-calculus [4], to which we refer for more examples and motivations of the definitions below. Features of the calculus includes a non-homomorphic definition of substitution that does not preserve sorts, and a sophisticated way of computing permitted pattern variables. This example highlights the flexibility of sorted psi-calculi in that such a specialized modelling language can be directly represented, in a form that is very close to the original.

We start from the term algebra T_Σ over the unsorted signature Σ consisting of the function symbols $()$, $(\cdot,\cdot)$, $\mathtt{eKey}(\cdot)$, $\mathtt{dKey}(\cdot)$, $\mathtt{enc}(\cdot,\cdot)$ and $\mathtt{enc}^{-1}(\cdot,\cdot)$. The operation $\mathtt{enc}^{-1}$ is "encryption with the inverse key", which is only permitted to occur in patterns. We add a sort system on T_Σ where $\mathtt{impl}$ denotes implementable terms not containing $\mathtt{enc}^{-1}$, and $\mathtt{pat}$ those that may only be used in patterns. The sort $\bot$ denotes ill-formed terms, which do not occur in well-formed processes. Substitution is defined homomorphically on the term algebra, except for $\mathtt{enc}^{-1}(M_1, M_2)\sigma$ which is $\mathtt{enc}(M_1\sigma, \mathtt{eKey}(N))$ when $M_2\sigma = \mathtt{dKey}(N)$, and $\mathtt{enc}^{-1}(M_1\sigma, M_2\sigma)$ otherwise. We let $\Vdash \subset \mathcal{P}(T_\Sigma) \times \mathcal{P}(T_\Sigma)$ be deducibility in the Dolev-Yao message algebra (for the precise definition, see [4]). The definition of $\textsc{vars}(X)$ below allows to bind only those names that can be deduced from X and the other names occurring in X. This excludes binding an unknown key, like in Example 4.

PMSPI
$\mathbf{T} = \mathbf{X} = T_\Sigma$
$\mathcal{S}_\mathcal{N} = \{\mathtt{impl}\}$ $\qquad \mathcal{S} = \{\mathtt{impl}, \mathtt{pat}, \bot\}$
$\prec = \overline{\propto} = \{(\mathtt{impl}, \mathtt{impl})\}$
$\underline{\propto} = \{(\mathtt{impl}, \mathtt{impl}), (\mathtt{impl}, \mathtt{pat})\}$
$\textsc{sort}(M) = \mathtt{impl}$ if $\forall N_1, N_2.\ \mathtt{enc}^{-1}(N_1, N_2) \not\preceq M$
$\textsc{sort}(M) = \bot$ if $\exists N_1, N_2.\ \mathtt{enc}^{-1}(N_1, \mathtt{dKey}(N_2)) \preceq M$
$\textsc{sort}(M) = \mathtt{pat}$ otherwise
$\textsc{match}(M, \widetilde{x}, X) = \{\widetilde{L} : M = X[\widetilde{x} := \widetilde{L}]\}$
$\textsc{vars}(X) = \{S \subseteq \mathrm{n}(X) : ((\mathrm{n}(X) \setminus S) \cup \{X\}) \Vdash S\}$

As an example, consider the following transitions in **PMSPI**:

$$
\begin{aligned}
&(\nu a, k, l)(\overline{a}\ \mathtt{enc}(\mathtt{dKey}(l), \mathtt{eKey}(k)).\overline{a}\ \mathtt{enc}(M, \mathtt{eKey}(l)) \\
&\qquad\qquad \mid \underline{a}(\lambda y)\mathtt{enc}(y, \mathtt{eKey}(k)) \,.\, \underline{a}(\lambda z)\mathtt{enc}^{-1}(z, y) \,.\, \overline{c}\ z) \\
&\quad \xrightarrow{\tau} (\nu a, k, l)(\overline{a}\ \mathtt{enc}(M, \mathtt{eKey}(l)) \mid \underline{a}(\lambda z)\mathtt{enc}(z, \mathtt{eKey}(l)) \,.\, \overline{c}\ z) \\
&\qquad\qquad\qquad\qquad\qquad\qquad \xrightarrow{\tau} (\nu a, k, l)\overline{c}\ M.
\end{aligned}
$$

Note that $\sigma = [y := \mathtt{dKey}(l)]$ resulting from the first input changed the sort of the second input pattern: $\textsc{sort}(\mathtt{enc}^{-1}(z, y)) = \mathtt{pat}$, but $\textsc{sort}(\mathtt{enc}^{-1}(z, y)\sigma) = \textsc{sort}(\mathtt{enc}(z, \mathtt{eKey}(l))) = \mathtt{impl}$. However, this is permitted by Definition 4, since $\mathtt{impl} \leq \mathtt{pat}$.

Example 6 (Nondeterministic computation). The previous examples considered total deterministic notions of computation on the term language. Here we consider a data term language equipped with partial non-deterministic evaluation: a lambda calculus with the erratic choice operator $\cdot \,[]\, \cdot$. Due to the non-determinism and partiality, evaluation cannot be part of the substitution function. Instead, the $\textsc{match}$ function collects all evaluations of the received term, which are non-deterministically selected from by the In rule. This example also highlights the use of object languages with binders, a common application of nominal logic.

We let substitution on terms be the usual capture-avoiding syntactic replacement, and define reduction contexts $\mathcal{R} ::= [] \mid \mathcal{R}\ M \mid (\boldsymbol{\lambda} x.M)\ \mathcal{R}$. Reduction $\rightarrow$ is the smallest pre-congruence for reduction contexts that contain the rules for β-reduction ($\boldsymbol{\lambda} x.M\ N \rightarrow M[x := N]$) and $\cdot \,[]\, \cdot$ (namely $M_1 \,[]\, M_2 \rightarrow M_i$ if $i \in \{1, 2\}$). We use the single-name patterns of Example 1, but include evaluation in matching.

NDLAM

$$\mathcal{S}_{\mathcal{N}} = \mathcal{S} = \{s\} \qquad \mathbf{X} = \mathcal{N}$$

$$M ::= a \mid M\ M \mid \boldsymbol{\lambda} x.M \mid M \,[]\, M$$

where x binds into M in $\boldsymbol{\lambda} x.M$

$$\textsc{match}(M, x, x) = \{N \;:\; M \rightarrow^{*} N \not\rightarrow\}$$

As an example, the agent $(\nu a)(\underline{a}(y) \,.\, \overline{c}\ y \,.\, \mathbf{0} \mid \overline{a}\ ((\boldsymbol{\lambda} x.x\ x) \,[]\, (\boldsymbol{\lambda} x.x)) \,.\, \mathbf{0})$ has two visible transitions, with labels $\overline{c}\ \boldsymbol{\lambda} x.x\ x$ and $\overline{c}\ \boldsymbol{\lambda} x.x$.

4 Conclusions and Further Work

We have described two features that taken together significantly improve the precision of applied process calculi: generalised pattern matching and substitution, which allow us to model computations on an arbitrary data term language, and a sort system which allows us to remove spurious data terms from consideration and to ensure that channels carry data of the appropriate sort. The well-formedness of processes is thereby guaranteed to be preserved by transitions. We have given examples of these features, ranging from the simple polyadic pi-calculus to the highly specialized pattern-matching spi-calculus, in the psi-calculi framework.

The meta-theoretic results carry over from the original psi formulations, and many have been machine-checked in Isabelle. We have also developed a tool for sorted psi-calculi [20], the Psi-calculi Workbench (Pwb), which provides an interactive simulator and automatic bisimulation checker. Users of the tool need only implement the parameters of their psi-calculus instances, supported by a core library.

Future work includes developing a symbolic semantics with pattern matching. For this, a reformulation of the operational semantics in the late style, where input objects are not instantiated until communication takes place, is necessary. We also aim to extend the use of sorts and generalized pattern matching to other variants of psi-calculi, including higher-order psi calculi [21] and reliable broadcast psi-calculi [22]. As mentioned in Sect. 2.6, further developments in Nominal Isabelle are needed for mechanizing theories with arbitrary but fixed sortings.

References

1. Bengtson, J., Johansson, M., Parrow, J., Victor, B.: Psi-calculi: a framework for mobile processes with nominal data and logic. LMCS 7(1:11) (2011)
2. Pitts, A.M.: Nominal logic, a first order theory of names and binding. Inf. Comput. **186**, 165–193 (2003)
3. Abadi, M., Fournet, C.: Mobile values, new names, and secure communication. In: Proceedings of POPL, pp. 104–115. ACM, January 2001
4. Haack, C., Jeffrey, A.: Pattern-matching spi-calculus. Inf. Comput. **204**(8), 1195–1263 (2006)
5. Gelernter, D.: Generative communication in Linda. ACM TOPLAS **7**(1), 80–112 (1985)
6. Schmitt, A., Stefani, J.-B.: The KELL calculus: a family of higher-order distributed process calculi. In: Priami, C., Quaglia, P. (eds.) GC 2004. LNCS, vol. 3267, pp. 146–178. Springer, Heidelberg (2005)
7. Milner, R.: The polyadic π-calculus: a tutorial. In: Bauer, F.L., Brauer, W., Schwichtenberg, H. (eds.) Logic and Algebra of Specification. NATO ASI, vol. 94, pp. 203–246. Springer, Heidelberg (1993)
8. Hüttel, H.: Typed ψ-calculi. In: Katoen, J.-P., König, B. (eds.) CONCUR 2011. LNCS, vol. 6901, pp. 265–279. Springer, Heidelberg (2011)
9. Blanchet, B.: Using Horn clauses for analyzing security protocols. In Cortier, V., Kremer, S., eds.: Formal Models and Techniques for Analyzing Security Protocols. Cryptology and Information Security Series, vol. 5, pp. 86–111. IOS Press (2011)
10. Fournet, C., Gordon, A.D., Maffeis, S.: A type discipline for authorization policies. In: Sagiv, M. (ed.) ESOP 2005. LNCS, vol. 3444, pp. 141–156. Springer, Heidelberg (2005)
11. Given-Wilson, T., Gorla, D., Jay, B.: Concurrent pattern calculus. In: Calude, C.S., Sassone, V. (eds.) TCS 2010. IFIP AICT, vol. 323, pp. 244–258. Springer, Heidelberg (2010)
12. Fournet, C., Gonthier, G.: The reflexive CHAM and the join-calculus. In: Proceedings of the POPL, pp. 372–385 (1996)
13. Gabbay, M.J., Pitts, A.M.: A new approach to abstract syntax with variable binding. Formal Aspects Comput. **13**, 341–363 (2001)
14. Johansson, M., Victor, B., Parrow, J.: Computing strong and weak bisimulations for psi-calculi. J. Logic Algebraic Program. **81**(3), 162–180 (2012)
15. Johansson, M., Bengtson, J., Parrow, J., Victor, B.: Weak equivalences in psi-calculi. In: Proceedings of LICS 2010, pp. 322–331. IEEE (2010)
16. Milner, R.: Communication and Concurrency. Prentice-Hall Inc., Upper Saddle River (1989)
17. Sangiorgi, D.: Expressing mobility in process algebras: first-order and higher-order paradigms. Ph.D thesis, University of Edinburgh, CST-99-93 (1993)
18. Carbone, M., Maffeis, S.: On the expressive power of polyadic synchronisation in π-calculus. Nord. J. Comput. **10**(2), 70–98 (2003)
19. Dolev, D., Yao, A.C.: On the security of public key protocols. IEEE Trans. Inf. Theor. **29**(2), 198–208 (1983)
20. Borgström, J., Gutkovas, R., Rodhe, I., Victor, B.: A parametric tool for applied process calculi. In: Proceedings of the 13th International Conference on Application of Concurrency to System Design (ACSD'13). IEEE (2013)
21. Parrow, J., Borgström, J., Raabjerg, P., Åman Pohjola, J.: Higher-order psi-calculi. Mathematical Structures in Computer Science FirstView (June 2013)

22. Åman Pohjola, J., Borgström, J., Parrow, J., Raabjerg, P., Rodhe, I.: Negative premises in applied process calculi. Technical Report 2013-014, Department of Information Technology, Uppsala University (2013)

Timed π-Calculus

Neda Saeedloei(✉) and Gopal Gupta

University of Texas at Dallas, Dallas, TX, USA
{neda.saeedloei,gupta}@utdallas.edu

Abstract. We extend π-calculus with real-time by adding clocks and assigning time-stamps to actions. The resulting formalism, timed π-calculus, provides a simple and novel way to annotate transition rules of π-calculus with timing constraints. Timed π-calculus is an expressive way of describing mobile, concurrent, real-time systems in which the behavior of systems is modeled by finite or infinite sequences of timed events. We develop an operational semantics as well as a notion of timed bisimilarity for the proposed language. We present the properties of timed bisimilarity; in particular, expansion theorem for real-time, concurrent, mobile processes is investigated.

1 Introduction

The π-calculus was introduced by Milner et al. [12] with the aim of modeling concurrent/mobile processes. The π-calculus provides a conceptual framework for describing systems whose components interact with each other. It contains an algebraic language for describing processes in terms of the communication actions they can perform. Theoretically, the π-calculus can model mobility, concurrency and message exchange between processes as well as infinite computation (through the infinite replication operator '!').

In many cases, processes run on controllers that control physical devices; therefore, they have to deal with physical quantities such as time, distance, pressure, acceleration, etc. Examples include communicating controller systems in cars (Anti-lock Brake System, Cruise Controllers, Collision Avoidance, etc.), automated manufacturing, smart homes, etc. Properties of such systems, which are termed cyber-physical systems (CPS) [6,9], cannot be fully expressed within π-calculus. In a real-time/cyber-physical system the correctness of the system's behavior depends not only on the tasks that the system is designed to perform, but also on the time instants at which these tasks are performed. While π-calculus can handle mobility and concurrency, it is not equipped to model real-time systems or CPS and support reasoning about their behavior related to time and other physical quantities. We extend π-calculus with real time so that these systems can be modeled and reasoned about.

Several extensions of π-calculus with time have been proposed [2,4,5,10]; all these approaches discretize time rather than represent it faithfully as a continuous quantity. Discretizing means that time is represented through finite time intervals. As a result, *infinitesimally small time intervals cannot be represented*

M. Abadi and A. Lluch Lafuente (Eds.): TGC 2013, LNCS 8358, pp. 119–135, 2014.
DOI: 10.1007/978-3-319-05119-2_8,

or reasoned about in these approaches. In practical real-time systems, e.g., a nuclear reactor, two or more events *can* occur within an infinitesimally small interval. Discretizing time can miss the modeling of such behavior which may be wholly contained within this infinitesimally small interval. In our approach for extending π-calculus with time, time is faithfully modeled as a continuous quantity. The most notable work on extending π-calculus with *real time* is the work of Chen [3]; however, the replication operator of the original π-calculus is not considered in this work. Therefore, it is unable to model infinite processes. In our approach the infinite behavior of timed precesses is modeled through thc infinite replication operator '!' as in original π-calculus.

We consider the extension of π-calculus with continuous time by adding finitely many real-valued clocks and assigning time-stamps to actions. The resulting formalism can be used for describing concurrent, mobile, real-time systems and CPS and reasoning about their behaviors.[1] In contrast to other extensions, in our work the notion of time and clocks is adopted directly from the well-understood formalism of timed automata [1]. For simplicity, the behavior of a real-time system is understood as a sequence (finite or infinite) of timed events, not states. The times of events are real numbers, which increase monotonically without bound.

2 Timed π-Calculus

2.1 Design Decisions

We define our timed π-calculus as an extension of the original π-calculus [12] with (local) clocks, clock operations and time-stamps. As in π-calculus, timed π-calculus processes use names (including clock names) to interact, and pass names to one another. These processes are identical to processes in π-calculus except that they have access to clocks which they can manipulate.

We assume an infinite set $\mathcal{N}$ of names (channel names and names passing through channels), an infinite set Γ of clock names (disjoint from $\mathcal{N}$) and an infinite set Θ of variables representing time-stamps (disjoint from $\mathcal{N}$ and Γ). When a process outputs a name through a channel, it also sends the time-stamp of the name and the clock that is used to generate the time-stamp. Inspired by the notion of name transmission in π-calculus, we can treat time-stamps and clocks just as other names and transmit them through/with channels. Just as channel transmission results in dynamic configuration of processes, clock and time-stamp transmission can result in dynamic temporal behavior of processes. Thus, messages are represented by triples of the form $\langle m, t_m, c\rangle$, where m is a name in $\mathcal{N}$, t_m is the time-stamp on m, and c is the clock that is used to generate t_m. It is important for the process to send its clock that is used to generate the time-stamp of the name, because the time-stamp of the incoming

[1] While we only focus on extending the π-calculus with continuous time, our method serves as a model for extending the π-calculus with other continuous quantities. An instance of this, though not in the context of π-calculus, can be found in [16].

name in conjunction with the clock received is used by the receiving process to reason about timing requirements of the system as well as *channel delays.*

In our timed π-calculus all the clocks are local clocks; however, their scope is changed as they are sent among processes. This will become clear when we explain how clock passing is performed in Sect. 2.5. Keeping the clocks local results in a considerably simpler design of the timed π-calculus without sacrificing its practical applicability. Note that all the clocks advance at the same rate. A clock can be set to zero simultaneously with any transition (transitions are defined formally in Sect. 2.4). At any instant, the *reading of a clock* is equal to the time that has elapsed since the last time the clock was reset. Following the semantics of timed automata [1], we only consider non-Zeno behaviors, that is, only a finite number of transitions can happen within a finite amount of time.

2.2 Clock Operations and Clock Interpretations

We consider two types of clock operations: resetting a clock and checking satisfaction of a clock constraint. Resetting a clock is used to remember the time at which a particular action in the system has taken place. Clock resets are represented by γ in the syntax of timed π-calculus. Clock constraints, denoted by δ, indicate timing constraints between actions that occur in the system. Note that if δ contains more than one constraint, then the conjunction of all constraints must be considered. δ and γ are defined by the following syntactic rules, in which c and $c_i, 1 \leq i \leq n$, are clock names, r is a constant in $\mathbb{R}_{\geq 0}$, t is a time-stamp and $\sim \in \{<, >, \leq, \geq, =\}$. ϵ represents an empty clock constraint or clock reset.

$$\delta ::= (c \sim r)\delta \mid (c - t \sim r)\delta \mid (t - c \sim r)\delta \mid \epsilon$$
$$\gamma ::= (c_1 := 0) \ldots (c_n := 0) \mid \epsilon$$

There are two ways to measure the passing of time while checking for a clock constraint. It can be measured and reasoned about against (i) the last time a clock was reset: e.g., a constraint $(c < 2)$ on sending m indicates that m must be sent out within two units of time since the clock c was reset, or (ii) the last time a clock c was reset in conjunction with a time-stamp t of a name. Note that in this case, the time-stamp t must be generated by clock c. For instance, suppose that a process P sends two consecutive names that are two units of time apart; if the time-stamp of the first name, generated by clock c is t_1, then the expression $c - t_1 = 2$ can be used to express this constraint.

For a process P, we define $c(P)$ to be the set of clock names in P. For every two processes P and Q we assume $c(P) \cap c(Q) = \emptyset$, initially. This property is also maintained all the time as transitions take place. A *clock interpretation* I for a set Γ of clocks is a mapping from Γ to $\mathbb{R}_{\geq 0}$. It assigns a real value to each clock in Γ. A clock interpretation I for Γ satisfies a clock constraint δ over Γ iff the expression obtained by applying I to δ evaluates to true. For $t \in \mathbb{R}_{\geq 0}$, $I + t$ denotes the clock interpretation which maps every clock c to the value $I(c) + t$. For $\gamma \subseteq \Gamma$, $[\gamma \mapsto t]I$ denotes the clock interpretation for Γ which assigns t to each $c \in \gamma$, and agrees with I over the rest of the clocks.

2.3 Syntax

The set of timed π-calculus processes is defined by the following syntactic rules in which, P, P', M and M' range over processes, x, y and z range over names in $\mathcal{N}$, c and d range over clock names in Γ, and t_y represents a time-stamp.

$$M ::= \delta\gamma\bar{x}\langle y, t_y, c\rangle.P \mid \delta\gamma x(\langle y, t_y, c\rangle).P \mid \delta\gamma\tau.P \mid 0 \mid M + M'$$
$$P ::= M \mid (P \mid P') \mid !P \mid (z)\ P \mid [x = y]\ P \mid [c = d]\ P$$

The expression $\delta\gamma\bar{x}\langle y, t_y, c\rangle.P$ represents a process that is capable of outputting name y on channel x. This process generates a time-stamp t_y using clock c and sends t_y and c along with y via the channel x, and evolves to P. The time-stamp t_y is the reading of clock c at the time of transition. *The assignment of a time-stamp to y and sending y is an atomic operation.* The clock constraint δ must be satisfied by the current value of clocks at the time of transition. γ specifies the clocks to be reset with this transition.

Example 1. The process $P = (c < 2)\bar{x}\langle y, t_y, c\rangle.P'$ is capable of sending name y on channel x within two units of time since clock c was last reset. Note that the time-stamp of y is the reading of clock c when the output takes place. Since the output can happen only within two units of time since c was last reset, then time-stamp t_y is a positive real number less than two ($t_y < 2$). t_y and c are both sent along with y through channel x.

The expression $\delta\gamma x(\langle y, t_y, c\rangle).P$ stands for a process which is waiting for a message on channel x. When a message arrives, the process will behave like $P\{z/y, t_z/t_y, d/c\}$ (substitution is formally defined in Definition 2) where z is the name received; t_z is the time-stamp of z; and d is the clock of the sending process that is used to generate t_z. The time-stamp t_z must satisfy the clock constraint expressed by δ; γ specifies the clocks to be reset with the transition.

Example 2. Assume process $Q = (e > 5)(d - t_z \leq 3)x(\langle z, t_z, d\rangle).Q'$ is the receiving process in Example 1. The received name, along with its time-stamp and the accompanying clock will be substituted for z, t_z and d, respectively. After substitution takes place, the constraint $c - t_y \leq 3$ specifies how long the received name was on transit. Any delay greater than three is not acceptable and cause the input action to not take place. Note that e is another local clock of Q. Both constraints $e > 5$ and $(d - t_z \leq 3)$ must be satisfied by the current value of clocks for the input action to take place.

Note that time-stamps are put on names only by the sending processes, that is no time-stamps are assigned to received names upon arrival. The value of a time-stamp generated by process P on sending name y, is the value of P's local clock c at the time of output. This value is generated such that it satisfies the clock constraint corresponding to the output action. Note that in Example 2, t_z gets bound to the time-stamp of the incoming name, as we do not assign time-stamps to the received names.

The expression $\delta\gamma\tau.P$ stands for a process that takes an internal action and evolves to P, and in doing so resets the clocks specified by γ, if the clock constraint δ is satisfied.

In each of three processes explained above, if the clock constraint δ is not satisfied by the value of clocks at the time of transition, then, the process becomes inactive. An inactive process, represented by 0, is a process that does nothing.

The operators + and | are used for nondeterministic *choice* and *composition* of processes, just as in π-calculus [12]. The *replication* $!P$, represents an infinite composition $P \mid P \mid \ldots$, just as in π-calculus. The *restriction* $(z)P, z \in \mathcal{N}$, behaves as P with z local to P. Therefore, z cannot be used as a channel over which to communicate with other processes or the environment. $[x = y]\, P, x, y \in \mathcal{N} \cup \Gamma$, evolves to P if x and y are the same name; otherwise, it becomes inactive.

Example 3. The timed π-calculus expression $x(\langle m, t_m, c\rangle).(c - t_m \leq 5)\bar{y}\langle n, t_n, c\rangle$ represents a process that is waiting for a message on channel x. The process upon receiving a name m with time-stamp t_m and its accompanying clock c on channel x, sends a name n with time-stamp t_n on channel y with the delay of at most 5 units of time since the time-stamp of m. The process will use the clock c to choose a time t_n on c such that $c - t_m \leq 5$.

In a process of the form $\delta\gamma x(\langle y, t, c\rangle).P$ the occurrences of y, t and c are binding occurrences, and the scope of the occurrences is P. In $(n)P, n \in \mathcal{N}$ the occurrence of n is a binding occurrence, and the scope of the occurrence is P.

Definition 1. *An occurrence of a (non-clock) name n in a process is* free *if it does not lie within the scope of a binding occurrence of n. An occurrence of a (non-clock) name in a process is* bound *if it is not free. All occurrences of a clock c in a process P are bound. The set of bound names of P, $bn(P)$, contains all names which occur bound in P. The set of names occurring free in P is denoted $fn(P)$. We write $n(P)$ for the set $fn(P) \cup bn(P)$ of names of P.*

Intuitively, the free (non-clock) names of a process, represent its (public) links to other processes. For instance, if processes P and Q share the same free name x, then, the channel x is shared between these two processes.

Example 4. Let $P = x(\langle y, t, c\rangle).0$ and $Q = (d > 1)(d < 5)\bar{x}\langle z, t', d\rangle.0$. Then, $fn(P) = \{x\}, bn(P) = \{y, t, c\}$, $fn(Q) = \{x, z, t'\}$, and $bn(Q) = \{d\}$. x is a channel that is shared between P and Q. This behavior can be represented for example in the parallel composition of P and Q: $(P \mid Q)$.

Definition 2. *[12] A substitution is a function θ from a set of names $\mathcal{N}$ to $\mathcal{N}$. If $x_i\theta = y_i$ for all i with $1 \leq i \leq n$ (and $x\theta = x$ for all other names x), we write $\{y_1/x_1, \ldots, y_n/x_n\}$ for θ.*

The effect of applying a substitution θ to a process P is to replace each free occurrence of each name x in P by $x\theta$, with change of bound names to avoid name capture (to preserve the distinction of bound names from the free names). Substitution for time-stamps can be defined similarly.

Definition 3. *A clock substitution is a function θ_c from a set of clock names Γ to Γ. If $c_i\theta_c = d_i$ for all i with $1 \leq i \leq n$ (and $c\theta_c = c$ for all other clock names c), we write $\{d_1/c_1, \ldots, d_n/c_n\}$ for θ_c.*

The effect of applying a substitution θ_c to a process P, $P\theta_c$, is to replace all occurrences of each clock name c in P by $c\theta_c$.

Definition 4. *Given a clock c, the function θ_f creates a fresh copy, f, of c (f does not appear in any process) and updates the interpretation with $I(f) = I(c)$. The application of θ_f to c is represented by $c\theta_f$.*

Definition 5. *A clock renaming θ_r is a clock substitution $\{f_1/c_1, \ldots, f_n/c_n\}$ in which $f_i = c_i\theta_f, 1 \leq i \leq n$.*

The effect of applying a clock renaming $\theta_r = \{f_1/c_1, \ldots, f_n/c_n\}$ to process P, $P\theta_r$, is to replace all occurrences of each name c in P by $c\theta_r$.

2.4 Operational Semantics

First, we define actions by the following syntactic rule:

$$\alpha ::= \bar{x}\langle y, t, c\rangle \mid \bar{x}\langle (y), t, c\rangle \mid x(\langle y, t, c\rangle) \mid \tau$$

The first two actions are the *bound output actions.* Bound output actions are used to carry names out of their scope. $\bar{x}\langle y, t, c\rangle$ is used for sending a name y, time-stamp of y, t, and the (local) clock that is used to generate t, via channel x. The process that gives rise to this action can be of the form $\bar{x}\langle y, t, d\rangle.P, c = d\theta_f$. In this action x, y and t are free and c is bound; c is the fresh copy of d. The expression $\bar{x}\langle (y), t, c\rangle$ is used by a process for sending its private name y (y is bound in the process) and its (local) clock c. The process that gives rise to this action can be of the form: $(y)\bar{x}\langle y, t, d\rangle.P, c = d\theta_f$. In this action x and t are free, while y and c are bound[2]; c is a fresh copy of d.

As we mentioned before all the clocks in the calculus are local clocks: the clocks of a process P are accessible only by P. However, the scope of the clocks is extended as they are sent to other processes. If d is sent to process Q by P, then both P and Q will have access to d. As a result, they both can reset d as part of their future transitions. To prevent processes interfering with each other by resetting a shared clock, P must create a fresh copy of d, let us call it c, and send c to Q. This is the reason of creating fresh copies of clocks in both output actions.

The third action is the *input action* $x(\langle y, t, c\rangle)$. This action is used for receiving any name z with its time-stamp t_z, and a clock d via x. y, t and c are place holders in the receiving process for values that will be received as inputs. In this action x is free, while y, t and c are bound names.

[2] Since all the clocks are local clocks and all clock names are bound, we do not use parenthesis as we do for regular names to distinguish them from free names.

The last action is the *silent action* τ, which is used to express performing an internal action. Silent actions can naturally arise from processes of the form $\tau.P$, or from communications within a process (e.g., rule COM in Table 1).

We use $fn(\alpha)$ for set of free names of α, $bn(\alpha)$ for set of bound names of α, and $n(\alpha)$ for the union of $fn(\alpha)$ and $bn(\alpha)$. Note that $fn(\tau) = \emptyset$ and $bn(\tau) = \emptyset$.

A transition in timed π-calculus is of the form $P \xrightarrow{\langle \delta,\alpha,\gamma\rangle} P'$. This transition is understood as follows: if δ is satisfied by the current values of clocks, P evolves into P', and in doing so performs the action α and resets the clocks specified by

Table 1. Timed π-calculus transition rules

$$\text{IN}\ \frac{}{\delta\gamma x(\langle z,t,c\rangle).P \xrightarrow{\langle \delta\{t'/t,d/c\},\, x(\langle y,t',d\rangle),\, \gamma\{d/c\}\rangle} P\{y/z,t'/t,d/c\}}\ y \notin fn((z)P)$$

$$\text{OUT}\ \frac{}{\delta\gamma \bar{x}\langle y,t,c\rangle.P \xrightarrow{\langle \delta,\bar{x}\langle y,t,d\rangle,\gamma\rangle} P}\ d = c\theta_f \qquad \text{TAU}\ \frac{}{\delta\gamma\tau.P \xrightarrow{\langle \delta,\tau,\gamma\rangle} P}$$

$$\text{PAR}\ \frac{P \xrightarrow{\langle \delta,\alpha,\gamma\rangle} P'}{(P \mid Q) \xrightarrow{\langle \delta,\alpha,\gamma\rangle} (P' \mid Q)}\ bn(\alpha) \cap fn(Q) = \emptyset \qquad \text{SUM}\ \frac{P \xrightarrow{\langle \delta,\alpha,\gamma\rangle} P'}{P + Q \xrightarrow{\langle \delta,\alpha,\gamma\rangle} P'}$$

$$\text{COM}\ \frac{P \xrightarrow{\langle \delta,\bar{x}\langle z,t,c\rangle,\gamma\rangle} P' \quad Q \xrightarrow{\langle \delta',x(\langle z,t,c\rangle),\gamma'\rangle} Q'}{(P \mid Q) \xrightarrow{\langle \delta\delta',\tau,\gamma\gamma'\rangle} (P' \mid Q')}$$

$$\text{OPEN}\ \frac{P \xrightarrow{\langle \delta,\bar{x}\langle y,t,c\rangle,\gamma\rangle} P'}{(y)P \xrightarrow{\langle \delta,\bar{x}\langle (u),t,c\rangle,\gamma\rangle} P'\{u/y\}}\ y \neq x \wedge u \notin fn((y)P')$$

$$\text{CLOSE}\ \frac{P \xrightarrow{\langle \delta,\bar{x}\langle (z),t,c\rangle,\gamma\rangle} P' \quad Q \xrightarrow{\langle \delta',x(\langle z,t,c\rangle),\gamma'\rangle} Q'}{(P \mid Q) \xrightarrow{\langle \delta\delta',\tau,\gamma\gamma'\rangle} (z)(P' \mid Q')}$$

$$\text{RES}\ \frac{P \xrightarrow{\langle \delta,\alpha,\gamma\rangle} P'}{(z)P \xrightarrow{\langle \delta,\alpha,\gamma\rangle} (z)P'}\ z \notin n(\alpha), z \in \mathcal{N}$$

$$\text{MATCH}\ \frac{P \xrightarrow{\langle \delta,\alpha,\gamma\rangle} P'}{[x = x]P \xrightarrow{\langle \delta,\alpha,\gamma\rangle} P'}\ x \in \mathcal{N} \text{ or } x \in \Gamma \qquad \text{REP}\ \frac{P \xrightarrow{\langle \delta,\alpha,\gamma\rangle} P'}{!P \xrightarrow{\langle \delta,\alpha,\gamma\rangle} (P'\theta_r \mid !P)}$$

$$\text{REP-COM}\ \frac{P \xrightarrow{\langle \delta,\bar{x}\langle z,t,c\rangle,\gamma\rangle} P' \quad P \xrightarrow{\langle \delta',x(\langle z,t,c\rangle),\gamma'\rangle} P''}{!P \xrightarrow{\langle \delta\delta',\tau,\gamma\gamma'\rangle} ((P'\theta'_r \mid P''\theta''_r) \mid !P)}$$

$$\text{REP-CLOSE}\ \frac{P \xrightarrow{\langle \delta,\bar{x}\langle (z),t,c\rangle,\gamma\rangle} P' \quad P \xrightarrow{\langle \delta',x(\langle z,t,c\rangle),\gamma'\rangle} P''}{!P \xrightarrow{\langle \delta\delta',\tau,\gamma\gamma'\rangle} ((z)(P'\theta'_r \mid P''\theta''_r) \mid !P)}$$

γ. With abuse of notation, we have used γ as a set of clocks to be reset. We call the triple $\langle \delta, \alpha, \gamma \rangle$ a timed action. The set of transition rules of timed π-calculus are represented in Table 1. These rules are labeled by timed actions.

In rule IN the incoming clock and time-stamp must satisfy the clock constraint in the receiving process, for transition to take place. The incoming clock might get reset upon arrival in the receiving process. These requirements are specified in the timed action for IN where t' and d (the received time-stamp and clock) are substituted for t and c, respectively. In rule OUT, d is a fresh copy of clock c which is created and sent along name y on outputting the name. The rule for COM is similar to that of original π-calculus; however, the clock c communicated between P and Q is a fresh clock name generated by rule OUT (the premise of COM).

The joint use of two rules OPEN and CLOSE is used for scope-extrusion of bound names (including clock names). A bound output combines with an input action, and once the bound name has been received, a restriction will be extended to the receiving process. This means the received name is still bound although its scope has grown. However, this restriction should not bind occurrences of free names in the receiving process. This is the reason for changing the name y to a fresh name u before sending y, as in the original π-calculus. Note that the OPEN rule does not changes the clock name c, as c is a fresh clock name generated by the rule OUT (the premise of OPEN).

Note that in the rule for REP the set of clock names in P' are *replaced* by fresh clock names by applying the renaming θ_r to P'. Similarly, in the rules for REP-COM and REP-CLOSE the clock names in the replicated processes are *replaced* by fresh clock names using θ'_r and θ''_r. Note also that there are two more rules for SUM and PAR where the process Q takes an action. These rules are symmetric to SUM and PAR rules of Table 1 and are eliminated.

Example 5. Using OUT and OPEN we can derive:

$$(y)\bar{x}\langle y, t, c\rangle.P \xrightarrow{\langle \epsilon, \bar{x}\langle (u), t, d\rangle, \epsilon\rangle} P\{u/y\}$$

For all u such that u is y or $u \notin fn(P)$ and $d = c\theta_f$. Using IN we have that

$$x(\langle z, t_z, e\rangle).Q \xrightarrow{\langle \epsilon, x(\langle u, t, d\rangle), \epsilon\rangle} Q\{u/z, t/t_z, d/e\}$$

For all u such that u is z or $u \notin fn(Q)$. By applying CLOSE we derive

$$((y)\bar{x}\langle y, t, c\rangle.P \mid x(\langle z, t_z, e\rangle).Q) \xrightarrow{\langle \epsilon, \tau, \epsilon\rangle} (u)(P\{u/y\} \mid Q\{u/z, t/t_z, d/e\})$$

Next, we formally define the operational semantics of timed π-calculus and how the transitions change the interpretation.

Definition 6. *[1] A time sequence $w = w_1 w_2 \ldots$ is a finite or infinite sequence of time values $w_i \in \mathbb{R}$ with $w_i > 0$, satisfying the following constraints:*

- *Monotonicity: w increases strictly monotonically; that is, $w_i < w_{i+1}$ for all $i \geq 1$.*
- *Progress: For every $w \in \mathbb{R}$, there is some $i \geq 1$ such that $w_i \geq w$.*

A system specified by set of timed π-calculus processes starts with all the clocks initialized to 0. Moreover, for every two processes P and Q, $c(P) \cap c(Q) = \emptyset$, initially. As time advances the value of all clocks advances, reflecting the elapsed time. At time w_i, a process P_{i-1} takes a timed action $\langle \delta_i, \alpha_i, \gamma_i \rangle$ and evolves to P_i, if the current values of clocks satisfy δ_i. The clocks specified by γ_i are reset to 0, and thus start counting time with respect to it. This behavior is captured by defining *runs* of timed π-calculus processes. A run for a process P, records the state (process expression) and the values of all the clocks at the transition points. For a time sequence $w = w_1 w_2 \ldots$ we define $w_0 = 0$.

Definition 7. *A run r, denoted by $(\bar{P}, \bar{I})$, of a timed π-calculus process P, is a finite or an infinite sequence of the form*

$$\langle P_0, I_0 \rangle \xrightarrow[w_1]{\langle \delta_1, \alpha_1, \gamma_1 \rangle} \langle P_1, I_1 \rangle \xrightarrow[w_2]{\langle \delta_2, \alpha_2, \gamma_2 \rangle} \langle P_2, I_2 \rangle \xrightarrow[w_3]{\langle \delta_3, \alpha_3, \gamma_3 \rangle} \ldots$$

where P_i is a process and $I_i \in [\Gamma \to \mathbb{R}_{\geq 0}]$, for all $i \geq 0$, satisfying the following requirements:

- *Initiation: P_0 is the initial process expression, and $I_0(c) = 0$ for all $c \in \Gamma$.*
- *Consecution: for all $i \geq 1$, there is a transition of the form $P_{i-1} \xrightarrow{\langle \delta_i, \alpha_i, \gamma_i \rangle} P_i$ such that $(I_{i-1} + w_i - w_{i-1})$ satisfies δ_i and $I_i = [\lambda_i \mapsto 0](I_{i-1} + w_i - w_{i-1})$.*

Along a run $r = (\bar{P}, \bar{I})$, the values of the clocks at time $w_i \leq w \leq w_{i+1}$ are given by the interpretation $(I_i + w - w_i)$. When the transition from P_i to P_{i+1} occurs, the value $(I_i + w_{i+1} - w_i)$ is used to check the clock constraint. At time w_{i+1}, the value of a clock that gets reset is defined to be 0.

When the transition from $P_i = \delta\gamma x(\langle z, t, c \rangle).P$ to $P_{i+1} = P\{y/z, t'/t, d/c\}$ occurs ($\langle y, t', d \rangle$ is the received name), we check the satisfiability of the clock constraint $\delta\{d/c, t'/t\}$, similarly we reset the clocks specified by $\gamma\{d/c\}$. Intuitively, this means that the values of the received clock and time-stamp should satisfy the constraint δ for the transition to take place. Moreover, the incoming clock might get reset upon arrival. These requirements are specified in the timed action of rule IN in Table 1. When the transition from $P_i = \delta\gamma\bar{x}\langle y, t, c \rangle.P$ to $P_{i+1} = P$ occurs in which, the timed action $\langle \delta, \bar{x}\langle y, t, d \rangle, \gamma \rangle, d = c\theta_f$ takes place, the time-stamp t in $\bar{x}\langle y, t, d \rangle$ gets bound to $(I_i(c) + w_{i+1} - w_i)$. Note that at this point $I_{i+1}(d) = I_{i+1}(c)$.

2.5 Passing Clocks and Channels

Link (channel) passing in timed π-calculus is handled in exactly the same manner as in π calculus, in the sense that a process P can send a public channel x to a process Q. However, if Q already has access to a private channel x before the

Table 2. Axioms of structural congruence

α-conversion:	
$P \equiv Q$ if Q can be obtained from P by finite number of changes of bound names.	
Parallel Composition:	*Restriction:*
$(P \mid Q) \mid R \equiv P \mid (Q \mid R)$	$(x)(y)\ P \equiv (y)(x)\ P$
$P \mid Q \equiv Q \mid P$	$(x)\ 0 \equiv 0$
$P \mid 0 \equiv P$	
	Replication:
Summation:	$!P \equiv P \mid !P$
$(P+Q)+R \equiv P+(Q+R)$	
$P+Q \equiv Q+P$	*Scope Extension:*
$P+0 \equiv P$	$((y)P \mid Q) \equiv (y)(P \mid Q)$ if $y \notin fn(Q)$

transition, the latter must be renamed to avoid confusion: this is called scope intrusion [12]. If P has a private link x that it sends to Q, the scope of restriction will be extended, this is called scope extrusion [12]. In this case, if Q already has access to a public link x, then the name of the private link must be changed before the transition (these are reflected in rules OPEN and CLOSE).

All clocks in timed π-calculus are local clocks; moreover, processes access disjoint sets of clocks. When a process P sends its (local) clock c to another process Q, it creates a fresh copy of c and sends this copy to Q.

Assume that $P = \delta\gamma\bar{y}\langle x, t_x, c\rangle.P'$ and $Q = \delta'\gamma' y(\langle z, t_z, d\rangle).Q'$. Furthermore, assume that P sends $\langle x, t_x, c\rangle$ to process Q. This behavior can be captured by the following timed π-calculus transition.

$$(P \mid Q) \xrightarrow{\langle \delta\delta', \tau, \gamma\gamma' \rangle} (P' \mid Q'\{x/z, t_x/t_z, e/d\}), \qquad e = c\theta_f$$

Next, we define the structural congruence for proposed timed π-calculus.

2.6 Structural Congruence

The notion of structural congruence for timed π-calculus processes is identical to that of original π-calculus [12]. Two timed π-calculus processes are structurally congruent if they are identical up to structure. Structural congruence, $\equiv$, is the least equivalence relation preserved by the process constructs that satisfy the axioms in Table 2.

2.7 Timed Bisimulation

We would like to identify two processes which cannot be distinguished by an observer. We assume that the observer is able to observe all kinds of actions and moreover, it can observe the times at which the actions are taken place.

Definition 8. *A binary relation S on timed π-calculus processes is a (strong) timed simulation if PSQ implies that:*

1. *If* $\langle P, I\rangle \xrightarrow[w]{\langle\delta,\tau,\gamma\rangle} \langle P', I'\rangle$, *then for some* Q', $\langle Q, I\rangle \xrightarrow[w]{\langle\delta,\tau,\gamma\rangle} \langle Q', I'\rangle$ *and* $P' \mathcal{S} Q'$,
2. *If* $\langle P, I\rangle \xrightarrow[w]{\langle\delta,\bar{x}\langle y,t,c\rangle,\gamma\rangle} \langle P', I'\rangle$, *then for some* Q', $\langle Q, I\rangle \xrightarrow[w]{\langle\delta,\bar{x}\langle y,t,c\rangle,\gamma\rangle} \langle Q', I'\rangle$ *and* $P' \mathcal{S} Q'$,
3. *If* $\langle P, I\rangle \xrightarrow[w]{\langle\delta,\bar{x}\langle(y),t,c\rangle,\gamma\rangle} \langle P', I'\rangle$ *and* $y \notin n(P, Q)$, *then for some* Q', $\langle Q, I\rangle \xrightarrow[w]{\langle\delta,\bar{x}\langle(y),t,c\rangle,\gamma\rangle} \langle Q', I'\rangle$ *and* $P' \mathcal{S} Q'$,
4. *If* $\langle P, I\rangle \xrightarrow[w]{\langle\delta,x(\langle y,t,c\rangle),\gamma\rangle} \langle P', I'\rangle$ *and* $y \notin n(P, Q)$, *then for some* Q', $\langle Q, I\rangle \xrightarrow[w]{\langle\delta,x(\langle y,t,c\rangle),\gamma\rangle} \langle Q', I'\rangle$ *and for all* z, $P'\{z/y\} \mathcal{S} Q'\{z/y\}$.

The relation $\mathcal{S}$ *is a (strong) timed bisimulation if both* $\mathcal{S}$ *and its inverse are timed simulation. The relation* $\dot{\sim}$, *(strong) bisimilarity, on timed processes is defined by* $P \dot{\sim} Q$ *if and only if there exists a timed bisimulation* $\mathcal{S}$ *such that* $P\mathcal{S}Q$.

Example 6. Assume P is a timed π-calculus process defined as:

$$(c < 2)(c := 0)\bar{x}\langle y, t_y, c\rangle \mid (d := 0)z(\langle w, t_w, d\rangle)$$

in which, $x \neq z$. Then,

$$\begin{aligned} P \dot{\sim}\ &(c < 2)(c := 0)\bar{x}\langle y, t_y, c\rangle.(d := 0)z(\langle w, t_w, d\rangle) + \\ &(d := 0)z(\langle w, t_w, d\rangle).(c < 2)(c := 0)\bar{x}\langle y, t_y, c\rangle \end{aligned}$$

Analogous to strong bisimilarity in π-calculus, $\dot{\sim}$ is not in general preserved by substitution of names. It follows that (strong) timed bisimilarity is not preserved by input prefix. As a result, (strong) timed bisimilarity is not a congruence.

Example 7. Assume P is defined as in Example 6, and $Q = u(\langle z, t_z, e\rangle).(P)$ Then,

$$\begin{aligned} Q \not\dot{\sim}\ u(\langle z, t_z, e\rangle).((c < 2)(c := 0)\bar{x}\langle y, t_y, c\rangle.(d := 0)z(\langle w, t_w, d\rangle) + \\ (d := 0)z(\langle w, t_w, d\rangle).(c < 2)(c := 0)\bar{x}\langle y, t_y, c\rangle) \end{aligned}$$

The reason is that, if z is instantiated to x (the channel name received in u is x), then $P\{x/z\}$ will have a τ transition which cannot be simulated by the right hand side of the equation.

Definition 9. *If* $x \neq y$, *then* $\delta\gamma\bar{x}\langle(y), t, c\rangle.P$ *means* $(y)\ \delta\gamma\bar{x}\langle y, t, c\rangle.P$, *and the prefix* $\bar{x}\langle(y), t, c\rangle$ *is called a derived prefix.*

A collection of algebraic laws for (strong) timed bisimilarity, which are extensions of algebraic laws for bisimilarity in π-calculus [12], is presented in Table 3. Note that ρ in proposition 5(d) denotes a prefix, including a derived prefix.

Table 3. Timed bisimilarity algebraic laws

Proposition 1 $\dot{\sim}$ is an equivalence relation.

Proposition 2.a If for all v in which $v \in fn(P) \cup fn(Q) \cup \{y\}$, $P\{v/y\} \dot{\sim} Q\{v/y\}$ then $\delta\gamma x(\langle y, t_y, c\rangle).P \dot{\sim} \delta\gamma x(\langle y, t_y, c\rangle).Q$

Proposition 2.b If $P \dot{\sim} Q$ then
(a) $P + R \dot{\sim} Q + R$
(b) $P \mid R \dot{\sim} Q \mid R$
(c) $[x = y]P \dot{\sim} [x = y]Q$
(d) $(u)P \dot{\sim} (u)Q$
(e) $\delta\gamma\tau.P \dot{\sim} \delta\gamma\tau.Q$
(f) $\delta\gamma\bar{x}\langle y, t_y, c\rangle.P \dot{\sim} \delta\gamma\bar{x}\langle y, t_y, c\rangle.Q$

Proposition 3 *Match*
(a) $[x = y]P \dot{\sim} 0$ if $x \neq y$
(b) $[x = x]P \dot{\sim} P$
(c) $[c = d]P \dot{\sim} 0$ if $c \neq d$
(d) $[c = c]P \dot{\sim} P$

Proposition 4 *Summation*
(a) $P + 0 \dot{\sim} P$
(b) $P + P \dot{\sim} P$
(c) $P + Q \dot{\sim} Q + P$
(d) $P + (Q + R) \dot{\sim} (P + Q) + R$

Proposition 5 *Restriction*
(a) $(y)\ P \dot{\sim} P$ $y \notin fn(P)$
(b) $(x)\ (y)\ P \dot{\sim} (y)\ (x)\ P$
(c) $(y)\ (P + Q) \dot{\sim} (y)\ P + (y)\ Q$
(d) $(y)\ \delta\gamma\rho.P \dot{\sim} \delta\gamma\rho.(y)\ P$ $y \notin n(\rho)$
(e) $(y)\ \delta\gamma\bar{y}\langle x, t, c\rangle.P \dot{\sim} 0$
(f) $(y)\ \delta\gamma y(\langle x, t, c\rangle).P \dot{\sim} 0$

Proposition 6 *Composition*
(a) $P \mid 0 \dot{\sim} P$
(b) $P_1 \mid P_2 \dot{\sim} P_2 \mid P_1$
(c) $(y)P_1 \mid P_2 \dot{\sim} (y)(P_1 \mid P_2)$ $y \notin fn(P_2)$
(d) $(P_1 \mid P_2) \mid P_3 \dot{\sim} P_1 \mid (P_2 \mid P_3)$
(e) $(y)(P_1 \mid P_2) \dot{\sim} (y)P_1 \mid (y)P_2$ $y \notin fn(P_1) \cap fn(P_2)$

Proposition 7 *Expansion*
Let $P \equiv \sum_i \delta_i\gamma_i\rho_i.P_i$ and $Q \equiv \sum_j \eta_j\lambda_j\phi_j.Q_j$ where δ_i and η_j are constraints, γ_i and λ_j specify the set of clocks to be reset and ρ_i and ϕ_j are prefixes; $bn(\rho_i) \cap fn(Q) = \emptyset$ for all i, and $bn(\phi_j) \cap fn(P) = \emptyset$ for all j; then

$$P \mid Q \dot{\sim} \sum_i \delta_i\gamma_i\rho_i.(P_i \mid Q) +$$

$$\sum_j \eta_j\lambda_j\phi_j.(P \mid Q_j) + \sum_{\rho_i \text{comp} \phi_j} \delta_i\eta_j\gamma_i\lambda_j\tau.R_{ij}$$

The relation ρ_i comp ϕ_j (ρ_i complements ϕ_j) holds in the following four cases, which also defines R_{ij}:

1. ρ_i is $\bar{x}\langle u, t, c\rangle$ and ϕ_j is $x(\langle v, t_v, d\rangle)$; then R_{ij} is $(P_i|Q_j\{u/v, t/t_v, e/d\})$ where $e = c\theta_f$,
2. ρ_i is $\bar{x}\langle(u), t, c\rangle$ and ϕ_j is $x(\langle v, t_v, d\rangle)$; then R_{ij} is $(w)(P_i\{w/u\}|Q_j\{w/v, t/t_v, e/d\})$ where w is not free in $(u)P_i$ or in $(v)Q_j$ and $e = c\theta_f$,
3. ρ_i is $x(\langle v, t_v, d\rangle)$ and ϕ_j is $\bar{x}\langle u, t, c\rangle$; then R_{ij} is $(P_i\{u/v, t/t_v, e/d\}|Q_j)$ where $e = c\theta_f$,
4. ρ_i is $x(\langle v, t_v, d\rangle)$ and ϕ_j is $\bar{x}\langle(u), t, c\rangle$; then R_{ij} is $(w)(P_i\{w/v, t/t_v, e/d\}|Q_j\{w/u\})$ where w is not free in $(v)P_i$ or in $(u)Q_j$ and $e = c\theta_f$.

Proofs of above propositions are extensions of the proofs for untimed π-calculus processes [12] (these extensions take clocks into account) which are not presented here due to lack of space.

3 Example: The Railroad Crossing Problem

The generalized railroad crossing (GRC) problem [7] describes a railroad crossing system with several tracks and an unspecified number of trains traveling through the tracks. The gate at the railroad crossing should be operated in a way that guarantees the *safety* and *utility* properties. The *safety* property stipulates that the gate must be down while there is a train in the crossing. The *utility* property states that the gate must be up (or going up) when there is no train in the crossing. The system is composed of three components: *train*, *controller* and *gate*. The components of the system which are specified via three timed automata in Fig. 1, communicate by sending and receiving signals. We specify the components of the system in timed π-calculus.

The controller at the railroad crossing might receive various signals from trains in different tracks. In order to avoid signals from different trains being mixed, each train communicates through a private channel with the controller. A new channel is established for each approaching train to the crossing area through which the communication between the train and the controller takes place. For simplicity of presentation we consider only one track in this example.

In our modeling of railroad crossing problem in timed π-calculus each component of the system is considered as a timed π-calculus process. This model is presented in Table 4. Note that the design of the railroad crossing problem shown in Fig. 1 (originally from [1]) does not account for the delay between the sending of *approach* (*exit*) signal by a train and receiving it by the controller. Similarly the delay between sending *lower* (*raise*) by the controller and receiving it by the gate is not taken into account. Arguably, in a correct design, the delay before *approach* is received by the controller should be taken into account. The *lower* signal must be sent within one unit of time since the time-stamp of the *original approach* but not the time at which the controller receives the signal (note that the controller resets its clock to remember the time it receives *approach*). In contrast, in our specification of the railroad crossing problem in timed π-calculus,

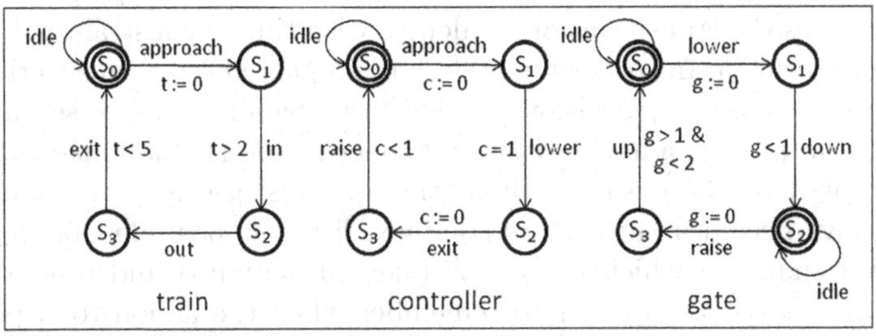

Fig. 1. Timed automata for train, controller, and gate in the railroad crossing problem

Table 4. The timed π-calculus expressions for components of the railroad crossing problem)

$train \equiv$	$controller \equiv$
$!(ch)\overline{ch1}\langle ch, t_c, t\rangle.$	$!ch1(\langle y, t_y, d\rangle).y(\langle x, t_x, c\rangle).$
$(t := 0)\overline{ch}\langle approach, t_a, t\rangle.$	$([x = approach](c = 1)(e := 0)\overline{ch2}\langle lower, t_l, e\rangle +$
$(t > 2)\tau.\tau.$	$[x = exit](c - t_x < 1)(e := 0)\overline{ch2}\langle raise, t_r, e\rangle)$
$(t < 5)\overline{ch}\langle exit, t_e, t\rangle)$	
$gate \equiv$	
$!ch2(\langle x, t_x, g\rangle).$	
$([x = lower](g < 1)\tau + [x = raise](g > 1)(g < 2)\tau)$	
$main \equiv train \mid controller \mid gate$	

we are considering the delays; therefore, all the time-related reasoning in the system is performed against *train*'s clock and the time-stamp of *approach* signal (sent by *train* to *controller*).

Note that in the π-calculus expression for *train* specified in Table 3, t is the local clock of *train* and the two consecutive τ actions correspond to *train*'s internal actions *in* and *out*. In the expression for *controller*, c is a place holder for the received clock t from *train*; while, e is the controller's clock that is reset before it is sent to *gate*. In the expression for *gate*, g is a place holder for the received clock e from *controller* and the two τ actions correspond to *gate*'s internal actions; the first τ represents *down*; while the second τ represents *up*.

Timed π-calculus allows the railroad crossing problem to be modeled more faithfully. Additionally, significantly more complex systems can be modeled. The timed π-calculus specification can be used for verification of the system as well as generating the implementation [15].

4 Discussions

Our proposed timed π-calculus extends the original π-calculus of Milner, while *preserving* the algebraic properties of the original π-calculus. The notion of timed bisimilarity and expansion in our calculus are also simple extensions of those found in the original π-calculus. Our calculus is a simple and powerful calculus which annotates the transitions of π-calculus with timing constraints. Our effort was driven by our desire to keep the design simple. The two most critical and fundamental assumptions/decisions made in this paper are discussed next.

First, on outputting a name we submit a clock and also the time-stamp of the name generated by the clock. Without time-stamps, precisely reasoning about channel delays becomes much more complex, if not impossible. As an example consider a scenario in which process P takes an action α and resets its clock c at the time of action in order to remember when the action took place. Let us assume that after t units of time (t is measured by c) have elapsed since α's occurrence, P sends a name n (along with clock c and time-stamp t_n generated by c) to process Q. Note that P did not reset the clock before this output, as it continues to need to measure the time since the occurrence of α. At this point if we wanted to know for how long the name n was in transit, we could not calculate it without t_n. However, on receiving n on Q, the expression $c - t_n$ could be used to calculate the exact time for which the name n was in transit.

The second fundamental design decision in our calculus is our choice of local clocks and how clocks are treated. Initially, processes have access to distinct set of clocks. Later, after transitions take place, the scope of local clocks may grow; however, we keep the distinction between clocks of different processes. We achieve this by having processes create fresh copies of their own clocks (and updating the interpretation accordingly) and sending these copies instead of their original clocks. Adopting this convention prevents processes from resetting each others' clocks, as the sending process may keep using (possibly resetting) the clock that was sent for measuring other subsequent events. Our choice of clocks and our careful treatment of clocks enabled us to extend the transition rules of the original π-calculus naturally in order to obtain the transition rules of our timed π calculus. It also made our expansion theorem an straightforward extension of the original one.

5 Conclusions and Related Work

Since the π-calculus was proposed by Milner et al. [12], many researchers have extended it for modeling distributed real-time systems. Berger has introduced timed π-calculus (π_t-calculus) [2], asynchronous π-calculus with timers and a notion of *discrete* time, locations, and message failure, and explored some of its basic properties. Olarte has studied temporal CCP (tcc) as a model of concurrency for mobile, timed reactive systems in his Ph.D thesis [13]. He has developed a process calculus called universal temporal CCP (utcc). His work can be seen as adding mobile operation to the tcc. In utcc, like tcc, time is conceptually divided into time intervals (or time units); therefore it is discretized. Lee et al. [10] introduced another timed extension of π-calculus called real-time π-calculus (πRT-calculus). They have introduced the time-out operator and considered a global clock, single observer as part of their design, as is common in other (static) real-time process algebras. They have used the set of natural numbers as the time domain, i.e., time is *discrete* and is strictly increasing. Ciobanu et al. [4] have introduced a model called timed distributed π-calculus in which they have considered timers for channels, by which they restrict access to channels. They use *decreasing* timers, and time is discretized in their approach also. Many other timed calculi have similar constructs which also discretize time [5,8,11]. In summary, all these approaches share some common features; they use a *discrete* time-stepping function or timers to increase/decrease the time-stamps after every action (they assume that every action takes exactly one unit of time). *In contrast, our approach for extending π-calculus with time faithfully treats time as continuous.*

Posse et al. [14] have proposed π_{klt}-calculus as a real-time extension of π-calculus and study a notion of time-bounded equivalence. They have developed an abstract machine for the calculus and developed an implementation based on this abstract machine for the π_{klt}-calculus in a language called `kiltera`. The replication operator of the original π-calculus is missing in this work.

The work of Yi [17] shows how to introduce time into Milner's CCS to model real-time systems. An extra variable t is introduced which records the time delay before a message on some channel α is available, and also a timer for calculating delays. The idea is to use delay operators to suspend activities. In our opinion, it is much harder to specify real-time systems using delays. Our approach provides a more direct way of modeling time in π-calculus via clocks, and also can be used to elegantly reason about delays.

The proposed timed π-calculus is an expressive, natural model for describing real-time, mobile, concurrent processes. It preserves the algebraic rules of the original π-calculus, while keeps the expansion theorem simple.

With respect to future work, we would like to extend our timed π-calculus with other continuous quantities; so that more complex systems as well as CPS can be expressed. While we have used our calculus for modeling and verifying the railroad crossing problem [15], we would like to model the generalized railroad crossing (GRC) problem in our calculus and use it for verifying properties of the system.

References

1. Alur, R., Dill, D.L.: A theory of timed automata. Theor. Comput. Sci. **126**(2), 183–235 (1994)
2. Berger, M.: Towards abstractions for distributed systems. Technical report, Imperial College London (2004)
3. Chen, J.: Timed extensions of π calculus. Theor. Comput. Sci. **11**(1), 23–58 (2006)
4. Ciobanu, G., Prisacariu, C.: Timers for distributed systems. Electr. Notes Theor. Comput. Sci. **164**(3), 81–99 (2006)
5. Degano, P., Loddo, J.V., Priami, C.: Mobile processes with local clocks. In: Dam, M. (ed.) LOMAPS-WS 1996. LNCS, vol. 1192, pp. 296–319. Springer, Heidelberg (1997)
6. Gupta, R.: Programming models and methods for spatiotemporal actions and reasoning in cyber-physical systems. In: NSF Workshop on CPS (2006)
7. Heitmeyer, C., Lynch, N.: The generalized railroad crossing: a case study in formal verification of real-time systems. In: IEEE Real-Time Systems Symposium, pp. 120–131. IEEE Computer Society Press, Los Alamitos (1994)
8. Laneve, C., Zavattaro, G.: Foundations of web transactions. In: Sassone, V. (ed.) FoSSaCS 2005. LNCS, vol. 3441, pp. 282–298. Springer, Heidelberg (2005)
9. Lee, E.A.: Cyber physical systems: design challenges. In: IEEE Symposium on Object Oriented Real-Time Distributed Computing, ISORC '08. IEEE Computer Society, Washington (2008)
10. Lee, J.Y., Zic, J.: On modeling real-time mobile processes. Aust. Comput. Sci. Commun. **24**(1), 139–147 (2002)
11. Mazzara, M.: Timing issues in web services composition. In: Bravetti, M., Kloul, L., Zavattaro, G. (eds.) EPEW/WS-EM 2005. LNCS, vol. 3670, pp. 287–302. Springer, Heidelberg (2005)

12. Milner, R., Parrow, J., Walker, D.: A calculus of mobile processes, parts i and ii. Inf. Comput. **100**(1), 1–77 (1992)
13. Olate, C.: Universal temporal concurrent constraint programming. Ph.D thesis, LIX, Ecole Polytechnique (2009)
14. Posse, E., Dingel, J.: Theory and implementation of a real-time extension to the π-calculus. In: Hatcliff, J., Zucca, E. (eds.) FMOODS/FORTE 2010, Part II. LNCS, vol. 6117, pp. 125–139. Springer, Heidelberg (2010)
15. Saeedloei, N.: Modeling and verification of real-time and cyber-physical systems. Ph.D. thesis, University of Texas at Dallas, Richardson, Texas (2011)
16. Saeedloei, N., Gupta, G.: A logic-based modeling and verification of CPS. SIGBED Rev. **8**, 31–34 (2011). http://doi.acm.org/10.1145/2000367.2000374
17. Yi, W.: CCS + time = an interleaving model for real time systems. In: Albert, J.L., Monien, B., Artalejo, M.R. (eds.) ICALP 1991. LNCS, vol. 510, pp. 217–228. Springer, Heidelberg (1991)

Towards Static Deadlock Resolution in the π-Calculus

Marco Giunti(✉) and António Ravara(✉)

CITI and DI-FCT, Universidade Nova de Lisboa, Lisbon, Portugal
m.giunti@campus.fct.unl.pt, aravara@fct.unl.pt

Abstract. Static analysis techniques based on session types discern concurrent programs that ensure the fidelity of protocol sessions – for each input (output) end point of a session there is exactly an output (input) end point available – being expressive enough to represent the standard π-calculus and several typing disciplines. More advanced type systems, enforcing properties as deadlock-freedom or even progress, sensibly reduce the set of typed processes, thus mining the expressiveness of the analysis. Herein, we propose a first step towards a compromise solution to this problem: a session based type checking algorithm that releases some deadlocks (when co-actions on the same channel occur in sequence in a thread). This procedure may help the software development process: the typing algorithm detects a deadlock, but instead of rejecting the code, fixes it by looking into the session types and producing new safe code that obeys the protocols and is deadlock-free.

1 Introduction

Background and related work. Session types, introduced for a dialect of the π-calculus of Milner et al. [1], allow a concise description of protocols by detailing the sequence of messages involved in each particular run of the protocol [2–5]. A key property is type-safety, which ensures that well-typed processes cannot go wrong in the sense that they do not reach neither the usual data errors, as those produced in this case by the use of base values as channels, nor *communication* errors, as those generated by two parallel processes waiting in input on a same session channel, or sending in output on the same session channel. An important feature is session delegation — the capacity to pass on the processing of a session. This is relevant for many purposes, e.g. it permits to design a FTP server that requires the presence of a daemon and of a pool of threads that will serve the client's request picked by the daemon [3].

While many session typing systems require a means to distinguish the two ends of a session channel in order to preserve type soundness [6–8], recently the first author and Vasconcelos have developed a session typing system [9,10] on top of the standard π-calculus. The main benefit is expressiveness: session delegation is described by the π-calculus communication mechanism; type-disciplines based on session [3,7] and linear [11] types can be embedded in the framework.

M. Abadi and A. Lluch Lafuente (Eds.): TGC 2013, LNCS 8358, pp. 136–155, 2014.
DOI: 10.1007/978-3-319-05119-2_9,

A drawback of most of these systems is accepting processes that exhibit various forms of deadlocks — although type safety is guaranteed, they do not ensure deadlock-freedom. For that aim, several proposals appeared recently, guaranteeing progress by inspecting causality dependencies in the processes [12–16]. Not surprisingly, these systems reduce the set of typed processes, rejecting (as usual in static analysis, which is not complete) deadlock-free processes.

Motivating example. To illustrate the problem that we are tackling in this paper, consider a synchronous π-calculus with session-based communication channels and boolean values. Take a process which behaviour consists in testing a boolean variable and, on success, in acknowledging the result on a received channel and then continuing the computation, like $a(x).b(z).\mathsf{if}\ z\ \mathsf{then}\ \overline{x}\langle\mathsf{true}\rangle.P'$. The process is well behaved and our type-system accepts it, but, the interaction with a process sending channel b can cause a runtime deadlock; in fact, several systems in the literature reject the process P below

$$P \stackrel{\text{def}}{=} (\nu a, b)(a(x).b(z).\mathsf{if}\ z\ \mathsf{then}\ \overline{x}\langle\mathsf{true}\rangle.P' \mid \overline{a}\langle b\rangle.\overline{a}\langle\mathsf{false}\rangle)$$

since

$$P \rightarrow (\nu a, b)(b(z).\mathsf{if}\ z\ \mathsf{then}\ \overline{b}\langle\mathsf{true}\rangle.P' \mid \overline{a}\langle\mathsf{false}\rangle)$$

The well-known problem of delegating a linear channel already in use by the receiver (cf. [8]) is avoided *a priori*; as a (unfortunate) by-product, legitimate processes of the form below are rejected as well:

$$LP \stackrel{\text{def}}{=} (\nu a, b)(a(x).\overline{d}\langle b\rangle.\overline{x}\langle\mathsf{true}\rangle \mid \overline{a}\langle b\rangle \mid P'')$$

The approach that we take is radically different: we aim at both type check P and at transform it in a process that is deadlock-free. To type P, we assign to a a pair type of the form $(?T_1.?\mathsf{bool.end}, !T_1.!\mathsf{bool.end})$, where the left entry says that an *end point* of a (actually, the one in the left thread of P) is used linearly to first receive a value of type T_1, and then to receive a boolean, while the right entry describes the dual behaviour of first sending a value of type T_1 and then a boolean, which occurs in the right thread. We assign to b the type $T \stackrel{\text{def}}{=} (?\mathsf{bool.end}, !\mathsf{bool.end})$; that is, we *split* T into $T_1 \stackrel{\text{def}}{=} (\mathsf{end}, !\mathsf{bool.end})$ and $T_2 \stackrel{\text{def}}{=} (?\mathsf{bool.end}, \mathsf{end})$, and let T_1 be delegated over a, and T_2 be used to type the input on b. The key idea towards the transformation of P into a deadlock-free process is to exploit the structure of the session type T, and check whether the end point channels described respectively by T_1 and T_2 are used sequentially, rather than in parallel.

In this paper, we still not deal with process P, but we handle processes resulting from it by a linear scan, using a constraint-based rewriting procedure.[1]

$$Q \stackrel{\text{def}}{=} (\nu a, b)(a(x).x(z).\mathsf{if}\ z\ \mathsf{then}\ \overline{x}\langle\mathsf{true}\rangle.P' \mid \overline{a}\langle b\rangle.\overline{a}\langle\mathsf{false}\rangle)$$

[1] The procedure is still at an experimental stage; we do not discuss it here.

Process Q above, resulting from P using the procedure, is typed by assigning to a the type $(?T.\mathsf{end}, !T.\mathsf{end})$. What is important is that our type checking algorithm, while typing Q and inferring that the variable x bound by the input on a has type T, detects that the two linear endpoints of x described respectively by T_1 and T_2 are used sequentially in i/o, and proposes a "fix". We generate new code for Q that mimics the behaviour described by the session type T, which, in principle, is the desired behaviour of (the communication channel of) Q. The type-assisted compositional translation $[\![\cdot]\!]$ maps the typed sequential continuation $Q' \stackrel{\text{def}}{=} x(z).\mathsf{if}\ z\ \mathsf{then}\ \overline{x}\langle\mathsf{true}\rangle.P'$ in a parallel process, using a forwarder (r) and a semaphore (m) (to impose, in the source and in the translated processes, the same order of communication); note that $v = \mathsf{true}$ is a parameter of the translation, obtained by a linear scan of Q.

$$[\![Q']\!]_v \stackrel{\text{def}}{=} (\nu r, m)(x(y).\overline{r}\langle y\rangle \mid r(z).\mathsf{if}\ z\ \mathsf{then}\ \overline{m}\langle\mathsf{true}\rangle.P' \mid \overline{x}\langle v\rangle.m(w))$$

After some confluent reduction steps, the channel sent over a is forwarded to the receiver, which can finally successfully pass the boolean test:

$$(\nu a, b)(a(x).[\![Q']\!]_v \mid \overline{a}\langle b\rangle.\overline{a}\langle\mathsf{false}\rangle) \rightarrow^* (\nu m)(\mathsf{if\ true\ then}\ \overline{m}\langle\mathsf{true}\rangle.P' \mid m(w) \mid \overline{a}\langle\mathsf{false}\rangle)$$

Note that the type checking algorithm does not apply any transformation to the legitimate (rewriting of) process LP (defined above), because the endpoint of channel x that corresponds to T_2 is not used in i/o (it is indeed delegated).

Contribution. Distributed programming is known to be very hard and one makes mistakes by not taking into consideration all possible executions of the code. Therefore, to assist in the software developing process, instead of simply rejecting a process that may contain a *resource self-holding deadlock* (*RSHDF*, i.e., one or more input and output on the same channel occur in sequence in a given thread, an instance of *Wait For* deadlocks [17,18]), we devise a type checking algorithm that produces a fix for this kind of deadlocked processes by a program transformation. We show that our program transformation is both *RSHDF*-deadlock-free and error-free. These properties are achieved by relying on automatic decoration of typed channels, and on light-weight verification of the format of decorations, thus avoiding the use of type contexts and systems.

Plan of the paper. In Sect. 2, we introduce a typed π-calculus with sessions obeying a linear discipline, and review the safety properties of the typing system. In Sect. 3, we define the class of resource-holding and of deadlock-free processes, showing the latter closed under reduction. In Sect. 4, we present an untyped π-calculus with decorated channels: as decorations are based on types, we do not need to rely on typing information to identify safe processes. In Sect. 5, we devise a split-free type checking algorithm that projects typed processes into decorated ones. The aim is two-fold: (i) assess the typability of a typed process given a context; and (ii) generate untyped, resource-deadlock free code. We conclude presenting the main results of the algorithm: it accepts processes typed by the split-based type system; and any process generated by the algorithm: (i) does not reach errors during the computation; (ii) is resource-holding deadlock-free. The proofs of the results presented herein are in a technical report (cf. [19]).

2 The Source Language: π-Calculus with Session Types

We present the syntax and the (static and dynamic) semantics of the monadic, choice-free, synchronous π-calculus, equipped with session types, our source language. Then we state the main properties ensured by the type system.

Syntax of processes and types. Let P, Q range over the set of *processes* $\mathcal{P}$, T range over *types* $\mathcal{T}$ and R, S over *session types*, and Γ range over *typing contexts* (or environments) $\mathcal{G}$, which are maps from variables x, y, z to types; *values* v, w are variables and the boolean constants true and false. The grammar in Fig. 1 defines the language, which is standard (cf. [1], but uses type annotations in restriction). We consider types T composed by channel types of the form (R, S), where R and S are session types, each describing an end point of a session, and the boolean type. An end point of a session S finishes with the type end. A type of the form $!T.S$ describes a channel that is used exactly once to send a value of type T, and then is used as prescribed by S, following a linear discipline. Similarly, $?T.S$ describes a channel that is used exactly once to receive a value of type T, and then is used as imposed by S. The type end describes an end point of a session on which no further interaction is possible.

Considering the usual notions of free and bound variables, α-conversion, as well as of substitution, cf. [20], we use $\mathrm{fv}(P)$ and $\mathrm{bv}(P)$ to indicate respectively the set of free and bound variables of P, which we assume disjoint by following Barendregt's variable convention [21], and let $\mathrm{var}(P)$ be the union of $\mathrm{fv}(P)$ and $\mathrm{bv}(P)$. A process P is *closed* whenever $\mathrm{var}(P) = \mathrm{bv}(P)$.

The processes of our language are thus synchronous output and input processes, in the forms $\overline{x}\langle v\rangle.P$ and $x(y).P$: the former sends a value v over channel x to P, the latter waits on x for a value v that will substitute the bound occurence of y in P, noted $P[v/y]$. Notice that substitution is not a total function; it is not defined, e.g., for $(\overline{y}\langle\mathsf{false}\rangle)[\mathsf{true}/y]$. When writing $P[v/y]$ we assume that the substitution operation involved is defined. The restricted process $(\nu y\colon T)P$ creates a variable y decorated with the type T; the occurrences of y in P are bound. Boolean values are contrasted using if-then-else. The remaining processes are parallel composition, replication, and inaction. We ignore trailing $\mathbf{0}$'s and write $(\nu\tilde{x}\colon\tilde{T})P$ as a shortcut for $(\nu\tilde{x}_1\colon T_1)\cdots(\nu\tilde{x}_n\colon T_n)P$, with $n \geq 0$.

Dynamic semantics: reduction. Following standard lines, we describe the operational semantics of processes through a reduction relation, and allow to rearrange processes with structural congruence. The congruence rules are standard; we note that the second rule in the second line allows to remove a restriction provided that the session type has been consumed.

The reduction rules are also standard. The only variation is that we record, as a label of the reduction arrow, the variable where the (free) synchronisation takes place (similarly to [7, 11]); this is convenient, and has no semantic impact, allowing to represent the progression of type decorations in restricted processes through the next operator over types. Let μ range over variables x, y and the symbol τ, which we assume reserved (not occurring in the syntax of processes).

Syntax of typed processes

T ::=	Types	P, Q ::=		Processes
(S, S)	session	$\overline{x}\langle v\rangle.P$		output
bool	boolean	$x(y).P$		input
S ::=	End point	$(\nu y\colon T)P$		restriction
$?T.S$	input	$\mathsf{if}\, v\, \mathsf{then}\, P\, \mathsf{else}\, Q$		conditional
$!T.S$	output	$(P \mid Q)$		composition
end	termination	$!P$		replication
v ::=	Values	$\mathbf{0}$		inaction
$\mathsf{true}, \mathsf{false}$	constant			
x, y	variable			

Operator for type progression

$$\mathsf{next}(?T.S) = S \qquad \mathsf{next}(!T.S) = S \qquad \mathsf{next}(\mathsf{end}) = \mathsf{end} \qquad \mathsf{next}((S_1, S_2)) = (\mathsf{next}(S_1), \mathsf{next}(S_2))$$

Rules for structural congruence

$$(P \mid Q) \equiv (Q \mid P) \qquad ((P_1 \mid P_2) \mid P_3) \equiv (P_1 \mid (P_2 \mid P_3)) \qquad (P \mid \mathbf{0}) \equiv P \qquad !P \equiv (P \mid !P)$$
$$((\nu y\colon T)P \mid Q) \equiv (\nu y\colon T)(P \mid Q), \;\; \text{if } y \notin \mathrm{fv}(Q) \quad (\nu y\colon (\mathsf{end}, \mathsf{end}))\mathbf{0} \equiv \mathbf{0}$$
$$(\nu y_1\colon T_1)(\nu y_2\colon T_2)P \equiv (\nu y_2\colon T_2)(\nu y_1\colon T_1)P \qquad P \equiv Q, \;\; \text{if } P =_\alpha Q$$

Rules for reduction

$$(\overline{x}\langle v\rangle.P \mid x(y).Q) \xrightarrow{x} (P \mid Q[v/y]) \qquad \text{[R-Com]}$$

$$\frac{P \xrightarrow{y} P' \qquad \mathsf{next}(T) = T'}{(\nu y\colon T)P \xrightarrow{\tau} (\nu y\colon T')P'} \qquad \frac{P \xrightarrow{\mu} P' \qquad \mu \neq y}{(\nu y\colon T)P \xrightarrow{\mu} (\nu y\colon T)P'} \qquad \text{[R-ResB],[R-Res]}$$

$$\mathsf{if\,true\,then}\, P\, \mathsf{else}\, Q \xrightarrow{\tau} P \qquad \mathsf{if\,false\,then}\, P\, \mathsf{else}\, Q \xrightarrow{\tau} Q \qquad \text{[R-IfT],[R-IfF]}$$

$$\frac{P \xrightarrow{\mu} P'}{(P \mid Q) \xrightarrow{\mu} (P' \mid Q)} \qquad \frac{P \equiv Q \quad Q \xrightarrow{\mu} Q' \quad Q' \equiv P'}{P \xrightarrow{\mu} P'} \qquad \text{[R-Par],[R-Struct]}$$

Fig. 1. Typed π-calculus

Moreover, let $\Rightarrow$ indicate the reflexive and transitive closure of $\xrightarrow{\mu}$, whenever the labels are irrelevant.

Static semantics: type system. The type system uses a notion of type and context split (cf. Walker's chapter in Pierce's book [22]), noted $\circ$, defined in Fig. 2. Formally, split is a three-argument relation. We write $\Gamma_1 \circ \Gamma_2$ to refer to a type environment Γ such that $\Gamma = \Gamma_1 \circ \Gamma_2$. Figure 3 contains a typing system with judgements of the form $\Gamma \vdash P$, where we assume that $\mathrm{fv}(P) \subseteq \mathrm{dom}(\Gamma)$ and $\mathrm{bv}(P) \cap \mathrm{dom}(\Gamma) = \emptyset$. We make use of predicates on types and contexts, *balanced* and *terminated* (noted respectively bal and term). Balancing relies on the standard duality notion of session types; we let $\overline{S}$ be the dual of S:

$$\overline{?T.S} = !T.\overline{S} \qquad \overline{!T.S} = ?T.\overline{S} \qquad \overline{\mathsf{end}} = \mathsf{end} \qquad \mathsf{bal}((S, \overline{S}))$$

Type split rules

$$S = S \circ \mathsf{end} \qquad S = \mathsf{end} \circ S$$

$$\frac{R = R_1 \circ R_2 \qquad S = S_1 \circ S_2}{(R, S) = (R_1, S_1) \circ (R_2, S_2)} \qquad \mathsf{bool} = \mathsf{bool} \circ \mathsf{bool}$$

Context split rules

$$\emptyset = \emptyset \circ \emptyset \qquad \frac{\Gamma = \Gamma_1 \circ \Gamma_2 \quad T = T_1 \circ T_2}{\Gamma, x\colon T = (\Gamma_1, x\colon T_1) \circ (\Gamma_2, x\colon T_2)}$$

Fig. 2. Type and context split

Typing rules for values

$$\frac{\mathsf{term}(\Gamma)}{\Gamma \vdash \mathsf{true}, \mathsf{false}\colon \mathsf{bool}} \qquad \frac{\mathsf{term}(\Gamma)}{\Gamma, x\colon T \vdash x\colon T} \qquad \text{[T-Bool],[T-Var]}$$

Typing rules for processes

$$\frac{\Gamma, x\colon (S,R), y\colon T \vdash P}{\Gamma, x\colon (?T.S, R) \vdash x(y).P} \qquad \frac{\Gamma_1 \vdash v\colon T \qquad \Gamma_2, x\colon (S,R) \vdash P}{\Gamma_1 \circ (\Gamma_2, x\colon (!T.S, R)) \vdash \overline{x}\langle v\rangle.P} \qquad \text{[T-In-L],[T-Out-L]}$$

$$\frac{\Gamma_1 \vdash v\colon \mathsf{bool} \qquad \Gamma_2 \vdash P \qquad \Gamma_2 \vdash Q}{\Gamma_1 \circ \Gamma_2 \vdash \mathsf{if}\, v\, \mathsf{then}\, P\, \mathsf{else}\, Q} \qquad \text{[T-If]}$$

$$\frac{\Gamma, x\colon T \vdash P \qquad \mathsf{bal}(T)}{\Gamma \vdash (\nu x\colon T)P} \qquad \frac{\Gamma \vdash P \qquad \mathsf{term}(\Gamma)}{\Gamma \vdash !P} \qquad \text{[T-Res],[T-Repl]}$$

$$\frac{\Gamma_1 \vdash P_1 \qquad \Gamma_2 \vdash P_2}{\Gamma_1 \circ \Gamma_2 \vdash P_1 \mid P_2} \qquad \frac{\mathsf{term}(\Gamma)}{\Gamma \vdash \mathbf{0}} \qquad \text{[T-Par],[T-Inact]}$$

Fig. 3. Type system

Note that booleans are not balanced, as we do not consider open processes of the form $\mathsf{if}\, y\, \mathsf{then}\, P\, \mathsf{else}\, Q$, or closed processes of the form $(\nu x\colon \mathsf{bool})P$. The terminated types are $(\mathsf{end}, \mathsf{end})$ and bool: $\mathsf{term}((\mathsf{end}, \mathsf{end}))$ $\mathsf{term}(\mathsf{bool})$.

The typing rules are inspired by the system of Giunti and Vasconcelos [9], and represent a subsystem of its recent re-formulation [10], to which we refer for all details. We note that (a) we have left and right rules for typing input and output processes, corresponding to the cases whether the type for the prefix is on the left or on the right: for compactness, we only indicate left rules; (b) Rule [T-Out-L] allow session delegation by means of context split: for instance, if $\Gamma \vdash P$ with $\Gamma = \Gamma_1 \circ (\Gamma_2, x\colon (!T_1.S, R))$, then v is both sent at type T_1 and used at type T_2 in the continuation, whereas $\Gamma(v) = T_1 \circ T_2$.

Results. The type system guarantees the usual type preservation and safety properties — basic values are not used as channels (for synchronisation) and channels are always used linearly — when considering *balanced* contexts, i.e., contexts mapping variables to balanced types (processes must send and receive values of the same type on both end points of a same channel). The proof of these results can be found in a recent work of Giunti [23].

Theorem 1 (Subject Reduction). *Let Γ be balanced. If $\Gamma \vdash P$ and $P \Rightarrow P'$ then there is Γ' balanced such that $\Gamma' \vdash P'$.*

The main result of this section is that typed processes do not reach errors during the computation. Besides basic errors of the form $\overline{x}\langle \mathsf{true}\rangle.P \mid x(y).y(z).P$, where true can be send through [R-COM] but the substitution is not defined, we consider errors due to non-linear use of channels, as in the parallel compositions $\overline{x}\langle v\rangle.P_1 \mid \overline{x}\langle w\rangle.P_2$ and $x(y).P_1 \mid x(y).P_2$.

Definition 1 (Error Process). *A process R is a* error, *if it is of the form $R \equiv (\nu\tilde{z}\colon \tilde{T})(P \mid Q)$, for some x, v and w, where (i) $P = \overline{x}\langle v\rangle.P_1 \mid \overline{x}\langle w\rangle.P_2$, or (ii) $P = x(y).P_1 \mid x(z).P_2$.*

Theorem 2 (Type Safety). *If $\Gamma \vdash P$ with Γ balanced, and $P \Rightarrow Q$, then Q is not an error.*

In short, although session type systems accept processes with non-deterministic behaviour (due to the behaviour of parallel composition), the behaviour of each session *is* deterministic, as communication channels (used for synchronisation) must be used *linearly.* In particular, a session type system rules out a process like $a(x).\mathbf{0} \mid \overline{a}\langle v\rangle.a(x).\mathbf{0} \mid \overline{a}\langle u\rangle$, since the communication order cannot be guaranteed, but accepts deadlocks like $\overline{a}\langle v\rangle.a(x).\mathbf{0}$, $a(x).\overline{a}\langle x\rangle$, or even like $a(x).\overline{b}\langle u\rangle \mid b(x).\overline{a}\langle v\rangle$.

3 Resource-Holding Deadlocks

The aim now is to introduce a syntactic (untyped) characterisation of processes that do not contain deadlocks due to the self-holding of resources; this is a simplified variant of *Hold and Wait* or *Resource-Holding* deadlocks. Our formulation of the property is such that it is preserved by reduction, and it has a simple, decidable, proof technique to verify if the property holds for a given process. In Sect. 6 we discuss how we envision to tackle the general deadlock resolution problem for the π-calculus. We motivate first the formal definition through examples. Then present it rigourously and develop the proof technique.

Resource self-holding deadlocks: motivation. In the following we analyse *balanced, typable, self-hold and wait* deadlocks while leaving type decorations implicit. Deadlocked processes like $(\nu a)(\nu b)(a(x).\overline{b}\langle \mathsf{true}\rangle \mid b(y).\overline{a}\langle \mathsf{false}\rangle)$ are *not* resource self-holding deadlocks, and are not addressed by our analysis technique. Intuitively, a process exhibits a resource self-holding deadlock if both ends of a (private) channel appear in sequence — communication on that channel is not possible. The basic examples[2] are the processes $(\nu a)\ \overline{a}\langle \mathsf{true}\rangle.a(y)$ and $(\nu a)\ a(y).\overline{a}\langle \mathsf{true}\rangle$, which

[2] While most of the examples do not require the use of restriction, we limit the scope of channels to help the comprehension of the reader.

contain a resource self-holding deadlock, since no communication on a can occur, as the co-actions appear in sequence, instead of in parallel. More intricate resource self-holding deadlocks include processes of the form $(\nu a)(\nu b)(\overline{b}\langle \mathsf{false}\rangle.(a(x).b(y) \mid \overline{a}\langle \mathsf{true}\rangle))$, or of the form

$$(\nu a)(\nu b)(a(x).b(y).\overline{x}\langle \mathsf{true}\rangle \mid \overline{a}\langle b\rangle) \tag{1}$$

$$a(x).b(y).\overline{a}\langle y\rangle.(x(z) \mid \overline{x}\langle \mathsf{true}\rangle) \mid \overline{b}\langle c\rangle \tag{2}$$

Process (1) is a simple variant of the process P of the introduction which delegates one end point of a session; process (2) describes a delicate situation involving binders. Our algorithm still not deal with these class of processes: in (1) we should predict that the left thread will receive b, while in (2) we cannot simply put the output on a in parallel, as the variable y would escape its scope. In Sect. 6 we envision how we could tackle these deadlocks.

Resource self-holding deadlocks: formally. We consider the following auxiliary notions on multisets, and let $\Cap$ be multiset intersection, $\Cup$ multiset union, $\Subset$ multiset inclusion, and $\setminus$ multiset difference. The *subject variables* of P, noted $\mathrm{subjv}(P)$, is the *multiset* with the occurrences of $x \in \mathrm{var}(P)$ identified by the rules (1) $\mathrm{subjv}(x(y).P) = \{x\} \Cup \mathrm{subjv}(P)$, and (2) $\mathrm{subjv}(\overline{x}\langle v\rangle.P) = \{x\} \Cup \mathrm{subjv}(P)$, the remaining productions being homomorphic. The *x-variables* of P, noted $x(P)$, is the subset identified by $\{x, x, \cdots\} \Cap \mathrm{subjv}(P)$, where $\{x, x, \dots\}$ is a countably infinite multiset of x.

Definition 2 (Sequential and Parallel Variables). *The* sequential variables *of a process* P*, noted* $\mathrm{sv}(P)$*, is the submultiset of* $\mathrm{subjv}(P)$ *identified by the rules (the remaining cases are homomorphic):*

1. $\mathrm{sv}(x(y).P) = \{x\} \Cup \mathrm{sv}(P)$
2. $\mathrm{sv}(\overline{x}\langle v\rangle.P) = \{x\} \Cup \mathrm{sv}(P)$
3. $\mathrm{sv}(P \mid Q) = \mathrm{sv}(P) \Cup \mathrm{sv}(Q) \setminus ((\mathrm{sv}(P) \Cap \mathrm{sv}(Q)) \Cup (\mathrm{sv}(P) \Cap \mathrm{sv}(Q)))$
4. $\mathrm{sv}(\mathsf{if}\, v\, \mathsf{then}\, P\, \mathsf{else}\, Q) = \mathrm{sv}(P) \Cup \mathrm{sv}(Q)$

The parallel variables *of a process* P*, noted* $\mathrm{pv}(P)$*, is* $\mathrm{pv}(P) \stackrel{def}{=} \mathrm{subjv}(P) \setminus \mathrm{sv}(P)$.

Parallel variables are those that occur as subjects in different threads. A process does not contain resource-holding deadlocks if every channel has a matching pair in another thread, giving it a chance to interact.

Definition 3 (Resource Self-Holding Deadlock Freedom). *A process* P *is* Resource Self-Holding Deadlock-Free (RSHDF)*, if* $\mathrm{sv}(P) = \emptyset$*, or, equivalently, if* $\mathrm{subjv}(P) = \mathrm{pv}(P)$.

Examples of (balanced typed) *RSHDF* processes include:

1. $\overline{a}\langle b\rangle.\overline{d}\langle c\rangle.a(x) \mid a(y).\overline{a}\langle \mathsf{true}\rangle \mid d(z)$ and
2. $(\nu a)(\nu b)(a(x).(\overline{x}\langle \mathsf{true}\rangle \mid b(z).x(y)) \mid \overline{b}\langle \mathsf{true}\rangle.\overline{a}\langle c\rangle)$.

Processes containing sequential variables (typed or not), and thus not *RSHDF*, are for instance:

1. $(\nu a)\overline{a}\langle \mathsf{true}\rangle \mid b(y)$, or $\overline{a}\langle b\rangle \mid a(x).(\overline{x}\langle \mathsf{true}\rangle \mid c(y))$, or even $(\nu a)(\overline{a}\langle b\rangle \mid \overline{c}\langle a\rangle)$;
2. $\mathsf{if\,true\,then}\,\overline{a}\langle b\rangle \mid a(y)\,\mathsf{else}\,\overline{a}\langle b\rangle.a(y)$.

We do not consider processes not typable by a balanced environment like:

1. $\overline{a}\langle b\rangle.\overline{d}\langle c\rangle.a(x) \mid \overline{a}\langle \mathsf{true}\rangle.a(y) \mid d(z)$, or $\overline{a}\langle \mathsf{true}\rangle \mid \overline{a}\langle \mathsf{false}\rangle$, or even
2. $a(x).P_1 \mid \overline{a}\langle \mathsf{true}\rangle.P_2 \mid a(y).P_3$,

which are *RSHDF*.

The main result of this section is that *RSHDF* is closed under reduction.

Theorem 3 (RSHDF preservation). *If $\Gamma \vdash P$ with Γ and P balanced, P is RSHDF, and $P \Rightarrow P'$, then P' is RSHDF.*

Strongly-balanced processes and environments. It is useful to analyse the shape of types of our interest. The invariant we rely on is that if a session type provides for sending/receiving a variable, then the type of the payload is balanced (i.e., when a process outputs a channel with an "active" session, it is forced to delegate *both* end points). We call such processes (types and type environments) *strongly-balanced.* In fact, processes of the form (1) above are not strongly-balanced, and are (still) not tackled by our analysis.

We have seen that balanced types guarantee subject reduction and type safety. Still, a balanced type permits to type a input process that waits for an unbalanced variable, what is useless since the process cannot receive such variable from a balanced process. To refine our analysis on type derivation trees, since in the forthcoming developments we work in an untyped setting, we identify the class of *strongly-balanced* types, processes and contexts, noted sbal.

4 The Target Language: Decorated π-Calculus

We use this new language in the type-checking and deadlock resolution algorithm. We adopt a constructive approach: the algorithm takes a typing context and a process and while building the type derivation creates a new process in the target language, decorating the channels with the types used up until that point. In fact, it transforms linearly used session channels into linear channels that synchronise in the same order, guaranteeing absence of races, as one session channel is mapped into a tuple of linear channels.

When, during type checking, the algorithm detects a (possible) deadlock, it launches the deadlock release function on the decorated version of the original process. Since we deal with sequential threads locally, transferring information from the global typing context to the channels occurring in that thread, the algorithm is *compositional* and *linear* in the size of the input process.

Syntax and semantics of the decorated π-calculus. In this section we introduce a variant of the polyadic π-calculus [20] where channels are decorated with session

Syntax of decorated processes

σ, ρ ::=	Decoration Types	H, K ::=	Processes
bool	boolean	$\overline{\phi}\langle\omega\rangle.H$	output
S	end point	$\phi(y_{\sigma_1}, \ldots, y_{\sigma_n}).H$	input
$\top$	top	$(\nu y_{\sigma_1}, \ldots, y_{\sigma_n})H$	restriction
ϕ, φ ::=	Prefixes	$\mathsf{if}\,\omega\,\mathsf{then}\,H\,\mathsf{else}\,K$	conditional
x_σ	decoration	$(H \mid K)$	composition
ω, ψ ::=	Values	$!H$	replication
$x_{\sigma_1}, \ldots, x_{\sigma_n}$	tuple	$\mathbf{0}$	inaction
$\mathsf{true}, \mathsf{false}$	constant		

Rules for reduction (extends Fig. 1)

$$\frac{S_1 = \overline{S_2} \qquad \tilde{\phi} = y_{\sigma_1}, \ldots, y_{\sigma_n} \qquad |\omega| = |\tilde{\phi}|}{(\overline{x_{S_1}}\langle\omega\rangle.H \mid x_{S_2}(\tilde{\phi}).K) \xrightarrow{x_{S_1}} (H \mid K[\omega/\tilde{\phi}])} \quad \text{[R-DCom]}$$

$$\frac{1 \leq i < j \leq n \qquad \sigma_i = S \qquad \sigma_j = \overline{S} \qquad H \xrightarrow{y_S} H'}{(\nu y_{\sigma_1}, \ldots, y_{\sigma_n})H \xrightarrow{\tau} (\nu y_{\sigma_1}, \ldots, y_{\sigma_{i-1}}, y_{\sigma_{i+1}}, \ldots, y_{\sigma_{j-1}}, y_{\sigma_{j+1}}, \ldots y_{\sigma_n})H'} \quad \text{[R-DResL]}$$

Fig. 4. Target language

types. The algorithm projects typed processes into decorated processes, as we explain ahead. We use polyadic channels to map a channel of type $(?T.S, !T.\overline{S})$ into a tuple of the form $x_{?T.S}, x_S, \ldots, x_{!T.\overline{S}}, x_{\overline{S}}, \ldots, x_\top$, where $\top \stackrel{\text{def}}{=} (\mathsf{end}, \mathsf{end})$.

The set of decorated processes $\mathcal{H}$, ranged by H, K, is defined in Fig. 4 by adorning processes of Fig. 1 with end point types S. There is a small difference, that is that we will never use end to decorate channels, and rely on $\top$ to decorate channels carrying void capabilities. We define free and bound variables of a process, noted respectively $\mathrm{fv}(H)$ and $\mathrm{bv}(H)$, in terms of multisets, and count the occurrences of a same decorated variable by means of a function $\mathsf{occurs} : \mathcal{F} \to \mathcal{N}$, where we let $\mathcal{F}$ be the set of decorated variables, ranged by ϕ, φ. We indicate tuples of prefixes with $\tilde{\phi}$. We use "\" to remove all occurrences of an entry in a multiset. For space limitations, we omit all the details and note that, for instance, $\mathrm{bv}((\nu y_\sigma, \ldots, y_\rho)P) = \{y_\sigma, \ldots, y_\rho\} \Cup (\{y_\sigma, \ldots, y_\rho\} \Cap \mathrm{fv}(P)) \Cup \mathrm{bv}(P)$ $= \mathrm{bv}(x_S(y_\sigma, \ldots, y_\rho).P)$. We assume that alpha-conversion preserve decorations, and define the usual rules for structural congruence, but for the axiom for the null process: $(\nu y_\top)\mathbf{0} \equiv \mathbf{0}$.

The main change to the π-calculus semantics [20] is the communication rule, [R-DCom]: two processes exchange a value only if the two end points of the channel are decorated with *dual types*; this is akin to the polarity-based communication [7], and can be easily implemented by pattern matching of decorations. Substitution of a prefix ϕ with a value ω of the same arity is noted as $[\omega/\phi]$:

whenever $\omega = x_{\sigma_1}, \ldots x_{\sigma_n}$ and $\tilde{\phi} = \phi_1, \ldots, \phi_n$, we write $P[\omega/\tilde{\phi}]$ to indicate the process $P[x_{\sigma_1}/\phi_1, \ldots, x_{\sigma_n}/\phi_n]$. As in Fig. 1, we record the prefix ϕ on the arrow, which is of help for practical purposes and has no semantic impact. We use η to range over ϕ and τ actions, and write $H \to K$ when the label is irrelevant. Rule [R-DResL] describes a reduction on a couple of dually decorated prefixes that are restricted, and its continuation where the two dual end point channels have been removed from the restriction declaration. This rule is meant to describe *linear* processes where a decoration S appears only once, as we will introduce below; for this very reason, the restriction can be removed after a synchronisation.

Sound decorations. Instead of relying on a type system to ensure safety, we exploit the decoration of variables to characterise processes that do not reach errors during the computation (henceforth called *sound* processes). This characterisation leads to a *static, syntax-directed* checking system. As we will show later, our algorithm converts well-typed processes into sound processes, as one would expect, so we do not need a static type system for decorated processes.

Sound processes H such that $z_{\mathsf{end}} \notin \text{var}(H)$, for any z, are determined through four syntactic conditions. First, we mimic the type system in Fig. 1 and enforce send and receive of values of the expected types by using a *coherence* inference system. The system not only checks the consistency between subject and object types, but also guarantees balanced payload types. However, it is not equivalent to the type system, since sequential and linear behaviour are checked separately Second, we check that processes have valid decorations for the same variable, i.e., types must form a chain (enforcing the sequential behaviour prescribed by the session types). Third, we check that each channel decorated with a type S is used exactly once. Fourth, we check that the order of the exchanges prescribed by the decorations are preserved. We omit the formal definition of sound process and refer the reader to the technical report [19] for all details.

The main result of this section says that sound processes do not reach errors, which are processes containing two processes prefixed with the same variable that *do not synchronise.*

Theorem 4. *If H is a sound process and $H \Rightarrow K$, then K is not of the form:*

1. $(\nu\tilde{\varphi})(\overline{x_S}\langle\omega\rangle.K_1 \mid \overline{x_R}\langle\psi\rangle.K_2 \mid K_3)$, *for some x_S, x_R, ω and ψ*
2. $(\nu\tilde{\varphi})(x_S(\tilde{\phi}).K_1 \mid x_R(\tilde{\phi}).K_2 \mid K_3)$, *for some x_S and x_R*
3. $(\nu\tilde{\varphi})(\overline{x_S}\langle\omega\rangle.K_1 \mid x_R(\tilde{\phi}).K_2 \mid K_3)$, *for some x_S, x_R, ω such that $R \neq \overline{S}$*

In the decorated setting, the notion of resource self-holding deadlock freedom is quite intuitive: prefixes with dual decorations must run in parallel. To this aim, we define a notion of set[3] intersection modulo dual type decorations, noted $\sqcap$: $(\{x_S\} \cup A) \sqcap (\{x_{\overline{S}}\} \cup B) = \{x_S, x_{\overline{S}}\} \cup (A \sqcap B)$, $x_S \sqcap x_R = \emptyset$ if $R \neq \overline{S}$, $x_S \sqcap y_R = \emptyset$ if $x \neq y$, and extend the definition of sequential variables as expected, e.g. $\text{sv}(H \mid K) = \text{sv}(H) \cup \text{sv}(K) \backslash (\text{sv}(H) \sqcap \text{sv}(K))$.

[3] The subject variables of a sound process is indeed a set.

Definition 4. *A sound process H is* Resource Self-Holding Deadlock-Free *(or* RSHDF*) if* $\mathrm{sv}(H) = \emptyset$.

Theorem 5. *If H is* RSHDF *and $H \to K$ then K is* RSHDF .

Canonical representation In this section we show that (strongly-balanced) typed π-calculus processes have a canonical representation in decorated π-calculus, and that this representation both preserves the operational semantics and is sound.

First, we formalise trough function dec the projection of a π-calculus variable having a strongly-balanced type T, or type bool, into a tuple of decorated variables. This assumption is needed to ensure that all type decorations generated by the projection are sound (cf. Theorem 7). The formal definition of strongly-balanced types and processes is in [19].

$$\mathsf{dec}(y, (?T.S, !T.\overline{S})) = \{y_{?T.S}, y_{!T.\overline{S}}\} \uplus \mathsf{dec}(y, (S, \overline{S})) \quad \mathsf{dec}(y, \mathsf{bool}) = y_{\mathsf{bool}}$$
$$\mathsf{dec}(y, (!T.S, ?T.\overline{S})) = \{y_{!T.S}, y_{?T.\overline{S}}\} \uplus \mathsf{dec}(y, (S, \overline{S})) \quad \mathsf{dec}(y, (\mathsf{end}, \mathsf{end})) = y_{\top}$$

Definition 5. *Let $\Gamma \vdash Q$ with Γ and Q strongly-balanced. The canonical representation of Q w.r.t. Γ, noted $\mathsf{dec}(\Gamma, Q)$, is obtained by*

1. $\mathsf{dec}(x(y).P) = x_{?T.S}(\mathsf{dec}(y, T)).\mathsf{dec}(\Gamma', P)$ *whenever* $\Gamma(x) = (?T.S, !T.\overline{S})$ *or* $\Gamma(x) = (!T.\overline{S}, ?T.S)$, *and $\Gamma' \vdash P$ is a sub-tree of $\Gamma \vdash x(y).P$;*
2. $\mathsf{dec}(\overline{x}\langle y\rangle.P) = x_{!T.S}(\mathsf{dec}(y, T)).\mathsf{dec}(\Gamma', P)$ *whenever* $\Gamma(x) = (!T.S, ?T.\overline{S})$ *or* $\Gamma(x) = (?T.\overline{S}, !T.S)$, *and $\Gamma' \vdash P$ is a sub-tree of $\Gamma \vdash \overline{x}\langle y\rangle.P$;*
3. $\mathsf{dec}((\nu x\colon T)P) = (\nu\, \mathsf{dec}(x, T))\mathsf{dec}((\Gamma, x\colon T), P)$.

The remaining cases are homomorphic.

Theorem 6 (Operational Correspondence). *Let $\Gamma \vdash P$ with Γ and P strongly-balanced.*

1. *if $P \to P'$ and $\Gamma' \vdash P'$ then* $\mathsf{dec}(\Gamma, P) \to \mathsf{dec}(\Gamma', P')$
2. *if* $\mathsf{dec}(\Gamma, P) \to H$ *then there are Γ', P' such that $P \to P'$ and* $H = \mathsf{dec}(\Gamma', P')$

Theorem 7 (Soundness). *If $\Gamma \vdash P$ with Γ and P strongly-balanced, then* $\mathsf{dec}(\Gamma, P)$ *is sound.*

5 Deadlock Resolution Algorithm

We finally present the type checking and disentangling algorithm that releases deadlocks from typed processes through a process transformation. This algorithm is implemented using an inductive function that projects couples in $\mathcal{G} \times \mathcal{P}$ of Sect. 2 into decorated processes in $\mathcal{H}$ of Sect. 4. For clarity, the implementation of this function is presented by means of pattern analysis rules: we note that the algorithmic rules do not rely on type and context split, which is inherently non-deterministic.

Our procedure resolves multiple, nested deadlocks, possibly on the same channel. It works in one linear pass (when analysing a sequential process) and it

Top-level call

$$\frac{\mathsf{sbal}(\Gamma) \qquad \Gamma; (\Gamma\downharpoonright) \vdash_{\mathsf{A}} P \triangleright \Gamma_1; \Delta_1; H \qquad \mathsf{term}(\Gamma_1) \qquad \mathsf{term}(\Delta_1)}{\Gamma \Vdash_{\mathsf{A}} P \triangleright H}$$

Patterns for variables

$$\frac{T = (S_1, S_2)}{\Gamma, x\colon T \vdash_{\mathsf{A}} x\colon T \triangleright \Gamma, x\colon \top} \qquad \frac{T = (S_1, S_2)}{\Gamma, x\colon T \vdash_{\mathsf{A}} x\colon \top \triangleright \Gamma, x\colon T} \qquad \text{[A-SESSION],[A-TOP]}$$

Patterns for output processes (excerpt)

$$\frac{\Gamma \vdash_{\mathsf{A}} y\colon T \triangleright \Gamma_1 \qquad \Gamma_1, x\colon (S, \mathsf{end}); \Delta_1, x\colon (\mathsf{start}, !T.S) \vdash_{\mathsf{A}} P \triangleright \Gamma_2, x\colon \top; \Delta_2, x\colon (\mathsf{start}, R); H \qquad (*)}{\Gamma, x\colon (!T.S, \overline{!T.S}); \Delta_1, x : \bot \vdash_{\mathsf{A}} \overline{x}\langle y\rangle.P \triangleright \Gamma_2, x\colon (\mathsf{end}, R); \Delta_2, x\colon \bot; K}$$
[A-OUTINIT-L]

$$\frac{\Gamma \vdash_{\mathsf{A}} y\colon T \triangleright \Gamma_1 \qquad \Gamma_1, x\colon (S, \mathsf{end}); \Delta_1, x\colon (\mathsf{start}, R) \vdash_{\mathsf{A}} P \triangleright \Gamma_2; \Delta_2; H \qquad (**)}{\Gamma, x\colon (!T.S, \mathsf{end}); \Delta_1, x\colon (\mathsf{start}, R) \vdash_{\mathsf{A}} \overline{x}\langle y\rangle.P \triangleright \Gamma_2; \Delta_2; K}$$
[A-OUTENV-L]

$$\frac{\Gamma \vdash_{\mathsf{A}} y\colon T \triangleright \Gamma_1 \qquad \Gamma_1, x\colon (\mathsf{end}, R); \Delta_1, x\colon (S, \mathsf{start}) \vdash_{\mathsf{A}} P \triangleright \Gamma_2; \Delta_2; H \qquad (***)}{\Gamma, x\colon (\mathsf{end}, R); \Delta_1, x\colon (!T.S, \mathsf{start}) \vdash_{\mathsf{A}} \overline{x}\langle y\rangle.P \triangleright \Gamma_2; \Delta_2; K}$$
[A-OUTPROJ-L]

(*) if $R = \overline{!T.S}$ then $K := \overline{x_{!T.S}}\langle \mathsf{dec}(y, T)\rangle.H$ else

if $R = \mathsf{end}$ then $K := [\![\overline{x_{!T.S}}\langle \mathsf{dec}(y, T)\rangle.H]\!]^{\mathsf{false}}$ else raise *fail*

(**) if $\Delta_2(x) = (\mathsf{start}, R)$ then $K := \overline{x_{!T.S}}\langle \mathsf{dec}(y, T)\rangle.H$ else $K := [\![\overline{x_{!T.S}}\langle \mathsf{dec}(y, T)\rangle.H]\!]^{\mathsf{false}}$

(***) if $\Gamma_2(x) = (\mathsf{end}, R)$ then $K := \overline{x_{!T.S}}\langle \mathsf{dec}(y, T)\rangle.H$ else $K := [\![\overline{x_{!T.S}}\langle \mathsf{dec}(y, T)\rangle.H]\!]^{\mathsf{false}}$

Fig. 5. Type checking function (part 1)

is compositional (with respect to parallel threads). We stress again that the class of deadlocks we disentangle is restricted to the *sequential* use of both end points of a channel in a given thread. Moreover, we consider herein only finite sessions (actually, we enforce total consumption of a session type when type-checking).

The top-level call of the algorithm, defined in Fig. 5, has the form $\Gamma \Vdash_{\mathsf{A}} P \triangleright H$, meaning that given in input a strongly-balanced environment Γ (cf. sbal) and a π-calculus process P, when the call is successful a decorated process H is returned in output; this implies that $\Gamma \vdash P$ (cf. Fig. 3), as we will show. In the rest of the presentation, let the $\triangleright$ symbol be the separator between the input (on the left) and the output (on the right) of the function. Note that the strongly-balanced hypothesis crucially permits to obtain deterministic and exhaustive pattern matching, as each free and bound variable is matched by an init pattern with a channel type formed by dual endpoints: balanced environments do not enforce this invariant for bound variables. However, we may need to use back-tracking (see below). Strongly-balanced (decoration) types also ease the program transformation and the proof of its soundness. The top level call $\Vdash_{\mathsf{A}}$ makes use of

Patterns for input processes (excerpt)

$$\frac{\Gamma_1, x\colon (S,\mathsf{end}), y\colon T; \Delta_1, x\colon (\mathsf{start}, R), y\colon \bot \vdash_{\mathsf{A}} P \triangleright \Gamma_2, x\colon \top, y\colon \top; \Delta_2, x\colon (\mathsf{start}, R), y\colon A; H \qquad \mathsf{term}(A) \qquad (\sharp)}{\Gamma_1, x\colon (?T.S, R); \Delta_1, x : \bot \vdash_{\mathsf{A}} x(y).P \triangleright \Gamma_2, x\colon (\mathsf{end}, R); \Delta_2, x\colon \bot; K}\ \text{[A-InInit-l]}$$

$$\frac{\Gamma_1, x\colon (S,\mathsf{end}), y\colon T; \Delta_1, x\colon (\mathsf{start}, R), y\colon \bot \vdash_{\mathsf{A}} P \triangleright \Gamma_2, y\colon \top; \Delta_2, y\colon A; H \qquad \mathsf{term}(A) \qquad (\sharp\sharp)}{\Gamma_1, x\colon (?T.S, \mathsf{end}); \Delta_1, x\colon (\mathsf{start}, R) \vdash_{\mathsf{A}} x(y).P \triangleright \Gamma_2; \Delta_2; K}\ \text{[A-InEnv-l]}$$

$$\frac{\Gamma_1, x\colon (\mathsf{end}, R), y\colon T; \Delta_1, x\colon (S, \mathsf{start}), y\colon \bot \vdash_{\mathsf{A}} P \triangleright \Gamma_2, y\colon \top; \Delta_2, y\colon A; H \qquad \mathsf{term}(A) \qquad (\sharp\sharp\sharp)}{\Gamma_1, x\colon (\mathsf{end}, R); \Delta_1, x\colon (?T.S, \mathsf{start}) \vdash_{\mathsf{A}} x(y).P \triangleright \Gamma_2; \Delta_2; K}\ \text{[A-InProj-l]}$$

($\sharp$) if $R = \overline{?T.S}$ then $K := x_{?T.S}(\mathtt{dec}(y,T)).H$ else if $R = \mathsf{end}$ then `Snippet` else raise *fail*

($\sharp\sharp$) if $\Delta_2(x) = (\mathsf{start}, R)$ then $K := x_{?T.S}(\mathtt{dec}(y,T)).H$ else `Snippet`

($\sharp\sharp\sharp$) if $\Gamma_2(x) = (\mathsf{end}, R)$ then $K := x_{?T.S}(\mathtt{dec}(y,T)).H$ else `Snippet`

`Snippet` if $e = \mathsf{findValue}(\overline{x_{!T.S}}, (\Gamma_1, x\colon \top), H)$ && $e \neq 0$ then $K := [\![x_{?T.S}(\mathtt{dec}(y,T)).H]\!]^e$
else $K := x_{?T.S}(\mathtt{dec}(y,T)).H$

Fig. 6. Type checking function (part 2)

the function $\vdash_{\mathsf{A}}$, which is the core of the type-checking and disentangling[4] mechanism. The formal definition of function $\vdash_{\mathsf{A}}$ is in Figs. 5, 6, and 7, where the rules are assumed to be executed in the given order. We introduce left rules for $\vdash_{\mathsf{A}}$ where the matched type for the subject does appear in the left of a type (S_1, S_2); the right rules follow the same schema. The inner call $\vdash_{\mathsf{A}}$ is a function with the following signature: $\vdash_{\mathsf{A}} : \mathcal{G} \times \mathcal{D} \times \mathcal{P} \to \mathcal{G} \times \mathcal{D} \times \mathcal{H}$. The set $\mathcal{D}$ contains *projections* Δ mapping variables to types $\mathcal{A} \stackrel{\text{def}}{=} \mathcal{T} \cup \{(S, \mathsf{start}), (\mathsf{start}, S), (\mathsf{start}, \mathsf{start})\}$; start is a new end-point type which plays a role "dual" to end. We use $\top$ as a short for $(\mathsf{end}, \mathsf{end})$, and $\bot$ as a short for $(\mathsf{start}, \mathsf{start})$. At the bootstrap, a projection Δ is generated from a type environment Γ by means of a *casting* function, noted $\lfloor$, which maps all types (S_1, S_2) in $\mathsf{range}(\Gamma)$ to type $(\mathsf{start}, \mathsf{start})$, and is idempotent over type bool. The top-level call $\Vdash_{\mathsf{A}}$ is then successful whenever the inner call $\vdash_{\mathsf{A}}$ returns Γ and Δ such that both are terminated, where we let any combination of end and start to form a terminated type.

Projections are used in $\vdash_{\mathsf{A}}$ to detect whether two end points of a same session are used sequentially, rather than in parallel. That is, in a projection a variable starts with type $(\mathsf{start}, \mathsf{start})$ and then it can possibly have assigned a type of the form (S, start) or (start, S), meaning that one of the two end points have been used sequentially. If at the end of the call the variable has a type of the form $(\mathsf{end}, \mathsf{start})$ or $(\mathsf{start}, \mathsf{end})$, we know that type S have been consumed, and we launch our program transformation by signalling where the deadlock may occur. While useful, projections are source of (light) non-determinism; for instance during type checking we may have Γ, Δ and x such that $\Gamma(x) = (?T_1.S_1, \mathsf{end})$

[4] When convenient, we will say "type disentangle" to mean resolution of a (typed) wait-for sequential deadlock.

Patterns for processes (excerpt)

$$\frac{\Gamma_1; \Delta_1 \vdash_{\mathsf{A}} P \triangleright \Gamma_2; \Delta_2; H \qquad \Gamma_2; \Delta_2 \vdash_{\mathsf{A}} Q \triangleright \Gamma_3; \Delta_3; K}{\Gamma_1; \Delta_1 \vdash_{\mathsf{A}} P \mid Q \triangleright \Gamma_3; \Delta_3; H \mid K} \quad \text{[A-Par]}$$

$$\frac{\mathsf{sbal}(T) \qquad \Gamma_1, x\colon T; \Delta_1, x\colon \top \vdash_{\mathsf{A}} P \triangleright \Gamma_2, x\colon \bot; \Delta_2, x\colon A; H \qquad \mathsf{term}(A)}{\Gamma_1; \Delta_1 \vdash_{\mathsf{A}} (\nu x\colon T)P \triangleright \Gamma_2; \Delta_2; (\nu \mathsf{dec}(x, T))H} \quad \text{[A-Res]}$$

$$\frac{\Gamma_1; \Delta_1 \vdash_{\mathsf{A}} y\colon \mathsf{bool} \triangleright \Gamma_2; \Delta_2 \qquad \Gamma_2; \Delta_2 \vdash_{\mathsf{A}} P \triangleright \Gamma_2; \Delta_2; H \qquad \Gamma_2; \Delta_2 \vdash_{\mathsf{A}} Q \triangleright \Gamma_2; \Delta_2; K}{\Gamma_1; \Delta_1 \vdash_{\mathsf{A}} \mathsf{if}\, y \,\mathsf{then}\, P \,\mathsf{else}\, Q \triangleright \Gamma_2; \Delta_2; \mathsf{if}\, y_{\mathsf{bool}} \,\mathsf{then}\, H \,\mathsf{else}\, K}$$

[A-If]

$$\frac{\Gamma; \Delta \vdash_{\mathsf{A}} P \triangleright \Gamma; \Delta; H}{\Gamma; \Delta \vdash_{\mathsf{A}} !P \triangleright \Gamma; \Delta; !H} \qquad \Gamma; \Delta \vdash_{\mathsf{A}} \mathbf{0} \triangleright \Gamma; \Delta; \mathbf{0} \qquad \text{[A-Repl],[A-Inact]}$$

Fig. 7. Type checking function (part 3)

and $\Delta(x) = (\mathsf{start}, ?T_2.S_2)$. In this case we use backtracking, and first try to use $(?T_1.S_1, \mathsf{end})$, and then, if an exception is raised, try to use $(\mathsf{start}, ?T_2.S_2)$.

We can now analyse the patterns of function $\vdash_{\mathsf{A}}$. The patterns for variables have the form $\Gamma_1 \vdash_{\mathsf{A}} x : T \triangleright \Gamma_2$ where Γ_1, x and T are respectively a context, a variable and a type received in input, and Γ_2 is a context returned in output. The patterns for processes $\Gamma_1; \Delta_1 \vdash_{\mathsf{A}} P_1 \triangleright \Gamma_2; \Delta_2; H_2$ follow in the same figure. For each input and output there are six rules: three matching the end point type on the left and three matching the end point type on the right. Consider one of the (six) rules for output, rule [A-OutInit-L]. The rule describes the pattern matched by the identified first, second and third parameter; the body invokes type-checking of variable y at the expected type by passing context Γ taken from the first parameter, and obtains as result Γ_1; a recursive call on the continuation is then invoked by "split" the continuation type of x in the context — $(S, \overline{!T.S})$ — between the context and the projection. To enforce termination of sessions, we check that the type of x in the return environment is $\top$. To see if x is deadlocked in P, we check the type (start, R) of x in the return projection: if R is different from $\overline{!T.S}$, then it has been used, and we invoke the disentangling function $[\![\cdot]\!]$ (cf. Fig. 8) passing as arguments the decorated process $\overline{x_{!T.S}}\langle \mathsf{dec}(y, T)\rangle.H$, where H is the return process, and the boolean constant false, which, in this case, is ignored: this second parameter will be used in the clauses for input. We can now read the side condition $(*)$ and understand the result forwarded in output: $K := \overline{x_{!T.S}}\langle \mathsf{dec}(y, T)\rangle.H$ when $R = \overline{!T.S}$, and $K := [\![\overline{x_{!T.S}}\langle \mathsf{dec}(y, T)\rangle.H]\!]^{\mathsf{false}}$ when $R = \mathsf{end}$. Note the failure when $R \neq \overline{!T.S}, \neq \mathsf{end}$, meaning that $\overline{!T.S}$ is partially consumed.

Pattern [A-OutEnv-L] is matched when the environment assigns to the output channel x a type of the form $(!T.S, \mathsf{end})$. The right end point type is equal to end since the channel has been used before (in input or output): in fact the type of x in the projection is (start, R), which is different from $\bot$. We type check the variable and launch the call for the continuation by passing the

Type disentangling encoding $[\![\cdot]\!] \colon \mathcal{H} \times \mathcal{V} \to \mathcal{H}$
($R = !T.S$, $I^T \stackrel{\text{def}}{=} ?T.\mathsf{end}$, $O^T = !T.\mathsf{end}$, y_T and z_T defined accordingly)

$$[\![\overline{x_R}\langle\omega\rangle.H]\!]^{\psi} \stackrel{\text{def}}{=} (\nu r_{O^T}, r_{I^T}, r_{\top}) \qquad (*)$$

$$(\overline{x_R}\langle\omega\rangle.\langle\!\langle H\rangle\!\rangle^{x_{\overline{R}}}_{r_{I^T}} \mid x_{\overline{R}}(y_T).\overline{r_{O^T}}\langle y_T\rangle)$$

$$[\![x_{\overline{R}}(y_U).H]\!]^{\psi} \stackrel{\text{def}}{=} (\nu r_{O^T}, r_{I^T}, r_{\top})(\nu m_{O^\top}, m_{I^\top}, m_{\top}) \qquad (**)$$

$$((x_{\overline{R}}(z_T).\overline{r_{O^T}}\langle z_T\rangle \mid r_{I^T}(y_U).\langle\!\langle H\rangle\!\rangle^{x_R}_{m_{O^\top}} \mid \overline{x_R}\langle\psi\rangle.m_{I^\top}()))$$

$(*)$ $\{r_{O^T}, r_{I^T}, r_{\top}, y_T\} \cap \mathrm{fv}(H) = \emptyset$ $\quad$ $(**)$ $\{r_{O^T}, r_{I^T}, r_{\top}, m_{O^\top}, m_{I^\top}, m_{\top}, z_T\} \cap \mathrm{fv}(H) = \emptyset$

Auxiliary function for processes, $\langle\!\langle\cdot\rangle\!\rangle \colon \mathcal{H} \times \mathcal{F} \times \mathcal{F} \to \mathcal{H}$

$$\langle\!\langle x_{\overline{R}}(y_U).H\rangle\!\rangle^{x_{\overline{R}}}_{\varphi} = \varphi(y_U).H$$

$$\langle\!\langle \phi(y_U).H\rangle\!\rangle^{\psi}_{\varphi} = \phi(y_U).\langle\!\langle H\rangle\!\rangle^{\psi}_{\varphi} \qquad \phi \neq \psi$$

$$\langle\!\langle \overline{x_R}\langle\omega\rangle.H\rangle\!\rangle^{x_R}_{\varphi} = \overline{\varphi}\langle\rangle.H$$

$$\langle\!\langle \overline{\phi}\langle\omega\rangle.H\rangle\!\rangle^{\psi}_{\varphi} = \overline{\phi}\langle\omega\rangle.\langle\!\langle H\rangle\!\rangle^{\psi}_{\varphi} \qquad \phi \neq \psi$$

The remaining cases are homomorphic

Fig. 8. Transformation of decorated processes

entry $x\colon (!T.S, \mathsf{end})$ for the environment and by forwarding the same projection received in input. Condition (**) is similarly to condition $(*)$ of [A-OutInit-L] and permit to check the shape of the return projection Δ in order to launch the code for disentangling: if $\Delta(x)$ is unchanged then we return the decorated process $\overline{x_{!T.S}}\langle\mathsf{dec}(y,T)\rangle.H$, otherwise we invoke disentangling on $\overline{x_{!T.S}}\langle\mathsf{dec}(y,T)\rangle.H$.

Pattern [A-OutProj-L] is matched when the type of the output channel x in the projection is of the form $(!T.S, \mathsf{start})$. In this case we invoke type checking for the continuation (after contrasting the variable) by passing the same environment received in input and by passing the entry $x\colon (S, \mathsf{start})$ for the projection. Dually to [A-OutEnv-L], in (***) we control the return environment Γ in order to launch disentangling: if $\Gamma(x)$ is unchanged then we forward in output $\overline{x_{!T.S}}\langle\mathsf{dec}(y,T)\rangle.H$, otherwise we return $[\![\overline{x_{!T.S}}\langle\mathsf{dec}(y,T)\rangle.H]\!]^{\mathsf{false}}$.

The rules for input, [A-InInit-L], [A-InEnv-L] and [A-InProj-L], follow in Fig. 6 and are analogous respectively to [A-OutInit-L], [A-OutEnv-L] and [A-OutProj-L] in Fig. 5. The main differences are:

(a) there is no variable to type-check;
(b) in the call for the continuation the variable y bound by the input is added to the context at the payload type of the channel, and to the projection at type $\bot$; the type of y must be terminated in both the return context

and environment (cf. condition $\mathsf{term}(A)$), to enforce a linear discipline for y whenever its type is different from bool and $\top$;

(c) function $[\![\cdot]\!]$ in Fig. 8 is invoked *after checking* that the value ω sent over the sequential output corresponding to the input prefix satisfies certain conditions (cf. `Snippet`). This is implemented through a linear scan function $\mathsf{findValue}$ (see below) which, when successful, returns a value different from 0. When successful, we invoke function $[\![\cdot]\!]$ by passing as arguments $x_{?T.S}(\mathtt{dec}(y,T)).H$ and ω, otherwise, we return $x_{?T.S}(\mathtt{dec}(y,T)).H$.

Function $\mathsf{findValue}$: $\mathcal{F} \times \mathcal{G} \times \mathcal{H} \to \mathcal{V} \cup \{0\}$ takes in input a prefix $x_S \in \mathcal{F}$, an environment $\Gamma \in \mathcal{G}$, and a decorated process $H \in \mathcal{H}$, and scans the structure of H to find the value ω sent over x_S. The function returns ω whenever ω is a boolean value, or is equal to the tuple $x_{\sigma_1}, \ldots, x_{\sigma_n}$, for some $x \in \mathrm{dom}(\Gamma)$, and 0 otherwise. See the technical report [19] for the formal definition.

In Fig. 7 we have rules for compositional processes. The interesting rule is the one for parallel composition, [A-PAR]. The first call on the left returns a triple (Γ_2, Δ_2, H), where Γ_2 and Δ_2 are obtained by setting to end the session end points used in P, and H is obtained by disentangling (the decoration of) P, through function $[\![\cdot]\!]$. The second call on the right uses the return context Γ_2 and the projection Δ_2 to generate the triple (Γ_3, Δ_3, K), where K is obtained by disentangling Q, using the same schema. Note that the deadlocks of P and Q are fixed compositionally: we detect whether P is deadlocked *before* analysing Q, and return the triple $(\Gamma_3, \Delta_3, H \mid K)$.

Program Transformation. The encoding $[\![\cdot]\!]$ in Fig. 8 maps decorated input and output processes in $\mathcal{H}$ into decorated processes in $\mathcal{H}$, given a parameter in $\mathcal{V}$. The partial operation $[\![\cdot]\!]$ is called only with prefixed arguments: when invoked, it disentangles the first prefix encountered. To this aim, it uses the auxiliary total function $\langle\!\langle \cdot \rangle\!\rangle$ which takes a decorated process and two prefixes and returns a process. In the *output first* case of $[\![\cdot]\!]$ (first line) we rely on a fresh (triple of) forwarder(s) r to carry the result to be received by the input prefix of x, now put in parallel; the deadlocked input occurrence of x is renamed to r by $\langle\!\langle \cdot \rangle\!\rangle$. Note that we ignore the ψ parameter; it is useful only in the case below. The *input first* case of $[\![\cdot]\!]$ (second line) follows a similar idea but is more elaborate, because of variable binding; in this case we need both a (triple of) forwarder(s) r and a (triple of) semaphore(s) m, to preserve the order of exchanges: the call $\langle\!\langle \cdot \rangle\!\rangle$ renames the deadlocked output occurrence of x in H with m, while the output on x is put in parallel by *instantiating* the tuples of values to be sent with the actual parameter of $[\![\cdot]\!]$, that is ψ. As introduced, this parameter is found (before invoking $[\![\cdot]\!]$) trough function $\mathsf{findValue}$: the function searches for the occurrence of an output prefix in a decorated process and returns the values sent in output, when these are a boolean constant or a tuple of free prefixes.

Results. The first result guarantees that the algorithm succeeds only when type-checking succeeds, that is when the process is accepted by the system in Fig. 3. The construction of the proof of the theorem is similar to the one in [23], as the process returned in output by $\Vdash_{\mathsf{A}}$ is ignored.

Theorem 8 (Typability). *If* $\Gamma \Vdash_{\mathsf{A}} P \rhd H$ *then* $\Gamma \vdash P$.

The second result is the main one of the paper: it ensures that the process returned by the algorithm is sound and *RSHDF*.

Theorem 9 (Deadlock Freedom). *If* $\Gamma \Vdash_{A} P \rhd H$ *then* H *is* RSHDF.

We have a stronger result for the sequential variables of P: such variables run in parallel *at the same level* in the process returned by the algorithm.

Theorem 10 (Mismatch Freedom). *If* $\Gamma \Vdash_{A} P \rhd H$ *and* $x \in \mathrm{sv}(P)$, *then for all* $x_s \in \mathrm{var}(H)$: $H \Longrightarrow K_{x_s}$ *with* $K_{x_s} \equiv (\nu\tilde{\varphi})(\overline{x_S}\langle\omega\rangle.K_1 \mid x_{\overline{S}}(\tilde{\phi}).K_2 \mid K_3)$.

6 Conclusions

We propose a new approach to tackle an old dilemma: can we do something to assist the programmer instead of simply reject code that does not type check? Founding on the π-calculus [1] and on a recent formulation of session types [9,10], we devised a type-checking algorithm that, when finds a particular form of deadlocks, which we refer to as resource self-holding deadlocks, automatically generates new type safe deadlock free code that mimics the original process intended behaviour as described by session types. We assessed the feasibility of our approach by implementing the algorithm (the code is available online, see [19]) and by analysing several examples of self-holding deadlocks. We believe that our approach is interesting since it can be used to release deadlocks in systems based on session and linear types, e.g. [3,7,11], which are represented by the type system of [10]. Moreover, we ensure deadlock freedom for well-typed processes not by restricting the set of typable processes, but by "fixing" those that exhibit the problem. If adapted to session based type systems of high-level languages, it may be an useful tool to assist the programmer in the software developing process, by (automatically) repairing program errors that can lead to runtime deadlocks. Our long-term goal is deadlock resolution for untyped processes, leaving the session type construction as a blackbox: the programmer writes the code; the algorithm infers the types, resolves the deadlocks, and provides error-free code.

For what concerns the limitations of our approach, we note that our notion of deadlock seems to be a specific instance of resource holding or *Hold and Wait* deadlocks [17,18], which is identified by considering resources (interpreted as π-calculus channels) blocked by the *same* thread; this notion is thus insensitive to the presence of cycles in waiting/releasing a resource. Specifically, there are four unmanaged classes of processes that we want to deal with: (1) we do not tackle processes of the form $a(x).\overline{x}\langle\mathsf{true}\rangle.b(z) \mid \overline{a}\langle b\rangle$ (which reduces in one step to the basic example $\overline{b}\langle\mathsf{true}\rangle.b(z)$), because the type of x is not balanced, which follows from a not having a strongly-balanced type; (2) we do not tackle processes like $a(x).c(z).\overline{a}\langle z\rangle.(\overline{x}\langle\mathsf{true}\rangle \mid x(y)) \mid \overline{c}\langle b\rangle$, because the actual object of the output on a is bound; (3) we do not tackle branching processes of the form $a(x).\mathsf{if}\, x\, \mathsf{then}\, \overline{a}\langle\mathsf{true}\rangle\, \mathsf{else}\, \overline{a}\langle\mathsf{false}\rangle$, i.e. they do not (algorithmically) type check, because we cannot resolve the non-determinism caused by the test; (4) we do not tackle processes with circular deadlocks like $a(x).\overline{b}\langle\mathsf{true}\rangle \mid b(y).\overline{a}\langle\mathsf{false}\rangle$. To solve (1) and (2), we plan to enhance function findValue and collect a series of constraints of the form $x = v$, (when possible) meaning that the (bound) variable x should be instantiated with v, *before* executing the algorithm. We can then pass as further parameter the constraints to be instantiated, e.g. (1) $x = b$, and (2) $z = b$, and re-use the pattern rules presented in this paper.

Issue (3) could be solved by considering the π-calculus with a non-deterministic choice operator, or by devising a communication protocol that implements a similar behaviour (cf. [24]), to transform the blocked processes by putting in parallel the choice $\overline{a}\langle\mathsf{true}\rangle + \overline{a}\langle\mathsf{false}\rangle$. The issue (4) seems orthogonal to our approach, and would require techniques to detect dependencies and circularities in message passing, similarly to many recent works (e.g. [12]). We leave this for future work, as well as a behavioural theory to relate the source and the resulting process of our tool.

Acknowledgments. This work is partially supported by the Portuguese Fundação para a Ciência e a Tecnologia via project "CITI/FCT/UNL 2011-2012" — grant PEst-OE/EEI/UI0527/2011 and project "Liveness, statically" — grant PTDC/EIA-CCO/117513/2010, and by the COST Action IC1201: Behavioural Types for Reliable Large-Scale Software Systems (BETTY). We would like to thank Adrian Francalanza for fruitful discussions and illuminating examples, and the anonymous reviewers for their careful reading and constructive criticisms.

References

1. Milner, R., Parrow, J., Walker, D.: A calculus of mobile processes, parts I and II. Inf. Comput. **100**(1), 1–77 (1992)
2. Honda, K.: Types for dyadic interaction. In: Best, E. (ed.) CONCUR 1993. LNCS, vol. 715, pp. 509–523. Springer, Heidelberg (1993)
3. Honda, K., Vasconcelos, V.T., Kubo, M.: Language primitives and type discipline for structured communication-based programming. In: Hankin, C. (ed.) ESOP 1998. LNCS, vol. 1381, pp. 122–138. Springer, Heidelberg (1998)
4. Takeuchi, K., Honda, K., Kubo, M.: An interaction-based language and its typing system. In: Halatsis, C., Maritsas, D., Philokyprou, G., Theodoridis, S. (eds.) PARLE 1994. LNCS, vol. 817, pp. 398–413. Springer, Heidelberg (1994)
5. Dezani-Ciancaglini, M., de'Liguoro, U.: Sessions and session types: an overview. In: Laneve, C., Su, J. (eds.) WS-FM 2009. LNCS, vol. 6194, pp. 1–28. Springer, Heidelberg (2010)
6. Dezani-Ciancaglini, M., Drossopoulou, S., Mostrous, D., Yoshida, N.: Objects and session types. Inf. Comput. **207**(5), 595–641 (2009)
7. Gay, S.J., Hole, M.J.: Subtyping for session types in the pi calculus. Acta Informatica **42**(2/3), 191–225 (2005)
8. Yoshida, N., Vasconcelos, V.T.: Language primitives and type discipline for structured communication-based programming revisited: two systems for higher-order session communication. In: SecReT. ENTCS, vol. 171(4), pp. 73–93 (2007)

9. Giunti, M., Vasconcelos, V.T.: A linear account of session types in the pi calculus. In: Gastin, P., Laroussinie, F. (eds.) CONCUR 2010. LNCS, vol. 6269, pp. 432–446. Springer, Heidelberg (2010)
10. Giunti, M., Vasconcelos, V.T.: Linearity, session types and the pi calculus. Math. Struct. Comput. Sci. (2013, in press)
11. Kobayashi, N., Pierce, B.C., Turner, D.N.: Linearity and the pi-calculus. ACM Trans. Program. Lang. Syst. **21**(5), 914–947 (1999)
12. Bettini, L., Coppo, M., D'Antoni, L., De Luca, M., Dezani-Ciancaglini, M., Yoshida, N.: Global progress in dynamically interleaved multiparty sessions. In: van Breugel, F., Chechik, M. (eds.) CONCUR 2008. LNCS, vol. 5201, pp. 418–433. Springer, Heidelberg (2008)
13. Caires, L., Pfenning, F.: Session types as intuitionistic linear propositions. In: Gastin, P., Laroussinie, F. (eds.) CONCUR 2010. LNCS, vol. 6269, pp. 222–236. Springer, Heidelberg (2010)
14. Caires, L., Vieira, H.T.: Conversation types. Theoret. Comput. Sci. **411**(51–52), 4399–4440 (2010)
15. Wadler, P.: Propositions as sessions. In: ICFP, pp. 273–286. ACM (2012)
16. Carbone, M., Montesi, F.: Deadlock-freedom-by-design: multiparty asynchronous global programming. In: POPL, pp. 263–274. ACM Press (2013)
17. Coffman, E.G., Elphick, M., Shoshani, A.: System deadlocks. ACM Comput. Surv. **3**(2), 67–78 (1971)
18. Knapp, E.: Deadlock detection in distributed databases. ACM Comput. Surv. **19**(4), 303–328 (1987)
19. Giunti, M.: (LockRes: a session type checker resolving deadlocks) http://ctp.di.fct.unl.pt/~mgiunti/lockres. The web page contains the SML/NJ prototype of the algorithm presented in this paper and the technical report.
20. Milner, R.: Communicating and Mobile Systems: The Pi-Calculus. Cambridge University Press, New York (1999)
21. Barendregt, H.: The Lambda Calculus - Its Syntax and Semantics, 1st edn. North-Holland, Amsterdam (1981, revised 1984)
22. Walker, D.: Substructural type systems. In: Pierce, B.C. (ed.) Advanced Topics in Types and Programming Languages, pp. 3–44. MIT Press, Cambridge (2005)
23. Giunti, M.: Algorithmic type checking for a pi-calculus with name matching and session types. J. Logic Algebraic Program. **82**(8), 263–281 (2013)
24. Nestmann, U., Pierce, B.C.: Decoding choice encodings. Inf. Comput. **163**(1), 1–59 (2000)

Information Flow

Fine-Grained and Coarse-Grained Reactive Noninterference

Pejman Attar and Ilaria Castellani(✉)

INRIA, 2004 route des Lucioles,
06902 Sophia Antipolis, France
{pejman.attar,ilaria.castellani}@inria.fr

Abstract. We study bisimilarity and the security property of *noninterference* in a core *synchronous reactive language* that we name *CRL*.

In the synchronous reactive paradigm, programs communicate by means of broadcast events, and their parallel execution is regulated by the notion of *instant*. Within each instant, programs may emit events and get suspended while waiting for events emitted by other programs. They may also explicitly return the control to the scheduler, thereby suspending themselves until the end of the instant. An instant is thus a period of time during which all programs compute until termination or suspension.

In *CRL* there is no memory, and the focus is on the control structure of programs. An *asymmetric parallel operator* is used to implement a deterministic scheduling. This scheduling is fair – in the sense that it gives its turn to each parallel component – if all components are *cooperative*, namely if they always return the control after a finite number of steps.

We first prove that *CRL* programs are indeed cooperative. This result is based on two features of the language: the semantics of loops, which requires them to yield the control at each iteration of their body; and a delayed reaction to the absence of events, which ensures the monotonicity of computations (viewed as I/O functions on event sets) during instants. Cooperativeness is crucial as it entails the *reactivity* of a program to its context, namely its capacity to input events from the context at the start of instants, and to output events to the context at the end of instants.

We define two bisimulation equivalences on programs, formalising respectively a *fine-grained observation* of programs (the observer is viewed as a program) and a *coarse-grained observation* (the observer is viewed as part of the context). As expected, the latter equivalence is more abstract than the former, as it only compares the I/O behaviours of programs at each instant, while the former also compares their intermediate results.

Based on these bisimulations, two properties of *reactive noninterference* (RNI) are proposed. Both properties are time-insensitive and termination-insensitive. Coarse-grained RNI is more abstract than fine-grained RNI, because it views the parallel operator as commutative and abstracts away from repeated emissions of the same event during an instant.

Work partially supported by the french ANR 08-EMER-010 grant PARTOUT.

M. Abadi and A. Lluch Lafuente (Eds.): TGC 2013, LNCS 8358, pp. 159–179, 2014.
DOI: 10.1007/978-3-319-05119-2_10,

Finally, a type system guaranteeing both security properties is presented. Thanks partly to a design choice of *CRL*, which offers two separate constructs for loops and iteration, this type system allows for a precise treatment of termination leaks, which are an issue in parallel languages.

1 Introduction

Many systems of widespread use, such as web browsers and web applications, may be modelled as *reactive programs*, that is programs that listen and react to their environment in a continuous way, by means of events. Since the environment may include mutually distrusting parties, such as a local user and a remote web server, reactive programs should be able to protect the confidentiality of the data they manipulate, by ensuring a *secure information flow* from the inputs they receive from one party to the outputs they release to another party.

Secure information flow is often formalised via the notion of *noninterference* (NI), expressing the absence of dependency between secret inputs and public outputs (or more generally, between inputs of some confidentiality level to outputs of lower or incomparable level). Originally introduced in [12], NI has been studied for a variety of languages, ranging from standard imperative and functional languages [16,18] to process calculi based on CCS or the pi-calculus [11]. On the other hand, little attention has been paid to noninterference for reactive programs, with the notable exception of [2,13] and [7].

We shall focus here on a particular brand of reactive programming, namely the *synchronous* one, which was first embodied in the synchronous language *SL* [9], an offspring of Esterel [6], and later incorporated into various programming environments, such as C, Java, Caml and Scheme. In the synchronous paradigm, the parallel execution of programs is regulated by a notion of *instant*. The model of *SL* departs from that of Esterel in that it assumes the reaction to the absence of an event to be postponed until the end of the instant. This assumption helps disambiguating programs and simplifying the implementation of the language. It is also essential to ensure the monotonicity of programs and their reactivity to the environment.

In this work, we will not explicitly model the interaction of a reactive program with the environment (this could be easily done but it would not bring any further insight). Instead, we concentrate on the interaction *within* a reactive program, making sure it regularly converges to a stable state (end of instant), in which the program is ready to interact with the environment. We call this property *cooperativeness* [1] or *internal reactivity*. In the sequel, we shall abandon the distinction between internal reactivity (among the components of a program) and *external reactivity* (towards the environment), to focus on the former.

This paper attempts to explore "secure reactive programming in a nutshell". To this end, we concentrate on a minimal reactive language without memory, consisting of standard sequential operators, an asymmetric parallel operator $\pitchfork$ (formalising a kind of *coroutine* parallelism under a deterministic scheduling), together with four typical reactive constructs, which we briefly describe next.

In our *Core Reactive Language* CRL, programs are made of parallel components s, s' – also called "threads" for simplicity in the following – combined with the operator $s \nmid s'$ and communicating by means of broadcast events. Threads may emit events, via a `generate` ev instruction, and get suspended while waiting for events to be emitted by other threads, through an `await` ev instruction. They may also explicitly yield the control to the scheduler, via a `cooperate` instruction, thereby suspending themselves until the end of the current instant. An instant is therefore a period of time during which all threads compute until termination or suspension. Clearly, this is a logical rather than a physical notion of instant, since the termination of instants is determined by the collective behaviour of threads rather than by some physical clock. At the end of an instant, all threads are inactive and share the same view of emitted events. At instant change, a preemption construct `do` s `watching` ev allows some suspended parts of threads to be pruned off, thus implementing a time-out mechanism. Interaction with the environment is limited to the start and the end of instants: the environment injects events at the start of instants and collects them at the end.

The starting point of our work is the paper [2], which laid the basis for the study of noninterference in a synchronous reactive language. The present work improves on [2] in several respects, which we summarise below.

The language examined in [2] is similar to CRL but strictly more expressive, including imperative constructs, local declarations and a memory. Indeed, our asymmetric parallel operator $\nmid$, which gives priority to its left component, is inspired by that of [2]. Here, however, we adopt a slightly different semantics for $s \nmid s'$, which preserves the position of threads within a program, while the semantics of [2] swapped the positions of s and s' in $s \nmid s'$ in case s was suspended, reducing it to $s' \nmid s$. This simple change forces the scheduler in CRL to serve the same thread at the start of each instant, thus avoiding the so-called *scheduling leaks* of [2], and allowing for a more relaxed typing rule for $\nmid$, which is just the standard rule for symmetric parallel composition.

Moreover, reactivity was not a concern in [2]: as soon as they contained *while loops*, programs were not guaranteed to terminate or suspend within an instant. Hence, it only made sense to consider a fine-grained notion of noninterference. By contrast, in CRL all programs are reactive, thanks to a clear separation between the loop construct `loop` s and the iteration construct `repeat` exp `do` s, and to our semantics for loops, which requires them to yield the control at each iteration of their body. This makes it possible to define a notion of coarse-grained *reactive noninterference* (RNI), which accounts only for the I/O behaviour of programs within each instant. The coarse-grained RNI property has an advantage over the fine-grained one: it exploits in a more direct way the structure of reactive computations, and it recovers the flavour of big-step semantics within each instant, offering a more abstract NI notion for reactive programs.

Finally, our type system is more permissive than that of [2], thanks to the relaxed typing rule for parallel composition and to refined typing rules for the conditional. Both improvements are made possible by design choices of CRL.

The main contributions of this paper are: (1) the reactivity result, (2) the definition of two bisimulation equivalences for synchronous reactive programs, of different granularity. To our knowledge, semantic equivalences for reactive programs have only been studied previously by Amadio [4]; (3) the proposal of two properties of reactive noninterference, based on the above bisimulations, and (4) the presentation of a type system ensuring both noninterference properties.

The rest of the paper is organised as follows. Sections 2 and 3 present the syntax and the semantics of the language *CRL*. Section 4 is devoted to proving reactivity of *CRL* programs. Section 5 introduces the two bisimulation equivalences and gives some properties of them. In Sect. 6 we define our two NI properties. Section 7 presents the security type system and the proof of its soundness. Finally, future and related work are briefly discussed in Sect. 8.

The proofs of the results are mostly omitted and may be found in [5].

2 Syntax

In this section we introduce the syntax of *CRL*. Let Val be a set of values, ranged over by v, v', Var a set of variables, ranged over by x, y, z, and $Events$ a set of events, ranged over by ev, ev'. A fixed valuation function $V : Var \rightarrow Val$ for open terms is assumed, which however will be left implicit until Sect. 6.

Expressions. An expression $exp \in Exp$ may be a basic value, a variable, or the value returned by a function. Letting $\overrightarrow{exp}$ denote a tuple of expressions $exp_1, \ldots, exp_n$, the syntax of expressions is:

$$exp \in Exp ::= v \mid x \mid f(\overrightarrow{exp})$$

The evaluation of a function call $f(\overrightarrow{exp})$ is assumed to be instantaneous, and therefore so is the evaluation of an expression exp, denoted by $exp \leadsto v$, which is formally defined by the three rules:

$$\frac{}{v \leadsto v} \qquad \frac{V(x) = v}{x \leadsto v} \qquad \frac{\forall i \in \{1, \ldots, n\} \,.\, exp_i \leadsto v_i \qquad f(v_1, \ldots, v_n) = v}{f(\overrightarrow{exp}) \leadsto v}$$

Programs. We now present the syntax of *CRL* programs. Alongside with typical sequential operators, *CRL* includes four operators that are commonly found in reactive languages, `cooperate`, `generate` ev, `await` ev and `do` s `watching` ev, as well as a binary *asymmetric parallel operator*, denoted by $\nmid$, which performs a deterministic scheduling on its components. This operator is very close to that used in [2] and, earlier on, in the implementation of *SugarCubes* [10]. However, while in [2] and [10] each parallel component was executing as long as possible, our operator $\nmid$ implements a form of *prioritised scheduling*, where the first component yields the control only when terminating or suspending (*late cooperation*), while the second yields it as soon as it generates an event that unblocks the first component (*early cooperation*). The syntax of programs is given by:

$$s \in \mathit{Programs} ::= \texttt{nothing} \mid s;s \mid (s \dagger s) \mid \texttt{cooperate} \mid \texttt{generate}\, ev \mid \texttt{await}\, ev \mid \texttt{do}\, s\, \texttt{watching}\, ev \mid (\texttt{loop}\, s) \mid (\texttt{repeat}\, exp\, \texttt{do}\, s) \mid (\texttt{if}\, exp\, \texttt{then}\, s\, \texttt{else}\, s)$$

Note that our language includes two different constructs for loops and iteration, in replacement of the standard *while loop* operator. This allows for a clear separation between nonterminating behaviours and iterative behaviours.

3 Semantics

This section presents the operational semantics of *CRL*. Programs proceed through a succession of instants, transforming sets of events. There are two transition relations, both defined on *configurations* of the form $\langle s, E\rangle$, where s is a program and $E \subseteq \mathit{Events}$ is an *event environment*, i.e. a set of present events.

Let us first give the general idea of these two transition relations:

1. The *small-step transition relation* describes the step-by-step execution of a configuration within a an instant. The general format of a transition is:
$$\langle s, E\rangle \rightarrow \langle s', E'\rangle$$
where:
   - s is the program to execute and s' is the residual program;
   - E is the starting event environment and E' is the resulting event environment: E' coincides with E if the transition does not generate any new event; otherwise $E' = E \cup \{ev\}$, where ev is the new generated event.
2. The *tick transition relation* describes the passage from one instant to the next, and applies only to suspended configurations. A transition of this kind has always the form:
$$\langle s, E\rangle \hookrightarrow \langle [s]_E, \emptyset\rangle$$
where the resulting event environment is empty and $[s]_E$ is a "reconditioning" of program s for the next instant, possibly allowing it to resume execution at the next instant even without the help of new events from the environment.

Before formally defining $\rightarrow$ and $\hookrightarrow$, we introduce the *suspension predicate* $\langle s, E\rangle\ddagger$, which holds when s is suspended in the event environment E, namely when all threads in s are waiting for events not contained in E, or have deliberately yielded the control for the current instant by means of a `cooperate` instruction.

The rules defining the predicate $\ddagger$ and the relations $\rightarrow$ and $\hookrightarrow$ are given in Fig. 1. The *reconditioning function* $[s]_E$ prepares s for the next instant: it erases all guarding `cooperate` instructions, as well as all guarding $\texttt{do}\, s'\, \texttt{watching}\, ev$ instructions whose time-out event ev belongs to E (i.e. has been generated).

We assume programs are well-typed with respect to a standard type system that ensures that in the commands $\texttt{if}\, exp\, \texttt{then}\, s_1\, \texttt{else}\, s_2$ and $\texttt{repeat}\, exp\, \texttt{do}\, s$ the expression exp evaluates respectively to a boolean and to an integer $n \geq 1$.

$$\langle cooperate, E\rangle\ddagger \;(coop) \qquad \frac{ev \notin E}{\langle \mathtt{await}\ ev, E\rangle\ddagger}\;(wait_s) \qquad \frac{\langle s, E\rangle\ddagger}{\langle \mathtt{do}\ s\ \mathtt{watching}\ ev, E\rangle\ddagger}\;(watch_s)$$

$$\frac{\langle s_1, E\rangle\ddagger}{\langle s_1; s_2, E\rangle\ddagger}\;(seq_s) \qquad \frac{\langle s_1, E\rangle\ddagger \quad \langle s_2, E\rangle\ddagger}{\langle s_1 \dagger s_2, E\rangle\ddagger}\;(par_s) \qquad \frac{\langle s, E\rangle\ddagger}{\langle s, E\rangle \hookrightarrow \langle [s]_E, \emptyset\rangle}\;(tick)$$

Suspension Predicate and Tick Transition Rule

$$[\mathtt{cooperate}]_E = \mathtt{nothing} \qquad [\mathtt{do}\ s\ \mathtt{watching}\ ev]_E = \begin{cases} \mathtt{nothing} & \textit{if } ev \in E \\ \mathtt{do}\ [s]_E\ \mathtt{watching}\ ev & \textit{otherwise} \end{cases}$$

$$[\mathtt{await}\ ev]_E = \mathtt{await}\ ev \qquad [s_1; s_2]_E = [s_1]_E\,; s_2 \qquad [s_1 \dagger s_2]_E = [s_1]_E \dagger [s_2]_E$$

Reconditioning Function

$$\frac{\langle s_1, E\rangle \to \langle s_1', E'\rangle}{\langle s_1; s_2, E\rangle \to \langle s_1'; s_2, E'\rangle}\;(seq_1) \qquad \langle \mathtt{nothing}\,; s, E\rangle \to \langle s, E\rangle \;(seq_2)$$

$$\frac{\langle s_1, E\rangle \to \langle s_1', E'\rangle}{\langle s_1 \dagger s_2, E\rangle \to \langle s_1' \dagger s_2, E'\rangle}\;(par_1) \qquad \langle \mathtt{nothing} \dagger s, E\rangle \to \langle s, E\rangle \;(par_2)$$

$$\frac{\langle s_1, E\rangle\ddagger \quad \langle s_2, E\rangle \to \langle s_2', E'\rangle}{\langle s_1 \dagger s_2, E\rangle \to \langle s_1 \dagger s_2', E'\rangle}\;(par_3) \qquad \frac{\langle s, E\rangle\ddagger}{\langle s \dagger \mathtt{nothing}, E\rangle \to \langle s, E\rangle}\;(par_4)$$

$$\langle \mathtt{generate}\ ev, E\rangle \to \langle \mathtt{nothing}, E \cup \{ev\}\rangle \;(gen) \qquad \frac{ev \in E}{\langle \mathtt{await}\ ev, E\rangle \to \langle \mathtt{nothing}, E\rangle}\;(wait)$$

$$\frac{\langle s, E\rangle \to \langle s', E'\rangle}{\langle \mathtt{do}\ s\ \mathtt{watching}\ ev, E\rangle \to \langle \mathtt{do}\ s'\ \mathtt{watching}\ ev, E'\rangle}\;(watch_1)$$

$$\langle \mathtt{do}\ \mathtt{nothing}\ \mathtt{watching}\ ev, E\rangle \to \langle \mathtt{nothing}, E\rangle \;(watch_2)$$

$$\langle \mathtt{loop}\ s, E\rangle \to \langle (s \dagger \mathtt{cooperate}); \mathtt{loop}\ s, E\rangle \;(loop)$$

$$\frac{exp \rightsquigarrow n}{\langle \mathtt{repeat}\ exp\ \mathtt{do}\ s, E\rangle \to \langle \underbrace{s; \ldots; s}_{n\ times}, E\rangle}\;(repeat)$$

$$\frac{exp \rightsquigarrow tt}{\langle \mathtt{if}\ exp\ \mathtt{then}\ s_1\ \mathtt{else}\ s_2, E\rangle \to \langle s_1, E\rangle}\;(if_1) \qquad \frac{exp \rightsquigarrow ff}{\langle \mathtt{if}\ exp\ \mathtt{then}\ s_1\ \mathtt{else}\ s_2, E\rangle \to \langle s_2, E\rangle}\;(if_2)$$

Small-step Transition Rules

Fig. 1. Operational Semantics of *CRL*

Let us comment on the most interesting transition rules. The execution of a parallel program always starts with its left branch (Rule (par_1)). Once the left branch is over, the program reduces to its right branch (Rule (par_2)). If the left branch is suspended, then the right branch executes (Rule (par_3)) until unblocking the left branch. Thus *early cooperation* is required in the right branch. To avoid nondeterminism, a terminated right branch can only be eliminated if the left branch is suspended (Rule (par_4)). A `loop` s program executes its body cyclically: a `cooperate` instruction is systematically added in parallel to its body to avoid *instantaneous loops*, i.e. divergence within an instant[1] (Rule ($loop$)). A `do` s `watching` ev program executes its body until termination or suspension (Rule ($watch_1$)), reducing to `nothing` when its body terminates (Rule ($watch_2$)).

The small-step transition relation satisfies two simple properties.

Proposition 1 (Determinism).
Let $s \in Programs$ *and* $E \subseteq Events$. *Then:*

$$s \neq \texttt{nothing} \quad \Rightarrow \quad \textit{either } \langle s, E\rangle \ddagger \ \textit{ or } \exists!\, s', E' \,.\, \langle s, E\rangle \rightarrow \langle s', E'\rangle$$

Proof By inspecting the suspension and transition rules, it is immediate to see that at most one transition rule applies to each configuration $\langle s, E\rangle$.

Proposition 2 (Event persistence).
Let $s \in Programs$ *and* $E \subseteq Events$. *Then:* $\quad \langle s, E\rangle \rightarrow \langle s', E'\rangle \Rightarrow E \subseteq E'$

Proof Straightforward, since the only transition rule that changes the event environment E is the rule for `generate` ev, which adds the event ev to E.

We define now the notion of *instantaneous convergence*, which is at the basis of the reactivity property of CRL programs. Let us first introduce some notation. The *timed multi-step transition relation* $\langle s, E\rangle \Rightarrow_n \langle s', E'\rangle$ is defined by:

$$\begin{array}{l}\langle s, E\rangle \Rightarrow_0 \langle s, E\rangle \\ \langle s, E\rangle \rightarrow \langle s', E'\rangle \wedge \langle s', E'\rangle \Rightarrow_n \langle s'', E''\rangle \quad \Rightarrow \quad \langle s, E\rangle \Rightarrow_{n+1} \langle s'', E''\rangle\end{array}$$

Then the *multi-step transition relation* $\langle s, E\rangle \Rightarrow \langle s', E'\rangle$ is given by:

$$\langle s, E\rangle \Rightarrow \langle s', E'\rangle \ \Leftrightarrow \ \exists n \,.\, \langle s, E\rangle \Rightarrow_n \langle s', E'\rangle$$

Note that the relation $\Rightarrow$ could also be defined as $\rightarrow^{\star}$.
The *immediate convergence* predicate is defined by:

$$\langle s, E\rangle \,\overset{\ddagger}{\curlyvee} \ \Leftrightarrow \ \langle s, E\rangle \ddagger \ \vee\ s = \texttt{nothing}$$

We may now define the relations and predicates of *instantaneous convergence* and *instantaneous termination*:

[1] In general, we shall call "instantaneous" any property that holds within an instant.

Definition 1 (Instantaneous convergence).

$$\begin{array}{lll} \langle s,E\rangle \Downarrow \langle s',E'\rangle & \text{if} & \langle s,E\rangle \Rightarrow \langle s',E'\rangle \ \wedge\ \langle s',E'\rangle \not\xrightarrow{} \\ \langle s,E\rangle \Downarrow & \text{if} & \exists s',E' .\ \langle s,E\rangle \Downarrow \langle s',E'\rangle \end{array}$$

Definition 2 (Instantaneous termination).

$$\begin{array}{lll} \langle s,E\rangle \mathbin{\overline{\Downarrow}} E' & \text{if} & \langle s,E\rangle \Downarrow \langle \mathtt{nothing},E'\rangle \\ \langle s,E\rangle \mathbin{\overline{\Downarrow}} & \text{if} & \exists E' .\ \langle s,E\rangle \mathbin{\overline{\Downarrow}} E' \end{array}$$

The *timed* versions $\Downarrow_n$ and $\overline{\Downarrow}_n$ of $\Downarrow$ and $\overline{\Downarrow}$ are defined in the expected way.

The relation $\langle s,E\rangle \Downarrow \langle s',E'\rangle$ defines the overall effect of the program s within an instant, starting with the set of events E. Indeed, $\Downarrow$ may be viewed as defining the *big-step semantics* of programs within an instant[2]. As an immediate corollary of Proposition 1, the relation $\Downarrow$ is a function.

In the next section we prove that every configuration $\langle s,E\rangle$ instantaneously converges. This property is called *reactivity*.

4 Reactivity

In this section we present our first main result, the reactivity of *CRL* programs. In fact, we shall prove a stronger property than reactivity, namely that every configuration $\langle s,E\rangle$ instantaneously converges in a number of steps which is bounded by the *instantaneous size* of s, denoted by $size(s)$. The intuition for $size(s)$ is that the portion of s that sequentially follows a `cooperate` instruction should not be taken into account, as it will not be executed in the current instant. Moreover, if s is a loop, $size(s)$ should cover a single iteration of its body.

To formally define the function $size(s)$, we first introduce an auxiliary function $dsize(s)$ (where"d" stands for "decorated") that assigns to each program an element of (**Nat** × **Bool**). Then $size(s)$ will be the first projection of $dsize(s)$. Intuitively, if $dsize(s) = (n,b)$, then n is an upper bound for the number of steps that s can execute within an instant; and b is *tt* or *ff* depending on whether or not a `cooperate` instruction is reached within the instant. For conciseness, we let $n^\wedge$ stand for (n, tt), n stand for $(n, f\!f)$, and n° range over $\{n^\wedge, n\}$.

The difference between $n^\wedge$ and n will essentially show when computing the size of a sequential composition: if the decorated size of the first component has the form $n^\wedge$, then a `cooperate` has been met and the counting will stop; if it has the form n, then n will be added to the decorated size of the second component.

Definition 3 (Instantaneous size).
The function size : Programs $\rightarrow$ **Nat** *is defined by:*

$$size(s) = n \quad \textit{if} \quad (dsize(s) = n \ \vee\ dsize(s) = n^\wedge)$$

[2] A direct definition of the big-step arrow $\Downarrow$ by a set of structural rules would be slightly more involved, as it would require calculating the output set E' as a fixpoint.

where the function dsize : *Programs* $\rightarrow$ (**Nat** $\times$ **Bool**) *is given inductively by:*

$$dsize(\texttt{nothing}) = 0 \qquad dsize(\texttt{cooperate}) = 0^{\wedge}$$
$$dsize(\texttt{generate}\ ev) = dsize(\texttt{await}\ ev) = 1$$
$$dsize(s_1; s_2) = \begin{cases} {n_1}^{\wedge} & \textit{if } dsize(s_1) = {n_1}^{\wedge} \\ (1 + n_1 + n_2)^{\circ} & \textit{if } dsize(s_1) = n_1 \ \wedge \ dsize(s_2) = {n_2}^{\circ} \end{cases}$$

$$dsize(s_1 \dagger s_2) = \begin{cases} (1 + n_1 + n_2)^{\wedge} & \textit{if } dsize(s_1) = {n_1}^{\wedge} \ \wedge \ dsize(s_2) = n_2 \\ (1 + n_1 + n_2)^{\wedge} & \textit{if } dsize(s_1) = n_1 \ \wedge \ dsize(s_2) = {n_2}^{\wedge} \\ (1 + n_1 + n_2)^{\circ} & \textit{if } dsize(s_1) = {n_1}^{\circ} \ \wedge \ dsize(s_2) = {n_2}^{\circ} \end{cases}$$

$$dsize(\texttt{repeat}\ exp\ \texttt{do}\ s) = (m + (m \times n))^{\circ} \qquad \textit{if } dsize(s) = n^{\circ} \ \wedge \ exp \rightsquigarrow m$$
$$dsize(\texttt{loop}\ s) = (2 + n)^{\wedge} \qquad \textit{if } \ dsize(s) = n^{\circ}$$
$$dsize(\texttt{do}\ s\ \texttt{watching}\ ev) = (1 + n)^{\circ} \quad \textit{if } dsize(s) = n^{\circ}$$
$$dsize(\texttt{if}\ exp\ \texttt{then}\ s_1\ \texttt{else}\ s_2) = \begin{cases} (1 + max\{n_1, n_2\})^{\wedge}, \textit{if } dsize(s_i) = {n_i}^{\wedge}, \\ (1 + max\{n_1, n_2\}), \textit{if for } \ i \neq j \\ \qquad\qquad dsize(s_i) = n_i \ \wedge \ dsize(s_j) = {n_j}^{\circ} \end{cases}$$

The following lemma establishes that $size(s)$ decreases at each step of a small-step execution:

Lemma 1 (Size reduction within an instant).

$$\forall s \, \forall E \quad (\langle s, E \rangle \rightarrow \langle s', E' \rangle \ \Rightarrow \ size(s') < size(s))$$

The proof of this result is not entirely straightforward because of the use of the decorated size *dsize* in the definition of $size(s)$. The proof may be found in [5].

We are now ready to prove our main result, namely that every program s instantaneously converges in a number of steps that is bounded by $size(s)$.

Theorem 1 (Reactivity). $\forall s, \forall E \quad (\exists n \leq size(s) \ \ \langle s, E \rangle \Downarrow_n)$

The proof proceeds by simultaneous induction on the structure and on the size of s. Induction on the size is needed for the case $s = s_1 \dagger s_2$. The detailed proof may be found in [5].

5 Fine-Grained and Coarse-Grained Bisimilarity

We now introduce two bisimulation equivalences (aka *bisimilarities*) on programs, which differ for the granularity of the underlying notion of observation. The first bisimulation formalises a *fine-grained observation* of programs: the observer is viewed as a program, which is able to interact with the observed program at any point of its execution. The second reflects a *coarse-grained observation* of programs: here the observer is viewed as part of the environment, which interacts with the observed program only at the start and the end of instants.

Let us start with an informal description of the two bisimilarities:

1. *Fine-grained bisimilarity* $\approx^{fg}$. In the bisimulation game, each small step must be simulated by a (possibly empty) sequence of small steps, and each instant change must be simulated either by an instant change, in case the continuation is observable (in the sense that it affects the event environment), or by an unobservable behaviour otherwise.
2. *Coarse-grained bisimilarity* $\approx^{cg}$. Here, each converging sequence of steps must be simulated by a converging sequence of steps, at each instant. For instant changes, the requirement is the same as for fine-grained bisimulation.

As may be expected, the latter equivalence is more abstract than the former, as it only compares the I/O behaviours of programs (as functions on sets of events) at each instant, while the former also compares their intermediate results.

Let us move now to the formal definitions of the equivalences $\approx^{fg}$ and $\approx^{cg}$. We first extend the reconditioning function to the program `nothing` as follows:

Notation. $\llcorner s \lrcorner_E \stackrel{\text{def}}{=} \begin{cases} [s]_E & \text{if } \langle s, E\rangle\ddagger \\ s & \text{if } s = \texttt{nothing} \end{cases}$

Definition 4 (Fine-grained bisimulation).
A symmetric relation $\mathcal{R}$ *on programs is a* fg-bisimulation *if* $s_1 \,\mathcal{R}\, s_2$ *implies, for any* $E \subseteq$ *Events:*

$$\begin{array}{l} 1)\ \langle s_1, E\rangle \rightarrow \langle s_1', E'\rangle \;\Rightarrow\; \exists\, s_2' \,.\, (\,\langle s_2, E\rangle \Rightarrow \langle s_2', E'\rangle \;\wedge\; s_1' \,\mathcal{R}\, s_2'\,) \\ 2)\ \langle s_1, E\rangle\ddagger \;\Rightarrow\; \exists\, s_2' \,.\, (\,\langle s_2, E\rangle \Downarrow \langle s_2', E\rangle \;\wedge\; \llcorner s_1 \lrcorner_E \,\mathcal{R}\, \llcorner s_2' \lrcorner_E\,) \end{array}$$

Then s_1, s_2 *are* fg-bisimilar, $s_1 \approx^{fg} s_2$, *if* $s_1 \,\mathcal{R}\, s_2$ *for some fg-bisimulation* $\mathcal{R}$.

The bisimilarity $\approx^{fg}$ is *weak*, in the terminology of process calculi, since it allows a single small step to be simulated by a (possibly empty) sequence of small steps. In the terminology of language-based security, an equivalence that abstracts away from the number of steps, thus allowing internal moves to be ignored, is called *time-insensitive.* Typically we have:

$$\texttt{nothing}\,;\,\texttt{generate}\; ev \quad \approx^{fg} \quad \texttt{generate}\; ev$$

$$\texttt{if}\; tt\; \texttt{then}\; s_1\; \texttt{else}\; s_2 \quad \approx^{fg} \quad s_1$$

The equivalence $\approx^{fg}$ is also *termination-insensitive*, as it cannot distinguish proper termination from suspension nor from internal divergence (recall that no divergence is possible within an instant and thus the execution of a diverging program always spans over an infinity of instants). For instance we have:

$$\texttt{nothing} \quad \approx^{fg} \quad \texttt{cooperate} \quad \approx^{fg} \quad \texttt{loop}\,\texttt{nothing}$$

Indeed, for any E the suspended behaviour $\langle \texttt{cooperate}, E\rangle\ddagger$ of the middle program can be simulated by the empty computation $\langle \texttt{nothing}, E\rangle \Downarrow \langle \texttt{nothing}, E\rangle$ of the left-hand program and by the two-step computation $\langle \texttt{loop}\,\texttt{nothing}, E\rangle \rightarrow$

$\langle(\texttt{nothing} \dagger \texttt{cooperate}) ; \texttt{loop nothing}, E\rangle \rightarrow \langle\texttt{cooperate} ; \texttt{loop nothing}, E\rangle\ddagger$ of the right-hand program, since $\llcorner\texttt{cooperate}\lrcorner_E = \texttt{nothing} = \llcorner\texttt{nothing}\lrcorner_E$, and $\llcorner\texttt{cooperate} ; \texttt{loop nothing}\lrcorner_E = \texttt{loop nothing}$.

The last example shows that, while it weakly preserves small-step transitions, $\approx^{fg}$ does *not* preserve tick transitions. On the other hand, it detects the instant in which events are generated. In other words, it is sensitive to the *clock-stamp* of events. For instance, we have:

$$\texttt{nothing} ; \texttt{generate}\ ev \not\approx^{fg} \texttt{cooperate} ; \texttt{generate}\ ev$$

because in the left-hand program ev is generated in the first instant, while in the right-hand program it is generated in the second instant. Incidentally, this example shows that $\approx^{fg}$ is not preserved by sequential composition (as was to be expected given that $\approx^{fg}$ is termination-insensitive).

On the other hand, we conjecture that $\approx^{fg}$ is *compositional*, that is, preserved by parallel composition, because in the bisimulation game the quantification on the event environment is renewed at each step, thus mimicking the generation of events by a parallel component.

Finally, $\approx^{fg}$ is sensitive to the order of generation of events and to repeated emissions of the same event ("stuttering"). Typical examples are:

$$(\texttt{generate}\ ev_1 \dagger \texttt{generate}\ ev_2) \quad \not\approx^{fg} \quad (\texttt{generate}\ ev_2 \dagger \texttt{generate}\ ev_1)$$

$$\texttt{generate}\ ev \quad \not\approx^{fg} \quad (\texttt{generate}\ ev ; \texttt{generate}\ ev)$$

In the last example, note that after generating the first event ev the right-hand program may be launched again in the event environment $E = \emptyset$, producing once more $E' = \{ev\}$. This cannot be mimicked by the left-hand program.

Definition 5 (Coarse-grained bisimulation).
A symmetric relation $\mathcal{R}$ on programs is a cg-bisimulation *if $s_1 \mathcal{R} s_2$ implies, for any $E \subseteq Events$:*

$$\langle s_1, E\rangle \Downarrow \langle s_1', E'\rangle \;\Rightarrow\; \exists\, s_2' . \,(\langle s_2, E\rangle \Downarrow \langle s_2', E'\rangle \;\wedge\; \llcorner s_1'\lrcorner_{E'} \,\mathcal{R}\, \llcorner s_2'\lrcorner_{E'})$$

Then s_1, s_2 are cg-bisimilar, *$s_1 \approx^{cg} s_2$, if $s_1 \mathcal{R} s_2$ for some cg-bisimulation $\mathcal{R}$.*

The bisimilarity $\approx^{cg}$ compares the overall effect of two programs at every instant. Therefore, one may argue that $\approx^{cg}$ makes full sense when coupled with reactivity. Indeed, if $\approx^{cg}$ were applied to programs that diverge within the first instant (or to programs that are bisimilar for the first k instants and diverge in the following instant), it would trivially equate all of them. In the absence of reactivity, it would seem preferable to focus on a fine-grained bisimilarity such as $\approx^{fg}$, which is able to detect intermediate results of instantaneously diverging computations.

Like $\approx^{fg}$, the bisimilarity $\approx^{cg}$ is both time-insensitive and termination-insensitive. Indeed, as will be established by Theorem 2, $\approx^{fg}$ implies $\approx^{cg}$. Moreover, $\approx^{cg}$ is *generation-order-insensitive* and *stuttering-insensitive*. Typically:

$$(\texttt{generate}\ ev_1 \nmid \texttt{generate}\ ev_2) \quad \approx^{cg} \quad (\texttt{generate}\ ev_2 \nmid \texttt{generate}\ ev_1)$$

$$\texttt{generate}\ ev \ \approx^{cg}\ (\texttt{generate}\ ev\, ;\ \texttt{generate}\ ev)$$

More generally, we can show that the equivalence $\approx^{cg}$ views the left-parallel composition $\nmid$ as a commutative operator:

Proposition 3 (Commutativity of $\nmid$ up to $\approx^{cg}$).

$$\forall s_1, s_2\,. \quad s_1 \nmid s_2 \ \approx^{cg}\ s_2 \nmid s_1$$

On the other hand, $\nmid$ is associative modulo both equivalences $\approx^{fg}$ and $\approx^{cg}$.

Proposition 4 (Associativity of $\nmid$ up to $\approx^{fg}$ and $\approx^{cg}$).

$$\forall s_1, s_2, s_3\,. \quad s_1 \nmid (s_2 \nmid s_3) \ \begin{matrix} \approx^{fg} \\ \approx_{cg} \end{matrix}\ (s_1 \nmid s_2) \nmid s_3$$

Let us recall that the asymmetric parallel operator $\Lsh$ of [2] was not associative up to fine-grained semantics (a simple example was given in [2]).

We show now that $\approx^{fg}$ is strictly included in $\approx^{cg}$ (the strictness of the inclusion being witnessed by the examples given above):

Theorem 2 (Relation between the bisimilarities).

$$\approx^{fg} \subset \approx^{cg}$$

Proof To prove $\approx^{fg} \subseteq \approx^{cg}$, it is enough to show that $\approx^{fg}$ is a cg-bisimulation. Let $s_1 \approx^{fg} s_2$. Suppose that $\langle s_1, E\rangle \Downarrow \langle s_1', E'\rangle$. This means that there exists $n \geq 0$ such that:

$$\langle s_1, E\rangle = \langle s_1^0, E^0\rangle \rightarrow \langle s_1^1, E^1\rangle \rightarrow \cdots \rightarrow \langle s_1^n, E^n\rangle = \langle s_1', E'\rangle \underset{\curlyvee}{\ddagger}$$

Since $s_1 \approx^{fg} s_2$, by Clauses 1 and 2 of Definition 4 we have correspondingly:

$$\langle s_2, E\rangle = \langle s_2^0, E^0\rangle \Rightarrow \langle s_2^1, E^1\rangle \Rightarrow \cdots \Rightarrow \langle s_2^n, E^n\rangle \Downarrow \langle s_2', E'\rangle \qquad (*)$$

where $s_1^i \approx^{fg} s_2^i$ for every $i < n$ and $\llcorner s_1' \lrcorner_{E'} \approx^{fg} \llcorner s_2' \lrcorner_{E'}$. Then we may conclude since $(*)$ can be rewritten as $\langle s_2, E\rangle \Downarrow \langle s_2', E'\rangle$.

Coarse-grained bisimilarity is very close to the semantic equivalence proposed by Amadio in [4] for a slightly different reactive language, equipped with a classical nondeterministic parallel operator. By contrast, the noninterference notion of [2] was based on a fine-grained bisimilarity (although bisimilarity was not explicitly introduced in [2], it was *de facto* used to define noninterference) which, however, was stronger than $\approx^{fg}$, since it acted as a strong bisimulation on programs with an observable behaviour (i.e. affecting the event environment).

As argued previously, coarse-grained bisimilarity is a natural equivalence to adopt when reactivity is guaranteed. It allows one to recover the flavour of big-step semantics within instants. On the other hand, fine-grained bisimilarity seems a better choice when reactivity is not granted. Note that reactivity was not a concern in either [2] or [4]. Nevertheless, it had been thoroughly studied in previous work by Amadio et al. [3].

Finally, it should be noted that, since our left-parallel composition operator $\nmid$ is deterministic, we could as well have used trace-based equivalences rather than bisimulation-based ones. However, defining traces is not entirely obvious for computations proceeding through instants, as it requires annotating with clock-stamps the events or event sets that compose a trace (depending on whether the trace is fine-grained or coarse-grained). Moreover, bisimulation provides a convenient means for defining noninterference in our concurrent setting, allowing the notion of clock-stamp to remain implicit. Lastly, as we aim to extend our study to a fully-fledged distributed reactive language, including a notion of site and asynchronous parallelism between sites, for which determinism would not hold anymore, we chose to adopt bisimulation-based equivalences from the start.

This concludes our discussion on semantic equivalences. We turn now to the definition of noninterference, which is grounded on that of bisimulation.

6 Security Property

In this section we define two noninterference properties for programs, which are based on the two bisimilarities introduced in Sect. 5. As usual when dealing with secure information flow, we assume a finite lattice $(\mathcal{S}, \leq)$ of *security levels*, ranged over by τ, σ, ϑ. We denote by $\sqcup$ and $\sqcap$ the join and meet operations on the lattice, and by $\bot$ and $\top$ its minimal and maximal elements.

In *CRL*, the objects that are assigned a security level are events and variables. An *observer* is identified with a downward-closed set of security levels (for short, a dc-set), i.e. a set $\mathcal{L} \subseteq \mathcal{S}$ satisfying the property: $(\tau \in \mathcal{L} \wedge \tau' \leq \tau) \Rightarrow \tau' \in \mathcal{L}$.

A type environment Γ is a mapping from variables and events to their types, which are just security levels τ, σ. Given a dc-set $\mathcal{L}$, a type environment Γ and an event environment E, the subset of E to which Γ assigns security levels in $\mathcal{L}$ is called the *$\mathcal{L}$-part* of E under Γ. Similarly, if $V : \mathit{Var} \rightarrow \mathit{Val}$ is a valuation, the subset of V whose domain is given levels in $\mathcal{L}$ by Γ is the *$\mathcal{L}$-part* of V under Γ.

Two event environments E_1, E_2 or two valuations V_1, V_2 are $=^{\Gamma}_{\mathcal{L}}$-equal, or indistinguishable by a $\mathcal{L}$-observer, if their $\mathcal{L}$-parts under Γ coincide:

Definition 6 ($\Gamma\mathcal{L}$-equality of event environments and valuations). *Let $\mathcal{L} \subseteq \mathcal{S}$ be a dc-set, Γ a type environment and V a valuation. Define:*

$$E_1 =^{\Gamma}_{\mathcal{L}} E_2 \;\; \text{if} \;\; \forall ev \in \mathit{Events} \;\; (\,\Gamma(ev) \in \mathcal{L} \;\Rightarrow\; (\,ev \in E_1 \Leftrightarrow ev \in E_2\,)\,)$$
$$V_1 =^{\Gamma}_{\mathcal{L}} V_2 \;\; \text{if} \;\; \forall x \in \mathit{Var} \;\; (\,\Gamma(x) \in \mathcal{L} \;\Rightarrow\; V_1(x) = V_2(x)\,)$$

Let $\rightarrow_V, \Rightarrow_V, \Downarrow_V$ denote our various semantic arrows under the valuation V. Then we may define the indistinguishability of two programs by a fine-grained or coarse-grained $\mathcal{L}$-observer, for a given Γ, by means of the following two notions of $\Gamma\mathcal{L}$-bisimilarity:

Definition 7 (Fine-grained $\Gamma\mathcal{L}$-bisimilarity).
A relation $\mathcal{R}$ on programs is a fg-$\Gamma\mathcal{L}$-V_1V_2-bisimulation *if $s_1 \mathcal{R} s_2$ implies, for any E_1, E_2 such that $E_1 =^{\Gamma}_{\mathcal{L}} E_2$:*

$$(1)\ \langle s_1, E_1\rangle \rightarrow_{V_1} \langle s_1', E_1'\rangle \Rightarrow \exists s_2', E_2' . (\langle s_2, E_2\rangle \Rightarrow_{V_2} \langle s_2', E_2'\rangle \wedge E_1' =^{\Gamma}_{\mathcal{L}} E_2' \wedge s_1' \mathcal{R} s_2')$$
$$(2)\ \langle s_1, E_1\rangle\ddagger \Rightarrow \exists s_2', E_2' . (\langle s_2, E_2\rangle \Downarrow_{V_2} \langle s_2', E_2'\rangle \wedge E_1 =^{\Gamma}_{\mathcal{L}} E_2' \wedge \llcorner s_1 \lrcorner_{E_1} \mathcal{R} \llcorner s_2' \lrcorner_{E_2'})$$
(3) and (4) : *Symmetric to* (1) *and* (2) *for* $\langle s_2, E_2\rangle$ *under valuation* V_2.

Then programs s_1, s_2 are fg-$\Gamma\mathcal{L}$-bisimilar, $s_1 \approx^{fg}_{\Gamma\mathcal{L}} s_2$, *if for any V_1, V_2 such that $V_1 =^{\Gamma}_{\mathcal{L}} V_2$, $s_1 \mathcal{R} s_2$ for some* fg-$\Gamma\mathcal{L}$-V_1V_2-bisimulation $\mathcal{R}$.

The *fg-$\Gamma\mathcal{L}$*-bisimilarity weakly preserves small-step transitions and convergence, while maintaining the $\Gamma\mathcal{L}$-equality on event environments. Note that, while in the definition of *fg*-bisimilarity it was possible to leave the valuation implicit, we need to make it explicit in the definition of *fg-$\Gamma\mathcal{L}$*-bisimilarity, as variables have security levels and are allowed to have different values if their level is not in $\mathcal{L}$. The reason why a *fg-$\Gamma\mathcal{L}$-V_1V_2*-bisimulation is parameterised on two valuations V_1 and V_2, and the quantification on valuations in $\approx^{fg}_{\Gamma\mathcal{L}}$ is only performed at the beginning of the bisimulation game, rather than at each step as for event environments, is that programs have no means to change the valuation. In a more expressive language where the valuation could change, it would be necessary to include the valuation in the environment that is quantified at each step.

Definition 8 (Coarse-grained $\Gamma\mathcal{L}$-bisimilarity).
A relation $\mathcal{R}$ on programs is a cg-$\Gamma\mathcal{L}$-V_1V_2-bisimulation *if $s_1 \mathcal{R} s_2$ implies, for any E_1, E_2 such that $E_1 =^{\Gamma}_{\mathcal{L}} E_2$:*
$$(1)\ \langle s_1, E_1\rangle \Downarrow_{V_1} \langle s_1', E_1'\rangle \Rightarrow \exists s_2', E_2' . (\ \langle s_2, E_2\rangle \Downarrow_{V_2} \langle s_2', E_2'\rangle \wedge E_1' =^{\Gamma}_{\mathcal{L}} E_2' \wedge \llcorner s_1' \lrcorner_{E_1'}\ \mathcal{R}\ \llcorner s_2' \lrcorner_{E_2'}\ )$$
(2) *Symmetric to* 1) *for* $\langle s_2, E_2\rangle$ *under valuation* V_2.
Two programs s_1, s_2 are cg-$\Gamma\mathcal{L}$-bisimilar, $s_1 \approx^{cg}_{\Gamma\mathcal{L}} s_2$, *if for any V_1, V_2 such that $V_1 =^{\Gamma}_{\mathcal{L}} V_2$, $s_1 \mathcal{R} s_2$ for some* cg-$\Gamma\mathcal{L}$-V_1V_2-bisimulation $\mathcal{R}$.

Our *reactive noninterference* (RNI) properties are now defined as follows:

Definition 9 (Fine-grained and Coarse-grained RNI).
A program s is fg-secure in Γ if $s \approx^{fg}_{\Gamma\mathcal{L}} s$ for every dc-set $\mathcal{L}$.
A program s is cg-secure in Γ if $s \approx^{cg}_{\Gamma\mathcal{L}} s$ for every dc-set $\mathcal{L}$.

The following example, where the superscripts indicate the security levels of variables and events, illustrates the difference between *fg*-security and *cg*-security.

Example 1. The following program is *cg*-secure but not *fg*-secure:

$$s = \texttt{if}\ x^{\top} = 0\ \texttt{then generate}\ ev_1^{\perp} \nmid \texttt{generate}\ ev_2^{\perp}$$
$$\texttt{else generate}\ ev_2^{\perp} \nmid \texttt{generate}\ ev_1^{\perp}$$

If we replace the second branch of s by **generate** $ev_1^{\perp}$; **generate** $ev_2^{\perp}$, then we obtain a program s' that is both *fg*-secure and *cg*-secure.

In general, from all the equivalences/inequivalences in page 11 we may obtain secure/insecure programs for the corresponding RNI property by plugging the two equivalent/inequivalent programs in the branches of a high conditional.

As expected, fine-grained security is stronger than coarse-grained security:

Theorem 3 (Relation between the RNI properties).

$$Let s \in Programs. \ If\ s\ is\ fg-secure\ then\ s\ is\ cg-secure.$$

Proof. The proof consists in showing that for any Γ and $\mathcal{L}$, we have $\approx^{fg}_{\Gamma\mathcal{L}} \subseteq \approx^{cg}_{\Gamma\mathcal{L}}$. To this end, it is enough to show that for any pair of valuations V_1 and V_2, any fg-$\Gamma\mathcal{L}$-V_1V_2-bisimulation $\mathcal{R}$ is also a cg-$\Gamma\mathcal{L}$-V_1V_2-bisimulation. The reasoning closely follows that of Theorem 2 and is therefore omitted.

We conclude this section with an informal discussion about *scheduling leaks*. We speak of scheduling leak when the position of the scheduler at the start of an instant may depend on secrets tested in previous instants. We have mentioned already that, unlike the "swapping" operator ↰ of [2], our operator ∤ preserves the spatial structure of programs. As a consequence, the same parallel component is scheduled at the beginning of each instant, and the position of the scheduler is independent of any previous test. Thus the scheduling leaks arising with the operator ↰, which implied a severe constraint in the type system of [2] (the addition of the condition $\sigma_i \leq \tau_j$ in Rule (Par)), cannot occur anymore with ∤. In particular, it may be shown that the scheduling leak example given in [2] does not arise if we replace ↰ by ∤. This point is explained in detail in [5].

7 Type System

We present now our security type system for *CRL*, which is based on those introduced in [8] and [17] for a parallel while language and already adapted to a reactive language in [2]. The originality of these type systems is that they associate pairs (τ, σ) of security levels with programs, where τ is a lower bound on the level of "writes" and σ is an upper bound on the level of "reads". This allows the level of reads to be recorded, and then to be used to constrain the level of writes in the remainder of the program. In this way, it is possible to obtain a more precise treatment of *termination leaks*[3] than in standard type systems.

Recall that a type environment Γ is a mapping from variables and events to security levels τ, σ. Moreover, Γ associates a type of the form $\overrightarrow{\tau} \rightarrow \tau$ to functions, where $\overrightarrow{\tau}$ is a tuple of types $\tau_1, \ldots, \tau_n$. Type judgements for expressions and programs have the form $\Gamma \vdash exp : \tau$ and $\Gamma \vdash s : (\tau, \sigma)$ respectively.

[3] Leaks due to different termination behaviours in the branches of a conditional. In classical parallel while languages, termination leaks may also arise in while loops. This is not possible in *CRL*, given the simple form of the `loop` construct. On the other hand, new termination leaks may originate from the possibility of suspension.

The intuition for $\Gamma \vdash exp : \tau$ is that τ is an *upper bound* on the levels of variables occurring in *exp*. According to this intuition, subtyping for expressions is *covariant*. The intuition for $\Gamma \vdash s : (\tau, \sigma)$ is that τ is a *lower bound* on the levels of events generated in s (the "writes"of s), and σ is an *upper bound* on the levels of events awaited or watched in s and of variables tested in s (the "reads" or *guards* of s, formally defined in Definition 11). Accordingly, subtyping for programs is *contravariant* in its first component, and *covariant* in the second.

The typing rules for expressions and programs are presented in Fig. 2. The rules that increase the guard type are (AWAIT), (WATCHING), (REPEAT) and (COND1), and those that check it against the write type of the continuation are (SEQ), (REPEAT) and (LOOP). Note that there are two more rules for the conditional, factoring out the cases where either both branches terminate in one instant or both branches are infinite: indeed, in these cases no termination leaks can arise and thus it is not necessary to increase the guard level. In Rule (COND2), *FIN* denotes the set of programs *terminating in one instant*, namely those built without using the constructs `await` *ev*, `cooperate` and `loop`. In Rule (COND3), *INF* denotes the set of infinite or *nonterminating* programs, defined inductively as follows[4]:

- $\texttt{loop}\, s \in INF$;
- $s \in INF \Rightarrow \texttt{repeat}\, exp\, \texttt{do}\, s \in INF$;
- $s_1 \in INF \ \vee\ s_2 \in INF \Rightarrow s_1; s_2 \in INF \ \wedge\ s_1 \nmid s_2 \in INF$
- $s_1 \in INF \ \wedge\ s_2 \in INF \Rightarrow \texttt{if}\, exp\, \texttt{then}\, s_1\, \texttt{else}\, s_2 \in INF$

Note that $FIN \cup INF \subset Programs$. Examples of programs that are neither in FIN nor in INF are: `await` *ev*, `if` *exp* `then nothing else` (`loop` s), and `do` (`loop` s) `watching` *ev*.

Definition 10 (Safe conditionals).
A conditional `if` *exp* `then` s_1 `else` s_2 *is* safe *if* $s_1, s_2 \in FIN$ *or* $s_1, s_2 \in INF$.

The reason for calling such conditionals "safe" is that they cannot introduce termination leaks, since their two branches have the same termination behaviour.

Note that the two sets FIN and INF only capture two specific *termination behaviours* of CRL programs, namely termination in one instant and nontermination. We could have refined further this classification of termination behaviours. Indeed, while only two termination behaviours are possible within each instant, due to reactivity (namely, proper termination and suspension), across instants there is an infinity of possible termination behaviours for programs: termination in a finite number k of instants, for any possible k, and nontermination. In other words, we could have defined a set FIN_k for each k and replaced Rule (COND2) by a Rule Schema (CONDK). The idea would remain the same: conditionals with uniform termination behaviours need not raise their guard level. For simplicity, we chose to focus on FIN and INF, leaving the finer analysis for future work.

We now prove that typability implies security via the classical steps:

[4] Recall that in a `repeat` *exp* `do` s program, *exp* is supposed to evaluate to some $n \geq 1$.

$$(\text{VAL})\quad \Gamma \vdash v : \bot \qquad (\text{VAR})\quad \frac{\Gamma(x) = \tau}{\Gamma \vdash x : \tau} \qquad (\text{SUBEXP})\quad \frac{\Gamma \vdash exp : \sigma, \quad \sigma \leq \sigma'}{\Gamma \vdash exp : \sigma'}$$

$$(\text{FUN})\quad \frac{\Gamma \vdash \overrightarrow{exp} : \overrightarrow{\tau}, \quad \Gamma(f) = \overrightarrow{\tau} \to \tau, \quad \forall i \,.\, \tau_i \leq \tau}{\Gamma \vdash f(\overrightarrow{exp}) : \tau}$$

Typing rules for expressions

$$(\text{NOTHING})\quad \Gamma \vdash \texttt{nothing} : (\top, \bot) \qquad (\text{COOPERATE})\quad \Gamma \vdash \texttt{cooperate} : (\top, \bot)$$

$$(\text{SEQ})\quad \frac{\Gamma \vdash s_1 : (\tau_1, \sigma_1), \quad \Gamma \vdash s_2 : (\tau_2, \sigma_2), \quad \sigma_1 \leq \tau_2}{\Gamma \vdash s_1 \,;\, s_2 : (\tau_1 \sqcap \tau_2, \sigma_1 \sqcup \sigma_2)}$$

$$(\text{PAR})\quad \frac{\Gamma \vdash s_1 : (\tau_1, \sigma_1), \quad \Gamma \vdash s_2 : (\tau_2, \sigma_2)}{\Gamma \vdash s_1 \nmid s_2 : (\tau_1 \sqcap \tau_2, \sigma_1 \sqcup \sigma_2)}$$

$$(\text{GENERATE})\quad \frac{\Gamma(ev) = \tau}{\Gamma \vdash \texttt{generate}\, ev : (\tau, \bot)} \qquad (\text{AWAIT})\quad \frac{\Gamma(ev) = \sigma}{\Gamma \vdash \texttt{await}\, ev : (\top, \sigma)}$$

$$(\text{WATCHING})\quad \frac{\Gamma(ev) = \vartheta, \quad \Gamma \vdash s : (\tau, \sigma), \quad \vartheta \leq \tau}{\Gamma \vdash \texttt{do}\, s\, \texttt{watching}\, ev : (\tau, \vartheta \sqcup \sigma)}$$

$$(\text{LOOP})\quad \frac{\Gamma \vdash s : (\tau, \sigma),\ \sigma \leq \tau}{\Gamma \vdash \texttt{loop}\, s : (\tau, \sigma)} \qquad (\text{REPEAT})\quad \frac{\Gamma \vdash exp : \vartheta,\ \Gamma \vdash s : (\tau, \sigma),\ \vartheta \sqcup \sigma \leq \tau}{\Gamma \vdash \texttt{repeat}\, exp\, \texttt{do}\, s : (\tau, \vartheta \sqcup \sigma)}$$

$$(\text{COND1})\quad \frac{\Gamma \vdash exp : \vartheta, \quad \Gamma \vdash s_i : (\tau, \sigma), \quad i = 1, 2, \quad \vartheta \leq \tau}{\Gamma \vdash \texttt{if}\, exp\, \texttt{then}\, s_1\, \texttt{else}\, s_2 : (\tau, \vartheta \sqcup \sigma)}$$

$$(\text{COND2})\quad \frac{\Gamma \vdash exp : \vartheta, \quad (\Gamma \vdash s_i : (\tau, \sigma) \ \wedge \ s_i \in FIN, \ i = 1, 2), \quad \vartheta \leq \tau}{\Gamma \vdash \texttt{if}\, exp\, \texttt{then}\, s_1\, \texttt{else}\, s_2 : (\tau, \sigma)}$$

$$(\text{COND3})\quad \frac{\Gamma \vdash exp : \vartheta, \quad (\Gamma \vdash s_i : (\tau, \sigma) \ \wedge \ s_i \in INF, \ i = 1, 2), \quad \vartheta \leq \tau}{\Gamma \vdash \texttt{if}\, exp\, \texttt{then}\, s_1\, \texttt{else}\, s_2 : (\tau, \sigma)}$$

$$(\text{SUBPROG})\quad \frac{\Gamma \vdash s : (\tau, \sigma), \quad \tau' \leq \tau, \quad \sigma \leq \sigma'}{\Gamma \vdash s : (\tau', \sigma')}$$

Typing rules for programs

Fig. 2. Security type system

Lemma 2 (Subject Reduction).
Let $\Gamma \vdash s : (\tau, \sigma)$. Then $\langle s, E\rangle \rightarrow \langle s', E'\rangle$ implies $\Gamma \vdash s' : (\tau, \sigma)$, and $\langle s, E\rangle\ddagger$ implies $\Gamma \vdash [s]_E : (\tau, \sigma)$.

Definition 11 (Guards and Generated Events).
(1) For any s, $Guards(s)$ is the union of the set of events ev such that s contains an `await` *ev or a* `do` *s'* `watching` *ev instruction (for some s'), together with the set of variables x that occur in s as argument of a function or in the control expression exp of an instruction* `repeat` *exp* `do` *s' or of an* unsafe *conditional* `if` *exp* `then` *s_1* `else` *s_2 in s.*

(2) For any s, $Gen(s)$ is the set of events ev such that `generate` *ev occurs in s.*

The following Lemma establishes that if $\Gamma \vdash s : (\tau, \sigma)$, then τ is a *lower bound* on the levels of events in $Gen(s)$ and σ is an *upper bound* on the levels of events and variables in $Guards(s)$.

Lemma 3 (Guard Safety and Confinement).

1. *If $\Gamma \vdash s : (\tau, \sigma)$ then $\Gamma(g) \leq \sigma$ for every $g \in Guards(s)$;*
2. *If $\Gamma \vdash s : (\tau, \sigma)$ then $\tau \leq \Gamma(ev)$ for every $ev \in Gen(s)$.*

We now state the main result of this section, namely the soundness of the type system for fine-grained reactive noninterference (and thus, by Theorem 3, also for coarse-grained reactive noninterference). The proof involves some additional definitions and preliminary results, which are not given here but reported in [5].

Theorem 4 (Typability $\Rightarrow$ Fine-grained RNI).
Let $s \in Programs$. If s is typable in Γ then s is fg-secure in Γ.

Note that programs s, s' of Example 1 are not typable (although *cg*-secure).

Example 2. The following programs are not typable and not secure, for any of the two security properties:

`await` $ev_1^\top$; `generate` $ev_2^\bot$
`loop` (`generate` $ev_2^\bot$; `await` $ev_1^\top$)
`repeat` $x^\top$ `do generate` $ev^\bot$
(`repeat` $x^\top$ `do cooperate`) ; `generate` $ev^\bot$
`do` (`cooperate` ; `generate` $ev_2^\bot$) `watching` $ev_1^\top$

The insecure flows in the first two programs are *termination leaks*, due to the possibility of suspension. The second program illustrates the need for the condition $\sigma \leq \tau$ in Rule (Loop) (to produce a similar example with `repeat` we need at least three security levels). The fourth program shows why the guard level of `repeat` should be raised in Rule (Repeat).

We conclude with some examples illustrating the use of the conditional rules.

Example 3. The following programs s_i and s are all typable, with the given type:

$s_1 = \texttt{if}\ (x^\top = 0)\ \texttt{then await}\ ev_1^\top\ \texttt{else cooperate}$ type $(\top, \top)$
$s_2 = \texttt{if}\ (x^\top = 0)\ \texttt{then nothing else generate}\ ev^\top$ type $(\top, \bot)$
$s_3 = \texttt{if}\ (x^\top = 0)\ \texttt{then nothing else (loop nothing)}$ type $(\top, \top)$
$s_4 = \texttt{if}\ (x^\top = 0)\ \texttt{then (loop nothing) else (loop cooperate)}$ type $(\top, \bot)$
$s = \texttt{generate}\ ev_2^\bot$ type $(\bot, \bot)$

Indeed, for all programs s_i the first component of the type (the write type) must be $\top$ because each of the Rules (Cond1) (Cond2) and (Cond3) prevents a "level drop" from the tested expression to the branches of the conditional, as in classical security type systems. On the other hand, the second component of the type (the guard type) will be $\bot$ for the safe conditionals s_2 and s_4, typed respectively using Rules (Cond2) and (Cond3), and $\top$ for the unsafe conditionals s_1 and s_3, typed using Rule (Cond1).

Then $s_2; s$ and $s_4; s$ are typable but not $s_1; s$ nor $s_3; s$.

8 Conclusion and Related Work

We have studied a core reactive language *CRL* and established a reactivity result for it, similar to those of [3,10] but based on different design choices. We also provided a syntactic bound for the length of the converging sequences.

We then proposed two RNI properties for the language, together with a security type system ensuring them. Our RNI properties rely on two bisimulation equivalences of different granularity. One of them, coarse-grained bisimilarity, is reminiscent of the semantic equivalence studied by Amadio in [4], which however was based on trace semantics. Our RNI properties also bear some analogy with the notions of *reactive noninterference* proposed in [7], and particularly with the termination-insensitive notion of ID-security (see also [15]), although the underlying assumptions of the model are quite different.

The model of cooperative threads of [1] is close in spirit to the model of *CRL*, but it is not concerned with synchronous parallelism. We should stress here that, to be appropriate for the study of a global computing setting, our synchronous model is intended to be part of a more general GALS model (Globally Asynchronous, Locally Synchronous), where various "synchronous areas" coexist and evolve in parallel, interacting with each other in an asynchronous way.

The idea of "slowing down" loops by forcing them to yield the control at each iteration, which is crucial for our reactivity result, was already used in [10] for a similar purpose. A similar instrumentation of loops was proposed in [14]. However, while in our work and in [10] a `cooperate` instruction is added *in parallel* with each iteration of the body of the loop, in [14] it is added *after* each iteration of the body. In a language that allows a parallel program to be followed in sequence by another program (which is not the case in [14]), our solution is more efficient in that it avoids introducing an additional suspension in case the body of the loop already contains one.

As regards future work, we expect some of our results - determinism, reactivity - to carry over smoothly to CRL extended with memory. However, some other properties like the commutativity of $\nmid$ will not hold anymore in such setting, at least if the memory is freely shared among threads. Nevertheless, our bisimilarities and security properties would continue to make sense in such extended language. In the longer run, we plan to extend our study to a fully-fledged distributed reactive language, where programs are executed on different sites and may migrate from one site to the other. In this setting, execution would still be synchronous and reactive within each site (each site would be a "synchronous area" within a GALS model), but it would be asynchronous among different sites. A migrating thread would be integrated in the destination site only when this would become ready to react to its environment (whence the importance of local reactivity in each site). In a more expressive language with I/O blocking operations or other forms of abnormal termination, the enforcement of the reactivity property as well as the treatment of termination channels is likely to become more complex (although the time-out mechanism provided by the watching statement could be of some help here).

Acknowledgments. We thank Frédéric Boussinot for insightful discussions and feedback, and Bernard Serpette for useful comments on a previous version of this paper. We also thank the anonymous referees for helpful remarks and suggestions.

References

1. Abadi, M., Plotkin, G.: A model of cooperative threads. In: Proceedings POPL 2009, pp. 29–40. ACM Press (2009)
2. Almeida Matos, A., Boudol, G., Castellani, I.: Typing noninterference for reactive programs. J. Logic Algebraic Program. **72**(2), 124–156 (2007)
3. Amadio, R.M., Dabrowski, F.: Feasible reactivity for synchronous cooperative threads. Electron. Notes Theoret. Comput. Sci. **154**(3), 33–43 (2006)
4. Amadio, R.M.: The SL synchronous language, revisited. J. Logic Algebraic Program. **70**(2), 121–150 (2007)
5. Attar, P., Castellani, I.: Fine-grained and coarse-grained reactive noninterference. INRIA Research Report (2013)
6. Berry, G., Gonthier, G.: The ESTEREL synchronous programming language: design, semantics, implementation. Sci. Comput. Program. **19**(2), 87–152 (1992)
7. Bohannon, A., Pierce, B. C., Sjöberg, V., Weirich, S., Zdancewic, S.: Reactive noninterference. In: Proceedings of the 16th ACM conference on Computer and communications security, pp. 79–90. ACM (2009)
8. Boudol, G., Castellani, I.: Noninterference for concurrent programs and thread systems. Theor. Comput. Sci. **281**(1), 109–130 (2002)
9. Boussinot, F., de Simone, R.: The SL synchronous language. Soft. Eng. **22**(4), 256–266 (1996)
10. Boussinot, F., Susini, J.F.: The SugarCubes tool box: a reactive Java framework. Sof. Pract. Experience **28**(14), 1531–1550 (1998)
11. Focardi, R., Gorrieri, R.: Classification of security properties. In: Focardi, R., Gorrieri, R. (eds.) FOSAD 2000. LNCS, vol. 2171, pp. 331–396. Springer, Heidelberg (2001)

12. Goguen, J. A., Meseguer, J.: Security policies and security models. In: Proceedings 1982 IEEE Symposium on Security and Privacy, pp. 11–20 (1982)
13. Goguen, J. A., Meseguer, J.: Unwinding and inference control. In: Proceedings 1984 IEEE Symposium on Security and Privacy (1984)
14. Russo, A., Sabelfeld, A.: Security for multithreaded programs under cooperative scheduling. In: Virbitskaite, I., Voronkov, A. (eds.) PSI 2006. LNCS, vol. 4378, pp. 474–480. Springer, Heidelberg (2007)
15. Russo, A., Zanarini, D., Jaskelioff, M.: Precise enforcement of confidentiality for reactive systems. In: Proceedings of the 26th IEEE Computer Security Foundations Symposium. IEEE (2013)
16. Sabelfeld, A., Myers, A.C.: Language-based information-flow security. IEEE J. Sel. Areas Commun. **21**(1), 5–19 (2003)
17. Smith, G.: A new type system for secure information flow. In: Proceedings of the 14th IEEE Computer Security Foundations Workshop. IEEE (2001)
18. Volpano, D., Smith, G., Irvine, C.: A sound type system for secure flow analysis. J. Comput. Secur. **4**(3), 167–187 (1996)

Information Flow Analysis for Valued-Indexed Data Security Compartments

Luísa Lourenço(✉) and Luís Caires

CITI e Departamento de Informática, Faculdade de Ciências e Tecnologia,
Universidade Nova de Lisboa, Lisboa, Portugal
kikentai@gmail.com, luis.caires@fct.unl.pt

Abstract. Data-intensive applications as popularised by cloud computing raise many security challenges, due to the large number of remote users involved and multi-tenancy. Frequently, the security compartment associated to data stored in shared containers, such as database tables, is not determined by the static structure of the database schema, but depends on runtime data values, as required to ensure so-called "row-level" security. In this paper, we investigate a programming language approach to these issues, based on a λ-calculus extended with data manipulation primitives. We develop a type-based information flow analysis introducing a notion of value-indexed security labels, representing value-indexed security levels, or compartments. Our results ensure that well-typed programs do not break confidentiality constraints imposed by a declared security discipline.

1 Introduction

Data-centricl applications have become a key component of IT infrastructures and, more recently, in the average user's daily tasks, due both to the internet's popularity and to the proliferation of cloud computing infrastructures on which most of these applications rely on nowadays. Unfortunately, such infrastructures, often based in relational database backends, do not provide enough support for the security requirements posed by such application scenarios. For instance, an app may inadvertently execute a query to extract sensitive information from the database and then insert that data in a table any user may read from, thus creating an insecure information flow, violating confidentiality. Such operation, however, may be deemed secure in a security model simply based on access control: a principal may have enough privileges to read the information and since the second table is public, he also has enough permissions to insert data there. To prevent such insecure flows, one may, at least in principle, apply to the application's code and database interface languages some form of information flow analysis[12, 15, 31].

However, data centric systems pose specific challenges on how to ensure confidentiality and integrity in the presence of multi-tenancy and container sharing. A key issue is that security compartments are not simply attached to the static

M. Abadi and A. Lluch Lafuente (Eds.): TGC 2013, LNCS 8358, pp. 180–198, 2014.
DOI: 10.1007/978-3-319-05119-2_11,

structure of the database schema, but are actually dynamic and dependent on runtime data, inducing so-called "row-level" security. For a typical example, consider within a social network app a database table holding for each user the list of her private photos. We would like to consider that the security level of the whole table is (say) `photos`, but that the security level of each row is `photos(id)`, where *id* is the actual userid value registered on it. Assuming that different userids give rise to incomparable security levels `photos(id)`, in the security lattice, we would then like to ensure that the app may never transfer private photos from one user to another, even if all photos are stored in the same database structure. A valued indexed security label such as `photos(id)` denotes a potential security compartment for each concrete `id` index value. Notice that since such indexes of security labels may be obtained by computation, or as the result of queries, they are not fixed or known at app design or construction time, and the same must be said of any indexed security label such as `photos(id)`. Nevertheless, our aim is to statically reason about information flows between the security compartments denoted by such indexed labels, so to invalidate code that break security policies. For this purpose, we introduce a type-based information flow analysis for a λ-calculus extended with a (SQL-like) data manipulation language (DML). As in classical approaches (e.g., [1,17]), both a type τ and a security label s are assigned to expressions by our typing judgment $\Delta \vdash e : \tau^{\mathsf{s}}$, reflecting the fact that the value of e will only be affected by computations interfering at security levels $\leq \mathsf{s}$. However, we are not aware of prior work exploring value-dependent security labels, as we do here. For example, $\Delta \vdash e : \tau^{\mathsf{photos(joe)}}$ states that e will not return a photo from any user other than `joe`, even if e may read a global table containing photos of all users. Value-dependency may be explicit, as in photos(joe), or implicit, captured by security-label dependent record types, useful to express row-level security.

We discuss our approach in more detail using a toy example inspired by a healthcare center software service that manages medical doctors and patients. The system requires information about doctors and patients, as well as patient's clinical records, to be stored in a database, according to the schema

```
entity Doctors(id_d, name, age, speciality) in
 entity Patients(id_p, name, age, address) in
  entity Records(id_p, date, clinical_info) in
   entity isPatientOf(id_p, id_d) in ...
```

which can be manipulated through usual SQL-like DML primitives. We are interested in statically ensuring confidentiality properties for the applications developed over this database. Suppose that data in the healthcare system is classified in three security levels `L`, `P`, and `D` where `L` represents data that can be disclosed to the general public, `P` data that patients can see, and `D` data that only doctors can observe. As expected, a partial order for these security levels would be `L<P<D`, expressing that `L` is the most permissive level and `D` the most restrictive. To describe a data security policy, we classify the database entities fields with these security levels (we omit data types for now): **`entity`** `Doctors(id_d: L, name: L, age: D, speciality: L)`, which states that a doctor's profile (represented

by a tuple in entity `Doctors`) is public except his age, that should remain secret and observable only to doctors; **entity** `Patients(id_p: L, name: P, age: P, address: P)`, stating a patient's profile is not public (except his identification number, which by itself does not disclose whose patient it belongs to), as well as his clinical record **entity** `Records(id_p: L, date: P, clinical_info: P)`, both visible to patients and to doctors (because `P<D`). A basic goal is then to guarantee that throughout the execution of any code manipulating these entities, the data stored in containers of security level `P` and `D` are not visible in a context with security level `L`, that is, this data is not made public. This may be achieved by an information flow analysis for a programming language with DML primitives, a first contribution of our work.

Yet, this basic approach is not enough to enforce the needed security policies. When we say that a patient can see his full profile we are stating something stronger than that: a patient can see *any* patient's full profile. This is clearly an undesirable limitation of the simple security label model adopted, which is not expressive enough to talk about individual tuples of an entity. In intuitive terms, the `P` security compartment needs to be partitioned (indexed) in many partitions `P(n)`, one for each patient `n`, e.g. `P(joe)`, `P(mary)`, etc, where `L<P(n) <P` for all n, and `P(m)≠P(n)` for all $n \neq m$. Now, all patient records are stored in the same data structure, the entity table Patients. To give to the table a uniform security type, we then introduce security-label dependent records, allowing us to express"row-level" security compartments:

```
entity Doctors(id_d: L, name: L, age: D(id_d), speciality: L) in
 entity Patients(id_p:L, name:P(id_p), age:P(id_p), address:P(id_p)) in
  entity Records(id_p: L, date: P(id_p), clinical_info: P(id_p)) in
   entity isPatientOf(id_p: L, id_d: L) in ...
```

In a security-label dependent record a field identifier may act as a binding occurrence for the value it might hold, and scopes over the security labels of the remaining fields. So by indexing security level `D` with the tuple's field `id_d`, we are stating that the age info of doctor with `id_d` = `house` belongs to level `D(house)`; and likewise by indexing security level `P` with a patient's identifier `id_p`, we are saying that this data is only visible to the patient (and no other patient) and, eventually, to any doctor (since `P<D`). Value dependent security labels allows us to talk about individual tuples and capture fine grained information flows. For instance, in the following code:

```
let info = first (from (x in Records)
                        where x.id_p=42 select x.clinical_info)
 in insert [id_p:42, date:today(), clinical_info:info] in Records
```

value `info` gets security level `P(42)` since we are projecting a tuple with `id_p` value `42`. This allows the insert operation to be deemed secure since we are inserting a tuple with `id_p=42`, and `clinical_info=info` and `date=today()` with security label `P(42)` (the latter by up-classification). On the other hand, if we replace the last line above by **insert** `[id_p:10, date:today(), clinical_info:info]` **in** `Records`, an insecure flow must be signalled, since data from patient `42` is being associated to patient `10`. In other words, we prevent information from patient with `id_p = 42` to be leaked to another patient's record. Such a fine grained flow analysis is possible in our runtime value indexed security label model. Notice that even if, in this example, labels are indexed by user ids, which may stand for principals, our model is completely general, as labels may be indexed by any data (for example, one may label by `secret(uid_to,uid_from)` the private message between users of identification numbers `uid_to, uid_from` in a message board). Moreover, our analysis is carried out for a higher-order language with a complete set of DML primitives, allowing stored procedures (higher-order store), and does not require runtime checks to infer the runtime values in our security labels.

The main technical contributions of our work are thus the development of a type-based information flow analysis for a λ-calculus extended with DML primitives, based on a useful notion of value-dependent (indexed) security label (Sect. 2 and Sect. 3). Our technical results include type preservation and the (key) non-interference theorem, which implies that well-typed programs do not break the confidentiality constraints imposed by the declared information flow discipline (Sect. 4). We conclude with an overview of related work (Sect. 5) and a final discussion (Sect. 6).

2 Programming Language

We carry out our development using a core programming language λ_{DB}, a typed λ-calculus with (imperative) data manipulation primitives, which we pick as a reasonable abstraction of commonly used language idioms for data centric programming [6,8,21]. The syntax of λ_{DB} language is given by the grammar in Fig. 1 where we assume an infinite set of *identifiers* (ranged over $x, y, t, \ldots$), an infinite set of *field names* (ranged over $s, n, m, \ldots$), and an infinite set of (store) *locations* (ranged over $l, l' \ldots$). We abbreviate indexed sets, in our syntax, with an overbar. So $\overline{[m:e]}$ stands for $[m_1{:}e_1, \ldots, m_n{:}e_n]$, $\overline{e}$ stands for $\{e_1, \ldots, e_n\}$, and **entity** $t(\overline{m{:}\tau^{\mathsf{s}}}\,)$ **in** e stands for **entity** $t(m_1{:}\tau_1^{\mathsf{s}_1}, \ldots, m_n{:}\tau_n^{\mathsf{s}_n})$ **in** e. Expressions in our language are identifiers, values, field access $e.m$, application $e_1(e_2)$, abstractions $\lambda(x{:}\tau_1^{\mathsf{s}_1}).e$, constant declaration, addition of an element to a list, list iteration, conditional, and primitives for data creation and manipulation. Values include booleans, unit value (), collections (lists) of values $\{v_1, \ldots, v_n\}$, records $[m_1{:}v_1, \ldots,\ m_n{:}v_n]$, and abstractions $\lambda(x{:}\tau_1^{\mathsf{s}_1}).e$. These are as expected. We assume other basic data types (integers, strings) and associated operations, such as **first**(-) and **rest**(-) for collections (but omit standard details).

The list iterator primitive computes an accumulated value from the list elements. For example, to compute the sum of all the elements in a list $c = \{v_1, \ldots, v_n\}$ of integers we could write **foreach**(c, 0,$x.y.(x + y)$). So the first expression in the list iterator primitive is the list to iterate on, and the second represents the initial value, and the third corresponds to the computation we want to perform on each iteration step. Identifiers x and y are binding occurrences and represent an element of the list and the current value of the accumulator, respectively.

$$
\begin{array}{lll}
e ::= & & \textit{(expression)} \\
 & \mid e.m & \text{(field access)} \\
 & \mid \textbf{let } x = e_1 \textbf{ in } e_2 & \text{(let)} \\
 & \mid e_1(e_2) & \text{(application)} \\
 & \mid \textbf{if } c \textbf{ then } e_1 \textbf{ else } e_2 & \text{(conditional)} \\
 & \mid [\overline{m : e}] & \text{(record)} \\
 & \mid \overline{e} & \text{(list)} \\
 & \mid e_1{::}e_2 & \text{(cons)} \\
 & \mid \textbf{foreach}(e_1, e_2, x.y.e_3) & \text{(iteration)} \\
 & \mid \textbf{entity } t\ (\overline{m : \tau^{s}}) \textbf{ in } e & \text{(entity)} \\
 & \mid \textbf{select}(t, x.c, x.e) & \text{(select)} \\
 & \mid \textbf{insert}(t, e) & \text{(insert)} \\
 & \mid \textbf{update}(t, x.e, x.c) & \text{(update)} \\
 & \mid \textbf{delete}(t, x.c) & \text{(delete)} \\
 & \mid x & \text{(identifier)} \\
 & \mid v & \text{(value)}
\end{array}
$$

$$
\begin{array}{lll}
c ::= & & \textit{(conditions)} \\
 & \mid \neg c & \text{(negation)} \\
 & \mid c_1 \vee c_2 & \text{(disjuction)} \\
 & \mid V = V & \text{(equality)} \\
 & \mid V & \text{(term)} \\
V ::= & & \textit{(terms)} \\
 & \overline{V} & \text{(list)} \\
 & \mid [\overline{m : V}] & \text{(record)} \\
 & \mid \lambda(x : \tau_1^{s_1}).e & \text{(abstraction)} \\
 & \mid \textbf{true} & \text{(true)} \\
 & \mid \textbf{false} & \text{(false)} \\
 & \mid x & \text{(identifier)} \\
 & \mid () & \text{(unit)} \\
 & \mid V.m & \text{(field access)} \\
v ::= & & \textit{(values)} \\
 & \overline{v} & \text{(list)} \\
 & \mid [\overline{m : v}] & \text{(record)} \\
 & \mid \lambda(x : \tau_1^{s_1}).e & \text{(abstraction)} \\
 & \mid \textbf{true} & \text{(true)} \\
 & \mid \textbf{false} & \text{(false)} \\
 & \mid () & \text{(unit)} \\
 & \mid l & \text{(locations)}
\end{array}
$$

Fig. 1. Syntax

In DML primitives we use the notation $x.c$ or $x.e$ to denote the condition c or body e under the entity cursor value x (which is bound in c and/or e). These primitives can be explained as follows: **entity** $t(m_1{:}\tau_1^{s_1},\ldots,m_n{:}\tau_n^{s_n})$ **in** e denotes the allocation of a new database relation named t with attributes m_1 to m_n; **select**$(t,x.c,x.e)$ denotes the projection of a set of attributes e in a relation t for which condition c holds; **insert**(t,e) denotes the insertion of a tuple denoted by expression e in the relation t; **update**$(t,x.e,x.c)$ denotes the replacement of each tuple in the relation t for which condition c holds by the tuple expressed by evaluating e, where x denotes the initial tuple value in c and e. Expression e is required to produce a tuple of the same type as the table, thus mentioning all of its fields. This does not limit the generality of the update primitive, since old values can be reused in the updated fields through x in e. Finally, **delete**$(t,x.c)$ denotes the deletion from relation t of the set of tuples for which the condition c is met.

For readability we sometimes use for DML primitives the natural concrete syntax adopted in Sect. 1. Logical conditions in syntax fragment c, used for conditionals and DML primitives, are side-effect free (pure). We distinguish a category of testable values V, used in logical conditions as terms, which denote the values v of our language plus field access and identifiers, necessary for expressing conditions in DML primitives. For decidability purposes, we assume intensional equality between lambda terms.

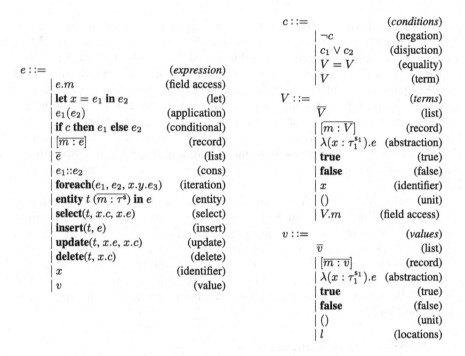

The operational semantics is defined using a reduction relation. Reduction is defined between configurations of the form $(S; e)$, where S is a store, and e is an expression. A reduction step of the form $(S; e) \longrightarrow (S'; e')$ states that expression e under state S evolves in one computational step to expression e' under state S'. Store S is a mapping from *locations* to collections of tuples, representing database tables. We provide an auxiliary definition for the evaluation of logical conditions.

Definition 1 (Conditional Expression Semantics). *The value of a closed condition c is given by the interpretation map $\mathcal{C}$:$c \rightarrow \{$***true**, **false***$\}$, as well as the auxiliary interpretation function for closed terms $\mathcal{T}$:$V \rightarrow v$ as follows:*
$\mathcal{C}[\![\neg c]\!] = \neg\mathcal{C}[\![c]\!] \qquad \mathcal{C}[\![c_1 \vee c_2]\!] = \mathcal{C}[\![c_1]\!] \vee \mathcal{C}[\![c_2]\!] \qquad \mathcal{C}[\![V_1 = V_2]\!] = (\mathcal{T}[\![V_1]\!] = \mathcal{T}[\![V_2]\!])$
$\mathcal{T}[\![\{V_1, \ldots, V_n\}]\!] = \{\mathcal{T}[\![V_1]\!], \ldots, \mathcal{T}[\![V_n]\!]\} \qquad \mathcal{T}[\![\lambda(x : \tau_1^{\mathsf{s}_1}).e]\!] = \lambda(x : \tau_1^{\mathsf{s}_1}).e$
$\mathcal{T}[\![[m_1{:}V_1, \ldots, m_n{:}V_n]]\!] = [m_1{:}\mathcal{T}[\![V_1]\!], \ldots, m_n{:}\mathcal{T}[\![V_n]\!]]$
$\mathcal{T}[\![\mathbf{true}]\!] = \mathbf{true} \qquad \mathcal{T}[\![\mathbf{false}]\!] = \mathbf{false} \qquad \mathcal{T}[\![()]\!] = ()$
$\mathcal{T}[\![V.m]\!] = \mathit{field}(\mathcal{T}[\![V]\!], m) \quad \mathit{field}([\ldots, m : v, \ldots], m) = v$

We now define our reduction relation, denoted as $(S; e) \longrightarrow (S'; e')$, as being inductively defined by the rules in Fig. 2 as well as the expected rules of a call-by-value λ-calculus for the non-DML expressions. For the complete definition see [20].

Rules in Fig. 2 capture the reductions for DML primitives. Rules (*foreach-left*) and (*foreach-right*) reduce the first and second expressions of the list iterator operator, respectively. These rules, together with rule (*foreach*), imply an evaluation order from left to right. Rule (*entity*) reduces to the continuation expression e and adds a fresh location l to the store, associating it with the empty list (empty table). Rule (*select*) states that, in order to evaluate a projection operation over entity t, we need to evaluate the logical condition c and then filter out all the rows that do not satisfy the condition. The first step is achieved by first creating a list of logical conditions, $\overline{c\{r_i/x\}}$, obtained by the substitution of all free occurrences of x in conditional expression c with each record r_i of entity t. Then, since for each conditional expression $c\{r_i/x\}$ corresponds a record r_i, the second step is achieved by creating a new list of expressions, $\overline{s}$, that will contain all records r_i for which their respective conditional expression $c\{r_i/x\}$ evaluated to `true`. Finally, we state that the projection operation **select** evaluates to a list of expressions obtained by replacing all free occurrences of x in e with the filtered records in $\overline{s}$. Rule (*insert-left*) reduces the expression in an insert operation while rule (*insert*) is applied when that expression is a record value, adding the value to the head of the list of records that represents entity t in the store. Rule (*update-init*) starts the computation of updated table contents by starting to compute the updating record $e\{r_i/x\}$ for each source record r_i such that the selecting condition $c\{r_i/x\}$ holds. Notice that the expression **updating**(l, e), where e is a collection expression, is not present in the source language and is only used in the operational semantics to express the (non-atomic) computation of the updated table contents, expressed by the collection e. When the the state **updating**(l, v) is reached, with a final updated collection, the table is updated

(*foreach-left*)
$$\frac{(S; e_1) \longrightarrow (S'; e_1')}{(S; \textbf{foreach}(e_1,\ e_2,\ x.y.e_3) \longrightarrow (S'; \textbf{foreach}(e_1',\ e_2,\ x.y.e_3))}$$

(*foreach-right*)
$$\frac{(S; e_2) \longrightarrow (S'; e_2')}{(S; \textbf{foreach}(v,\ e_2,\ x.y.e_3) \longrightarrow (S'; \textbf{foreach}(v,\ e_2',\ x.y.e_3))}$$

(*foreach*)
$$\frac{v_l = h{::}hs}{(S; \textbf{foreach}(v_l,\ v,\ x.y.e_3) \longrightarrow (S; \textbf{foreach}(hs,\ e_3\{^h/_x\}\{^v/_y\},\ x.y.e_3))}$$

(*foreach-base*)
$$(S; \textbf{foreach}(\{\},\ v,\ x.y.e_3) \longrightarrow (S; v)$$

(*entity*)
$$\frac{l \notin dom(S) \cup fn(e)}{(S; \textbf{entity}\ t\ (\overline{m : \tau^{\mathsf{s}}})\ \textbf{in}\ e) \longrightarrow (S \cup \{l \mapsto \emptyset\};\ e\{^l/_t\})}$$

(*select*)
$$\frac{S(l) = \{r_1, \ldots, r_n\} \quad \overline{s} = \{r_i \mid \mathcal{C}[\![c\{^{r_i}/_x\}]\!]\} \quad 1 \leq k \leq k' \leq n}{(S; \textbf{select}(l,\ x.c,\ x.e)) \longrightarrow (S; \{e\{^{s_k}/_x\}, \ldots, e\{^{s_{k'}}/_x\}\})}$$

(*insert-left*)
$$\frac{(S; e) \longrightarrow (S'; e')}{(S; \textbf{insert}(l,\ e)) \longrightarrow (S'; \textbf{insert}(l, e'))}$$

(*insert*)
$$\frac{S(l) = \overline{r} \quad \overline{s} = v{::}\overline{r}}{(S; \textbf{insert}(l,\ v)) \longrightarrow (S[l \mapsto \overline{s}], ())}$$

(*update-init*)
$$\frac{S(l) = \{r_1, \ldots, r_n\} \quad \overline{e'} = \{r_i' \mid r_i' = (\mathcal{C}[\![c\{^{r_i}/_x\}]\!]?\ e\{^{r_i}/_x\}\ :\ r_i)\}}{(S; \textbf{update}(l,\ x.e,\ x.c)) \longrightarrow (S; \textbf{updating}(l,\ \overline{e'}))}$$

(*updating*)
$$\frac{(S; e) \longrightarrow (S'; e')}{(S; \textbf{updating}(l,\ e)) \longrightarrow (S'; \textbf{updating}(l,\ e'))}$$

(*update*)
$$\frac{}{(S; \textbf{updating}(l, v) \longrightarrow (S[l \mapsto v];\ ())}$$

(*delete*)
$$\frac{S(l) = \{r_1, \ldots, r_n\} \quad \overline{s} = \{r_i \mid \neg\mathcal{C}[\![c\{^{r_i}/_x\}]\!]\}}{(S; \textbf{delete}(l, x.c)) \longrightarrow (S[l \mapsto \overline{s}];\ ())}$$

Fig. 2. Reduction rules for DML core

in one step, using rule (*update*). Rule (*delete*) removes from the relevant entity all records r for which condition $c\{r/x\}$ holds.

3 Type System

In this section we present our type system, which ensures the intended non-interference property. The syntax of types is defined in Fig. 4. Our types are annotated with value dependent security labels s, thus always of the form τ^{s} where τ is a standard type and s is a (possibly indexed) security label.

Security labels, which may be in general value dependent, have the form $\ell(\mathsf{v})$, where v is a security label index given by the grammar in Fig. 3. A security label

$$
\begin{array}{lll}
\mathsf{v} ::= & & \textit{(label indexes)} \\
& \overline{v} & \text{(collection)} \\
& \mid \overline{[m : v]} & \text{(record)} \\
& \mid \textbf{true} & \text{(true)} \\
& \mid \textbf{false} & \text{(false)} \\
& \mid \top & \text{(top)} \\
& \mid \bot & \text{(bot)} \\
& \mid m & \text{(field identifier)}
\end{array}
$$

Fig. 3. Syntax of label indexes

$$
\begin{array}{lll}
\mathsf{s}, \mathsf{r}, \mathsf{t} ::= \ell(\mathsf{v}) & & \text{value dependent label} \\
\tau^{\mathsf{s}} ::= & \tau^{*\mathsf{s}} & \text{collection type} \\
& \mid (\tau^{\mathsf{s}} \to \tau'^{\mathsf{r}})^{\mathsf{t}} & \text{arrow type} \\
& \mid \overline{[m : \tau^{\mathsf{s}}]}^{\mathsf{r}} & \text{record type} \\
& \mid \mathtt{cmd}^{\mathsf{s}} & \text{command type} \\
& \mid \mathtt{Bool}^{\mathsf{s}} & \text{bool type}
\end{array}
$$

Fig. 4. Syntax of types

$$
\textit{(s-reflex)}\ \frac{}{\tau^{\mathsf{s}} <: \tau^{\mathsf{s}}}
\qquad
\textit{(s-trans)}\ \frac{\tau^{\mathsf{s}} <: \tau^{\mathsf{s}''} \quad \tau^{\mathsf{s}''} <: \tau^{\mathsf{s}'}}{\tau^{\mathsf{s}} <: \tau^{\mathsf{s}'}}
$$

$$
\textit{(s-arrow)}\ \frac{\tau^{\mathsf{s}'} <: \tau^{\mathsf{s}} \quad \tau'^{\mathsf{r}} <: \tau'^{\mathsf{r}'}}{(\tau^{\mathsf{s}} \to \tau'^{\mathsf{r}})^{\mathsf{t}} <: (\tau^{\mathsf{s}'} \to \tau'^{\mathsf{r}'})^{\mathsf{t}}}
\qquad
\textit{(s-record)}\ \frac{\forall_i\ \tau_i^{\mathsf{s}_i} <: \tau_i^{\mathsf{s}'_i} \quad \sqcup \mathsf{s}'_i \leq \mathsf{s}'}{\overline{[m : \tau^{\mathsf{s}}]}^{\mathsf{s}} <: \overline{[m : \tau^{\mathsf{s}'}]}^{\mathsf{s}'}}
\qquad
\textit{(s-expr)}\ \frac{\mathsf{s} \leq \mathsf{s}'}{\tau^{\mathsf{s}} <: \tau^{\mathsf{s}'}}
$$

Fig. 5. Subtyping rules

is *concrete* if its index is a value v, not a field identifier m. A label $\ell(m)$ where m is a field identifier only makes sense in the scope of a record type declaration, as explained below. Concrete security labels form a lattice, with $\top$ the top element (the most restrictive security level), and $\bot$ the bottom element (the most permissive security level), and $\sqcup$, $\sqcap$, denoting join and meet respectively. The lattice partial order is noted $\leq$ and $<$ its strict part; we write $\mathsf{s}\#\mathsf{s}'$ to say that neither $\mathsf{s} \leq \mathsf{s}'$ nor $\mathsf{s}' \leq \mathsf{s}$. We use $|\cdot|^{\uparrow}$ to denote the concrete upwards approximation of a label where $|\ell(m)|^{\uparrow} = \ell(\top)$ and $|\ell(v)|^{\uparrow} = \ell(v)$, and $|\cdot|^{\downarrow}$ to denote the concrete downwards approximation where $|\ell(m)|^{\downarrow} = \ell(\bot)$ and $|\ell(v)|^{\downarrow} = \ell(v)$. By convention, dependent security labels $\ell(\bot)$ and $\ell(\top)$ are interpreted as approximations to the (standard, non-value dependent) security label ℓ. We then require that for any value v, $\ell(\bot) \leq \ell(v) \leq \ell(\top)$ holds in the security lattice $\mathcal{L}$. Apart from this, we do not pose any extra assumptions of the security lattice, except that the ordering between labels is well defined and satisfies the lattice property (e.g., well defined meets and joins, etc).

Our type structure includes the boolean type, the unit type, (security-label dependent) record types, functional types, and collection types. We also assume other basic types, such as integers and strings, with associated operations, useful for examples and any practical needs. In a record type $[m_1{:}\tau_1^{\mathsf{s}_1}, \ldots, m_n{:}\tau_n^{\mathsf{s}_n}]^{\mathsf{s}'}$ any label s_i with $i > 1$ may be dependent on a previous field, and thus be of the form $\ell(m_j)$ with $j < i$. These are the only allowed occurrences of non-concrete security labels in types and programs: in the context of security-label dependent records. Moreover, for every such record type occurring in a valid typing we always have $\sqcup \mathsf{s}_i' \leq \mathsf{s}'$, where s_i' is the concrete security level of field m_i since a record value depends on all fields, its security level cannot be lower than the level of any of its fields. This differs from traditional approaches, [17,25], that classify data structures with a security level representing the lower bound of the elements' labels. With our approach, since a projection of a record field may have a lower security level than its record, we end up having an implicit but controlled form of declassification. The collection type $\tau^{*\mathsf{s}}$ states that each collection element has type τ^{s}, so security labels of a collection's elements are homogenous.

The typing judgment is of the form $\Delta \vdash_{\mathcal{S}}^{\mathsf{r}} e : \tau^{\mathsf{s}}$, stating that expression e has type τ under typing environment Δ, and given the constraint set $\mathcal{S}$. The label s states that value of expression e does not depend on data classified with security levels above s or incomparable with s. Thus the type system ensures that only information flow from a level l to a level h such that $\mathsf{l} \leq \mathsf{h}$ is allowed. Label r expresses the security level of the computational context (cf. the "program counter" [22,25]), a standard technical device to capture implicit flows. Our type system uses a constraint system to approximate runtime values, necessary to eliminate or capture value dependencies in security labels, and approximate reasoning about runtime values. We restrict constraints to talk about *pure* expressions, without side-effects (all non-DML expressions).

Definition 2. *A constraint set $\mathcal{S}$ is a finite set of constraints of the form $e \doteq e'$ where e, e' are pure expressions. We assume given a decidable and sound equational theory and write $S \models e \doteq e'$ to mean that $\mathcal{S}$ entails $e \doteq e'$. We require $\doteq$ to be compatible with reduction in the sense that for any e, e' pure if $(S; e) \rightarrow (S; e')$ then $\models e \doteq e'$.*

We denote by $\mathcal{S}\{x \doteq e\}$ the set $\mathcal{S} \cup \{x \doteq e\}$ if e is a pure expression, and $\mathcal{S}$ otherwise. We give some examples of expected equational axioms:

$$(c \wedge c') \doteq \texttt{true} \Rightarrow c \doteq \texttt{true} \qquad [\ldots, m_i{:}v_i, \ldots].m_i \doteq v_i$$
$$(x \doteq v) \wedge e \doteq e' \Rightarrow e\{v/x\} \doteq e'\{v/x\} \quad v \doteq v$$

So, for example, $\{x.m_1 \doteq 2, x.m_1 \doteq y{+}1\} \models y \doteq 1$. As for any equational theory, we assume that $S \models E$ and $\mathcal{S} \cup \{E\} \models E'$ implies $S \models E'$ (deduction closure). For our purposes, we abstract away from the particular equational theory used: the precise formulation of the equational theory is orthogonal to our approach, as long as a sound and decidable system is adopted (clearly, the more complete the theory the better). Typing declarations assign types to identifiers $x : \tau^{\mathsf{s}}$, and collection types of record types to locations, $t : \tau^{\mathsf{s}}$. A typing environment Δ is a list of typing declarations.

Definition 3 (Type System). *Typing is expressed by the judgment* $\Delta \vdash^{\mathsf{r}}_{\mathcal{S}} e : \tau^{\mathsf{s}}$*, stating that expression* e *is well-typed by* τ^{s} *in environment* Δ*, given constraints in* $\mathcal{S}$*, and concrete context security level* r.

Key typing rules are given in Figs. 6 and 7, see [20] for the complete set of rules. We also define a simple subtyping relation (Fig. 5) denoted $<:$. Notice the role of $\leq$ in subtyping, allowing up-classification. Before discussing our typing rules, we present some useful notions related to security-label dependent record fields.

Definition 4 (Label approximation). *Let* $\mathcal{S}$ *be a constraint set,* s *a label, and* x *an identifier. We define the label approximation* $\theta_x(\mathcal{S}, \mathsf{s})$ *to be the concrete label given by*

$$\theta_x(\mathcal{S}, \ell(\mathsf{v})) \triangleq \begin{cases} \ell(v) & if\ \mathsf{v} = m \ and \ \mathcal{S} \models x.m \doteq v \\ |\ell(\mathsf{v})|^{\downarrow} & otherwise \end{cases}$$

$\theta_x(\mathcal{S}, \mathsf{s})$ approximates (from below) the runtime value associated to the index of the security label s, given the information provided by the constraints $\mathcal{S}$. The interesting case is when the index v is a field identifier m_i of record x (typically, is used in typing rules for constructs where x denotes a query or update cursor of a database entity). In this case, the runtime value v may be approximated by solving $\mathcal{S} \models e \doteq v$ for v. For example, $\theta_x(\{x.m_1 \doteq 2, x.m_2 \doteq x.m_1 + 3\}, \ell(m_2)) = \ell(5)$ because $\{x.m_1 \doteq 2, x.m_2 \doteq x.m_1 + 3\} \models x.m_2 \doteq 5$. But $\theta_x(\{x.m_1 \doteq 2, x.m_2 \doteq x.m_1 + 3\}, \ell(m_3)) = \ell(\bot)$ since there is no v such that $\{x.m_1 \doteq 2, x.m_2 \doteq x.m_1 + 3\} \models x.m_3 \doteq v$.

We now discuss our key typing rules, omitting the standard ones for any typed λ-calculus. Rule (*t-refineRecord*) can be used to introduce a field dependent security label for a field m_j, given that we can derive that the indexing field contains a runtime value v_j (via relation $\models$). The converse is achieved with rule (*t-unrefineRecord*). In Fig. 7 we present the typing rules for DML primitives. Type rule (*t-entity*) adds the entity's identifier to the type context, assigning to it a collection type of record types where each field's type corresponds to the ones declared, and types the continuation expression with the extended typing context. To approximate the table record security level, we use $|\mathsf{s}|^{\uparrow}$.

In rule (*t-select*), to prevent implicit flows, we force the security label of the conditional expression to be the same as the one for body expression e and change the computational context label r to the least upper bound between the current context security label and the conditional expression's label. Rule (*t-insert*) states that an insert primitive is well-typed if the expression has exactly the same security type as the entity's elements, this prevents explicit flows from occurring. Moreover, in order to prevent implicit flows, we check if the current computational context is lower than or equal to all the fields' security labels. But since these labels may mention field identifiers, we use θ_x to approximate the concrete levels (x fresh in the conclusion). In rules (*t-update*) and (*t-delete*) we apply the same principles of rule (*t-insert*) to prevent explicit flows, and of rules (*t-select*) and (*t-insert*) to account for implicit flows. In rule (*t-update*) one needs to make sure that the least upper bound between the current context security

(t-app)

$$\frac{\Delta \vdash^{\mathsf{r}}_{\mathcal{S}} e_1 : (\tau'^{\mathsf{s}'} \to \tau^{\mathsf{s}})^{\mathsf{t}} \quad \Delta \vdash^{\mathsf{r}}_{\mathcal{S}} e_2 : \tau'^{\mathsf{s}'}}{\Delta \vdash^{\mathsf{r}}_{\mathcal{S}} e_1(e_2) : \tau^{\mathsf{s} \sqcup \mathsf{t}}}$$

(t-lambda)

$$\frac{\Delta, x : \tau^{\mathsf{s}} \vdash^{\mathsf{r}}_{\mathcal{S}} e : \tau'^{\mathsf{s}'}}{\Delta \vdash^{\mathsf{r}}_{\mathcal{S}} \lambda(x : \tau^{\mathsf{s}}).e : (\tau^{\mathsf{s}} \to \tau'^{\mathsf{s}'})^{\perp}}$$

(t-field)

$$\frac{\Delta \vdash^{\mathsf{r}}_{\mathcal{S}} e : [\ldots, m_i{:}\tau_i^{\mathsf{s}_i}, \ldots]^{\mathsf{s}'} \quad \mathsf{s}_i \in \mathcal{L}}{\Delta \vdash^{\mathsf{r}}_{\mathcal{S}} e.m_i : \tau_i^{\mathsf{s}_i}}$$

(t-record)

$$\frac{\forall_i \quad \Delta \vdash^{\mathsf{r}}_{\mathcal{S}} e_i : \tau_i^{\mathsf{s}_i}}{\Delta \vdash^{\mathsf{r}}_{\mathcal{S}} [\ldots, m_i{:}e_i, \ldots] : [\ldots, m_i{:}\tau_i^{\mathsf{s}_i}, \ldots]^{\sqcup \mathsf{s}_i}}$$

(t-refineRecord)

$$\frac{\begin{array}{c}\Delta \vdash^{\mathsf{r}}_{\mathcal{S}} e : [\ldots, m_j{:}\tau_j^{\mathsf{s}_j}, \ldots, m_i{:}\tau_i^{\ell_i(v_j)}, \ldots]^{\mathsf{s}} \\ \mathcal{S}\{x \doteq e\} \models x.m_j \doteq v_j\end{array}}{\Delta \vdash^{\mathsf{r}}_{\mathcal{S}} e : [\ldots, m_j : \tau_j^{\mathsf{s}_j}, \ldots, m_i : \tau_i^{\ell_i(m_j)}, \ldots]^{\mathsf{s}}}$$

(t-id)

$$\frac{}{\Delta, x : \tau^{\mathsf{s}} \vdash^{\mathsf{r}}_{\mathcal{S}} x : \tau^{\mathsf{s}}}$$

(t-unrefineRecord)

$$\frac{\begin{array}{c}\Delta \vdash^{\mathsf{r}}_{\mathcal{S}} e : [\ldots, m_j{:}\tau_j^{\mathsf{s}_j}, \ldots, m_i{:}\tau_i^{\ell_i(m_j)}, \ldots]^{\mathsf{s}} \\ \mathcal{S}\{x \doteq e\} \models x.m_j \doteq v_j\end{array}}{\Delta \vdash^{\mathsf{r}}_{\mathcal{S}} e : [\ldots, m_j : \tau_j^{\mathsf{s}_j}, \ldots, m_i : \tau_i^{\ell_i(v_j)}, \ldots]^{\mathsf{s}}}$$

(t-sub)

$$\frac{\Delta \vdash^{\mathsf{r}}_{\mathcal{S}} e : \tau^{\mathsf{s}} \quad \tau^{\mathsf{s}} <: \tau^{\mathsf{s}'} \quad \mathsf{r}' \leq \mathsf{r}}{\Delta \vdash^{\mathsf{r}'}_{\mathcal{S}} e : \tau^{\mathsf{s}'}}$$

(t-let)

$$\frac{\Delta \vdash^{\mathsf{r}}_{\mathcal{S}} e_1 : \tau^{\mathsf{s}} \quad \Delta, x : \tau^{\mathsf{s}} \vdash^{\mathsf{r}}_{\mathcal{S}\{x \doteq e_1\}} e_2 : \tau'^{\mathsf{s}'}}{\Delta \vdash^{\mathsf{r}}_{\mathcal{S}} \textbf{let } x = e_1 \textbf{ in } e_2 : \tau'^{\mathsf{s}'}}$$

(t-if)

$$\frac{\begin{array}{c}\Delta \vdash^{\mathsf{r}}_{\mathcal{S}} c : \mathtt{Bool}^{\mathsf{s}} \\ \Delta \vdash^{\mathsf{r} \sqcup \mathsf{s}}_{\mathcal{S} \cup \{c \doteq \mathtt{true}\}} e_1 : \tau^{\mathsf{s}} \\ \Delta \vdash^{\mathsf{r} \sqcup \mathsf{s}}_{\mathcal{S} \cup \{c \doteq \mathtt{false}\}} e_2 : \tau^{\mathsf{s}}\end{array}}{\Delta \vdash^{\mathsf{r}}_{\mathcal{S}} \textbf{if } c \textbf{ then } e_1 \textbf{ else } e_2 : \tau^{\mathsf{s}}}$$

Fig. 6. Typing rules for (pure) expressions (sample rules)

label ("program counter" security level) and the conditional expression's label is below or equal to the greatest lower bound of the security levels of both the "old" records and "updated" records, so to make sure only up-flows are allowed. In (*t-update*), y is required fresh in the conclusion. As already mentioned, expression e is required to produce a tuple of the same type as the table elements, updating all fields. This does not limit the generality of the update primitive, since the old values may be used in the updated fields through x in e and is in fact convenient for the expressiveness of our information flow analysis.

4 Type Preservation and Non-Interference

In this section we present the soundness results for our type system, which ensures that well-typed programs do not leak confidential information to security compartments unrelated by the assumed security lattice. Main statements are Theorem 1 (Type Preservation) - types are preserved by the reduction relation - Theorem 2 (Progress) - well-typed expressions are either a value or have a reduction step - and 3 (Noninterference) - well-typed expressions satisfy the noninterference property.

(t-foreach)

$$\frac{\Delta \vdash^{\mathsf{r}}_{\mathcal{S}} e_1 : \tau^{*\mathsf{s}} \quad \Delta \vdash^{\mathsf{r}}_{\mathcal{S}} e_2 : \tau'^{\mathsf{s}} \qquad \Delta, x : \tau^{\mathsf{s}}, y : \tau'^{\mathsf{s}} \vdash^{\mathsf{r}}_{\mathcal{S}} e_3 : \tau'^{\mathsf{s}}}{\Delta \vdash^{\mathsf{r}}_{\mathcal{S}} \textbf{foreach}\ (e_1,\ e_2,\ x.y.e_3) : \tau'^{\mathsf{s}}}$$

(t-entity)

$$\frac{\Delta, t : [m_1 : \tau_1^{\mathsf{s}_1}, \ldots, m_n : \tau_n^{\mathsf{s}_n}]^{*\sqcup|\mathsf{s}_i|^{\uparrow}} \vdash^{\mathsf{r}}_{\mathcal{S}} e : \tau^{\mathsf{s}'}}{\Delta \vdash^{\mathsf{r}}_{\mathcal{S}} \textbf{entity}\ t(m_1 : \tau_1^{\mathsf{s}_1}, \ldots, m_n : \tau_n^{\mathsf{s}_n})\ \textbf{in}\ e : \tau^{\mathsf{s}'}}$$

(t-select)

$$\frac{\Delta(t) = [\ldots, m_i{:}\tau_i^{\mathsf{s}_i}, \ldots]^{*\mathsf{s}} \qquad \mathcal{S}' = \mathcal{S} \cup \{c \doteq \mathtt{true}\} \qquad \Delta, x : [\ldots, m_i{:}\tau_i^{\mathsf{s}_i}, \ldots]^{\mathsf{s}} \vdash^{\mathsf{r}}_{\mathcal{S}} c : \mathtt{Bool}^{\mathsf{s}'} \qquad \Delta, x : [\ldots, m_i{:}\tau_i^{\mathsf{s}_i}, \ldots]^{\mathsf{s}} \vdash^{\mathsf{r}\sqcup\mathsf{s}'}_{\mathcal{S}'} e : \tau^{\mathsf{s}'}}{\Delta \vdash^{\mathsf{r}}_{\mathcal{S}} \textbf{select}(t,\ x.c,\ x.e) : \tau^{*\mathsf{s}'}}$$

(t-insert)

$$\frac{\Delta(t) = [\ldots, m_i{:}\tau_i^{\mathsf{s}_i}, \ldots]^{*\mathsf{s}} \qquad \Delta \vdash^{\mathsf{r}}_{\mathcal{S}} e : [\ldots, m_i{:}\tau_i^{\mathsf{s}_i}, \ldots]^{\mathsf{s}} \quad \forall_i\ \mathsf{r} \leq \theta_x(\mathcal{S}\{x \doteq e\}, \mathsf{s}_i)}{\Delta \vdash^{\mathsf{r}}_{\mathcal{S}} \textbf{insert}(t,\ e) : \mathtt{cmd}^{\bot}}$$

(t-update)

$$\frac{\Delta(t) = [\ldots, m_i{:}\tau_i^{\mathsf{s}_i}, \ldots]^{*\mathsf{s}} \qquad \mathcal{S}' = \mathcal{S} \cup \{c \doteq \mathtt{true}\} \qquad \Delta, x : [\ldots, m_i{:}\tau_i^{\mathsf{s}_i}, \ldots]^{\mathsf{s}} \vdash^{\mathsf{r}}_{\mathcal{S}} c : \mathtt{Bool}^{\mathsf{s}'} \qquad \Delta, x : [\ldots, m_i{:}\tau_i^{\mathsf{s}_i}, \ldots]^{\mathsf{s}} \vdash^{\mathsf{r}}_{\mathcal{S}'} e : [\ldots, m_i{:}\tau_i^{\mathsf{s}_i}, \ldots]^{\mathsf{s}'} \qquad \forall_i\ \mathsf{r} \sqcup \mathsf{s}' \leq \theta_x(\mathcal{S}', \mathsf{s}_i) \sqcap \theta_y(\mathcal{S}\{y \doteq e\}, \mathsf{s}_i)}{\Delta \vdash^{\mathsf{r}}_{\mathcal{S}} \textbf{update}(t,\ x.e,\ x.c) : \mathtt{cmd}^{\bot}}$$

(t-delete)

$$\frac{\Delta(t) = [\ldots, m_i{:}\tau_i^{\mathsf{s}_i}, \ldots]^{*\mathsf{s}} \qquad \Delta, x : [\ldots, m_i{:}\tau_i^{\mathsf{s}_i}, \ldots]^{\mathsf{s}} \vdash^{\mathsf{r}}_{\mathcal{S}} c : \mathtt{Bool}^{\mathsf{s}'} \qquad \forall_i\ \mathsf{r} \sqcup \mathsf{s}' \leq \theta_x(\mathcal{S} \cup \{c \doteq \mathtt{true}\}, \mathsf{s}_i)}{\Delta \vdash^{\mathsf{r}}_{\mathcal{S}} \textbf{delete}(t,\ x.c) : \mathtt{cmd}^{\bot}}$$

Fig. 7. Typing rules for DML core

We now introduce notions of store consistency and well-typed configurations, and define an expression equivalence relation.

Definition 5 (Store Consistency). *Given a typing environment Δ and a store S, we say store S is consistent with respect to typing environment Δ, denoted as $\Delta \vdash S$, if $dom(S) \subseteq dom(\Delta)$ and $\forall l \in dom(S)$ then $\Delta \vdash^{\mathsf{r}}_{\mathcal{S}} S(l) : \Delta(l)$.*

Definition 6 (Well-typed Configuration). *A configuration $(S; e)$ is well-typed in Δ if $\Delta \vdash S$ and $\Delta \vdash^{\mathsf{r}}_{\mathcal{S}} e : \tau^{\mathsf{s}}$.*

To prove type preservation, we introduce the substitution lemma on which it relies.

Lemma 1 (Substitution Lemma).
If $\Delta \vdash^{\mathsf{r}}_{\mathcal{S}} v{:}\tau'^{\mathsf{s}'}$ and $\Delta, x{:}\tau'^{\mathsf{s}'} \vdash^{\mathsf{r}}_{\mathcal{S}} e{:}\tau^{\mathsf{s}}$ then $\Delta \vdash^{\mathsf{r}}_{\mathcal{S}\{v/x\}} e\{v/x\}{:}\tau^{\mathsf{s}}$.
Proof: Induction on the derivation of $\Delta, x{:}\tau'^{\mathsf{s}'} \vdash^{\mathsf{r}}_{\mathcal{S}} e{:}\tau^{\mathsf{s}}$, see [20].

Theorem 1 states that any reduction step of a well-typed configuration leads to a well-typed configuration, where the typing of the final configuration is possibly extended with new locations of entities (via **`entity`**) in the state.

Theorem 1 (Type Preservation).
Let $\Delta \vdash S$ and $\Delta \vdash^{\mathsf{r}}_{\mathcal{S}} e{:}\tau^{\mathsf{s}}$. If $(S; e) \longrightarrow (S'; e')$ then there is Δ' such that $\Delta' \vdash^{\mathsf{r}}_{\mathcal{S}} e' : \tau^{\mathsf{s}}$, $\Delta' \vdash S'$ and $\Delta \subseteq \Delta'$.
Proof: Induction on the derivation of $\Delta \vdash^{\mathsf{r}}_{\mathcal{S}} e{:}\tau^{\mathsf{s}}$, see [20].

(e-val)

$$\frac{\Delta \vdash^{\mathsf{r}}_{S_1} v : \tau^{\mathsf{s}'} \quad \Delta \vdash^{\mathsf{r}}_{S_2} v : \tau^{\mathsf{s}'}}{\Delta \vdash^{\mathsf{r}}_{S_1,S_2} v \cong_{\mathsf{s}} v : \tau^{\mathsf{s}'}}$$

(e-valOpaque)

$$\frac{\Delta \vdash^{\mathsf{r}}_{S_1} v_1 : \tau^{\mathsf{s}'} \quad \Delta \vdash^{\mathsf{r}}_{S_2} v_2 : \tau^{\mathsf{s}'} \quad \mathsf{s} < \mathsf{s}'}{\Delta \vdash^{\mathsf{r}}_{S_1,S_2} v_1 \cong_{\mathsf{s}} v_2 : \tau^{\mathsf{s}'}}$$

(e-sub)

$$\frac{\Delta \vdash^{\mathsf{r}'}_{S_1,S_2} e \cong_{\mathsf{s}} e' : \tau^{\mathsf{s}''} \quad \tau^{\mathsf{s}''} <: \tau^{\mathsf{s}'} \quad \mathsf{r} \leq \mathsf{r}'}{\Delta \vdash^{\mathsf{r}}_{S_1,S_2} e \cong_{\mathsf{s}} e' : \tau^{\mathsf{s}'}}$$

(e-refineRecord)

$$\frac{\Delta \vdash^{\mathsf{r}}_{S_1,S_2} e \cong_{\mathsf{s}} e' : [\ldots, m_j : \tau_j^{\mathsf{s}_j}, \ldots, m_i : \tau_i^{\ell_i(v_j)}, \ldots]^{\mathsf{s}'} \quad S_1\{x \doteq e\} \models x.m_j \doteq v_j \quad S_2\{x \doteq e'\} \models x.m_j \doteq v_j}{\Delta \vdash^{\mathsf{r}}_{S_1,S_2} e \cong_{\mathsf{s}} e' : [\ldots, m_j : \tau_j^{\mathsf{s}_j}, \ldots, m_i : \tau_i^{\ell_i(m_j)}, \ldots]^{\mathsf{s}'}}$$

Fig. 8. Equivalence of expressions up to level s (sample rules)

The next result says that in a well-typed configuration $(S; e)$ either e is a value, or e has a reduction step. Theorem 2 says that well-typed programs never get stuck.

Theorem 2 (Progress).
Let $\Delta \vdash^{\mathsf{r}}_{S} e{:}\tau^{\mathsf{s}}$ and $\Delta \vdash S$. If e is not a value then $(S; e) \longrightarrow (S'; e')$.
Proof: Induction on the derivation of $\Delta \vdash^{\mathsf{r}}_{S} e : \tau^{\mathsf{s}}$, see [20].

In order to formulate our main result (non-interference), we need to present some auxiliary definitions, namely store equivalence and expression equivalence up to a security level. To define store equivalence we use the *filter* function *filter*(Δ, S, s) that given store S returns the store obtained from S by redacting (replace by $\star$) all stored values classified at levels above security level s or incomparable to s (see [20]). Stores S_1, S_2 such that $\Delta \vdash S_i$ are said equivalent up to level s if *filter*$(\Delta, S_1, \mathsf{s}) =$ *filter*$(\Delta, S_2, \mathsf{s})$.

Definition 7 *P*(Expression Equivalence).
Expression equivalence of e_1 and e_2 up to s is asserted by $\Delta \vdash^{\mathsf{r}}_{S_1,S_2} e_1 \cong_{\mathsf{s}} e_2{:}\tau^{\mathsf{s}'}$.

Intuitively, two expressions are equivalent up to level s if they yield the same result under stores equivalent up to s. Such formulations of equivalence are usual for expressing non-interference, and always relate expressions at the same type and security level. Notice that two expressions may be equivalent up to level s even if they are classified at a different level s′. Technically, expressions e_1 and e_2 are equivalent up to level s if they only differ in subexpressions classified at higher (or incomparable) security levels (so they cannot be distinguished by attackers constrained to see only up to level s). We show key defining rules for expression equivalence in Fig. 8 (full set of rules in [20]).

We can, at last, present our final main result: the non-interference theorem.

Theorem 3 (Non-Interference).
Let $\Delta \vdash S_1$, $\Delta \vdash S_2$, $S_1 =_{\mathsf{s}} S_2$, and $\Delta \vdash^{\mathsf{r}}_{S_1,S_2} e_1 \cong_{\mathsf{s}} e_2 : \tau^{\mathsf{s}'}$.
If $(S_1, e_1) \longrightarrow (S_1', e_1')$, and $(S_2, e_2) \longrightarrow (S_2', e_2')$ then there is Δ' such that $\Delta \subseteq \Delta'$, $\Delta' \vdash S_1'$, $\Delta' \vdash S_2'$, $S_1' =_{\mathsf{s}} S_2'$, and $\Delta' \vdash^{\mathsf{r}}_{S_1,S_2} e_1' \cong_{\mathsf{s}} e_2' : \tau^{\mathsf{s}'}$.
Proof: Induction on the derivation of $\Delta \vdash^{\mathsf{r}}_{S_1,S_2} e_1 \cong_{\mathsf{s}} e_2 : \tau^{\mathsf{s}'}$, see [20].

The non-interference states that if we execute two equivalent instances of the same program under stores that differ only on information with higher (or incomparable) security level than s, then the resulting stores remain indistinguishable up to security level s. As a consequence we have

Corollary 1. *Assume* $\Delta \vdash^{\mathsf{r}}_{\mathcal{S}} e{:}\tau^{\mathsf{s}'}$, $\Delta \vdash S_1$, $\Delta \vdash S_2$ *and* $S_1 =_{\mathsf{s}} S_2$.
If $(S_1, e) \xrightarrow{*} (S_1', v_1)$, *and* $(S_2, e) \xrightarrow{*} (S_2', v_2)$ *then there is* Δ' *such that* $\Delta \subseteq \Delta'$, $\Delta' \vdash S_1'$, $\Delta' \vdash S_2'$, $S_1' =_{\mathsf{s}} S_2'$ *and* $\Delta' \vdash^{\mathsf{r}}_{\mathcal{S}_1,\mathcal{S}_2} v_1 \cong_{\mathsf{s}} v_2{:}\tau^{\mathsf{s}'}$.
Also, for all s *if* $\mathsf{s} \not\leq \mathsf{s}'$ *then* $v_1 = v_2$.

The above result precisely express the fact that an attacker "located" at security level s cannot distinguish between evaluations of a program taking place in environments that only differ in data that should be considered confidential for level s, e.g., data classified at any level l such that $\mathsf{l} \not\leq s$. To illustrate the non-interference theorem, we use **entity** `Records (id_p:int`^{L}`, date:Date`$^{\mathsf{P(id\_p)}}$`, clinical_info:tinfo`$^{\mathsf{P(id\_p)}}$`)`.

```
let info= first( from (x in Records)
                 where x.id_p=42 select x.clinical_info)
 in insert [id_p:42, date:today(), clinical_info:info] in Records
```

Assume P(10)#P(42) Let S_1 and S_2 be stores such that S_1(Records) = {(10,d$_1$,X), (42,d$_2$, A)} and S_2(Records) = {(10,d$_1$,X), (42,d$_2$,B)} with $A \neq B$. We have $S_1 =_{P(10)} S_2$ since the values A and B, classified as P(42), are not visible at level P(10). We have $\Delta \vdash^{\mathsf{r}}_{\mathcal{S}_1,\mathcal{S}_2}$ **insert** [id_p: 42, date: today(), clinical_info: info] **in** Records$\cong_{P(10)}$**insert** [id_p: 42, date: today(), clinical_info: info] **in** Records:cmd$^{\perp}$. Consider the reductions (S_1;**insert** [id_p: 42, date: today(), clinical_info: info] **in** Records) $\longrightarrow$(S_1'; ()) and (S_2;**insert** [id_p: 42,date:today(), clinical_info:info] **in** Records) $\longrightarrow$ (S_2; ()). Then S_1(Records) = {(10,d$_1$,X), (42,d$_2$,A), (42, d$_3$,A)} and S_2(Records)= {(10,d$_1$,X), (42,d$_2$,B), (42,d$_3$,B)} meaning the property is satisfied, since *filter*(Δ, S_1,P(10)) = {(10,d$_1$,X), (42,⋆,⋆), (42,⋆,⋆)} = *filter*(Δ, S_2,P(10)), that is $S_1' =_{P(10)} S_2'$. So, the effects of the above command are not visible at security level P(10). Now consider the following slight modification of the code above:

```
let info= first (from (x in Records)
                 where x.id_p=42 select x.clinical_info)
 in insert [id_p: 10, date: today(), clinical_info: info] in Records
```

We have $\Delta \vdash^{\mathsf{r}}_{\mathcal{S}_1,\mathcal{S}_2}$ **insert** [id_p: 10, date: today(), clinical_info: info] **in** Records$\cong_{P(10)}$ **insert** [id_p: 10, date: today(), clinical_info: info] **in** Records: cmd$^{\perp}$. After reduction steps (S_1;**insert** [id_p:10, date: today(), clinical_info:info] **in** Records)$\longrightarrow$(S_1; ()) and (S_2;**insert** [id_p:10, date: today(), clinical_info:info] **in** Records)$\longrightarrow$ (S_2; ()) we have S_1(Records)={(10,d$_1$,X), (42,d$_2$, A), (10,d$_3$,A)} and S_2(Records)={(10,d$_1$,X), (42,d$_2$,B), (10,d$_3$,B)}. But now $S_1 \neq_{P(10)} S_2$ since, upon the insertion of the tuple [id_p: 10, date: today(), clinical_info: info], the values A and B are observable at level P(10). This is captured by the notion of store equivalence since *filter*(Δ, S_1,P(10)) = {(10,d$_1$,X), (42,⋆,⋆), (10, d$_3$,A)} and *filter*(Δ, S_2,P(10)) = {(10,d$_1$,X), (42,⋆,⋆), (10, d$_3$,B)}. Thus, the thesis of the noninterference theorem is not satisfied, and this program is rejected by the type system. Clearly, it is not possible to give the appropriate (security-label dependent record) type [id_p:int^{L}, date:$\text{Date}^{P(\texttt{id\_p})}$, clinical_info:$\text{tinfo}^{P(\texttt{id\_p})}$] to the record [id_p:10, date: today(), clinical_info:info] (using rule (*t-unrefineRecord*)) since the security level of info is P(42) but the value of id_p is 10.

5 Related Work

Our core typed λ-calculus equipped with SQL-like DML primitives is inspired in proposals such as [5,9,21] and provides a natural vehicle to investigate information flow security analyses for data-centric software systems. There is a huge body of work on language-based information flow analysis (see e.g., [25]). Early works [26,31] focus on simple imperative languages. [17] presents an information flow analysis for a λ-calculus with references, sums, and product types. The dependency calculus [1] generalises [17] and is shown to be able to encode the languages of [17,31], as well as the respective noninterference results.

Several proposals for information flow analysis on web-based or data-centric applications were put forward. In [2] a dynamic information flow mechanism for a Javascript-like language based on a notion of faceted values is proposed. Faceted values offer different views of a value given the execution context's principal. Other recent work [16] proposes a dynamic information flow analysis for a subset of the ECMA standard for Javascript. In [13] a taint analysis for mobile applications is proposed, where implicit flows are not taken into account to minimise performance overhead, and in [11] a dynamic analysis to prevent insecure cross-application information flows is developed. The framework presented in [14] offers confinement mechanisms at both the OS and browser level via both Mandatory Access Control and information flow analysis. Interestingly, their security labels (represented by a set of principals) allow for "row-level" policies, specified through functions from a tuple (of the document whose policy we're specifying) to a set of readers. Other works based on dynamic analysis include [7,19,27,33]. Our work is instead based on static analysis, as we seek to obtain compile time security guarantees, and avoid possible information leaks due to exceptional behavior (dynamic security errors).

Several works on static language-based analysis of information flow policies for web and data-centric software systems have also been proposed. In [18] the authors present a static type-based information flow analysis for a web scripting language based on PHP that ensures confidentiality of its data but no formalization of a security result is given. The (seminal) decentralised label model of [23] supports static analysis of information flow policies based on labelling data elements with policies that specifies allowed reader and writer principals, but which cannot easily express value-dependent "row-level" security compartments as we do. In [10] the authors present a static analysis to enforce label-based security policies in the web programming language SELinks. Their analysis is able to enforce relevant information flow policies in web applications although the authors do not discuss the noninterference property. Examples of other works aiming to statically enforce data security on DML-based applications are [8] and [5]. The approach taken by the former consists in adding program specifications expressed by SQL-queries which are then typechecked, while the latter uses refinement types and semantic subtyping to enforce properties that may be relevant for security. Unlike our approach, these works do not provide a value-dependent information flow analysis leading to non-interference results, as we have done here. An interesting work tackling dynamic issues within an statically verified information flow framework is [30], which addresses the manipulation of runtime first-class representations of principals. In [34] an information flow analysis is introduced where security labels can actually be changed at runtime and case-analysed by a conditional-construct. In our work we do not consider dynamically changing labels but, instead, use runtime values to index security labels to ensure "row-level" security. In [6] a refinement type-based approach for data security for a DML, which can handle policies depending on the database state, is proposed. To some extent, the work in this paper can be seen as recasting some ideas of [6] in the setting of a much more expressive information flow analysis framework. Several recent works explore applications of refinement types [3,4] and dependent types [28,29] to language-based security. For instance, in [28] the authors present a general-purpose language that allows for encodings of high-level security concerns such as information flow and access control policies. To formulate the former, a user-defined security lattice must be defined via a CanFlow relation, as opposed to assuming a security lattice as we do in this work, and a dependent-type tracked is used to associate security labels to data, which also records its provenance. A confidentiality result is showed stating that a program without the correct privileges cannot distinguish values protected by them, and so, as a corollary, cannot interfere with the behavior of programs with the right privileges. This result resembles the notion of our non-interference theorem, although the authors only take into account side-effect free expressions (so nothing is said about stored values). Moreover, privileges are principals that are authorized to access data instead of a security level compartment, as in our case, but the authors claim to be possible to formulate a non-interference result. Despite all these works, however, we are not aware of prior work exploring value-dependent security labels within an information flow framework, in the sense introduced in this paper.

6 Concluding Remarks

We have developed an expressive type-based information flow analysis for a core λ-calculus augmented with SQL-like primitives. Our core language may be seen as a convenient abstraction for practical data-manipulating programming languages. A key novelty of our work consists in the introduction of a notion of value-indexed security label, which allows us to parametrize security compartments on the values of computations or on dynamically stored data, thus enabling the enforcement of so-called "row-level" security policies within shared containers, relevant to address several realistic security concerns of data-centric software services. Our main technical results are type preservation and noninterference theorems, which ensure the soundness of our information flow analysis: well-typed programs do not disclose information for security compartments unauthorised by the security lattice.

As information flow analysis per se is not enough in general to provide complete security guarantees [24], we would like to combine our value dependent type-based information flow analysis with a suitable form of role-based access control. Some of the techniques used in this paper relate to the general notion of dependent types. It certainly deserves further study and generalisation, namely regarding its connection with more standard dependent type systems [29,32]. In particular, the introduction of first-order dependent function types in our language, which would add to the expressiveness of our approach, should be further investigated.

Acknowledgements. We thank the anonymous reviewers for their insightful comments. This work is supported by CITI, and FCT/MEC under grant SFRH/BD/68801/2010.

References

1. Abadi, M., Banerjee, A., Heintze, N., Riecke, J.G.: A core calculus of dependency. In: Appel, A.W., Aiken, A. (eds.) POPL '99, pp. 147–160. ACM (1999)
2. Austin, T.H., Flanagan, C.: Multiple facets for dynamic information flow. In: Field, J., Hicks, M. (eds.) POPL 2012, pp. 165–178. ACM (2012)
3. Baltopoulos, I.G., Borgström, J., Gordon, A.D.: Maintaining database integrity with refinement types. In: Mezini, M. (ed.) ECOOP 2011. LNCS, vol. 6813, pp. 484–509. Springer, Heidelberg (2011)
4. Bengtson, J., Bhargavan, K., Fournet, C., Gordon, A.D., Maffeis, S.: Refinement types for secure implementations. ACM Trans. Program. Lang. Syst. **33**(2), 8 (2011)
5. Bierman, G.M., Gordon, A.D., Hritcu, C., Langworthy, D.E.: Semantic subtyping with an SMT solver. J. Funct. Program. **22**(1), 31–105 (2012)
6. Caires, L., Pérez, J.A., Seco, J.C., Vieira, H.T., Ferrão, L.: Type-based access control in data-centric systems. In: Barthe, G. (ed.) ESOP 2011. LNCS, vol. 6602, pp. 136–155. Springer, Heidelberg (2011)
7. Cheng, W., Ports, D.R.K., Schultz, D., Popic, V., Blankstein, A., Cowling, J., Curtis, D., Shrira, L., Liskov, B.: Abstractions for usable information flow control in aeolus. In: USENIX Annual Technical Conference (2012)
8. Chlipala, A.: Static checking of dynamically-varying security policies in database-backed applications. In: Arpaci-Dusseau, R.H., Chen, B. (eds.) OSDI 2010, pp. 105–118. USENIX Association (2010)
9. Cooper, E., Lindley, S., Wadler, P., Yallop, J.: Links: web programming without tiers. In: de Boer, F.S., Bonsangue, M.M., Graf, S., de Roever, W.-P. (eds.) FMCO 2006. LNCS, vol. 4709, pp. 266–296. Springer, Heidelberg (2007)
10. Corcoran, B.J., Swamy, N., Hicks, M.W.: Cross-tier, label-based security enforcement for web applications. In: Çetintemel, U., Zdonik, S.B., Kossmann, D., Tatbul, N. (eds.) SIGMOD 2009, pp. 269–282. ACM (2009)
11. Davis, B., Chen, H.: DBTaint: cross-application information flow tracking via databases. In: WebApps'10, p. 12. USENIX Association (2010)
12. Denning, D.E., Denning, P.J.: Certification of programs for secure information flow. Commun. ACM **20**(7), 504–513 (1977)

13. Enck, W., Gilbert, P., Chun, B.G., Cox, L.P., Jung, J., McDaniel, P., Sheth, A.: TaintDroid: an information-flow tracking system for realtime privacy monitoring on smartphones. In: Arpaci-Dusseau, R.H., Chen, B. (eds.) OSDI 2010, pp. 393–407. USENIX Association (2010)
14. Giffin, D.B., Levy, A., Stefan, D., Terei, D., Mazières, D., Mitchell, J., Russo, A. : Hails: protecting data privacy in untrusted web applications. In: OSDI 2012, pp. 47–60. USENIX (2012)
15. Goguen, J. A., Meseguer, J.: Security policies and security models. In: IEEE Symposium on Security and Privacy, pp. 11–20 (1982)
16. Hedin, D., Sabelfeld, A.: Information-flow security for a core of JavaScript. In: Chong, S. (eds.) CSF 2012, pp. 3–18. IEEE (2012)
17. Heintze, N., Riecke, J.G.: The SLam calculus: programming with secrecy and integrity. In: MacQueen, D.B., Cardelli, L. (eds.) POPL '98, pp. 365–377. ACM (1998)
18. Li, P., Zdancewic, S.: Practical information-flow control in web-based information systems. In: CSFW 2005, pp. 2–15. IEEE Computer Society (2005)
19. Liu, J., George, M.D., Vikram, K., Qi, X., Waye, L., Myers, A.C.: Fabric: a platform for secure distributed computation and storage. In: Matthews, J.N., Anderson, T.E. (eds.) SOSP 2009, pp. 321–334. ACM (2009)
20. Lourenço, L., Caires, L.: Information flow analysis for valued-indexed aata security compartments. Technical report, UNL. http://ctp.di.fct.unl.pt/luisal/resources/techreportDLIF13.pdf (2013)
21. Meijer, E., Beckman, B., Bierman, G.M.: LINQ: reconciling object, relations and XML in the.NET framework. In: Chaudhuri, S., Hristidis, V., Polyzotis, N. (eds.) Proceedings of the ACM SIGMOD International Conference on Management of Data, p. 706. ACM (2006)
22. Myers, A.C.: JFlow: practical mostly-static information flow control. In: Appel, A.W., Aiken, A. (eds) POPL '99, pp. 228–241. ACM (1999)
23. Myers, A.C., Liskov, B.: A decentralized model for information flow control. In: SOSP, pp. 129–142 (1997)
24. Nanevski, A., Banerjee, A., Garg, D.: Verification of information flow and access control policies with dependent types. In: S&P 2011, pp. 165–179. IEEE Computer Society (2011)
25. Sabelfeld, A., Myers, A.C.: Language-based information-flow security. IEEE J. Sel. Areas Commun. (Spec. Issue Formal Methods Secur.) **21**(1), 5–19 (2003)
26. Sabelfeld, A., Sands, D.: A per model of secure information flow in sequential programs. Higher-Order Symbolic Comput. **14**(1), 59–91 (2001)
27. Schultz, D., Liskov, B., IFDB: decentralized information flow control for databases. In: Hanzálek, Z., Härtig, H., Castro, M., Kaashoek, M.F. (eds.) EuroSys 2013. ACM (2013)
28. Swamy, N., Chen, J., Chugh, R.: Enforcing stateful authorization and information flow policies in FINE. In: Gordon, A.D. (ed.) ESOP 2010. LNCS, vol. 6012, pp. 529–549. Springer, Heidelberg (2010)
29. Swamy, N., Chen, J., Fournet, C., Strub, P-Y., Bhargavan, K., Yang, J.: Secure distributed programming with value-dependent types. In: Chakravarty, M.M.T., Hu, Z., Danvy, O. (eds.) ICFP 2011, pp. 266–278. ACM (2011)
30. Tse, S., Zdancewic, S.: Run-time principals in information-flow type systems. ACM Trans. Program. Lang. Syst. **30**(1), 1–44 (2007)
31. Volpano, D.M., Irvine, C.E., Smith, G.: A sound type system for secure flow analysis. J. Comput. Secur. **4**(2/3), 167–188 (1996)

32. Xi, H., Pfenning, F.: Dependent types in practical programming. In: Appel, A.W., Aiken, A. (eds.) POPL '99, pp. 214–227. ACM (1999)
33. Zeldovich, N., Boyd-Wickizer, S., Mazières, D.: Securing distributed systems with information flow control. In: Crowcroft, J., Dahlin, M. (eds.) NSDI 2008, pp. 293–308. USENIX Association (2008)
34. Zheng, L., Myers, A.C.: Dynamic security labels and static information flow control. Int. J. Inf. Sec. **6**(2–3), 67–84 (2007)

A Library for Removing Cache-Based Attacks in Concurrent Information Flow Systems

Pablo Buiras[1](✉), Amit Levy[2], Deian Stefan[2], Alejandro Russo[1], and David Mazières[2]

[1] Chalmers University of Technology, Göteborg, Sweden
buiras@chalmers.se
[2] Stanford University, Stanford, USA

Abstract. Information-flow control (IFC) is a security mechanism conceived to allow untrusted code to manipulate sensitive data without compromising confidentiality. Unfortunately, untrusted code might exploit some covert channels in order to reveal information. In this paper, we focus on the LIO concurrent IFC system. By leveraging the effects of hardware caches (e.g., the CPU cache), LIO is susceptible to attacks that leak information through the *internal timing covert channel.* We present a *resumption*-based approach to address such attacks. Resumptions provide fine-grained control over the interleaving of thread computations at the library level. Specifically, we remove cache-based attacks by enforcing that every thread yield after executing an "instruction," i.e., atomic action. Importantly, our library allows for porting the full LIO library—our resumption approach handles local state and exceptions, both features present in LIO. To amend for performance degradations due to the library-level thread scheduling, we provide two novel primitives. First, we supply a primitive for securely executing pure code in parallel. Second, we provide developers a primitive for controlling the granularity of "instructions"; this allows developers to adjust the frequency of context switching to suit application demands.

1 Introduction

Popular website platforms, such as Facebook, run third-party applications (apps) to enhance the user experience. Unfortunately, in most of today's platforms, once an app is installed it is usually granted full or partial access to the user's sensitive data—the users have no guarantees that their data is not arbitrarily ex-filtrated once apps are granted access to it [18]. As demonstrated by Hails [9], information-flow control (IFC) addresses many of these limitations by restricting how sensitive data is disseminated. While promising, IFC systems are not impervious to attacks; the presence of *covert channels* allows attackers to leak sensitive information.

Covert channels are mediums not intended for communication, which nevertheless can be used to carry and, thus, reveal information [19]. In this work, we focus on the *internal timing covert channel* [33]. This channel emanates from the

M. Abadi and A. Lluch Lafuente (Eds.): TGC 2013, LNCS 8358, pp. 199–216, 2014.
DOI: 10.1007/978-3-319-05119-2_12,

mere presence of concurrency and shared resources. A system is said to have an internal timing covert channel when an attacker, as to reveal sensitive data, can alter *the order of public events* by affecting the timing behavior of threads. To avoid such attacks, several authors propose decoupling computations manipulating sensitive data from those writing into public resources (e.g., [4,5,27,30,35]).

Decoupling computations by security levels only works when all shared resources are modeled. Similar to most IFC systems, the concurrent IFC system LIO [35] only models shared resources at the programming language level and does not explicitly consider the effects of hardware. As shown in [37], LIO threads can exploit the underlying CPU cache to leak information through the internal timing covert channel.

We propose using *resumptions* to model interleaved computations. (We refer the interested reader to [10] for an excellent survey of resumptions.) A resumption is either a (computed) value or an atomic action which, when executed, returns a new resumption. By expressing thread computations as a series of resumptions, we can leverage resumptions for controlling concurrency. Specifically, we can interleave atomic actions, or "instructions," from different threads, effectively forcing each thread to yield at deterministic points. This ensures that scheduling is not influenced by underlying caches and thus cannot be used to leak secret data. We address the attacks on the recent version of LIO [35] by implementing a Haskell library which ports the LIO API to use resumptions. Since LIO threads possess local state and handle exceptions, we extend resumptions to account for these features.

In principle, it is possible to force deterministic interleaving by means other than resumptions; in [37] we show an instruction-based scheduler that achieves this goal. However, Haskell's monad abstraction allows us to easily model resumptions as a library. This has two consequences. First, and different from [37], it allows us to deploy a version of LIO that does not rely on changes to the Haskell compiler. Importantly, LIO's concurrency primitives can be modularly redefined, with little effort, to operate on resumptions. Second, by effectively implementing "instruction based-scheduling" at the level of library primitives, we can address cache attacks not covered by the approach described in [37] (see Sect. 5).

In practice, a library-level interleaved model of computations imposes performance penalties. With this in mind, we provide primitives that allow developers to execute code in parallel, and means for securely controlling the granularity of atomic actions (which directly affects performance).

Although our approach addresses internal timing attacks in the presence of shared hardware, the library suffers from leaks that exploit the termination channel, i.e., programs can leak information by not terminating. However, this channel can only be exploited by brute-force attacks that leak data external to the program—an attacker cannot leak data within the program, as can be done with the internal timing covert channel.

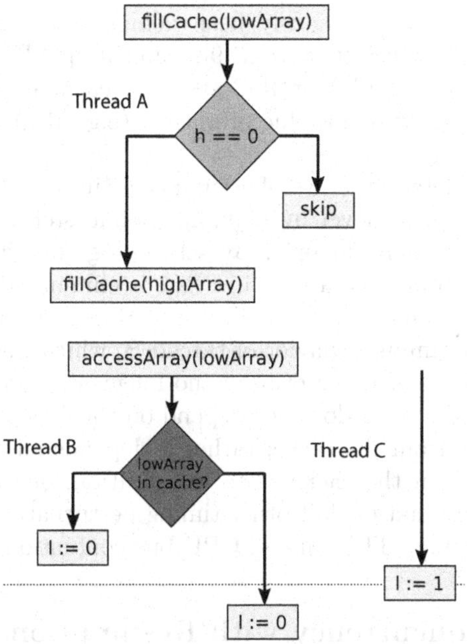

Fig. 1. Cache attack

2 Cache Attacks on Concurrent IFC Systems

Figure 1 shows an attack that leverages the timing effects of the underlying cache in order to leak information through the internal timing covert channel. In isolation, all three threads are secure. However, when executed concurrently, threads B and C race to write to a public, shared variable `l`. Importantly, the race outcome depends on the state of the secret variable `h`, by changing the contents of underlying CPU cache according to its value (e.g., by creating and traversing a large array as to fill the cache with new data).

The attack proceeds as follows. First, thread A fills the cache with the contents of a public array `lowArray`. Then, depending on the secret variable `h`, it evicts data from the cache (by filling it with arbitrary data) or leaves it intact. Concurrently, public threads B and C delay execution long enough for A to finish. Subsequently, thread B accesses elements of the public array `lowArray`, and writes 0 to public variable `l`; if the array has been evicted from the cache (`h==0`), the amount of time it takes to perform the read, and thus the write to `l`, will be much longer than if the array is still in the cache. Hence, to leak the value of `h`, thread C simply needs to delay writing 1 to `l` long enough so that it is above the case where the cache is full (with the public array), but shorter than it take to refill the cache with the (public) array. Observing the contents of `l`, the attacker directly learns the value of `h`.

This simple attack has previously been demonstrated in [37], where confidential data from the GitStar system [9], build atop LIO, was leaked. Such attacks are not limited to LIO or IFC systems; cache-based attacks against many system, including cryptographic primitives (e.g., RSA and AES), are well known [1,23,26,40].

The next section details the use of resumptions in modeling concurrency at the programming language level by defining atomic steps, which are used as the thread scheduling quantum unit. By scheduling threads according to the number of executed atoms, the attack in Fig. 1 is eliminated. As in [37], this is the case because an atomic step runs till completion, regardless of the state of the cache. Hence, the timing behavior of thread B, which was previously leaked to thread C by the time of preemption, is no longer disclosed. Specifically, the scheduling of thread C's `l:=1` does not depend on the time it takes thread B to read the public array from the cache; rather it depends on the atomic actions, which do not depend on the cache state. In addition, our use of resumptions also eliminates attacks that exploit other timing perturbations produced by the underlying hardware, e.g., TLB misses, CPU bus contention, etc.

3 Modeling Concurrency with Resumptions

In pure functional languages, computations with side-effects are encoded as values of abstract data types called *monads* [22]. We use the type $m\ a$ to denote computations that produce results of type a and may perform side-effects in monad m. Different side-effects are often handled by different monads. In Haskell, there are monads for performing inputs and outputs (monad *IO*), handling errors (monad *Error*), etc. The IFC system LIO simply exposes a monad, *LIO*, in which security checks are performed before any IO side-effecting action.

Resumptions are a simple approach to modeling interleaved computations of concurrent programs. A resumption, which has the form $res ::= x \mid \alpha \triangleright res$, is either a computed value x or an atomic action α followed by a new resumption res. Using this notion, we can break down a program that is composed of a series of instructions into a program that executes an atomic action and yields control to a scheduler by giving it its subsequent resumption. For example, program $P := i_1; i_2; i_3$, which performs three side-effecting instructions in sequence, can be written as $res_P := i_1; i_2 \triangleright i_3 \triangleright ()$, where $()$ is a value of a type with just one element, known as *unit*. Here, an atomic action α is any sequence of instructions. When executing res_P, instructions i_1 and i_2 execute atomically, after which it yields control back to the scheduler by supplying it the resumption $res'_P := i_3 \triangleright ()$. At this point, the scheduler may schedule atomic actions from other threads or execute res'_P to resume the execution of P. Suppose program $Q := j_1; j_2$, rewritten as $j_1 \triangleright j_2 \triangleright ()$, runs concurrently with P. Our concurrent execution of P and Q can be modeled with resumptions, under a round-robin scheduler, by writing it as $P || Q := i_1; i_2 \triangleright j_1 \triangleright i_3 \triangleright j_2 \triangleright () \triangleright ()$. In other words, resumptions allow us to implement a scheduler that executes $i_1; i_2$, postponing the execution of i_3, and executing atomic actions from Q in the interim.

$$
\begin{array}{l}
\mathbf{data}\ \mathit{Thread}\ m\ a\ \mathbf{where} \\
\quad \mathit{Done} :: a \rightarrow \mathit{Thread}\ m\ a \\
\quad \mathit{Atom} :: m\ (\mathit{Thread}\ m\ a) \rightarrow \mathit{Thread}\ m\ a \\
\quad \mathit{Fork}\ \ :: \mathit{Thread}\ m\ () \rightarrow \mathit{Thread}\ m\ a \\
\qquad\qquad \rightarrow \mathit{Thread}\ m\ a
\end{array}
$$

Fig. 2. Threads as Resumptions

Implementing threads as resumptions. As previously done in [10,11], Fig. 2 defines threads as resumptions at the programming language level. The thread type ($\mathit{Thread}\ m\ a$) is parametric in the resumption computation value type (a) and the monad in which atomic actions execute (m)[1]. (Symbol :: introduces type declarations and $\rightarrow$ denotes function types.) The definition has several value constructors for a thread. Constructor *Done* captures computed values; a value $\mathit{Done}\ a$ represents the computed value a. Constructor *Atom* captures a resumption of the form $\alpha \triangleright \mathit{res}$. Specifically, *Atom* takes a monadic action of type $m\ (\mathit{Thread}\ m\ a)$, which denotes an atomic computation in monad m that returns a new resumption as a result. In other words, *Atom* captures both the atomic action that is being executed (α) and the subsequent resumption (res). Finally, constructor *Fork* captures the action of spawning new threads; value $\mathit{Fork}\ \mathit{res}\ \mathit{res}'$ encodes a computation wherein a new thread runs resumption res and the original thread continues as res'.[2] As in the standard Haskell libraries, we assume that a fork does not return the new thread's final value and thus the type of the new thread/resumption is simply $\mathit{Thread}\ m\ ()$.

Programming with resumptions. Users do not build programs based on resumptions by directly using the constructors of $\mathit{Thread}\ m\ a$. Instead, they use the interface provided by Haskell monads: $\mathit{return} :: a \rightarrow \mathit{Thread}\ m\ a$ and $(\gg\!=) :: \mathit{Thread}\ m\ a \rightarrow (a \rightarrow \mathit{Thread}\ m\ b) \rightarrow \mathit{Thread}\ m\ b$. The expression $\mathit{return}\ a$ creates a resumption which consists of the computed value a, i.e., it corresponds to $\mathit{Done}\ a$. The operator $(\gg\!=)$, called *bind*, is used to sequence atomic computations. Specifically, the expression $\mathit{res} \gg\!= f$ returns a resumption that consists of the execution of the atomic actions in res followed by the atomic actions obtained from applying f to the result produced by res. We sometimes use Haskell's **do**-notation to write such monadic computations. For example, the expression $\mathit{res} \gg\!= (\lambda a \rightarrow \mathit{return}\ (a{+}1))$, i.e., actions described by the resumption res followed by $\mathit{return}\ (a+1)$ where a is the result produced by res, is written as $\mathbf{do}\ a \leftarrow \mathit{res}; \mathit{return}\ (a+1)$.

Scheduling computations. We use round-robin to schedule atomic actions of different threads. Fig. 3 shows our scheduler implemented as a function from a list of threads into an interleaved computation in the monad m. The scheduler behaves

[1] In our implementation, atomic actions α (as referred as in $\alpha \triangleright \mathit{res}$) are actions described by the monad m.

[2] Spawning threads could also be represented by a equivalent constructor $\mathit{Fork}' :: \mathit{Thread}\ m\ () \rightarrow \mathit{Thread}\ m\ a$, we choose *Fork* for pedagogical reasons.

$$\begin{array}{l}
\mathbf{sch} :: [\mathit{Thread}\ m\ ()] \rightarrow m\ () \\
\mathbf{sch}\ [\,] \qquad\qquad\qquad\quad = \mathit{return}\ () \\
\mathbf{sch}\ ((\mathit{Done}\ _) : \mathit{thrds}) \ = \mathbf{sch}\ \mathit{thrds} \\
\mathbf{sch}\ ((\mathit{Atom}\ m) : \mathit{thrds}) = \\
\quad \mathbf{do}\ \mathit{res} \leftarrow m; \mathbf{sch}\ (\mathit{thrds} +\!\!+ [\mathit{res}]) \\
\mathbf{sch}\ ((\mathit{Fork}\ \mathit{res}\ \mathit{res}') : \mathit{thrds}) = \\
\quad \mathbf{sch}\ ((\mathit{res} : \mathit{thrds}) +\!\!+ [\mathit{res}'])
\end{array}$$

Fig. 3. Simple round-robin scheduler

as follows. If there is an empty list of resumptions, the scheduler, and thus the program, terminates. If the resumption at the head of the list is a computed value ($\mathit{Done}\ \_$), the scheduler removes it and continues scheduling the remaining threads (**sch** *thrds*). (Recall that we are primarily concerned with the side-effects produced by threads and not about their final values.) When the head of the list is an atomic step ($\mathit{Atom}\ m$), **sch** runs it ($\mathit{res} \leftarrow m$), takes the resulting resumption (*res*), and appends it to the end of the thread list ($\mathbf{sch}\ (\mathit{thrds} +\!\!+ [\mathit{res}])$). Finally, when a thread is forked, i.e., the head of the list is a $\mathit{Fork}\ \mathit{res}\ \mathit{res}'$, the spawned resumption is placed at the front of the list ($\mathit{res} : \mathit{thrds}$). Observe that in both of the latter cases the scheduler is invoked recursively—hence we keep evaluating the program until there are no more threads to schedule. We note that although we choose a particular, simple scheduling approach, our results naturally extend for a wide class of deterministic schedulers [28,38].

4 Extending Resumptions with State and Exceptions

LIO provides general programming language abstrations (e.g., state and exceptions), which our library must preserve to retain expressiveness. To this end, we extend the notion of resumptions and modify the scheduler to handle thread local state and exceptions.

Thread local state. As described in [34], the *LIO* monad keeps track of a *current label*, L_{cur}. This label is an upper bound on the labels of all data in lexical scope. When a computation C, with current label L_C, observes an object labeled L_O, C's label is raised to the least upper bound or *join* of the two labels, written $L_C \sqcup L_O$. Importantly, the current label governs where the current computation can write, what labels may be used when creating new channels or threads, etc. For example, after reading an object O, the computation should not be able to write to a channel K if L_O is more confidential than L_K—this would potentially leak sensitive information (about O) into a less sensitive channel. We write $L_C \sqsubseteq L_K$ when L_K at least as confidential as L_C and information is allowed to flow from the computation to the channel.

Using our resumption definition of Sect. 3, we can model concurrent LIO programs as values of type $\mathit{Thread}\ \mathit{LIO}$. Unfortunately, such programs are overly restrictive—since LIO threads would be sharing a single current label—and do

$$
\begin{aligned}
&\mathbf{sch}\ ((Atom\ m) : thrds) = \\
&\quad \mathbf{do}\ res \leftarrow m \\
&\qquad\ st \ \ \leftarrow get \\
&\qquad\ \mathbf{sch}\ (thrds +\!\!+ [put\ st \succ res]) \\
&\mathbf{sch}\ ((Fork\ res\ res') : thrds) = \\
&\quad \mathbf{do}\ st \leftarrow get \\
&\qquad\ \mathbf{sch}\ ((res : thrds) +\!\!+ [put\ st \succ res'])
\end{aligned}
$$

Fig. 4. Context-switch of local state

not allow for the implementation of many important applications. Instead, and as done in the concurrent version of LIO [35], we track the state of each thread, independently, by modifying resumptions, and the scheduler, with the ability to context-switch threads with state.

Figure 4 shows these changes to **sch**. The context-switching mechanism relies on the fact that monad m is a state monad, i.e., provides operations to retrieve (get) and set (put) its state. LIO is a state monad,[3] where the state contains (among other things) L_{cur}. Operation $(\succ) :: m\ b \rightarrow Thread\ m\ a \rightarrow Thread\ m\ a$ modifies a resumption in such a way that its first atomic step ($Atom$) is extended with $m\ b$ as the first action. Here, $Atom$ consists of executing the atomic step ($res \leftarrow m$), taking a snapshot of the state ($st \leftarrow get$), and restoring it when executing the thread again ($put\ st \succ res$). Similarly, the case for $Fork$ saves the state before creating the child thread and restores it when the parent thread executes again ($put\ st \succ res'$).

Exception handling. As described in [36], LIO provides a secure way to throw and catch exceptions—a feature crucial to many real-world applications. Unfortunately, simply using LIO's *throw* and *catch* as atomic actions, as in the case of local state, results in non-standard behavior. In particular, in the interleaved computation produced by **sch**, an atomic action from a thread may throw an exception that would propagate outside the thread group and crash the program. Since we do not consider leaks due to termination, this does not impact security; however, it would have non-standard and restricted semantics. Hence, we first extend our scheduler to introduce a top-level *catch* for every spawned thread.

Besides such an extension, our approach still remains quite limiting. Specifically, LIO's *catch* is defined at the level of the monad LIO, i.e., it can only be used inside atomic steps. Therefore, catch-blocks are prevented from being extended beyond atomic actions. To address this limitation, we lift exception handling to work at the level of resumptions.

To this end, we consider a monad m that handles exceptions, i.e., a monad for which $throw :: e \rightarrow m\ a$ and $catch :: m\ a \rightarrow (e \rightarrow m\ a) \rightarrow m\ a$, where e

[3] For simplicity of exposition, we use *get* and *set*. However, LIO only provides such functions to trusted code. In fact, the monad *LIO* is not an instance of *MonadState* since this would allow untrusted code to arbitrarily modify the current label—a clear security violation.

$$
\begin{aligned}
&\mathit{throw}\ e = \mathit{Atom}\ (\mathit{LIO.throw}\ e)\\
&\mathit{catch}\ (\mathit{Done}\ a)\ \_ = \mathit{Done}\ a\\
&\mathit{catch}\ (\mathit{Atom}\ a)\ \mathit{handler} =\\
&\quad \mathit{Atom}\ (\mathit{LIO.catch}\\
&\qquad (\mathbf{do}\ \mathit{res} \leftarrow a\\
&\qquad\qquad \mathit{return}\ (\mathit{catch}\ \mathit{res}\ \mathit{handler}))\\
&\qquad (\lambda e \rightarrow \mathit{return}\ (\mathit{handler}\ e)))\\
&\mathit{catch}\ (\mathit{Fork}\ \mathit{res}\ \mathit{res}')\ \mathit{handler} =\\
&\quad \mathit{Fork}\ \mathit{res}\ (\mathit{catch}\ \mathit{res}'\ \mathit{handler})
\end{aligned}
$$

Fig. 5. Exception handling for resumptions

is a type denoting exceptions, are accordingly defined. Function *throw* throws the exception supplied as an argument. Function *catch* runs the action supplied as the first argument $(m\ a)$, and if an exception is thrown, then executes the handler $(e \rightarrow m\ a)$ with the value of the exception passed as an argument. If no exceptions are raised, the result of the computation (of type a) is simply returned.

Figure 5 shows the definition of exception handling for resumptions. Since *LIO* defines *throw* and *catch* [36], we qualify these underlying functions with *LIO* to distinguish them from our resumption-level *throw* and *catch*. When throwing an exception, the resumption simply executes an atomic step that throws the exception in *LIO* (*LIO.throw e*).

The definitions of *catch* for *Done* and *Fork* are self explanatory. The most interesting case for *catch* is when the resumption is an *Atom*. Here, *catch* applies *LIO.catch* step by step to each atomic action in the sequence; this is necessary because exceptions can only be caught in the *LIO* monad. As shown in Fig. 5, if no exception is thrown, we simply return the resumption produced by m. Conversely, if an exception is raised, *LIO.catch* will trigger the exception handler which will return a resumption by applying the top-level *handler* to the exception e. To clarify, consider catching an exception in the resumption $\alpha_1 \triangleright \alpha_2 \triangleright x$. Here, *catch* executes α_1 as the first atomic step, and if no exception is raised, it executes α_2 as the next atomic step; on the other hand, if an exception is raised, the resumption $\alpha_2 \triangleright x$ is discarded and *catch*, instead, executes the resumption produced when applying the exception handler to the exception.

5 Performance Tuning

Unsurprisingly, interleaving computations at the library-level introduces performance degradation. To alleviate this, we provide primitives that allow developers to control the granularity of atomic steps—fine-grained atoms allow for more flexible programs, but also lead to more context switches and thus performance degradation (as we spend more time context switching). Additionally, we provide a primitive for the parallel execution of pure code. We describe these features—which do not affect our security guarantees—below.

Granularity of atomic steps. To decrease the frequency of context switches, programmers can treat a complex set of atoms (which are composed using monadic bind) as a single atom using $singleAtom :: Thread\ m\ a \rightarrow Thread\ m\ a$. This function takes a resumption and "compresses" all its atomic steps into one. Although *singleAtom* may seem unsafe, e.g., because we do not restrict threads from adjust the granularity of atomic steps according to secrets, in Sect. 6 we show that this is not the case—it is the atomic execution of atoms, regardless of their granularity, that ensures security.

Parallelism. As in [37], we cannot run one scheduler **sch** per core to gain performance through parallelism. Threads running in parallel can still race to public resources, and thus vulnerable to internal timing attacks (that may, for example, rely on the L3 CPU cache). In principle, it is possible to securely parallelize arbitrary side-effecting computations if races (or their outcomes) to shared public resource are eliminated. Similar to *observational low-determinism* [41], our library could allow parallel computations to compute on disjoint portions of the memory. However, whenever side-effecting computations follow parallel code, we would need to impose synchronization barriers to enforce that all side-effects are performed in a pre-determined order. It is precisely this order, and LIO's safe side-effecting primitives for shared-resources, that hides the outcome of any potential dangerous parallel race. In this paper, we focus on executing pure code in parallel; we leave side-effecting code to future work.

Pure computations, by definition, cannot introduce races to shared resources since they do not produce side effects.[4] To consider such computations, we simply extend the definition of *Thread* with a new constructor: $Parallel :: pure\ b \rightarrow (b \rightarrow Thread\ m\ a) \rightarrow Thread\ m\ a$. Here, *pure* is a monad that characterizes pure expressions, providing the primitive $runPure :: pure\ b \rightarrow b$ to obtain the value denoted by the code given as argument. The monad *pure* could be instantiated to *Par*, a monad that parallelizes pure computations in Haskell [21], with *runPure* set to *runPar*. In a resumption, *Parallel p f* specifies that p is to be executed in a separate Haskell thread—potentially running on a different core than the interleaved computation. Once p produces a value x, f is applied to x to produce the next resumption to execute.

Figure 6 defines **sch** for pure computations, where interaction between resumptions and Haskell-threads gets regulated. The scheduler relies on well-established synchronization primitives called MVars [13]. A value of type *MVar* is a mutable location that is either empty or contains a value. Function *putMVar* fills the MVar with a value if it is empty and blocks otherwise. Dually, *takeMVar* empties an MVar if it is full and returns the value; otherwise it blocks. Our scheduler implementation **sch** simply takes the resumption produced by the *sync* function and schedules it at the end of the thread pool. Function *sync*, internally creates a fresh MVar v and spawns a new Haskell-thread to execute

[4] In the case of Haskell, lazy evaluation may pose a challenge since whether or not a thunk has been evaluate is indeed an effect on a cache [24]. Though our resumption-based approach handles this for the single-core case, handling this in general is part of our ongoing work.

$$
\begin{array}{l}
\textbf{sch}\ (Parallel\ p\ f : thrds) = \\
\quad \textbf{do}\ res \leftarrow sync\ (\lambda v \rightarrow putMVar\ v\ (runPure\ p)) \\
\qquad\qquad\qquad\quad (\lambda v \rightarrow takeMVar\ v) \\
\qquad\qquad\qquad\quad f \\
\qquad \textbf{sch}\ (thrds +\!\!+ [res])
\end{array}
$$

Fig. 6. Scheduler for parallel computations

putMVar v (runPure p). This action will store the result of the parallel computation in the provided MVar. Subsequently, *sync* returns the resumption *res*, whose first atomic action is to read the parallel computation's result from the MVar (*takeMVar v*). At the time of reading, if a value is not yet ready, the atomic action will block the whole interleaved computation. However, once a value x is produced (in the separate thread), f is applied to it and the execution proceeds with the produced resumption $(f\ x)$.

6 Soundness

In this section, we extend the previous formalization of LIO [34] to model the semantics of our concurrency library. We present the syntax extensions that we require to model the behavior of the *Thread* monad:

Expression: $e ::= \ldots \mid \textbf{sch}\ e_s \mid Atom\ e \mid Done\ e \mid Fork\ e\ e \mid Parallel\ e\ e$

where e_s is a list of expressions. For brevity, we omit a full presentation of the syntax and semantics, since we rely on previous results in order to prove the security property of our approach. The interested reader is referred to [6].

Expressions are the usual λ-calculus expressions with special syntax for monadic effects and LIO operations. The syntax node **sch** e_s denotes the scheduler running with the list of threads e_s as its thread pool. The nodes $Atom\ e$, $Done\ e$, $Fork\ e\ e$ and $Parallel\ e\ e$ correspond to the constructors of the *Thread* data type. In what follows, we will use metavariables x, m, p, t, v and f for different kinds of expressions, namely values, monadic computations, pure computations, threads, MVars and functions, respectively.

We consider a global environment Σ which contains the current label of the computation ($\Sigma.\texttt{lbl}$), and also represents the resources shared among all threads, such as mutable references. We start from the one-step reduction relation[5] $\langle \Sigma, e \rangle \longrightarrow \langle \Sigma', e' \rangle$, which has already been defined for LIO [34]. This relation represents a single evaluation step from e to e', with Σ as the initial environment and Σ' as the final one. Presented as an extension to the $\longrightarrow$ relation, Figure 7 shows the reduction rules for concurrent execution using **sch**. The configurations for this relation are of the form $\langle \Sigma, \textbf{sch}\ t_s \rangle$, where Σ is a runtime

[5] As in [35], we consider a version of $\longrightarrow$ which does not include the operation *toLabeled*, since it is susceptible to internal timing attacks.

(DONE)

$$\frac{}{\langle \Sigma, \mathbf{sch}\ (\mathit{Done}\ x : t_s)\rangle \longrightarrow \langle \Sigma, \mathbf{sch}\ t_s\rangle}$$

(ATOM)

$$\frac{\langle \Sigma, m\rangle \longrightarrow^{*} \langle \Sigma', (e)^{\text{LIO}}\rangle}{\langle \Sigma, \mathbf{sch}\ (\mathit{Atom}\ (\mathit{put}\ \Sigma.\mathtt{lbl} \gg m) : t_s)\rangle \longrightarrow \langle \Sigma', \mathbf{sch}\ (t_s +\!\!+ [\mathit{put}\ \Sigma.\mathtt{lbl} \succ e])\rangle}$$

(FORK)

$$\frac{}{\langle \Sigma, \mathbf{sch}\ (\mathit{Fork}\ m_1\ m_2 : t_s)\rangle \longrightarrow \langle \Sigma, \mathbf{sch}\ ((m_1 : t_s) +\!\!+ [\mathit{put}\ \Sigma.\mathtt{lbl} \succ m_2])\rangle}$$

Fig. 7. Semantics for **sch** expressions.

(SEQ)

$$\frac{\langle \Sigma, e\rangle \longrightarrow \langle \Sigma', e'\rangle \qquad P \Rightarrow P'}{\langle \Sigma, e \parallel P\rangle \hookrightarrow \langle \Sigma', e' \parallel P'\rangle}$$

(PURE)

$$\frac{P \Rightarrow P' \qquad v_s \text{ fresh MVar} \qquad s = \Sigma.\mathtt{lbl}}{\begin{array}{c}\langle \Sigma, \mathbf{sch}\ (\mathit{Parallel}\ p\ f : t_s) \parallel P\rangle \hookrightarrow \\ \langle \Sigma, \mathbf{sch}\ (t_s +\!\!+ [\mathit{Atom}\ (\mathit{takeMVar}\ v_s \ggg f)]) \parallel P' \parallel (\mathit{putMVar}\ v_s\ (\mathit{runPure}\ p))_s\rangle\end{array}}$$

(SYNC)

$$\frac{P \Rightarrow P'}{\begin{array}{c}\langle \Sigma, \mathbf{sch}\ (\mathit{Atom}\ (\mathit{takeMVar}\ v_s \ggg f) : t_s) \parallel (\mathit{putMVar}\ v_s\ x)_s \parallel P\rangle \hookrightarrow \\ \langle \Sigma, \mathbf{sch}\ (f\ x : t_s) \parallel P'\rangle\end{array}}$$

Fig. 8. Semantics for **sch** expressions with parallel processes.

environment and t_s is a list of *Thread* computations. Note that the computation in an *Atom* always begins with either *put* $\Sigma.\mathtt{lbl}$ for some label $\Sigma.\mathtt{lbl}$, or with *takeMVar* v for some MVar v. Rules (DONE), (ATOM), and (FORK) basically behave like the corresponding equations in the definition of **sch** (see Figs. 3 and 4). In rule (ATOM), the syntax node $(e)^{\text{LIO}}$ represents an LIO computation that has produced expression e as its result. Although **sch** applications should expand to their definitions, for brevity we show the unfolding of the resulting expressions into the next recursive call. This unfolding follows from repeated application of basic λ-calculus reductions.

Figure 8 extends relation $\longrightarrow$ into $\hookrightarrow$ to express pure parallel computations. The configurations for this relation are of the form $\langle \Sigma, \mathbf{sch}\ t_s \| P\rangle$, where P is an abstract process representing a pure computation that is performed in parallel. These abstract processes would be reified as native Haskell threads. The operator $(\|)$, representing parallel process composition, is commutative and associative.

As described in the previous section, when a *Thread* evaluates a *Parallel* computation, a new native Haskell thread should be spawned in order to run it.

Rule (PURE) captures this intuition. A fresh MVar v_s (where s is the current label) is used for synchronization between the parent and the spawned thread. A process is denoted by *putMVar* v_s followed by a pure expression, and it is also tagged with the security level of the thread that spawned it.

Pure processes are evaluated in parallel with the main threads managed by **sch**. The relation $\Rightarrow$ nondeterministically evaluates one process in a parallel composition and is defined as follows.

$$\frac{\mathit{runPure}\ p \longrightarrow^{*} x}{(\mathit{putMVar}\ v_s\ (\mathit{runPure}\ p))_s \| P \Rightarrow (\mathit{putMVar}\ v_s\ x)_s \| P}$$

For simplicity, we consider the full evaluation of one process until it yields a value as just one step, since the computations involved are pure and therefore cannot leak data. Rule (SEQ) in Fig. 8 represents steps where no parallel forking or synchronization is performed, so it executes one $\longrightarrow$ step alongside a $\Rightarrow$ step.

Rule (SYNC) models the synchronization barrier technique from Sect. 5. When an *Atom* of the form ($\mathit{takeMVar}\ v_s \gg\!= f$) is evaluated, execution blocks until the pure process with the corresponding MVar v_s completes its computation. After that, the process is removed and the scheduler resumes execution.

Security guarantees. We show that programs written using our library satisfy termination-insensitive non-interference, i.e., an attacker at level L cannot distinguish the results of programs that run with indistinguishable inputs. This result has been previously established for the sequential version of LIO [34]. As in [20,31,34], we prove this property by using the *term erasure* technique.

In this proof technique, we define function ε_L in such a way that $\varepsilon_L(e)$ contains only information below or equal to level L, i.e., the function ε_L replaces all the information more sensitive than L or incomparable to L in e with a hole ($\bullet$). We adapt the previous definition of ε_L to handle the new constructs in the library. In most of the cases, the erasure function is simply applied homomorphically (e.g., $\varepsilon_L(e_1\ e_2) = \varepsilon_L(e_1)\ \varepsilon_L(e_2)$). For **sch** expressions, the erasure function is mapped into the list; all threads with a current label above L are removed from the pool ($\mathit{filter}\ (\not\equiv \bullet)\ (\mathit{map}\ \varepsilon_L\ t_s)$), where $\equiv$ denotes syntactic equivalence). Analogously, erasure for a parallel composition consists of removing all processes using an MVar tagged with a level not strictly below or equal to L. The computation performed in a certain *Atom* is erased if the label is not strictly below or equal than L. This is given by

$$\varepsilon_L(\mathit{Atom}\ (\mathit{put}\ s \gg m)) = \begin{cases} \bullet & , s \not\sqsubseteq L \\ \mathit{put}\ s \gg \varepsilon_L\ (m) & , \text{otherwise} \end{cases}$$

A similar rule exists for expressions of the form $\mathit{Atom}\ (\mathit{takeMVar}\ v_s \gg\!= f)$. Note that this relies on the fact that an atom must be of the form $\mathit{Atom}\ (\mathit{put}\ s \gg m)$ or $\mathit{Atom}\ (\mathit{takeMVar}\ v_s \gg\!= f)$ by construction. For expressions of the form *Parallel* $p\ f$, erasure behaves homomorphically, i.e. $\varepsilon_L(\mathit{Parallel}\ p\ f) = \mathit{Parallel}\ \varepsilon_L(p)\ (\varepsilon_L \circ f)$.

Following the definition of the erasure function, we introduce the a new evaluation relation $\hookrightarrow_L$ as follows: $\langle \Sigma, t \| P \rangle \hookrightarrow_L \varepsilon_L(\langle \Sigma', t' \| P' \rangle)$ if $\langle \Sigma, t \| P \rangle \hookrightarrow \langle \Sigma', t' \| P' \rangle$. The relation $\hookrightarrow_L$ guarantees that confidential data, i.e., data not below or equal-to level L, is erased as soon as it is created. We write $\hookrightarrow_L^*$ for the reflexive and transitive closure of $\hookrightarrow_L$.

In order to prove non-interference, we will establish a simulation relation between $\hookrightarrow^*$ and $\hookrightarrow_L^*$ through the erasure function: erasing all secret data and then taking evaluation steps in $\hookrightarrow_L$ is equivalent to taking steps in $\hookrightarrow$ first, and then erasing all secret values in the resulting configuration. In the rest of this section, we consider well-typed terms to avoid stuck configurations.

Proposition 1 (Many-step simulation). *If* $\langle \Sigma, \mathbf{sch}\ t_s \| P \rangle \hookrightarrow^* \langle \Sigma', \mathbf{sch}\ t_s' \| P' \rangle$, *then it holds that* $\varepsilon_L(\langle \Sigma, \mathbf{sch}\ t_s \| P \rangle) \hookrightarrow_L^* \varepsilon_L(\langle \Sigma', \mathbf{sch}\ t_s' \| P' \rangle)$.

The L-equivalence relation $\approx_L$ is an equivalence relation between configurations and their parts, defined as the equivalence kernel of the erasure function ε_L: $\langle \Sigma, \mathbf{sch}\ t_s \| P \rangle \approx_L \langle \Sigma', \mathbf{sch}\ r_s \| Q \rangle$ iff $\varepsilon_L(\langle \Sigma, \mathbf{sch}\ t_s \| P \rangle) = \varepsilon_L(\langle \Sigma', \mathbf{sch}\ r_s \| Q \rangle)$.

If two configurations are L-equivalent, they agree on all data below or at level L, i.e., an attacker at level L is not able to distinguish them.

The next theorem shows the non-interference property. The configuration $\langle \Sigma, \mathbf{sch}\ [] \rangle$ represents a final configuration, where the thread pool is empty and there are no more threads to run.

Theorem 1 (Termination-insensitive non-interference). *Given a computation* e, *inputs* e_1 *and* e_2, *an attacker at level* L, *runtime environments* Σ_1 *and* Σ_2, *then for all inputs* e_1, e_2 *such that* $e_1 \approx_L e_2$, *if* $\langle \Sigma_1, \mathbf{sch}\ [e\ e_1] \rangle \hookrightarrow^* \langle \Sigma_1', \mathbf{sch}\ [] \rangle$ *and* $\langle \Sigma_2, \mathbf{sch}\ [e\ e_2] \rangle \hookrightarrow^* \langle \Sigma_2', \mathbf{sch}\ [] \rangle$, *then* $\langle \Sigma_1', \mathbf{sch}\ [] \rangle \approx_L \langle \Sigma_2', \mathbf{sch}\ [] \rangle$.

This theorem essentially states that if we take two executions from configurations $\langle \Sigma_1, \mathbf{sch}\ [e\ e_1] \rangle$ and $\langle \Sigma_2, \mathbf{sch}\ [e\ e_2] \rangle$, which are indistinguishable to an attacker at level L ($e_1 \approx_L e_2$), then the final configurations for the executions $\langle \Sigma_1', \mathbf{sch}\ [] \rangle$ and $\langle \Sigma_2', \mathbf{sch}\ [] \rangle$ are also indistinguishable to the attacker ($\langle \Sigma_1', \mathbf{sch}\ [] \rangle \approx_L \langle \Sigma_2', \mathbf{sch}\ [] \rangle$). This result generalizes when constructors *Done*, *Atom*, and *Fork* involve exception handling (see Fig. 5). The reason for this lies in the fact that *catch* and *throw* defer all exception handling to *LIO.throw* and *LIO.catch*, which have been proved secure in [36].

7 Case Study: Classifying Location Data

We evaluated the trade-offs between performance, expressiveness and security through an LIO case study. We implemented an untrusted application that performs K-means clustering on sensitive user location data, in order to classify GPS-enabled cell phone into locations on a map, e.g., home, work, gym, etc. Importantly, this app is untrusted yet computes clusters for users without leaking their location (e.g., the fact that Alice frequents the local chapter of the Rebel Alliance). K-means is a particularly interesting application for evaluating our scheduler as the classification phase is highly parallelizable—each data point can be evaluated independently.

We implemented and benchmarked three versions of this app: (i) A baseline implementation that does not use our scheduler and parallelizes the computation using Haskell's *Par* Monad [21]. Since in this implementation, the scheduler is not modeled using resumptions, it leverages the parallelism features of *Par*. (ii) An implementation in the resumption based scheduler, but pinned to a single core (therefore not taking advantage of parallelizing pure computations). (iii) A parallel implementation using the resumption-based scheduler. This implementation expresses the exact same computation as the first one, but is not vulnerable to cache-based leaks, even in the face of parallel execution on multiple cores.

We ran each implementation against one month of randomly generated data, where data points are collected each minute (so, 43200 data points in total). All experiments were run ten times on a machine with two 4-core (with hyperthreading) 2.4 Ghz Intel Xeon processors and 48 GB of RAM. The secure, but non-parallel implementation using resumptions performed extremely poorly. With mean 204.55 s (standard deviation 7.19 s), it performed over eight times slower than the baseline at 17.17 s (standard deviation 1.16 s). This was expected since K-means is highly parallelizable. Conversely, the parallel implementation in the resumption based scheduler performed more comparably to the baseline, at 17.83 s (standard deviation 1.15 s).

To state any conclusive facts on the overhead introduce by our library, it is necessary to perform a more exhaustive analysis involving more than a single case study.

8 Related work

Cryptosystems. Attacks exploiting the CPU cache have been considered by the cryptographic community [16]. Our attacker model is weaker than the one typically considered in cryptosystems, i.e., attackers with access to a stopwatch. As a countermeasure, several authors propose partitioning the cache (e.g., [25]), which often requires special hardware. Other countermeasures (e.g. [23]) are mainly implementation-specific and, while applicable to cryptographic primitives, they do not easily generalize to arbitrary code (as required in our scenario).

Resumptions. While CPS can be used to model concurrency in a functional setting [7], resumptions are often simpler to reason about when considering security guarantees [10,11]. The closest related work is that of Harrison and Hook [11]; inspired by a secure multi-level operating system, the authors utilize resumptions to model interleaving and layered state monads to represent threads. Every layer corresponds to an individual thread, thereby providing a notion of local state. Since we do not require such generality, we simply adapt the scheduler to context-switch the local state underlying the *LIO* monad. We believe that authors overlooked the power of resumptions to deal with timing perturbations produced by the underlying hardware. In [10], Harrison hints that resumptions could handle exceptions; in this work, we consummate his claim by describing precisely how to implement *throw* and *catch*.

Language-based IFC. There is been considerable amount of literature on applying programming languages techniques to address the internal timing covert channel (e.g. [28,33,35,39,41]). Many of these works assume that the execution of a single step, i.e., a reduction step in some transition system, is performed in a single unit of time. This assumption is often made so that security guarantees can be easily shown using programming language semantics. Unfortunately, the presence of the CPU cache (or other hardware shared state) breaks this correspondence, making cache attacks viable. Our resumption approach establishes a correspondence between atomic steps at the implementation-level and reduction step in a transition system. Previous approaches can leverage this technique when implementing systems, as to avoid the reappearance of the internal timing channel.

Agat [2] presents a code transformation for sequential programs such that both code paths of a branch have the same memory access pattern. This transformation has been adapted in different works (e.g., [32]). Agat's approach, however, focuses on avoiding attacks relying on the data cache, while leaving the instruction cache unattended.

Russo and Sabelfeld [29] consider non-interference for concurrent while-like-programs under cooperative and deterministic scheduling. Similar to our work, this approach eliminates cache-attacks by restricting the use of yields. Differently, our library targets a richer programming languages, i.e., it supports parallelism, exceptions, and dynamically adjusting the granularity of atomic actions.

Secure multi-execution [8] preserves confidentiality of data by executing the same sequential program several times, one for each security level. In this scenario, cache-based attacks can only be removed in specific configurations [14] (e.g., when there are as many CPU cores as security levels).

Hedin and Sands [12] present a type-system for preventing external timing attacks for bytecode. Their semantics is augmented to incorporate history, which enables the modeling of cache effects. Zhang et al. [42] provide a method for mitigating external events when their timing behavior could be affected by the underlying hardware. Their semantics focusses on sequential programs, wherein attacks due to the cache arise in the form of externally visible events. Their solution is directly applicable to our system when considering external events.

System security. In order to achieve strong isolation, Barthe et al. [3] present a model of virtualization which flushes the cache upon switching between guest operating systems. Flushing the cache in such scenarios is common and does not impact the already-costly context-switch. Although this technique addresses attacks that leverage the CPU cache, it does not address the case where a shared resource cannot be controlled (e.g., CPU bus).

Allowing some information leakage, Kopft et al. [17] combines abstract interpretation and quantitative information-flow to analyze leakage bounds for cache attacks. Kim et al. [15] propose StealthMem, a system level protection against cache attacks. StealthMem allows programs to allocate memory that does not get evicted from the cache. StealthMem is capable of enforcing confidentiality for a stronger attacker model than ours, i.e., they consider programs with access to a stopwatch and running on multiple cores. However, we suspect that StealthMem is not adequate for scenarios with arbitrarily complex security lattices, wherein not flushing the cache would be overly restricting.

9 Conclusion

We present a library for LIO that leverages resumptions to expose concurrency. Our resumption-based approach and "instruction"- or atom-based scheduling removes internal timing leaks induced by timing perturbations of the underlying hardware. We extend the notion of resumptions to support state and exceptions and provide a scheduler that context-switches programs with such features. Though our approach eliminates internal-timing attacks that leverage hardware caches, library-level threading imposes considerable performance penalties. Addressing this, we provide programmers with a safe mean for controlling the context-switching frequency, i.e., allowing for the adjustment of the "size" of atomic actions. Moreover, we provide a primitive for spawning computations in parallel, a novel feature not previously available in IFC tools. We prove soundness of our approach and implement a simple case study to demonstrate its use. Our techniques can be adapted to other Haskell-like IFC systems beyond LIO. The library, case study, and details of the proofs can be found at [6].

Acknowledgments. We would like to thank Josef Svenningsson and our colleagues in the ProSec and Functional Programming group at Chalmers for useful comments. This work was supported by the Swedish research agency VR, STINT, the Barbro Osher foundation, DARPA CRASH under contract #N66001-10-2-4088, and multiple gifts from Google. Deian Stefan is supported by the DoD through the NDSEG Fellowship Program.

References

1. Aciiçmez, O.: Yet another microarchitectural attack:: exploiting I-cache. In: Proceedings of the 2007 ACM workshop on Computer security architecture, CSAW '07. ACM (2007)
2. Agat, J.: Transforming out timing leaks. In: Proceedings of the ACM Symposium on Principles of Programming Languages, pp. 40–53, January 2000
3. Barthe, G., Betarte, G., Campo, J., Luna, C.: Cache-leakage resilient OS isolation in an idealized model of virtualization. In: Proceedings of the IEEE Computer Security Foundations Symposium. IEEE Computer Society, June 2012
4. Boudol, G., Castellani, I.: Noninterference for concurrent programs. In: Orejas, F., Spirakis, P.G., van Leeuwen, J. (eds.) ICALP 2001. LNCS, vol. 2076, pp. 382–395. Springer, Heidelberg (2001)
5. Boudol, G., Castellani, I.: Non-interference for concurrent programs and thread systems. Theor. Comput. Sci. **281**(1), 109–130 (2002)

6. Buiras, P., Levy, A., Stefan, D., Russo, A., Mazières, D.: A library for removing cache-based attacks in concurrent information flow systems: Extended version. http://www.cse.chalmers.se/~buiras/resLIO.html (2013)
7. Claessen, K.: A poor man's concurrency monad. J. Funct. Program. **9**(3), 313–323 (1999)
8. Devriese, D., Piessens, F.: Noninterference through secure multi-execution. In: Proceedings of the 2010 IEEE Symposium on Security and Privacy, SP '10. IEEE Computer Society (2010)
9. Giffin, D.B., Levy, A., Stefan, D., Terei, D., Mazières, D., Mitchell, J., Russo, A.: Hails: protecting data privacy in untrusted web applications. In: Proceedings of the 10th Symposium on Operating Systems Design and Implementation, October 2012
10. Harrison, B.: Cheap (but functional) threads. J. Funct. Program. http://people.cs.missouri.edu/~harrisonwl/drafts/CheapThreads.pdf (2004)
11. Harrison, W.L., Hook, J.: Achieving information flow security through precise control of effects. In: Proceedings of the IEEE Computer Security Foundations Workshop. IEEE Computer Society (2005)
12. Hedin, D., Sands, D.: Timing aware information flow security for a JavaCard-like bytecode. Electron. Notes Theor. Comput. Sci. **141**(1), 163–182 (2005)
13. Jones, S.P., Gordon, A., Finne, S.: Concurrent Haskell. In: Proceedings of the 23rd ACM SIGPLAN-SIGACT Symposium on Principles of Programming Languages. ACM (1996)
14. Kashyap, V., Wiedermann, B., Hardekopf, B.: Timing- and termination-sensitive secure information flow: exploring a new approach. In: Proceedings of the IEEE Symposium on Security and Privacy. IEEE (2011)
15. Kim, T., Peinado, M., Mainar-Ruiz, G.: STEALTHMEM: system-level protection against cache-based side channel attacks in the cloud. In: Proceedings of the USENIX Conference on Security Symposium, Security'12. USENIX Association (2012)
16. Kocher, P.C.: Timing attacks on implementations of Diffie-Hellman, RSA, DSS, and other systems. In: Koblitz, N. (ed.) CRYPTO 1996. LNCS, vol. 1109, pp. 104–113. Springer, Heidelberg (1996)
17. Köpf, B., Mauborgne, L., Ochoa, M.: Automatic quantification of cache side-channels. In: Madhusudan, P., Seshia, S.A. (eds.) CAV 2012. LNCS, vol. 7358, pp. 564–580. Springer, Heidelberg (2012)
18. Krohn, M., Yip, A., Brodsky, M., Morris, R., Walfish, M.: A world wide web without walls. In: 6th ACM Workshop on Hot Topics in Networking (Hotnets), Atlanta, November 2007
19. Lampson, B.W.: A note on the confinement problem. Commun. ACM **16**(10), 613–615 (1973)
20. Li, P., Zdancewic, S.: Arrows for secure information flow. Theor. Comput. Sci. **411**(19), 1974–1994 (2010)
21. Marlow, S., Newton, R., Jones, S.L.P.: A monad for deterministic parallelism. In: Proceedings of the ACM SIGPLAN Symposium on Haskell (2011)
22. Moggi, E.: Notions of computation and monads. Inf. Comput. **93**(1), 55–92 (1991)
23. Osvik, D.A., Shamir, A., Tromer, E.: Cache attacks and countermeasures: the case of AES. In: Pointcheval, D. (ed.) CT-RSA 2006. LNCS, vol. 3860, pp. 1–20. Springer, Heidelberg (2006)
24. Pablo, B., Russo, A.: Lazy programs leak secrets. In: The Pre-proceedings of the 18th Nordic Conference on Secure IT Systems (NordSec), October 2013

25. Page, D.: Partitioned cache architecture as a side-channel defence mechanism. IACR Cryptology ePrint Archive 2005 (2005)
26. Percival, C.: Cache missing for fun and profit. In: Proceedings of BSDCan 2005 (2005)
27. Pottier, F.: A simple view of type-secure information flow in the π-calculus. In: Proceedings of the 15th IEEE Computer Security Foundations Workshop (2002)
28. Russo, A., Sabelfeld, A.: Securing interaction between threads and the scheduler. In: Proceedings of the IEEE Computer Security Foundations Workshop, July 2006
29. Russo, A., Sabelfeld, A.: Security for multithreaded programs under cooperative scheduling. In: Virbitskaite, I., Voronkov, A. (eds.) PSI 2006. LNCS, vol. 4378, pp. 474–480. Springer, Heidelberg (2007)
30. Russo, A., Hughes, J., Naumann, D.A., Sabelfeld, A.: Closing internal timing channels by transformation. In: Okada, M., Satoh, I. (eds.) ASIAN 2006. LNCS, vol. 4435, pp. 120–135. Springer, Heidelberg (2007)
31. Russo, A., Claessen, K., Hughes, J.: A library for light-weight information-flow security in Haskell. In: Proceedings of the ACM SIGPLAN Symposium on Haskell, pp. 13–24. ACM Press, September 2008
32. Sabelfeld, A., Sands, D.: Probabilistic noninterference for multi-threaded programs. In: Proceedings of the IEEE Computer Security Foundations Workshop, July 2000
33. Smith, G., Volpano, D.: Secure information flow in a multi-threaded imperative language. In: Proceedings of the ACM Symposium on Principles of Programming Languages, January 1998
34. Stefan, D., Russo, A., Mitchell, J.C., Mazières, D.: Flexible dynamic information flow control in Haskell. In: Haskell Symposium. ACM SIGPLAN, September 2011
35. Stefan, D., Russo, A., Buiras, P., Levy, A., Mitchell, J.C., Mazières, D.: Addressing covert termination and timing channels in concurrent information flow systems. In: The 17th ACM SIGPLAN International Conference on Functional Programming (ICFP), pp. 201–213. ACM, September 2012
36. Stefan, D., Russo, A., Mitchell, J.C., Mazières, D.: Flexible dynamic information flow control in the presence of exceptions. Arxiv preprint arXiv:1207.1457 (2012)
37. Stefan, D., Buiras, P., Yang, E.Z., Levy, A., Terei, D., Russo, A., Mazières, D.: Eliminating cache-based timing attacks with instruction-based scheduling. In: Proceedings of the European Symposium on Research in Computer Security, pp. 718–735 (2013)
38. Swierstra, W.: A Functional specification of effects. Ph.D. thesis, University of Nottingham, November 2008
39. Volpano, D., Smith, G.: Probabilistic noninterference in a concurrent language. J. Comput. Secur. **7**(2–3), 231–253 (1999)
40. Wong, W.H.: Timing attacks on RSA: revealing your secrets through the fourth dimension. Crossroads **11**(3), p. 5 (2005)
41. Zdancewic, S., Myers, A.C.: Observational determinism for concurrent program security. In: Proceedings of the IEEE Computer Security Foundations Workshop, June 2003
42. Zhang, D., Askarov, A., Myers, A.C.: Language-based control and mitigation of timing channels. In: Proceedings of PLDI. ACM (2012)

Models, Specifications, and Proofs

Specification of Asynchronous Component Systems with Modal I/O-Petri Nets

Serge Haddad[1(✉)], Rolf Hennicker[2], and Mikael H. Møller[3]

[1] LSV, ENS Cachan & CNRS & Inria, Cachan, France
haddad@lsv.ens-cachan.fr
[2] Ludwig-Maximilians-Universität München, Munich, Germany
[3] Aalborg University, Aalborg, Denmark

Abstract. Modal transition systems are an elegant way to formalise the design process of a system through refinement and composition. Here we propose to adapt this methodology to asynchronous composition via Petri nets. The Petri nets that we consider have distinguished labels for inputs, outputs, internal communications and silent actions and "must" and "may" modalities for transitions. The input/output labels show the interaction capabilities of a net to the outside used to build larger nets by asynchronous composition via communication channels. The modalities express constraints for Petri net refinement taking into account observational abstraction from silent transitions. Modal I/O-Petri nets are equipped with a modal transition system semantics. We show that refinement is preserved by asynchronous composition and by hiding of communication channels. We study compatibility properties which express communication requirements for composed systems and we show that these properties are decidable, they are preserved in larger contexts and also by modal refinement. On this basis we propose a methodology for the specification of distributed systems in terms of modal I/O-Petri nets which supports incremental design, encapsulation of components, stepwise refinement and independent implementability.

1 Introduction

Component-based design is an important field in software engineering. Crucial tasks in the design process concern the stepwise refinement of specifications towards implementations and the formation of component assemblies by composition. Many approaches and formalisms have been proposed for rigorous component-based design supporting different communication styles and different notions of refinement. Among them particular attention has been attracted by modal transition systems introduced by Larsen and Thomsen in 1988 [15] which use distinguished may- and must-transitions to specify allowed and obligatory behaviour and thus provide a flexible basis for refinement. While refinement concerns the vertical dimension of system development, composition concerns the

This work has been partially sponsored by the EU project ASCENS, 257414.

M. Abadi and A. Lluch Lafuente (Eds.): TGC 2013, LNCS 8358, pp. 219–234, 2014.
DOI: 10.1007/978-3-319-05119-2_13,

horizontal dimension in which larger systems are built from smaller ones such that communication requirements must be respected. Communication properties are important when reasoning about distributed mechanisms, algorithms and applications (e.g. management of sockets in UNIX, maintaining unicity of a token in a ring based algorithm, guarantee of email reading, etc).

Petri nets are a natural model for the design of concurrent and distributed systems. They have received a great attention w.r.t. the composition and refinement issues including communication properties. Composition of nets has been addressed via several paradigms. The process algebra approach has been investigated by several works leading to the Petri net algebra [5]. Such an approach is closely related to synchronous composition. In [20] and [21] asynchronous composition of nets is performed via a set of places or, more generally, via a subnet modelling some medium. Then structural restrictions on the subnets are proposed in order to preserve global properties like liveness or deadlock-freeness. In [18] a general composition operator is proposed and its associativity is established. A closely related concept to composition is the one of open Petri nets which has been used in different contexts like the analysis of web services [22]. In parallel, very early works have been done for defining and analyzing refinement of nets; see [6] for a survey. Looking at more recent works, [19] (which is the closest to our contribution) studies the refinement in the context of circuit design. In [19] a notion of correct implementation is introduced which is shown to be compositional. Several works also use an abstraction/refinement paradigm to propose efficient verification methods; see e.g. [8].

In our contribution we want to combine the advantages of modal transition systems with the ability of Petri nets to represent infinite state systems, with their decidability potential and with their way how asynchronous composition is achieved. A natural candidate are *modal Petri nets* introduced in [7] (and later in [2] as a special case of Modal Process Rewrite Systems) which studies modal refinement and decidability results. Surprisingly, to the best of our knowledge, no other approaches to modal Petri nets exist yet. On the other hand, for asynchronous communication, we have recently introduced in [10] *asynchronous I/O-Petri nets*, for which we have analysed several communication properties from the compositionality and decidability point of view. Hence it is an obvious goal to combine, adjust and extend the results achieved in [7] and [10] to a rigorous design methodology that supports the vertical and the horizontal dimension of software development in a uniform and compatible way.

Concerning the vertical dimension we consider modal refinement; for the horizontal dimension we consider asynchronous composition and we focus on the *message consuming* and the *necessarily message consuming* properties which are important requirements to ensure that previously sent messages can or must necessarily be consumed by the communication partner. It turns out that the necessarily message consuming property defined in [10] is in general not preserved by modal refinement. This is due to the fact that our refinement notion supports observational abstraction. Therefore we investigate the new notion of an *observationally weakly fair run* and show that necessarily message consuming is indeed preserved by modal refinement if we restrict the consumption requirement to all observational weakly fair runs. Due to the fairness requirement the necessarily consuming property is also preserved on the horizontal layer when components are put in compatible contexts. We also show that the new variants of the communication properties are decidable.

This paper is structured as follows: In Sect. 2, we summarise our proposal by means of an illustrating example. Section 3 presents the underlying formal defintions of modal asynchronous I/O-Petri nets (MAIOPNs) and their semantics in terms of modal asynchronous I/O-transition systems (MAIOTSs). In Sect. 4, we consider modal refinement and show that it is compositional. We also show that modal refinement is preserved by channel hiding. In Sect. 5, we study (necessarily) message consuming systems and we present the results on the preservation of the communication properties by composition and by refinement. As a consequence, our framework supports the principle of independent implementability in the sense of [1]. We finish with some concluding remarks in Sect. 6.

2 Illustrating Example

We introduce an illustrating example to motivate our notions of modal asynchronous I/O-Petri nets (MAIOPNs), their composition, hiding and refinement. For this purpose we consider a top down approach to the design of a simple compressing system (inspired by [3]) which is able to receive files for compression and outputs either zip- or jpg-files. We start with an interface specification of the system modelled by the CompressorInterface in Fig. 1a.

The interface specification is presented by a labelled Petri net with distinguished input and output labels and with modalities on the transitions. The label file suffixed with "?" indicates an input action and the labels comprJpg, comprZip suffixed with "!" indicate output actions. Following the idea of modal transition systems introduced by Larsen and Thomsen in [15] transitions are equipped with "must" or "may" modalities. A must-transition, drawn black, indicates that this transition is required for any refinement while a may-transition, drawn white, may also be removed or turned into a must-transition. Models containg only must-transitions represent implementations. In the example it is required that input files must always be received and that the option to produce zipped text files is always available while a refinement may or may not support the production of compressed jpg-files for graphical data. Our interface specification models an infinite state system since an unbounded number of files can be received.

In the next step we propose an architecture for the realisation of the compressing system as shown in Fig. 1b. It is given by an assembly of three connected components, a Controller component which delegates the compression tasks, a GifCompressor component which actually performs the compression of gif-files into jpg-files and a TxtCompressor component which produces zip-files from text files. The single components are connected by unbounded and unordered channels gif, jpg, ... for asynchronous communication.

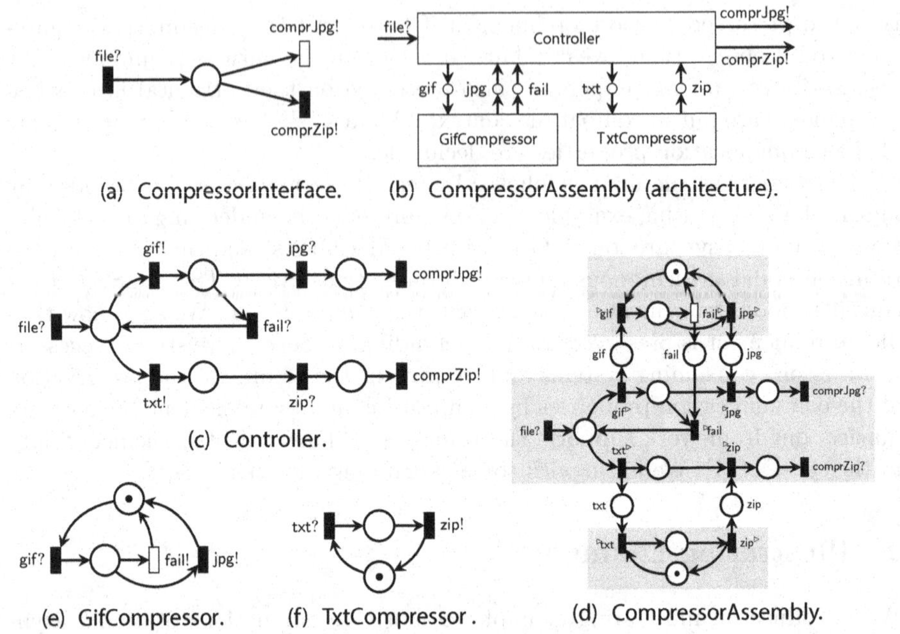

Fig. 1. **a** CompressorInterface, **b** Compressor Assembly (architecture), **c** Controller, **d** Compressor Assembly, **e** GifCompressor, **f** TxtCompressor.

The behaviour of the single components is modelled by the MAIOPNs shown in Fig. 1c, e, f. The behaviour of the CompressorAssembly is given by the asynchronous composition of the single Petri nets shown in Fig. 1d. For each pair of shared input and output actions a new place is introduced, called communication channel. Transitions with a shared output label a (of a given component) are connected to the new place a and the transition label is renamed to $a^{\rhd}$ in the composition. Similarly the place a is connected to transitions with the corresponding input label a which is then renamed to ${}^{\rhd}a$ in the composition. The result of our composition is very similar to the composition of open Petri nets, see e.g. [16], which relies on matching of interface places. But our approach is methodologically different since we introduce the communication places only when the composition is constructed. In that way our basic components are not biased to asynchronous composition but could be used for synchronous composition as well. In this work we focus on asynchronous composition and we are particularly interested in the analysis of generic communication properties ensuring that messages pending on communication channels are eventually consumed. Therefore our notion of modal asynchronous I/O-Petri net will comprise an explicit discrimination of channel places and, additionally to input/output labels we use, for each channel a, distinguished communication labels $a^{\rhd}$ for putting messages on the channel and ${}^{\rhd}a$ for consuming messages from the channel. If the set of channels is empty a MAIOPN models an interface or a primitive component from which larger systems can be constructed by asynchronous composition.

In our example the behaviour of the CompressorAssembly is given by the asynchronous composition Controller $\otimes_{pn}$ TxtCompressor $\otimes_{pn}$ GifCompressor shown in Fig. 1d. It models a highly parallel system such that compressing of files can be executed concurrently and new files can be obtained at the same time. Each single compressing tool, however, is working sequentially. Its behaviour should be clear from the specifications. The GifCompressor in Fig. 1e has an optional behaviour modelled by a may-transition to indicate a compressing failure and then the controller will submit the file again.

After the assembly has been established we are interested in whether communication works properly in the sense that pending messages on communication channels will be consumed. We will distinguish between two variants of consumption requirements (see Sect. 5) expressing that for non-empty channels there must be a possibility for consumption or, more strongly, that consumption must always happen on each (observationally weakly fair) run. The fairness assumption is essential to support incremental design (Theorem 9); for instance we can first check that Controller $\otimes_{pn}$ TxtCompressor has the desired communication properties for the channels {txt, zip}, then we check that the full assembly has the desired communication properties for its channel subset {gif, jpg, fail} and from this we can automatically derive that the assembly has the properties for *all* its channels.

It remains to show that the CompressorAssembly is indeed a realisation of the CompressorInterface. For this purpose we consider the black-box behaviour of the assembly obtained by hiding the communication channels. This is done by applying our hiding operator to the CompressorAssembly denoted by CompressorAssembly$\backslash_{pn}${gif, jpg, fail, txt, zip}; see Fig. 2. Hiding moves all communication labels $a^{\triangleright}$ and ${}^{\triangleright}a$ for the hidden channels a to the invisible action τ. In this way producing and consuming messages from hidden channels become silent transitions. Now we have to establish a refinement relation between CompressorAssembly$\backslash_{pn}${gif, jpg, fail, txt, zip} and the CompressorInterface by taking into account the modalities on the transitions such that must-transitions of the abstract specification must be available in the refinement and all transitions of the refinement must be allowed by corresponding may-transitions of the abstract specification. In our example the assembly has implemented the optional jpg compression of the interface by a must-transition. Obviously we must also deal with silent transitions which, in our example, occur in CompressorAssembly$\backslash_{pn}${gif, jpg, fail, txt, zip}. For this purpose we use a modal refinement relation, denoted by $\leq_{\mathrm{m}}^{*}$, which supports observational abstraction. In our case study this is expressed by the proof obligation (1) in Fig. 2.

Figure 2 illustrates that after the assembly is proven to be a correct realisation of the interface one can still further refine the assembly by component-wise refinement of its constituent parts. For instance, we can locally refine the GifCompressor by resolving the may-modality for producing failures. There are basically two possibilities: Either the failure option is removed or it is turned into

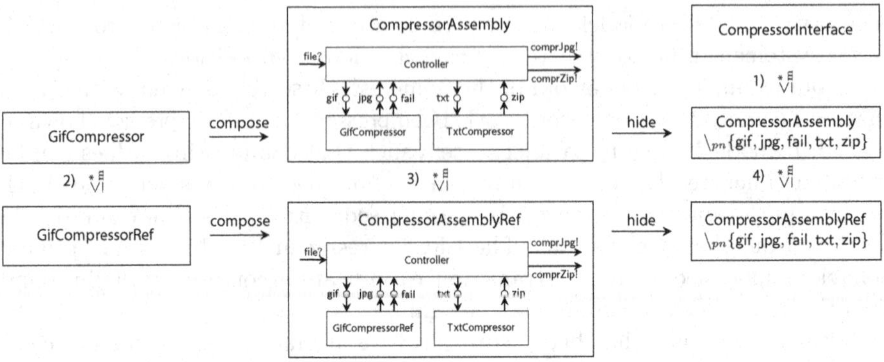

Fig. 2. System development methodology.

a must-transition. The component GifCompressorRef in Fig. 2 represents such a refinement of GifCompressor indicated by (2). We will show in Theorem 3.1 that refinement is compositional, i.e. we obtain automatically that the assembly CompressorAssemblyRef obtained by composition with the new gif compressor is a refinement of CompressorAssembly indicated by (3) in Fig. 2. As a crucial result we will also show in Theorem 10 that refinement preserves communication properties which then can be automatically derived for CompressorAssemblyRef. Finally, we must be sure that the refined assembly provides a realisation of the original interface specification CompressorInterface. This can be again automatically achieved since hiding preserves refinement (Theorem 3.2) which leads to (4) in Fig. 2 and since refinement is transitive.

In the next sections we will formally elaborate the notions discussed above. We hope that their intended meaning is already sufficiently explained such that we can keep the presentation short. An exception concerns the consideration of the message consuming properties in Sect. 5 which must still be carefully studied to ensure incremental design and preservation by refinement.

3 Modal Asynchronous I/O-Petri Nets

In this section we formalise the syntax of MAIOPNs and we define their transition system semantics. First we recall some basic definitions for modal Petri nets and modal transition systems.

3.1 Modal Petri Nets and Modal Transition Systems

In the following we consider labelled Petri nets such that transitions are equipped with labels of an alphabet Σ or with the symbol τ that models silent transitions. We write Σ_τ for $\Sigma \uplus \{\tau\}$. We assume the reader to be familiar with the basic notions of labelled Petri nets consisting of a finite set P of places, a finite set T of transitions, a set of arcs between places and transitions (transitions and places resp.), formalised by incidence matrices W^- and W^+, an initial marking m^0 and a labelling function $\lambda : T \to \Sigma_\tau$. In [7] we have introduced *modal Petri nets* $\mathcal{N} = (P, T, T^\Box, \Sigma, W^-, W^+, \lambda, m^0)$ such that $T^\Box \subseteq T$ is a distinguished subset of must-transitions. We write $m \overset{t}{\dashrightarrow} m'$ if a transition $t \in T$ is firable from a marking m leading to a marking m'. If $t \in T^\Box$ we write $m \overset{t}{\longrightarrow} m'$. If $\lambda(t) = a$ we write $m \overset{a}{\dashrightarrow} m'$ and for $t \in T^\Box$ we write $m \overset{a}{\longrightarrow} m'$. The notation is extended as usual to firing sequences $m \overset{\sigma}{\dashrightarrow} m'$ with $\sigma \in T^*$ and to $m \overset{\sigma}{\longrightarrow} m'$ with $\sigma \in (T^\Box)^*$. A marking m is reachable if there exists a firing sequence $\sigma \in T^*$ such that $m^0 \overset{\sigma}{\dashrightarrow} m$.

Modal transition systems have been introduced in [15]. We will use them to provide semantics for modal Petri nets. A modal transition system is a tuple $\mathcal{S} = (\Sigma, Q, q^0, \dashrightarrow, \longrightarrow)$, such that Σ is a set of labels, Q is a set of states, $q^0 \in Q$ is the initial state, $\dashrightarrow \subseteq Q \times \Sigma_\tau \times Q$ is a may-transition relation, and $\longrightarrow \subseteq \dashrightarrow$ is a must-transition relation. We explicitly allow the state space Q to be infinite which is needed to give interpretations to modal Petri nets that model infinite state systems.

The semantics of a modal Petri net $\mathcal{N} = (P, T, T^\Box, \Sigma, W^-, W^+, \lambda, m^0)$ is given by the modal transition system $\mathsf{mts}(\mathcal{N}) = (\Sigma, Q, q^0, \dashrightarrow, \longrightarrow)$ representing the reachability graph of the net by taking into account modalities: $Q \subseteq \mathbb{N}^P$ is the set of reachable markings of $\mathcal{N}$, $\dashrightarrow\; = \{(m, a, m') \mid a \in \Sigma_\tau \text{ and } m \overset{a}{\dashrightarrow} m'\}$, $\longrightarrow\; = \{(m, a, m') \mid a \in \Sigma_\tau \text{ and } m \overset{a}{\longrightarrow} m'\}$, and $q^0 = m^0$.

In the sequel we will use the following notations for modal transition systems. We write may-transitions as $q \overset{a}{\dashrightarrow} q'$ for $(q, a, q') \in \dashrightarrow$ and similarly must-transitions as $q \overset{a}{\longrightarrow} q'$. The notation is extended in the usual way to finite sequences $\sigma \in \Sigma_\tau^*$ by the notations $q \overset{\sigma}{\dashrightarrow} q'$ and $q \overset{\sigma}{\longrightarrow} q'$. The set of reachable states of $\mathcal{S}$ is given by $\mathrm{Reach}(\mathcal{S}) = \{q \mid \exists \sigma \in \Sigma_\tau^* \,.\, q^0 \overset{\sigma}{\dashrightarrow} q\}$. For a sequence $\sigma \in \Sigma_\tau^*$ the observable projection $\mathrm{obs}(\sigma) \in \Sigma^*$ is obtained from σ by removing all occurrences of τ. Let $a \in \Sigma$ be a visible action and $q, q' \in Q$. We write $q \overset{a}{=\!=\!\Rightarrow} q'$ if $q \overset{\sigma}{\dashrightarrow} q'$ with $\mathrm{obs}(\sigma) = a$ and we call $q \overset{a}{=\!=\!\Rightarrow} q'$ a weak may-transition. Similarly we write $q \overset{a}{\Longrightarrow} q'$ if all transitions are must-transitions and call $q \overset{a}{\Longrightarrow} q'$ a weak must-transition. The notation is extended as expected to finite sequences $\sigma \in \Sigma^*$ of visible actions by the notations $q \overset{\sigma}{=\!=\!\Rightarrow} q'$ and $q \overset{\sigma}{\Longrightarrow} q'$. In particular, $q \overset{\epsilon}{=\!=\!\Rightarrow} q'$ means that there is a (possibly empty) sequence of silent may-transitions from q to q' and similarly $q \overset{\epsilon}{\Longrightarrow} q'$ expresses a finite sequence of silent must-transitions.

3.2 Modal Asynchronous I/O-Petri Nets, Composition and Hiding

In this paper we consider systems which may be open for communication with other systems and may be composed to larger systems. The open actions are modelled by input labels (for the reception of messages from the environment) and output labels (for sending messages to the environment) while communication inside an asynchronously composed system takes place by removing or putting messages to distinguished communication channels. Given a finite set C

of channels, an *I/O-alphabet over* C is the disjoint union $\Sigma = \mathsf{in} \uplus \mathsf{out} \uplus \mathsf{com}$ of pairwise disjoint sets of input labels, output labels and communication labels, such that $\mathsf{com} = \{{}^{\rhd}a, a^{\rhd} \mid a \in C\}$. For each channel $a \in C$, the label ${}^{\rhd}a$ represents consumption of a message from a and $a^{\rhd}$ represents putting a message on a. A *modal asynchronous I/O-Petri net* (MAIOPN) $\mathcal{N} = (C, P, T, T^{\Box}, \Sigma, W^{-}, W^{+}, \lambda, m^{0})$ is a modal Petri net such that $C \subseteq P$ is a set of channel places which are initially empty, $\Sigma = \mathsf{in} \uplus \mathsf{out} \uplus \mathsf{com}$ is an I/O-alphabet over C, and for all $a \in C$ and $t \in T$, there exists an (unweighted) arc from a to t iff $\lambda(t) = {}^{\rhd}a$ and there exists an (unweighted) arc from t to a iff $\lambda(t) = a^{\rhd}$.

The *asynchronous composition* of MAIOPNs works as for asynchronous I/O-Petri nets considered in [10] by introducing new channel places and appropriate transitions for shared input/output labels. The non-shared input and output labels remain open in the composition. Moreover, we require that the must-transitions of the composition are the union of the must-transitions of the single components. The asynchronous composition of two MAIOPNs $\mathcal{N}$ and $\mathcal{M}$ is denoted by $\mathcal{N} \otimes_{pn} \mathcal{M}$. It is commutative and also associative under appropriate syntactic restrictions on the underlying alphabets. An example of a composition of three MAIOPNs is given in Fig. 1d.

We introduce a *hiding operator* on MAIOPNs which allows us to hide communication channels. In particular, it allows us to compute the black-box behaviour of an assembly when all channels are hidden. Let $\mathcal{N}$ be a MAIOPN with I/O-alphabet $\Sigma_{\mathcal{N}} = \mathsf{in}_{\mathcal{N}} \uplus \mathsf{out}_{\mathcal{N}} \uplus \mathsf{com}_{\mathcal{N}}$, and let $H \subseteq C_{\mathcal{N}}$ be a subset of its channels. The *channel hiding of* H in $\mathcal{N}$ is the MAIOPN $\mathcal{N} \setminus_{pn} H$ with channels $C = C_{\mathcal{N}} \setminus H$, with I/O-alphabet $\Sigma = \mathsf{in}_{\mathcal{N}} \uplus \mathsf{out}_{\mathcal{N}} \uplus \mathsf{com}$ such that $\mathsf{com} = \{{}^{\rhd}a, a^{\rhd} \mid a \in C\}$, and with the labelling function:

$$\lambda(t) = \begin{cases} \tau & \text{if } \exists a \in H \;.\; \lambda_{\mathcal{N}}(t) = {}^{\rhd}a \text{ or } \lambda_{\mathcal{N}}(t) = a^{\rhd}, \\ \lambda_{\mathcal{N}}(a) & \text{otherwise.} \end{cases}$$

3.3 Semantics: Modal Asynchronous I/O-Transition Systems

We extend the transition system semantics of modal Petri nets defined in Sect. 3.1 to MAIOPNs. For this purpose we introduce *modal asynchronous I/O-transition system* (MAIOTS) $\mathcal{S} = (C, \Sigma, Q, q^{0}, \dashrightarrow, \longrightarrow, \mathrm{val})$ which are modal transition systems such that C is a finite set of channels, $\Sigma = \mathsf{in} \uplus \mathsf{out} \uplus \mathsf{com}$ is an I/O-alphabet over C, and $\mathrm{val} : Q \longrightarrow \mathbb{N}^{C}$ is a channel valuation function which determines for each state $q \in Q$ how many messages are actually pending on each channel $a \in C$. Instead of $\mathrm{val}(q)(a)$ we write $\mathrm{val}(q, a)$. We require that initially all channels are empty, i.e. $\mathrm{val}(q^{0}, a) = 0$ for all $a \in C$, that for each $a \in C$ putting $a^{\rhd}$ and consuming ${}^{\rhd}a$ messages from a has the expected behaviour, and that the open input/output actions have no effect on a channel[1], i.e.

[1] $\mathrm{val}(q)[a{+}{+}]$ ($\mathrm{val}(q)[a{-}{-}]$ resp.) denotes the update of val which increments (decrements) the value of a and leaves the values of all other channels unchanged.

$$q \xrightarrow{a^{\triangleright}} q' \implies \text{val}(q') = \text{val}(q)[a{+}{+}],$$

$$q \xrightarrow{{}^{\triangleright}a} q' \implies \text{val}(q, a) > 0 \text{ and } \text{val}(q') = \text{val}(q)[a - -], \text{ and}$$

$$\text{for all } x \in (\mathsf{in} \cup \mathsf{out}), q \xrightarrow{x} q' \implies \text{val}(q') = \text{val}(q).$$

The semantics $\mathsf{maiots}(\mathcal{N})$ of a modal asynchronous I/O-Petri net $\mathcal{N}$ is given by the transition system semantics of modal Petri nets such that the reachable markings are the states. Additionally we define the associated channel valuation function val : $Q \longrightarrow \mathbb{N}^C$ such that the valuation of a channel a in a current state m is given by the number of tokens on a under the marking m, i.e. $\text{val}(m, a) = m(a)$. For instance, the semantics of the CompressorInterface in Sect. 2 and of the Controller leads to infinite state transition systems; the transition systems associated with the two compressor components have two reachable states and the transitions between them correspond directly to their Petri net representations in Fig. 1e, f.

The *asynchronous composition* $\mathcal{S} \otimes \mathcal{T}$ of two MAIOTSs $\mathcal{S}$ and $\mathcal{T}$ works as for asynchronous I/O-transition systems in [10] taking additionally care that must-transitions of $\mathcal{S}$ and $\mathcal{T}$ induce must-transitions of $\mathcal{S} \otimes \mathcal{T}$. The composition introduces new channels $C_{\mathcal{ST}} = \Sigma_{\mathcal{S}} \cap \Sigma_{\mathcal{T}}$ for shared input/output labels. Every transition with a shared output label a becomes a transition with the communication label $a^{\triangleright}$, and similarly transitions with input labels a become transitions with label ${}^{\triangleright}a$. The state space of the composition is (the reachable part of) the Cartesian product of the underlying state spaces of $\mathcal{S}$ and $\mathcal{T}$ together with the set $\mathbb{N}^{C_{\mathcal{ST}}}$ of valuations for the new channels such that transitions labelled by $a^{\triangleright}$ and ${}^{\triangleright}a$ have the expected effect on the new channels; for details see [10]. The asynchronous composition of two MAIOTSs is commutative and also associative under appropriate syntactic restrictions on the underlying alphabets.

We also introduce a *hiding operator* on MAIOTSs that hides communication channels and moves all corresponding communication labels to τ. Let $\mathcal{S} = (C_{\mathcal{S}}, \Sigma_{\mathcal{S}}, Q_{\mathcal{S}}, q^0_{\mathcal{S}}, \dashrightarrow_{\mathcal{S}}, \longrightarrow_{\mathcal{S}}, \text{val}_{\mathcal{S}})$ be a MAIOTS with I/O-alphabet $\Sigma_{\mathcal{S}} = \mathsf{in}_{\mathcal{S}} \uplus \mathsf{out}_{\mathcal{S}} \uplus \mathsf{com}_{\mathcal{S}}$, and let $H \subseteq C_{\mathcal{S}}$ be a subset of its channels. The *channel hiding of* H in $\mathcal{S}$ is the MAIOTS $\mathcal{S} \setminus H = (C, \Sigma, Q_{\mathcal{S}}, q^0_{\mathcal{S}}, \dashrightarrow, \longrightarrow, \text{val})$, such that $C = C_{\mathcal{S}} \setminus H$, $\Sigma = \mathsf{in}_{\mathcal{S}} \uplus \mathsf{out}_{\mathcal{S}} \uplus \mathsf{com}$ with $\mathsf{com} = \{{}^{\triangleright}a, a^{\triangleright} \mid a \in C\}$, $\text{val}(q, a) = \text{val}_{\mathcal{S}}(q, a)$ for all $q \in Q, a \in C$, and the may-transition relation is given by:

$$\dashrightarrow \; = \{(q, a, q') \mid a \in (\Sigma_\tau \setminus \{{}^{\triangleright}a, a^{\triangleright} \mid a \in H\}) \text{ and } q \overset{a}{\dashrightarrow}_{\mathcal{S}} q'\} \cup$$

$$\{(q, \tau, q') \mid \exists a \in H \text{ such that either } q \overset{a^{\triangleright}}{\dashrightarrow}_{\mathcal{S}} q' \text{ or } q \overset{{}^{\triangleright}a}{\dashrightarrow}_{\mathcal{S}} q'\},$$

The must-transition relation $\longrightarrow$ is defined analogously.

For the results developed in the next sections it is important that our transition system semantics is compositional and compatible with hiding as stated in the next theorem. The proof is given in Appendix A of [11].

Theorem 1. *Let $\mathcal{N}$ and $\mathcal{M}$ be two composable MAIOPNs and let $H \subseteq C_{\mathcal{N}}$ be a subset of the channels of $\mathcal{N}$. The following holds:*

1. $\mathsf{maiots}(\mathcal{N} \otimes_{pn} \mathcal{M}) = \mathsf{maiots}(\mathcal{N}) \otimes \mathsf{maiots}(\mathcal{M})$ *(up to isomorphic state spaces),*
2. $\mathsf{maiots}(\mathcal{N} \setminus_{pn} H) = \mathsf{maiots}(\mathcal{N}) \setminus H$.

4 Modal Refinement

The refinement relation between MAIOPNs will be defined by considering their semantics, i.e. MAIOTSs. For this purpose we adapt the weak modal refinement relation for modal transition systems introduced in [13] which is based on a simulation relation in both directions. It says that must-transitions of an abstract specification must be preserved by the refinement while may-transitions of a concrete specification must be allowed by the abstract one. In any case silent transitions labelled with τ can be inserted, similarly to weak bisimulation, but respecting modalities. Observational abstraction from silent transitions is indeed important in many examples; e.g. when relating the encapsulated behaviour of an assembly to a requirements specification as discussed in Sect. 2. If all transitions of the abstract specification are must-transitions, modal refinement coincides with weak bisimulation. Obviously, the modal refinement relation defined as follows is reflexive and transitive.

Definition 2 (Modal refinement). *Let $\mathcal{S} = (C, \Sigma, Q_\mathcal{S}, q^0_\mathcal{S}, \dashrightarrow_\mathcal{S}, \longrightarrow_\mathcal{S}, \mathrm{val}_\mathcal{S})$ and $\mathcal{T} = (C, \Sigma, Q_\mathcal{T}, q^0_\mathcal{T}, \dashrightarrow_\mathcal{T}, \longrightarrow_\mathcal{T}, \mathrm{val}_\mathcal{T})$ be two MAIOTSs with the same I/O-alphabet Σ over channels C. A relation $R \subseteq Q_\mathcal{S} \times Q_\mathcal{T}$ is a* modal refinement relation *between $\mathcal{S}$ and $\mathcal{T}$ if for all $(q_\mathcal{S}, q_\mathcal{T}) \in R$ and $a \in \Sigma$:*

1. $q_\mathcal{T} \xrightarrow{a}_\mathcal{T} q'_\mathcal{T} \implies \exists q'_\mathcal{S} \in Q_\mathcal{S} \,.\, q_\mathcal{S} \stackrel{a}{\Longrightarrow}_\mathcal{S} q'_\mathcal{S} \wedge (q'_\mathcal{S}, q'_\mathcal{T}) \in R$,
2. $q_\mathcal{T} \xrightarrow{\tau}_\mathcal{T} q'_\mathcal{T} \implies \exists q'_\mathcal{S} \in Q_\mathcal{S} \,.\, q_\mathcal{S} \stackrel{\epsilon}{\Longrightarrow}_\mathcal{S} q'_\mathcal{S} \wedge (q'_\mathcal{S}, q'_\mathcal{T}) \in R$,
3. $q_\mathcal{S} \stackrel{a}{\dashrightarrow}_\mathcal{S} q'_\mathcal{S} \implies \exists q'_\mathcal{T} \in Q_\mathcal{T} \,.\, q_\mathcal{T} \stackrel{a}{\Rrightarrow}_\mathcal{T} q'_\mathcal{T} \wedge (q'_\mathcal{S}, q'_\mathcal{T}) \in R$,
4. $q_\mathcal{S} \stackrel{\tau}{\dashrightarrow}_\mathcal{S} q'_\mathcal{S} \implies \exists q'_\mathcal{T} \in Q_\mathcal{T} \,.\, q_\mathcal{T} \stackrel{\epsilon}{\Rrightarrow}_\mathcal{T} q'_\mathcal{T} \wedge (q'_\mathcal{S}, q'_\mathcal{T}) \in R$.

We say that $\mathcal{S}$ is a modal refinement *of $\mathcal{T}$, written $\mathcal{S} \leq^*_\mathrm{m} \mathcal{T}$, if there exists a modal refinement relation R between $\mathcal{S}$ and $\mathcal{T}$ such that $(q^0_\mathcal{S}, q^0_\mathcal{T}) \in R$. We write $q_\mathcal{S} \leq^*_\mathrm{m} q_\mathcal{T}$ when $(q_\mathcal{S}, q_\mathcal{T}) \in R$ for a modal refinement relation R.* ◇

The next theorem shows that modal refinement is preserved by asynchronous composition and by channel hiding. The compositionality result stems in principle from [13] and is proved in Appendix B of [11] in the context of MAIOTS. The second result is also proved in Appendix B of [11] similarly to a result in [12] for hiding in synchronous systems.

Theorem 3. *Let $\mathcal{S}, \mathcal{T}, \mathcal{E}$ and $\mathcal{F}$ be MAIOTSs such that C is the set of channels of $\mathcal{S}$ and of $\mathcal{T}$ and let $H \subseteq C$.*

1. *If $\mathcal{S} \leq^*_\mathrm{m} \mathcal{T}$, $\mathcal{E} \leq^*_\mathrm{m} \mathcal{F}$ and $\mathcal{S}$ and $\mathcal{E}$ are composable, then $\mathcal{T}$ and $\mathcal{F}$ are composable and $\mathcal{S} \otimes \mathcal{E} \leq^*_\mathrm{m} \mathcal{T} \otimes \mathcal{F}$.*
2. *If $\mathcal{S} \leq^*_\mathrm{m} \mathcal{T}$ then $\mathcal{S} \setminus H \leq^*_\mathrm{m} \mathcal{T} \setminus H$.*

The refinement definition and results are propagated to modal asynchronous I/O-Petri nets in the obvious way: A MAIOPN $\mathcal{M}$ is a *modal refinement of* a MAIOPN $\mathcal{N}$, also denoted by $\mathcal{M} \leq^*_\mathrm{m} \mathcal{N}$, if $\mathsf{maiots}(\mathcal{M}) \leq^*_\mathrm{m} \mathsf{maiots}(\mathcal{N})$. The counterparts of Theorem 3.1 and 3.2 for MAIOPNs are consequences of the semantic compatibility results in Theorem 1.1. Examples for modal refinements of MAIOPNs and applications of the theorem are pointed out in Sect. 2.

The decidability status of the modal refinement problem for MAIOPNs depends on the kind of Petri nets one considers. Observing that there is a simple reduction from the bisimilarity problem to the modal refinement problem and that the former problem is undecidable for Petri nets [14], one gets that the latter problem is also undecidable; for an evolved discussion see [2]. However when one restricts Petri nets to be modally weakly deterministic, the modal refinement problem becomes decidable. The modal weak determinism of Petri nets is a behavioural property which can also be decided (see [7] for both proofs). In addition, determinism is a desirable feature for a specification (when possible). For instance modal language specification is an alternative to modal transition systems that presents such a behaviour [17].

5 Message Consuming Systems

In this section we consider generic properties concerning the asynchronous communication via channels inspired by the various channel properties studied in [10].

We focus on the *message consuming* and the *necessarily message consuming* properties and generalise them to take into account modalities and observational abstraction w.r.t. silent transitions. Our goal is that the properties scale up to larger contexts (to support incremental design) and that they are preserved by modal refinement. Moreover we consider their decidability. For the definitions we rely on the semantics of MAIOPNs, i.e. on MAIOTSs.

Let us first discuss the message consuming property (a) of Definition 4 for a MAIOTS $\mathcal{S}$ and a subset B of its channels. It requires, for each channel $a \in B$, that if in an arbitrary reachable state q of $\mathcal{S}$ there is a message on a, then $\mathcal{S}$ must be able to consume it, possibly after some delay caused by the execution of autonomous must-transitions. All transitions that do not depend on the environment, i.e. are not related to input labels, are considered to be autonomous. Our approach follows a "pessimistic" assumption taking into account arbitrary environments that can let the system go where it wants and can also stop to provide inputs at any moment. It is important that we require must-transitions since the consuming property should be preserved by modal refinement. It is inspired by the notion of "output compatibility" studied for synchronously composed transition systems in [12].

A central role when components run in parallel is played by fairness assumptions; see, e.g., [4]. First we must define what we mean by a run and then we will explain our fairness notion. A run is a finite or infinite sequence of state transitions which satisfies a maximality condition. In principle a run can only stop when a deadlock is reached. However we must be careful since (1) we are dealing with open systems whose executions depend on the input from the environment, (2) we must take into account that transitions with a may-modality can be skipped in a refinement, and (3) we must be aware that also silent must-transitions without successive mandatory visible actions can be omitted in a refinement; cf. Definition 2, rule 2. In particular divergence in an abstract state could be implemented by a deadlock. If one of the above conditions holds in a certain state it is called a *potential deadlock state.*

Formally, let $\mathcal{S} = (C, \Sigma, Q, q^0, \dashrightarrow, \longrightarrow, \mathrm{val})$ be a MAIOTS with $\Sigma = \mathsf{in} \uplus \mathsf{out} \uplus \mathsf{com}$. A state $q \in Q$ is a potential deadlock state if for all $a \in (\Sigma \setminus \mathsf{in})$, there is no state $q' \in Q$ such that $q \overset{a}{\Longrightarrow} q'$. A *run* of $\mathcal{S}$ starting in a state $q_1 \in Q$ is a finite or infinite sequence $\rho = q_1 \overset{a_1}{\dashrightarrow} q_2 \overset{a_2}{\dashrightarrow} q_3 \overset{a_3}{\dashrightarrow} \cdots$ with $a_i \in \Sigma_\tau$ and $q_i \in Q$ such that, if the sequence is finite, its last state is a potential deadlock state. We assume that system runs are executed in a runtime infrastructure which follows a fair scheduling policy. In our context this means that any visible autonomous action a, that is always enabled by a weak must-transition from a certain state on, will infinitely often be executed. Formally, a run $\rho = q_1 \overset{a_1}{\dashrightarrow} q_2 \overset{a_2}{\dashrightarrow} \cdots$ is called *observationally weakly fair* if it is finite or if it is infinite and then for all $a \in (\Sigma \setminus \mathsf{in})$ the following holds:

$$(\exists k \geq 1 \,.\, \forall i \geq k \,.\, \exists q' \,.\, q_i \overset{a}{\Longrightarrow} q') \implies (\forall k \geq 1 \,.\, \exists i \geq k \,.\, a_i = a).$$

We denote the set of all observationally weakly fair runs of $\mathcal{S}$ starting from q_1 by $\mathrm{owfruns}_{\mathcal{S}}(q_1)$. For instance, for the MAIOPN $\mathcal{M}$ in Fig. 3b on page xx an infinite run which always executes $a^{\triangleright}, {}^{\triangleright}a, \ldots$ is observationally weakly fair. A (diverging) run of $\mathcal{M}$ which always executes τ from a certain state on is not observationally weakly fair since ${}^{\triangleright}a$ is then always enabled by a weak must-transition but never taken.

Note that for our results it is sufficient to use a weak fairness property instead of strong fairness. We are now ready to define also the necessarily consuming property 4 which requires that whenever a message is pending on a communication channel then the message must eventually be consumed on all observationally weakly fair runs.

Definition 4 (Message consuming). *Let* $\mathcal{S} = (C, \Sigma, Q, q^0, \dashrightarrow, \longrightarrow, \mathrm{val})$ *be a MAIOTS with I/O-alphabet* $\Sigma = \mathsf{in} \uplus \mathsf{out} \uplus \mathsf{com}$ *and let* $B \subseteq C$ *be a subset of its channels.*

(a) $\mathcal{S}$ *is* message consuming *w.r.t.* B *if for all* $a \in B$ *and all* $q \in \mathrm{Reach}(\mathcal{S})$,

$$\mathrm{val}(q, a) > 0 \implies \exists q', q'' \in Q \,.\, \exists \sigma \in (\Sigma \setminus \mathsf{in})^* \,.\, q \overset{\sigma}{\Longrightarrow} q' \overset{{}^{\triangleright}a}{\longrightarrow} q''.$$

(b) $\mathcal{S}$ *is* necessarily message consuming *w.r.t.* B *if for all* $a \in B, q \in \mathrm{Reach}(\mathcal{S})$,

$$\mathrm{val}(q, a) > 0 \implies \forall \rho \in \mathrm{owfruns}_{\mathcal{S}}(q) \,.\, {}^{\triangleright}a \in \rho \,.^{2}$$

$\mathcal{S}$ *is* (necessarily) message consuming *if* $\mathcal{S}$ *is (necessarily) message consuming w.r.t.* C. ◇

In the special case, in which all may-transitions are must-transitions and no silent transitions occur observationally weakly fair runs coincide with weakly fair runs and the two consuming properties coincide with the corresponding properties in [10].

---

[2] i.e. there is a transition in ρ labelled by ${}^{\triangleright}a$.

Proposition 5. *Let $\mathcal{S}$ be a MAIOTS. If $\mathcal{S}$ is necessarily message consuming w.r.t B then $\mathcal{S}$ is message consuming w.r.t B.*

The proof can found in Appendix C of [11]. It is an adoptation of the one in [9].

The definitions and the proposition are propagated to modal asynchronous I/O-Petri nets in the obvious way. For instance, a MAIOPN $\mathcal{N}$ is *(necessarily) message consuming* if $\mathsf{maiots}(\mathcal{N})$ is (necessarily) message consuming. All MAIOPNs considered in Sect. 2 are necessarily message consuming.

As stated in the introduction, Petri nets are a useful model since (1) they model infinite state systems and (2) several relevant properties of transition systems are decidable. The following proposition whose proof is an adaption of the one in [10] establishes that one can decide both consuming properties. For sake of completeness, its proof can be found in Appendix C of [11].

Proposition 6. *Let $\mathcal{N}$ be a MAIOPN and let $B \subseteq C$ be a subset of its channels. The satisfaction by $\mathcal{N}$ of the message consuming and the necessarily message consuming properties w.r.t. B are decidable.*

Both message consuming properties are compositional; they are preserved when systems are put into larger contexts. The proof of the compositionality of the message consuming property 4 relies on the fact that autonomous executions of constituent parts (not involving inputs) can be lifted to executions of compositions. To prove compositionality of the necessarily consuming property 4 one shows that projections of observationally weakly fair runs to constituent parts of a composition are again observationally weakly fair runs. Both facts and the following consequences are proved in Appendix C of [11]. The proof has the same shape as the proof of Proposition 15 in [10] which is given in [9].

Proposition 7. *Let $\mathcal{S}$ and $\mathcal{T}$ be two composable MAIOTSs such that $C_{\mathcal{S}}$ is the set of channels of $\mathcal{S}$. Let $B \subseteq C_{\mathcal{S}}$. If $\mathcal{S}$ is (necessarily) consuming w.r.t. B, then $\mathcal{S} \otimes \mathcal{T}$ is (necessarily) consuming w.r.t. B.*

Proposition 7 leads directly to the desired modular verification result which allows us to check consuming properties in an incremental manner: To show that a composed system $\mathcal{S} \otimes \mathcal{T}$ is (necessarily) message consuming it is sufficient to know that both constituent parts $\mathcal{S}$ and $\mathcal{T}$ have this property and to check that $\mathcal{S} \otimes \mathcal{T}$ is (necessarily) message consuming w.r.t. the new channels established for the communication between $\mathcal{S}$ and $\mathcal{T}$, i.e. that $\mathcal{S}$ and $\mathcal{T}$ are compatible.

Definition 8 (Compatibility). *Two composable MAIOTSs $\mathcal{S}$ and $\mathcal{T}$ with shared labels $\Sigma_{\mathcal{S}} \cap \Sigma_{\mathcal{T}}$ are* (necessarily) message consuming compatible *if $\mathcal{S} \otimes \mathcal{T}$ is (necessarily) message consuming w.r.t. $\Sigma_{\mathcal{N}} \cap \Sigma_{\mathcal{M}}$.* ◇

Theorem 9 (Incremental Design). *Let $\mathcal{S}$ and $\mathcal{T}$ be (necessarily) message consuming compatible. If both $\mathcal{S}$ and $\mathcal{T}$ are (necessarily) message consuming, then $\mathcal{S} \otimes \mathcal{T}$ is (necessarily) message consuming.*

All results hold analogously for asynchronous I/O-Petri nets due to the compositional semantics of MAIOPNs; see Theorem 1.1 An application of incremental design has been discussed in Sect. 2.

An important issue concerns the preservation of the message consuming properties by refinement. We can show that this holds for modal refinement which is not considered in [10]. The preservation of the message consuming property relies on the fact that for any "concrete" reachable state there is a related "abstract" state with the same number of messages on each channel. To prove the preservation of the necessarily consuming property the essential point is to show that for any observationally weakly fair run of a concrete MAIOTS there is a corresponding observationally weakly fair run of the abstract MAIOTS with the same visible actions. Both facts and the following consequences are proved in Appendix C of [11].

Theorem 10. *Let $\mathcal{S}$, $\mathcal{T}$ be two MAIOTSs with channels C and let $\mathcal{S} \leq^*_{\mathrm{m}} \mathcal{T}$. Let $B \subseteq C$. If $\mathcal{T}$ is (necessarily) message consuming w.r.t. B, then $\mathcal{S}$ is (necessarily) message consuming w.r.t. B. By definition, the theorem propagates to MAIOPNs.*

Example 11. The nets in Fig. 3 show an abstract MAIOPN $\mathcal{N}$ and a concrete MAIOPN $\mathcal{M}$ with silent τ-transitions. Both nets have a single channel place a. Obviously, $\mathcal{M} \leq^*_{\mathrm{m}} \mathcal{N}$ is a modal refinement. It is also clear that $\mathcal{N}$ is necessarily message consuming. By Theorem 10, $\mathcal{M}$ is necessarily message consuming as well. Indeed, as pointed out above, a diverging run of $\mathcal{M}$ which always executes τ from a certain state on is not observationally weakly fair and therefore needs not to be considered. This shows also why weakly fair runs are not appropriate here since a diverging run of $\mathcal{M}$ is weakly fair (it always visits a state in which ${}^{\triangleright}a$ is not immediately enabled) but does not consume.

As a consequence of Theorems 3.1 and 10 our theory supports the principle of independent implementability in the sense of [1]. This fact is applied in Sect. 2 to obtain the global refinement (3) in Fig. 2 from the local refinement (2) preserving the necessarily consuming property.

Corollary 12 (Independent Implementability). *Let $\mathcal{S}, \mathcal{T}, \mathcal{E}$ and $\mathcal{F}$ be MAIOTSs. If $\mathcal{T}$ and $\mathcal{F}$ are (necessarily) message consuming compatible and $\mathcal{S} \leq^*_{\mathrm{m}} \mathcal{T}$ and $\mathcal{E} \leq^*_{\mathrm{m}} \mathcal{F}$, then $\mathcal{S}$ and $\mathcal{E}$ are (necessarily) message consuming compatible and $\mathcal{S} \otimes \mathcal{E} \leq^*_{\mathrm{m}} \mathcal{T} \otimes \mathcal{F}$. This holds analogously for MAIOPNs.*

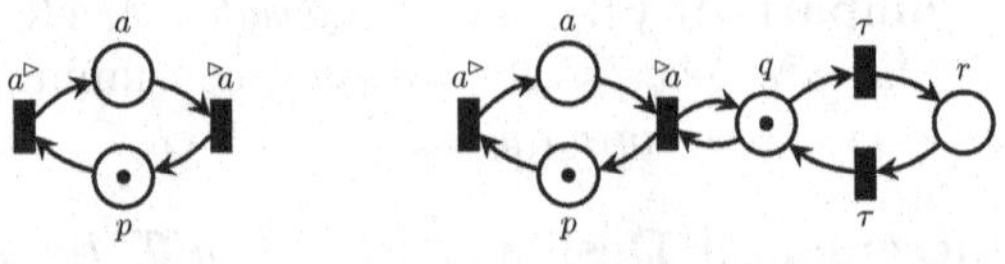

(a) Abstract MAIOPN $\mathcal{N}$ (b) Concrete MAIOPN $\mathcal{M}$

Fig. 3. Necessarily consuming nets and modal refinement

6 Conclusion and Future Work

We have developed a fully integrated approach for the design of asynchronously composed component systems based on the formalism of MAIOPNs. Our approach ensures that the communication properties are preserved by asynchronous composition and by modal refinement, the basic ingredients of the design process. Several continuations of this work are possible. First, it would be interesting to see how our approach works in larger case studies and concrete applications. The "Assume/Guarantee" approach is a standard way to substitute a component by a behavioural interface in order to make easier the compositional verification. We plan to investigate how this approach can be integrated in our framework. Also it would be interesting to consider further operators on specifications like quotients. For the latter we would be faced with the problem to find mild conditions for the existence of quotients in the context of modal refinement which supports observational abstraction. Finally, broadcasting is an appropriate communication mechanism in the asynchronous environment. So it would be interesting to investigate how our approach can be adapted to this communication operator.

References

1. de Alfaro, L., Henzinger, T.A.: Interface-based design. Engineering Theories of Software-intensive Systems, NATO Science Series: Mathematics, Physics, and Chemistry, vol. 195. Springer, pp. 83–104 (2005)
2. Beneš, N., Křetínský, J.: Modal process rewrite systems. In: Proceedings of the International Conference on Theoretical Aspects of Computing (ICTAC 2012), vol. LNCS 7521, pp 120–135, Springer (2012)
3. Bernardo, M., Ciancarini, P., Donatiello, L.: Architecting families of software systems with process algebras. ACM Trans. Softw. Eng. Meth. **11**(4), 386–426 (2002)
4. Bérard, B., Bidoit, M., Finkel, A., Laroussinie, F., Petit, A., Petrucci, L., Schnoebelen, P.: Systems and Software Verification: Model-Cheking Techniques and Tools. Springer, Heidelberg (2001)
5. Best, E., Devillers, R., Koutny, M.: Petri Net Algebra. Springer Monographs in Theoretical Computer Science (2001)
6. Brauer, W., Gold, R., Vogler, W.: A survey of behaviour and equivalence preserving refinements of Petri nets. Applications and Theory of Petri Nets, pp. 1–46 (1989)
7. Elhog-Benzina, D., Haddad, S., Hennicker, R.: Refinement and asynchronous composition of modal Petri Nets. In: Jensen, K., Donatelli, S., Kleijn, J. (eds.) Transactions on Petri Nets and Other Models of Concurrency V. LNCS, vol. 6900, pp. 96–120. Springer, Heidelberg (2012)
8. Ganty, P., Raskin, J.-F., Van Begin, L.: From many places to few: automatic abstraction refinement for Petri Nets, ATPN 2007. LNCS **4546**, 124–143 (2007)
9. Haddad, S., Hennicker, R., Møller, M.H.: Channel properties of asynchronously composed Petri Nets. In: Colom, J.-M., Desel, J. (eds.) Petri Nets 2013. LNCS, vol. 7927, pp. 369–388. Springer, Heidelberg (2013)
10. Haddad, S., Hennicker, R., Møller, M.H.: Channel properties of asynchronously composed Petri Nets. Research Report LSV-13-05, Laboratoire Spécification et Vérification, ENS Cachan, France (2013)

11. Haddad, S., Hennicker, R., Møller, M.H.: Specification of asynchronous component systems with modal I/O-Petri Nets. Research Report LSV-13-16, Laboratoire Spécification et Vérification. ENS Cachan, France (2013)
12. Hennicker, R., Knapp, A.: Modal interface theories for communication-safe component assemblies. In: Cerone, A., Pihlajasaari, P. (eds.) ICTAC 2011. LNCS, vol. 6916, pp. 135–153. Springer, Heidelberg (2011)
13. Hüttel, H., Larsen, K.G.: The use of static constructs in a modal process logic. In: Logic at Botik 1989, pp. 163–180 (1989)
14. Jancar, P.: Undecidability of bisimilarity for Petri Nets and related problems. Theor. Comput. Sci. **148**, 281–301 (1995)
15. Larsen, K.G., Thomsen, B.; A modal process logic. In: 3rd Annual Symposium on Logic in Computer Science (LICS), IEEE Computer Society, pp. 203–210 (1988)
16. Lohmann, N., Massuthe, P., Wolf, K.: Operating guidelines for finite-state services. In: Kleijn, J., Yakovlev, A. (eds.) ICATPN 2007. LNCS, vol. 4546, pp. 321–341. Springer, Heidelberg (2007)
17. Raclet, J.-B.: Residual for component specifications. In: Proceedings of the 4th International Workshop on Formal Aspects of Component Software (FACS07), Sophia-Antipolis, France (2007)
18. Reisig, W.: Simple composition of nets. In: Franceschinis, G., Wolf, K. (eds.) Petri Nets 2009. LNCS, vol. 5606, pp. 23–42. Springer, Heidelberg (2009)
19. Schäfer, M., Vogler, W.: Component refinement and CSC-solving for STG decomposition. Theor. Comput. Sci. **388**(1–3), 243–266 (2007)
20. Souissi, Y.: On liveness preservation by composition of nets via a set of places. In: 11th International Conference on Applications and Theory of Petri Nets, LNCS 524, pp. 277–295 (1990)
21. Souissi, Y., Memmi, G.: Composition of nets via a communication medium. In: 10th International Conference on Applications and Theory of Petri Nets, LNCS 483, pp. 457–470 (1989)
22. Stahl, C., Wolf, K.: Deciding service composition and substitutability using extended operating guidelines. Data Knowl. Eng. **68**(9), 819–833 (2009)

A Formal Model for the Deferred Update Replication Technique

Andrea Corradini[1(✉)], Leila Ribeiro[2],
Fernando Dotti[3], and Odorico Mendizabal[3]

[1] Dipartimento di Informatica, Università di Pisa, Pisa, Italy
andrea@di.unipi.it
[2] Instituto de Informática, Universidade Federal do Rio Grande do Sul, Porto Alegre, Brazil
leila@inf.ufrgs.br
[3] Faculdade de Informática, Pontifícia Universidade Católica do Rio Grande do Sul, Porto Alegre, Brazil
fernando.dotti@pucrs.br, omendizabal@gmail.com

Abstract. Database replication is a technique employed to enhance both performance and availability of database systems. The Deferred Update Replication (DUR) technique offers strong consistency (i.e. serializability) and uses an optimistic concurrency control with a lazy replication strategy relying on atomic broadcast communication. Due to its good performance, DUR has been used in the construction of several database replication protocols and is often chosen as a basic technique for several extensions considering modern environments. The correctness of the DUR technique, i.e. if histories accepted by DUR are serializable, has been discussed by different authors in the literature. However, a more comprehensive discussion involving the completeness of DUR w.r.t. serializability was lacking. As a first contribution, this paper provides an operational semantics of the DUR technique which serves as foundation to reason about DUR and its derivatives. Second, using this model the correctness of DUR w.r.t. serializability is shown. Finally, we discuss the completeness of DUR w.r.t. serializability and show that for any serializable history there is an equivalent history accepted by DUR. Moreover, we show that transactions aborted by DUR could not be accepted without changing the order of already committed transactions.

1 Introduction

For the past several decades, database management systems have been of paramount importance to safely keep users data. A database system is typically manipulated by concurrent transactions from several users. The common correctness criterion used to validate consistency in databases is *serializability* (or *strong consistency*) [3,11]. Roughly, an interleaved execution of several concurrent transactions is *serializable* if it has the same effect on a database as some

Partially supported by FAPERGS and CNPq.

M. Abadi and A. Lluch Lafuente (Eds.): TGC 2013, LNCS 8358, pp. 235–253, 2014.
DOI: 10.1007/978-3-319-05119-2_14,

serial execution of these transactions. The preservation of database consistency is one key aspect which is usually ensured by schedulers responsible for the implementation of concurrency control mechanisms. While early approaches to assuring database integrity where based on some form of locking, hindering concurrency and thus transaction throughput, optimistic methods for concurrency control emerged to take advantage from both the low conflict rate among transactions and the hardware architectures allowing better performance [9]. According to such methods, a transaction is executed under the optimistic assumption that no other transaction will conflict with it. At the end of the execution, a validation phase takes place, in order to either commit or invalidate the transaction [4].

Further seeking to enhance performance, replication techniques for database systems have been thoroughly studied in past years [3]. Several replication techniques emerged in the database community which can be classified according to two basic characteristics: where updates take place (primary copy vs. update anywhere) and kind of interaction for update synchronization (eager vs. lazy) [7]. While database replication is aimed primarily at performance, in distributed systems replication has high availability as a major concern. Examples of replication approaches developed for distributed systems are the primary-backup [5] and the state machine replication [15] approaches.

The search for highly available and high performance databases leads to consider the combination of replication and optimistic concurrency control. Since with optimistic concurrency control transactions progress independently and are validated at the end of the execution, and since in a distributed setting communication costs and delays are to be avoided, a natural configuration to consider is the primary copy approach with lazy update. The Deferred Update Replication (DUR) approach [12] uses these ideas with multiple primary copies. According to DUR, the servers fully replicate the database while clients choose any server to submit a transaction. Transaction processing at the server takes place without coordinating with other servers. Upon transaction termination issued by the client, a certification test is performed to assure database consistency. The finalization protocol is based on atomic broadcast to submit the modifications of a local transaction to all other servers in total delivery order. Each server will receive the same finalization requests in the same order, apply the same certification tests, leading to the same sequence of coherent modifications in each server.

The DUR technique is currently being extended in different ways, such as to support byzantine faults, to enhance throughput of update transactions and to support in-memory transaction execution [13,16,17]. The correctness of the basic technique, i.e. if DUR accepted histories are serializable, is discussed by different authors [6,8,12,13]. In [14] the authors use TLA^+ to validate serializability of DUR based protocols. A similar approach is adopted by [1], where the authors present a formal specification and correctness proof for replicated database systems using I/O automata.

In this paper we contribute to the analysis of the DUR technique in three main aspects: (i) We provide an operational semantics of the DUR technique, which serves as a foundation to discuss its correctness and completeness, as well as a solid contribution for future extensions to represent variations of DUR as mentioned before; (ii) Based on this model the correctness of DUR is shown w.r.t. serializability; (iii) Furthermore we show the completeness of DUR w.r.t. serializable histories: for any serializable history there is an equivalent history accepted by DUR; moreover it is shown that if a transaction would be aborted by the execution of DUR, then the history obtained by including this transaction in a history recasting exactly the execution of the algorithm up to this point would not be serializable in the strict sense, that is, without changing the order of already committed transactions. While (ii) is, to some extent, closely related to previous works, contributions (i) and (iii) bring new elements to the discussion of DUR and the theory of concurrency control.

This paper is structured as follows: in Sect. 2 we present several concepts from [3] on serializability theory; in Sect. 3 we present the DUR technique based on [17]; in Sect. 4 the operational semantics of DUR is presented; in Sect. 5 both correctness and completeness of DUR as mentioned above are discussed; finally in Sect. 6 we review the results achieved and discuss possible directions for future work.

2 Serializability Theory

In this section we review some of the main definitions of serializability theory [3].

Definition 1 (Database actions). *Given a set of variables X, a* ***database action*** *may be* $\mathbf{r}[\mathbf{x}]$, *a* **read** *of variable $x \in X$;* $\mathbf{w}[\mathbf{x}]$, *a* **write** *on variable $x \in X$;* $\mathbf{c}$, *a commit; or* $\mathbf{a}$, *an abort. The set of actions over variables in X will be denoted by* $\boldsymbol{Act}(X)$. *We say that two actions are* ***conflicting*** *is they operate on the same variable and at least one of them is a* **write**.

Definition 2 (Transaction). *A* ***transaction*** *is a pair $\langle T, \leq_T\rangle$ where T:* $\boldsymbol{Act}(X) \to \mathbb{N}$ *is a multiset of actions mapping each action to the number of its occurrences; we often identify T with its* extension, *i.e. with the set*

$$\{\mathbf{o}^{\mathbf{i}}_{\mathbf{T}}[\mathbf{x}] \mid \mathbf{o} \in \{\mathbf{r}, \mathbf{w}\}, x \in X, 0 < i \leq T(\mathbf{o}[\mathbf{x}])\} \cup \{\mathbf{o}^{\mathbf{i}}_{\mathbf{T}} \mid \mathbf{o} \in \{\mathbf{a}, \mathbf{c}\}, 0 < i \leq T(\mathbf{o})\}.$$

Furthermore, $\leq_T \subseteq T \times T$ is a finite partial order relation, and the following conditions must hold:

1. *either $T(\mathbf{c}) = 1$ and $T(\mathbf{a}) = 0$, or $T(\mathbf{c}) = 0$ and $T(\mathbf{a}) = 1$;*
2. *T has at least one* **read** *or* **write** *action;*
3. *either $\mathbf{c}^{\mathbf{1}}_{\mathbf{T}}$ or $\mathbf{a}^{\mathbf{1}}_{\mathbf{T}}$ must be maximal wrt $\leq_T$ (we drop this superscript from now on);*
4. *if $\mathbf{w}^{\mathbf{i}}_{\mathbf{T}}[\mathbf{x}] \in T$ then for any action $\mathbf{o}^{\mathbf{k}}_{\mathbf{T}}[\mathbf{x}]$ that reads or writes variable x, either $\mathbf{o}^{\mathbf{k}}_{\mathbf{T}}[\mathbf{x}] \leq_T \mathbf{w}^{\mathbf{i}}_{\mathbf{T}}[\mathbf{x}]$ or $\mathbf{w}^{\mathbf{i}}_{\mathbf{T}}[\mathbf{x}] \leq_T \mathbf{o}^{\mathbf{k}}_{\mathbf{T}}[\mathbf{x}]$*

We often denote transaction $\langle T, \leq_T\rangle$ simply by T, leaving the partial order understood. We denote by vars(T) the set of variables used in T, namely vars(T) $= \{x \in X \mid T(\mathbf{r}[\mathbf{x}]) + T(\mathbf{w}[\mathbf{x}]) > 0\}$. We also introduce the following auxiliary notations:

- $T[x] = T \cap \{\mathbf{r}^{\mathbf{i}}_{\mathbf{T}}[\mathbf{x}], \mathbf{w}^{\mathbf{i}}_{\mathbf{T}}[\mathbf{x}]\}$ *is the subset of actions of* T *involving variable* x*;*
- $\leq^x_T = \leq_T \cap (T[x] \times T[x])$.

We consider three subsets of vars(T). The set of ***local variables*** *is defined as* $\mathbf{loc}(T) = \{x \mid \exists i \,.\, \mathbf{w}^{\mathbf{i}}_{\mathbf{T}}[\mathbf{x}] = min(\leq^x_T)\}$*. Intuitively, if the first action over* x *in* T *is a write (often called a "blind write"), then* x *is handled as a local variable and its value before* T *is irrelevant. By the condition on* $\leq_T$*, if the minimum of* $\leq^x_T$ *is a* **write** *then it is unique.*

The ***readset*** *of* T *is defined as* $\mathbf{rs}(T) = \{x \mid \exists i \,.\, \mathbf{r}^{\mathbf{i}}_{\mathbf{T}}[\mathbf{x}] \in min(\leq^x_T)\}$*. Thus the readset of* T *consists of all the variables of the transaction whose original value was read outside* T*. Note that* $\mathbf{rs}(T)$ *and* $\mathbf{loc}(T)$ *form a partition of vars(T).*

The ***writeset*** *of* T *is defined as* $\mathbf{ws}(T) = \{x \mid T(\mathbf{w}[\mathbf{x}]) > 0\}$*, i.e. the set of variables modified by* T*. A transaction with an empty writeset is called a* ***read-only transaction****; we shall use the predicate* **ro** *defined as* $\mathbf{ro}(T) \equiv (\mathbf{ws}(T) = \varnothing)$*. Note that* $\mathbf{loc}(T) \subseteq \mathbf{ws}(T)$*.*

Histories represent concurrent executions of transactions. Actions of different transactions can never be the same, but they may act on shared data (variables). Therefore, a history must carry information about the order in which conflicting actions shall occur. Moreover, it may define also relationships among other (non-conflicting) actions.

Definition 3 (History). *Given a set of transactions* $S = \{T_1, \ldots, T_n\}$*, a* ***complete history*** *over* S *is a partial order* $\langle H, \leq \rangle$ *where*

1. $H = \bigcup_{i=1}^n T_i$*;*
2. $\leq \supseteq \bigcup_{i=1}^n \leq_i$*;*
3. *for any conflicting actions* o_1 *and* o_2 *in* H*, either* $o_1 \leq o_2$ *or* $o_2 \leq o_1$*.*

A ***history*** *is a prefix of a complete history. A transaction* T_i *is* ***committed*** */* ***aborted*** *in a history* H *if* $\mathbf{c}_{\mathbf{T_i}} \in H$ */* $\mathbf{a}_{\mathbf{T_i}} \in H$*. If a transaction is neither committed nor aborted, it is* ***active*** *in a history. The* ***committed projection*** *of a history* H *is denoted by* $C(H)$ *and is obtained by removing from* H *all actions that belong to active or aborted transactions. The* ***non-aborted projection*** *of a history* H *is denoted by* $NA(H)$ *and is obtained by removing from* H *all actions of aborted transactions.*

The set of variables used (written or read) in a history H *is denoted by vars(H). Given a history* $(H, \leq_H)$*, the* ***induced dependency relation*** *on transactions* $\leq^T_H$ *is defined as:* $T_1 \leq^T_H T_2$ *if there are actions* $o_1 \in T_1$ *and* $o_2 \in T_2$ *such that* $o_1 \leq_H o_2$*. A history is* ***strict*** *if whenever there are actions* $\mathbf{w}_{\mathbf{T_j}}[\mathbf{x}] \leq_H \mathbf{o}_{\mathbf{T_i}}[\mathbf{x}]$*, with* $T_i, T_j \in H$ *and* $i \neq j$*, either* $\mathbf{a}_{\mathbf{T_j}} \leq_H \mathbf{o}_{\mathbf{T_i}}[\mathbf{x}]$ *or* $\mathbf{c}_{\mathbf{T_j}} \leq_H \mathbf{o}_{\mathbf{T_i}}[\mathbf{x}]$*.*

Strictness implies that if a transaction T writes a variable, no other transaction can read/write it before T is terminated. This is commonly required in applications since histories that are not strict allow serializations that are rather counterintuitive (that would "undo the past"), and also implies recoverability and avoids cascading aborts.

The following equivalence notion on histories is known as conflict-equivalence, since it is based on the compatibility between conflicting items of histories. In this paper we will stick to this kind of equivalence.

Definition 4 (History Equivalence). *Given two histories $(H_1, \leq_{H_1})$ and $(H_2, \leq_{H_2})$, we say that they are* ***equivalent*** *if*

1. *$H_1 = H_2$ (they have the same actions);*
2. *they order conflicting actions of non-aborted transactions in the same way: for all $o_1, o_2 \in NA(H_1)$ such that o_1 and o_2 are conflicting, $o_1 \leq_{H_1} o_2$ if and only if $o_1 \leq_{H_2} o_2$.*

Note that this definition of equivalence poses no restriction on the dependencies of non-conflicting actions.

Definition 5 (Serial History). *A complete history $(H, \leq_H)$ is* ***serial*** *if for every two transactions $T_i, T_j \in H$, either for all $o_i \in T_i$ we have $end_j \leq_H o_i$, or for all $o_j \in T_j$ it holds $end_i \leq_H o_j$, where end_j (end_i) is the commit or abort action of T_j (T_i).*

Note that the induced dependency relation on transactions of a serial history is a total order, even if $\leq_H$ does not need to be total.

Definition 6 (Serializable History). *A history $(H, \leq_H)$ is (conflict)* ***serializable*** *if there is a serial history $(H_s, \leq_{H_s})$ that is equivalent to the committed projection $C(H)$.*

For a proof of the following theorem, see [3] (Serializability Theorem, Sect. 2.3).

Theorem 1. *Let $(H, \leq_H)$ be a history and $G(H)$ be the graph whose nodes are the transactions of H and arcs represent the relationship between the conflicting actions in $\leq_H$, lifted to the corresponding transactions. A history is serializable iff $G(H)$ is acyclic.*

3 The Deferred Update Replication

The Deferred Update Replication (DUR) technique coordinates transaction processing on a group of servers that fully replicate the database. It provides fault-tolerance due to replication while offering good performance. Clients submit transactions to any server. Servers execute transactions locally, without coordination with other servers, in a so-called execution phase. The concurrency control strategy is optimistic. When the client requests the transaction's termination, the respective server broadcasts updates to all servers which then have to certify that the transaction can be serialized with other committed transactions that executed concurrently. When the client requests the transaction's commit, it broadcasts its local updates to all servers which then have to certify that the transaction can be serialized with other committed transactions that were executed concurrently. The termination phase uses an atomic broadcast protocol that ensures that all servers receive the same termination messages in the same order. Since all execute the same certification procedures, they decide homogeneously, accepting (committing and updating the local states) or not (aborting) the transaction, and thus progress over the same (replicated) states. The good performance is achieved since: update transactions progress independently in each server during the execution phase; read-only transactions can be certified locally; communication is restricted to the dissemination of updates for certification at the end of the transaction (lazy approach) which implies a lower overhead if compared to propagation of updates during the transaction (eager approach).

Since in the following sections we provide an operational semantics for DUR, we adopt and explain here the main DUR algorithms at client and server sides from [17]. Each transaction t has a unique identifier id, a readset rs keeping the variables read by t; a writeset ws keeping both the variables and the values updated by t; and a snapshot identifier st that records the snapshot of the database when t started reading values.

According to the client algorithm of [17] (see Fig. 1, left), after a transaction t is initiated (lines 1–4), the client may request a read, a write or a commit operation. For brevity, it is not shown in the algorithm the case in which the client executes an abort operation. A read operation by transaction t on variable k will add k to $t.rs$. If k belongs to $t.ws$ it means that k has been previously written and the read operation returns the local value (lines 7, 8). Otherwise the value has to be read from one server s from the set of servers S (lines 10, 11). If this was the first read of this transaction, the snapshot identifier returned by the server is stored in $t.st$. A write operation simply adds locally to $t.ws$ the value written on the variable. A commit of a read-only transaction is decided locally. In case of an update transaction, a request for certification of transaction t is atomically broadcast to all servers and an answer from one of the servers is awaited. The transaction certification decision is based on the readset of the transaction and on the writesets of the already committed concurrent transactions.

Notice that the algorithm does not distinguish between local and non-local variables: when a variable is read it is added to the readset even if it was initialized with a blind write.

According to the server algorithm, a server has a snapshot counter SC recording the number of committed transactions (line 17) and a writeset for each snapshot $WS[i]$ that records the writeset of the transaction committed at snapshot i. When a read request arrives, if it is the first read of a transaction (line 5) then the server assigns to the transaction's snapshot identifier st the current value of the snapshot counter, that the client will keep for future reads. Then the server retrieves from the database the most recent value v for variable k before or at the same snapshot identified by st (line 6). When client c requests a commit

DUR, Client *c*'s code

```
1: begin(t):
2: t.rs ← ∅
3: t.ws ← ∅
4: t.st ← ⊥
5: read(t, k):
6: t.rs ← t.rs ∪ k
7: if (k, *) ∈ t.ws then
8:     return v s.t. (k, v) ∈ t.ws
9: else
10:    send(read, k, t.st) to some s ∈ S
11:    wait until receive(k, v, st) from s
12:    if t.st = ⊥ then t.st = st
13:    return v
14: write(t, k, v):
15: t.ws ← t.ws ∪ k, v
16: commit(t):
17: if t.ws = ∅ then
18:    return commit
19: else
20:    abcast(c, t)
21:    wait until receive(outcome) from s
22:    return outcome
```

DUR, Server *s*'s code

```
1: initialization:
2: SC ← 0
3: WS[..] ← ∅
4: when receive(read, k, st) from c
5: if st = ⊥ then st ← SC
6: retrieve(k, v, st) from database
7: send(k, v, st) to c
8: when adeliver(c, t)
9: outcome ← certify(t)
10: if outcome = commit then
11:    apply t.ws to database
12: send(outcome) to c
13: function certify(t)
14: for i ← t.st to SC do
15:    if WS[i] ∩ t.rs ≠ ∅ then
16:        return abort
17: SC ← SC + 1
18: WS[SC] ← items(t.ws)
19: return commit
```

Fig. 1. DUR algorithms

(using the atomic broadcast primitive *adeliver* - line 8) all servers will run the certification test (line 9) and in case the outcome is *commit* the writeset is used to update the database (lines 10, 11). Any outcome is sent to client c (line 12). The certification of t verifies if any committed transaction concurrent with t (line 14) updated variables of the readset of t (line 15). In such case t has to be aborted. Otherwise t is committed, a new snapshot is generated at the server (line 17) and the server keeps track of the variables updated in the last commit (line 18).

As one can observe, the certification of a transaction t depends only on whether the values read ($t.rs$) are valid upon termination, i.e. if no committed concurrent transaction has written on a value after it has been read by t.

Certification of read-only transactions is straightforward since all read values are consistent with the snapshot *st* of the first read, assuring that no update happened on the variables until after *st* - the transaction is considered to happen atomically at *st*, reading a consistent state even if snapshot *st* is in the past.

We can observe that since updates are deferred to the moment of termination, and actually updates and commit of one transaction are performed atomically, no updates and commits of different transactions interleave. The database progresses over states where updates are from a single transaction.

4 The DUR Algorithm, Formally

We present here a formalization of the behaviour of the server, as described in the previous section, using a transition system. This will be exploited for a proof of correctness and completeness of the **DUR Server** algorithm.

We assume that there is a fixed set of transactions $\mathcal{T}$ which includes all transactions that will ever interact with the server. Since at most a finite number of transactions can be terminated in each state of the server's evolution, to make the formalization easier we assume $\mathcal{T}$ to be finite. Notice that the readset and the writeset of a transaction are built in the client's code, and are used by the server only when the transaction is completed. Therefore we consider them as statically known, and denote them as $\mathbf{rs}(T)$ and $\mathbf{ws}(T)$, respectively. Note however that $\mathbf{rs}(T)$ denotes the readset as defined in Definition 2, while the readset of a transaction according to the algorithm of Fig. 1 also includes the local variables, and could be denoted as $\mathbf{rs}(T) \cup \mathbf{loc}(T)$: we will discuss later the consequences of this assumption.

The snapshot identifier, identifying the snapshot of the database that a transaction accesses, is assigned dynamically by the server at the first read operation. Therefore the state of a server includes, besides the snapshot counter SC and a vector of committed writesets WS (see lines 2–3 of the server's code), a function ST defined on $\mathcal{T}$ returning the snapshot identifier, if defined, and $\perp$ otherwise. The state also includes an additional function on transactions, the *commit index* CI, which is defined only on terminated transactions and records whether the transaction is aborted or not, and in case it is not read-only the index of its committed writeset in vector WS.

The components of a well-formed server state have to satisfy several constraints, listed in the next definition, most of which are pretty obvious: as shown in Theorem 2, well-formedness will guarantee reachability. We just stress that the commit index of a read-only transaction is set, quite arbitrarily, to its snapshot identifier plus 0.5. In this way it is smaller than the commit index of any transaction that could modify the variables in the readset after being accessed.

Definition 7 (Server State). *A* ***server state*** *over a finite set of transactions* $\mathcal{T}$ *is a four-tuple* $D = \langle SC, WS, ST, CI \rangle$*, where*

- SC *is an integer, the* snapshot counter*;*
- WS *is a vector of (committed) writesets* $WS : \{0, \ldots, SC\} \to \mathcal{P}(X)$*;*
- $ST : \mathcal{T} \to \{0, \ldots, SC\} \cup \{\perp\}$ *maps each transaction in* $\mathcal{T}$ *to its* snapshot identifier*, i.e. an integer* $ST(T) \leq SC$ *which is the index of the writeset from which the first value of* T *is read, if any, and* $\perp$ *otherwise;*
- $CI : \mathcal{T} \to \{0.5, 1, 1.5, \ldots, SC, SC + 0.5\} \cup \{\perp, abort\}$ *maps each transaction to its* commit index*. A transaction* T *is* aborted *if* $CI(T) = abort$*; it is* active *if* $CI(T) = \perp$ *and* $ST(T) \neq \perp$*; and it is* committed *if* $CI(T) \in \mathbb{Z}$*. We shall denote by* $Comm(D)$ *the set of transactions committed in* D*, and by* $RO(D)$ *its subset of read-only transactions.*

We will denote by $\bot$ *the constant function mapping all transactions to* $\bot$. *A server state is* ***well-formed*** *if the following conditions are satisfied:*

1. $WS(0) = X$, *that is, the first writeset of WS includes all variables (it represents their initial values);*
2. *every other writeset in WS corresponds to exactly one committed, non-read-only transaction; formally, CI restricts to a bijection*

$$Comm(D) \setminus RO(D) \leftrightarrow \{1, 2, \ldots, SC\}, \text{ and}$$

$$\forall T \in Comm(D) \setminus RO(D)\,.\, WS(CI(T)) = \boldsymbol{ws}(T)$$

3. *if the snapshot identifier of a transaction is defined then its readset is not empty:*

$$ST(T) \neq \bot \Rightarrow \boldsymbol{rs}(T) \neq \varnothing$$

4. *an aborted transaction has a defined snapshot identifier and its readset has been modified by a committed transaction:*

$$CI(T) = abort \Rightarrow ST(T) \neq \bot \wedge (\exists i \in [ST(T)+1, SC]\,.\, WS(i) \cap \boldsymbol{rs}(T) \neq \varnothing)$$

5. *the snapshot identifier of a non-read-only committed transaction, if defined, is less than the commit index, and in this case its readset was not modified before committing:*

$$\neg \boldsymbol{ro}(T) \wedge CI(T) \notin \{abort, \bot\} \wedge ST(T) \neq \bot \Rightarrow$$

$$0 \leq ST(T) < CI(T) \wedge (\forall i \in [ST(T)+1, CI(T)-1]\,.\, WS(i) \cap \boldsymbol{rs}(T) = \varnothing)$$

6. *a read-only transaction cannot abort, and if committed its commit index is one half more than its snapshot identifier:*

$$\boldsymbol{ro}(T) \Rightarrow (CI(T) \neq abort) \wedge (CI(T) \neq \bot \Rightarrow ST(T) \neq \bot \wedge CI(T) = ST(T) + 0.5)$$

The behaviour of the server can be represented as a transition systems where transitions are triggered by the interactions with the clients. Every client, while executing a transaction $T \in \mathcal{T}$, interacts with the server to read the values of the variables in its readset and to deliver the values of the variables in its writeset upon completion. From the server's side, as described in algorithm **DUR Server** (Fig. 1, right), this corresponds to receiving a sequence of *receive* (briefly *rec*) requests, followed by one *adeliver* (*adel*) request, which depending on the situation can cause the transaction to be committed or to abort. The first *rec* request is handled in a special way, as it will fix the snapshot of the data repository which is relevant for transaction T.

For our goals, the concrete values of the variables are irrelevant, as it is the name of the variable read with a *rec* request, assuming that it belongs to the readset of the transaction. We will therefore disregard this information assuming that *rec* requests will have only the transaction issuing the request as argument, exactly as the *adel* request.

Definition 8 (Server as Transition System). *A server $\mathcal{S}$ over a set of transactions $\mathcal{T}$ is a transition system having as states the well-formed server states of Definition 7, as initial state the state $D_0 = \langle SC_0 = 0, WS_0 = [0 \mapsto X], ST_0 = \bot, CI_0 = \bot] \rangle$, and where transitions are generated by the following inference rules (for the sake of readability, the components of states that are not changed in a rule are represented by an underscore):*

$$[read\text{-}\bot]\frac{ST(T) = \bot, \boldsymbol{rs}(T) \neq \varnothing}{\langle \_, \_, ST, \_ \rangle \xrightarrow{rec(T)} \langle \_, \_, ST[T \mapsto SC], \_ \rangle}$$

$$[read]\frac{ST(T) \neq \bot}{\langle \_, \_, \_, \_ \rangle \xrightarrow{rec(T)} \langle \_, \_, \_, \_ \rangle}$$

[commit]

$$\frac{CI(T) = \bot, \neg \boldsymbol{ro}(T), \neg (\exists x \in \boldsymbol{rs}(T), i \in \{ST(T)+1, \ldots, SC\} \,.\, x \in WS(i))}{\langle SC, WS, \_, CI \rangle \xrightarrow{adel(T)} \langle SC+1, WS[SC+1 \mapsto \boldsymbol{ws}(T)], \_, CI[T \mapsto SC+1] \rangle}$$

$$[commit\text{-}RO]\frac{CI(T) = \bot, \boldsymbol{ro}(T)}{\langle \_, \_, \_, CI \rangle \xrightarrow{adel(T)} \langle \_, \_, \_, CI[T \mapsto ST(T) + 0.5] \rangle}$$

$$[abort]\frac{CI(T) = \bot, \neg \boldsymbol{ro}(T), (\exists x \in \boldsymbol{rs}(T), i \in \{ST(T)+1, \ldots, SC\} \,.\, x \in WS(i))}{\langle \_, \_, \_, CI \rangle \xrightarrow{adel(T)} \langle \_, \_, \_, CI[T \mapsto abort] \rangle}$$

Rules *[read]*-$\bot$ and *[read]* encode lines 4–7 of algorithm **DUR Server** (Fig. 1): since we abstract from variables values, and variable names are recorded by functions **rs** and **ws**, the only visible effect in the server state is the assignment of a snapshot identifier to a transaction, if missing. Rules *[commit]* and *[abort]* encode lines 8–19 of the algorithm. Note that in the premises of these rules we used the set $\mathbf{rs}(T)$ instead of the larger set $\mathbf{rs}(T) \cup \mathbf{loc}(T)$, as used in the algorithm in Fig. 1. This means that our model has less abort transitions than the algorithm would have, and we will show in Theorem 4 that our definition characterises exactly the histories that should be aborted because they would lead to non-serializable histories. Rule *[commit-RO]* records the completion of a read-only transaction, that has no visible effect for the server in the DUR algorithm, but is necessary in our encoding to keep function *CI* up to date.

It is worth stressing that we implicitly assume that the server receives a *rec*(T) request only if the readset of transaction T is not empty, and that it receives at most one *adel*(T) request for each transaction T: condition $\mathbf{rs}(T) \neq \varnothing$ in rule *[read*$-\bot$*]* and condition $CI(T) = \bot$ in the last three rules guarantee that requests violating these conditions will not be processed.

Note that a transaction T may terminate (commit or abort) even if $ST(T)$ is undefined. The snapshot identifier of T is undefined if and only if the execution of T never generates a *rec*(T) transition, i.e. if the readset $\mathbf{rs}(T)$ is empty. In this case, T is not read-only (because transactions without any action are forbidden by Definition 2) and thus the last premise of rule *[commit]* is vacuously satisfied, while the premise of the *[abort]* rule is vacuously false.

We shall often represent transitions by labeling them with both the request of the client (over the arrow) and with the applied rule (under), as in $D \xrightarrow[\text{[read-}\bot\text{]}]{rec(T)}$. Furthermore, we write $D \Rightarrow D'$ if there is a transition from D to D' using the rules of Definition 8.

To conclude this section, we state that the well-formedness of a server state guarantees its reachability. The lengthy proof is in the appendix.

Theorem 2 (Well-formed server states are reachable). *A server state over a set of transactions $\mathcal{T}$ is reachable if and only if it is well-formed.*

5 Correctness and Completeness of Deferred Update Replication

We show now that the server as previously specified guarantees the serializability of the transactions that it committed. This is a pretty straightforward correctness result. More interestingly, thanks to the rigorous formalization we are also able to prove that the server is "complete", in the sense that it never happens that a transaction is aborted if it was serializable.

Note that it is sufficient to verify one server, since all servers receive the actions in the same order, and thus should arrive to the same commit/abort decision for each transaction since they run the same algorithm. The same order of actions is guaranteed by an atomic broadcast protocol, that is assumed to be available in the underlying distributed platform. Also, it is not necessary to formalize the clients because, besides the mild constraints that they issue a *rec* request only if the readset is not empty and at most one *adel* request for each transaction, we do not make any further assumption on the order of actions that can be generated by them. Again, what is important is that the *adel* actions of all clients are received in the same order by all servers, and this is provided by the atomic broadcast protocol. There are many ways to implement this protocol: for the results of this paper we assume that the distributed platform executing the DUR technique provides this service.

Since by Theorem 2 all and only the well-formed states are reachable in an execution of the server, the correctness of the server can be proved by showing that in any well-formed state, the dependencies among committed transactions that are recorded in the state are compatible with a history including them *only if* the history is serializable. In other words, a non-serializable history could not be executed by the server.

Therefore let us define when a complete history containing a set of committed transactions is consistent with a well-formed state of the server.

Definition 9 (History-state consistency). *Let $D = \langle SC, WS, ST, CI \rangle$ be a wellformed server state over a set of transactions $\mathcal{T}$, and $\langle H, \leq_H \rangle$ be a complete history. Then H and D are* ***consistent*** *if*

1. *$\langle H, \leq_H \rangle$ is a history over Comm(D), i.e. over the transactions of $\mathcal{T}$ which committed in D;*

2. *for each pair $T \neq T' \in Comm(D)$, for each pair of conflicting actions* $\mathbf{a} \in T$ *and* $\mathbf{b} \in T'$, *we have:*
   (a) $\mathbf{a} <_H \mathbf{b}$ *implies* $CI(T) < CI(T')$;
   (b) *if* $x \in \boldsymbol{rs}(T')$ *and* $\mathbf{b} = \mathbf{r_{T'}[x]}$ *(and thus* $\mathbf{a} = \mathbf{w_T[x]}$*), then* $\mathbf{w_T[x]} <_H \mathbf{r_{T'}[x]}$ *if and only if* $CI(T) \leq ST(T')$.

Condition *2(a)* states that the causality among conflicting actions belonging to distinct transactions in H is consistent with the commit ordering of transactions. Condition *2(b)* guarantees that the history correctly records the values read by a transaction for the variables in its readset, imposing that such values are those available at the database snapshot $ST(T)$. In fact, each read action in the readset must depend on all and only the write actions for the same variable in transactions that committed not later than the snapshot identifier. Note that since all pairs of conflicting events have to be causally related in a history, it follows that $\mathbf{r_{T'}[x]} <_H \mathbf{w_T[x]}$ if and only if $ST(T') < CI(T)$. In this case, since by *2(a)* we also know that $CI(T') < CI(T)$, we can conclude that $ST(T') \leq CI(T') < CI(T)$, as $ST(T') \leq CI(T')$ because D is well-formed.

The next result states the correctness of DUR algorithm.

Proposition 1 (Consistent histories are serializable). *Let* $\langle H, \leq \rangle$ *be a complete history consistent with a well-formed server state* $D = \langle SC, WS, ST, CI \rangle$. *Then* H *is serializable.*

Proof. Let $\sqsubseteq'_D$ be the commit ordering on $Comm(D)$, i.e. $T \sqsubseteq'_D T'$ if $CI(T) \leq CI(T')$; it is a partial order because two read-only transactions may have the same commit index. Let $\sqsubseteq_D$ be any total order compatible with $\sqsubseteq'_D$, ordering such read-only transactions in an arbitrary way. Then by condition *2(a)* above for each pair of conflicting actions $\mathbf{a_T[x]} \leq_H \mathbf{b_{T'}[x]}$ in H with $T \neq T'$, we have $T \sqsubseteq_D T'$. Therefore H is serializable, because it is equivalent to a serial history where all actions of a transaction T are caused by the commit action of a transaction T' if and only if $T' \sqsubseteq_D T$. □

Viceversa, completeness can be proved by showing that any serializable history is consistent with a well-formed server state. The following theorem is stated only for serialisable histories without aborted transactions because a history may have arbitrary aborts (transactions that deliberately choose to abort - see Definition 2), whereas a DUR-server only has "necessary" aborts - the ones that happened due to conflicts in concurrent updates.

Theorem 3 (Serializable histories and consistent states). *Let* H *be a complete serializable history without aborted transactions. Then there is a well-formed server state* D *that is consistent with* H.

Proof. The proof is by induction on the number of committed transactions in H.

For the base case, the initial state of Definition 8 is clearly consistent with the empty history since there are no aborted/active transactions in H.

Now suppose we have a complete serializable history H_{n+1} with $n+1$ transactions. Let H_n be obtained by removing one transaction, say T, that is maximal with respect to the transaction order induced by $\leq_{H_{n+1}}$. H_n is a complete serializable history because H_{n+1} is. By induction hypothesis there is a well-formed server state $D_n = \langle SC, WS, ST, CI\rangle$ that is compatible with H_n. A well-formed server state D_{n+1} can be obtained in the following way. If T is not read-only and $\mathbf{rs}(T) \neq \varnothing$

$$D_{n+1} = \langle SC+1, WS[T \mapsto \mathbf{ws}(T)], ST[T \mapsto i], CI[T \mapsto SC+1]\rangle$$

where $i \in [SC_U, SC]$ and SC_U is the last snapshot in which some variable in $\mathbf{rs}(T)$ was updated ($SC_U = max\{CI(T_i) \mid WS(T_i) \cap \mathbf{rs}(T) \neq \varnothing\}$). This state clearly satisfies all conditions of Definition 7. If the transaction does not read any value, ST maps T to $\perp$, and also in this case all conditions are satisfied. If T is read-only, we define the server state as

$$D_{n+1} = \langle SC, WS, ST[T \mapsto i], CI[T \mapsto i+0.5]\rangle$$

Again, this state satisfies all conditions of Definition 7. In particular, in this case T must read some value by point 2 of Definition 2. □

To conclude, let us exploit the proposed formalization to show that the server causes a transaction to abort only when allowing it to commit would result in a non-serializable history. Interestingly, this property would not hold if in the premise of rule *[abort]* of Definition 8 we would have used as readset $\mathbf{rs}(T) \cup \mathbf{loc}(T)$ instead of $\mathbf{rs}(T)$.

For a given server state, it is possible to define a history corresponding to the execution of the transactions within this state. This history contains dependencies that enforce an order on the committed transactions according to the *CI* order, and otherwise would relate conflicting events of active/committed transactions according to the way they are related in *ST* and *CI*. Note that there can not be any dependency between active transactions because such transactions only have read actions in D (all write actions of a transaction T are recorded in the server state implicitly at commit time, when the writeset of T is added to *WS*).

Definition 10 (Execution history). *Let D be a well-formed server state over a set of transactions $\mathcal{T}$ without aborted transactions. Then we define the* ***execution history consistent with*** *D, denoted by $execHist(D)$, as $\langle H, \leq_H\rangle$ where*

- *H contains all actions of committed transactions of D, and only the minimal read actions from variables in $\mathbf{rs}(T)$ of active transactions of D;*
- *$\leq_H$ is the transitive closure of the relation containing all dependencies of transactions in $\mathcal{T}$ plus the pairs (we consider CI and ST whenever they are defined):*
  - $\langle \mathbf{c_{T_i}}, \mathbf{c_{T_j}}\rangle$, *if $CI(T_i) < CI(T_j)$;*
  - $\langle \mathbf{c_{T_i}}, \mathbf{o_{T_j}[x]}\rangle$, *if $CI(T_i) < CI(T_j)$ and $o_{T_j}[x]$ conflicts with an action $w_{T_i}[x]$;*
  - $\langle \mathbf{w_{T_i}[x]}, \mathbf{r_{T_j}[x]}\rangle$ *if $CI(T_i) \leq ST(T_j)$; and*
  - $\langle \mathbf{r_{T_i}[x]}, \mathbf{w_{T_j}[x]}\rangle$ *if $ST(T_i) < CI(T_j)$.*

The conditions on well-formed states (Definition 7) assure that $\leq_H$ is a partial order. By construction, if D has no active/aborted transactions, *execHist*(D) is strict. The following theorem states that if a transaction T will be aborted at server state D, then the corresponding history, that is, the history that contains all committed and active transactions until that moment plus the writeset and commit of T would not be serializable.

Theorem 4 (Abort is necessary). *Given a well-formed server state D without aborted transactions, the corresponding execution history $execHist(D) = \langle EH, \leq_{EH}\rangle$ and an active transaction T from D. Let $\langle H, \leq_H\rangle$ be defined as*

- $H = EH \cup T$;
- *$\leq_H$ is the transitive closure of the relation containing $\leq_{EH}$, $\leq_T$ plus the pairs $\langle \mathbf{c_i}, \mathbf{o_T}\rangle$, if an action of transaction T conflicts with some action of transaction $T_i \in EH$.*

If rule [abort] is enabled for a transaction T then H is not serializable.

Proof. If rule *[abort]* is enabled then T is not read-only and its read-set is not empty. Moreover, there is at least one transaction, say T_i, that committed in D and that updated a variable x read by T with an action $\mathbf{r_T[x]}$, with $ST(T) < CI(T_i)$. Let $i = CI(T_i)$ and let $\mathbf{w_i[x]}$ be the action of T_i that updated x. This means that actions $\mathbf{w_i[x]}$ and $\mathbf{r_T[x]}$ are in EH and $\mathbf{r_T[x]} \leq_{EH} \mathbf{w_i[x]}$ by Definition 10. But by definition of H, we must have that $\mathbf{c_i} \leq_H \mathbf{r_T[x]}$ and thus $\mathbf{w_i[x]} \leq_H \mathbf{r_T[x]}$ (because all actions of a transaction are related to the commit of the transaction and $\leq_H$ is transitive). Therefore, since $\leq_H$ includes $\leq_{EH}$, $\leq_H$ induces a cycle $T \leq_H^T T_i$ and $T_i \leq_H^T T$ and is therefore not serializable (actually $\leq_H$ is not even a history, since $\leq_H$ is not a partial order). □

The proof of the last result is crucially based on the fact that each variable x in the readset of T has its initial value set by an action $\mathbf{r_T[x]}$: if this value is overwritten by a concurrent transaction that commits before T, then T has to abort because its addition to the current history would cause a cycle of dependencies. If in the precondition of rule *[abort]* we would have used $\mathbf{rs}(T) \cup \mathbf{loc}(T)$ (as in the algorithm of Fig. 1) instead of $\mathbf{rs}(T)$, the result would not hold. In fact, if the variable overwritten by a concurrent transaction that commits before T is a local one, i.e. it is initialized in T by a blind write $\mathbf{w_T[x]}$, then the corresponding action $\mathbf{r_T[x]}$ would not belong to the execution history EH, and in the resulting history H it would be larger than any conflicting event in EH, giving rise to a serializable history. Thus in this situation the algorithm of Fig. 1 would cause an unnecessary failure of the transaction, that is avoided in our model thanks to a careful definition of readset.

6 Discussion

In this paper we have analyzed the Deferred Update Replication (DUR) technique, providing a formal model as a transition system that described the behaviour of the algorithm. In the construction of this transition system we used a slightly more permissive premise for committing transactions than the algorithm presented in [17], allowing transactions to commit even if some update was performed in some of its read variables, as long as the first action on this variable in the committing transaction was a write (thus, the variable was considered to be local). We showed that for this model all reachable states correspond to serialisable histories involving the corresponding transactions. Moreover, we showed that for all serialisable histories, it is possible that the DUR algorithm generates an execution containing all these transactions. But note that, given a server state D and a transaction T that is trying to commit, if the algorithm suggest the abortion, this does not mean that there is no serialisable history containing all committed transaction plus T, what it means is that it is not possible to find a serialisation without changing the order of some already committed transaction. This was stated as a theorem relating abort transitions and strict histories.

Besides being used to show the correctness and completeness of DUR, the formal model can be used as a basis to reason about other extensions of DUR that have been proposed recently in the literature, for example, considering replicated database partitions to enhance overall throughput [17], byzantine fault tolerance [13], and in-memory transaction execution [16]. Such extensions are very much attractive to modern computational environments (cloud computing; open systems and untrusted parties; modern architectures) and a formal analysis involving correctness and completeness is highly desired. In addition to the directly related family of DUR protocols, the contribution is also relevant to many other existing systems using replication and optimistic concurrency control, a frequent combination.

Another interesting line of research would be to check to which extent the theory of concurrency can be applied in this setting. The serialisability theory was very well-studied mainly in the 80s and 90s, and to a great extent results are based on very basic definitions of switching transactions to obtain equivalence notions over histories. To handle more complex scenarios, like the ones arising e.g. from unreliable systems, cloud computing or adaptive systems, it might be necessary to reason using more abstract notions of histories and equivalences. The use of concurrency models explicitly handling causality like event structures [10] or asymmetric event structures [2] about database updates in such settings.

7 Appendix

We present here the proof of Theorem 2.

Theorem 5 (Well-formed server states are reachable). *A server state over a set of transactions $\mathcal{T}$ is reachable if and only if it is well-formed.*

Proof. **Only if part** We must show that the initial state D_0 of Definition 8 is well-formed, and that if D is well-formed and there is a transition $D \Rightarrow D'$, then D' is well-formed as well. Let us consider the six conditions for well-formedness of Definition 7.

1. By definition $WS_0(0) = X$ holds in D_0, and the only rule that modifies vector WS, that is *[commit]*, changes it at index $CI+1 > 0$; therefore the first condition is satisfied by each reachable state.
2. D_0 satisfies the second condition because $CI_0 = \bot$. The only rule that modifies WS is *[commit]*, which also changes SC and CI in a way that maintains the invariant described by the second condition.
3. The only rule that modifies the snapshot identifier $ST(T)$ of a transaction is *[read−⊥]*: its second premise guarantees the third condition.
4. Finally, conditions 4, 5 and 6 are clearly satisfied by D_0 because $CI_0 = \bot$, and they express invariants that are easily checked to be maintained by rules *[abort]*, *[commit]* and *[commit-RO]*, respectively.

If part Let $D = \langle SC_D, WS_D, ST_D, CI_D \rangle$ be a well-formed server state over $\mathcal{T}$. We proceed by induction on the cardinality of $Comm(D)$.

If $|Comm(D)| = 0$, no transaction of $\mathcal{T}$ committed, and therefore we must have $SC_D = 0$, $WS_D = [0 \mapsto X]$, and $CI_D = \bot$, as no transaction could have aborted either, by condition 4 of Definition 7. Furthermore, $ST_D(T) \in \{\bot, 0\}$ for all $T \in \mathcal{T}$, i.e. some transactions may already have 0 as snapshot identifier. Let us show that D is reachable, i.e. $D_0 \Rightarrow^* D$ where D_0 is as in Definition 8. In fact, if $\{T_i\}_{1 \le i \le k} = \{T \mid ST_D(T) = 0\}$, by condition 3 of Definition 7 we know that $\mathbf{rs}(T_i)$ is not empty for $1 \le i \le k$, and thus there exists a sequence of transitions $D_0 \xrightarrow[\text{[read−⊥]}]{rec(T_1)} D_0^1 \cdots D_0^{k-1} \xrightarrow[\text{[read−⊥]}]{rec(T_k)} D_0^k = D$, where for all $i \in [1,k]$ it holds $ST_{D_0^i}(T) = 0 \iff T \in \{T_1, \ldots, T_i\}$.

Suppose now that $|Comm(D)| = n+1$. We first show that, without loss of generality, we may assume that no transaction aborted yet in D. In fact, if $\{T_i\}_{1 \le i \le k} = \{T \mid CI_D(T) = aborted\}$, then D is reachable from a state D' where those transactions are still active (i.e. $CI_{D'}(T_i) = \bot$), with a sequence of k *[abort]* transitions, one for each element of $\{T_i\}_{1 \le i \le k}$. The preconditions of such *[abort]* transitions are satisfied by condition 4 of 7.

Now, assuming that D has no aborted transactions, let T be one of the transactions in $Comm(D)$ with maximal commit index. We have two cases: either T is read-only or not.

If T is read-only, by conditions 6 and 2 of Definition 7 we have $CI_D(T) = ST_D(T) + 0.5 = SC + 0.5$. Consider the server state $D' = \langle SC, WS, ST', CI' \rangle$ where

$$ST'(x) = \begin{cases} ST(x) & \text{if } x \neq T \\ \bot & \text{if } x = T \end{cases} \qquad CI'(x) = \begin{cases} CI(x) & \text{if } x \neq T \\ \bot & \text{if } x = T \end{cases}$$

State D' represents a snapshot of the system where all transactions but T are as in state D, while T did not start yet (its snapshot identifier is $\bot$). It is easily shown that D' is well-formed, therefore by inductive hypothesis D' is reachable from D_0.

It remains to show that D is reachable from D' by accepting all the requests generated by the execution of T, i.e. $D' \xrightarrow[\text{read−⊥}]{rec(T)} D'' \xrightarrow[\text{[read]}]{rec(T)} D'' \cdots D'' \xrightarrow[\text{[commit-RO]}]{adel(T)} D$;

in fact the first transition sets $ST(T)$ to SC, and the last one sets $CI(T)$ to $SC+0.5$.

If T is not read-only, by condition 2 of Definition 7 we have that $CI_D(T) = SC_D$. Let us additionally assume that $ST_D(T) = CI_D(T)-1$. The idea, as in the case just seen, is to remove T from D obtaining a state D' with less committed transactions. But if there are transactions with $ST_D(T') = SC_D = CI_D(T)$, the resulting state would not be well-formed because $ST_D(T') > SC_{D'} = SC_D - 1$.

Therefore let us consider state D' obtained from D by setting $ST_{D'}(T) = \bot$ for all transactions in $\{T\}_{1\leq i\leq k} = \{T \mid ST_D(T) = CI_D\}$. We clearly have $D' \Rightarrow^* D$ with a sequence of transitions $D' \xrightarrow[read-\bot]{rec(T_1)} D'_1 \cdots D'_{k-1} \xrightarrow[read-\bot]{rec(T_k)} D'_k = D$, which are possible by condition 3 of Definition 7.

Consider now the server state $D'' = \langle SC'', WS'', ST'', CI'' \rangle$ where

$$SC'' = SC' - 1, \qquad WS''(x) = \begin{cases} WS'(x) & \text{if } x \neq SC' \\ \bot & \text{if } x = SC' \end{cases}$$

$$ST''(x) = \begin{cases} ST'(x) & \text{if } x \neq T \\ \bot & \text{if } x = T \end{cases} \qquad CI''(x) = \begin{cases} CI'(x) & \text{if } x \neq T \\ \bot & \text{if } x = T \end{cases}$$

State D'' is the server state before transaction T has started, and it is easily shown to be well-formed. Therefore by induction hypothesis D'' is reachable from D_0. To show that $D'' \Rightarrow^* D'$, we consider two cases, depending on the readset of T.

1. $\mathbf{rs}(T) = \varnothing$: In this case, the premise of *[commit]* is satisfied because T is not read-only, thus $D'' \xrightarrow[[commit]]{adel(T)} \hat{D}$. The resulting state is

   $$\hat{D} = \langle SC''+1, WS''[SC''+1 \mapsto \mathbf{ws}(T)], ST'', CI''[T \mapsto SC''+1] \rangle$$

   and using $SC'' = SC' - 1$, $CI'(T) = SC'$, $\mathbf{rs}(T) = \varnothing$ we conclude that

   $$\hat{D} = \langle SC', WS''[CI'(T) \mapsto \mathbf{ws}(T)], ST', CI''[T \mapsto SC'] \rangle$$

   and thus $D' = \hat{D}$ is reachable.
2. $\mathbf{rs}(T) \neq \varnothing$: Here, analogously to the case of read-only transactions, we may start by an application of rule *[read]*$-\bot$ followed by some applications of rule *[read]* until all variables in $\mathbf{rs}(T)$ are read, leading to state $\hat{D}$. Since state D was well-formed, it is easy to check that rule *[commit]* is enabled for T in $\hat{D}$, and that its application yields state D'.

It remains to consider the last case, where the transaction with highest commit index in D, say T, is not read-only and where $ST_D(T) < CI_D(T) - 1$. We argue as follows. Let D' be exactly like D, but with $ST_{D'}(T) = CI_D(T) - 1$. By the argument just presented we know that D' is reachable from D_0, i.e. there is a sequence of transitions $D_0 \Rightarrow D_1 \cdots D_{n-1} \Rightarrow D_n = D'$. In this sequence, the transition $\cdot \xrightarrow[\mathit{read}-\bot]{\mathit{rec}(T)} \cdot$, that sets the value of $ST(T)$, must occur after transition $\cdot \xrightarrow[\mathit{[commit]}]{\mathit{adel}(T')} \cdot$, which sets $CI(T') = CI(T) - 1$. Between the two transitions, there could be other *[read]*, *[read]*$-\bot$ and *[commit-RO]* transitions only. Now, it is easy to show that $\cdot \xrightarrow[\mathit{read}-\bot]{\mathit{rec}(T)} \cdot$ can be anticipated by switching it with all these transitions, without affecting the well-formedness of the states and without changing the final state. Finally, when we have the consecutive transitions $\cdot \xrightarrow[\mathit{[commit]}]{\mathit{adel}(T')} \cdot \xrightarrow[\mathit{read}-\bot]{\mathit{rec}(T)} \cdot$, we can switch them by obtaining $\cdot \xrightarrow[\mathit{read}-\bot]{\mathit{rec}(T)} \cdot \xrightarrow[\mathit{[commit]}]{\mathit{adel}(T')} \cdot$. This is possible, again, because the well-formedness of state D ensures that $\mathbf{ws}(T') \cap \mathbf{rs}(T) = \varnothing$. In the resulting final state only the value of $ST(T)$ is changed, and it is $CI(T') = CI(T) - 2$. By iterating this transformation of the sequence of transitions we can show that the original state D is reachable. □

References

1. Armendáriz-Iñigo, J.E., de Mendívil, J.R.G., Garitagoitia, J.R., Muñoz-Escoí, F.D.: Correctness proof of a database replication protocol under the perspective of the I/O automaton model. Acta Inf. **46**(4), 297–330 (2009)
2. Baldan, P., Corradini, A., Montanari, U.: Contextual Petri Nets, asymmetric event structures and processes. Inf. Comput. **171**(1), 1–49 (2001)
3. Bernstein, P.A., Hadzilacos, V., Goodman, N.: Concurrency Control and Recovery in Database Systems. Addison-Wesley, San Diego (1987)
4. Bhargava, B.K.: Concurrency control in database systems. IEEE Trans. Knowl. Data Eng. **11**(1), 3–16 (1999)
5. Budhiraja, N., Marzullo, K., Schneider, F.B., Toueg, S.: The primary-backup approach. Distrib. Syst. **2**, 199–216 (1993)
6. Garcia, R., Rodrigues, R., Preguiça, N.M.: Efficient middleware for byzantine fault tolerant database replication. In: Kirsch, C.M., Heiser, G. (eds.) EuroSys, pp. 107–122. ACM (2011)
7. Gray, J., Helland, P., O'Neil, P.E., Shasha, D.: The dangers of replication and a solution. In: Jagadish, H.V., Mumick, I.S. (eds.) SIGMOD Conference. pp. 173–182, ACM Press (1996)
8. Kemme, B., Alonso, G.: A new approach to developing and implementing eager database replication protocols. ACM Trans. Datab. Syst. **25**(3), 333–379 (2000)
9. Kung, H.T., Robinson, J.T.: On optimistic methods for concurrency control. ACM Trans. Datab. Syst. (TODS) **6**(2), 213–226 (1981)
10. Nielsen, M., Plotkin, G., Winskel, G.: Petri nets, event structures and domains, part I. Theor. Comput. Sci. **13**(1), 85–108 (1981)
11. Papadimitriou, C.H.: The serializability of concurrent database updates. J. ACM **26**(4), 631–653 (1979)
12. Pedone, F., Guerraoui, R., Schiper, A.: Transaction reordering in replicated databases. In: 16th IEEE Symposium on Reliable Distributed Systems (SRDS), pp. 175–182. IEEE (1997)
13. Pedone, F., Schiper, N.: Byzantine fault-tolerant deferred update replication. J. Brazil. Comput. Soc. **18**, 3–18 (2012)

14. Schmidt, R., Pedone, F.: A Formal Analysis of the Deferred Update Technique. In: Tovar, E., Tsigas, P., Fouchal, H. (eds.) OPODIS. LNCS, vol. 4878, pp. 16–30. Springer, Heidelberg (2007)
15. Schneider, F.B.: Implementing fault-tolerant services using the state machine approach: A tutorial. ACM Comput. Surv. (CSUR) **22**(4), 299–319 (1990)
16. Sciascia, D., Pedone, F.: RAM-DUR: In-memory deferred update replication. In: 31st IEEE Symposium on Reliable Distributed Systems (SRDS), pp. 81–90. IEEE (2012)
17. Sciascia, D., Pedone, F., Junqueira, F.: Scalable deferred update replication. In: 42nd Annual IEEE/IFIP International Conference on Dependable Systems and Networks (DSN), pp. 1–12. IEEE (2012)

Studying Operational Models of Relaxed Concurrency

Gustavo Petri(✉)

Purdue University, West Lafayette, USA
gpetri@cs.purdue.edu

Abstract. We study two operational semantics for relaxed memory models. Our first formalization is based on the notion of write-buffers which is pervasive in the memory models literature. We instantiate the (Total Store Ordering) TSO and (Partial Store Ordering) PSO memory models in this framework. Memory models that support more aggressive relaxations (e.g. read-to-read reordering) are not easily described with write-buffers. Our second framework is based on a general notion of speculative computation. In particular we allow the prediction of function arguments, and execution ahead of time (e.g. by branch prediction). While technically more involved than write-buffers, this model is more expressive and can encode all the Sparc family of memory models: TSO, PSO and (Relaxed Memory Ordering) RMO. We validate the adequacy of our instantiations of TSO and PSO by formally comparing their write-buffer and speculative formalizations. The use of operational semantics techniques is paramount for the tractability of these proofs.

1 Introduction

Current trends in multi-core architectures have raised interest in the formalization of relaxed memory models. While most works on the area concentrate on axiomatic definitions of such models [1,13,18] in this work we concentrate on the operational formalization of such models and the techniques that they enable.

Some recent works – including ours – have addressed the operational semantics of relaxed memory models [4,7,8,10,19], to mention but a few. In [7] we consider the operational semantics of *write-buffering* (see [1]). In these models writes to the memory are delayed in buffers, and are later updated into the memory. When a write is buffered, the issuing process is able to continue executing provided that its execution does not conflict with the suspended writes. Buffering a thread write has, from another thread perspective, the effect of delaying its execution w.r.t. subsequent actions of that thread. Write buffering is only one of the many memory order relaxations of common machine architectures and programming languages [1]. In [8] we consider the semantics of *speculative computation*, where actions in a thread can be performed in advance – or in parallel – without waiting for prior actions to be completed. Speculations are more

Research supported by NSF 1237923.

M. Abadi and A. Lluch Lafuente (Eds.): TGC 2013, LNCS 8358, pp. 254–272, 2014.
DOI: 10.1007/978-3-319-05119-2_15,

$$\begin{bmatrix} p := 1\,; \\ r_0 := (!q) \end{bmatrix} \parallel \begin{bmatrix} q := 1\,; \\ r_1 := (!p) \end{bmatrix} \qquad \begin{bmatrix} p := 1\,; \\ q := 1 \end{bmatrix} \parallel \begin{bmatrix} r_0 := (!q)\,; \\ r_1 := (!p) \end{bmatrix}$$

(a) TSO & PSO: $r_0 = r_1 = 0$ (b) PSO: $r_0 = 1$ & $r_1 = 0$

Fig. 1. TSO and PSO examples

general than write buffering, since more behaviors are possible. This additional expressivity comes at the cost of a more elaborate formalism. Here we provide a uniform presentation and a formal comparison of instances of the frameworks justifying that claim. To do so, we present instances of both frameworks describing the TSO (Total Store Ordering) and PSO (Partial Store Ordering) memory models of Sparc [20]. However, the RMO (Relaxed Memory Ordering) model cannot be encoded with write-buffers.

Let us focus on TSO and PSO. Both models can reorder a read instruction with respect to a previous write. Figure 1a illustrates this behavior, where we assume that p and q are pointers in the memory initialized to 0, r_0 and r_1 refer to local "registers" (private to a thread), and we use the ML syntax $(!p)$ for dereferencing p. If we execute these threads according to their interleaving semantics [11] the final result $r_0 = r_1 = 0$ is not possible. However, if any of the reads is allowed to execute before its previous write (since they are on different references), the result is possible. PSO additionally allows two subsequent writes to be reordered. The result in Fig. 1b can happen if the write of q takes place before the one of p. Another relaxation of these models is the capability of a thread to *read its own writes early*, according to [1]. Thus a thread can see its own writes before any other thread in the system.

In this work we formalize TSO and PSO with write buffers and speculations. For completeness we present a formalization of RMO with speculations. We then prove the adequacy of our formalizations of TSO and PSO with write-buffers and speculation. To that end we develop a third calculus, including both, write buffers and speculations, and prove their equivalence. This proof is based on the same basic concepts of true concurrency that we use to define the frameworks [7,8], where we distinguish as particularly important, the equivalence by permutation of independent steps, first introduced for the λ-calculus in [6].

In summary we make the following contributions: (1) We present in a uniform language two frameworks to describe relaxed memory models extending the ideas of [7,8]. (2) We present a speculative semantics that allows for *argument speculation*. While this is not our first attempt at speculative semantics [8], this addition generalizes the calculus presented in that work. In particular, branch prediction can be considered as a particular case of argument speculation where the condition is the argument. (3) As an example of the frameworks we instantiate the memory models of Sparc [20], which inspired some of the changes to [8]. (4) Using standard true concurrency techniques we prove the adequacy of the instantiations with the two frameworks of PSO and TSO. (5) This equivalence proof enables the reuse of the proof of the *fundamental property* of memory models, which we proved in [8] for buffered models, in the context of the speculative calculus. While the simulation argument of [8] is not surprising, a similar argument in the calculus of speculations would require nonstandard techniques which is leveraged using our adequacy proof.

2 Two Frameworks of Relaxed Memory

To avoid clutter and focus on the memory model related aspects of programming languages we consider the syntax of a simple imperative call-by-value λ-calculus, extended with constructs for atomic operations and barriers to impose ordering among actions as typically found in the instruction set of machine architectures. We remark that the choice of a λ-like language constraints in no way the memory model arguments that follow.

$$\begin{array}{rcll} v \in \mathcal{V}al & ::= & x \mid \lambda x e \mid tt \mid \mathit{ff} \mid () & \textit{values} \\ e \in \mathcal{E}xpr & ::= & v \mid (ve) \mid (\mathsf{ref}\, v) \mid (!\, v) \mid (v_0 := v_1) & \textit{expressions} \\ & \mid & (\mathsf{cas}\ v) \mid \langle \mathtt{wr}|\mathtt{rd}\rangle \mid \langle \mathtt{wr}|\mathtt{wr}\rangle & \end{array}$$

The memory model relevant instructions are writes to the memory, reads from the memory, atomic actions that use the memory and ordering instructions, all of them present in our language. Moreover we consider the language in quasi-Administrative Normal Form (ANF) [9][1].

Let us briefly discuss the intuitive semantics of the language. Our values are: λ-abstractions, booleans and the value () to represent termination. We adopt the syntax $e_0\,; e_1$ to denote the expression $(\lambda x e_1 e_0)$ where x is not free in e_1. The expression $(\mathsf{ref}\, v)$ allocates a new memory location with the value v returning the reference where the value was allocated. The expression $(!p)$ reads the memory retrieving the value at the location p. The expression $(p := v)$ updates the memory at location p with v. We also have a simple compare-and-swap construct $(\mathsf{cas}\ p)$ that atomically reads and modifies the reference p. In fact, this is a very primitive version of a standard read-modify-write construct. It reads the reference p and if the result of the read is ff it updates the location with value tt atomically; if the result of the read is tt it leaves the location unmodified. The returned value signals to the success or failure of the test. One could think of $(\mathsf{cas}\ p)$ as executing the following code atomically: (if $(!p)$ then ff else $(p := tt)\,; tt$). To finish with the language we have the barrier constructs $\langle \mathtt{wr}|\mathtt{rd}\rangle$ and $\langle \mathtt{wr}|\mathtt{wr}\rangle$ which are used to impose ordering on the evaluation of instructions of threads. These barrier instructions will not be of interest until the introduction of the relaxed semantics. We anticipate that the barrier $\langle \mathtt{wr}|\mathtt{rd}\rangle$ prevents write actions previous to the barrier (in the program syntax) from being delayed past read actions following the barrier. And similarly, the $\langle \mathtt{wr}|\mathtt{wr}\rangle$ barrier imposes constraints on two write instructions.

We present the technical tools that we will use throughout the paper alongside the standard semantics of this programming language. The operational

[1] A more complete language is considered in [15].

semantics is given in two steps. First we provide rules that allow individual expressions to execute, where the values obtained from dereferencing a pointer are *predicted* (i.e. unconstrained). In a second step, we compose all the expressions (threads) into a single configuration that synchronizes them and interacts with the memory.

As it is common practice, we decompose expressions into a *redex* (reducible expression) and an evaluation context, that is an expression where a subexpression has been replaced with a hole denoted here by $[]$. To describe the dynamics of our language we need to include pointers $p, q \in \mathcal{R}ef$ which are runtime values, and the runtime expression $(\lambda v^? e_0 e_1)$ which we use to decompose the β-reduction rule of the λ-calculus in two steps: $(\lambda x e_0 v) \xrightarrow{\beta_v} (\lambda v^? \{x/v\} e_0 v) \xrightarrow{\beta} \{x/v\} e_0$, where we include labels that will shortly be explained. The extended language is as follows:

$$
\begin{array}{rcll}
e & ::= & \ldots \mid (\lambda v^? e_0\, e_1) & \textit{expressions} \\
v & ::= & \ldots \mid p \mid (\lambda v^? e_0) & \textit{values} \\
r & ::= & (\lambda x e v) \mid (\lambda v^? e v) \mid (\mathsf{ref}\, v) \mid (!\, p) \mid (p := v) & \textit{redexes} \\
 & \mid & (\mathsf{cas}\; p) \mid \langle \mathtt{wr}|\mathtt{rd}\rangle \mid \langle \mathtt{wr}|\mathtt{wr}\rangle & \\
\mathbf{E} & ::= & [] \mid (v\mathbf{E}) & \textit{evaluation contexts}
\end{array}
$$

To describe the interaction of several threads and the memory, we label the transitions with the *actions* being taken at each step. Actions are sampled from the syntax:

$$
\begin{array}{l}
a \in \mathcal{A}ct ::= \beta_v \mid \beta \mid \nu_{p,v} \mid \mathsf{wr}_{p,v} \mid \mathsf{rd}_{p,v} \mid \mathsf{rd}^{\circ}_{p,v} \mid \mathsf{cas}_{p,v} \mid b \\
b \in \mathcal{B}ar ::= \mathtt{wr} \mid \mathtt{ww}
\end{array}
$$

The meaning of these symbols is better understood by looking at the semantics of single expressions in Fig. 2. As we anticipated, β_v and β are the actions that result from a function application. Notice how the standard β-reduction rule is split into two steps. The actions concerning the memory are: $\nu_{p,v}$, which results from creating a new pointer p with value v, $\mathsf{wr}_{p,v}$ for writing on p, and similarly for $\mathsf{rd}_{p,v}$ where the value v is unconstrained. The action $\mathsf{cas}_{p,v}$ results from a compare-and-swap and $\mathtt{wr}$ and $\mathtt{ww}$ result from write-read barriers and a write-write barriers respectively. The special action $\mathsf{rd}^{\circ}_{p,v}$ notifies, in the relaxed semantics that follows, that the value v has been obtained from a buffer, or speculated.

The semantics of thread systems is given by means of transitions between configurations $C = (S, T)$ containing a *store* S, which represents the memory,

$$
\begin{array}{lll}
\mathbf{E}[(\lambda x e v)] \xrightarrow{\beta_v} \mathbf{E}[(\lambda v^? \{x/v\} e\; v)] & \mathbf{E}[(p := v)] \xrightarrow{\mathsf{wr}_{p,v}} \mathbf{E}[()] & \mathbf{E}[(!\, p)] \xrightarrow{\mathsf{rd}^{\circ}_{p,v}} \mathbf{E}[v] \\
\mathbf{E}[(\lambda v^? e v)] \xrightarrow{\beta} \mathbf{E}[e] & \mathbf{E}[(!\, p)] \xrightarrow{\mathsf{rd}_{p,v}} \mathbf{E}[v] & \mathbf{E}[\langle \mathtt{wr}|\mathtt{rd}\rangle] \xrightarrow{\mathtt{wr}} \mathbf{E}[()] \\
\mathbf{E}[(\mathsf{ref}\, v)] \xrightarrow{\nu_{p,v}} \mathbf{E}[p] & \mathbf{E}[(\mathsf{cas}\; p)] \xrightarrow{\mathsf{cas}_{p,v}} \mathbf{E}[v] & \mathbf{E}[\langle \mathtt{wr}|\mathtt{wr}\rangle] \xrightarrow{\mathtt{ww}} \mathbf{E}[()]
\end{array}
$$

Fig. 2. Semantics of single expressions

$$\frac{e \xrightarrow{a} e'}{(S, e_t \| T) \xrightarrow{a} (S', e'_t \| T)} (*) \begin{cases} a = \nu_{p,v} & \Rightarrow p \notin \mathsf{dom}(S) \ \&\ S' = S \cup \{p \mapsto v\} \\ a \in \{\mathsf{rd}_{p,v}, \mathsf{rd}^{\circ}_{p,v}\} & \Rightarrow S(p) = v \\ a = \mathsf{wr}_{p,v} & \Rightarrow S' = S[p \leftarrow v] \\ a \in \{\mathsf{cas}_{p,tt}\} & \Rightarrow S(p) = \mathit{ff} \ \&\ S' = S[p \leftarrow tt] \\ a \in \{\mathsf{cas}_{p,\mathit{ff}}\} & \Rightarrow S(p) = tt \end{cases}$$

Fig. 3. Multithreaded semantics (interleaving, or *strong*)

and is formally a mapping from the set $\mathsf{dom}(S) \subseteq \mathcal{R}ef$ into values, and a thread system T which is a set of elements e_t where $t \in \mathcal{T}id$ is a thread identifier and $e \in \mathcal{E}xpr$ is the actual code of the thread. Of course, a thread identifier occurs at most once in T. We denote by $(e_t \| T)$ the thread system that contains all the threads in T as well as the thread e_t.

The semantics of the full thread system is given in Fig. 3, where we only make explicit in the constraint $(*)$ the cases where store changes (i.e. $S' \neq S$), or where the action depends on S. We will consider this to be the *standard* semantics of our language. We will call this semantics the *strong* semantics, as opposed to the ones of the following sections, which we shall call *relaxed*, or *weak*.

2.1 Write Buffering Models

To formalize the semantics of TSO and PSO we add *write buffers* to the strong semantics. Buffers are FIFO queues of pending memory updates and barriers, defined by the syntax:

$$B ::= \epsilon \ \mid\ B \triangleleft [p \mapsto v] \ \mid\ B \triangleleft [b]$$

The empty buffer is denoted by ϵ, and nonempty buffers contain pending memory updates $[p \leftarrow v]$, or pending barriers $[b]$. We will use the notation $B(p)$ to denote the (ordered) sequence of values pending in the buffer B for the reference p, as well as any pending barriers on that buffer. The auxiliary function $B \downarrow p$ represents the buffer B where the first (in FIFO order) update to the reference p has been popped. We will also use the notation $a \triangleright B$ to represent the buffer whose first element is a and then continues like B.

We augment the thread systems of the previous section with buffers. In particular, since we are only concerned with the PSO and TSO memory models of Sparc there is no need to consider thread creation. The buffers are local to a thread, meaning that pending updates on buffers cannot be shared among different threads. Thus, configurations have now the form $C = (S, (B_t, e_t) \| T)$ where B_t is the buffer associated to the thread t. We will use new actions that result from updates pertaining buffers.

$$a \in \mathcal{A}ct \ ::= \ \ldots \ \mid\ \mathsf{bu}_{p,v} \ \mid\ \bar{b}$$

The action $\mathsf{bu}_{p,v}$ corresponds to an update of the memory by a write that was pending in a buffer, and the action $\bar{b}$ corresponds to the removal of a barrier

$$\frac{e \xrightarrow{a} e'}{(S,(B,e_t)\|T) \xrightarrow[t]{a} (S',(B',e_t')\|T)}(*) \qquad \frac{B = b \rhd B' \qquad b \in \mathcal{B}ar}{(S,(B,e_t)\|T) \xrightarrow[t]{\bar{b}} (S,(B',e_t)\|T)}$$

$$\frac{B = [p \mapsto v] \rhd B' \quad S' = S[p \leftarrow v]}{(S,(B,e_t)\|T) \xrightarrow[t]{\mathsf{bu}_{p,v}} (S',(B',e_t)\|T)}\text{TSO} \qquad \frac{B(p) = \mathtt{wr}^n \cdot v \cdot s \quad S' = S[p \leftarrow v]}{(S,(B,e_t)\|T) \xrightarrow[t]{\mathsf{bu}_{p,v}} (S',(B{\downarrow}p,e_t)\|T)}\text{PSO}$$

$$(*)\begin{cases} a = \nu_{p,v} \Rightarrow p \notin \mathsf{dom}(S)\ \& \\ \qquad\qquad S' = S \cup \{p \mapsto v\} \\ a = \mathsf{wr}_{p,v} \Rightarrow B' = B \lhd [p \mapsto v] \\ a = \mathsf{rd}_{p,v} \Rightarrow S(p) = v\ \&\ \ulcorner B(p) \urcorner = \epsilon \\ a = \mathsf{rd}^{\mathsf{o}}_{p,v} \Rightarrow \ulcorner B(p) \urcorner = v \end{cases} \qquad \begin{array}{l} a \in \mathcal{B}ar \Rightarrow B' = B \lhd [a] \\ a = \mathsf{cas}_{p,ff} \Rightarrow S(p) = tt\ \&\ B = \epsilon \\ a = \mathsf{cas}_{p,tt} \Rightarrow S(p) = ff\ \&\ B = \epsilon \\ \qquad\qquad \&\ S' = S[p \leftarrow v] \end{array}$$

Fig. 4. PSO & TSO with write buffers

$b \in \mathcal{B}ar$ from a buffer. We refer to these actions as the commit of a previous write or barrier that originated the buffer item. We can now present the semantics of PSO and TSO in Fig. 4. For convenience, we use the following notation on sequences[2] of pending writes and barriers: $\ulcorner s \urcorner = \epsilon$ if $s = \mathtt{ww}^n$; and $\ulcorner s \urcorner = v$ if $s = s' \cdot v \cdot \mathtt{ww}^n$; and $\mathtt{wr}$ does not occur in s', being undefined otherwise.

There are many rules that change from the strong semantics presented previously. Importantly, write and barrier actions have as their only effect appending the update or barrier to the end of the buffer. Notice as well that the rules for actions $\mathsf{rd}_{p,v}$ and $\mathsf{rd}^{\mathsf{o}}_{p,v}$ are now different from each other. On the one hand, the action $\mathsf{rd}_{p,v}$ reads the contents from the memory, requiring that the buffer be empty for the reference p, and moreover, that there are no pending $\mathtt{wr}$ barriers. In fact, it is in this way that barrier symbols constrain the execution of some actions, disallowing particular reorderings. On the other hand, the action $\mathsf{rd}^{\mathsf{o}}_{p,v}$ retrieves its value from the buffer, or reads its *own write*. The three new rules (i.e. the new actions) update the contents of the memory by emptying the buffers. These rules are nondeterministically triggered and model the asynchronous working of the memory architecture. In the rule for $\bar{b}$, the barrier symbol is removed from the buffer only when it reaches its top, that is, when all actions that were buffered previous to the barrier have been committed. Similarly, for TSO, a buffered write is updated into the memory upon reaching the top of the buffer. The only modification necessary to obtain PSO is the rule that updates the memory (that is the action $\mathsf{bu}_{p,v}$), where a buffered write can be committed into the store even if there are previously buffered writes on *different* references. These are the final two rules in Fig. 4.

Let us reconsider the example program of Fig. 1a. The following is a possible computation that justifies the result $r_0 = r_1 = 0$, where we demark the buffers

[2] Throughout the paper we use the notations $a \cdot b$ for the concatenation of sequences a and b, and $\leq$ for the prefix ordering.

with $\langle\rangle$, and implicitly name the thread to the left t_0 and the one to the right t_1 (we leave the PSO example Fig. 1b to the reader):

$$\langle\epsilon\rangle(p := 1\,;(!q)) \| \langle\epsilon\rangle(q := 1\,;(!p)) \xrightarrow[t_0]{\mathsf{wr}_{p,1}} \langle\epsilon \triangleleft [p \mapsto 1]\rangle(!q) \| \langle\epsilon\rangle(q := 1\,;(!p)) \xrightarrow[t_1]{\mathsf{wr}_{q,1}}$$
$$\langle\epsilon \triangleleft [p \mapsto 1]\rangle(!q) \| \langle\epsilon \triangleleft [q \mapsto 1]\rangle(!p) \xrightarrow[t_0]{\mathsf{rd}_{q,0}} \langle\epsilon \triangleleft [p \mapsto 1]\rangle(0) \| \langle\epsilon \triangleleft [q \mapsto 1]\rangle(!p)$$
$$\xrightarrow[t_1]{\mathsf{rd}_{p,0}} \xrightarrow[t_0]{\mathsf{bu}_{p,1}} \langle\epsilon\rangle 0 \parallel \langle\epsilon \triangleleft [q \mapsto 1]\rangle 0 \xrightarrow[t_1]{\mathsf{bu}_{q,1}} \langle\epsilon\rangle 0 \parallel \langle\epsilon\rangle 0$$

Importantly, both these memory models satisfy the *fundamental property* of relaxed memory models [2,17]. This property states that programs that are free of data races in their interleaving semantics only exhibit sequentially consistent behaviors in their relaxed semantics. We now make these claims precise.

Definition 1 (Data-Race). *A configuration C is said to contain a data race if $C = \big(S, (\mathbf{E}[(p := v)]_t \parallel \mathbf{E}'[r]_{t'} \parallel T')\big)$ and $r \in \{(!p), (p := w) \mid w \in \mathcal{V}al\}$.*

The definition of data-race can be easily lifted to programs.

Definition 2 (DRF Program). *We say a configuration C is data-race free (DRF for short) if every configuration C' reachable from C by the interleaving semantics (i.e. $C \xrightarrow{*} C'$) contains no data-race. A parallel program $\mathsf{e}_0 \| \ldots \| \mathsf{e}_n$ is data-race free if the configuration $(\emptyset, \mathsf{e}_0 \| \ldots \| \mathsf{e}_n)$ is data-race free.*

We can now prove the fundamental property for the models with write buffers.

Theorem 3 (Fundamental Property). *The weak memory models TSO and PSO implement the interleaving semantics for data-race free programs. More precisely, the configurations where all buffers are empty (c.f. Fig. 4) reachable from a DRF regular configuration C in the semantics with write buffers coincide with the configurations reachable from the same configuration C in the interleaving semantics (c.f. Fig. 3).*

We eschew the proof since it very closely follows the one in [7] with the simplification that here we do not consider thread creation. Moreover, since we do not consider locks (we are concerned with architectural models), the only means to establish ordering between concurrent conflicting accesses is through the use of cas instructions. Although the DRF result of TSO and PSO is well known, we emphasize here that our proof is a mostly standard bisimulation, which we can do due to the operational semantics. Most other proofs of this result are non-constructive (e.g. [13]).

As we anticipated, write buffers alone are not sufficient to model the read-read reorderings exhibited by RMO. This is typically illustrated by the IRIW (Independent Reads Independent Writes) example that follows, where we assume that p and q are initially 0:

$$\begin{bmatrix} r_0 := (!p)\,; \\ r_1 := (!q) \end{bmatrix} \parallel \begin{bmatrix} r_2 := (!q)\,; \\ r_3 := (!p) \end{bmatrix} \parallel p := 1 \parallel q := 1$$
$$\text{RMO: } r_0 = r_2 = 1 \;\&\; r_1 = r_3 = 0$$

It is clear that no write buffer behavior can produce this result since the writing threads have just one write each, and the reading threads do not use their write buffers in any way. It is therefore necessary to consider another kind of relaxation to capture RMO behaviors. If we allow any of the reading threads to speculate their second read before the first one, the behavior becomes possible (without recourse to any buffering argument). To see this, imagine that the second reads of the reading threads are executed first, then the writes of the writing threads, and finally the first reads of the reading threads. This kind of behavior is typical of *speculative* execution models which motivates our next semantics.

2.2 Speculative Models

We now consider the specification of relaxed memory models by means of speculations. We previously addressed the speculative semantics of programming languages in [8,15] where we generally discussed about the modeling of relaxed memory models. Let us briefly introduce a modified framework from [8] and show how TSO, PSO and RMO[3] can be modeled with it.

The two ingredients introduced for the speculative framework are *speculation contexts* and the *prediction of arguments* in applications. Speculation contexts generalize the evaluation contexts previously defined, by allowing the reduction of expressions that are otherwise not enabled in the strong semantics of Sect. 2, and have the following syntax:

$$\mathbf{\Sigma} ::= [] \mid (v\mathbf{\Sigma}) \mid (\lambda x \mathbf{\Sigma} e) \mid (\lambda v^? \mathbf{\Sigma} e) \qquad \textit{speculation contexts}$$

Notice that in an expression like $(\lambda x(!p)e)$ one can reduce the redex $(!p)$, by choosing the speculative context $(\lambda x[]e)$. In particular, this means that one can execute e_1 before e_0 in $(e_0\,;e_1)$. The second ingredient, the prediction of arguments, not present in [8], requires to extend the syntax for redexes with the new redex $(\lambda x e_0 e_1) \in r$, where the expression e_1 is not required to be a value. The speculative semantics for this redex is then:

$$\mathbf{\Sigma}[(\lambda x e_0 e_1)] \xrightarrow{\beta_v} \mathbf{\Sigma}[(\lambda v^? \; \{x/v\}e_0 \; e_1)] \tag{1}$$

The reason why we need this type of speculation can be seen with the expression $(\lambda y\, p := y\; (q := 1\,; 0))$. If we consider this example under the semantics of PSO with write buffers (cf. the previous section), it is clear that the write of p can be updated into the memory before the one of q, since they are on different references. However, if we are not able to predict that the expression $(q := 1\,; 0)$

[3] Since most proofs in this paper are not concerned with RMO we will just present its formalization for completeness, but we will otherwise ignore it.

invariably returns 0, the write of p cannot proceed until the one of q has been performed with speculations. To solve this issue we add the possibility to predict the arguments (the reduction labeled β_v), which are later validated in the actual application (the reduction labeled β). Then, in the example above we can have:

$$(\lambda y\, p := y\ (q := 1\,;0)) \xrightarrow{\beta_0} (\lambda 0^?\ p := 0\ (q := 1\,;0))$$
$$\xrightarrow{\mathsf{wr}_{p,0}} (\lambda 0^? ()(q := 1\,;0)) \xrightarrow{*} (\lambda 0^? ()0) \xrightarrow{\beta} ()$$

modeling the reordering of write buffers. Notice that if an argument is mispredicted, the speculation gets stuck, and therefore the computation is disregarded.

In fact, not all speculations will be considered legitimate. To define which ones we will regard as valid, we need to identify in the transitions *where* in the expression the reduction is taking place. To that end, we shall use *occurrences*, defined as sequences of symbols sampled from the set $\mathcal{SOcc} = \mathcal{Occ} \cup \{(\lambda\_[]\_)\}$ where $\mathcal{Occ} = \{(\_[])\}$. An occurrence $o \in \mathcal{Occ}^*$ is called *normal* in contrast with occurrences in the set $\mathcal{SOcc}^*/\mathcal{Occ}^*$ which we shall name *speculative*. Normal computations – that is computations that do not speculate – involve only normal occurrences. We can recover the occurrence $@\mathbf{\Sigma}$ of the hole in a speculation context $\mathbf{\Sigma}$ by means of the following inductive definition, where z in the last case can be a variable in $\mathcal{Var}$ or a tagged value $v^?$:

$$@[] = \varepsilon \qquad @(v\mathbf{\Sigma}) = (\_[]) \cdot @\mathbf{\Sigma} \qquad @(\lambda z \mathbf{\Sigma} e) = (\lambda\_[]\_) \cdot @\mathbf{\Sigma}$$

We will denote by $e@o$ the subexpression of e whose occurrence is o in case that is defined. The inductive definition is obvious.

The semantics of expressions is similar to the one given in Fig. 2 with the evaluation contexts $\mathbf{E}$ replaced by a speculation contexts $\mathbf{\Sigma}$ and the occurrence label ($@\mathbf{\Sigma}$) in the transitions. For example, the rule for β-reduction becomes: $\mathbf{\Sigma}[(\lambda v^? ev)] \xrightarrow[@\mathbf{\Sigma}]{\beta} \mathbf{\Sigma}[e]$. Only one rule is added, the one we presented in (1) for the redex $(\lambda x e_0 e_1)$ where e_1 is potentially not a proper value. In the example below one can see that these rules effectively achieve computing in advance w.r.t. the strong semantics of Sect. 2.

$$(!q)\,; p := tt \quad \xrightarrow{\mathsf{wr}_{p,tt}} \quad (!q)\,;() \quad \xrightarrow{\mathsf{rd}_{q,tt}} \quad tt\,;() \quad \xrightarrow{*} \quad ()$$

We can see that the write of p is performed before the read of q although the program text has them in the reverse order.

The semantics of thread systems is almost identical to the strong semantics presented in Fig. 3. In fact the configurations are exactly the same, and the only rule that changes is the one for $\mathsf{rd}^{\mathsf{o}}_{p,v}$, where the value is speculated at this stage of the semantics. The intention is that these values will be served by *own* writes of the same thread (cf. write buffers). The necessary conditions on this action will be imposed in the definition of valid computation. The semantics of thread systems, given in Fig. 5, is almost identical to that of Fig. 3 with the exception

$$\frac{e \xrightarrow[o]{a} e'}{(S, e_t \| T) \xrightarrow[t,o]{a} (S', e'_t \| T)} (*) \begin{cases} a \in \{\beta_v, \mathsf{rd}^{\circ}_{p,v}\} \Rightarrow \mathsf{FRef}(v) \subseteq \mathsf{dom}(S) \\ \cdots \end{cases}$$

Fig. 5. Speculative semantics

of the rules explicitly mentioned, where $\mathsf{FRef}(e)$ is the set of references occurring in e. The transitions are labeled with the thread identifier, which will be used in the sequel.

We revisit the example program of Fig. 1a, with a possible speculative computation justifying $r_0 = r_1 = 0$ (omitting the occurrences):

$$(p := 1\,;\,(!q))\|(q := 1\,;\,(!p)) \xrightarrow[t_0]{\mathsf{rd}_{q,0}} (p := 1\,;\,0)\|(q := 1\,;\,(!p)) \xrightarrow[t_1]{\mathsf{rd}_{p,0}}$$
$$(p := 1\,;\,0)\|(q := 1\,;\,0) \xrightarrow[t_1]{\mathsf{wr}_{q,1}}\xrightarrow[t_0]{\mathsf{wr}_{p,1}}\xrightarrow{*} 0\|0$$

Validity Condition. The speculative computations presented so far are too permissive for our purposes, since the rules do not take into account possible data dependencies present in the program. The following speculation is an example:

$$r := (!p)\,; p := tt \quad \xrightarrow{\mathsf{wr}_{p,tt}} \quad r := (!p)\,;() \quad \xrightarrow{\mathsf{rd}_{p,tt}} \quad r := tt\,;() \quad \xrightarrow{*} \quad ()$$

where we can see that the reordering of the write on p and the read on p causes the read to see a value that has been put in the memory by a write that should follow the read in normal (sequential) computations. It is clear that this speculation violates the programmers intention, and therefore, this speculation should not be permitted. Intuitively, speculations will be considered valid if they do not violate the sequential semantics of expressions, and all read own actions have a preceding write with the same value. To express that a speculation does not violate the sequential semantics of the original expression we will strongly rely on the notion of speculations that are similar up to the reordering of independent steps, a concept borrowed from the early work by Berry and Lévy in the λ-calculus [6].

To define the permutation of steps formally, which is central to our result, we need to introduce some technical machinery, which might be familiar from a "true concurrency" perspective. Let us define the residual of an occurrence o' after a step with action a at occurrence o in the expression e, which indicates where a subexpression at o' in e remains (if any) after a step a at o:

$$o'/_e(a, o) \triangleq \begin{cases} o' & \text{if } o \not\leq o',\ \text{or } o' = o \cdot (\_[]) \cdot o'' \ \&\ a = \beta_v \\ & \quad \text{or } o' = o \cdot (\lambda\_[]\_) \cdot o'' \ \&\ a = \beta_v \ \&\ e@o' \text{ is a redex} \\ o \cdot o'' & \text{if } o' = o \cdot (\lambda\_[]\_) \cdot o'' \ \&\ a = \beta \\ \texttt{undef} & \text{otherwise} \end{cases}$$

In the following we write $o'/_e(a,o) \equiv o''$ to mean that the residual of o' after (a,o) is defined, and it is o''. Notice that if $o'/_e(a,o) \equiv o''$ with $o' \in \mathcal{O}cc^*$ then $o'' = o'$ and $o \not\leq o'$.

We now prove that if two consecutive actions are not related by redex creation (i.e. they have residuals after each other), then reordering their steps in the speculation leads to the same result. This property is key to the definition of *valid* speculations[4]:

Lemma 4 (Reordering Lemma). *If* $e_0 \xrightarrow[o_0]{a_0} e \xrightarrow[o_1]{a_1} e_1$ *with* $o_1 \equiv o_1'/_{e_0}(a_0, o_0)$ *and* $o_0' \equiv o_0/_{e_0}(a_1, o_1')$, *then there exists* e' *(unique up to α-conversion) such that* $e_0 \xrightarrow[o_1']{a_1} e' \xrightarrow[o_0']{a_0} e_1$.

To take into account the dependencies in the program we need a notion of conflict. We introduce the notations $\mathcal{MRd}_p \triangleq \{\mathsf{rd}_{p,v}, \mathsf{cas}_{p,v} | v \in \mathcal{V}al\}$ for the read actions on reference p that effectively use the memory, and $\mathcal{MWr}_p \triangleq \{\mathsf{wr}_{p,v}, \mathsf{cas}_{p,tt} | v \in \mathcal{V}al\}$ for write actions that modify the memory and define then the conflict relation.

Definition 5 (Conflicting Actions). *We denote by # the following relation on actions:*

$$\# \triangleq \bigcup_{p \in \mathcal{R}ef} (\mathcal{MWr}_p \times \mathcal{MWr}_p) \cup (\mathcal{MWr}_p \times \mathcal{MRd}_p) \cup (\mathcal{MRd}_p \times \mathcal{MWr}_p)$$

Notice that we explicitly have that speculative read actions are not conflicting with write actions on the same thread. Formally: $(\mathsf{wr}_{p,v}, \mathsf{rd}^{\circ}_{p,w}) \notin \#$.

We now define a *reordering relation* establishing when two speculations correspond to each other up to the reordering of intermediate steps. This definition is parametric on a *dependency* relation $\mathcal{D}$. We only require that $\# \subseteq \mathcal{D}$.

Definition 6 (Reordering Relation). *Given a dependency relation* $\mathcal{D}$ *we define a reordering relation between speculations, called* $\mathcal{D}$*-reordering, to be the least preorder* $\propto^{\mathcal{D}}$ *such that if* $e_0 \xrightarrow[o_0]{a_0} e \xrightarrow[o_1]{a_1} e_1$ *with* $o_0' \equiv o_0/_e(a_1, o_1')$ *and* $o_1'/_e(a_0, o_0) \equiv o_1$, *and* $\neg(a_0 \mathcal{D} a_1)$, *then* $\sigma_0 \cdot e_0 \xrightarrow[o_1']{a_1} e' \xrightarrow[o_0']{a_0} e_1 \cdot \sigma_1 \propto^{\mathcal{D}} \sigma_0 \cdot e_0 \xrightarrow[o_0]{a_0} e \xrightarrow[o_1]{a_1} e_1 \cdot \sigma_1$ *where* e' *is determined by Reordering Lemma.*

A speculation will be considered valid if it is a reordering of a normal speculation. In other words, if it can be reordered to a speculation where all actions take place in program order. In addition, we will check that the actions $\mathsf{rd}^{\circ}_{p,v}$ return the last value written to p in the normal speculation, conforming the semantics of write buffering. To do so, we need to identify steps that represent the same transition in reordering related speculations. We use the notions of a *step* and *step family*, originally introduced as "redex-with-history" in [6,12].

[4] The proof of this and subsequent results can be found in the extended version [16].

Definition 7 (Step and Step Family). *A* step *is a pair* $[\sigma, (a, o)]$ *of a speculation* $\sigma : e \xrightarrow{*} e'$ *and an action* a *at occurrence* o *such that* $e' \xrightarrow[o]{a} e''$ *for some expression* e''*. The binary relation* $\sim^{\mathcal{D}}$ *on steps, meaning that two steps are in the* same family, *is the equivalence relation generated by the rule*

$$\frac{\exists \sigma''.\ \sigma' \propto^{\mathcal{D}} \sigma \cdot \sigma'' \text{ or } \sigma \cdot \sigma'' \propto^{\mathcal{D}} \sigma' \ \&\ o' \equiv o/\sigma''}{[\sigma, (a, o)] \sim^{\mathcal{D}} [\sigma', (a, o')]}$$

We now define the validity of speculations, where we see that $\mathsf{rd}^{\circ}_{p,v}$ actions take their value from the last write on p in the corresponding normal speculation.

Definition 8 (Speculation Validity). *A speculation* σ *is* $\mathcal{D}$*-valid if there is a normal speculation* σ' *such that* $\sigma \propto^{\mathcal{D}} \sigma'$*, and if* $\sigma' = \sigma'_0 \cdot \xrightarrow[o]{\mathsf{rd}^{\circ}_{p,v}} \cdot \sigma'_1$ *then there exists* σ''_0*,* σ'''_0 *and* o' *such that* $\sigma'_0 = \sigma''_0 \cdot \xrightarrow[o']{\mathsf{wr}_{p,v}} \cdot \sigma'''_0$ *where* σ'''_0 *contains no* $\mathsf{wr}_{p,-}$ *actions. We call the step* $[\sigma''_0, (\mathsf{wr}_{p,v}, o')]$ *the matching write of* $[\sigma'_0, (\mathsf{rd}^{\circ}_{p,v}, o)]$*, and we denote it* $\mathsf{match}([\sigma'_0, (\mathsf{rd}^{\circ}_{p,v}, o)])$.

We now specialize the speculative semantics to TSO and PSO, by particularizing the dependency relations that characterize them. We introduce the notations $\mathcal{R}d_p \triangleq \mathcal{MR}d_p \cup \{\mathsf{rd}^{\circ}_{p,v} \mid v \in \mathcal{V}al\}$ and $\mathcal{W}r_p \triangleq \mathcal{MW}r_p \cup \{\mathsf{cas}_{p,ff}\}$ of read and write actions on location p (not necessarily accessing the memory as opposed to $\mathcal{MR}d_p$ and $\mathcal{MW}r_p$), and $\mathcal{R}d \triangleq \bigcup_{p \in \mathcal{R}ef} \mathcal{R}d_p$ and $\mathcal{W}r \triangleq \bigcup_{p \in \mathcal{R}ef} \mathcal{W}r_p$. As a step towards the dependencies of TSO, PSO and RMO we define the dependencies induced by barrier actions denoted by $\ltimes^{TSO}$, $\ltimes^{PSO}$ and $\ltimes^{RMO}$ where we assume the barrier actions $\mathtt{rr}$ and $\mathtt{rw}$ generated by the barriers $\langle \mathtt{rd}|\mathtt{rd} \rangle$ and $\langle \mathtt{rd}|\mathtt{wr} \rangle$ respectively which prevent the reordering of reads with subsequent reads and writes respectively, wich are allowed by RMO.

$$\begin{aligned}
\ltimes^{TSO} &\triangleq (\mathcal{W}r \times \{\mathtt{wr}\}) \cup (\{\mathtt{wr}\} \times \mathcal{R}d)\\
\ltimes^{PSO} &\triangleq \ltimes^{TSO} \cup (\mathcal{W}r \times \{\mathtt{ww}\}) \cup (\{\mathtt{ww}\} \times \mathcal{W}r)\\
\ltimes^{RMO} &\triangleq \ltimes^{PSO} \cup (\mathcal{R}d \times \{\mathtt{rr}, \mathtt{rw}\}) \cup (\{\mathtt{rw}\} \times \mathcal{W}r) \cup (\{\mathtt{rr}\} \times \mathcal{R}d)
\end{aligned}$$

Definition 9 (TSO, PSO and RMO). *The TSO, PSO and RMO memory models are characterized by the following dependency relations:*

$$\begin{aligned}
\mathcal{D}^{RMO} &\triangleq \# \cup \ltimes^{RMO}\\
\mathcal{D}^{PSO} &\triangleq \# \cup \ltimes^{PSO} \cup (\mathcal{R}d \times \mathcal{R}d) \cup (\mathcal{R}d \times \mathcal{W}r)\\
\mathcal{D}^{TSO} &\triangleq \# \cup \ltimes^{TSO} \cup (\mathcal{R}d \times \mathcal{R}d) \cup (\mathcal{R}d \times \mathcal{W}r) \cup (\mathcal{W}r \times \mathcal{W}r)
\end{aligned}$$

The semantic definition of RMO is here only given for completeness, we shall not refer to it in the rest of the paper.

Finally, we need a notion of when a write should, or should not, be considered committed (cf. write buffers). To do that we need to know when two steps in a speculation are inherently ordered; that is, they are ordered similarly for all possible valid reorderings of the speculation.

Definition 10 (Step Ordering). *Given a speculation* $\sigma = \sigma_0 \cdot \xrightarrow[o_0]{a_0} \cdot \sigma_1 \cdot \xrightarrow[o_1]{a_1} \cdot \sigma_2$, *we have* $[\sigma_0, (a_0, o_0)] \prec_\sigma [\sigma_0 \cdot \xrightarrow[o_0]{a_0} \cdot \sigma_1, (a_1, o_1)]$, *iff for all* σ' *with* $\sigma' \propto^{\mathcal{D}} \sigma$ *then* $\sigma' = \sigma'_0 \cdot \xrightarrow[o'_0]{a_0} \cdot \sigma'_1 \cdot \xrightarrow[o'_1]{a_1} \cdot \sigma'_2$ *with* $[\sigma_0, (a_0, o_0)] \sim [\sigma'_0, (a_0, o'_0)]$ *and* $[\sigma_0 \cdot \xrightarrow[o_0]{a_0} \cdot \sigma_1, (a_1, o_1)] \sim [\sigma'_0 \cdot \xrightarrow[o'_0]{a_0} \cdot \sigma'_1, (a_1, o'_1)]$.

Now we can define when, in a speculative computation, a write has to be considered committed. We denote by $\gamma|_t$ the projection of thread t over γ.

Definition 11. *Given* $\gamma = \gamma_0 \cdot \xrightarrow[t,o]{\mathsf{wr}_{p,v}} \cdot \gamma_1$, *the step* $[\gamma_0|_t, (\mathsf{wr}_{p,v}, o)]$ *is* committed *in* γ *if there are* γ'_1, γ''_1, t', o',w *such that* $\gamma_1 = \gamma'_1 \cdot \xrightarrow[t',o']{\mathsf{rd}_{p,w}} \cdot \gamma''_1$, *or* $\gamma_1 = \gamma'_1 \cdot \xrightarrow[t,o']{\mathsf{wr}_{q,w}} \cdot \gamma''_1$ *with* $[\gamma_0|_t, (\mathsf{wr}_{p,v}, o)] \prec_{\gamma|_t} [\gamma_0 \cdot \xrightarrow[t,o]{\mathsf{wr}_{p,v}} \cdot \gamma'_1|_t, (\mathsf{wr}_{q,w}, o')]$ *and* $[\gamma_0 \cdot \xrightarrow[t,o]{\mathsf{wr}_{p,v}} \cdot \gamma'_1, (\mathsf{wr}_{p,q}, o')]$ *is committed in* γ.

To see why we require this condition for validity, consider the following thread system in PSO where we depict only threads:

$$\begin{bmatrix} p := tt\,; \\ \langle \mathtt{wr}|\mathtt{wr}\rangle\,; \\ q := tt\,; \\ (!p) \end{bmatrix} \parallel \big[(!q)\big] \xrightarrow[t_0]{\mathsf{wr}_{p,tt}} \begin{bmatrix} \langle \mathtt{wr}|\mathtt{wr}\rangle\,; \\ q := tt\,; \\ (!p) \end{bmatrix} \parallel \big[(!q)\big] \xrightarrow[t_0]{\mathtt{ww}} \begin{bmatrix} q := tt\,; \\ (!p) \end{bmatrix} \parallel \big[(!q)\big]$$
$$\xrightarrow[t_0]{\mathsf{wr}_{q,tt}} \big[(!p)\big] \parallel \big[(!q)\big] \xrightarrow[t_1]{\mathsf{rd}_{q,tt}} \big[(!p)\big] \parallel \big[\ tt\ \big]$$

It is clear that the final read of p by t_0 cannot be a $\mathsf{rd}^{\circ}_{p,v}$ (that is a read of an uncommitted write), since the write of q has already been made globally visible, and there is a $\langle \mathtt{wr}|\mathtt{wr}\rangle$ between the write of p and the one of q. This is obvious in the semantic with write-buffers but has to be required for speculations.

We can now give the definition of validity for TSO and PSO speculative computations.

Definition 12 (Valid Speculative Computation). *A speculative computation* γ *is* $\mathcal{D}$-valid *iff for every thread* t *we have that* $\gamma|_t$ *is a* $\mathcal{D}$*-valid speculation, and additionally, if* $\gamma = \gamma' \cdot \xrightarrow[t,o']{\mathsf{rd}^{\circ}_{p,v}} \cdot \gamma_2$ *where* $\gamma' = \gamma_0 \cdot \xrightarrow[t,o]{\mathsf{wr}_{p,v}} \cdot \gamma_1$, *and* $\mathsf{match}([\gamma'|_t, (\mathsf{rd}^{\circ}_{p,v}, o')]) \sim [\gamma_0|_t, (\mathsf{wr}_{p,v}, o)]$ *then* $[\gamma_0|_t, (\mathsf{wr}_{p,v}, o)]$ *is not committed in* γ'.

Hence, $\mathcal{D}^{TSO}$-valid speculative computations describe TSO, and similarly $\mathcal{D}^{PSO}$-valid speculative computations describe PSO. Thus, the examples of Fig. 1 are valid.

3 A Formal Comparison

We prove that both instances of PSO are equivalent by showing how a computation with write buffers can be transformed into an equivalent one with speculations, and vice versa. A similar result for TSO is obtained as a corollary observing that the semantic rules for PSO are a superset of the rules of TSO.

Since the mechanisms used in these formalizations are very different, we introduce a *third calculus* incorporating both, write buffers and speculations. We consider this calculus merely as a tool for the proof. We then show that computations of PSO with write buffers can be embedded in this third calculus, and so can computations of PSO with speculations. Our proof of coincidence amounts to proving that: starting from a computation of the third calculus embedding a computation with write buffers (or speculations) one can reorder actions, with an appropriate instance of the reordering equivalence relation, to get a computation that is an embedding of a speculative (respectively write buffers) PSO computation. To simplify the results we disregard $\mathsf{cas}_{p,v}$ observing that its treatment can be deduced from similar conditions on read and write actions.

Let us formalize this third calculus, which we call *merge*. The semantic rules for single expressions are exactly the same as for the semantics of speculations; that is, the rules of Fig. 2 with speculation contexts $\mathbf{\Sigma}$ instead of $\mathbf{E}$. For example, the rule for read in Fig. 2 is translated in the merge calculus to:

$$\mathbf{\Sigma}[(!\,p)] \xrightarrow{\mathsf{rd}_{p,v}} \mathbf{\Sigma}[v]$$

To cope with speculation we further add the redex $(\lambda x e_0 e_1)$ and its associated reduction rule presented in Eq. (1).

Configurations, and the rules for thread systems are the same as presented for the semantics of write buffers in Fig. 4 with the exception of the rule $\mathsf{rd}^{\circ}_{p,v}$ which in merge has no constraints. As we did in the semantics of speculations the transitions will be labeled with the occurrence and the thread performing the action. Let us refresh the semantics of Fig. 4, emphasizing the only change we make:

$$\frac{e \xrightarrow[o]{a} e'}{(S,(B,e_t)\|T) \xrightarrow[t,o]{a} (S',(B',e'_t)\|T)}\ (*)\ \begin{cases} a = \mathsf{rd}^{\circ}_{p,v} & \Rightarrow\ S' = S\ \&\ B' = B \\ \dots \end{cases}$$

where the conditions not mentioned are similar to the ones of $(*)$ in Fig. 4.

As we have done before, we now define an equivalence by reordering of independent steps for merge, which allows us to compare its executions. Importantly the addition of buffers to the calculus of the previous section makes the definition of conflict, and hence dependency, change. This is because in merge the actual memory update is done by the buffer update rule $(\mathsf{bu}_{p,v})$ rather than the write rule $(\mathsf{wr}_{p,v})$. Moreover, memory update only affects reads from the memory $(\mathsf{rd}_{p,v})$ unlike buffer reads $(\mathsf{rd}^{\circ}_{p,v})$ which are retrieved from the thread local buffer. The definitions of conflict and dependency for the merge calculus are then:

$$\#^{MG} = \{(\mathsf{bu}_{p,v},\mathsf{bu}_{p,w}),(\mathsf{rd}_{p,v},\mathsf{bu}_{p,w}),(\mathsf{bu}_{p,v},\mathsf{rd}_{p,w}) \mid p \in \mathcal{R}\mathit{ef},\ v,w \in \mathcal{V}\mathit{al}\}$$

$$\mathcal{D}^{MG} \triangleq \#^{MG} \cup \ltimes^{PSO} \cup (\mathcal{R}d \times \mathcal{R}d) \cup (\mathcal{R}d \times \mathcal{W}r)$$

It is not hard to see that every computation of a program in the semantics of PSO with write buffers is strictly included the semantics of that program in merge. This is obvious since the configurations are the same, and the set of semantic rules of write buffer PSO is strictly included in the set of rules of merge. Similarly any computation of PSO with speculation can be trivially embedded into merge by simply forcing a buffer update (by the $\mathsf{bu}_{p,v}$ rule) after every write ($\mathsf{wr}_{p,v}$). We shall denote the merge trace resulting from the speculation trace γ by this forcing semantics by $\lceil\gamma\rceil$. Conversely, a computation γ of the merge-calculus can be related with PSO speculations by "erasing" all the buffer update actions that immediately follow its generating write. We shall denote by $\lfloor\gamma\rfloor$ this operation in the sequel. The following remark establishes these trivial embeddings.

Remark 13. Every computation $\gamma : C \xrightarrow{*} C'$ of PSO with write buffers (as in Fig. 4) is also a legal execution of the merge-calculus. For every valid speculative computation $\gamma : C \xrightarrow{*} C'$ (as in Fig. 5), $\lceil\gamma\rceil : C \xrightarrow{*} C'$ is a computation of the merge-calculus.

This remark provides us with embeddings and projections from, and to, the merge-calculus for both write buffers and speculations. The rest of the proof only deals with the reordering of steps in the merge-calculus. To that end, we reproduce the result of Lemma 4, this time for the merge-calculus.

Lemma 14 (Merge Reordering). *If* $e_0 \xrightarrow[o_0]{a_0} e \xrightarrow[o_1']{a_1} e_1$, *then there exists* e' *such that* $e_0 \xrightarrow[o_1]{a_1} e' \xrightarrow[o_0']{a_0} e_1$ *such that* $o_1' \equiv o_1/_{e_0}(a_0, o_0)$ *and* $o_0' \equiv o_0/_{e_0}(a_1, o_1)$.

We can then instantiate the reordering relation (Definition 6) of the previous section using the merge reordering lemma, and we denote by $\propto^{MG}$ the merge reordering relation: $\propto^{\mathcal{D}^{MG}}$.

Much can be said about the merge-calculus equivalence by reordering relation. However the merge-calculus is just a tool in our proof, with little practical interest for the memory models we consider in this paper. We point the interested reader to the extended version of the paper [16, Appendix B] for a detailed account of the merge-calculus intermediate results. Suffice it to say here that the equivalence by reordering of merge allows us to transform, by reorderings independent steps, the embedding in merge of a trace of PSO with write-buffers (or PSO with speculations) into a an embedding in merge of a trace of PSO with speculations (or PSO with write-buffers respectively). These are the main results that we consider next.

From Buffers to Speculations. In the following theorem we show how to transform the a PSO write-buffers computation (embedded in the merge-calculus) into an equivalent merge-computation where the buffers have no effect. By this we mean that each write in the resulting computation is immediately followed by its update into memory. The resulting computation corresponds to the embedding of a PSO speculation in the merge-calculus, and therefore erasing the buffer updates we obtain a PSO speculative computation.

The intuition behind this proof is that, while writes in the write-buffer calculus are executed in program order – that is, respecting the program text –, their effects are only visible at the time when the buffer is updated into memory. Based on this observation we conclude that in the semantics with write buffers, a write does not affect the behavior of other threads until its buffer update. Therefore, we can push the write to happen at a later time, by introducing speculations that execute instructions that follow the write in program order. In fact, doing so we prove that we can postpone executing the write up to the point where its buffer update is executed. For a simplified example consider a trace γ of PSO with write buffers where we stand out an occurrence of a write and its subsequent corresponding buffer update:

$$\gamma = \gamma_0 \cdot \xrightarrow[t]{\mathsf{wr}_{p,v}} \cdot \gamma_1 \cdot \xrightarrow[t]{\mathsf{bu}_{p,v}} \cdot \gamma_2$$

The following theorem is based on an intermediate result proving that the merge segment γ_1 can be permuted by the merge reordering relation to render an equivalent trace:

$$\gamma \propto^{MG} \gamma_0 \cdot \gamma_1' \cdot \xrightarrow[t]{\mathsf{wr}_{p,v}} \cdot \xrightarrow[t]{\mathsf{bu}_{p,v}} \cdot \gamma_1'' \cdot \gamma_2$$

where $\gamma_1' \cdot \xrightarrow[t]{\mathsf{wr}_{p,v}} \cdot \xrightarrow[t]{\mathsf{bu}_{p,v}} \cdot \gamma_1''$ has speculative behavior (as permitted by the merge calculus). Notice that all actions in γ_1 by threads other than t are independent of the write, and for actions on t we show that there is at least one such write that can be speculated upon (the formalization can be found in [16, Appendix B]).

The inductive application of the intuition stated above renders a computation where all writes and barrier actions are immediately followed by their corresponding commit. The proof is by induction on the number of write and barrier actions that are not immediately committed.

Theorem 15 (Write Buffers $\Rightarrow$ Speculations). *For any computation $\gamma : C \xrightarrow{*} C'$ of the formalization of PSO with write-buffers there exists a merge computation $\gamma' : C \xrightarrow{*} C'$ such that for every thread t, $\gamma'|_t \propto^{MG} \gamma|_t$. Moreover, $\lfloor \gamma' \rfloor$ is a $\mathcal{D}^{PSO}$-valid speculative computation.*

From Speculations to Buffers. As the reader might expect, the converse argument follows the same idea in the opposite direction. As a simplified example, suppose that we start with a PSO speculative computation of the form

$$\gamma = \gamma_0 \cdot \xrightarrow[t]{\mathsf{wr}_{p,v}} \cdot \gamma_1$$

Our embedding of γ into the merge would render:

$$\lceil \gamma \rceil = \lceil \gamma_0 \rceil \cdot \xrightarrow[t]{\mathsf{wr}_{p,v}} \cdot \xrightarrow[t]{\mathsf{bu}_{p,v}} \cdot \lceil \gamma_1 \rceil$$

Moreover, $\lceil \gamma_0 \rceil$ can be decomposed to obtain:

$$\lceil \gamma \rceil \propto^{MG} \lceil \gamma_0' \rceil \cdot \xrightarrow[t]{\mathsf{wr}_{p,v}} \cdot \lceil \gamma_0'' \rceil \cdot \xrightarrow[t]{\mathsf{bu}_{p,v}} \cdot \lceil \gamma_1 \rceil$$

such that the occurrence of the write $\mathsf{wr}_{p,v}$ is no longer speculative – that is, respects the program order. The details of this construction can be found in the extended version of the paper [16, Appendix B].

Using this argument inductively we conclude that given a merge calculus computation where all thread projections are valid, there is a merge computation with the same initial and final configurations such that the steps are reordered by pushing write and barrier actions to their normal occurrence – that is, respecting the program order –, and is therefore a PSO write buffer computation.

Theorem 16 (Speculations ⇒ Write Buffers). *Given $\gamma : C \xrightarrow{*} C'$ a $\mathcal{D}^{PSO}$-valid speculative computation of the formalization of PSO with speculations, there exists a merge computation $\gamma' : C \xrightarrow{*} C$ such that for all $t \in \mathcal{T}id$, $\lceil \gamma \rceil|_t \propto^{MG} \gamma'|_t$. Moreover, γ' is a computation of the calculus with buffers.*

Notice that although the proofs we provided are stated for PSO, nothing in the proof themselves is PSO specific. On the contrary, they are stated using generic notions of conflict/dependency. Therefore the same result holds for TSO.

Corollary 17. *The semantics of TSO with write buffers and speculations are equivalent.*

As a final corollary of the proof of equivalence of the semantics we get the proof of the fundamental property for the speculative semantics of TSO and PSO, which we did not prove in Sect. 2.2 nor in [8]. This illustrates the power of these different presentations of the semantics. While the proof of the fundamental property for write-buffering semantics was studied in [7], its proof for the semantics with speculations was missing in [8]. Hence, our equivalence result establishes the fundamental property for speculations without needing a new proof strategy.

Corollary 18 (Fundamental Property). *The speculative semantics of TSO and PSO satisfy the fundamental property of relaxed memory models.*

The proof is an immediate consequence of Theorems 3, 16 and 15.

4 Related Work and Conclusions

Related Work. Our semantics of TSO and PSO with write buffers instantiates our framework [7]. In [14] a TSO-like semantics with write buffers is given for x86 architectures. This semantics is very similar to the semantics of TSO we present here, which results as a natural consequence of instantiating [7]. The speculative semantics of TSO, PSO and RMO are based on our framework of [8]. However, although the principle of speculation is the same, value-speculation was not considered in [8] which greatly simplifies, and subsumes the technical treatment of that paper. In that sense, the speculation calculus of this paper supersedes the framework of [8]. The equivalence between the formalizations of TSO and PSO in the different frameworks are new to this paper and were developed as part of the thesis [15] but are otherwise unpublished. Importantly [7,8] focus on high-level programming languages whereas in this work we focus on architectures through the use of those frameworks.

There are many formalizations of TSO, PSO and RMO in the literature, each with a specific goal in mind. Of the axiomatic definitions of these architectures we distinguish [3,18]. There are as well other operational formalizations, e.g. [4, 5]. Most of these leave the programming language abstract. In particular [4,5] focus on decidability rather than on the programming language semantics, and therefore the language is immaterial. Our work is unique in its focus is on a programming languages semantics and programming languages techniques for relaxed memory models.

Conclusions. We provided two different formalizations of the TSO and PSO memory models using different operational frameworks. We prove that these instantiations are equivalent using standard programming languages techniques based on the permutation equivalence of [6]. The more sophisticated model of speculations proves to be more general than the one of write buffers. Our proofs show the potential of operational formalizations of relaxed memory models to support technical developments. We speculate that operational models should also be well suited to support verification techniques.

References

1. Adve, S.V., Gharachorloo, K.: Shared memory consistency models: a tutorial. Computer **29**, 66–76 (1996)
2. Adve, S.V., Hill, M.D.: Weak ordering – a new definition. In: ISCA, pp. 2–14. ACM, New York (1990)
3. Alglave, J.: A shared memory poetics. Ph.D. thesis, Université Paris 7 (2010)
4. Atig, M.F., Bouajjani, A., Burckhardt, S., Musuvathi, M.: On the verification problem for weak memory models. In: POPL '10, pp. 7–18 (2010)
5. Atig, M.F., Bouajjani, A., Burckhardt, S., Musuvathi, M.: What's decidable about weak memory models? In: Seidl, H. (ed.) ESOP 2012. LNCS, vol. 7211, pp. 26–46. Springer, Heidelberg (2012)
6. Berry, G., Lévy, J.-J.: Minimal and optimal computations of recursive programs. J. ACM **26**(1), 148–175 (1979)
7. Boudol, G., Petri, G.: Relaxed memory models: an operational approach. In: POPL, pp. 392–403. ACM, New York (2009)
8. Boudol, G., Petri, G.: A theory of speculative computation. In: Gordon, A.D. (ed.) ESOP 2010. LNCS, vol. 6012, pp. 165–184. Springer, Heidelberg (2010)
9. Flanagan, C., Sabry, A., Duba, B.F., Felleisen, M.: The essence of compiling with continuations. In: PLDI, pp. 237–247. ACM, New York (1993)
10. Jagadeesan, R., Pitcher, C., Riely, J.: Generative operational semantics for relaxed memory models. In: Gordon, A.D. (ed.) ESOP 2010. LNCS, vol. 6012, pp. 307–326. Springer, Heidelberg (2010)

11. Lamport, L.: How to make a multiprocessor computer that correctly executes multiprocess progranm. IEEE Trans. Comput. **28**(9), 690–691 (1979)
12. Lévy, J.-J.: Optimal reductions in the lambda calculus. In: Seldin, J.P., Hindley, J.R. (eds.) To H. B. Curry: Essays on Combinatory Logic, Lambda Calculus and Formalism, pp. 159–191. Academic Press, London (1980)
13. Manson, J., Pugh, W., Adve, S.V.: The Java memory model. In: POPL '05, pp. 378–391. ACM, New York (2005)
14. Owens, S., Sarkar, S., Sewell, P.: A better x86 memory model: x86-TSO. In: Berghofer, S., Nipkow, T., Urban, C., Wenzel, M. (eds.) TPHOLs 2009. LNCS, vol. 5674, pp. 391–407. Springer, Heidelberg (2009)
15. Petri, G.: Operational semantics of relaxed memory models. Ph.D. thesis, Nice (2010). http://www.cs.purdue.edu/homes/gpetri/publis/thesisPetri.pdf
16. Petri, G.: Studying operational models of relaxed concurrency (extended version) (2013). http://www.cs.purdue.edu/homes/gpetri/publis/opsem-long.pdf
17. Saraswat, V.A., Jagadeesan, R., Michael, M.M., von Praun, C.: A theory of memory models. In: PPOPP, pp. 161–172 (2007)
18. Sarkar, S., Sewell, P., Nardelli, F.Z., Owens, S., Ridge, T., Braibant, T., Myreen, M.O., Alglave, J.: The semantics of x86-CC multiprocessor machine code. In: POPL, pp. 379–391. ACM, New York (2009)
19. Sewell, P., Sarkar, S., Owens, S., Nardelli, F.Z., Myreen, M.O.: x86-TSO: a rigorous and usable programmer's model for x86 multiprocessors. CACM **53**(7), 89–97 (2010)
20. CORPORATE SPARC Inc.: The SPARC Architecture Manual (version 9). Prentice-Hall Inc., Upper Saddle River (1994)

Certificates and Separation Logic

Martin Nordio[1(✉)], Cristiano Calcagno[1,2,3], and Bertrand Meyer[1]

[1] ETH Zurich, Zurich, Switzerland
martin.nordio@inf.ethz.ch
[2] Imperial College London, London, UK
[3] Monoidics Ltd, London, UK
ccris@doc.ic.ac.uk, bertrand.meyer@inf.ethz.ch

Abstract. Modular and local reasoning about object-oriented programs has been widely studied for programing languages such as C# and Java. Once source programs have been proven, the next verification challenge is to ensure that the code produced by the compiler is correct. Since verifying a compiler can be extremely complex, this paper uses *proof-transforming compilation*, an alternative approach which automatically generates *certificates*, a bytecode proof, from proofs in the source language. The paper develops a bytecode logic using separation logic, and proof translation from proofs of object-oriented programs to bytecode. The translation also handles proofs for concurrent programs. The bytecode logic and the proof transformation are proven sound.

Keywords: Software verification · Program proofs · Separation logic · Proof-carrying code

1 Introduction

Object-oriented programming has been increasingly attractive in the last decades, however, it has also introduced new verification challenges. Solutions have been proposed, for example, separation logic [19] has extended Hoare logics to reason about programs with mutable data structures; ownership [7] has introduced a technique to reason about the heap structure.

Once the object-oriented programs have been proven correct with respect to their specifications, the verification process should ensure that the code produced by the compiler is correct. Since verifying the compiler is complex [11], techniques such as *translation validation* [21] have been proposed. In *translation validation*, instead of proving that the compiler always generates a correct target code, each translation is validated showing that the target code correctly implements the source program. The *translation validation* approach compares the input and the output, using an analyzer, independently of how the compiler is implemented. Together with a source proof, this gives an indirect correctness proof for the bytecode program.

Expanding the ideas of Proof-Carrying Code [13], Barthe et al. [4][1] and Nordio et al. [17] have proposed an alternative verification process based on

[1] Barthe et al. called this approach *preservation of proof obligations.*

M. Abadi and A. Lluch Lafuente (Eds.): TGC 2013, LNCS 8358, pp. 273–293, 2014.
DOI: 10.1007/978-3-319-05119-2_16,

proof-transforming compilation (PTC). The PTC approach consists of translating proofs of object-oriented programs to bytecode proofs. The verification process is performed at the level of the source program taking advantage of already developed verification techniques. Then, a *proof-transforming compiler* translates automatically a program and its proof into bytecode representing both the program and the proof. The main advantage of PTC is that it addresses full functional correctness as expressed by the original specifications.

Previous work on proof-transforming compilation [1,3,12] has developed the basics of the technique, using either Hoare-style logics or verification condition generators. The main limitation of these works lies on the properties that can be proven in the source program. Those logics cannot prove programs with mutable data structures, for example the programs presented by Distefano et al. [8], which include a visitor pattern example. This restriction is produced by the techniques used to verify the source program.

This paper presents a bytecode logic using separation logic, and proof transformation from Java to bytecode. The translation takes a proof of object-oriented programs written using Parkinson and Bierman's logic [20], and produces a bytecode proof in separation logic style. The bytecode logic introduces dynamic and static specifications for bytecode methods, and framing for bytecode instructions. The use of separation logic allows us to handle proofs that previous works [1,3,12] could not. The definition of the bytecode logic using separation logic makes the translation feasible. In this paper, we also extend the proof transformation to handle proofs for concurrent programs.

Outline. Section 2 presents an overview of separation logic. Section 3 describes the bytecode logic. The proof transformation is developed in Sect. 4. The approach is extended to handle concurrency in Sect. 5. Section 6 shows an example of the proof-transforming compilation approach; soundness is discussed in Sect. 7. Sections 8 and 9 describe related work and conclusions respectively.

2 Overview of Separation Logic

Separation logic [19] provides an elegant approach to reasoning about programs with mutable data structures. It extends Hoare logic with spatial connectives which allow assertions to define separation between parts of the heap. In this paper, we use Parkinson and Bierman's logic [20], which we briefly describe next.

2.1 The Core Language

The programming language used in this paper is a common subset of C# and Java extended with static and dynamic specifications. The syntax is:

L	$::=$	**class** C [**extends** C_1] { **public** $\overline{D}\ \overline{f}$; $\overline{A}\ \overline{M}$ }	*Class Definition*
A	$::=$	**define** $\alpha_C(\overline{x})$ **as** P	*Abstract Predicate Family*
M	$::=$	**public virtual** $C\ m(\overline{D}\ \overline{p})\ DSspec\ \overline{D}\ \overline{x};\ s;$	*Method Definition*
	$\mid$	**public override** $C\ m(\overline{D}\ \overline{p})\ DSspec\ \overline{D}\ \overline{x};\ s;$	
$DSspec$	$::=$	**dynamic** $Spec$; **static** $Spec$	*Dynamic and Static Spec.*
$Spec$	$::=$	$\{P\}\_\{Q\} \mid Spec$ **also** $\{P\}\_\{Q\}$	*Specification Combination*
s	$::=$	$x = e \mid s; s \mid x = y.f \mid x.f = e$	*Statements*
	$\mid$	$x = y.m(\overline{e}) \mid x = y.C :: m(\overline{e}) \mid x = \texttt{new}\ C()$	

Programs are defined as a set of classes, where each class consists of a collection of methods and field definitions; a class can specify at most one superclass. The class definition also contains abstract predicates families (APF). A method declaration includes the method name, parameters with type and name, method specifications, as well as a method body. Method specifications include a static specification and a dynamic specification. Static specifications are used to verify the implementation of a method and direct method calls (in Java this would be with a **super** call); dynamic specifications are used for calls that are dynamically dispatched. The specifications consist of a sequence of pre- and postconditions separated by the keyword **also**: $\{P_1\}\_\{Q_1\}$ **also** $\{P_2\}\_\{Q_2\}$ is defined as $\{P_1 \wedge P_2\}\_\{Q_1 \wedge Q_2\}$. The return statement is not supported in the source language; the return value is assigned to a local variable result. The notation we use is the following: f ranges over field names, m ranges over method names, $\overline{x}$ over sequences of variables, $\overline{p}$ for sequences of method call parameters, C, C_1, D over class names; $\overline{e}$ denotes a sequence of expressions.

An *abstract predicate* is defined with a name, a definition, and a scope. The abstract predicate's name and its definition can be swapped within the scope; outside the scope, the abstract predicate is handled atomically, i.e. by its name. For example, in a class *Cell*, we define the abstract predicate $Val_{Cell}(x, y)$ as $x.val \mapsto y$. The scope of the predicate is inside of the class *Cell*; in the implementation of *Cell*, the predicate $Val_{Cell}(x, y)$ and its definition can be swapped; outside the class, the predicate is handled by its name.

To accommodate inheritance, Parkinson and Bierman [20] introduce *abstract predicates families*. Each class can define its own entry predicate for an APF; this definition allows weakening preconditions, and strengthening postconditions for method overriding. The relationship between the family and entry is given by $x{:}C \Rightarrow (\alpha(x, \overline{x}) \Leftrightarrow \alpha_c(x, \overline{x}))$ where α is an abstract predicate, and α_C is the definition of the predicate for the class C.

2.2 Separation Logic for the Source Language

Memory Model and Assertion Language. Program states are mappings from local variables and parameters to values, and from locations to values: $State \equiv Store \times Heap$, where $Store \equiv Var \rightharpoonup Value$, and $Heap \equiv Location \rightharpoonup Value$. The formulae of assertion language are given by the following grammar:

$$P, Q := true \mid false \mid P \wedge Q \mid P \vee Q \mid P \Rightarrow Q \mid \forall x.P \mid \exists x.P \mid P * Q \mid e{=}e \mid x.f \mapsto e' \mid \alpha(\overline{e}) \mid \alpha_c(\overline{e})$$
$$e \quad := x \mid \texttt{null} \mid e\ \texttt{op}\ e$$

The semantics of formulae is defined as follows:

$$\sigma, h \models P * Q \stackrel{def}{=} \exists h_0, h_1 . h_0 \perp h_1 \textit{ and } h_0 \cdot h_1 = h \textit{ and } \sigma, h_0 \models P \textit{ and } \sigma, h_1 \models Q$$
$$\sigma, h \models e = e' \stackrel{def}{=} \sigma(e) = \sigma(e') \qquad \sigma, h \models \alpha(\overline{x}) \stackrel{def}{=} h \in (\Lambda(\alpha)(\sigma(\overline{x})))$$
$$\sigma, h \models x.f \mapsto e' \stackrel{def}{=} h(\sigma(x)).f = \sigma(e')$$

For $\sigma \in Store$, $\sigma(e)$ denotes the evaluation of the expression e in the store σ. For $h \in Heap$, $h(e).f$ denotes the evaluation of the field f of the expression e. The connectives $(\wedge, \vee)$ and quantifiers $(\exists, \forall)$ are interpreted in the usual way, and omitted here. The formula $P * Q$ allows us to assert that two portions of the heap are disjoint in which P and Q hold respectively. The interpretation of abstract predicates is given by the function Λ, which maps predicate names to predicate definitions.

Method and Statement Specifications. Properties of methods are written as $\Delta; \Gamma \vdash C.m(\overline{x})$ **dynamic** $\{P_C\}\_\{Q_C\}$ **static** $\{R_C\}\_\{S_C\}$ where Δ is the environment containing the logical assumptions about APFs that are available in the scope of the method m, and Γ is the environment containing the dynamic and static method specifications. This specification informally means that the method m in class C can be verified to meet its specification. In particular, Γ is used to handle recursion; Γ is initialized at the beginning of the proof with all the static and dynamic specifications.

The environments are given by the following grammar

$$\Gamma ::= \epsilon \ \mid \ \{P\}C.m(\overline{p})\{Q\}, \Gamma \ \mid \ \{P\}C :: m(\overline{p})\{Q\}, \Gamma$$
$$\Delta ::= \epsilon \ \mid \ \alpha_C \stackrel{def}{=} \lambda(x; \overline{x})P, \Delta$$

where dynamic specifications are denoted by $\{P\}\ C.m(\overline{p})\ \{Q\}$; static specification are denoted by $\{P\}\ C :: m(\overline{p})\ \{Q\}$.

Properties of statements are expressed by Hoare triples of the form $\Delta; \Gamma \vdash \{P\}\ s\ \{Q\}$. This triple defines the following refined partial correctness property [15]: if s's execution starts in a state satisfying P, then (1) s terminates normally in a state where Q holds, or (2) s aborts due to errors or actions than are beyond the semantics of the programming language, e.g., memory problem, or (3) s runs forever.

2.3 Proof Rules

The proof rules, taken from Parkinson and Bierman's work [20], for a subset of the source language is defined as follows:

Field Write
$$\frac{}{\Delta; \Gamma \vdash \{x.f \mapsto \_\}\ x.f := e\ \{x.f \mapsto e\}}$$

Dynamic Dispatch
$$\frac{C.m(\overline{p}) :\ \{P\}\ \_\ \{Q\} \in \Gamma}{\Delta; \Gamma \vdash \{P[x, \overline{e}/\mathtt{this}, \overline{p}] \wedge \mathtt{this} \neq \mathtt{null}\}\ z = x.m(\overline{e})\ \{Q[z, x, \overline{e}/\mathsf{result}, \mathtt{this}, \overline{p}]\}}$$
where x has a static type C.

Direct Method Call

$$\frac{C\!::\!m(\overline{p}):\ \{R\}\ \_\ \{S\} \in \Gamma}{\Delta;\Gamma \vdash \{R[x,\overline{e}/\mathtt{this},\overline{p}] \wedge \mathtt{this} \neq \mathtt{null}\}\ z = x.C\!::\!m(\overline{e})\ \{S[z,x,\overline{e}/\mathsf{result},\mathtt{this},\overline{p}]\}}$$

Method

$$\frac{\begin{array}{c}\Delta;\Gamma \vdash \{R_C\}\ \mathit{body}\ \{S_C\} \quad \text{(Body verification)}\\ \Delta \vdash \{R_C\}\_\{S_C\} \ \Rightarrow\ \{P_C * \mathit{this}\!:\!C\}\_\{Q_C\} \quad \text{(Dynamic dispatch)}\end{array}}{\Delta;\Gamma \vdash \textbf{public virtual}\ C.m(\overline{x})\ \textbf{dynamic}\ \{P_C\}\_\{Q_C\}\ \textbf{static}\ \{R_C\}\_\{S_C\}\ \mathit{body}}$$

The rule for field write is standard. The rule for direct method call uses the static specification; $C::m(\overline{p}):\ \{R\}\ \_\ \{S\} \in \Gamma$ denotes that Γ contains the static specification $\{R\}\_\{S\}$, which is associated with the method m in class C. The rule for dynamic dispatch is similar to the direct method call but uses the dynamic specification; $C.m(\overline{p}):\ \{P\}\ \_\ \{Q\} \in \Gamma$ denotes that Γ contains the dynamic specification $\{P\}\_\{Q\}$ that is associated with the method m. The connection between the method body proofs and the method specifications is formalized with the *Method* rule. This rule has two proof obligations showing that (1) the method body satisfies its static specification; and (2) the use of the dynamic specification is valid for dynamic dispatch. The implication $\Delta \vdash \{R_C\}\_\{S_C\} \ \Rightarrow\ \{P_C * \mathit{this}:C\}\_\{Q_C\}$ means that the static precondition R_C implies the dynamic precondition $P_C * \mathit{this}:C$, and the dynamic postcondition Q_C implies the static postcondition S_C. Note that to handle recursion, the logic does not add any dynamic and static specifications to the environment Γ; Γ is initialized at the beginning with all these specifications. The logic also has a rule for overridden methods, which is similar to the *Method* rule and adds a proof obligation that shows the new dynamic specification is a valid behavioral subtype. This rule is omitted here.

To prove a class, the following *Class* rule is used:

$$\frac{\mathit{for\ all}\ M_i\ \mathit{in}\ \overline{M} : \Delta;\Gamma \vdash M_i}{\Delta;\Gamma \vdash \textbf{class}\ C : D\ \{\textbf{public}\ \ \overline{T}\ \overline{f};\overline{M}\ \}}$$

To be able to fold and unfold the definition of an abstract predicate, the logic has two axioms. These axioms allows folding and unfolding if and only if the abstract predicate is in scope. The axioms are:

$$\mathit{Open}\text{: } (\alpha(\overline{x}) \stackrel{def}{=} P), \Lambda \models \alpha(\overline{e}) \Rightarrow P[\overline{e}/\overline{x}]$$
$$\mathit{Close}\text{: } (\alpha(\overline{x}) \stackrel{def}{=} P), \Lambda \models P[\overline{e}/\overline{x}] \Rightarrow \alpha(\overline{e})$$

One of the most important rules for separation logic is the *Frame* rule. This rule is defined as follows:

$$\frac{\Delta;\Gamma \vdash \{P\}\ \overline{s}\ \{Q\}}{\Delta;\Gamma \vdash \{P * R\}\ \overline{s}\ \{Q * R\}}\ \text{where } \mathit{Mod}(\overline{s}) \cap \mathit{FV}(R) = \emptyset$$

The expression $\mathit{Mod}(\overline{s}) \cap \mathit{FV}(R) = \emptyset$ expresses that $\overline{s}$ does not modify the free variables of R. The logic also has rules for weakening and elimination of abstract predicates. Space prevents us from presenting these rules, for a complete description of the logic see [20].

```
class Cell {
    public int val;
    public virtual void set(int x)
        dynamic {Val(this,_)} _ {Val(this,x)}
        static {this.val ↦ _}_{this.val ↦ x)}
        { val = x; }
    public virtual int get()
        dynamic {Val(this,v)} _ {Val(this,v) * result=v }
        static {this.val ↦ _}_{this.val ↦ x) * result=v}
        { ret := val; }
}
class Recell extends Cell {
    public int bak;
    public override void set(int x)
        dynamic {Val(this,v,_)}_{Val(this,x,v)}
        static {this.val ↦ v}_{this.val ↦ x * this.bak ↦ v}
        { bak = super.get(); super.set(x); }
}
```

(a) Cell Example

$\{ Val_{Recell}(this, v, \_) \}$ [*Open Axiom*]
$\{ Val_{Cell}(this, v) * this.bak \mapsto \_ \}$
this.*bak* = **super**.*get*();
$\{ Val_{Cell}(this, v) * this.bak \mapsto v \}$ [*Direct Method Call*]
super.*set*(*x*);
$\{ Val_{Cell}(this, x) * this.bak \mapsto v \}$ [*Direct Method Call*]
$\{ Val_{Recell}(this, x, v) \}$ [*Close Axiom*]

(b) Sketch of the Proof for the Method *set*

Fig. 1. Example using static and dynamic specifications.

2.4 Example

Figure 1a shows an example from Parkinson and Bierman [20], which illustrates the use of static and dynamic specifications, and abstract predicates. The class *Cell* implements a single cell with an integer value; the class *Recell* extends the implementation of *Cell* storing the previous value of the cell. Each method has two specifications: a *dynamic specification*, that is used for dynamic method calls, and a *static specification*, that is used to verify the implementation and direct method calls. To define the dynamic specification of the method *set*, the abstract predicate family $Val(x, y)$ is used; the definition of this predicate for the class *Cell* is $Val_{Cell}(x, y) \stackrel{def}{=} x.val \mapsto y$. This predicate expresses that the field *val* of the object x points to the object y. In the class *Recell*, the method *set* is overridden. Its specification is extended, and the predicate Val takes an extra argument. The definition is $Val_{Recell}(x, y, z) \stackrel{def}{=} Val_{Cell}(x, y) * x.bak \mapsto z$. In this definition, the operator $*$ is used to express non-interference.

The proof of the source example consists of a proof for the classes *Cell* and *Recell*. The proof of the class *Recell* consist of the proof of the method *set*; these proofs are constructed applying the *Class* rule and the *Method* rule respectively. A sketch of the proof of the method *set* is presented in Fig. 1b. It applies the rules *Direct Method Call* as well as the *Open and Close axioms.*

3 A Separation Logic for Bytecode

3.1 The Bytecode Language

The bytecode language consists of classes with methods and fields. Methods are implemented as method bodies consisting of a sequence of labeled bytecode instructions. Bytecode instructions operate on the operand stack, local variables (which also include parameters), and the heap. Each method body ends with a return instruction, which return the control flow to the caller; a method returns the value stored in a special local variable result. This language is extended with dynamic and static specifications. We also introduced abstract predicates families to the bytecode language. This extension to the bytecode language makes the translation feasible. The syntax is:

$$\begin{aligned}
&L, A, \overline{M}, \overline{DSspec}, Spec ::= as\ defined\ in\ Sect. 2.1\\
&s ::= \overline{l : Inst}\\
&Inst ::= \mathsf{pop}\ x \mid \mathsf{push}\ v \mid \mathsf{goto}\ l' \mid \mathsf{nop} \mid \mathsf{return} \mid \mathsf{brtrue}\ l' \mid\\
&\qquad\quad \mathsf{putfld}\ f \mid \mathsf{newobj}\ C \mid \mathsf{invokespecial}\ C{::}m
\end{aligned}$$

This language is similar to Java bytecode. We treat local variables and method parameters using the same instructions. Instead of using an array of local variables like in Java Bytecode, we use the name of the source variable. To simplify the proof translation, we assume the bytecode language has a boolean type.

The semantics of the instructions is as follows: the instruction pop x removes the top element of the stack and assigns it to x; push v puts the value v on top of the stack; goto transfers control the program point l'; nop has no effect; return returns to caller; brtrue transfers control to the label l' if the top of the stack is *true* removing this value from the stack; the instruction putfld f updates the field f; newobj creates an object of type C. The instruction invokespecial is used to call private methods and super methods.

3.2 Memory Model

Bytecode program states are a triple consisting of an operand stack, a local store, and a heap:

$$\begin{aligned}
State &\equiv Stack \times Store \times Heap\\
Stack &\equiv Value^*\\
Store &\equiv Var \rightharpoonup Value\\
Heap &\equiv Location \rightharpoonup Value
\end{aligned}$$

The *Stack* type is defined as a list of values; *Store* is a mapping from local variables and parameters to values; *Heap* is a mapping from locations to values. In the following section, we present the axiomatic semantics.

3.3 Axiomatic Semantics

Assertion Language. Formulae for the assertion language of bytecode method specifications are the same as for the source language (described in Sect. 2.2). The formulae for the assertion language for preconditions of bytecode instructions are extended because the precondition can refer to the stack. Formulae are defined as $S \bullet P$ where S is a stack of values, and P is a formula defined as in the source language. The definition is $BytecodePre := S \bullet P$ where $S := e^*$, and P and e are defined as in Sect. 2.2. The formal semantics of formulae is defined as follows:

$$\begin{aligned} s, \sigma, h \models S \bullet P \quad &\stackrel{def}{=} s, \sigma \models S \text{ and } \sigma, h \models P \\ (v_1, ..., v_n), \sigma \models (e_1, ...e_m) &\stackrel{def}{=} n = m \text{ and } \sigma(e_i) = v_i \\ \sigma, h \models P \quad &\stackrel{def}{=} \text{as defined in Sect. 2.2} \end{aligned}$$

Following, we define the implication operator for bytecode preconditions:

Definition 1. *Given the stacks* S_1 *and* S_2 *and the expressions* P *and* Q*, then* $s, \sigma, h \models S_1 \bullet P \Rightarrow S_2 \bullet Q$ *iff* $s, \sigma, h \models S_1 \bullet P$ *implies* $s, \sigma, h \models S_2 \bullet Q$*. We write* $S_1 \bullet P \Rightarrow S_2 \bullet Q$ *to mean validity:* $\forall s, \sigma, h: \; s, \sigma, h \models S_1 \bullet P \Rightarrow S_2 \bullet Q$*.*

Proof Rules for Classes. A bytecode proof consists of a list of proofs for the bytecode classes. To prove the bytecode classes, the logic has the same *Class* rule and *Frame* rule as in the source language.

Proof Rules for Method Specifications. Properties of bytecode methods are defined as $\Delta; \Gamma \vdash C.m(\overline{x})$ **dynamic** $\{P_C\}\_\{Q_C\}$ **static** $\{R_C\}\_\{S_C\}$. This definition is the same as in the source language. In particular the treatment of recursion is the same as in the source logic: the environment Γ contains the static and dynamic specifications, and it is initialized at the beginning of the proof.

The logic has a similar *Method* rule and *Override* rule to the logic for the source language. The bytecode *Method* rule is defined as follows:

$$\frac{\begin{array}{ll} & \Delta \vdash \{R_C\}\_\{S_C\} \Rightarrow \{P_C * this{:}C\}\_\{Q_C\} \text{ (Dynamic dispatch)} \\ R_C \Rightarrow E_1 & E_j \Rightarrow S_C \quad body = \{E_1\}\ 1 : I_1, \ldots \{E_j\}\ j : \mathsf{return} \quad \Psi = (l_1, E_1) \ldots (l_j, E_j) \\ & \forall i \in 1, \ldots j : \Delta; \Gamma; \Psi \vdash \{E_i\}\ i : I_i \text{ (Bytecode body verification)} \end{array}}{\Delta; \Gamma \vdash \textbf{public } C.m(\overline{x}) \textbf{ dynamic } \{P_C\}\_\{Q_C\} \textbf{ static } \{R_C\}\_\{S_C\}\ body}$$

This rule, besides showing that the use of dynamic dispatch is valid, has three extra proof obligations: we need to verify that (1) the precondition of the method implies the precondition of the first bytecode instruction (E_1); (2) the postcondition of the last bytecode instruction (E_j) implies the method postcondition, and (3) all the instruction specifications of the method m hold. Note that the body of the method m, denoted by *body*, is a list of bytecode specifications of the form $\Delta; \Gamma; \Psi \vdash \{E_i\}\ i : I_i$.

Proof Rules for Instruction Specifications. The bytecode logic treats instructions individually since control can be transferred into the middle of a sequence. Each instruction at the label l has a precondition E_l. Bytecode specifications have the form $\Delta; \Gamma; \Psi \vdash \{E_l\}\ l : inst$ where Δ is the environment containing the APF, Γ is the environment containing the dynamic and static method specifications (as in the source logic), and Ψ is a mapping from labels to preconditions. We use the environment Ψ to make explicit the list of successor preconditions. This environment is used, in particular for the application of the *Frame* rule.

The semantics of $\Delta; \Gamma; \Psi \vdash \{E_l\}\ l{:}inst$ is: if the precondition E_l holds when the program counter is at the label l, then the preconditions of the successor instructions hold after successful execution of instruction *inst*.

The rules for the bytecode instructions except for the instructions invokespecial are defined as follows:

$$\frac{S \bullet \exists x'.x = v[x'/x] \wedge P[x'/x] \ \Rightarrow\ E_{l+1}}{\Delta; \Gamma; \Psi, (l{+}1, E_{l+1}) \vdash \{(S,v) \bullet P\}\ l{:}\mathsf{pop}\ x} \qquad \frac{(S,v) \bullet P \ \Rightarrow\ E_{l+1}}{\Delta; \Gamma; \Psi, (l{+}1, E_{l+1}) \vdash \{S \bullet P\}\ l{:}\mathsf{push}\ v}$$

$$\frac{S \bullet P \Rightarrow\ E_{l'}}{\Delta; \Gamma; \Psi, (l', E_{l'}) \vdash \{S \bullet P\}\ \ l : \mathsf{goto}\ l'} \qquad \frac{S \bullet P \Rightarrow\ E_{l+1}}{\Delta; \Gamma; \Psi, (l{+}1, E_{l+1}) \vdash \{S \bullet P\}\ \ l{:}\mathsf{nop}}$$

$$\frac{S \bullet P\ \wedge\ v = true \Rightarrow E_{l'} \qquad S \bullet P\ \wedge\ v = false \Rightarrow E_{l+1}}{\Delta; \Gamma; \Psi, (l', E_l'), (l+1, E_{l+1}) \vdash \{(S,v) \bullet P\}\ \ l : \mathsf{brtrue}\ l'}$$

$$\frac{S \bullet P * (r.f \mapsto v)\ \Rightarrow\ E_{l+1}}{\Delta; \Gamma; \Psi, (l+1, E_{l+1}) \vdash \{(S,r,v) \bullet P * r.f \mapsto \_\}\ l{:}\mathsf{putfld}\ f}$$

In the rule of the instruction pop, the precondition assumes that the operand stack is not empty. The implication $S \bullet \exists x'.x = v[x'/x] \wedge P[x'/x] \ \Rightarrow\ E_{l+1}$ expresses that one has to show that the formula $S \bullet \exists x'.x = v[x'/x] \wedge P[x'/x]$ implies the precondition of the next instruction. In this formula, the operand stack is S since the value v has been popped and assigned to x. The replacements are similar to the assignment rule in the source language. The environment $\Psi, (l+1, E_{l+1})$ expresses that the precondition of the instruction at label $l+1$ is E_{l+1}. The rule for push adds a value v on top of the stack S, then one has to show that $(S,v) \bullet P$ implies the next instruction's precondition. The rule for putfld assigns the value v of to the field $r.f$.

Below, we present the rule for invokespecial (the rule for invokevirtual is similar). Similar to the source logic, this rule uses the static specifications.

$$\frac{C{::}m(\overline{p}) : \{T\}\_\{R\} \in \Gamma \qquad (S,v) \bullet R[y/\mathtt{this}, \overline{z}/\overline{p}, v/result] \Rightarrow E_{l+1}}{\Delta; \Gamma; \Psi, (l+1, E_{l+1}) \vdash \{(S,y,\overline{z}) \bullet T[y/\mathtt{this}, \overline{z}/\overline{p}] \wedge y \neq \mathtt{null}\}\ l{:}\mathsf{invokespecial}\ C{:}m}$$

where v is a logical variable.

Frame Rule for Bytecode Instructions. The *Frame* rule of the logic of the source language can be applied to both method specifications and instructions. For example, the *Frame* rule could be applied to a triple where the instruction is an assignment. In our bytecode logic, we have developed a *Frame* rule for bytecode specifications. This rule is needed to translate the *Frame* rule from the source language. The rule is defined as follows:

$$\frac{\Delta;\Gamma;\Psi \vdash \{S\bullet P\}\, l : inst \quad \Psi' = Succ(l,\Psi) \quad \Psi = \Psi',\Psi''}{\Delta;\Gamma;(\Psi' * R),\Psi'' \vdash \{S \bullet P * R\} \quad l : inst} \quad \text{where } Mod(inst) \cap FV(R) = \emptyset$$

Bytecode specifications can have several successors. For example, the bytecode branching instruction brtrue l has two successors: the next instruction and the instruction at label l. The standard *Frame* rule (in the source logic) strengthens both the precondition and the postcondition of the triple. Since bytecode specifications can have several successors, we need to strengthen all successor preconditions. The successor instructions are contained in the environment Ψ'. It is constructed using the function *Succ*, which yields the environment with the label l and its precondition, and l's successors. The environment $\Psi' * R$ is obtained from the successor instructions of l in Ψ', by adding $*R$ to each precondition. These separating conjunctions are only added to the preconditions of l and the successor instructions, so the environment Ψ'' is not modified.

Language-Independent Rules. The bytecode logic also has language-independent rules such as stack-disjointness. In this section, we present the most important language-independent rules. The following rule is used in the proof translation to embed a local proof transformation in a wider context, for example to combine the results of applying the *Frame* rule to single instructions.

$$\textit{Env-weakening} \quad \frac{\Delta;\Gamma;\Psi \vdash \{P\} \quad l : inst}{\Delta;\Gamma;\Psi,\Psi' \vdash \{P\} \quad l : inst}$$

Another language-independent rule is the *stack-disjointness* rule, which allows reasoning about stacks that might have different values and sizes. For example, this rule allows reasoning about a program that might push either a value v_1 or a value v_2 into the stack, and therefore, the top of the stack is either v_1 or v_2. The rule is defined as:

$$\textit{stack-disjointness} \quad \frac{\Delta;\Gamma;\Psi \vdash \{(S,v_1) \bigvee (S,v2) \bullet P\} \quad l : inst}{\Delta;\Gamma;\Psi \vdash \{(S,(v_1 \bigvee v_2)) \bullet P\} \quad l : inst}$$

The semantics of the formulae, denoted as $\models$, is extended to support stack disjointness: $S_1 \bigvee S_2 \bullet P$, and expression disjointness: $x = (v_1 \bigvee v_2)^2$. The semantics is:

$$\begin{array}{lll} s,\sigma & \models S_1 \bigvee S_2 & \stackrel{def}{=} (s,\sigma \models S_1 \ or\ s,\sigma \models S_2) \\ (s,e),\sigma & \models (S_1,(v1 \bigvee v_2)) & \stackrel{def}{=} (s,\sigma \models S_1 \ and\ (e = \sigma(v_1)\ or\ e = \sigma(v_2)\ ) \\ s,h & \models x = (v_1 \bigvee v_2) & \stackrel{def}{=} s,\sigma \models (x = v_1) \vee (x = v_2) \end{array}$$

2 The expression disjointness is used when the value $v_1 \bigvee v_2$ is popped from the stack and assigned to a variable x

3.4 Examples

This subsection presents two examples illustrating the application of the frame rule and disjointness rule for bytecode.

Example Applying the Frame Rule. Assume the following valid bytecode proof:

$$\begin{array}{ll}
\Delta;\Gamma;(l_2,S_2\bullet P_2) & \vdash \{S_1\bullet P_1\}\ l_1 : \ \mathsf{push}\ x\\
\Delta;\Gamma;(l_3,S_3\bullet P_3),(l_5,S_5\bullet P_5) & \vdash \{S_2\bullet P_2\}\ l_2 : \ \mathsf{brtrue}\ l_5\\
\Delta;\Gamma;(l_4,S_4\bullet P_4) & \vdash \{S_3\bullet P_3\}\ l_3 : \ \mathsf{push}\ y\\
\Delta;\Gamma;(l_5,S_5\bullet P_5) & \vdash \{S_4\bullet P_4\}\ l_4 : \ \mathsf{goto}\ l_6\\
\Delta;\Gamma;(l_6,S_6\bullet P_6) & \vdash \{S_5\bullet P_5\}\ l_5 : \ \mathsf{push}\ z\\
\Delta;\Gamma;\epsilon & \vdash \{S_6\bullet P_6\}\ l_6 : \ \mathsf{return}
\end{array}$$

where P_i is the precondition at label l_i. The application of the *Frame* rule to the instructions at labels $l_1...l_6$ adds $*R$ to each precondition. Given that each instruction specification contains a list of the successors, the rule also adds $*R$ to each precondition in the environment Ψ. After applying the *Frame* rule, we obtain the following proof:

$$\begin{array}{ll}
\Delta;\Gamma;(l_2,S_2\bullet P_2*R) & \vdash \{S_1\bullet P_1*R\}\ l_1{:}\,\mathsf{push}\ x\\
\Delta;\Gamma;(l_3,S_3\bullet P_3*R),(l_5,S_5\bullet P_5*R) & \vdash \{S_2\bullet P_2*R\}\ l_2{:}\,\mathsf{brtrue}\ l_5\\
\Delta;\Gamma;(l_4,S_4\bullet P_4*R) & \vdash \{S_3\bullet P_3*R\}\ l_3{:}\,\mathsf{push}\ y\\
\Delta;\Gamma;(l_6,S_6\bullet P_6*R) & \vdash \{S_4\bullet P_4*R\}\ l_4{:}\,\mathsf{goto}\ l_6\\
\Delta;\Gamma;(l_6,S_6\bullet P_6*R) & \vdash \{S_5\bullet P_5*R\}\ l_5{:}\,\mathsf{push}\ z\\
\Delta;\Gamma;\epsilon & \vdash \{S_6\bullet P_6*R\}\ l_6{:}\,\mathsf{return}
\end{array}$$

Note that the instruction l_2 has two successors: l_3 and l_5. Thus, the application of the *frame* rule changes the environment $(l_3,P_3),(l_5,P_5)$ to $(l_3,P_3*R),(l_5,P_5*R)$. Applying the *Env-weakening* rule, we obtain the following proof:

$$\begin{array}{l}
\Delta;\Gamma;\Psi\vdash\{S_1\bullet P_1*R\}\ l_1 : \ \mathsf{push}\ x\\
\Delta;\Gamma;\Psi\vdash\{S_2\bullet P_2*R\}\ l_2 : \ \mathsf{brtrue}\ l_5\\
\Delta;\Gamma;\Psi\vdash\{S_3\bullet P_3*R\}\ l_3 : \ \mathsf{push}\ y\\
\Delta;\Gamma;\Psi\vdash\{S_4\bullet P_4*R\}\ l_4 : \ \mathsf{goto}\ l_6\\
\Delta;\Gamma;\Psi\vdash\{S_5\bullet P_5*R\}\ l_5 : \ \mathsf{push}\ z\\
\Delta;\Gamma;\Psi\vdash\{S_6\bullet P_6*R\}\ l_6 : \ \mathsf{return}\\
\mathit{where}\ \Psi \stackrel{def}{=} (l_1,P_1*R)\ ...\ (l_6,P_6*R)
\end{array}$$

Example Applying the Disjointness Rule. Assume we want to prove the following program:

$$\begin{array}{l}
l_1 : \ \mathsf{push}\ b\\
l_2 : \ \mathsf{brtrue}\ l_5\\
l_3 : \ \mathsf{push}\ 0\\
l_4 : \ \mathsf{goto}\ l_6\\
l_5 : \ \mathsf{push}\ 1\\
l_6 : \ \mathsf{pop}\ x\\
l_7 : \ \mathsf{nop}
\end{array}$$

where at the instruction l_7 the expression $x = 0 \lor x = 1$ holds. To simplify the proof, the omit the details of the environments $\Delta; \Gamma; \Psi$ and we write $\Delta; \Gamma; \Psi$ without defining the successor instructions in Ψ. The preconditions for these instructions are as follows (assuming the stack is S before the execution of this code):

$$
\begin{array}{ll}
\Delta; \Gamma; \Psi \vdash \{S \bullet True\} & l_1 : \ \mathsf{push}\ b \\
\Delta; \Gamma; \Psi \vdash \{(S, b) \bullet True\} & l_2 : \ \mathsf{brtrue}\ l_5 \\
\Delta; \Gamma; \Psi \vdash \{S \bullet True\} & l_3 : \ \mathsf{push}\ 0 \\
\Delta; \Gamma; \Psi \vdash \{(S, 0) \bullet True\} & l_4 : \ \mathsf{goto}\ l_6 \\
\Delta; \Gamma; \Psi \vdash \{S \bullet True\} & l_5 : \ \mathsf{push}\ 1 \\
\Delta; \Gamma; \Psi \vdash \{(S, (0 \bigvee 1)) \bullet True\} & l_6 : \ \mathsf{pop}\ x \\
\Delta; \Gamma; \Psi \vdash \{S \bullet x = 0 \lor x = 1\} & l_7 : \ \mathsf{nop}
\end{array}
$$

The preconditions at labels l_1 to l_5 hold by applying the push, brtrue, push, and goto rules. The interesting part of the proof is at labels l_6 and l_7. Applying the *stack disjointness* rule we can prove:

$$
stack\text{-}disjointness \quad \frac{\Delta; \Gamma; \Psi \vdash \{(S, 0) \bigvee (S, 1) \bullet True\} \quad l : inst}{\Delta; \Gamma; \Psi \vdash \{(S, (0 \bigvee 1)) \bullet True\} \quad l : inst}
$$

Now, we need to prove that the instructions at labels l_4 and l_5 satisfy the precondition $(S, 0) \bigvee (S, 1) \bullet True$. By definition of $(S, 0) \bigvee (S, 1) \bullet True$, the precondition $\{(S, 0) \bullet True\}$ implies $(S, 0) \bigvee (S, 1) \bullet True$, and the precondition $\{(S, 1) \bullet True\}$ implies $(S, 0) \bigvee (S, 1) \bullet True$. Then, applying the goto and pop rules, the instructions at labels l_4 and l_5 hold.

To prove the instruction of line l_7, we apply the pop rule, obtaining:

$$
\frac{S \bullet x = (0 \bigvee 1) \land True \ \Rightarrow \ S \bullet x = 0 \lor x = 1}{\Delta; \Gamma; \Psi \vdash \{(S, (0 \bigvee 1)) \bullet True\} l_6 : \ \mathsf{pop}\ x}
$$

The implication holds by definition of $x = 0 \bigvee 1$ which is defined as $x = 0 \lor x = 1$. Therefore, the proof is a valid proof.

4 Proof Transformation for Separation Logic

The proof translation takes a proof in the source language (Sect. 2), and produces a proof in the bytecode logic (Sect. 3). The proof translation is developed using the translation functions ∇_C, ∇_M ∇_S, and ∇_E, which translate classes, methods, instructions, and expressions respectively. The signature of these functions are as follows:

$$
\begin{array}{l}
\nabla_C : ProofTree \rightarrow BytecodeProofTree \\
\nabla_M : ProofTree \rightarrow BytecodeProofTree \\
\nabla_S : ProofTree \rightarrow List[BytecodeSpec] \\
\nabla_E : Pre \times Exp \times Post \rightarrow List[BytecodeSpec]
\end{array}
$$

A *ProofTree* is a derivation in the logic of the source language. A *Bytecode-ProofTree* is a derivation in the bytecode logic; the function ∇_S produces the proof for the body of a bytecode method; it consists of a list of bytecode specifications. The postcondition in the function ∇_E is used to prove soundness of the translation. In the following sections, we present the translation for method specifications, the *Frame* rule, and statements.

Proof Translation for Method Specifications. A source proof for a class C consists of a list of method names with a dynamic and static specification, and proofs for the method bodies. The source logic uses the *Class rule* to prove the method bodies. Since the source and the bytecode logic treat the heap in the same way, use the same abstract predicate definitions, and have the same method specifications, these environments are not modified by the translation. To translate classes, the translation applies the *Class* rule in the bytecode. The translation is defined as follows:

$$\nabla_C\left(\frac{\textit{for all } M_i \textit{ in } \overline{M} : \Delta;\Gamma \vdash M_i}{\Delta;\Gamma \vdash \textbf{class } C{:}D\{\textbf{public } \overline{T}\ \overline{f};\overline{M}\}}\right) = \frac{\textit{for all } M_i \textit{ in } \overline{M} : \nabla_M(\Delta;\Gamma \vdash M_i)}{\Delta;\Gamma \vdash \textbf{class } C{:}D\{\textbf{public } \overline{T}\ \overline{f};\overline{M}\ \}}$$

The function ∇_M maps proofs of methods in Java to proofs of methods in bytecode. Given that the signature of the methods in Java and bytecode are the same (both use dynamic and static specifications), the translation does not modify the signature of the methods. The resulting bytecode proof uses the *Method* rule in bytecode where the body of the method is produced by the translation ∇_S. The translation is defined as follows:

$$\nabla_M\left(\frac{\begin{array}{c}\Delta;\Gamma \vdash \{R_C\}\ \textit{body}\ \{S_C\}\ \ \text{(Body verification)}\\ \Delta \vdash \{R_C\}\_\{S_C\} \Rightarrow \{P_C * \textit{this}{:}C\}\_\{Q_C\}\ \ \text{(Dynamic dispatch)}\end{array}}{\begin{array}{l}\Delta;\Gamma \vdash \textbf{public virtual } C.m(\overline{x})\\ \qquad \textbf{dynamic } \{P_C\}\_\{Q_C\}\ \textbf{static } \{R_C\}\_\{S_C\}\ \textit{body}\end{array}}\right) =$$

$$\frac{\begin{array}{c}\Delta \vdash \{R_C\}\_\{S_C\} \Rightarrow \{P_C * \textit{this}{:}C\}\_\{Q_C\}\ \ \text{(Dynamic dispatch)}\\ R_C \Rightarrow E_1 \quad E_j \Rightarrow S_C \quad \textit{body\_bytecode} = \nabla_S(\textit{body})\ \ \text{(Bytecode body verification)}\end{array}}{\Delta;\Gamma \vdash \textbf{public } C.m(\overline{x})\ \textbf{dynamic } \{P_C\}\_\{Q_C\}\ \textbf{static } \{R_C\}\_\{S_C\}\ \textit{body\_bytecode}}$$

Proof Translation of the Frame Rule. To translate the *Frame* rule applied to statements, first we apply the translation ∇_S to the triple $\Delta;\Gamma \vdash \{P\}\ s\ \{Q\}$ producing the bytecode derivations

$$\Delta;\Gamma;\Psi_1 \vdash \{S_1 \bullet P_1\}\ \ l_1 : i_1\ \ \ldots\ \ \Delta;\Gamma;\Psi_n \vdash \{S_n \bullet P_n\}\ \ l_n : i_n$$

where Ψ_k only contains the labels and preconditions relevant to instruction i_k

Then, we apply the frame rule for bytecode instructions (p. XXX) to add the predicate $*R$ to the conjunction to the precondition of each derivation, and to the environment Ψ_i. Finally, we use the *Env-weakening* rule to unify the environments resulting from the application of the *Frame* rule into a single environment for the whole block of instructions. The translation produces the following proof:

$$\Delta;\Gamma;\Psi \vdash \{S_1 \bullet P_1 * R\}\ \ l_1 : i_1\ \ \ldots\ \ \Delta;\Gamma;\Psi \vdash \{S_n \bullet P_n * R\}\ \ l_n : i_n$$

where $\Psi \stackrel{def}{=} \Psi_1 * R, \Psi_2 * R, \ldots, \Psi_k * R$

Proof Translation of Statements. In this section, we present the translation functions for compound and direct method call. The translation of a compound is defined as:

$$\nabla_S\left(\frac{\{P\}s_1\{Q\} \quad \{Q\}s_2\{R\}}{\{P\}s_1;s_2\{R\}}\right) = \nabla_S(\{P\}s_1\{Q\}) + \nabla_S(\{Q\}s_2\{R\})$$

The direct method call translation is as follows:

$$\nabla_S\left(\frac{C.m(\overline{p}):\ \{P\}\_\{Q\} \in \Gamma}{\Delta;\Gamma \vdash \{P'\}\ z = x.C::m(\overline{e})\ \{Q[z,x,\overline{e}/\mathsf{result},\mathtt{this},\overline{p}]\}}\right) =$$

$$\begin{array}{ll}
\Delta;\Gamma;\Psi_1 \vdash \{\epsilon \bullet P'\} & L_A:\ \mathsf{push}\ x \\
 & \nabla_E(\ x \bullet P'\ ,\ \overline{e},\ \ (x,\overline{e}) \bullet P'\ ) \\
\Delta;\Gamma;\Psi_2 \vdash \{\ (x,\overline{e}) \bullet P'\} & L_B:\ \mathsf{invokespecial}\ C::m \\
\Delta;\Gamma;\Psi_3 \vdash \{\ \mathsf{result} \bullet Q[x,\overline{e}/\mathtt{this},\overline{p}]\ \} & L_C:\ \mathsf{pop}\ z
\end{array}$$

where P' is defined as $P[x,\overline{e}/\mathtt{this},\overline{p}] \wedge \mathtt{this} \neq \mathtt{null}$, and Ψ_1, Ψ_2, Ψ_3 only contain the labels relevant to the instructions at labels L_A, L_B, and L_C respectively.

The translation of direct method call first pushes the target object on top of the stack; then it translates the list of expressions $\overline{e}$ using the function ∇_E; the method m is invoked using the instruction invokespecial, and finally the result of the invocation is stored in the variable z.

5 Proof Transformation for Concurrent Programs

This section extends the PTC approach to handle concurrent programs. We first present the source logic, the bytecode logic and its proof transformation for disjoint concurrency. Then, we expand the approach to critical regions.

5.1 Basic Concurrency

In Java, concurrency is implemented using the *Thread* class. This class contains methods such as *start*: to execute a thread, and *join*: to wait for the termination of a thread. To handle critical regions, the instruction synchronized is used. To simplify the semantics, we assume an instruction $s_1 \parallel s_2$ in the source language, which runs the instructions s_1 and s_2 concurrently. This instruction is equivalent to execute $s_1.start()$; $s_2.start()$;$s_1.join()$;$s_2.join()$. For the bytecode language, we also assume the threads are first run and then joined; thus, we assume an instruction invokeStartJoin.

Concurrency for the Source Logic. In this paper, we use the axiomatic semantics of the instruction $s_1 \parallel s_2$ defined by O'Hearn [18]. The rule, called the *Disjoint Concurrency* rule, is defined as follows:

$$\frac{\Delta;\Gamma \vdash \{P_1\}\ s_1\ \{Q_1\} \quad \Delta;\Gamma \vdash \{P_2\}\ s_2\ \{Q_2\}}{\Delta;\Gamma \vdash \{P_1 * P_2\}\ s_1 \parallel s_2\ \{Q_1 * Q_2\}}$$

where s_1 does not modify any variables free in P_2, s_2, Q_2, and conversely.

Concurrency for the Bytecode Logic. Let $C_1{:}run$ and $C_2{:}run$ be bytecode methods. The instruction invokeStartJoin $C_1{:}run$ $C_2{:}run$ executes the *run* methods concurrently and waits for the termination of both. To simplify the semantics, we assume these methods are procedures. The rule for invokeStartJoin extends the rule for invokespecial (Sect. 3.3) to concurrency.

Let P_1', P_2', Q_1' and Q_2' be:

$$\begin{aligned}
P_1' &\stackrel{def}{=} P_1[y_1/\mathtt{this}] \wedge y_1 \neq \mathtt{null}\\
Q_1' &\stackrel{def}{=} Q_1[y_1/\mathtt{this}]\\
P_2' &\stackrel{def}{=} P_2[y_2/\mathtt{this}] \wedge y_2 \neq \mathtt{null},\ \mathit{and}\\
Q_2' &\stackrel{def}{=} Q_2[y_2/\mathtt{this}]
\end{aligned}$$

The rule is defined as follows:

$$\frac{\begin{array}{c} C_1{::}run : \{P_1\}\_\{Q_1\} \in \Gamma \qquad C_2{::}run : \{P_2\}\_\{Q_2\} \in \Gamma \\ S \bullet Q_1' * Q_2' \Rightarrow E_{l+1} \end{array}}{\Delta; \Gamma; \Psi, (l+1, E_{l+1}) \vdash \{(S, y_1, y_2) \bullet P_1' * P_2'\} \quad l : \mathsf{invokeStartJoin}\ C_1{:}run\ C_2{:}run}$$

where $C_1{:}run$ does not modify any variables free in $P_2, C_2{:}run, Q_2$, and conversely.

Proof Transformation. The proof translator takes a proof using the *Disjoint Concurrency* rule, and generates a bytecode proof. To translate it, we first extend the definition of the translation function ∇_C. This function applies the translation function ∇_M to all the methods M_i in a class C, and also uses a new function ∇_P. The function ∇_P produces classes C_1 and C_2 with a method *run* for each use of the instruction $s_1 \parallel s_2$. The function ∇_C is defined as follows:

$$\nabla_C\left(\frac{\mathit{forall}\ M_i : \Delta; \Gamma \vdash M_i}{\Delta; \Gamma \vdash \{P_1\}\ \mathbf{class}\ C{:}D\ \{\mathbf{public}\ \overline{M}\}}\right) = \frac{\mathit{forall}\ M_i\ \nabla_M(\Delta; \Gamma \vdash M_i); \nabla_P(\Delta; \Gamma \vdash M_i)}{\Delta; \Gamma \vdash \{P_1\}\ \mathbf{class}\ C{:}D\ \{\mathbf{public}\ \overline{M}\}}$$

The function ∇_P generates method proofs only when the *Disjoint Concurrency* rule is used. For other rules, this function is applied recursively. The definition of ∇_P for the case of the *Disjoint Concurrency* rule is as follows:

$$\nabla_P\left(\frac{\Delta; \Gamma \vdash \{P_1\}\ s_1\ \{Q_1\} \qquad \Delta; \Gamma \vdash \{P_2\}\ s_2\ \{Q_2\}}{\Delta; \Gamma \vdash \{P_1 * P_2\}\ s_1 \parallel s_2\ \{Q_1 * Q_2\}}\right) =$$

$$\frac{b = \nabla_S(\Delta; \Gamma \vdash \{P_1\}\ s_1\ \{Q_1\}) \ \ \text{(Bytecode body verification)}}{\Delta; \Gamma \vdash \mathbf{public}\ C_1.run(\overline{p_1})\ \mathbf{dynamic}\ \{P_1\}\_\{Q_1\}\ \mathbf{static}\ \{P_1\}\_\{Q_1\}\ b}$$

$$\frac{b = \nabla_S(\Delta; \Gamma \vdash \{P_2\}\ s_2\ \{Q_2\}) \ \ \text{(Bytecode body verification)}}{\Delta; \Gamma \vdash \mathbf{public}\ C_2.run(\overline{p_2})\ \mathbf{dynamic}\ \{P_2\}\_\{Q_2\}\ \mathbf{static}\ \{P_2\}\_\{Q_2\}\ b}$$

The translation function ∇_S is extended to handle concurrency; the translation first creates two objects of type C_1 and C_2, and then applies the invokeStartJoin rule. The translation is:

$$\nabla_S \left(\frac{\Delta; \Gamma \vdash \{P_1\}\ s_1\ \{Q_1\} \quad \Delta; \Gamma \vdash \{P_2\}\ s_2\ \{Q_2\}}{\Delta; \Gamma \vdash \{P_1 * P_2\}\ s_1 \parallel s_2\ \{Q_1 * Q_2\}} \right) =$$

$$\Delta; \Gamma; \Psi_1 \vdash \{\epsilon \bullet P_1 * P_2\}\ \ L_A : \ \mathsf{newobj}\ C_1$$
$$\Delta; \Gamma; \Psi_2 \vdash \{y_1 \bullet P_1 * P_2\}\ L_B : \ \mathsf{newobj}\ C_2$$

$$\frac{C_1{::}run : \{P_1\}\_\{Q_1\} \in \Gamma \qquad C_2{::}run : \{P_2\}\_\{Q_2\} \in \Gamma \qquad (y_1, y_2) \bullet Q_1' * Q_2' \Rightarrow E_{L_C+1}}{\Delta; \Gamma; \Psi_3 \vdash \{(y_1, y_2) \bullet P_1' * P_2'\}\ \ L_C : \mathsf{invokeStartJoin}\ C_1{:}run\ C_2{:}run}$$

where $P_1' \stackrel{def}{=} P_1[y_1/\mathtt{this}] \wedge y_1 \neq \mathtt{null}$ $\quad P_2' \stackrel{def}{=} P_2[y_2/\mathtt{this}] \wedge y_2 \neq \mathtt{null}$
$Q_1' \stackrel{def}{=} Q_1[y_1/\mathtt{this}]$ $\quad Q_2' \stackrel{def}{=} Q_2[y_2/\mathtt{this}]$
y_1 and y_2 are fresh objects of type C_1 and C_2 resp.,
and Ψ_1, Ψ_2, Ψ_3 only contain the labels relevant to the instructions at L_A, L_B, L_C resp.

5.2 Critical Regions

Critical Regions in the Source Logic. To access a resource in a critical region, O'Hearn's work [18] uses a statement `with` r `do` s. This statement can be implemented in Java using synchronized statements. O'Hearn's rule, adapted to Java, is defined as follows:

$$\frac{\Delta; \Gamma \vdash \{P * RI_r\}\ s_1\ \{Q * RI_r\}}{\Delta; \Gamma \vdash \{P\}\ \mathsf{synchronized}\ (r)\ s_1\ \{Q\}}$$ where no other process modifies variables free in P or Q.

In this rule, the code in the critical region can see the state RI_r associated with the resource r. However, outside this region, reasoning proceeds without this knowledge. The state RI_r is called *resource invariant*; it is fixed for each resource r.

Critical Regions for the Bytecode Logic. To model critical regions, Java Bytecode provides two instructions: monitorenter and monitorexit to entering and leaving a critical region. To simplify the semantics and the proof transformation, we assume these instructions take a given resource r as argument (in Java Bytecode, these resources are pushed onto the stack). The rules for these instructions are defined as follows:

$$\frac{S \bullet P * RI_r \Rightarrow\ E_{l+1}}{\Delta; \Gamma; \Psi, (l{+}1, E_{l+1}) \vdash \{S \bullet P\}\ \ l : \mathsf{monitorenter}\ r}$$

$$\frac{S \bullet Q \Rightarrow\ E_{l+1}}{\Delta; \Gamma; \Psi, (l{+}1, E_{l+1}) \vdash \{S \bullet Q * RI_r\}\ \ l : \mathsf{monitorexit}\ r}$$

The first rule adds the *resource invariant* RI_r to the precondition P; the second rule removes this *resource invariant* from the precondition $S \bullet Q * RI_r$.

Proof Transformation. The translation of critical regions uses the bytecode instructions monitorenter and monitorexit. The translation is:

$$\nabla_S\left(\frac{\Delta;\Gamma \vdash \{P * RI_r\}\ s_1\ \{Q * RI_r\}}{\Delta;\Gamma \vdash \{P\}\ \textsf{synchronized}\ (r)\ s_1\ \{Q\}}\right) =$$

$$\begin{array}{ll} \Delta;\Gamma;\Psi_1 \vdash \{\epsilon \bullet P\} & L_A : \textsf{monitorenter}\ r \\ & \nabla_S(\ \Delta;\Gamma \vdash \{P * RI_r\}\ s_1\ \{Q * RI_r\}\ ) \\ \Delta;\Gamma;\Psi_2 \vdash \{\epsilon \bullet Q * RI_r\} & L_B : \textsf{monitorexit}\ r \end{array}$$

where Ψ_1 and Ψ_2 only contain the labels relevant to the instructions at labels L_A and L_B respectively.

To check the validity of the translation, we need to show the validity of each generated instruction. Since the precondition of the first instruction of s_1 is $P * RI_r$, then the instruction monitorenter is valid because $P * RI_r \Rightarrow P * RI_r$. The postcondition of s_1 is $Q * RI_r$, which is the precondition of monitorexit. By the definition of monitorexit, we need to show Q implies the postcondition of s_1, which is Q. Therefore, the translation is valid.

6 Example

Our proof translation takes the proof of the cell example (Fig. 1), and produces a bytecode proof. The source proof consist of the proof for the classes *Cell* and *Recell* where each proof contains the proof of their methods. The proof translation is performed in two steps. In the first step, the rules for classes and method specifications are translated using the functions ∇_C and ∇_M. In the second step, the method bodies are translated using the function ∇_S. This function takes the proof of Fig. 1b, and produces the bytecode proof of Fig. 2.

The static and dynamic specifications, highlighted in Fig. 2, express the same properties as in the source program. The body of the method consists of a sequence of precondition, label, and instruction. Bytecode preconditions are pairs $S \bullet P$ where S is a list of expressions representing the stack, and P is a formula in separation logic. For example, the precondition at label 03 expresses that the object `this` is on the top of the stack and that the property $Val(this, v) * this.bak \mapsto \_$ holds. The stack grows to the right, e.g. in $(this, x)$ the top element is x; we denote the empty stack with ϵ. The translation function ∇_S first applies the *Open axiom*[3] generating the bytecode proof at label 01. Then, the triple for the assignment $bak = super.get()$ is translated, producing the proof at labels 02–05. Then, the triple for the method invocation $super.set(x)$; is translated producing the proof at labels 05–07. Finally, the *Close axiom* is translated producing the proof at label 09. The last instruction of the proof is the return instruction.

[3] The *Open axiom* allows unfolding the abstract predicate $Val_{Recell}(this, v, \_)$ to its definition $Val_{Cell}(this, v) * this.bak \mapsto \_$.

public override void *set*(**int** *x*)

$\textbf{dynamic}\ \{Val(\textbf{this}, v, \_)\}\ \_\ \{Val(\textbf{this}, x, v)\}$
$\textbf{static}\ \ \{\textbf{this}.val \mapsto v\}\ \_\ \{\textbf{this}.val \mapsto x * \textbf{this}.bak \mapsto v\}$

$\{\ \epsilon \bullet Val_{Recell}(this, v, \_)\}$	01: **nop**
$\{\ \epsilon \bullet Val_{Cell}(this, v) * this.bak \mapsto \_\ \}$	02: **push** *this*
$\{\ this \bullet Val_{Cell}(this, v) * this.bak \mapsto \_\ \}$	03: **invokespecial** *Cell:get*
$\{\ ret' \bullet Val_{Cell}(this, v) * this.bak \mapsto \_ *\ ret' = v\}$	04: **push** *this*
$\{\ (ret', this) \bullet Val_{Cell}(this, v) * this.bak \mapsto \_ *\ ret' = v\}$	05: **putfld** *bak*
$\{\ \epsilon \bullet Val_{Cell}(this, v) * this.bak \mapsto v\ \}$	06: **push** *this*
$\{\ this \bullet Val_{Cell}(this, v) * this.bak \mapsto v\ \}$	07: **push** *x*
$\{\ (this, x) \bullet Val_{Cell}(this, v) * this.bak \mapsto v\ \}$	08: **invokespecial** *Cell:set*
$\{\ \epsilon \bullet Val_{Cell}(this, x) * this.bak \mapsto v\ \}$	09: **nop**
$\{\ \epsilon \bullet Val_{Recell}(this, x, v)\}$	10: **ret**

Fig. 2. Example of the application of proof-transforming compilation.

7 Soundness of the Proof-Transforming Compiler

In this section, we present the soundness theorems for the proof-transforming compiler. Soundness informally means that the translation produces valid bytecode proofs. Soundness is defined with three theorems for the translation of classes, methods, and instructions.

The following theorem expresses that if the *class* rule in the source logic is a valid derivation, then the translation produces a valid derivation in the bytecode logic.

Theorem 1 (Soundness of the Class Translator).

$$\frac{\textit{for all } M_i \textit{ in } \overline{M} : \Delta; \Gamma \vdash M_i}{\Delta;\Gamma \vdash \textbf{\textit{class}}\ C{:}D\ \{\textbf{\textit{public}}\ \ \overline{T}\ \overline{f}; \overline{M}\ \}} \Rightarrow \nabla_C\left(\frac{\textit{for all } M_i \textit{ in } \overline{M} : \Delta; \Gamma \vdash M_i}{\Delta;\Gamma \vdash \textbf{\textit{class}}\ C{:}D\ \{\textbf{\textit{public}}\ \ \overline{T}\ \overline{f}; \overline{M}\ \}}\right)$$

The soundness theorem for the method translator expresses that if the proof of the method m is a valid derivation, then the proof translation produces a valid bytecode proof. It is defined as follows:

Theorem 2 (Soundness of the Method Translator). *Let $Tree_1$ be the derivation tree of the Method rule. Then,*

$$\frac{Tree_1}{\Delta; \Gamma \vdash \begin{array}{l}\textbf{\textit{public virtual}}\ C.m(\overline{x})\\ \textbf{\textit{dynamic}}\ \{P_C\}\_\{Q_C\}\ \textbf{\textit{static}}\ \{R_C\}\_\{S_C\}\ \ body\end{array}} \Rightarrow$$

$$\nabla_M\left(\frac{Tree_1}{\Delta; \Gamma \vdash \begin{array}{l}\textbf{\textit{public virtual}}\ C.m(\overline{x})\\ \textbf{\textit{dynamic}}\ \{P_C\}\_\{Q_C\}\ \textbf{\textit{static}}\ \{R_C\}\_\{S_C\}\ \ body\end{array}}\right)$$

The following theorem, for instruction translation, states that if (1) we have a valid source proof for the instruction s, and (2) we have a proof translation from the source proof that produces the instructions $I_{l_{start}} ... I_{l_{end}}$, and their respective preconditions $E_{l_{start}} ... E_{l_{end}}$, and (3) the postcondition in the source logic implies the next precondition of the last generated instruction (if the last generated instruction is the last instruction of the method, we use the postcondition in the source logic), then every bytecode specification holds: $\Delta; \Gamma; \Psi \vdash \{E_l\}\ l : I_l$. The theorem is the following:

Theorem 3 (Soundness of the Instruction Translator). *Let $Tree_1$ be the derivation tree used to prove the instruction s. Then,*

$$\frac{Tree_1}{\Delta; \Gamma \vdash \{P\}\ s\ \{Q\}} \quad \wedge$$
$$(\ (E_{l_{start}}, I_{l_{start}}) ... (E_{l_{end}}, I_{l_{end}})\ ) = \nabla_S \left(\frac{Tree_1}{\Delta; \Gamma \vdash \{P\}\ s\ \{Q\}} \right) \wedge$$
$$(Q \ \Rightarrow \ E_{l_{end+1}})$$
$$\Rightarrow$$
$$\forall\, l \ \in \ l_{start} \ ... \ l_{end} : \ \Delta; \Gamma; \Psi \vdash \{E_l\}\ \ l : I_l$$

The proof runs by induction on the structure of the derivation tree of

$$\frac{Tree_1}{\Delta; \Gamma \vdash \{P\}\ s\ \{Q\}}$$

8 Related Work

Bytecode Analysis. Several logics for bytecode have been developed. Stata and Abadi [23] first introduced a type system for Java bytecode. To verify bytecode with frame properties, Benton [5] has developed compositional logic for a stack-based abstract machine. The logic is a separation style logic and uses shifting operations to reindex stack assertions. Chin et al. [6] also present a heap model for a bytecode language to support separation logic. Dong et al. [9] develop a modular reasoning technique for low-level intermediate programs. However, those works do not support object-oriented features. Bannwart and Müller [1] present a Hoare-style logic for a bytecode language with object-oriented features similar to the JVM language. Dynamic and static specifications are treated in their logic, however, their inter-relationship is not considered.

Proof-Transforming Compilation. There has been several works on proof-transforming compilation [1,3,12,17,22]. The closest related work to our proof-transforming compiler are the works by Barthe *et al.* [3,4] on proof preserving compilation. They prove the preservation of proof obligations from Java programs to JVM programs; thus, they show that if the certificate proves the verification condition in the source, then this certificate can be used to prove the verification condition in the bytecode. Our bytecode logic and proof transformation can handle more complex examples that those works cannot; for example, programs using mutable data structures such as the programs proven by Distefano et al. [8], which include the factory, observer, and visitor patterns. The limitation on those works is given by the techniques used to verify the source program. Our work introduces a bycode logic using separation logic and its proof transformation, which makes possible to translate the proofs of programs using mutable data structures.

Kunz [10] presents proof preserving compilation for concurrent programs using an Owicki/Gries-like proof system. Our work handles non-interference and concurrent programs using separation logic.

Compared to our earlier effort on proof transformation [12,16,17], this work has a cleaner treatment of the stack, develops a more powerful bytecode logic, uses a different and more powerful source code proof system, and supports concurrency. Barthe et al. [2] implemented an infrastructure for Proof Carrying Code (PCC). Our current implementation [14] of the PCC infrastructure consist of proof transforming compiler for a Hoare-style logic, and a proof checker formalized in Isabelle. As future work, we plan to extend this implementation to handle separation logic.

9 Conclusions

We have developed a separation logic for bytecode; the logic adapts Parkinson and Bierman's work on abstract predicates [20] for bytecode. We also present proof transforming compilation from a separation logic for object-oriented programs to our bytecode logic. The bytecode logic and the proof transformation are sound. To prove soundness of the proof translation, we show that the translation of a valid source proof yields a valid bytecode proof. The use of a separation logic for bytecode allows us to translate more complex source proofs that previous works cannot handle, for example, programs using mutable data structures. The results show that the proof transformation can be extended to handle proofs of concurrent programs.

Acknowledgements. We thank Stephan van Staden, Sebastian Nanz, Scott West, and Mei Tang for their insightful comments on drafts of this paper. The research leading to these results has received funding from the European Research Council under the European Union's Seventh Framework Programme (FP7/2007-2013)/ERC Grant agreement no. 291389.

References

1. Bannwart, F.Y., Müller, P.: A program logic for bytecode. In: Spoto, F. (ed.) BYTECODE. ENTCS, vol. 141(1), pp. 255–273. Elsevier, Amsterdam (2005)
2. Barthe, G., Crégut, P., Grégoire, B., Jensen, T., Pichardie, D.: The MOBIUS proof carrying code infrastructure. In: de Boer, F.S., Bonsangue, M.M., Graf, S., de Roever, W.-P. (eds.) FMCO 2007. LNCS, vol. 5382, pp. 1–24. Springer, Heidelberg (2008)

3. Barthe, G., Grégoire, B., Pavlova, M.I.: Preservation of proof obligations from Java to the Java virtual machine. In: Armando, A., Baumgartner, P., Dowek, G. (eds.) IJCAR 2008. LNCS(LNAI), vol. 5195, pp. 83–99. Springer, Heidelberg (2008)
4. Barthe, G., Rezk, T., Saabas, A.: Proof obligations preserving compilation. In: Third International Workshop on Formal Aspects in Security and Trust, Newcastle, UK, pp. 112–126 (2005)
5. Benton, N.: A typed, compositional logic for a stack-based abstract machine. In: Yi, K. (ed.) APLAS 2005. LNCS, vol. 3780, pp. 364–380. Springer, Heidelberg (2005)
6. Chin, W., David, C., Nguyen, H., Qin, S.: Enhancing modular OO verification with separation logic. In: POPL '08, pp. 87–99. ACM (2008)
7. Clarke, D., Drossopoulou, S.: Ownership, encapsulation and the disjointness of type and effect. In: OOPSLA '02, vol. 37. ACM (2002)
8. Distefano, D., Parkinson, M.J.: jStar: towards practical verification for Java. In: OOPSLA '08, pp. 213–226 (2008)
9. Dong, Y., Wang, S., Zhang, L., Yang, P.: Modular certification of low-level intermediate representation programs. In: ICSAC, pp. 563–570. IEEE Computer Society (2009)
10. Kunz, C.: Certificate translation for the verification of concurrent programs. In: Wirsing, M., Hofmann, M., Rauschmayer, A. (eds.) TGC 2010. LNCS, vol. 6084, pp. 237–252. Springer, Heidelberg (2010)
11. Zhou, Z., Chindaro, S., Deravi, F.: Face recognition using balanced pairwise classifier training. In: Weerasinghe, D. (ed.) ISDF 2009. LNICST, vol. 41, pp. 42–49. Springer, Heidelberg (2010)
12. Müller, P., Nordio, M.: Proof-transforming compilation of programs with abrupt termination. In: SAVCBS '07, pp. 39–46 (2007)
13. Necula, G.: Compiling with proofs. Ph.D. thesis, School of Computer Science, Carnegie Mellon University (1998)
14. Nordio, M.: Proofs and proof transformations for object-oriented programs. Ph.D. thesis, ETH Zurich (2009)
15. Nordio, M., Calcagno, C., Müller, P., Meyer, B.: A sound and complete program logic for Eiffel. In: Oriol, M., Meyer, B. (eds.) TOOLS EUROPE 2009. LNBIP, vol. 33, pp. 195–214. Springer, Heidelberg (2009)
16. Nordio, M., Müller, P., Meyer, B.: Formalizing proof-transforming compilation of Eiffel programs. Technical report 587, ETH Zurich (2008)
17. Nordio, M., Müller, P., Meyer, B.: Proof-transforming compilation of Eiffel programs. In: Paige, R.F., Meyer, B. (eds.) TOOLS-EUROPE 2008. LNBIP, vol. 11, pp. 316–335. Springer, Heidelberg (2008)
18. O'Hearn, P.W.: Resources, concurrency, and local reasoning. Theor. Comput. Sci. **375**, 271–307 (2007)
19. O'Hearn, P.W., Yang, H., Reynolds, J.C.: Separation and information hiding. In: POPL '04, pp. 268–280. ACM (2004)
20. Parkinson, M.J., Bierman, G.M.: Separation logic, abstraction and inheritance. In: POPL '08, pp. 75–86. ACM (2008)
21. Pnueli, A., Siegel, M., Singerman, E.: Translation validation. In: Steffen, B. (ed.) TACAS 1998. LNCS, vol. 1384, pp. 151–166. Springer, Heidelberg (1998)
22. Saabas, A., Uustalu, T.: Program and proof optimizations with type systems. J. Logic Algebr. Program. **77**(1–2), 131–154 (2008)
23. Stata, R., Abadi, M.: A type system for Java bytecode subroutines. In: POPL '98, pp. 149–160. ACM (1998)

Quantitative Analysis

On-the-fly Fast Mean-Field Model-Checking

Diego Latella[1(✉)], Michele Loreti[2], and Mieke Massink[1]

[1] Istituto di Scienza e Tecnologie dell'Informazione 'A. Faedo', CNR, Pisa, Italy
Diego.Latella@isti.cnr.it
[2] Università di Firenze, Firenze, Italy

Abstract. A novel, scalable, on-the-fly model-checking procedure is presented to verify bounded PCTL properties of selected individuals in the context of very large systems of independent interacting objects. The proposed procedure combines on-the-fly model checking techniques with deterministic mean-field approximation in discrete time. The asymptotic correctness of the procedure is shown and some results of the application of a prototype implementation of the FlyFast model-checker are presented.

Keywords: Probabilistic model-checking · On-the-fly model-checking · Mean-field approximation · Discrete time Markov chains

1 Introduction

Model checking has been widely recognised as a powerful approach to the automatic verification of concurrent and distributed systems. It consists of an efficient procedure that, given an abstract model $\mathcal{M}$ of the system, decides whether $\mathcal{M}$ satisfies a logical formula Φ, typically drawn from a temporal logic. Despite the success of model-checking procedures, their scalability have always been a concern due to the potential combinatorial explosion of the state space that needs to be searched.

The main contribution of this paper is a novel model-checking procedure, based on an original combination of local, on-the-fly model-checking techniques and mean field approximation in discrete time [26]. The procedure can be used to verify bounded PCTL [18] properties of selected individuals in the context of systems consisting of a large number of similar but independent interacting objects. It is scalable in the sense that it is insensitive to the size of the population the system consists of. The asymptotic correctness of the model-checking procedure is proven and a prototype implementation of the model-checker, FlyFast, is applied to a bench-mark example from computer epidemics that was also studied extensively in [7], to which we refer for a detailed discussion. To the best of our knowledge, this is the first implementation of an *on-the-fly mean field* model-checker for *discrete time, probabilistic, time-synchronous* models.

This research has been partially funded by the EU projects ASCENS (nr. 257414) and QUANTICOL (nr. 600708), and the IT MIUR project CINA.

M. Abadi and A. Lluch Lafuente (Eds.): TGC 2013, LNCS 8358, pp. 297–314, 2014.
DOI: 10.1007/978-3-319-05119-2_17,

Following the approach in [26] we consider a model for interacting objects, where the evolution of each object is given by a finite state discrete time Markov chain. The transition matrix of each object may depend on the distribution of states of all objects in the system. Each object can be in one of its local states at any point in time and all objects proceed in discrete time and in a clock-synchronous fashion. When the number of objects is large, the overall behaviour of the system in terms of its 'occupancy measure', i.e. the fraction of objects that are in a particular local state at a particular time, can be approximated by the (deterministic) solution of a *difference equation* which is called the 'mean field'[1]. This convergence result has been extended in [26] to obtain a 'fast' way to stochastically simulate the evolution of a selected, limited number of specific objects in the context of the overall behaviour of the population.

We show that the deterministic iterative procedure of [26], to compute the average overall behaviour of the system and that of individual objects in the context of the overall system, combines well with an *on-the-fly* probabilistic model-checking procedure for the verification of bounded PCTL formulas addressing selected objects of interest[2]. An on-the-fly recursive approach also provides a natural way to address nested path formulae and time-varying truth values of such formulae. The algorithm presented in this paper is parametric w.r.t. the semantic interpretation of the language. In particular we present two different interpretations; one based on the standard, *exact probabilistic semantics* of a simple probabilistic population description language, and the other one on the *mean-field approximation in discrete time* of such a semantics. The latter is the main contribution of the current paper. The considered PCTL formulae can be extended along the lines proposed in [21,22] with properties that address the overall status of the system. We show a simple instance of that.

The models we consider are also known as SIO-models (System of Independent Objects) [7]. These are time-synchronous models in which each object performs a probabilistic step in each discrete time unit, possibly looping to the same state. This is a class of models that is frequently encountered in various research disciplines ranging from telecommunication to computational biology. The objects interact in an indirect way via the global state of the overall system.

2 Related Work

Traditionally, model checking approaches are divided into two broad categories: *global* approaches that determine the set of *all* states in $\mathcal{M}$ that satisfy Φ, and *local* approaches that, given a state s in $\mathcal{M}$, determine whether s satisfies Φ [5,11].

[1] The term 'mean field' has its origin in statistical physics and is sometimes used with slightly different meaning in the literature. Here we intend the meaning as defined in [26].

[2] Note that the transition probabilities of these selected objects at time t may depend on the occupancy measure of the system at t and therefore also the truth-values of the formulas may vary with time.

Global symbolic model checking algorithms are popular because of their computational efficiency and can be found in many model checkers, both in a qualitative (see e.g. [10]) and in a stochastic setting (see e.g. [2,23]). The set of states that satisfy a formula is constructed recursively in a *bottom-up* fashion following the syntactic structure of the formula. Depending on the particular formula to verify, usually the underlying model can be reduced to fewer states before the algorithm is applied. Moreover, as is shown e.g. in [2] for stochastic model checking, the model checking algorithm can be reduced to combinations of existing well-known and optimised algorithms for CTMCs such as transient analysis.

Local model checking algorithms have been proposed to mitigate the state space explosion problem using a so called 'on-the-fly' approach (see e.g. [5,11, 15,20]). On-the-fly algorithms are following a *top-down* approach that does not require global knowledge of the complete state space. For each state that is encountered, starting from a given state, the outgoing transitions are followed to adjacent states, constructing step by step local knowledge of the state space until it is possible to decide whether the given state satisfies the formula. For qualitative model checking, local model-checking algorithms have been shown to have the same worst-case complexity as the best existing global procedures for the above mentioned logics. However, in practice, they have better performance when only a subset of the system states need to be analysed to determine whether a system satisfies a formula. Furthermore, local model-checking may still provide some results in case of systems with a very large or even infinite state space where global model checking approaches would be impossible to use. In the context of stochastic model checking several on-the-fly approaches have been proposed, among which [13] and [17]. The former is a probabilistic model checker for bounded PCTL formulas. The latter uses an on-the-fly approach to detect a maximal relevant search depth in an infinite state space and then uses a *global* model-checking approach to verify bounded CSL [1,2] formulas in a continuous time setting on the selected subset of states. An on-the-fly approach by itself however, does not solve the challenging scalability problems that arise in truly large parallel systems, such as collective adaptive systems, e.g., gossip protocols [9], self-organised collective decision making [28], computer epidemics [8] and foreseen smart urban transportation systems and decentralised control strategies for smart grids.

To address this type of scalability challenges in probabilistic model-checking, recently, several approaches have been proposed. In [16,19] approximate probabilistic model-checking is introduced. This is a form of statistical model-checking that consists in the generation of random executions of an *a priori* established maximal length. On each execution the property of interest is checked and statistics are performed over the outcomes. The number of executions required for a reliable result depends on the maximal error-margin of interest. The approach relies on the analysis of individual execution traces rather than a full state space exploration and is therefore memory-efficient. However, the number of execution traces that may be required to reach a desired accuracy may be large and therefore time-consuming. The approach works for general models, i.e., not necessarily populations of similar objects, but is not independent of the number of objects involved.

To analyse properties of large scale mobile communication networks mean field approximations in discrete time have also been used e.g., in Bakshi et al. [3]. In that work an automatised method is proposed and applied to the analysis of dynamic gossip networks. A general convergence result to a deterministic difference equation is used, similar to that in [26], but not its extension to analyse individual behaviour in the context of a large population, nor its exploitation in model-checking algorithms.

In Chaintreau et al. [9], mean field convergence in *continuous time* is used to analyse the distribution of the age of information that objects possess when using a mix of gossip and broadcast for information distribution in situations where objects are not homogeneously distributed in space. An overview of mean field interaction models for computer and communication systems by Benaïm et al. can be found in [4].

Preliminary ideas on the exploitation of mean field convergence in *continuous time* for model-checking mean field models, and in particular for an extension of the logic CSL, were informally sketched in a presentation at QAPL 2012 [21], but no model-checking algorithms were presented. Follow-up work on the above mentioned approach can be found in [22] which relies on earlier results on fluid model checking by Bortolussi and Hillston [6]. In the latter a *global CSL* model-checking procedure is proposed for the verification of properties of a selection of individuals in a population. This work is perhaps the most closely related to our work, however their procedure exploits mean field convergence and fast simulation [12,14] in a *continuous* time setting rather than in a discrete time setting and is based on an *interleaving* model of computation, rather than a clock-synchronous one; furthermore, a *global* model-checking approach, rather than an on-the-fly approach, is followed. The modelling language used in [6] is PEPA. Earlier work by Stefanek et al. [29] on the use of mean field convergence in *continuous time* for grouped PEPA has investigated the quality of the convergence results when the related differential equations are derived directly from the process algebraic model. Potential issues with accuracy were found concerning the parallel composition operator of PEPA that involves a (non-linear) minimum function applied to rates originating from synchronising populations. This could, in some circumstances, give rise to inaccuracies in the approximation. It is however possible to detect such situations.

3 Time Bounded PCTL and On-the-fly Model-Checking

In this section we recall the definition of the *time bounded* fragment of PCTL[3] and we present an on-the-fly model-checking algorithm. The algorithm is parametric in the sense that it can be used for different languages and semantic

[3] For notational simplicity we call the fragment PCTL as well.

Table 1. Satisfaction relation for Time Bounded PCTL.

$s \models_{\mathcal{M}} a$	iff $a \in \ell(s)$
$s \models_{\mathcal{M}} \neg\Phi$	iff not $s \models_{\mathcal{M}} \Phi$
$s \models_{\mathcal{M}} \Phi_1 \vee \Phi_2$	iff $s \models_{\mathcal{M}} \Phi_1$ or $s \models_{\mathcal{M}} \Phi_2$
$s \models_{\mathcal{M}} \mathcal{P}_{\bowtie p}(\varphi)$	iff $\mathbb{P}\{\sigma \in Paths_{\mathcal{M}}(s) \mid \sigma \models_{\mathcal{M}} \varphi\} \bowtie p$
$\sigma \models_{\mathcal{M}} \mathcal{X}\,\Phi$	iff $\sigma[1] \models_{\mathcal{M}} \Phi$
$\sigma \models_{\mathcal{M}} \Phi_1 \mathcal{U}^{\leq k} \Phi_2$	iff $\exists 0 \leq h \leq k\ s.t.\ \sigma[h] \models_{\mathcal{M}} \Phi_2 \ \wedge\ \forall 0 \leq i < h\ .\ \sigma[i] \models_{\mathcal{M}} \Phi_1$

interpretations. In this paper we use two instantiations of the algorithm; one is on a DTMC semantics of a simple language of object populations (Sect. 4) and the other is on a mean-field approximation semantics of the same language, for "fast model-checking" (Sect. 5). For the sake of readability, we present only a schema of the algorithm for time *bounded* PCTL, that is the same as that proposed in [13]. The interested reader is referred to [25] where a novel algorithm is defined and implemented for *the full* logic.

3.1 Time Bounded PCTL

Given a set $\mathscr{P}$ of atomic propositions, the syntax of PCTL is defined below, where $a \in \mathscr{P}$, $k \geq 0$ and $\bowtie \in \{\geq, >, \leq, <\}$:

$$\Phi ::= a \mid \neg\Phi \mid \Phi \vee \Phi \mid \mathcal{P}_{\bowtie p}(\varphi) \qquad \text{where } \varphi ::= \mathcal{X}\,\Phi \mid \Phi\,\mathcal{U}^{\leq k}\,\Phi.$$

PCTL formulae are interpreted over *state labelled* DTMCs. A state labelled DTMC is a pair $\langle \mathcal{M}, \ell \rangle$ where $\mathcal{M}$ is a DTMC with state set $\mathcal{S}$ and $\ell : \mathcal{S} \to 2^{\mathscr{P}}$ associates each state with a set of atomic propositions; for each state $s \in \mathcal{S}$, $\ell(s)$ is the set of atomic propositions true in s. In the following, we assume $\mathbf{P}$ be the one step probability matrix for $\mathcal{M}$; we abbreviate $\langle \mathcal{M}, \ell \rangle$ with $\mathcal{M}$, when no confusion can arise. A path σ over $\mathcal{M}$ is a non-empty sequence of states $s_0, s_1, \cdots$ where $\mathbf{P}_{s_i, s_{i+1}} > 0$ for all $i \geq 0$. We let $Paths_{\mathcal{M}}(s)$ denote the set of all infinite paths over $\mathcal{M}$ starting from state s. By $\sigma[i]$ we denote the i-th element s_i of path σ. Finally, in the sequel we will consider DTMCs equipped with an initial state s_0, i.e. the probability mass is initially all in s_0. For any such a DTMC $\mathcal{M}$, and for all $t \in \mathbb{N}$ we let the set $L_{\mathcal{M}}(t) = \{\sigma[t] \mid \sigma \in Paths_{\mathcal{M}}(s_0)\}$.

We define the satisfaction relation on $\mathcal{M}$ and the logic in Table 1.

3.2 On-the-fly PCTL Model-Checking Algorithm

In this section we introduce a local on-the-fly model-checking algorithm for time-bounded PCTL formulae. The basic idea of an on-the-fly algorithm is simple: while the state space is generated in a stepwise fashion from a term s of the language, the algorithm considers only the relevant prefixes of the paths while they

Table 2. Function Check

1	Check(s : proc, Φ : formula)=
2	match Φ
3	with
4	$\mid a \rightarrow$ (lab_eval s a)
5	$\mid \neg\Phi_1 \rightarrow \neg$Check($s,\Phi_1$)
6	$\mid \Phi_1 \vee \Phi_2 \rightarrow$ Check(s,ϕ_1) $\vee$ Check(s,Φ_2)
7	$\mid \mathcal{P}_{\langle\text{relop}\rangle p}(\varphi) \rightarrow$ CheckPath(s,φ)$\langle\text{relop}\rangle p$

are generated. For each of them it updates the information about the satisfaction of the formula that is checked. In this way, only that part of the state space is generated that can provide information on the satisfaction of the formula and irrelevant parts are not taken into consideration.

In the case of probabilistic process population languages, for large populations, a mean-field approximated semantics can be defined. In Sect. 5 we show how a drastic reduction of the state space can be obtained, by using the same algorithm on such semantic models. We call such a combined use of on-the-fly model-checking and mean-field semantics "Fast model-checking" after "Fast simulation", introduced in [26].

The algorithm abstracts from any specific language and different semantic interpretations of a language. We only assume an abstract interpreter function that, given a generic process term, returns a probability distribution over the set of terms. Below, we let proc be the (generic) type of *probabilistic process terms* while we let formula and path_formula be the types of *state-* and *path-* PCTL formulae. Finally, we use lab to denote the type of *atomic propositions*.

The abstract interpreter can be modelled by means of two functions: next and lab_eval. Function next associates a list of pairs (proc, float) to each element of type proc. The list of pairs gives the terms, i.e. states, that can be reached in one step from the given state and their one-step transition probability. We require that for each s of type proc it holds that $0 < p' \leq 1$, for all $(s',p') \in$ next(s) and $\sum_{(s',p')\in\text{next}(s)} p' = 1$. Function lab_eval returns for each element of type proc a function associating a bool to each atomic proposition a in lab. Each instantiation of the algorithm consists in the appropriate definition of next and lab_eval, depending on the language at hand and its semantics.

The local model-checking algorithm is defined as a function, Check, shown in Table 2. On atomic state-formulae, the function returns the value of lab_eval; when given a non-atomic state-formula, Check calls itself recursively on sub-formulae, in case they are state-formulae, whereas it calls function CheckPath, in case the sub-formula is a path-formula. In both cases the result is a Boolean value that indicates whether the state satisfies the formula.

Function CheckPath, shown in Table 3, takes a state $s \in$ proc and a PCTL path-formula $\varphi \in$ path_formula as input. As a result, it produces the probability measure of the set of paths, starting in state s, which satisfy path-formula φ.

Table 3. Function CheckPath

```
CheckPath( s : proc , φ : path_formula )=
match φ with
|𝒳Φ → let p = 0.0 and lst = next(s) in
    for (s',p') ∈ lst do if Check(s',Φ) then p ← p+p'
    done;
    p
|Φ1 𝒰≤k Φ2 → if Check(s,Φ2) then 1.0
         else if Check(s,¬Φ1) then 0.0
         else if k>0 then
              begin
                  let p = 0.0 and lst = next(s) in
                  for (s',p') ∈ lst do
                      p ← p+p' * CheckPath(s',Φ1 𝒰≤k−1 Φ2)
                  done;
                  p
              end
         else 0.0
```

Following the definition of the formal semantics of PCTL, two different cases can be distinguished. If φ has the form $\mathcal{X}\,\Phi$ then the result is the sum of the probabilities of the transitions from s to those next states s' that satisfy Φ. To verify the latter, function Check is recursively invoked on such states. If φ has the form $\Phi_1\,\mathcal{U}^{\leq k}\,\Phi_2$ then we first check if s satisfies Φ_2, then 1 is returned, since φ is trivially satisfied. If s does not satisfy Φ_1 then 0 is returned, since φ is trivially violated. For the remaining case we need to recursively invoke CheckPath for the states reachable in one step from s, i.e. the states in the set $\{s' | \exists p' : (s',p') \in \mathsf{next}(s)\}$. Note that these invocations of CheckPath are made on $\varphi' = \Phi_1\,\mathcal{U}^{\leq k-1}\,\Phi_2$ if $k > 0$. If $k \leq 0$ then the formula is trivially not satisfied by s and the value 0 is returned.

Let s be a term of a probabilistic process language and $\mathcal{M}$ the complete discrete time stochastic process associated with s by the formal semantics of the language. The following theorem is easily proved by induction on Φ [25].

Theorem 1. $s \models_{\mathcal{M}} \Phi$ *if and only if* $\mathsf{Check}(s, \Phi) = \mathsf{true}$. •

4 Modelling Language

In this section we define a simple population description language. The language is essentially a textual version of the graphical notation used in [26]. A *system* is defined as a population of N identical interacting processes or objects[4]. At any point in time, each object can be in any of its finitely many states and the evolution of the system proceeds in a *clock-synchronous* fashion: at each clock

[4] In [26] *object* is used instead of *process*. We consider the two terms synonyms here.

tick each member of the population must either execute one of the transitions that are enabled in its current state, or remain in such a state.[5]

Syntax. Let $\mathcal{A}$ be a denumerable non-empty set of *actions*, ranged over by $a, a', a_1, \ldots$ and $\mathcal{S}$ be a denumerable non-empty set of *state constants*, ranged over by $C, C', C_1, \ldots$ An *object specification* Δ is a set $\{D_i\}_{i \in I}$, for finite index set I, where each *state definition* D_i has the form $C_i := \sum_{j \in J_i} a_{ij}.C_{ij}$, with J_i a finite index set, states $C_i, C_{ij} \in \mathcal{S}$, and $a_{ij} \in \mathcal{A}$, for $i \in I$ and $j \in J_i$. Intuitively, the notation $\sum_{j \in J_i} a_{ij}.C_{ij}$ is to be intended as the n-ary extension of the standard process algebraic binary non-deterministic choice operator. We require that $a_{ij} \neq a_{ij'}$, for $j \neq j'$ and that for each state constant C_{ij} occurring in the r.h.s. of a state definition D_i of Δ there is a *unique* $k \in I$ such that C_{ij} is the l.h.s. of D_k.

Example 1 (*An epidemic model* [7]). We consider a network of computers that can be infected by a worm. Each node in the network can acquire infection from two sources, i.e. by the activity of a worm of an infected node (`inf_sus`) or by an external source (`inf_ext`). Once a computer is infected, the worm remains latent for a while, and then activates (`activate`). When the worm is active, it tries to propagate over the network by sending messages to other nodes. After some time, an infected computer can be patched (`patch`), so that the infection is recovered. New versions of the worm can appear; for this reason, recovered computers can become susceptible to infection again, after a while (`loss`). The object specification of the epidemic model is the following:

```
S := inf_ext.E + inf_sus.E
E := activate.I
I := patch.R
R := loss.S
```

The set of all actions occurring in object specification Δ is denoted by $\mathcal{A}_\Delta$. Similarly, the set of states is denoted by $\mathcal{S}_\Delta$, ranged over by $c, c', c_1 \cdots$. In Example 1, we have $\mathcal{A}_{\mathtt{EM}} = \{\mathtt{inf\_ext}, \mathtt{inf\_sus}, \mathtt{activate}, \mathtt{patch}, \mathtt{loss}\}$ and $\mathcal{S}_{\mathtt{EM}} = \{\mathtt{S}, \mathtt{E}, \mathtt{I}, \mathtt{R}\}$. A system is assumed composed of N interacting instances of an object. Interaction among objects is modelled probabilistically, as described below. Each action in $\mathcal{A}_\Delta$ is assigned a probability value, that may depend on the global state of the system. This is achieved by means of a *probability function definition*, that takes the following form: $a{::}E$, where $a \in \mathcal{A}_\Delta$ and E is an expression, i.e. an element of Exp, defined according to the following grammar:

$$E ::= v \mid \mathsf{frc}\, C \mid \langle \mathrm{uop} \rangle\, E \mid E\, \langle \mathrm{bop} \rangle\, E \mid (E)$$

where $v \in [0, 1]$ and for each state C, $\mathsf{frc}\, C$ denotes the fraction of objects, over the total number of objects N, in the system, that are currently in state C. Operators $\langle \mathrm{uop} \rangle$ and $\langle \mathrm{bop} \rangle$ are standard arithmetic unary and binary operators.

Example 2 (Probability function definitions). For the *epidemic model* of Example 1 we assign the following probability function definitions:

[5] For the purpose of the present paper, language expressivity is not a main concern.

```
inf_ext :: αe;
inf_sus :: αi * (frc I);
activate :: αa;
patch :: αr;
loss :: αs;
```

where α_e, α_i, α_a, α_r and α_s are model parameters in $[0,1]$, with $\alpha_e + \alpha_i \leq 1$.

A *system specification* is a triple $\langle \Delta, A, \mathbf{C}_0 \rangle^{(N)}$ where Δ is an object specification, A is a set of probability function definitions containing exactly one definition for each $a \in \mathcal{A}_\Delta$, and $\mathbf{C}_0 = \langle c_{0_1}, \ldots, c_{0_N} \rangle$ is the *initial system state*, with $c_{0_n} \in \mathcal{S}_\Delta$, for $n = 1 \ldots N$; we say that N is the *population size*[6]; in the sequel, we will omit the explicit indication of the size N in $\langle \Delta, A, \mathbf{C}_0 \rangle^{(N)}$, and elements thereof or related functions, writing simply $\langle \Delta, A, \mathbf{C}_0 \rangle$, when this cannot cause confusion.

Semantics. Let $\langle \Delta, A, \mathbf{C}_0 \rangle$ be a system specification. We associate with Δ the Labelled Transition System (LTS) $\langle \mathcal{S}_\Delta, \mathcal{A}_\Delta, \rightarrowtail \rangle$, where $\mathcal{S}_\Delta$ and $\mathcal{A}_\Delta$ are the states and labels of the LTS, respectively, and the transition relation $\rightarrowtail \subseteq \mathcal{S}_\Delta \times \mathcal{A}_\Delta \times \mathcal{S}_\Delta$ is the smallest relation induced by rule (1).

$$\frac{C := \sum_{j \in J} a_j.C_j \quad k \in J}{C \overset{a_k}{\rightarrowtail} C_k} \tag{1}$$

In the following we let $\mathcal{U}^S = \{\mathbf{m} \in [0,1]^S \mid \sum_{i=1}^S \mathbf{m}_{[i]} = 1\}$ be the unit simplex of dimension S; furthermore, we let $c, c', C, C' \ldots$ range over $\mathcal{S}_\Delta$ and for generic vector $\mathbf{v} = \langle v_1, \ldots, v_r \rangle$ we let $\mathbf{v}_{[j]}$ denote the j-th component v_j of $\mathbf{v}$, for $j = 1, \ldots, r$. A (system) *global state* is a tuple $\mathbf{C}^{(N)} \in \mathcal{S}_\Delta^N$. W.l.g., we assume that $\mathcal{S}_\Delta = \{C_1, \ldots, C_S\}$ and that a total order is defined on state constants $C_1, \ldots, C_S$ so that we can unambiguously associate each component of a vector $\mathbf{m} = \langle m_1, \ldots, m_S \rangle \in \mathcal{U}^S$ with a distinct element of $\{C_1, \ldots, C_S\}$. With each global state $\mathbf{C}^{(N)}$ an *occupancy measure* vector $\mathbf{M}^{(N)}(\mathbf{C}^{(N)}) \in \mathcal{U}^S$ is associated where $\mathbf{M}^{(N)}(\mathbf{C}^{(N)}) = \langle M_1^{(N)}, \ldots, M_S^{(N)} \rangle$ with

$$M_i^{(N)} = \frac{1}{N} \sum_{n=1}^{N} \mathbf{1}_{\{\mathbf{C}_{[n]}^{(N)} = C_i\}}$$

for $i = 1, \ldots, S$, and the value of $\mathbf{1}_{\{\alpha=\beta\}}$ is 1, if $\alpha = \beta$, and 0 otherwise.

A probability function definition $a{::}E$ associates a real value to action a by evaluating E in the current global state, via the interpretation function $\mathscr{E}$. In practice the occupancy measure representation of the state is used in $\mathscr{E}$.

The expressions interpretation function $\mathscr{E} : \mathrm{Exp} \to \mathcal{U}^S \to \mathbb{R}$ is defined as usual:

$$\mathscr{E}[\![v]\!]_{\mathbf{m}} = v$$
$$\mathscr{E}[\![\mathsf{frc}\, C_i]\!]_{\mathbf{m}} = \mathbf{m}_{[i]}$$

[6] Appropriate syntactical shorthands can be introduced for describing the initial state, e.g. $\langle \mathtt{S[2000]}, \mathtt{E[100]}, \mathtt{I[200]}, \mathtt{R[0]} \rangle$ for 2000 objects initially in state S etc.

$\mathscr{E}[\![\langle \text{uop} \rangle\, E]\!]_{\mathbf{m}} = \langle \text{uop} \rangle\, (\mathscr{E}[\![E]\!]_{\mathbf{m}})$
$\mathscr{E}[\![E_1 \,\langle \text{bop} \rangle\, E_2]\!]_{\mathbf{m}} = (\mathscr{E}[\![E_1]\!]_{\mathbf{m}})\,\langle \text{bop} \rangle\,(\mathscr{E}[\![E_2]\!]_{\mathbf{m}})$
$\mathscr{E}[\![(E)]\!]_{\mathbf{m}} = (\mathscr{E}[\![(E)]\!]_{\mathbf{m}})$

The set A of probability function definitions characterises a function π with type $\mathcal{U}^S \to \mathcal{A}_\Delta \to \mathbb{R}$ as follows: for each $a::E$ in A, we have $\pi(\mathbf{m}, a) = \mathscr{E}[\![E]\!]_{\mathbf{m}}$.

For a system specification of size N, we define the *object transition matrix* as follows: $\mathbf{K}^{(N)} : \mathcal{U}^S \times \mathcal{S}_\Delta \times \mathcal{S}_\Delta \to \mathbb{R}$, with

$$\mathbf{K}^{(N)}(\mathbf{m})_{c,c'} = \begin{cases} \sum_{a:c \overset{a}{\rightarrowtail} c'} \pi(\mathbf{m}, a), & \text{if } c \neq c', \\ 1 - \sum_{a \in I(c)} \pi(\mathbf{m}, a), & \text{if } c = c'. \end{cases} \tag{2}$$

where $I(c) = \{a \in \mathcal{A}_\Delta | \exists c' \in \mathcal{S}_\Delta : c \overset{a}{\rightarrowtail} c' \neq c\}$. We say that a state $c \in \mathcal{S}_\Delta$ is *probabilistic* in $\mathbf{m}$ if $0 \leq \sum_{a \in I^*(c)} \pi(\mathbf{m}, a) \leq 1$ where set $I^*(c)$ is defined as follows: $I^*(c) = I(c) \cup \{a \in \mathcal{A}_\Delta | c \overset{a}{\rightarrowtail} c\}$. Note that whenever all states in $\mathcal{S}_\Delta$ are probabilistic in $\mathbf{m}$, matrix $\mathbf{K}^{(N)}(\mathbf{m})$ is a one step transition probability matrix. We define the (system) *global state transition matrix* $\mathbf{S}^{(N)} : \mathcal{U}^S \times \mathcal{S}_\Delta^N \times \mathcal{S}_\Delta^N \to \mathbb{R}$, as

$$\mathbf{S}^{(N)}(\mathbf{m})_{\mathbf{C},\mathbf{C}'} = \Pi_{n=1}^N \mathbf{K}^{(N)}(\mathbf{m})_{\mathbf{C}_{[n]},\mathbf{C}'_{[n]}}.$$

Note that whenever all states in $\mathcal{S}_\Delta$ are probabilistic in $\mathbf{m}$, matrix $\mathbf{S}^N(\mathbf{m})$ is a one step transition probability matrix modelling a possible single step of the system as result of the parallel execution of a single step of each of the N instances of the object. In this case, the $S^N \times S^N$ matrix $\mathbf{P}^{(N)}$ with

$$\mathbf{P}^{(N)}_{\mathbf{C},\mathbf{C}'} = \mathbf{S}^{(N)}(\mathbf{M}^{(N)}(\mathbf{C}))_{\mathbf{C},\mathbf{C}'} \tag{3}$$

is the one-step transition matrix of a (finite state) DTMC, namely the DTMC of the system composed on N objects specified by Δ. In this case, we let $\mathbf{X}^{(N)}(t)$ denote the Markov process with transition probability matrix $\mathbf{P}^{(N)}$ as above and $\mathbf{X}^{(N)}(0) = \mathbf{C}_0^{(N)}$, i.e. with initial probability distribution $\boldsymbol{\delta}_{\mathbf{C}_0^{(N)}}$, where $\mathbf{C}_0^{(N)}$ is the initial system state and $\boldsymbol{\delta}_{\mathbf{C}_0^{(N)}}$ is the Dirac distribution with the total mass on $\mathbf{C}_0^{(N)}$. With a little bit of notational overloading, we define the 'occupancy measure DTMC' as $\mathbf{M}^{(N)}(t) = \mathbf{M}^{(N)}(\mathbf{X}^{(N)}(t))$; for $\mathbf{m} = \mathbf{M}^{(N)}(\mathbf{C})$, for some state $\mathbf{C}$ of DTMC $\mathbf{X}(t)$, we have:

$$\mathbb{P}\{\mathbf{M}^{(N)}(t+1) = \mathbf{m}' \mid \mathbf{M}^{(N)}(t) = \mathbf{m}\} = \sum_{\mathbf{C}':\mathbf{M}^{(N)}(\mathbf{C}')=\mathbf{m}'} \mathbf{P}^{(N)}_{\mathbf{C},\mathbf{C}'} \tag{4}$$

Note that the above definition is a good definition; in fact, if $\mathbf{M}^{(N)}(\mathbf{C}) = \mathbf{M}^{(N)}(\mathbf{C}'')$, then $\mathbf{C}$ and $\mathbf{C}''$ are just two permutations of the same local states. This implies that for all $\mathbf{C}'$ we have $\mathbf{P}^{(N)}_{\mathbf{C},\mathbf{C}'} = \mathbf{P}^{(N)}_{\mathbf{C}'',\mathbf{C}'}$.

PCTL local Model-checking. For the purpose of expressing system properties in PCTL, we partition the set of atomic propositions $\mathscr{P}$ into sets $\mathscr{P}_1$and $\mathscr{P}_g$. Given system specification $\langle \Delta, A, \mathbf{C}_0^{(N)} \rangle^{(N)}$, we extend it with a *state labelling function definition* that associates each state $c \in \mathcal{S}_\Delta$ with a (possibly empty) finite set $\ell_1(c)$ of propositions from $\mathscr{P}_1$. We extend ℓ_1 to global states with $\ell_1(\langle c_1, \ldots, c_N \rangle) = \ell_1(c_1)$; this way, we can express *local* properties of the first object in the system, in the *context* of the complete population[7]. In order to express also (a limited class of) *global* properties of the population, we use set $\mathscr{P}_g$. The system specification is further enriched by associating labels $a \in \mathscr{P}_g$ with expressions bexp in the class BExp of restricted boolean expressions. We assume a sublanguage of function specifications be given[8] and for function symbol F, $\mathscr{E}[\![F]\!]_{\mathbf{m}} : [0,1]^q \mapsto \mathbb{R}$ continuous in $[0,1]^q$, with $\mathscr{E}[\![F]\!]_{\mathbf{m}} = \mathscr{E}[\![F]\!]_{\mathbf{m}'}$ for all $\mathbf{m}, \mathbf{m}' \in \mathcal{U}^S$; then BExp is the set of expressions of the form $F(E_1, \ldots, E_q)\,\langle\text{relop}\rangle\, r$, where each E_j is of the form $\mathsf{frc}\, C$, $\langle\text{relop}\rangle \in \{>, <\}$, $r \in \mathbb{R}$ and $\mathscr{E}[\![F(E_1, \ldots, E_q)]\!]_{\mathbf{m}} = \mathscr{E}[\![F]\!]_{\mathbf{m}}(\mathscr{E}[\![E_1]\!]_{\mathbf{m}}, \ldots, \mathscr{E}[\![E_q]\!]_{\mathbf{m}})$.

We define the state global labelling function ℓ_g as

$$\ell_g(\langle c_1, \ldots, c_N \rangle) = \{a \in \mathscr{P}_g \mid \mathscr{E}[\![\text{bexp}_a]\!]_{\mathbf{M}^{(N)}(\langle c_1, \ldots, c_N \rangle)} = \text{tt}\}.$$

We obtain the state labelled DTMC $\mathcal{D}^{(N)}(t)$ from $\mathbf{X}^{(N)}(t)$, with transition matrix $\mathbf{P}^{(N)}$ above, by enriching it with labelling function $\ell_{\mathcal{D}^{(N)}}$ such that $\ell_{\mathcal{D}^{(N)}}(\mathbf{C}) = \ell_1(\mathbf{C}) \cup \ell_g(\mathbf{C})$.

The definition of $Paths_{\mathcal{D}^{(N)}}(\mathbf{C}^{(N)})$ as well as that of the satisfaction relation $\models_{\mathcal{D}^{(N)}}$ are obtained by instantiating those given in Sect. 3.1 to $\mathcal{D}^{(N)}$. For $\sigma \in Paths_{\mathcal{D}^{(N)}}(\mathbf{C}^{(N)})$, $\sigma[j]_{[n]}$ denotes the n-th local state of global state $\sigma[j]$.

For model-checking a system specification $\langle \Delta, A, \mathbf{C}_0^{(N)} \rangle^{(N)}$ we instantiate proc with[9] $\mathcal{S}_\Delta^N$ and lab with $\mathscr{P}_1 \cup \mathscr{P}_g$. Function next is instantiated to the function $\mathsf{next}_{\mathcal{D}^{(N)}}$, where

$$\mathsf{next}_{\mathcal{D}^{(N)}}(\mathbf{C}) = [(\mathbf{C}', p') \mid \mathbf{P}^{(N)}_{\mathbf{C},\mathbf{C}'} = p' > 0].$$

Given a vector $\mathbf{C}$, $\mathsf{next}_{\mathcal{D}^{(N)}}(\mathbf{C})$ computes a list corresponding to the positive elements of the row of matrix $\mathbf{P}^{(N)}$ associated with $\mathbf{C}$. Of course, only those elements of $\mathbf{P}^{(N)}$ that are necessary for $\mathsf{next}_{\mathcal{D}^{(N)}}$ are actually computed. Function $\mathsf{lab\_eval}$ is instantiated with the function $\mathsf{lab\_eval}_{\mathcal{D}^{(N)}} : \mathcal{S}_\Delta^N \times \mathcal{A}_\Delta \to \mathbb{B}$ with $\mathsf{lab\_eval}_{\mathcal{D}^{(N)}}(\mathbf{C}, a) = a \in \ell_{\mathcal{D}^{(N)}}(\mathbf{C})$.

Example 3 (Properties). For the epidemic model of Example 1 we can consider the following properties, where $i, e, r \in \mathscr{P}_1$ are labelling states I, E and R, respectively, and $LowInf \in \mathscr{P}_g$ is defined as $(\mathsf{frc}\, I) < 0.25$:

---

[7] Of course, the choice of the *first* object is purely conventional. Furthermore, all the results which in the present paper are stated w.r.t. the *first* object of a system, are easily extended to finite subsets of objects in the system. For the sake of notation, in the rest of the paper, we stick to the *first object* convention.

[8] The specific features of the sublanguage are not relevant for the purposes of the present paper and we leave their treatment out for the sake of simplicity.

[9] Strictly speaking, the relevant components of the algorithm are instantiated to *representations* of the terms, sets and functions mentioned in this section. For the sake of notational simplicity, we often use the same notation both for mathematical objects and for their representations.

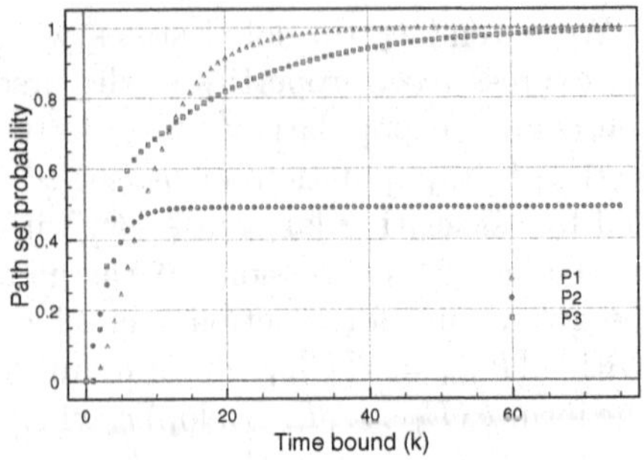

	PRISM	Exact on-the-fly
$P1$	$108.479s$	$29.587s$
$P2$	$51.816s$	$3.409s$
$P3$	$216.952s$	$85.579s$

Model parameter values:
$\alpha_e = 0.1$, $\alpha_i = 0.2$, $\alpha_r = 0.2$
$\alpha_a = 0.4$, $\alpha_s = 0.1$

Fig. 1. Exact model-checking results (left) and verification time (right).

P1 the worm will be active in the first component within k steps with a probability that is at most p: $\mathcal{P}_{\leq p}(\ true\ \mathcal{U}^{\leq k}\ i\ )$;

P2 the probability that the first component is infected, but latent, in the next k steps while the worm is active on less then 25% of the components is at most p: $\mathcal{P}_{\leq p}(LowInf\ \mathcal{U}^{\leq k}\ e\ )$;

P3 the probability to reach, within k steps, a configuration where the first component is not infected but the worm will be activated with probability greater than 0.3 within 5 steps is at most p:

$$\mathcal{P}_{\leq p}(\ true\ \mathcal{U}^{\leq k}\ (!e \wedge !i \wedge \mathcal{P}_{>0.3}(\ true\ \mathcal{U}^{\leq 5}\ i\ ))).$$

In Fig. 1 the result of exact PCTL model-checking of Example 1 is reported. On the left the probability of the set of paths that satisfy the path-formulae used in the three formulae above is shown for a system composed of eight objects each in initial state S, for k from 0 to 70. On the right the time needed to perform the analysis using PRISM [23] and using exact on-the-fly PCTL model checking are presented[10], showing that the latter has comparable performance. Worst-case complexity of both algorithms are also comparable. The local model-checker has been instantiated with the model defined by the (exact) operational semantics of the language, where each state $\mathbf{C} \in S_{\Delta}^{N}$ is a *global* system state. In Sect. 5 we instantiate the procedure with the mean-field, approximated, semantics of the language, leading to a scalable, 'fast', model-checker, insensitive to the population size.

5 Fast Mean-Field Model-Checking

Given a system specification $\langle \Delta, A, \mathbf{C}_0^{(N)} \rangle^{(N)}$ with initial state $\mathbf{C}_0$, we want to focus on the behaviour of the first object, starting in the initial state $\mathbf{C}_{0[1]}$,

[10] We use a $1.86GHz$ Intel Core 2 Duo with 4 GB. State space generation time of PRISM is not counted. The experiments are available at http://rap.dsi.unifi.it/~loreti/OFPMC/).

when in execution with all the other objects for (very) large population size N. We define a mapping $\mathcal{H}^{(N)} : \mathcal{S}_\Delta^N \to (\mathcal{S}_\Delta \times \mathcal{U}^S)$ such that $\mathcal{H}^{(N)}(\mathbf{C}^{(N)}) = \langle \mathbf{C}_{[1]}^{(N)}, \mathbf{M}^{(N)}(\mathbf{C}^{(N)})\rangle$. Note that $\mathcal{H}^{(N)}$ and $\mathcal{D}^{(N)}(t)$ together define a state labelled DTMC, denoted $\mathcal{HD}^{(N)}(t)$, and defined as $\mathcal{H}^{(N)}(\mathbf{X}^{(N)}(t))$, with $\ell_1(\langle c, \mathbf{m}\rangle) = \ell_1(c)$, $\ell_g(\langle c, \mathbf{m}\rangle) = \{a \in \mathscr{P}_g \mid \mathscr{E}[\![\mathrm{bexp}_a]\!]_{\mathbf{m}} = \mathrm{tt}\}$, and $\ell_{\mathcal{HD}^{(N)}}(\langle c, \mathbf{m}\rangle)$ defined as $\ell_1(\langle c, \mathbf{m}\rangle) \cup \ell_g(\langle c, \mathbf{m}\rangle)$, where $\mathscr{P}_1, \mathscr{P}_g$ and bexp_a are defined in a similar way as in Sect. 4. The one-step matrix of $\mathcal{HD}^{(N)}(t)$ is:

$$\mathbf{H}^{(N)}_{\langle c,\mathbf{m}\rangle,\langle c',\mathbf{m}'\rangle} = \sum_{\mathbf{C}':\mathcal{H}^{(N)}(\mathbf{C}')=\langle c',\mathbf{m}'\rangle} \mathbf{P}^{(N)}_{\mathbf{C},\mathbf{C}'} \tag{5}$$

where $\mathbf{C}$ is such that $\mathcal{H}^{(N)}(\mathbf{C}) = \langle c, \mathbf{m}\rangle$.[11] The definitions of paths for state $\langle c, \mathbf{m}\rangle$ of $\mathcal{HD}^{(N)}$, $Paths_{\mathcal{HD}^{(N)}}(\langle c, \mathbf{m}\rangle)$, of $L_{\mathcal{HD}^{(N)}}(t)$ and of the satisfaction relation $\models_{\mathcal{HD}^{(N)}}$ of PCTL formulas against $\mathcal{HD}^{(N)}(t)$, are obtained by instantiating the relevant definitions of Sect. 3.1 to the model $\mathcal{HD}^{(N)}(t)$. Furthermore, we let $L_{\mathcal{HD}^{(N)}}(t, c) = \{\langle c', \mathbf{m}'\rangle \in \mathrm{L}_{\mathcal{HD}^{(N)}}(t) \mid c' = c\}$.

We extend mapping $\mathcal{H}^{(N)}$ to sets and paths in the obvious way: for set X of states, let $\mathcal{H}^{(N)}(X) = \{\mathcal{H}^{(N)}(x) \mid x \in X\}$, and for $\sigma \in Paths_{\mathcal{D}^{(N)}}(\mathbf{C}^{(N)})$, let $\mathcal{H}^{(N)}(\sigma) = \mathcal{H}^{(N)}(\sigma[0])\mathcal{H}^{(N)}(\sigma[1])\mathcal{H}^{(N)}(\sigma[2])\cdots$

The following lemma relates the two interpretations of the logic, and can be easily proved by induction on formulae Φ [24].

Lemma 1. *For all $N > 0$, states $\mathbf{C}^{(N)}$ and formulas Φ the following holds: $\mathbf{C}^{(N)} \models_{\mathcal{D}^{(N)}} \Phi$ iff $\mathcal{H}^{(N)}(\mathbf{C}^{(N)}) \models_{\mathcal{HD}^{(N)}} \Phi$.* •

We now consider the stochastic process $\mathcal{HD}(t)$ defined below, for $c_0, c, c' \in \mathcal{S}_\Delta$, $\boldsymbol{\mu}_0, \mathbf{m}, \mathbf{m}' \in \mathcal{U}^S$ and function $\mathbf{K}(\mathbf{m})_{c,c'}$, continuous in $\mathbf{m}$:

$$\begin{aligned} &\mathbb{P}\{\mathcal{HD}(0) = \langle c, \mathbf{m}\rangle\} = \boldsymbol{\delta}_{\langle c_0, \boldsymbol{\mu}_0\rangle}(\langle c, \mathbf{m}\rangle), \\ &\mathbb{P}\{\mathcal{HD}(t+1) = \langle c', \mathbf{m}'\rangle \mid \mathcal{HD}(t) = \langle c, \mathbf{m}\rangle\} = \begin{cases} \mathbf{K}(\mathbf{m})_{c,c'}, & \text{if } \mathbf{m}' = \mathbf{m}\cdot\mathbf{K}(\mathbf{m}) \\ 0, & \text{otherwise.} \end{cases} \end{aligned} \tag{6}$$

The definition of the labeling function $\ell_{\mathcal{HD}}$ is the same as that of $\ell_{\mathcal{HD}^{(N)}}$. Note that $\mathcal{HD}$ is a DTMC with initial state $\langle c_0, \boldsymbol{\mu}_0\rangle$; memoryless-ness as well as time homogeneity directly follow from the definition of the process (6). The definitions of paths for state $\langle c, \mathbf{m}\rangle$ of $\mathcal{HD}$, $Paths_{\mathcal{HD}}(\langle c, \mathbf{m}\rangle)$, of $L_{\mathcal{HD}}(t)$ and of the satisfaction relation $\models_{\mathcal{HD}}$ of PCTL formulas against $\mathcal{HD}(t)$ are obtained by instantiating the relevant definitions of Sect. 3.1 to the model $\mathcal{HD}(t)$. Furthermore, define function $\boldsymbol{\mu}(t)$ as follows: $\boldsymbol{\mu}(0) = \boldsymbol{\mu}_0$ and $\boldsymbol{\mu}(t+1) = \boldsymbol{\mu}(t)\cdot\mathbf{K}(\boldsymbol{\mu}(t))$; then, for $t \geq 0$ and for $\langle c, \mathbf{m}\rangle \in L_{\mathcal{HD}}(t)$ we have $\mathbf{m} = \boldsymbol{\mu}(t)$.

In the following we use the fundamental result stated below, due to Le Boudec et al. [26].

Theorem 4.1 of [26] *Assume that for all $c, c' \in \mathcal{S}_\Delta$, there exists function* $\mathbf{K}(\mathbf{m})_{c,c'}$, continuous in $\mathbf{m}$, *such that, for $N \to \infty$, $\mathbf{K}^{(N)}(\mathbf{m})_{c,c'}$ converges*

[11] With a similar argument as for definition (4), noting that $\mathbf{M}^{(N)}(\mathbf{C}) = \mathbf{M}^{(N)}(\mathbf{C}'')$ and $\mathbf{C}_{[1]} = \mathbf{C}''_{[1]}$, it can be easily seen that also definition (5) is a good definition.

uniformly in $\mathbf{m}$ *to* $\mathbf{K}(\mathbf{m})_{c,c'}$. *Assume, furthermore, that there exists* $\boldsymbol{\mu}_0 \in \mathcal{U}^S$ *such that* $\mathbf{M}^{(N)}(\mathbf{C}_0^{(N)})$ *converges almost surely to* $\boldsymbol{\mu}_0$. *Define function* $\boldsymbol{\mu}(t)$ *of* t *as follows:* $\boldsymbol{\mu}(0) = \boldsymbol{\mu}_0$ *and* $\boldsymbol{\mu}(t+1) = \boldsymbol{\mu}(t) \cdot \mathbf{K}(\boldsymbol{\mu}(t))$. *Then, for any fixed* t, *almost surely* $\lim_{N\to\infty} \mathbf{M}^{(N)}(t) = \boldsymbol{\mu}(t)$. •

Remark 1. We observe that, as direct consequence of Theorem 4.1 of [26] and of the restrictions on the definition of BExp, for any fixed t and for all $\epsilon > 0$, there exists $\bar{N}$ such that, for all $N \geq \bar{N}$, almost surely

$$| \mathscr{E}[\![\mathrm{bexp}]\!]_{\mathbf{m}} - \mathscr{E}[\![\mathrm{bexp}]\!]_{\boldsymbol{\mu}(t)} | < \epsilon$$

for all $\langle c, \mathbf{m}\rangle \in L_{\mathcal{HD}^{(N)}}(t)$ and bexp $\in$ BExp. In other words, for N large enough and $\langle c, \mathbf{m}\rangle \in L_{\mathcal{HD}^{(N)}}(t)$, $\ell_g(\langle c, \mathbf{m}\rangle) = \ell_g(\langle c, \boldsymbol{\mu}(t)\rangle)$, and, consequently, $\ell(\langle c, \mathbf{m}\rangle) = \ell(\langle c, \boldsymbol{\mu}(t)\rangle)$. •

In the rest of the paper we will focus on sequences $\left(\langle \Delta, A, \mathbf{C}_0\rangle^{(N)}\right)_{N\geq N_0}$ of system specifications, for some $N_0 > 0$. In particular, we will consider only sequences $\left(\mathcal{HD}^{(N)}(t)\right)_{N\geq N_0}$ such that for all $N \geq N_0$, $\mathbf{C_0}_{[1]}^{(N)} = \mathbf{C_0}_{[1]}^{(N_0)}$; in other words we want the population size increase with N, while the (initial state of the) first object of the system is left unchanged.

Let us now go back to process $\mathcal{HD}(t)$, where, in Eq. (6) we use function $\mathbf{K}(\mathbf{m})_{c,c'}$ of the hypothesis of the theorem recalled above; similarly, for the initial distribution we use $\boldsymbol{\delta}_{\langle \mathbf{C}_{0[1]}^{(N)}, \boldsymbol{\mu}(0)\rangle}$.

The following is a corollary of Theorem 4.1 and Theorem 5.1 (Fast simulation) presented in [26], when considering sequences $\left(\mathcal{HD}^{(N)}(t)\right)_{N\geq N_0}$ as above (see also Remark 1):

Corollary 1. *Under the assumptions of Theorem 4.1 of [26], for any fixed* t, *almost surely,* $\lim_{N\to\infty} \mathcal{HD}^{(N)}(t) = \mathcal{HD}(t)$. •

Remark 2. A consequence of Corollary 1 is that, under the assumptions of Theorem 4.1 of [26], for any fixed t, almost surely, for N to ∞, we have that, for all $\langle c, \mathbf{m}\rangle \in L_{\mathcal{HD}^{(N)}}(t, c)$ and $c' \in \mathcal{S}_\Delta$, $\sum_{\langle c', \mathbf{m}'\rangle : L_{\mathcal{HD}^{(N)}}(t+1, c')} \mathbf{H}^{(N)}_{\langle c,\mathbf{m}\rangle,\langle c',\mathbf{m}'\rangle}$ approaches $\mathbf{K}(\boldsymbol{\mu}(t))_{c,c'}$, i.e. for all $\epsilon > 0$ there exists N_0 s.t. for all $N \geq N_0$

$$\left| \left(\sum_{\langle c', \mathbf{m}'\rangle : L_{\mathcal{HD}^{(N)}}(t+1, c')} \mathbf{H}^{(N)}_{\langle c,\mathbf{m}\rangle,\langle c',\mathbf{m}'\rangle} \right) - \mathbf{K}(\boldsymbol{\mu}(t))_{c,c'} \right| < \epsilon$$

•

In the sequel we state the main theorem of the present paper, that relies on the notion of *formulae safety*, with w.r.t. $\mathcal{HD}(t)$: a formula Φ is *safe* for a model $\mathcal{M}$ iff for all sub-formulae Φ' of Φ and states s of $\mathcal{M}$, if Φ' is of the form $\mathcal{P}_{\bowtie p}(\varphi)$ then $\mathbb{P}\{\eta \in Paths_{\mathcal{M}}(s) \mid \eta \models_{\mathcal{M}} \varphi\} \neq p$.

The theorem, together with Theorem 1 and Lemma 1, establishes the formal relationship between the satisfaction relation on the exact semantics of the language and that on its mean-field approximation, thus justifying the fast local model-checking instantiation we will show in the sequel.

Theorem 2. *Under the assumptions of Theorem 4.1 of [26], for all safe formulas Φ, for any fixed t and $\mathcal{H}^{(N)}(\mathbf{C}^{(N)}) \in L_{\mathcal{HD}^{(N)}}(t)$, almost surely, for N large enough, $\mathcal{H}^{(N)}(\mathbf{C}^{(N)}) \models_{\mathcal{HD}^{(N)}} \Phi$ iff $\langle \mathbf{C}^{(N)}_{[1]}, \boldsymbol{\mu}(t)\rangle \models_{\mathcal{HD}} \Phi$.* •

Proof. The proof is carried out by induction on Φ; in the proof we write $\mathbf{C}$ instead of $\mathbf{C}^{(N)}$ for the sake of readability.

For brevity, we show only the case for $\mathcal{P}_{\bowtie p}(\mathcal{X}\ \Phi)$; for the complete proof we refer to [24]. By definition of $\models_{\mathcal{HD}^{(N)}}$ and $\models_{\mathcal{HD}}$, we have to show that, for any fixed t and $\mathcal{H}^{(N)}(\mathbf{C}) \in L_{\mathcal{HD}^{(N)}}(t)$, a.s., for N large enough,

$$\mathbb{P}\{\rho \in Paths_{\mathcal{HD}^{(N)}}(\mathcal{H}^{(N)}(\mathbf{C})) \mid \rho \models_{\mathcal{HD}^{(N)}} \mathcal{X}\ \Phi\} \bowtie p$$

iff

$$\mathbb{P}\{\eta \in Paths_{\mathcal{HD}}(\langle \mathbf{C}_{[1]}, \boldsymbol{\mu}(t)\rangle) \mid \eta \models_{\mathcal{HD}} \mathcal{X}\ \Phi\} \bowtie p.$$

Below, we actually prove that, for any fixed t and $\mathcal{H}^{(N)}(\mathbf{C}) \in L_{\mathcal{HD}^{(N)}}(t)$, a.s., for N large enough, the probabilities of the two sets of paths are approaching each other, which implies the assert.

$\mathbb{P}\{\rho \in Paths_{\mathcal{HD}^{(N)}}(\mathcal{H}^{(N)}(\mathbf{C})) \mid \rho \models_{\mathcal{HD}^{(N)}} \mathcal{X}\ \Phi\}$ is defined as

$$p_{\mathbf{H}}^{(N)} = \sum_{\mathcal{H}^{(N)}(\mathbf{C}'):\mathcal{H}^{(N)}(\mathbf{C}')\models_{\mathcal{HD}^{(N)}}\Phi} \mathbf{H}^{(N)}_{\mathcal{H}^{(N)}(\mathbf{C}),\mathcal{H}^{(N)}(\mathbf{C}')} \tag{7}$$

and $\mathbb{P}\{\eta \in Paths_{\mathcal{HD}}(\langle \mathbf{C}_{[1]}, \boldsymbol{\mu}(t)\rangle) \mid \eta \models_{\mathcal{HD}} \mathcal{X}\ \Phi\}$ is defined as

$$p(t)_{\mathbf{K}} = \sum_{\mathbf{C}'_{[1]}:\langle \mathbf{C}'_{[1]},\boldsymbol{\mu}(t+1)\rangle\models_{\mathcal{HD}}\Phi} \mathbf{K}(\boldsymbol{\mu}(t))_{\mathbf{C}_{[1]},\mathbf{C}'_{[1]}}. \tag{8}$$

The I.H. ensures that, a.s., for $N \geq \bar{N}_{\mathbf{C}'}$, $\mathcal{H}^{(N)}(\mathbf{C}') \models_{\mathcal{HD}^{(N)}} \Phi$ if and only if $\langle \mathbf{C}'_{[1]}, \boldsymbol{\mu}(t+1)\rangle \models_{\mathcal{HD}} \Phi$, with $\mathcal{H}^{(N)}(\mathbf{C}') \in L_{\mathcal{HD}^{(N)}}(t+1)$. In particular, it holds that, for any specific value $\bar{c}$ of $\mathbf{C}'_{[1]}$ above and $\mathcal{H}^{(N)}(\mathbf{C}') \in L_{\mathcal{HD}^{(N)}}(t+1,\bar{c})$, $\mathcal{H}^{(N)}(\mathbf{C}') \models_{\mathcal{HD}^{(N)}} \Phi$ if and only if $\langle \bar{c}, \boldsymbol{\mu}(t+1)\rangle \models_{\mathcal{HD}} \Phi$, that is: either *all* elements of $L_{\mathcal{HD}^{(N)}}(t+1,\bar{c})$ satisfy Φ or *none* of them does it. Furthermore, for such $\bar{c}$, by Corollary 1, for all $\epsilon_{\bar{c}} > 0$ there exists $N_{\bar{c}}$ s.t. for all $N \geq N_{\bar{c}}$

$$\left| \left(\sum_{\langle \bar{c},\overline{\mathbf{m}}\rangle:L_{\mathcal{HD}^{(N)}}(t+1,\bar{c})} \mathbf{H}^{(N)}_{\mathcal{H}^{(N)}(\mathbf{C}),\langle \bar{c},\overline{\mathbf{m}}\rangle} \right) - \mathbf{K}(\boldsymbol{\mu}(t))_{\mathbf{C}_{[1]},\bar{c}} \right| < \epsilon_{\bar{c}}$$

(see Remark 2). So, for any $\epsilon > 0$ there exists an $\hat{N}$ larger than any of such $\bar{N}_{\mathbf{C}'}$ and $N_{\bar{c}}$, such that for all $N \geq \hat{N}$ $\left|p_{\mathbf{H}}^{(N)} - p(t)_{\mathbf{K}}\right| < \epsilon$ i.e. the value $p_{\mathbf{H}}^{(N)}$ of sum (7) approaches the value $p(t)_{\mathbf{K}}$ of sum (8). Finally, safety of $\mathcal{P}_{\bowtie p}(\mathcal{X}\ \Phi)$, implies that the value $p(t)_{\mathbf{K}}$ of (8) is different from p. If $p(t)_{\mathbf{K}} > p$ then we can choose ϵ small enough that also $p_{\mathbf{H}}^{(N)} > p$ and, similarly, if $p(t)_{\mathbf{K}} < p$, we get also $p_{\mathbf{H}}^{(N)} < p$, which proves the assert. □

Finally, using Lemma 1 we get the following

Corollary 2. *Under the assumptions of Theorem 4.1 of [26], for all safe formulas Φ, for any fixed t and $\mathbf{C}^{(N)} \in L_{\mathcal{D}^{(N)}}(t)$, almost surely, for N large enough $\mathbf{C}^{(N)} \models_{\mathcal{D}^{(N)}} \Phi$ iff $\langle \mathbf{C}_{[1]}^{(N)}, \boldsymbol{\mu}(t)\rangle \models_{\mathcal{HD}} \Phi$.* •

Fast local model-checking. On-the-fly *fast* PCTL model-checking on the limit DTMC $\mathcal{HD}(t)$ is obtained by instantiating proc with $\mathcal{S}_{\Delta} \times \mathcal{U}^{S}$ and lab with $\mathscr{P}_1 \cup \mathscr{P}_g$; next is instantiated with $\mathsf{next}_{\mathcal{HD}}$ defined as follows:

$$\mathsf{next}_{\mathcal{HD}}(\langle c, \mathbf{m}\rangle) = [(\langle c', \mathbf{m}\cdot \mathbf{K}(\mathbf{m})\rangle, p') \mid \mathbf{K}(\mathbf{m})_{c,c'} = p' > 0],$$

with $\mathbf{K}(\mathbf{m})_{c,c'}$ as in Theorem 4.1 of [26]; lab_eval is instantiated as expected: $\mathsf{lab\_eval}_{\mathcal{HD}}(\langle c, \mathbf{m}\rangle, a) = a \in \ell_{\mathcal{HD}}(\langle c, \mathbf{m}\rangle)$. The instantiation is implemented in FlyFast.

Remark 3. Although in the hypothesis of the theorem we require formulae safety, for all practical purposes, it is actually sufficient to require that

$$\mathbb{P}\{\eta \in Paths_{\mathcal{HD}}(s') \mid \eta \models_{\mathcal{HD}} \varphi\} \neq p$$

for all formulae $\mathcal{P}_{\bowtie p}(\varphi)$ and states s' such that $\mathsf{CheckPath}(s', \varphi)$ is computed during the execution of $\mathsf{Check}(s, \Phi)$ (see Table 2). This (weaker) safety check is readily added to the algorithm. •

Example 4 (FlyFast *results*). Figure 2 shows the result of FlyFast on the model of Example 1 for the first object of a large population of objects, each initially in state S. In Fig. 2 (left) the same properties are considered as in Example 3. The analysis takes less than a second and is *insensitive* to the total population size. Fig. 2 (right) shows how the probability measure of the set of paths satisfying formula $true\ \mathcal{U}^{\leq k}\ (!e \wedge !i \wedge \mathcal{P}_{>0.3}(\ true\ \mathcal{U}^{\leq 5}\ i\ ))$ of property $P3$ on page 12, (for $k = 3$), changes for initial time $t0$ varying from 0 to 10.

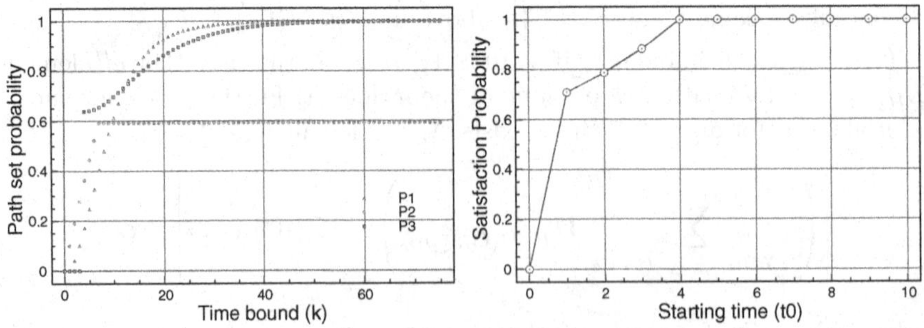

Fig. 2. Fast model-checking results.

6 Conclusions and Future Work

In this paper we have presented a fast PCTL model-checking approach that builds upon *local, on-the-fly* model-checking and *mean-field* approximation, allowing for scalable analysis of selected objects in the context of very large systems. The model-checking algorithm is parametric w.r.t. the specific semantic model of interest. We presented related correctness results, an example of application of a prototype implementation and briefly discussed complexity of the algorithm. The results can be trivially extended in order to consider multiple selected objects. Following approaches similar to those presented in [26], we plan to extend our work to heterogeneous systems and systems with memory. We are interested in extensions that address spatial distribution of objects as well as more expressive logics, combining local and global properties, and languages (e.g. [22,27]) and to study the exact relation between mean field convergence results for continuous interleaving models and discrete, time-synchronous ones.

References

1. Aziz, A., Sanwal, K., Singhal, V., Brayton, R.: Model checking continuous time Markov chains. ACM Trans. Comput. Logic **1**(1), 162–170 (2000)
2. Baier, C., Haverkort, B., Hermanns, H., Katoen, J.P.: Model-checking algorithms for continuous-time Markov chains. IEEE Trans. Softw. Eng. **29**(6), 524–541 (2003). IEEE CS
3. Bakhshi, R., Endrullis, J., Endrullis, S., Fokkink, W., Haverkort, B.: Automating the mean-field method for large dynamic gossip networks. In: QEST 2010, pp. 241–250. IEEE Computer Society (2010)
4. Benaïm, M., Le Boudec, J.Y.: A class of mean field interaction models for computer and communication systems. Perform. Eval. **65**(11–12), 823–838 (2008)
5. Bhat, G., Cleaveland, R., Grumberg, O.: Efficient on-the-fly model checking for CTL*. In: LICS, pp. 388–397. IEEE Computer Society (1995)
6. Bortolussi, L., Hillston, J.: Fluid model checking. In: Koutny, M., Ulidowski, I. (eds.) CONCUR. LNCS, vol. 7454, pp. 333–347. Springer, Heidelberg (2012)
7. Bortolussi, L., Hillston, J., Latella, D., Massink, M.: Continuous approximation of collective system behaviour: a tutorial. Perform. Eval. **70**(5), 317–349 (2013). http://www.sciencedirect.com/science/article/pii/S0166531613000023
8. Bradley, J.T., Gilmore, S.T., Hillston, J.: Analysing distributed internet worm attacks using continuous state-space approximation of process algebra models. J. Comput. Syst. Sci. **74**(6), 1013–1032 (2008)
9. Chaintreau, A., Le Boudec, J.Y., Ristanovic, N.: The age of gossip: spatial mean field regime. In: Douceur, J.R., Greenberg, A.G., Bonald, T., Nieh, J. (eds.) SIGMETRICS/Performance, pp. 109–120. ACM, Seattle (2009)
10. Clarke, E.M., Emerson, E.A., Sistla, A.P.: Automatic verification of finite-state concurrent systems using temporal logic specifications. ACM Trans. Program. Lang. Syst. **8**(2), 244–263 (1986)
11. Courcoubetis, C., Vardi, M., Wolper, P., Yannakakis, M.: Memory-efficient algorithms for the verification of temporal properties. Form. Methods Syst. Des. **1**(2–3), 275–288 (1992)

12. Darling, R., Norris, J.: Differential equation approximations for Markov chains. Probab. Surv. **5**, 37–79 (2008)
13. Della Penna, G., Intrigila, B., Melatti, I., Tronci, E., Zilli, M.V.: Bounded probabilistic model checking with the murφ verifier. In: Hu, A.J., Martin, A.K. (eds.) FMCAD 2004. LNCS, vol. 3312, pp. 214–229. Springer, Heidelberg (2004)
14. Gast, N., Gaujal, B.: A mean field model of work stealing in large-scale systems. In: Misra, V., Barford, P., Squillante, M.S. (eds.) SIGMETRICS. pp. 13–24. ACM (2010)
15. Gnesi, S., Mazzanti, F.: An abstract, on the fly framework for the verification of service oriented systems. In: Wirsing, M., Hölzl, M. (eds.) SENSORIA. LNCS, vol. 6582, pp. 390–407. Springer, Heidelberg (2011)
16. Guirado, G., Hérault, T., Lassaigne, R., Peyronnet, S.: Distribution, approximation and probabilistic model checking. Electr. Notes Theor. Comput. Sci. **135**(2), 19–30 (2006). http://dx.doi.org/10.1016/j.entcs.2005.10.016
17. Hahn, E.M., Hermanns, H., Wachter, B., Zhang, L.: INFAMY: an infinite-state Markov model checker. In: Bouajjani, A., Maler, O. (eds.) CAV 2009. LNCS, vol. 5643, pp. 641–647. Springer, Heidelberg (2009)
18. Hansson, H., Jonsson, B.: A logic for reasoning about time and reliability. Formal Aspects Comput. **6**, 512–535 (1994)
19. Hérault, T., Lassaigne, R., Magniette, F., Peyronnet, S.: Approximate probabilistic model checking. In: Steffen, B., Levi, G. (eds.) VMCAI 2004. LNCS, vol. 2937, pp. 73–84. Springer, Heidelberg (2004)
20. Holzmann, G.J.: The SPIN Model Checker: Primer and Reference Manual. Addison-Wesley, Reading (2004)
21. Kolesnichenko, A., Remke, A., de Boer, P.T.: A logic for model-checking of mean-field models. Technical report TR-CTIT-12-11. http://doc.utwente.nl/80267/ (2012)
22. Kolesnichenko, A., Remke, A., de Boer, P.T.: A logic for model-checking of mean-field models. In: Dependable Systems and Networks DSN13 (2013)
23. Kwiatkowska, M., Norman, G., Parker, D.: Probabilistic symbolic model checking using PRISM: a Hybrid approach. STTT **6**(2), 128–142 (2004)
24. Latella, D., Loreti, M., Massink, M.: On-the-fly fast mean-field model-checking: full version. Technical report. http://arxiv.org/abs/1312.3416 (2013)
25. Latella, D., Loreti, M., Massink, M.: On-the-fly probabilistic model-checking: full version. Technical report. http://goo.gl/uVkPP6/ (2013)
26. Le Boudec, J.Y., McDonald, D., Mundinger, J.: A generic mean field convergence result for systems of interacting objects. In: QEST07. pp. 3–18. IEEE Computer Society Press (2007). ISBN 978-0-7695-2883-0
27. McCaig, C., Norman, R., Shankland, C.: From individuals to populations: a mean field semantics for process algebra. Theor. Comput. Sci. **412**(17), 1557–1580 (2011)
28. Montes de Oca, M.A., Ferrante, E., Scheidler, A., Pinciroli, C., Birattari, M., Dorigo, M.: Majority-rule opinion dynamics with differential latency: a mechanism for self-organized collective decision-making. Swarm Intell. **5**(3–4), 305–327 (2011)
29. Stefanek, A., Hayden, R.A., Bradley, J.T.: A new tool for the performance analysis of massively parallel computer systems. In: QAPL 2010. EPTCS, vol. 28. pp. 159–181 (2010)

Group-by-Group Probabilistic Bisimilarities and Their Logical Characterizations

Marco Bernardo[1], Rocco De Nicola[2], and Michele Loreti[3](✉)

[1] Dipartimento di Scienze di Base e Fondamenti, Università di Urbino, Urbino, Italy
[2] IMT, Institute for Advanced Studies Lucca, Lucca, Italy
[3] Dipartimento di Statistica, Informatica, Applicazioni, Università di Firenze, Firenze, Italy
michele.loreti@unifi.it

Abstract. We provide two interpretations, over nondeterministic and probabilistic processes, of PML, the probabilistic version of Hennessy-Milner logic used by Larsen and Skou to characterize bisimilarity of probabilistic processes without internal nondeterminism. We also exhibit two new bisimulation-based equivalences, which are in full agreement with the two different interpretations of PML. The new equivalences are coarser than the bisimilarity for nondeterministic and probabilistic processes proposed by Segala and Lynch, which instead is in agreement with a version of Hennessy-Milner logic extended with an additional probabilistic operator interpreted over state distributions rather than over individual states. The modal logic characterizations provided for the new equivalences thus offer a uniform framework for reasoning on purely nondeterministic processes, reactive probabilistic processes, and nondeterministic and probabilistic processes.

1 Introduction

Modal logics and behavioral equivalences play a key rôle in the specification and verification of concurrent systems. The former are useful for model checking, in that they can be employed for specifying the properties to be verified. The latter are ancillary to the former, in the sense that they enable the transformation/minimization of the models to be checked while guaranteeing that specific properties are preserved.

Because of this, whenever a new behavioral relation is proposed, the quest starts for the associated modal logic, i.e., for a logic such that two systems are behaviorally equivalent if and only if they satisfy the same logical formulae. The first result along this line is due to Hennessy and Milner [13]. They showed that *bisimilarity* over *fully nondeterministic processes*, modeled as a labeled transition system (LTS) [16], is in full agreement with a very simple modal logic, now known as HML. This logic has only four operators: true, $\cdot \wedge \cdot$, $\neg \cdot$, and $\langle a \rangle \cdot$, the last one

Work partially supported by the FP7-IST-FET Project ASCENS, grant no. 257414, and the MIUR-PRIN Project CINA.

M. Abadi and A. Lluch Lafuente (Eds.): TGC 2013, LNCS 8358, pp. 315–330, 2014.
DOI: 10.1007/978-3-319-05119-2_18,

called *diamond* and used to describe the existence of a-labeled transitions. After this result, whenever any of the many quantitative variants of process description languages and process models has been introduced, other behavioral equivalences and modal logics have been defined and analogous results have been established to handle features such as probability and time.

Most of the works along the lines outlined above take as starting point a behavioral equivalence and then look for the logic in agreement with it. Obviously, it is also interesting, once one has fixed a model and a logic to reason about it, to find out the "right" behavioral relation. A first work in this direction was [5]; it showed that bisimilarity and stuttering bisimilarity are, respectively, in full agreement with the logical equivalences induced by CTL* and by CTL* without the next-time operator when interpreted over Kripke structures (state-labeled transition systems) [6]. In a subsequent work, it was shown that the equivalence induced by the probabilistic temporal logic PCTL*, interpreted over probabilistic Kripke structures, coincides with probabilistic bisimilarity [1]. A more recent work is [26], which introduces new probabilistic bisimilarities that are in full agreement with the logical equivalences induced by PCTL, PCTL*, and their variants without the next-time operator interpreted over nondeterministic and probabilistic Kripke structures [4].

In this paper, we concentrate on the results obtained for extended LTS models that have been developed to deal with *probabilistic systems*. We look for bisimilarities that are in agreement with a probabilistic variant of HML known as PML [17,18]. This logic is obtained by simply decorating the diamond operator with a probability bound. Formula $\langle a \rangle_p \phi$ is satisfied by state s if an a-labeled transition is possible from s after which a set of states satisfying ϕ is reached with probability at least p.

Modal logic characterizations for probabilistic bisimilarities have been studied for the first time by Larsen and Skou [17,18]. They introduced a probabilistic bisimilarity for *reactive probabilistic processes* [28] and showed that the considered probabilistic bisimilarity is in full agreement with PML. Subsequently, Desharnais et al. [10] showed that PML without negation is sufficient to characterize probabilistic bisimilarity for the same class of processes. Reactive probabilistic processes being LTS-based models where (i) every action-labeled transition reaches a probability distribution over states and (ii) the actions labeling transitions departing from the same state are all different from each other.

Segala and Lynch [23] defined, instead, a probabilistic bisimilarity for a more expressive model that also admits *internal nondeterminism*, i.e., the possibility for a state to have several outgoing transitions labeled with the same action. For this probabilistic bisimilarity over *nondeterministic and probabilistic processes*, Segala and collaborators [14,19] exhibited a logical characterization in terms of an extension of HML, in which formulae satisfaction is defined over *probability distributions on states* rather than over single states. The logic is obtained from HML by giving the diamond operator a universal interpretation (all states in the support of a distribution must satisfy the formula) and by adding a unary operator $[\cdot]_p$ such that $[\phi]_p$ is true on a state distribution whenever the probability of the set of states that satisfy formula ϕ is at least p. Recently, Crafa and Ranzato [7] showed an equivalent formulation of the logic that retrieves the HML interpretation of the diamond operator by lifting the transition relation to state distributions. Following a similar lifting, Hennessy [12] proposed an alternative logical characterization based on what he calls pHML, where a binary operator $\cdot \oplus_p \cdot$ is added to HML (instead of the unary operator $[\cdot]_p$) such that $\phi_1 \oplus_p \phi_2$ asserts decomposability of a state distribution to satisfy the two subformulae.

Now, the difference between PML and the two probabilistic extensions of HML in [19] and [12] is quite striking. It is thus interesting to understand whether such a difference is due to the different expressive power of the models in [17] and [23] – i.e., the absence or the presence of internal nondeterminism – or to the way probabilistic bisimilarity was defined on those two models. Since in [19] it was shown that PML characterizes the probabilistic bisimilarity over processes *alternating* nondeterminism and probability defined in [11,20], we feel it is worth exploring alternative definitions of probabilistic bisimilarity rather than alternative models.

The aim of this paper is to show that it is possible to define new probabilistic bisimilarities for *non-alternating* nondeterministic and probabilistic processes [22] that are characterized by PML. Our result is somehow similar to the one established in [26], where new probabilistic bisimilarities over nondeterministic and probabilistic Kripke structures were exhibited that are characterized by PCTL and its variants. In both cases, the starting point for defining the new probabilistic bisimilarities is the consideration (see also [8]) that sometimes the definition of Segala and Lynch [23] might be over discriminating and thus differentiate processes that, according to intuition, should be identified.

Indeed, to compare systems where both nondeterminism and probabilistic choices coexist, in [22,23] the notion of *scheduler* (or *adversary*) is used to resolve internal nondeterminism. A scheduler can be viewed as an external entity that selects the next action to perform according to the current state and the past history. When a scheduler is applied to a system, a fully probabilistic model called a *resolution* is obtained. The basic idea is deeming equivalent two systems if and only if for each resolution of one system (the *challenger*) there exists a resolution of the other (the *defender*) such that the two resolutions are probabilistic bisimilar in the sense of [17] (*fully matching resolutions*).

Let us consider two scenarios modeling the offer to Player1 and Player2 of three differently biased dice. The game is conceived in such a way that if the outcome of a throw gives 1 or 2 then Player1 wins, while if the outcome is 5 or 6 Player2 wins. In case of 3 or 4, the result is a draw. The two scenarios are reported in Fig. 1. For instance, with the biased die associated with the leftmost branch of the first scenario, it happens that 3 or 4 (draw) will appear with probability 0.4, while 1 or 2 (Player1 wins) will appear with probability 0.6. Numbers 5 and 6 will never appear (no chance for Player2 to win).

The probabilistic bisimilarity proposed in [23] differentiates the models in Fig. 1 even if in both scenarios each player has the *same set of probabilities* of winning/drawing/losing, which is $\{0.6, 0.4, 0\}$. To identify these systems, from a

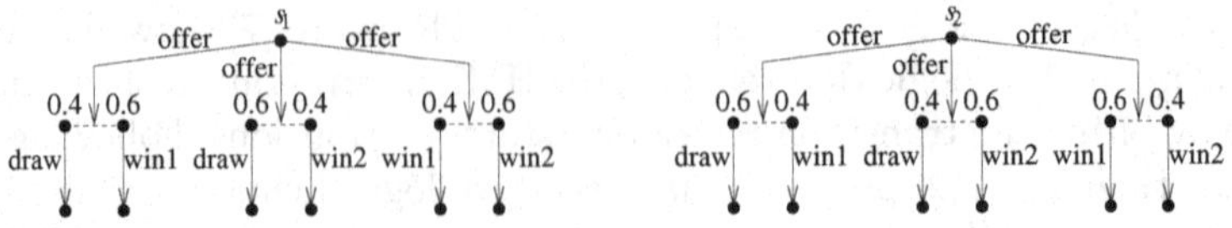

Fig. 1. Two games guaranteeing the same winning probabilities ($\sim_{\text{PB,gbg},=}$).

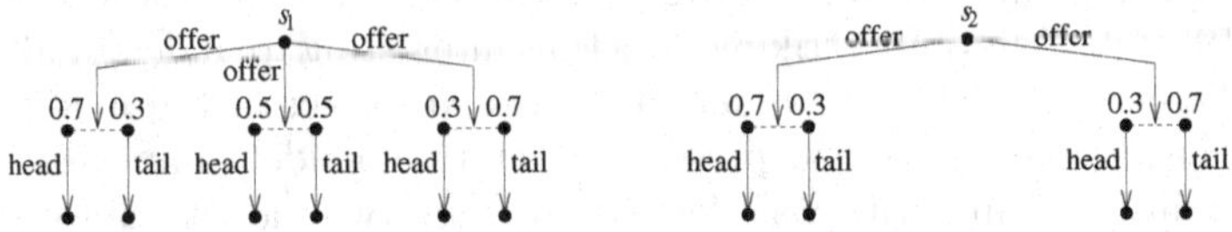

Fig. 2. Two games guaranteeing the same extremal head/tail probabilities ($\sim_{\text{PB,gbg},\leq}$).

bisimulation perspective it is needed to weaken the impact of schedulers. Indeed, while in [23] the challenger and the defender must stepwise behave the same along two fully matching resolutions, here, in the same vein as [27], we admit bisimulation games with *partially matching resolutions*.

Other two systems differentiated (under deterministic schedulers) by the probabilistic bisimilarity in [23] are those in Fig. 2. In the first scenario, the two players are offered a choice among a fair coin and two biased ones. In the second scenario, the players can simply choose between the two biased coins of the former scenario. In both scenarios, Player1 wins with head while Player2 wins with tail. In our view, the two scenarios could be identified if what matters is that in both of them each player has exactly the *same extremal – i.e., minimal and maximal – probabilities* of winning (0.3 and 0.7).

The first probabilistic bisimilarity we will introduce – denoted by $\sim_{\text{PB,gbg},=}$ – identifies the two systems in Fig. 1, but distinguishes those in Fig. 2. Our second probabilistic bisimilarity – denoted by $\sim_{\text{PB,gbg},\leq}$ – instead identifies both the two systems in Fig. 1 and the two systems in Fig. 2. Notably, the same identifications are induced by one of the probabilistic bisimilarities in [26]. Indeed, once the appropriate transformations (eliminating actions from transitions and labeling each state with the set of possible next-actions) are applied to get nondeterministic and probabilistic Kripke structures from the four systems in Figs. 1 and 2, we have that no PCTL* formula distinguishes the two systems in Fig. 1 and the two systems in Fig. 2. However, it is worth pointing out that neither $\sim_{\text{PB,gbg},=}$ nor $\sim_{\text{PB,gbg},\leq}$ coincides with the probabilistic bisimilarities in [26].

We shall show that $\sim_{\text{PB,gbg},\leq}$ is precisely characterized by the original PML as defined by Larsen and Skou [17,18], with the original interpretation of the diamond operator: state s satisfies $\langle a \rangle_p \phi$ if s has an a-transition that reaches with probability at least p a set of states satisfying ϕ. In contrast, $\sim_{\text{PB,gbg},=}$ is characterized by a variant of PML having an interval-based operator $\langle a \rangle_{[p_1,p_2]}\cdot$ instead of $\langle a \rangle_p\cdot$: state s satisfies $\langle a \rangle_{[p_1,p_2]}\phi$ if s has an a-transition that reaches with probability between p_1 and p_2 a set of states satisfying ϕ. We shall refer to the interpretation of these two diamond operators as *existential* because it simply requires that there exists a way to resolve internal nondeterminism that guarantees satisfaction of formula ϕ within a certain probability range.

For both logics, we shall also provide an alternative interpretation of the diamond operator, which is inspired by the actual interpretation of PCTL* in [4]. We shall call *universal* this interpretation that might appear more appropriate in a nondeterministic and probabilistic setting. With this interpretation, state s satisfies $\langle a \rangle_p \phi$ (resp. $\langle a \rangle_{[p_1,p_2]} \phi$) if it has an a-transition that enjoys the same property as before and each a-transition departing from s enjoys that property, meaning that the formula is satisfied by s *no matter how internal nondeterminism is resolved.* We shall see that both universally interpreted variants of the logic lead to the same equivalence as the one characterized by the original interpretation of the original PML. Indeed, $\sim_{\mathrm{PB,gbg},\leq}$ has also many other characterizations (see [3]), and this leads us to the convincement that it is an interesting behavioral relation for nondeterministic and probabilistic processes.

The rest of the paper is organized as follows. In Sect. 2, we provide the necessary background. The interpretations of PML over the non-alternating model are introduced in Sect. 3 and the new probabilistic bisimilarities that they characterize are presented in Sect. 4. Finally, Sect. 5 draws some conclusions. Due to space limitation, all proofs are omitted; they can be found in [3].

2 Background

In this section, we define a model for nondeterministic and probabilistic processes. Then, we recast in this general model the bisimilarity in [13] and the probabilistic bimilarity in [17], together with their HML and PML characterizations. Finally, we recall the probabilistic bisimilarity in [23] and its modal logic characterization for both the non-alternating case and the alternating case.

2.1 The NPLTS Model

Processes combining nondeterminism and probability are typically described by means of extensions of the LTS model, in which every action-labeled transition goes from a source state to a *probability distribution over target states* rather than to a single target state. The resulting processes are essentially Markov decision processes [9] and are representative of a number of slightly different probabilistic computational models including internal nondeterminism such as, e.g., concurrent Markov chains [29], strictly alternating models [11], probabilistic automata in the sense of [22], and the denotational probabilistic models in [15] (see [25] for an overview). We formalize them as a variant of simple probabilistic automata [22].

Definition 1. *A nondeterministic and probabilistic labeled transition system, NPLTS for short, is a triple* $(S, A, \longrightarrow)$ *where:*

- *S is an at most countable set of states.*
- *A is a countable set of transition-labeling actions.*
- *$\longrightarrow \subseteq S \times A \times Distr(S)$ is a transition relation, where $Distr(S)$ is the set of probability distributions over S.* ■

A transition $(s, a, \mathcal{D})$ is written $s \xrightarrow{a} \mathcal{D}$. We say that $s' \in S$ is not reachable from s via that a-transition if $\mathcal{D}(s') = 0$, otherwise we say that it is reachable with probability $p = \mathcal{D}(s')$. The reachable states form the support of $\mathcal{D}$, i.e., $supp(\mathcal{D}) = \{s' \in S \mid \mathcal{D}(s') > 0\}$. We write $s \xrightarrow{a}$ to indicate that s has an a-transition. The choice among all the transitions departing from s is external and nondeterministic, while the choice of the target state for a specific transition is internal and probabilistic.

The notion of NPLTS yields a non-alternating model [22] and embeds the following restricted models:

- *Fully nondeterministic processes*: every transition is Dirac, i.e., it leads to a distribution that concentrates all the probability mass into one target state.
- *Fully probabilistic processes*: every state has at most one outgoing transition.
- *Reactive probabilistic processes*: no state has two or more outgoing transitions labeled with the same action [28]. These processes include the probabilistic automata in the sense of [21].
- *Alternating processes*: every state that enables a non-Dirac transition enables only that transition. Similar to [20,30], these processes consist of a non-strict alternation of fully nondeterministic states and fully probabilistic states, with the addition that transitions departing from fully probabilistic states are labeled with actions.

An NPLTS can be depicted as a directed graph-like structure in which vertices represent states and action-labeled edges represent action-labeled transitions. Given a transition $s \xrightarrow{a} \mathcal{D}$, the corresponding a-labeled edge goes from the vertex representing state s to a set of vertices linked by a dashed line, each of which represents a state $s' \in supp(\mathcal{D})$ and is labeled with $\mathcal{D}(s')$ – label omitted if $\mathcal{D}(s') = 1$. Four NPLTS models are shown in Figs. 1 and 2.

We say that an NPLTS $(S, A, \longrightarrow)$ is *image finite* iff for all $s \in S$ and $a \in A$ the set $\{\mathcal{D} \in Distr(S) \mid s \xrightarrow{a} \mathcal{D}\}$ is finite. Following [17], we say that it satisfies the *minimal probability assumption* iff there exists $\epsilon \in \mathbb{R}_{>0}$ such that, whenever $s \xrightarrow{a} \mathcal{D}$, then for all $s' \in S$ either $\mathcal{D}(s') = 0$ or $\mathcal{D}(s') \geq \epsilon$; this implies that $supp(\mathcal{D})$ is finite because it can have at most $\lceil 1/\epsilon \rceil$ elements. If $\mathcal{D}(s')$ is a multiple of ϵ for all $s' \in S$, then the *minimal deviation assumption* is also satisfied.

Sometimes, instead of ordinary transitions, we will consider *combined transitions* [23], each being a convex combination of equally labeled transitions. Given an NPLTS $(S, A, \longrightarrow)$, $s \in S$, $a \in A$, and $\mathcal{D} \in Distr(S)$, in the following we write $s \xrightarrow{a}_{\mathrm{c}} \mathcal{D}$ iff there exist $n \in \mathbb{N}_{>0}$, $\{p_i \in \mathbb{R}_{]0,1]} \mid 1 \leq i \leq n\}$, and $\{s \xrightarrow{a} \mathcal{D}_i \mid 1 \leq i \leq n\}$ such that $\sum_{i=1}^{n} p_i = 1$ and $\sum_{i=1}^{n} p_i \cdot \mathcal{D}_i = \mathcal{D}$.

2.2 Bisimilarity for Fully Nondeterministic Processes

We recast in the NPLTS model the definition of bisimilarity for fully nondeterministic processes in [13]. In this case, the target of each transition is a Dirac distribution δ_s for $s \in S$, i.e., $\delta_s(s) = 1$ and $\delta_s(s') = 0$ for all $s' \in S \setminus \{s\}$.

Definition 2. *Let $(S, A, \longrightarrow)$ be an NPLTS in which the target of each transition is a Dirac distribution. A relation $\mathcal{B}$ over S is a* bisimulation *iff, whenever $(s_1, s_2) \in \mathcal{B}$, then for all actions $a \in A$ it holds that:*

- *For each $s_1 \xrightarrow{a} \delta_{s'_1}$ there exists $s_2 \xrightarrow{a} \delta_{s'_2}$ such that $(s'_1, s'_2) \in \mathcal{B}$.*
- *For each $s_2 \xrightarrow{a} \delta_{s'_2}$ there exists $s_1 \xrightarrow{a} \delta_{s'_1}$ such that $(s'_1, s'_2) \in \mathcal{B}$.*

We denote by $\sim_{\mathrm{B}}$ the largest bisimulation. ■

Given an image-finite NPLTS $(S, A, \longrightarrow)$ in which the target of each transition is a Dirac distribution, the relation $\sim_{\mathrm{B}}$ is characterized by the so-called Hennessy-Milner logic (HML) [13]. The set $\mathbb{F}_{\mathrm{HML}}$ of its formulae is generated by the following grammar ($a \in A$):

$$\phi ::= \mathsf{true} \mid \neg\phi \mid \phi \wedge \phi \mid \langle a \rangle \phi$$

The semantics of HML can be defined through an interpretation function $\mathcal{M}_{\mathrm{HML}}$ that associates with any formula in $\mathbb{F}_{\mathrm{HML}}$ the set of states satisfying the formula:

$$\begin{aligned}
\mathcal{M}_{\mathrm{HML}}[\![\mathsf{true}]\!] &= S \\
\mathcal{M}_{\mathrm{HML}}[\![\neg\phi]\!] &= S \setminus \mathcal{M}_{\mathrm{HML}}[\![\phi]\!] \\
\mathcal{M}_{\mathrm{HML}}[\![\phi_1 \wedge \phi_2]\!] &= \mathcal{M}_{\mathrm{HML}}[\![\phi_1]\!] \cap \mathcal{M}_{\mathrm{HML}}[\![\phi_2]\!] \\
\mathcal{M}_{\mathrm{HML}}[\![\langle a \rangle \phi]\!] &= \{s \in S \mid \exists s' \in \mathcal{M}_{\mathrm{HML}}[\![\phi]\!].s \xrightarrow{a} \delta_{s'}\}
\end{aligned}$$

2.3 Bisimilarity for Reactive Probabilistic Processes

We recast in the NPLTS model also the definition of probabilistic bisimilarity for reactive probabilistic processes in [17]. In the following, we let $\mathcal{D}(S') = \sum_{s' \in S'} \mathcal{D}(s')$ for $\mathcal{D} \in \mathit{Distr}(S)$ and $S' \subseteq S$.

Definition 3. *Let $(S, A, \longrightarrow)$ be an NPLTS in which the transitions of each state have different labels. An equivalence relation $\mathcal{B}$ over S is a* probabilistic bisimulation *iff, whenever $(s_1, s_2) \in \mathcal{B}$, then for all actions $a \in A$ and equivalence classes $C \in S/\mathcal{B}$ it holds that for each $s_1 \xrightarrow{a} \mathcal{D}_1$ there exists $s_2 \xrightarrow{a} \mathcal{D}_2$ such that $\mathcal{D}_1(C) = \mathcal{D}_2(C)$. We denote by $\sim_{\mathrm{PB}}$ the largest probabilistic bisimulation.* ■

Given an NPLTS $(S, A, \longrightarrow)$ satisfying the minimal deviation assumption in which the transitions of each state have different labels, the relation $\sim_{\mathrm{PB}}$ is characterized by PML [17,18]. The set $\mathbb{F}_{\text{PML}}$ of its formulae is generated by the following grammar ($a \in A$, $p \in \mathbb{R}_{[0,1]}$):

$$\phi ::= \mathsf{true} \mid \neg\phi \mid \phi \wedge \phi \mid \langle a \rangle_p \phi$$

The semantics of PML can be defined through an interpretation function $\mathcal{M}_{\text{PML}}$ that differs from $\mathcal{M}_{\text{HML}}$ only for the last clause, which becomes as follows:

$$\mathcal{M}_{\text{PML}}[\![\langle a \rangle_p \phi]\!] = \{s \in S \mid \exists \mathcal{D} \in \mathit{Distr}(S). s \xrightarrow{a} \mathcal{D} \wedge \mathcal{D}(\mathcal{M}_{\text{PML}}[\![\phi]\!]) \geq p\}$$

Note that, in this reactive setting, if an a-labeled transition exists that goes from s to $\mathcal{D}$, then it is the only a-labeled transition departing from s, and hence $\mathcal{D}$ is unique. In [10], it was subsequently shown that probabilistic bisimilarity for reactive probabilistic processes can be characterized by PML without negation and that the existence of neither a minimal deviation nor a minimal probability needs to be assumed to achieve the characterization result.

2.4 Bisimilarity for Non-Alternating and Alternating Processes

For NPLTS models in their full generality, we now recall two probabilistic bisimulation equivalences defined in [23]. Both of them check whether the probabilities of *all* classes of equivalent states – i.e., the *class distributions* – reached by the two transitions considered in the bisimulation game are equal.

The first equivalence relies on deterministic schedulers for resolving nondeterminism. This means that, when responding to an a-transition of the challenger, the defender can only select a single a-transition (if any).

Definition 4. *Let $(S, A, \longrightarrow)$ be an NPLTS. An equivalence relation $\mathcal{B}$ over S is a* class-distribution probabilistic bisimulation *iff, whenever $(s_1, s_2) \in \mathcal{B}$, then for all actions $a \in A$ it holds that for each $s_1 \xrightarrow{a} \mathcal{D}_1$ there exists $s_2 \xrightarrow{a} \mathcal{D}_2$ such that, for all equivalence classes $C \in S/\mathcal{B}$, $\mathcal{D}_1(C) = \mathcal{D}_2(C)$. We denote by $\sim_{\text{PB,dis}}$ the largest class-distribution probabilistic bisimulation.* ■

While in Def. 3 the quantification over $C \in S/\mathcal{B}$ can be placed before or after the transitions because s_1 and s_2 can have at most one outgoing a-transition each, in Def. 4 it is important for the quantification to be after the transitions.

The second equivalence relies instead on randomized schedulers. This means that, when responding to an a-transition of the challenger, the defender can select a convex combination of a-transitions (if any). In the following, the acronym ct stands for "based on combined transitions".

Definition 5. *Let $(S, A, \longrightarrow)$ be an NPLTS. An equivalence relation $\mathcal{B}$ over S is a* class-distribution ct-probabilistic bisimulation *iff, whenever $(s_1, s_2) \in \mathcal{B}$, then for all actions $a \in A$ it holds that for each $s_1 \xrightarrow{a} \mathcal{D}_1$ there exists $s_2 \xrightarrow{a}_{\text{c}} \mathcal{D}_2$ such that, for all equivalence classes $C \in S/\mathcal{B}$, $\mathcal{D}_1(C) = \mathcal{D}_2(C)$. We denote by $\sim_{\text{PB,dis}}^{\text{ct}}$ the largest class-distribution ct-probabilistic bisimulation.* ■

In order to obtain a modal logic characterization for $\sim_{\text{PB,dis}}$ and $\sim^{\text{ct}}_{\text{PB,dis}}$, in [14,19] an extension of HML much richer than PML was defined. The main differences are that (i) formulae are interpreted over probability distribution on states rather than over single states and (ii) the modal operator $\langle a \rangle_p \cdot$ is split into the original modal operator $\langle a \rangle \cdot$ of HML and an additional unary operator $[\cdot]_p$ such that state distribution $\mathcal{D}$ satisfies $[\phi]_p$ if $\mathcal{D}$ associates with the set of states satisfying ϕ a probability that is at least p.

In [12], the same equivalences (lifted to state distributions) were differently characterized by adding to HML a binary operator $\cdot \oplus_p \cdot$, where $\phi_1 \oplus_p \phi_2$ asserts decomposability of a state distribution to satisfy the two subformulae.

For alternating processes, i.e., NPLTS models in which every state that enables a non-Dirac transition enables only that transition, the following holds:

- $\sim_{\text{PB,dis}}$ and $\sim^{\text{ct}}_{\text{PB,dis}}$ collapse into a single equivalence that coincides with those defined in [11,20] for alternating processes, as shown in [24].
- $\sim_{\text{PB,dis}}$ is again characterized by the original PML, as shown in [19].

3 Interpreting PML over NPLTS Models

PML was originally interpreted in [17,18] on reactive probabilistic processes and then in [19] on alternating processes. The same interpretation can be applied to general NPLTS models by establishing that state s satisfies formula $\langle a \rangle_p \phi$ iff *there exists* a resolution of internal nondeterminism such that s can perform an a-transition and afterwards reaches with probability at least p a set of states that satisfy ϕ. This *existential interpretation* only provides a *weak guarantee* of fulfilling properties, as it depends on how internal nondeterminism is resolved.

A different interpretation can be adopted by following [4]: s satisfies $\langle a \rangle_p \phi$ iff, *for each* resolution of internal nondeterminism, s can perform an a-transition and afterwards reaches with probability at least p a set of states that satisfy ϕ. The resulting *universal interpretation* provides a *strong guarantee* of fulfilling properties because, no matter how internal nondeterminism is resolved, a certain behavior is ensured.

We denote by $\text{PML}_{\exists,\geq}$ and $\text{PML}_{\forall,\geq}$ the logics resulting from the two different interpretations of the diamond operator, which we formalize as follows:

$$\mathcal{M}_{\text{PML}_{\exists,\geq}}[\![\langle a \rangle_p \phi]\!] = \{s \in S \mid \exists \mathcal{D}. s \xrightarrow{a} \mathcal{D} \wedge \mathcal{D}(\mathcal{M}_{\text{PML}_{\exists,\geq}}[\![\phi]\!]) \geq p\}$$

$$\mathcal{M}_{\text{PML}_{\forall,\geq}}[\![\langle a \rangle_p \phi]\!] = \{s \in S \mid s \xrightarrow{a} \wedge \forall \mathcal{D}. s \xrightarrow{a} \mathcal{D} \Longrightarrow \mathcal{D}(\mathcal{M}_{\text{PML}_{\forall,\geq}}[\![\phi]\!]) \geq p\}$$

Finally, we denote by $\text{PML}_{\exists,\text{I}}$ and $\text{PML}_{\forall,\text{I}}$ two further variants generalizing the previous two logics, in which the probability value p is replaced by a probability interval $[p_1, p_2]$ – where $p_1, p_2 \in \mathbb{R}_{[0,1]}$ are such that $p_1 \leq p_2$ – and the resulting diamond operator is interpreted as follows:

$$\mathcal{M}_{\mathrm{PML}_{\exists,\mathrm{I}}}[\![\langle a\rangle_{[p_1,p_2]}\phi]\!] = \{s \in S \mid \exists \mathcal{D}. s \xrightarrow{a} \mathcal{D} \wedge p_1 \leq \mathcal{D}(\mathcal{M}_{\mathrm{PML}_{\exists,\mathrm{I}}}[\![\phi]\!]) \leq p_2\}$$

$$\mathcal{M}_{\mathrm{PML}_{\forall,\mathrm{I}}}[\![\langle a\rangle_{[p_1,p_2]}\phi]\!] = \{s \in S \mid s \xrightarrow{a} \wedge \forall \mathcal{D}. s \xrightarrow{a} \mathcal{D} \Longrightarrow p_1 \leq \mathcal{D}(\mathcal{M}_{\mathrm{PML}_{\forall,\mathrm{I}}}[\![\phi]\!]) \leq p_2\}$$

Note that $\langle a\rangle_p\phi$ can be encoded as $\langle a\rangle_{[p,1]}\phi$ because p is a lower bound.

In the following, if L is one of the above variants of PML, then we denote by $\mathcal{F}_{\mathrm{L}}(s)$ the set of formulae in $\mathbb{F}_{\mathrm{L}}$ satisfied by state s and we let $s_1 \sim_{\mathrm{L}} s_2$ iff $\mathcal{F}_{\mathrm{L}}(s_1) = \mathcal{F}_{\mathrm{L}}(s_2)$. Interestingly enough, the equivalences induced by the universally interpreted variants are the same and coincide with the equivalence induced by the existentially interpreted variant with probabilistic bound. In contrast, the equivalence induced by $\mathrm{PML}_{\exists,\mathrm{I}}$ is finer (see [3]).

4 Bisimilarities Characterized by PML

In this section, we introduce the probabilistic bisimilarities for NPLTS models that are characterized by PML as interpreted in the previous section. Before presenting their definition, we highlight the differences with respect to $\sim_{\mathrm{PB,dis}}$.

Firstly, instead of comparing the probability distributions over all classes of equivalent states reached by the transitions considered in the bisimulation game, the new equivalences focus on *a single equivalence class at a time*. Therefore, similar to [27], given an action a the probability distribution over all classes of equivalent states reached by an a-transition of the challenger can now be matched by means of *several* (not just by one) a-transitions of the defender, each taking care of a different class.

Secondly, the new equivalences take into account the probability of reaching *groups of equivalence classes* rather than individual classes. This would make no difference in the case of $\sim_{\mathrm{PB,dis}}$, while here it significantly changes the discriminating power (see [3]). Due to the previous and the current difference with respect to $\sim_{\mathrm{PB,dis}}$, we call these equivalences *group-by-group probabilistic bisimilarities*.

Thirdly, the new equivalences come in several variants depending on whether, in the bisimulation game, the probabilities of reaching a certain group of classes of equivalent states are compared based on $=$ or $\leq$. Again, this would make no difference in the case of $\sim_{\mathrm{PB,dis}}$.

In the following, we let $\bigcup \mathcal{G} = \bigcup_{C \in \mathcal{G}} C$ when $\mathcal{G} \in 2^{S/\mathcal{B}}$ is a group of equivalence classes with respect to an equivalence relation $\mathcal{B}$ over S.

Definition 6. *Let $(S, A, \longrightarrow)$ be an NPLTS and the relational operator $\bowtie \in \{=, \leq\}$. An equivalence relation $\mathcal{B}$ over S is a* $\bowtie$-group-by-group probabilistic bisimulation *iff, whenever $(s_1, s_2) \in \mathcal{B}$, then for all actions $a \in A$ and groups of equivalence classes $\mathcal{G} \in 2^{S/\mathcal{B}}$ it holds that for each $s_1 \xrightarrow{a} \mathcal{D}_1$ there exists $s_2 \xrightarrow{a} \mathcal{D}_2$ such that $\mathcal{D}_1(\bigcup \mathcal{G}) \bowtie \mathcal{D}_2(\bigcup \mathcal{G})$. We denote by $\sim_{\mathrm{PB,gbg},\bowtie}$ the largest $\bowtie$-group-by-group probabilistic bisimulation.* ■

The definition of $\sim_{\text{PB,gbg},\bowtie}$ assumes the use of deterministic schedulers, but it can be easily extended to the case of randomized schedulers by analogy with $\sim^{\text{ct}}_{\text{PB,dis}}$, thus yielding $\sim^{\text{ct}}_{\text{PB,gbg},\bowtie}$.

Note that, while in Def. 4 the quantification over $C \in S/\mathcal{B}$ is after the transitions, in Def. 6 the quantification over $\mathcal{G} \in 2^{S/\mathcal{B}}$ is before the transitions thus allowing a transition of the challenger to be matched by several transitions of the defender depending on the target groups.

The relation $\sim_{\text{PB,gbg},=}$ identifies the two systems in Fig. 1, whilst the relation $\sim_{\text{PB,gbg},\leq}$ also identifies the two systems in Fig. 2. The following theorem shows that $\sim_{\text{PB,dis}}$ is finer than $\sim_{\text{PB,gbg},=}$ and that the latter is finer than $\sim_{\text{PB,gbg},\leq}$.

Theorem 1. *Let $(S, A, \longrightarrow)$ be an NPLTS and $s_1, s_2 \in S$. Then:*

1. $s_1 \sim_{\text{PB,dis}} s_2 \implies s_1 \sim_{\text{PB,gbg},=} s_2$.
2. $s_1 \sim_{\text{PB,gbg},=} s_2 \implies s_1 \sim_{\text{PB,gbg},\leq} s_2$. ■

The two implications above cannot be reversed: Fig. 1 shows that $\sim_{\text{PB,dis}}$ is strictly finer than $\sim_{\text{PB,gbg},=}$ and Fig. 2 shows that $\sim_{\text{PB,gbg},=}$ is strictly finer than $\sim_{\text{PB,gbg},\leq}$.

In [23], it is also shown that $\sim^{\text{ct}}_{\text{PB,dis}}$, the variant of $\sim_{\text{PB,dis}}$ that relies on randomized schedulers (see Def. 5), is strictly finer than $\sim_{\text{PB,dis}}$. On the contrary, we have that $\sim_{\text{PB,gbg},\leq}$ coincides with its ct-variant, and hence it is insensitive to the choice between deterministic or randomized schedulers used to resolve nondeterminism. This is not the case for $\sim_{\text{PB,gbg},=}$. Indeed, the ct-variants of $\sim_{\text{PB,gbg},=}$ coincides with $\sim_{\text{PB,gbg},\leq}$, meaning that, in the bisimulation game, randomized schedulers reduce the discriminating power of the =-comparison of probabilities to that of the ≤-comparison. As expected, the ct-variant of $\sim_{\text{PB,dis}}$ is coarser than that of $\sim_{\text{PB,gbg},=}$, and thus also coarser than $\sim_{\text{PB,gbg},\leq}$ and $\sim^{\text{ct}}_{\text{PB,gbg},\leq}$.

Theorem 2. *Let $\mathcal{U} = (S, A, \longrightarrow)$ be an NPLTS and $s_1, s_2 \in S$. Then:*

1. $s_1 \sim_{\text{PB,gbg},=} s_2 \implies s_1 \sim^{\text{ct}}_{\text{PB,gbg},=} s_2$.
2. $s_1 \sim^{\text{ct}}_{\text{PB,dis}} s_2 \implies s_1 \sim^{\text{ct}}_{\text{PB,gbg},=} s_2$.
3. $s_1 \sim_{\text{PB,gbg},\leq} s_2 \iff s_1 \sim^{\text{ct}}_{\text{PB,gbg},\leq} s_2 \iff s_1 \sim^{\text{ct}}_{\text{PB,gbg},=} s_2$ *when $\mathcal{U}$ is image-finite.* ■

The inclusions of $\sim_{\text{PB,gbg},=}$ in $\sim^{\text{ct}}_{\text{PB,gbg},=}$ is strict. This can be proved by using the systems in Fig. 2. Indeed, $s_1 \not\sim_{\text{PB,gbg},=} s_2$ while $s_1 \sim^{\text{ct}}_{\text{PB,gbg},=} s_2$; the latter holds because the central offer-transition of s_1 can be matched by a convex combination of the two offer-transitions of s_2 both weighted by 0.5. Also the inclusion of $\sim^{\text{ct}}_{\text{PB,dis}}$ in $\sim_{\text{PB,gbg},\leq}$ is strict. This is evidenced by the systems in Fig. 1; no transition of s_1 can be obtained as the convex combination of transitions of s_2 and thus $s_1 \not\sim^{\text{ct}}_{\text{PB,dis}} s_2$. Finally, it also holds that $\sim^{\text{ct}}_{\text{PB,dis}}$ and $\sim_{\text{PB,gbg},=}$ are incomparable. Indeed, the two systems in Fig. 1 are equated by $\sim_{\text{PB,gbg},=}$ and distinguished by $\sim^{\text{ct}}_{\text{PB,dis}}$, while the two systems in Fig. 2 are distinguished by $\sim_{\text{PB,gbg},=}$ and equated by $\sim^{\text{ct}}_{\text{PB,dis}}$. These results are summarized in Fig. 3.

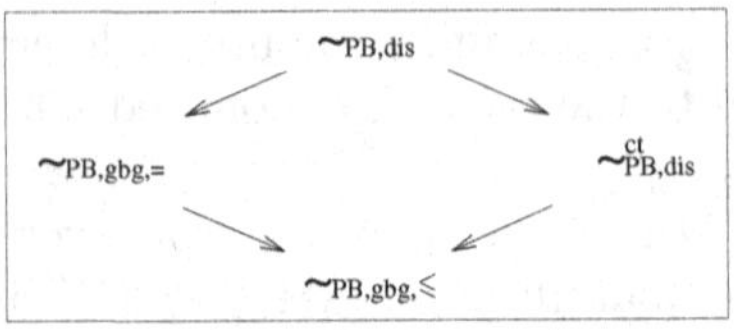

Fig. 3. Relating group-by-group and distribution-based probabilistic bisimilarities

For the new probabilistic bisimilarities, different alternative definitions can be obtained by varying the requirements on the comparison between sets of probabilities by considering not only $=$ and $\leq$ but also $\geq$, or by comparing only extremal probabilities ($\sqcup$ and/or $\sqcap$). Quite surprisingly, all relations but the one based on $=$ do collapse. Due to lack of space, we do not consider these variants in the present paper (see [3]).

Before moving to the modal logic characterization results, we show that the two group-by-group probabilistic bisimilarities and their ct-variants collapse on existing bisimilarities when one considers NPLTS models with a restricted interplay between probabilistic and non-determinism. In particular they coincide with: (i) the bisimilarity in [13] for fully nondeterministic processes (see Definition 2); (ii) the probabilistic bisimilarity in [17] for reactive probabilistic processes (see Definition 3); (iii) the probabilistic bisimilarities in [23] when alternating processes are considered. These results provide additional evidences that PML can be a uniform framework for reasoning on different classes of processes including probability and various degrees of nondeterminism.

Theorem 3. *Let $(S, A, \longrightarrow)$ be an NPLTS in which the target of each transition is a Dirac distribution. Let $s_1, s_2 \in S$ and $\bowtie \in \{=, \leq\}$. Then:*

$$s_1 \sim_{\text{PB,gbg},\bowtie} s_2 \iff s_1 \sim^{\text{ct}}_{\text{PB,gbg},\bowtie} s_2 \iff s_1 \sim_{\text{B}} s_2 \qquad \blacksquare$$

Theorem 4. *Let $(S, A, \longrightarrow)$ be an NPLTS in which the transitions of each state have different labels. Let $s_1, s_2 \in S$ and $\bowtie \in \{=, \leq\}$. Then:*

$$s_1 \sim_{\text{PB,gbg},\bowtie} s_2 \iff s_1 \sim^{\text{ct}}_{\text{PB,gbg},\bowtie} s_2 \iff s_1 \sim_{\text{PB}} s_2 \qquad \blacksquare$$

Theorem 5. *Let $(S, A, \longrightarrow)$ be an NPLTS in which every state that enables a non-Dirac transition enables only that transition. If $s_1, s_2 \in S$ and $\bowtie \in \{=, \leq\}$ then:*

$$s_1 \sim_{\text{PB,gbg},\bowtie} s_2 \iff s_1 \sim_{\text{PB,dis}} s_2$$
$$s_1 \sim^{\text{ct}}_{\text{PB,gbg},\bowtie} s_2 \iff s_1 \sim^{\text{ct}}_{\text{PB,dis}} s_2 \qquad \blacksquare$$

We are now ready to establish our logical characterization results and to show that $\sim_{\text{PB,gbg},=}$ is characterized by $\text{PML}_{\exists,\text{I}}$ while $\sim_{\text{PB,gbg},\leq}$ is characterized by $\text{PML}_{\exists,\geq}$, under the image finiteness and minimal probability assumptions.

Theorem 6. *Let $(S, A, \longrightarrow)$ be an image-finite NPLTS satisfying the minimal probability assumption. Let $s_1, s_2 \in S$. Then:*

$$s_1 \sim_{\text{PB,gbg,=}} s_2 \iff s_1 \sim_{\text{PML}_{\exists,\text{I}}} s_2$$

■

Theorem 7. *Let $(S, A, \longrightarrow)$ be an image-finite NPLTS satisfying the minimal probability assumption. Let $s_1, s_2 \in S$. Then:*

$$s_1 \sim_{\text{PB,gbg,}\leq} s_2 \iff s_1 \sim_{\text{PML}_{\exists,\geq}} s_2$$

■

Given the importance of these results in the economy of the paper, below we sketch the proof of Thm. 6; the one for Thm. 7 follows the same pattern. First, we need to provide an alternative characterization of $\sim_{\text{PB,gbg,=}}$ as the limit of a sequence of equivalence relations $\sim^i_{\text{PB,gbg,=}}$.

For an NPLTS $(S, A, \longrightarrow)$, the family $\{\sim^i_{\text{PB,gbg,=}} \mid i \in \mathbb{N}\}$ of equivalence relations over S is inductively defined as follows:

- $\sim^0_{\text{PB,gbg,=}} = S \times S$.
- $\sim^{i+1}_{\text{PB,gbg,=}}$ is the set of all pairs $(s_1, s_2) \in \sim^i_{\text{PB,gbg,=}}$ such that for all actions $a \in A$ and groups of equivalence classes $\mathcal{G} \in 2^{S/\sim^i_{\text{PB,gbg,=}}}$ it holds that for each $s_1 \xrightarrow{a} \mathcal{D}_1$ there exists $s_2 \xrightarrow{a} \mathcal{D}_2$ such that $\mathcal{D}_1(\bigcup \mathcal{G}) = \mathcal{D}_2(\bigcup \mathcal{G})$.

Each equivalence relation $\sim^i_{\text{PB,gbg,=}}$ identifies those states that cannot be distinguished within i steps of computation. The following lemma guarantees that two states of an image-finite NPLTS are equivalent according to $\sim_{\text{PB,gbg,=}}$ iff they are equivalent according to all the relations $\sim^i_{\text{PB,gbg,=}}$.

Lemma 1. *Let $(S, A, \longrightarrow)$ be an image-finite NPLTS. Then:*

$$\sim_{\text{PB,gbg,=}} = \bigcap_{i \in \mathbb{N}} \sim^i_{\text{PB,gbg,=}}$$

■

The second step of the proof is to show that two states are equated by $\sim^i_{\text{PB,gbg,=}}$ iff they satisfy the same formulae in $\mathbb{F}^i_{\text{PML}_{\exists,\text{I}}}$, which is the set of formulae in $\mathbb{F}_{\text{PML}_{\exists,\text{I}}}$ whose maximum number of nested diamond operators is at most i.

Lemma 2. *Let $(S, A, \longrightarrow)$ be an image-finite NPLTS satisfying the minimal probability assumption. Let $s_1, s_2 \in S$. Then for all $i \in \mathbb{N}$:*

$$s_1 \sim^i_{\text{PB,gbg,=}} s_2 \iff \mathcal{F}^i_{\text{PML}_{\exists,\text{I}}}(s_1) = \mathcal{F}^i_{\text{PML}_{\exists,\text{I}}}(s_2)$$

■

Now Theorem 6 directly follows from Lemma 1 and Lemma 2. The same result would not hold if $\text{PML}_{\exists,\geq}$ was used. For instance, the two states s_1 and s_2 in Fig. 2, which are not related by $\sim_{\text{PB,gbg,=}}$ as can be seen by considering the $\text{PML}_{\exists,\text{I}}$ formula $\langle \text{offer} \rangle_{[0.5,0.5]} \langle \text{head} \rangle_{[1,1]} \texttt{true}$, cannot be distinguished by any $\text{PML}_{\exists,\geq}$ formula.

It is easy to see that $\sim^{\text{ct}}_{\text{PB,gbg,=}}$ and $\sim^{\text{ct}}_{\text{PB,gbg,}\leq}$ are respectively characterized by $\text{PML}^{\text{ct}}_{\exists,\text{I}}$ and $\text{PML}^{\text{ct}}_{\exists,\geq}$, in which the interpretation of the diamond operator relies on combined transitions instead of ordinary ones.

5 Conclusion

We have addressed the problem of defining behavioral relations for nondeterministic and probabilistic processes that are characterized by modal logics as close as possible to PML, the natural probabilistic version of the by now standard HML for fully nondeterministic processes. We have introduced two new probabilistic bisimilarities ($\sim_{\text{PB,gbg},\leq}$ and $\sim_{\text{PB,gbg},=}$) following a group-by-group approach and studied their relationships with an existential and a universal interpretation of two variants of PML, in which the diamond is respectively decorated with a probability lower bound and a probability interval. All the resulting logical equivalences, except the one based on existential interpretation and probability intervals, do coincide with $\sim_{\text{PB,gbg},\leq}$. Interestingly enough, $\sim_{\text{PB,gbg},=}$, which is finer than $\sim_{\text{PB,gbg},\leq}$, has naturally emerged in a framework recently developed to provide a uniform model and uniformly defined behavioral equivalences for different classes of (nondeterministic, stochastic, probabilitic) processes [2].

These results, together with backward compatibility of our equivalences with those already defined for models with a restricted interplay between probability and nondeterminism, provide additional evidences that PML can be a uniform framework for reasoning on different classes of processes including probability and various degrees of nondeterminism.

We have also considered variants of our equivalences that rely on combined transitions and have proved that all such variants collapse on $\sim_{\text{PB,gbg},\leq}$. This suggests that, in the group-by-group approach, resolving nondeterminism with deterministic or randomized schedulers leads to the same identifications except when checking for equality of probabilities.

Our work has some interesting points in common with [26], where new probabilistic bisimilarities over nondeterministic and probabilistic Kripke structures have been defined that are in full agreement with PCTL, PCTL*, and their variants without the next-time operator. Indeed, both [26] and our work witness that, in order to characterize the equivalences induced by PCTL/PCTL*/PML in a nondeterministic and probabilistic setting, it is necessary to: (1) Anticipate the quantification over the sets of equivalent states to be reached in the bisimulation game, as done in [27]; (2) Consider groups of classes of equivalent states rather than only classes; (3) Compare for equality only the extremal probabilities of reaching certain sets of states rather than all the probabilities.

It is, however, worth noting that both our equivalences differ from those of [26]. There, to define probabilistic bisimilarities a multistep and inductive approach has been used and only their strong multistep 1-depth bisimulation is strongly related to $\sim_{\text{PB,gbg},\leq}$. In contrast, the general probabilistic bisimilarity of [26], obtained as the limit of the chain of n-depth bisimulations, is provably finer than both our group-by-group probabilistic bisimilarities once the appropriate model transformation from Kripke structures to NPLTS is performed.

Our results and those in [26] also show that, in the case of nondeterministic and probabilistic processes, it is not possible to define a single probabilistic bisimilarity that is characterized by both PML – as interpreted in this paper – and PCTL* – as interpreted in [4]. Thus, for nondeterministic and probabilistic processes the situation is quite different from the case of fully nondeterministic processes, where probabilistic bisimilarity is characterized by both HML [13] and CTL* [5], and from the case of reactive probabilistic processes, where probabilistic bisimilarity is characterized by both PML [17,18] and PCTL* [1].

References

1. Aziz, A., Singhal, V., Balarin, F., Brayton, R., Sangiovanni-Vincentelli, A.: It usually works: the temporal logic of stochastic systems. In: Wolper, P. (ed.) CAV 1995. LNCS, vol. 939, pp. 155–165. Springer, Heidelberg (1995)
2. Bernardo, M., De Nicola, R., Loreti, M.: A uniform framework for modeling nondeterministic, probabilistic, stochastic, or mixed processes and their behavioral equivalences. Inf. Comput. **225**, 29–82 (2013)
3. Bernardo, M., De Nicola, R., Loreti, M.: Revisiting bisimilarity and its modal logic for nondeterministic and probabilistic processes. Technical report 06/2013, IMT Institute for Advanced Studies Lucca (2013). http://eprints.imtlucca.it/1553/
4. Bianco, A., de Alfaro, L.: Model checking of probabilistic and nondeterministic systems. In: Thiagarajan, P.S. (ed.) FSTTCS 1995. LNCS, vol. 1026, pp. 499–513. Springer, Heidelberg (1995)
5. Browne, M., Clarke, E., Grümberg, O.: Characterizing finite Kripke structures in propositional temporal logic. Theor. Comput. Sci. **59**, 115–131 (1988)
6. Clarke, E., Emerson, E., Sistla, A.: Automatic verification of finite-state concurrent systems using temporal logic specifications. ACM Trans. Program. Lang. Syst. **8**, 244–263 (1986)
7. Crafa, S., Ranzato, F.: A spectrum of behavioral relations over LTSs on probability distributions. In: Katoen, J.-P., König, B. (eds.) CONCUR 2011. LNCS, vol. 6901, pp. 124–139. Springer, Heidelberg (2011)
8. de Alfaro, L., Majumdar, R., Raman, V., Stoelinga, M.: Game refinement relations and metrics. Logical Meth. Comput. Sci. **4**(3–7), 1–28 (2008)
9. Derman, C.: Finite State Markovian Decision Processes. Academic Press, New York (1970)
10. Desharnais, J., Edalat, A., Panangaden, P.: Bisimulation for labelled Markov processes. Inf. Comput. **179**, 163–193 (2002)
11. Hansson, H., Jonsson, B.: A calculus for communicating systems with time and probabilities. In: Proceedings of RTSS 1990, pp. 278–287. IEEE-CS Press (1990)
12. Hennessy, M.: Exploring probabilistic bisimulations, part I. Formal Aspects Comput. **24**, 749–768 (2012)
13. Hennessy, M., Milner, R.: Algebraic laws for nondeterminism and concurrency. J. ACM **32**, 137–162 (1985)
14. Hermanns, H., Parma, A., Segala, R., Wachter, B., Zhang, L.: Probabilistic logical characterization. Inf. Comput. **209**, 154–172 (2011)
15. Jifeng, H., Seidel, K., McIver, A.: Probabilistic models for the guarded command language. Sci. Comput. Program. **28**, 171–192 (1997)
16. Keller, R.: Formal verification of parallel programs. Commun. ACM **19**, 371–384 (1976)
17. Larsen, K., Skou, A.: Bisimulation through probabilistic testing. Inf. Comput. **94**, 1–28 (1991)
18. Larsen, K., Skou, A.: Compositional verification of probabilistic processes. In: Cleaveland, W.R. (ed.) CONCUR 1992. LNCS, vol. 630, pp. 456–471. Springer, Heidelberg (1992)

19. Parma, A., Segala, R.: Logical characterizations of bisimulations for discrete probabilistic systems. In: Seidl, H. (ed.) FOSSACS 2007. LNCS, vol. 4423, pp. 287–301. Springer, Heidelberg (2007)
20. Philippou, A., Lee, I., Sokolsky, O.: Weak bisimulation for probabilistic systems. In: Palamidessi, C. (ed.) CONCUR 2000. LNCS, vol. 1877, pp. 334–349. Springer, Heidelberg (2000)
21. Rabin, M.: Probabilistic automata. Inf. Control **6**, 230–245 (1963)
22. Segala, R.: Modeling and verification of randomized distributed real-time systems. Ph.D. thesis (1995)
23. Segala, R., Lynch, N.: Probabilistic simulations for probabilistic processes. In: Jonsson, B., Parrow, J. (eds.) CONCUR 1994. LNCS, vol. 836, pp. 481–496. Springer, Heidelberg (1994)
24. Segala, R., Turrini, A.: Comparative analysis of bisimulation relations on alternating and non-alternating probabilistic models. In: Proceedings of QEST 2005, pp. 44–53. IEEE-CS Press (2005)
25. Sokolova, A., de Vink, E.: Probabilistic automata: system types, parallel composition and comparison. In: Baier, C., Haverkort, B.R., Hermanns, H., Katoen, J.P., Siegle, M. (eds.) Validation of Stochastic Systems. LNCS, vol. 2925, pp. 1–43. Springer, Heidelberg (2004)
26. Song, L., Zhang, L., Godskesen, J.C.: Bisimulations meet PCTL equivalences for probabilistic automata. In: Katoen, J.-P., König, B. (eds.) CONCUR 2011. LNCS, vol. 6901, pp. 108–123. Springer, Heidelberg (2011)
27. Tracol, M., Desharnais, J., Zhioua, A.: Computing distances between probabilistic automata. In: Proceedings of QAPL 2011. EPTCS, vol. 57, pp. 148–162 (2011)
28. van Glabbeek, R., Smolka, S., Steffen, B.: Reactive, generative and stratified models of probabilistic processes. Inf. Comput. **121**, 59–80 (1995)
29. Vardi, M.: Automatic verification of probabilistic concurrent finite-state programs. In: Proceedings of FOCS 1985, pp. 327–338. IEEE-CS Press (1985)
30. Yi, W., Larsen, K.: Testing probabilistic and nondeterministic processes. In: Proceedings of PSTV 1992, pp. 47–61. North-Holland (1992)

Author Index

Author Index